SHORT STORIES
for Students

Advisors

Jayne M. Burton: Language Arts Teacher, Samuel V. Champion High School, Boerne, Texas. B.A. from Christopher Newport University. Member of National Council of Teachers of English and Sigma Tau Delta International English Honor Society; Chapter President of Delta Kappa Gamma International Society for Key Women Educators.

Kate Hamill: English Teacher, Catonsville High School, Catonsville, Maryland. B.A. from Pomona College; M.A. from University of Virginia; MSEd from University of Maryland.

Mary Beth Maggio: Language Arts Teacher, Schaumburg District No. 54, Schaumburg, Illinois. B.A. from Illinois State University; M.A. from Northern Illinois University.

Thomas Shilts: Youth Librarian, Capital Area District Library, Okemos, Michigan. M.S.L.S. from Clarion University of Pennsylvania; M.A. from University of North Dakota.

Amy Spade Silverman: Taught at independent schools in California, Michigan, Texas, and New York. B.A. from University of Michigan; M.F.A. from University of Houston. Member of National Council of Teachers of English, Teachers and Writers, and NCTE Opinion Panel. Exam Reader, Advanced Placement Literature and Composition. Poet, published in *North American Review*, *Nimrod*, and *Michigan Quarterly Review*, among other publications.

Mary Turner: English and AP Literature and Composition Teacher. B.S. from East Texas University; MEd from Western Kentucky University.

Laura Jean Waters: Certified School Library Media Specialist, Wilton High School, Wilton, Connecticut. B.A. from Fordham University; M.A. from Fairfield University.

SHORT STORIES
for Students

Presenting Analysis, Context, and Criticism on
Commonly Studied Short Stories

VOLUME 32

Sara Constantakis, Project Editor

Foreword by Thomas E. Barden

GALE
CENGAGE Learning™

Detroit • New York • San Francisco • New Haven, Conn • Waterville, Maine • London

GALE
CENGAGE Learning

Short Stories for Students, Volume 32

Project Editor: Sara Constantakis

Rights Acquisition and Management: Tracie Richardson, Tim Sisler, Robyn Young

Composition: Evi Abou-El-Seoud

Manufacturing: Rhonda A. Dover

Imaging: John Watkins

Product Design: Pamela A. E. Galbreath, Jennifer Wahi

Content Conversion: Katrina Coach

Product Manager: Meggin Condino

Gale
27500 Drake Rd.
Farmington Hills, MI, 48331-3535

ISBN-13: 978-1-4144-6696-5
ISBN-10: 1-4144-6696-X

ISSN 1092-7735

This title is also available as an e-book.
ISBN-13: 978-1-4144-7458-8
ISBN-10: 1-4144-7458-X
Contact your Gale, a part of Cengage Learning sales representative for ordering information.

Printed in Mexico
1 2 3 4 5 6 7 15 14 13 12 11

Table of Contents

Why Study Literature At All?

Short Stories for Students is designed to provide readers with information and discussion about a wide range of important contemporary and historical works of short fiction, and it does that job very well. However, I want to use this guest foreword to address a question that it does *not* take up. It is a fundamental question that is often ignored in high school and college English classes as well as research texts, and one that causes frustration among students at all levels, namely why study literature at all? Isn't it enough to read a story, enjoy it, and go about one's business? My answer (to be expected from a literary professional, I suppose) is no. It is not enough. It is a start; but it is not enough. Here's why.

First, literature is the only part of the educational curriculum that deals directly with the actual world of lived experience. The philosopher Edmund Husserl used the apt German term *die Lebenswelt*, "the living world," to denote this realm. All the other content areas of the modern American educational system avoid the subjective, present reality of everyday life. Science (both the natural and the social varieties) objectifies, the fine arts create and/or perform, history reconstructs. Only literary study persists in posing those questions we all asked before our schooling taught us to give up on them. Only literature gives credibility to personal perceptions, feelings, dreams, and the "stream of consciousness" that is our inner voice. Literature wonders about infinity, wonders why God permits evil, wonders what will happen to us after we die. Literature admits that we get our hearts broken, that people sometimes cheat and get away with it, that the world is a strange and probably incomprehensible place. Literature, in other words, takes on all the big and small issues of what it means to be human. So my first answer is that of the humanist we should read literature and study it and take it seriously because it enriches us as human beings. We develop our moral imagination, our capacity to sympathize with other people, and our ability to understand our existence through the experience of fiction.

My second answer is more practical. By studying literature we can learn how to explore and analyze texts. Fiction may be about *die Lebenswelt*, but it is a construct of words put together in a certain order by an artist using the medium of language. By examining and studying those constructions, we can learn about language as a medium. We can become more sophisticated about word associations and connotations, about the manipulation of symbols, and about style and atmosphere. We can grasp how ambiguous language is and how important context and texture is to meaning. In our first encounter with a work of literature, of course, we are not supposed to catch all of these things. We are spellbound, just as the writer wanted us to be. It is as serious students of the writer's art that we begin to see how the tricks are done.

Seeing the tricks, which is another way of saying "developing analytical and close reading skills," is important above and beyond its intrinsic literary educational value. These skills transfer to other fields and enhance critical thinking of any kind. Understanding how language is used to construct texts is powerful knowledge. It makes engineers better problem solvers, lawyers better advocates and courtroom practitioners, politicians better rhetoricians, marketing and advertising agents better sellers, and citizens more aware consumers as well as better participants in democracy. This last point is especially important, because rhetorical skill works both ways when we learn how language is manipulated in the making of texts the result is that we become less susceptible when language is used to manipulate us.

My third reason is related to the second. When we begin to see literature as created artifacts of language, we become more sensitive to good writing in general. We get a stronger sense of the importance of individual words, even the sounds of words and word combinations. We begin to understand Mark Twain's delicious proverb "The difference between the right word and the almost right word is the difference between lightning and a lightning bug." Getting beyond the "enjoyment only" stage of literature gets us closer to becoming makers of word art ourselves. I am not saying that studying fiction will turn every student into a Faulkner or a Shakespeare. But it will make us more adaptable and effective writers, even if our art form ends up being the office memo or the corporate annual report.

Studying short stories, then, can help students become better readers, better writers, and even better human beings. But I want to close with a warning. If your study and exploration of the craft, history, context, symbolism, or anything else about a story starts to rob it of the magic you felt when you first read it, it is time to stop. Take a break, study another subject, shoot some hoops, or go for a run. Love of reading is too important to be ruined by school. The early twentieth century writer Willa Cather, in her novel *My Antonia*, has her narrator Jack Burden tell a story that he and Antonia heard from two old Russian immigrants when they were teenagers. These immigrants, Pavel and Peter, told about an incident from their youth back in Russia that the narrator could recall in vivid detail thirty years later. It was a harrowing story of a wedding party starting home in sleds and being chased by starving wolves. Hundreds of wolves attacked the group's sleds one by one as they sped across the snow trying to reach their village. In a horrible revelation, the old Russians revealed that the groom eventually threw his own bride to the wolves to save himself. There was even a hint that one of the old immigrants might have been the groom mentioned in the story. Cather has her narrator conclude with his feelings about the story. "We did not tell Pavel's secret to anyone, but guarded it jealously as if the wolves of the Ukraine had gathered that night long ago, and the wedding party had been sacrificed, just to give us a painful and peculiar pleasure." That feeling, that painful and peculiar pleasure, is the most important thing about literature. Study and research should enhance that feeling and never be allowed to overwhelm it.

Thomas E. Barden
Professor of English and Director
of Graduate English Studies,
The University of Toledo

Introduction

Purpose of the Book

The purpose of *Short Stories for Students* (*SSfS*) is to provide readers with a guide to understanding, enjoying, and studying short stories by giving them easy access to information about the work. Part of Gale's "For Students" Literature line, *SSfS* is specifically designed to meet the curricular needs of high school and undergraduate college students and their teachers, as well as the interests of general readers and researchers considering specific short fiction. While each volume contains entries on "classic" stories frequently studied in classrooms, there are also entries containing hard-to-find information on contemporary stories, including works by multicultural, international, and women writers.

The information covered in each entry includes an introduction to the story and the story's author; a plot summary, to help readers unravel and understand the events in the work; descriptions of important characters, including explanation of a given character's role in the narrative as well as discussion about that character's relationship to other characters in the story; analysis of important themes in the story; and an explanation of important literary techniques and movements as they are demonstrated in the work.

In addition to this material, which helps the readers analyze the story itself, students are also provided with important information on the literary and historical background informing each work. This includes a historical context essay, a box comparing the time or place the story was written to modern Western culture, a critical overview essay, and excerpts from critical essays on the story or author. A unique feature of *SSfS* is a specially commissioned critical essay on each story, targeted toward the student reader.

To further help today's student in studying and enjoying each story, information on audiobooks and other media adaptations is provided (if available), as well as reading suggestions for works of fiction and nonfiction on similar themes and topics. Classroom aids include ideas for research papers and lists of critical and reference sources that provide additional material on the work.

Selection Criteria

The titles for each volume of *SSfS* were selected by surveying numerous sources on teaching literature and analyzing course curricula for various school districts. Some of the sources surveyed include: literature anthologies, *Reading Lists for College-Bound Students: The Books Most Recommended by America's Top Colleges*; *Teaching the Short Story: A Guide to Using Stories from around the World*, by the National Council of Teachers of English (NCTE); and "A Study of High School Literature Anthologies," conducted by Arthur Applebee at the Center for the Learning and Teaching of Literature and sponsored by the National Endowment for the Arts and the Office of Educational Research and Improvement.

Input was also solicited from our advisory board, as well as educators from various areas. From these discussions, it was determined that each volume should have a mix of "classic" stories (those works commonly taught in literature classes) and contemporary stories for which information is often hard to find. Because of the interest in expanding the canon of literature, an emphasis was also placed on including works by international, multicultural, and women authors. Our advisory board members—educational professionals—helped pare down the list for each volume. Works not selected for the present volume were noted as possibilities for future volumes. As always, the editor welcomes suggestions for titles to be included in future volumes.

How Each Entry Is Organized

Each entry, or chapter, in *SSfS* focuses on one story. Each entry heading lists the title of the story, the author's name, and the date of the story's publication. The following elements are contained in each entry:

Introduction: a brief overview of the story which provides information about its first appearance, its literary standing, any controversies surrounding the work, and major conflicts or themes within the work.

Author Biography: this section includes basic facts about the author's life, and focuses on events and times in the author's life that may have inspired the story in question.

Plot Summary: a description of the events in the story. Lengthy summaries are broken down with subheads.

Characters: an alphabetical listing of the characters who appear in the story. Each character name is followed by a brief to an extensive description of the character's role in the story, as well as discussion of the character's actions, relationships, and possible motivation.

Characters are listed alphabetically by last name. If a character is unnamed—for instance, the narrator in "The Eatonville Anthology"—the character is listed as "The Narrator" and alphabetized as "Narrator." If a character's first name is the only one given, the name will appear alphabetically by that name.

Themes: a thorough overview of how the topics, themes, and issues are addressed within the story. Each theme discussed appears in a separate subhead.

Style: this section addresses important style elements of the story, such as setting, point of view, and narration; important literary devices used, such as imagery, foreshadowing, symbolism; and, if

applicable, genres to which the work might have belonged, such as Gothicism or Romanticism. Literary terms are explained within the entry, but can also be found in the Glossary.

Historical Context: this section outlines the social, political, and cultural climate in which the author lived and the work was created. This section may include descriptions of related historical events, pertinent aspects of daily life in the culture, and the artistic and literary sensibilities of the time in which the work was written. If the story is historical in nature, information regarding the time in which the story is set is also included. Long sections are broken down with helpful subheads.

Critical Overview: this section provides background on the critical reputation of the author and the story, including bannings or any other public controversies surrounding the work. For older works, this section may include a history of how the story was first received and how perceptions of it may have changed over the years; for more recent works, direct quotes from early reviews may also be included.

Criticism: an essay commissioned by *SSfS* which specifically deals with the story and is written specifically for the student audience, as well as excerpts from previously published criticism on the work (if available).

Sources: an alphabetical list of critical material used in compiling the entry, with bibliographical information.

Further Reading: an alphabetical list of other critical sources which may prove useful for the student. Includes full bibliographical information and a brief annotation.

Suggested Search Terms: a list of search terms and phrases to jumpstart students' further information seeking. Terms include not just titles and author names but also terms and topics related to the historical and literary context of the works.

In addition, each entry contains the following highlighted sections, set apart from the main text as sidebars:

Media Adaptations: if available, a list of audiobooks and important film and television adaptations of the story, including source information. The list also includes stage adaptations, musical adaptations, etc.

Topics for Further Study: a list of potential study questions or research topics dealing with the story. This section includes questions related to other disciplines the student may be studying, such as American history, world history, science, math, government, business, geography, economics, psychology, etc.

Compare and Contrast: an "at-a-glance" comparison of the cultural and historical differences between the author's time and culture and late twentieth century or early twenty-first century Western culture. This box includes pertinent parallels between the major scientific, political, and cultural movements of the time or place the story was written, the time or place the story was set (if a historical work), and modern Western culture. Works written after 1990 may not have this box.

What Do I Read Next?: a list of works that might give a reader points of entry into a classic work (e.g., YA or multicultural titles) and/or complement the featured story or serve as a contrast to it. This includes works by the same author and others, works from various genres, YA works, and works from various cultures and eras.

Other Features

SSfS includes "Why Study Literature At All?," a foreword by Thomas E. Barden, Professor of English and Director of Graduate English Studies at the University of Toledo. This essay provides a number of very fundamental reasons for studying literature and, therefore, reasons why a book such as *SSfS*, designed to facilitate the study of literture, is useful.

A Cumulative Author/Title Index lists the authors and titles covered in each volume of the *SSfS* series.

A Cumulative Nationality/Ethnicity Index breaks down the authors and titles covered in each volume of the *SSfS* series by nationality and ethnicity.

A Subject/Theme Index, specific to each volume, provides easy reference for users who may be studying a particular subject or theme rather than a single work. Significant subjects from events to broad themes are included.

Each entry may include illustrations, including photo of the author, stills from film adaptations (if available), maps, and/or photos of key historical events.

Citing Short Stories for Students

When writing papers, students who quote directly from any volume of *SSfS* may use

the following general forms to document their source. These examples are based on MLA style; teachers may request that students adhere to a different style, thus, the following examples may be adapted as needed.

When citing text from *SSfS* that is not attributed to a particular author (for example, the Themes, Style, Historical Context sections, etc.), the following format may be used:

"The Celebrated Jumping Frog of Calavaras County." *Short Stories for Students*. Ed. Kathleen Wilson. Vol. 1. Detroit: Gale, 1997. 19–20.

When quoting the specially commissioned essay from *SSfS* (usually the first essay under the Criticism subhead), the following format may be used:

Korb, Rena. Critical Essay on "Children of the Sea." *Short Stories for Students*. Ed. Kathleen Wilson. Vol. 1. Detroit. Gale, 1997. 39–42.

When quoting a journal or newspaper essay that is reprinted in a volume of *SSfS*, the following form may be used:

Schmidt, Paul. "The Deadpan on Simon Wheeler." *Southwest Review* 41.3 (Summer, 1956): 270–77. Excerpted and reprinted in *Short Stories for Students*. Vol. 1. Ed. Kathleen Wilson. Detroit: Gale, 1997. 29–31.

When quoting material from a book that is reprinted in a volume of *SSfS*, the following form may be used:

Bell-Villada, Gene H. "The Master of Short Forms." *García Márquez: The Man and His Work*. University of North Carolina Press, 1990. 119–36. Excerpted and reprinted in *Short Stories for Students*. Vol. 1. Ed. Kathleen Wilson. Detroit: Gale, 1997. 89–90.

We Welcome Your Suggestions

The editorial staff of *Short Stories for Students* welcomes your comments and ideas. Readers who wish to suggest short stories to appear in future volumes, or who have other suggestions, are cordially invited to contact the editor. You may contact the editor via E-mail at: **ForStudents Editors@cengage.com.** Or write to the editor at:

Editor, *Short Stories for Students*
Gale
27500 Drake Road
Farmington Hills, MI 48331-3535

Literary Chronology

1809: Nikolai Vasil'evich Gogol is born on March 20 in Velikie Sorochintsy, Russia.

1836: Nikolai Vasil'evich Gogol's short story "The Nose" is published in the journal *Sovremennik*.

1852: Nikolai Vasil'evich Gogol dies of self-starvation on February 9 in Moscow, Russia.

1865: Joseph Rudyard Kipling is born on December 30 in Bombay, India.

1882: James Joyce is born February 2 in Dublin, Ireland.

1888: Joseph Rudyard Kipling's short story "The Man Who Would Be King" is published in the collection *The Phantom Rickshaw*.

1893: Carl Stephenson is born in Vienna, Austria.

1899: Jorge Luis Borges is born on August 24 in Buenos Aires, Argentina.

1907: Joseph Rudyard Kipling is awarded the Nobel Prize for Literature.

1912: Tillie Olsen is born on January 14 in Omaha, Nebraska.

1914: James Joyce's short story "The Sisters" is published in *Dubliners* after appearing in draft form in the *Irish Homestead* in 1904.

1917: Carson McCullers is born on February 19 in Columbus, Georgia.

1936: Joseph Rudyard Kipling dies of a perforated duodenal ulcer on January 18 in London, England.

1938: Carl Stephenson's short story "Leiningen Versus the Ants" is published in *Esquire* magazine.

1938: Joyce Carol Oates is born on June 16 in Lockport, New York.

1938: Raymond Carver is born on May 25 in Clatskanie, Oregon.

1940: Bharati Mukherjee is born on July 27 in Calcutta, India.

1941: James Joyce dies following surgery for a perforated ulcer on January 13 in Zurich, Switzerland.

1946: Tim O'Brien is born on October 1 in Austin, Minnesota.

1949: Jorge Luis Borges's short story "The House of Asterion" is published in the collection *El Aleph*.

1954: Sandra Cisneros is born on December 29 in Chicago, Illinois.

1955: Carson McCullers's short story "The Haunted Boy" is published in *Mademoiselle* magazine.

1956: Ha Jin is born as Xuefei Jin on February 21 in Jinzhou, China.

1957: Tony Romano is born on June 30 in Chicago, Illinois.

1957: Tillie Olsen's short story "O Yes" is published as "Baptism" in *Prairie Schooner*. It is later published as "O Yes" in *Tell Me a Riddle* in 1961.

1967: Carson McCullers dies of a stroke on September 29 in Nyack, New York.

1968: Joyce Carol Oates's short story "Stalking" is published in *American Review* magazine and is published in the 1972 reissue of the collection *Marriages and Infidelities*.

1981: Raymond Carver's short story "Popular Mechanics" is published in the collection *What We Talk About When We Talk About Love*. It is first published as "Mine" in the 1977 collection *Furious Seasons*.

1986: Jorge Luis Borges dies on June 14 in Geneva, Switzerland.

1988: Bharati Mukherjee's short story "The Tenant" is published in *The Middleman, and Other Stories*.

1988: Raymond Carver dies of lung cancer on August 2 in Port Angeles, Washington.

1990: Tim O'Brien's short story "On the Rainy River" is published in the collection *The Things They Carried*.

1991: Sandra Cisneros's short story "My Lucy Friend Who Smells Like Corn" is published in the collection *Woman Hollering Creek*.

2000: Ha Jin's short story "Saboteur" is published in the collection *The Bridegroom*.

2007: Tillie Olsen dies of Alzheimer's disease on January 1 in Oakland, California.

2009: Tony Romano's short story "If You Eat, You Never Die" is published in the collection *If You Eat, You Never Die: Chicago Tales*.

Acknowledgements

The editors wish to thank the copyright holders of the excerpted criticism included in this volume and the permissions managers of many book and magazine publishing companies for assisting us in securing reproduction rights. We are also grateful to the staffs of the Detroit Public Library, the Library of Congress, the University of Detroit Mercy Library, Wayne State University Purdy/Kresge Library Complex, and the University of Michigan Libraries for making their resources available to us. Following is a list of the copyright holders who have granted us permission to reproduce material in this volume of *SSFS*. Every effort has been made to trace copyright, but if omissions have been made, please let us know.

COPYRIGHTED EXCERPTS IN *SSFS*, VOLUME 32, WERE REPRODUCED FROM THE FOLLOWING PERIODICALS:

Bloomsbury Review, v. 8, no. 1, January-February 1988. Copyright © 1998 by William L. Stull. Reproduced by permission.—*Booklist* v. 90, no. 1, September 1, 1993. Reproduced by permission.—*Booklist*, v. 103, no. 16, April 15, 2007. Reproduced by permission.—*Booklist*, v. 105, no. 18, December 15, 2008. Reproduced by permission.—*Chicagoist. com*, March 9, 2010. Copyright © Gothamist, LLC. Reproduced by permission.—*Commonweal*, v. 130, no. 3, February 14, 2003. Copyright © 2003 by *Commonweal*. Reproduced by permission.—*Contemporary Literature*, v. 32, no. 1, Spring 1991. Copyright © 1991. Reproduced by permission of the University of Wisconsin Press.—*Contemporary Literature*, v. 39, no. 1, Spring 1998. Copyright © 1998 by the University of Wisconsin Press. Reproduced by permission of the University of Wisconsin Press.—*English Journal*, v. 71, no. 6, October 1982. Copyright © 1982 by the National Council of Teachers of English. Reproduced by permission.—Frisch, Mark. From "Introduction: 'El Aleph' (The Aleph) and 'La Casa de Asterion' (The House of Asterion): Between Monism and Chaos," in *You Might Be Able to Get There from Here: Reconsidering Borges and the Postmodern*. Farleigh Dickinson University Press, 2004. Copyright © 2004 by Farleigh Dickinson University Press. Reproduced by permission.—*Georgia Review*, Summer 1974. Copyright © 1974 by *The Georgia Review*. Reproduced by permission.—*Great Lakes Review*, v. 5, no. 2, Winter 1979. Copyright © 1979 by the Michigan Historial Review. Reproduced by permission.—*International Fiction Review*, v. 29, no. 1-2, January 2002. Copyright © 2002 by Alexandra Fitts. Reproduced by permission.—*Journal of American Studies*, v. 29, no. 3, December 1995. Copyright © 1995 by Cambridge University Press. Reproduced by permission.—*Journal of Narrative Technique*, v. 2, no. 2, May 1972. Copyright © 1972 by Eastern Michigan University. Reproduced by permission.—*Kirkus Reviews*, October 15, 2008. Copyright © 2008 by Kirkus Media. Reproduced by permission.—*Library Journal*, v. 132, no. 9, May 15, 2007. Copyright © 2007 Library Journals LLC. Reproduced by permission.—*Monthly Review*, v.

55, no. 6, November 2003. Copyright © 2003 by the *Monthly Review*. Reproduced by permission.—*New Zealand Herald*, November 10, 2001. Copyright © 2001 by the *New Zealand Herald*. Reproduced by permission.—*Northwest Review*, v. 37, no. 3, 1999. Copyright © 1999 by the *Northwest Review*. Reproduced by permission.—*Publishers Weekly*, v. 255, no. 42, October 20, 2008. Copyright © 2008 by PWXYZ, LLC. Reproduced by permission.—*South China Morning Post*, September 30, 2000. Copyright © 2000 South China Morning Post Ltd. Reproduced by permission.—*Southern Literary Journal*, v. 34, no. 1, Fall 2001. Copyright © 2001 by the University of North Carolina Press. Reproduced by permission.—*Studies in American Jewish Literature*, no. 5, 1986. Copyright © 1986 by *Studies in American Jewish Literature*. Reproduced by permission.—*Studies in Short Fiction*, v. 1, no. 1, Fall 1963. Copyright © 1963 by Studies in Short Fiction, Inc. Reproduced by permission.—*Studies in Short Fiction*, v. 27, no. 1, Winter 1990. Copyright © 1990 by *Studies in Short Fiction*. Reproduced by permission.—*Studies in Short Fiction*, v. 29, no. 1, Winter 1992. Copyright © 1992 by Studies in Short Fiction, Inc. Reproduced by permission.—*Studies in Short Fiction*, v. 31, no. 3, Summer 1994. Copyright © 1994 by *Studies in Short Fiction*. Reproduced by permission.—*Studies in Short Fiction*, v. 31, no. 4, Fall 1994. Copyright © 1994 by Studies in Short Fiction, Inc. Reproduced by permission.—*Studies in Short Fiction*, v. 32, no. 3, Summer 1995. Copyright © by Studies in Short Fiction, Inc. Reproduced by permission.—Sultan, Stanley. From "Dublin Boy and Man in 'The Sisters'," in *Joyce and the City: The Significance of Place*. Edited by Michael Begnal. Syracuse University Press, 2002. Copyright © 2002 by Syracuse University. Reproduced by permission.—*The Massachusetts Review*, v. 24, Number 3, Autumn 1983. Copyright © 1983 by the *Massachusetts Review*. Reproduced by permission.—*The Massachusetts Review*, Volume 29, Number 4, Winter 1988. Copyright © 1988 by the *Massachusetts Review*. Reproduced by permission.—*Women's Review of Books*, v. 6, no. 12, September 1989. Copyright © by Old City Publishing. Reproduced by permission.—*World Literature Today*, v. 64, no. 2, Spring 1990. Copyright © 1990 *World Literature Today*. Reproduced by permission.—

COPYRIGHTED EXCERPTS IN *SSFS*, VOLUME 32, WERE REPRODUCED FROM THE FOLLOWING BOOKS:

Buhs, Joshua Blu. From "Grins a Prohibitive Fracture, 1945-1957," in *The Fire Ants War: Nature, Science, and Public Policy in Twentieth-century America*. University of Chicago Press, 2004. Copyright © 2004 by the University of Chicago. Reproduced by permission.—Carr, Virginia Spencer. From "The Short Fiction," in *Understanding Carson McCullers*. University of South Carolina Press, 1990. Copyright © 1990 University of South Carolina Press. Reproduced by permission.—Fletcher, John. From "Joyce, Beckett, and the Short Story in Ireland," in *Re: Joyce'n Beckett*. Edited by Phyllis Carey and Ed Jewinski. Fordham University Press, 1992. Copyright © 1992 by Fordham University Press. Reproduced by permission.—Gotwald, Jr., William H. From "Army Ants and the Military Metaphor," in *Army Ants: The Biology of Social Predation*. Cornell University Press, 1995. Copyright © 1995 by Cornell University. Reproduced by permission.—Johnson, Greg. From "Understanding Joyce Carol Oates," in *Understanding Joyce Carol Oates*. University of South Carolina Press, 1987. Copyright © 1987 by the University of South Carolina Press. Reproduced by permission.—Yalom, Marilyn. From "Tillie Olsen," in *Women Writers of the West Coast: Speaking of Their Lives and Careers*. Edited by Marilyn Yalom. Capra Press, 1983. Reproduced by permission.

Contributors

Susan Andersen: Andersen is a writer and teacher with a Ph.D. in English literature. Entry on "The Man Who Would Be King." Original essay on "The Man Who Would Be King."

Bryan Aubrey: Aubrey holds a Ph.D. in English. Entries on "The Haunted Boy" and "Leiningen Versus the Ants." Original essays on "The Haunted Boy" and "Leiningen Versus the Ants."

Catherine Dominic: Dominic is a novelist and a freelance writer and editor. Entry on "The Nose." Original essays on "The Nose" and "Leiningen Versus the Ants."

Joyce Hart: Hart is a published author and teacher of creative writing. Entry on "My Lucy Friend Who Smells Like Corn." Original essay on "My Lucy Friend Who Smells Like Corn."

Diane Andrews Henningfeld: Diane Andrews Henningfeld holds the rank of professor emerita at Adrian College and publishes widely on literary topics. Entry on "On the Rainy River." Original essay on "On the Rainy River."

Michael Allen Holmes: Holmes is a writer and editor. Entries on "Saboteur," "The Tenant," and "The House of Asterion." Original essays on "Saboteur," "The Tenant," and "The House of Asterion."

Sheri Karmiol: Karmiol teaches literature and drama at the University of New Mexico, where she is a lecturer in the University Honors Program. Entry on "O Yes." Original essay on "O Yes."

David Kelly: Kelly is a teacher of creative writing in Illinois. Entry on "Popular Mechanics." Original essay on "Popular Mechanics."

Michael J. O'Neal: O'Neal holds a Ph.D. in English. Entry on "Stalking." Original essay on "Stalking."

Leah Tieger: Tieger is a freelance writer and editor. Entry on "The Sisters." Original essay on "The Sisters."

Rebecca Valentine: Valentine is a writer and editor whose focus includes American history and the humanities. Entry on "If You Eat, You Never Die." Original essay on "If You Eat, You Never Die."

The Haunted Boy

CARSON McCULLERS

1955

"The Haunted Boy" is a short story by twentieth-century southern American writer Carson McCullers. It was first published in the magazines *Mademoiselle* and *Botteghe Oscure* in 1955, and then reprinted in McCullers's *Collected Short Stories* in 1955. It appeared again in McCullers's *Collected Stories* in 1987. It is currently available in *Collected Stories of Carson McCullers*, published by Mariner Books in 1998, and in *The Mortgaged Heart: Selected Writings*, edited by Margarita G. Smith and published by Mariner Books in 2005. The story takes place on a single afternoon and is told through the eyes of Hugh, a boy of about fourteen. Hugh is deeply concerned when he returns from school to find that his mother, whose mental health has recently been unstable, is not at home. As the story unfolds, McCullers explores issues of love, anger, and guilt in the relationship between the boy and his mother. Although the story is not considered one of McCullers's major works, it is typical of her work in that it deals with the complexity of the feelings people have when in close relationships with others.

AUTHOR BIOGRAPHY

McCullers was born Lulu Carson Smith on February 19, 1917, in Columbus, Georgia, to Marguerite and Lamar Smith. As a child, Carson wanted to

Carson McCullers (Leonard Mccombe | Time and Life Pictures | Getty Images)

be a concert pianist and practiced for six to eight hours every day, but she gave up that ambition before she was fifteen. In 1932, McCullers contracted pneumonia and rheumatic fever, although the latter was undiagnosed at the time. These illnesses were to prove the first of many for her.

Her desire to become a writer led her, at the age of seventeen, to New York, where she supported herself with odd jobs and studied creative writing at Columbia University and New York University in the evenings. Sometimes forced by ill health to return to Georgia, on one such trip in 1935 she met Reeves McCullers, who was in the U.S. Army and was also a writer. They married in 1937, after Reeves left the army, and lived in Charlotte, North Carolina, and then Fayetteville, North Carolina.

In 1940, McCullers published her first novel, *The Heart Is a Lonely Hunter*, which was favorably received by reviewers and remains one of her best-known works. After this success, McCullers became part of a literary and artistic circle of friends that included the poet W. H. Auden, and

was centered in Brooklyn Heights, New York. Her second novel, *Reflections in a Golden Eye*, was published in 1941. McCullers and Reeves had separated several times and divorced in 1942. The couple reconciled and remarried in 1945, after Reeves returned from Army service in World War II. The marriage did not succeed, however, and Reeves, who was an alcoholic, committed suicide in Paris in November 1953.

In 1942, McCullers received a Guggenheim Fellowship and stayed for six months at Yaddo, the famous writers' colony in Saratoga Springs, New York, a place she returned to several times. Her third novel, *The Member of the Wedding*, appeared in 1946.

In 1947, McCullers suffered a series of strokes, leading to the loss of vision in one eye, temporary loss of speech, and permanent paralysis on her left side. In 1948, discouraged by her poor health, she made a suicide attempt and was hospitalized in a psychiatric clinic. However, in time she began to write again, and in 1950, her dramatization of *The Member of the Wedding* opened and ran for 501 performances on Broadway. It received the New York Drama Critics Circle Award, and a film version appeared in 1951.

In the same year, her novella *The Ballad of the Sad Café* was published, and in 1955, "The Haunted Boy" was published in *Mademoiselle*. This story was included in McCullers's *Collected Stories* in the same year. Another play, *The Square Root of Wonderful*, was performed on Broadway in 1957, but only for seven weeks and was widely considered a failure. McCullers continued to have health problems, and in 1961 she had surgery for breast cancer. In that year, her final novel, *Clock without Hands*, was published but did not receive favorable reviews.

In 1964 McCullers fractured her right hip and left elbow. Three years later, she suffered a stroke and was comatose for seven weeks until she died on September 29, 1967, in Nyack, New York, at the age of fifty.

PLOT SUMMARY

"The Haunted Boy" is set in April, perhaps somewhere in the South, although no exact location is specified. Hugh, who is in his first year of high school, returns home from school with his friend John. Hugh calls out to his mother, but there is no reply, and he senses that something might be wrong. He expects his mother to be at home. He and John go into the kitchen, where a lemon pie that Hugh's mother has made sits on the table. Feeling somewhat reassured, Hugh calls out again for his mother, but again there is no reply, and his feeling of unease returns.

Hugh cuts slices of the pie for himself and John. He feels very anxious, and John notices his discomfort. However, he tells Hugh that he cannot stay long because he has to sell some tickets for the Glee Club. Hugh is disappointed and tries to persuade John to stay longer. He does not want to be in the house alone. He calls for his mother a third time, but again there is no reply. Usually when she goes out, she leaves a note, but on this occasion, there is no note. He decides he must go upstairs, but the sight of the closed bathroom door reminds him of something from the past, and he feels dizzy.

After he returns to the kitchen, the dizziness passes. He pours two glasses of milk, and John asks him why he is so worried about his mother—is she sick? Hugh replies in an oblique way. He tells John of a fight he had with another boy who had been telling everyone that Hugh's mother was in Milledgeville and was crazy. Milledgeville is a state hospital for the mentally ill. Hugh tells John that his mother had been sick for a while and had been admitted to Milledgeville, but she was not crazy. He explains that the previous year his mother had been pregnant, but she had needed surgery for a tumor and she lost the baby. After this she became depressed. One day she tried to take her own life, and Hugh found her when he returned from school.

John listens sympathetically. Again he says he must leave, and Hugh tries to persuade him to stay. They talk for a while and then Hugh takes a basketball outside and he and John play for a while. The physical activity relieves the accumulated tension. Feeling happy for the moment, Hugh thinks up the first two lines of a poem, but his happiness soon fades. John says he must go, but once more Hugh tries to persuade him to stay. He tells his friend that his mother is always at home when he returns from school. He tries to get John to accompany him upstairs, telling him, untruthfully, that he is assembling hi-fi equipment up there. He knows John does not believe him. John finally insists that he must leave, and Hugh is left alone in the house.

Hugh climbs the stairs, full of dread, his heart pounding. He opens the bathroom door

and for a moment sees things the way they were when his mother had tried to kill herself. He had found his mother lying on the floor in a pool of blood. But as he steadies himself, he realizes that everything is perfectly normal in the bathroom. His mother is not there. He goes to the bedroom, lies down on the bed, and cries. He did not cry the whole time his mother was in the hospital and he was living at home with just his father, but he cries now.

He is still crying when his mother returns. She asks him what is wrong, but he cannot tell her. He finally blurts out a question asking her why she did it, but she mistakenly thinks he is referring to the new silk dress she is wearing. She tells him she decided to buy some new clothes, and she bought two dresses and two petticoats. Hugh says he hates the new clothes. He is angry at her because she tried to kill herself, but instead of confessing to that, he directs the anger at his mother's choice of new clothes. Then she points out the new blue shoes she bought. Hugh says he does not like the new purchases because they make it look as if she is trying to look younger than she is. But when he sees that this remark has hurt her feelings, his anger vanishes, and he apologizes. He says he likes the clothes and shoes. His mother responds by kissing him on the cheek and asks him again why he was crying. He starts to tell her about how he had come home and found her gone, and that there was no note, but he cannot confess the terror he had felt. He just says that all afternoon he had felt "odd."

When Hugh's father returns, he calls Hugh out to the backyard. Hugh's mother has told him that Hugh was crying earlier, and now it is Hugh's father's turn to ask him why he was crying. Hugh says he does not know but thinks he was just nervous. His father puts his arm around Hugh's shoulder and tells him that his mother looks very well, better than she has looked for years. Soon it will be summer, and they will all go on picnics together, his father says. He then tells Hugh that he thinks Hugh did very well during the time his mother was ill. Hugh is not used to hearing compliments from his father, and after his father has returned to the house Hugh feels a warm glow. When it starts to gets dark, Hugh sees his mother preparing dinner in the lighted kitchen. His emotions have calmed and he feels he will never cry again. He is no longer afraid.

CHARACTERS

Hugh Brown

Hugh is a normal kid of about fourteen, in his first year of high school. He is a bright, sensitive, loving boy. He likes to play basketball, and he even writes poetry. He seems mature for his age, preferring the company of his friend John, who is two years older, to that of boys of his own age. Hugh is very attached to his mother, and her mental instability, involving a suicide attempt, has had a devastating effect on him. This may not be surprising since he endured the shock of discovering her after she had slashed her wrists. In the past few months, while his mother was in the hospital being treated for depression, he has been withdrawn, not wanting to make many friends at school. He does not want anyone to find out about his mother. When a boy taunted him that his mother was crazy, Hugh became angry and beat him up. He tells John he wanted to kill the boy. Generally speaking, however, Hugh represses his emotions regarding his mother. During the last few months he has not permitted himself to cry once, even though his father did. But the tension in him builds up and comes to a head on the afternoon the story relates. He loves his mother dearly, but there is also anger in him because she deserted him, and he knows that he needs her so much. Hugh's relationship with his father is less intimate, but they appear to get along well enough, although his father rarely compliments him on anything.

Hugh's Father

Hugh's father is not a central character in the story until the end. The reader learns snippets of information about him as the narrator tells what happened in the family over the previous few months. When his wife was in the hospital, he took Hugh hunting nearly every Saturday, and they killed many quail and doves, although they lived mostly on a monotonous diet of steak or hot dogs and let the kitchen get messy. On occasion he had talked with Hugh about Hugh's mother but not very often, only when they were doing something else together, such as carpentry or washing dishes. Hugh's father is obviously fond of his son, but he appears to be a rather remote figure who finds it difficult to express emotions. He is strict with his son, never allowing him to leave tools out of place, for example, and he never praises Hugh or offers compliments. Hugh's deepest relationship is therefore with his mother, not his father. Only at the end does the father become more prominent. He inquires about his son's well-being and puts his arm around his shoulder. He offers Hugh a rare compliment and implies that he will soon be a man.

Hugh's Mother

Hugh's forty-two-year-old mother has recently been suffering from some mental instability. It appears that, at least from what Hugh knows, the trouble began when she had a failed pregnancy. This left her depressed and rundown. She is also going through menopause, referred to in the story as a change of life. After she made a suicide attempt she was admitted to a hospital for the mentally ill. She remained there for several months but on the afternoon the story the takes place, she has been out of the hospital for about a month. She appears to have recovered from her illness. The fact that she wanted to go out and buy new clothes is a sign of this recovery. She is ready once more to participate fully in life. Hugh's mother loves her son, and the two are close. She shows physical affection for him and has a couple of pet names for him—Shelley-Poe (in reference to the poets Percy Bysshe Shelley and Edgar Allan Poe) and Loveyboy, the latter being a name she called him when he was much younger. She does not realize that he is angry with her for what she did, and he is unable to talk to her openly about it.

John Laney

John Laney is Hugh's friend. He is two years older than Hugh and is the most able student in his class. He is clever with words. He is also the best athlete in his class. Hugh thinks John is the best friend he has ever had. Sitting with John at the kitchen table makes him feel safer; his friend has a calming influence on him. John is indeed a good friend to Hugh. He is sensitive to and considerate of his friend's feelings. He senses that all is not right with Hugh. When Hugh tells him about his mother's suicide attempt, John strokes his arm over his sweater. Unfortunately, John is unable to help his friend more by staying longer, because he has agreed to sell tickets for the Glee Club's operetta, and he feels strongly that he must meet his obligations.

THEMES

Coming of Age

Hugh is experiencing emotional turmoil that neither Hugh nor his parents really understand. Yet this is part of the process of growing up for him; he is becoming consciously aware of the place his mother has in his life and the complex emotions he has for her. He has also experienced the trauma of finding his mother after her suicide attempt, which has left him emotionally scarred. Although the reader sees Hugh only in an acutely nervous state, because he fears his mother may again have tried to kill herself, a new perspective is provided on Hugh's experience and progress in the scene with his father at the end of the story. His father compliments Hugh on how the boy has handled the situation over the previous few months: "I just want you to know that I realize how fine you were all that bad time. How fine, how damn fine." Hugh feels as if his father is speaking to him as if he, Hugh, were grown up, and this is a sign of how the difficult time Hugh has been through has helped him to mature. He has, at a young age, been tested, but he has come through it well, perhaps better than he realizes. The coming-of-age implications of this incident at the end of the story become even more clear when the father remarks, just as he is about to walk back into the house, "You'll be taller than your old man in a year or so." Hugh has been through the crucible of emotional pain, but he has weathered the storm and is growing up fast.

Mother-child Relationships

The story provides insight into the complexities of love, in this case the love between a mother and her teenage son, as seen from the point of view of the son. The theme, however, might apply to other types of relationship in which two people are close. In this case, Hugh is very close to his mother. He is deeply attached to her, as might be expected in any such loving relationship. But because his mother attempted suicide and was temporarily taken away from him—she spent several months in the hospital—an element of insecurity has entered the relationship, mixed also with anger and guilt on the part of Hugh. The insecurity can be seen immediately in the unease that Hugh feels when his mother is not home when he returns from school. She normally considers his feelings in such a situation by leaving a note, but on this occasion she has not done so. This puts Hugh into an extreme

TOPICS FOR FURTHER STUDY

- Select another short story by McCullers and write an essay in which you compare it to "The Haunted Boy." Do the stories contain similar themes and characters, and in what ways do they differ?

- In the story, Hugh's mother suffers from depression and has attempted suicide. Working with another student, research the topic of suicide. What are the signs that someone may be contemplating suicide? How can suicide be prevented? Is suicide more common in women or men? The old or the young? Give a class presentation in which you present your findings. Use PowerPoint and share your presentation with your classmates via slideshare.net.

- Read *The Struggle to be Strong: True Stories by Teens about Overcoming Tough Times*, edited by Al Desetta and Sybil Wolin (Free Spirit Publishing, 2000). This is a book written mostly by African American, Latino, and Asian teens, in which they discuss how they have dealt with difficult issues in their lives, including relationships with parents. Write a short review of the book, commenting on what you learned from it, and which stories you liked best, and why. Publish the review on Amazon.com, your Web page, or on your social networking site.

- Write a short story that centers around the relationship a teenage boy or girl has with his or her mother or father. Perhaps there are issues that the teenagers cannot discuss with their parents. But what happens when strong emotions or feelings cannot be expressed? Consult *Seize the Story: A Handbook for Teens Who Like to Write*, by Victoria Handley, published by Cottonwood Press in 2008. You can also consult StoryJumper.com for a seven-step process for writing a story.

state of anxiety because he fears she may have made another attempt on her life. His absent mother is on his mind all the time that his friend

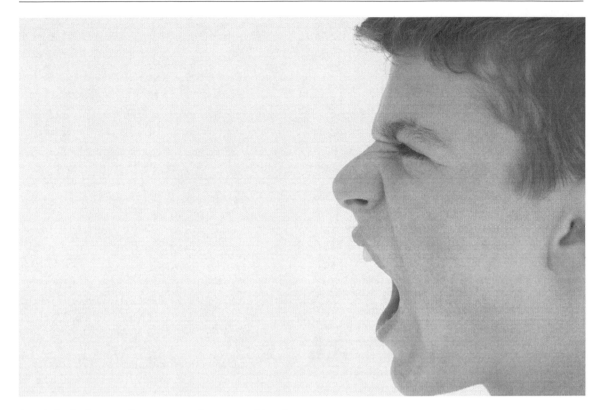

Hugh lashed out at her in anger because of his fear. (*Monkey Business Images | Shutterstock.com*)

John is in the house with him. Hugh is obviously proud of his mother, since he tells John about what a great cook she is. But her actions have also left him with unresolved feelings of anger.

The tension of the afternoon, during which he swings from moments of great anxiety to a few carefree moments (when he plays basketball) and then back again, brings all these unresolved feelings to a head, and he breaks down in tears, which he never did during all the months of the crisis. The relief he feels when his mother finally returns crystallizes the difficult feelings he is experiencing. He thinks back to the moment he discovered her bleeding from her self-inflicted wound and acknowledges that from that moment he felt a "grudge" against her, and asked himself *"why did she do this to me?"* His mother has done violence to herself, but she is perceived by the boy as having done something to him—deserted him, bewildered him, left him in turmoil and loneliness. However, as happens in many close relationships, Hugh finds it impossible to directly speak the truth. It is too difficult, too painful, to say. Only in the immediate aftermath of the traumatic afternoon, when his mother returns, is he able to

blurt out the question that has been haunting him: "Why did you do it?" But when his mother misunderstands his meaning, he cannot bring himself to follow through and explain his real feelings. However, the truth, if it cannot be spoken directly, comes out in other ways, in his criticism of his mother's new clothes. Although the flash of anger soon goes, and the loving relationship is reestablished, Hugh's mother never gets to hear the real truth about what her son is going through. Close they may be, but they are unable to communicate honestly with each other. The intense incident shows the net of dependency on which this relationship is based—not unusual for a boy who is still a child—and the anger, and then guilt at experiencing the anger, that is felt when expectations are violated and, in consequence, deep emotional needs go unmet.

STYLE

Point of View
The story is told from Hugh's point of view by a limited third-person narrator. This means that

the narrator has insight only into the thoughts and feelings of Hugh. For example, in the third paragraph, the narrator states that "Hugh felt there was something wrong." The remainder of the story explores and develops Hugh's thoughts and emotions from this point of view. What this means is that all the other characters—John, and Hugh's mother and father—are seen only, so to speak, from the outside, from the perspective of how Hugh sees them. Their own thoughts are not disclosed. They reveal themselves to the reader through their words and their actions, but not through their thoughts. McCullers observes this point of view strictly and does not deviate from it. Even a passage such as, "Laney was calling him by his ordinary first name; he thought he was a sissy . . . " refers to Hugh's perceptions of what his friend John Laney is thinking; it does not offer insight directly into John's thoughts. The choice of this point of view is extremely effective. It keeps the story focused entirely on the state of mind of the boy and allows the feeling of tension and dread to build inexorably and not be dissipated by a switch in point of view to that of another character. The mother's story is thus told obliquely, through Hugh's involvement in it and his thoughts about it. Had the story been told by an omniscient narrator, the reader would have had access to the thoughts of all the characters. However, this would have widened the scope of the story beyond the author's intentions.

Foreshadowing

Foreshadowing occurs in a work of fiction when something appears that offers a hint at future events. The foreshadowing may be an image, an event, a piece of dialogue, or anything else that, seen in retrospect, hints at or obliquely predicts some future event. Foreshadowing occurs in this story in the use of an image featuring the color red. It comes in the third paragraph and is not difficult to spot. Hugh has just returned from school and feels that something is wrong. He happens to glance at the rug on the sitting room floor: "The sun shone on a red piece in the flowered rug. Red-bright, red-dark, red-dead—Hugh sickened with a sudden chill remembrance of the 'other time.'" The red patch in the rug serves here not only as a symbolic reminder of a past event, but foreshadows what Hugh now fears may be waiting for him upstairs: his mother once again lying in a pool of her own blood. The image of the red in the carpet, the color of blood, helps to

establish the mood of dread and terror right at the beginning of the story and also contributes to a sense of mystery because the reader does not yet know that the color red is reminding Hugh of blood.

HISTORICAL CONTEXT

Attitudes about Mental Illness

In the 1950s less was known about mental illness than is known today. In the story, Hugh feels the stigma attached to mental illness. He was taunted by a boy at school who said his mother was "crazy," because he knew she had been admitted to the state hospital for the mentally ill. Hugh is determined to defend her against such a false allegation. His mother was suffering from depression following surgery for a tumor that caused a miscarriage and the onset of menopause as a result. In those days, however, even a common mental illness like depression was not fully understood by the general public and people did not like to talk about it (an attitude that is far less common in the twenty-first century but does still exist). In the 1950s, those who were perceived as mentally ill were generally rejected by the public, who thought of mental illness as something quite different from other illnesses. People returning from hospitals for the mentally ill often found it hard to find a job and a place to live and to have a social life. Such people often led isolated lives, unable to fully participate in society. The problem was that society was fearful of those labeled mentally ill. The public associated mental illness with extreme conditions and assumed such people would exhibit unpredictable and violent behavior.

Studies done in the 1950s confirmed these negative perceptions. Several of these studies were reported in Judith Rabkin's article "Public Attitudes toward Mental Illness: A Review of the Literature." One study conducted in a rural Canadian town in 1951 showed that although people were prepared to accept that the range of normal behavior was quite wide, they could not accept the proposition that "normal and abnormal behavior fall within a single continuum and are not qualitatively distinct." In other words, people believed that the mentally ill were set apart from those who were normal; there was something different about them, and people wanted to protect themselves from the notion

COMPARE
&
CONTRAST

- **1950s:** Mental illnesses such as depression are treated with newly developed antidepressant drugs that target imbalances in brain chemistry. Another treatment is electroconvulsive therapy (ECT), also known as electric shock therapy. Electrodes are attached to the scalp and an electrical pulse induces a seizure in the brain. Although controversial, ECT is effective in many cases although it can lead to memory loss. American poet Sylvia Plath undergoes electric shock therapy in the 1950s and is temporarily cured of depression. She writes about it in her autobiographical novel, *The Bell Jar* (1963).

  Today: Depression is treated in many ways, most often through a combination of antidepressant drugs such as Prozac, Zoloft, and Paxil, and psychotherapy. The drugs raise the level of chemicals like serotonin in the brain to restore normal mood. ECT is still used, although far more infrequently than in the 1950s, usually in cases of severe depression that have not responded to any other treatment.

- **1950s:** Television increases in popularity. Popular shows include Westerns like *Gunsmoke* and *Wagon Train*, comedies such as *I Love Lucy* and *Amos 'n' Andy*, drama shows like *Dragnet*, and variety shows including the *Bob Hope Show* and the *Ed Sullivan Show*. The courtroom drama *Perry Mason* is also very popular. Various drama anthologies, such as the *Kraft Television Theatre*, *Goodyear Television Playhouse*, and *Fireside Theater* present sixty- to ninety-minute plays.

Viewers have a choice of just three television networks: NBC, ABC, and CBS.

  Today: Even though it is competing with other forms of entertainment available on the Internet, television has lost none of its appeal in the twenty-first century. Among the most popular TV shows in 2010 are reality shows like *Dancing with the Stars*, *American Idol*, and *Big Brother*. Unlike in the 1950s, viewers have a choice of hundreds of different channels.

- **1950s:** McCullers is one of several female southern writers making an impact on American literary culture along with Eudora Welty and Flannery O'Connor, both of whom, like McCullers, publish most of their major works in the twenty-year period from 1940 to 1960. Other distinguished Southern female writers of the day include Katherine Anne Porter and Caroline Gordon.

  Today: Women writers continue the tradition of southern literature. The work of Mary Hood, from Georgia, has a distinctly southern flavor. She writes *Familiar Heat* (1995) and two short-story collections. Olympia Vernon, raised in Louisiana and Mississippi, wins the Ernest J. Gaines Award for Literary Excellence in 2007 for her novel, *A Killing in This Town* (2006). Lee Smith's work often reflects the Virginia culture in which she grew up. Her novel, *The Last Girls* (2003), about a raft trip down the Mississippi River, is a best seller.

---

that anyone might, under certain circumstances, become mentally ill. In another study, conducted by J. Nunnally in the 1950s and published in 1961 as part of Rabkin's article, showed that, in Nunnally's words, "the mentally ill are regarded with fear, distrust and dislike by the general public." This attitude applied to people

from all age groups and levels of education; "all tend to regard the mentally ill as relatively dangerous, dirty, unpredictable and worthless." In a 1956 study of 2,001 Louisiana residents conducted by Shirley Star, also cited by Rabkin, only 15 percent of respondents to a survey answered yes to the question "If I needed a babysitter, I would be willing to hire a woman who had been going to see a psychiatrist." Over the next few decades, public attitudes slowly began to change as more information about mental illness was disseminated, although many people still find it difficult to accept the notion that mental illness is an illness like any other and can be treated without any stigma attaching to the patient.

Television, Film, and Radio

The story provides a glimpse of how people kept themselves entertained in the 1950s. Television was still in its early days, but John says he could not live without it. In his house, the television is on from seven in the morning until late at night when the family goes to bed. However, Hugh's family does not yet own a television. Hugh tells John that his father plans to buy one when he has paid off the medical bills incurred by his mother's illness. This shows that ownership of television was not universal in the 1950s, as it is today when almost every home owns at least one. However, in the 1950s the television industry was experiencing explosive growth. In 1945, at the end of World War II, there were less than 7,000 TVs in the United States, and only nine television stations. In 1949, only 10 percent of U.S. households owned a television, but by 1959, that figure had risen to 90 percent. The earliest television networks were the same as today, with one exception. While NBC, CBS, and ABC thrived, DuMont went out of business in 1956. Television offered a wide variety of programming, and the period is sometimes known as the golden age of television. In "The Haunted Boy," John enthusiastically tells Hugh that on TV "There're plays and skits and gags going on continually."

The rapid growth of television was a challenge to the film industry, which feared that the new medium would drastically reduce audiences in cinemas. It was also a challenge to producers of live entertainment, such as plays and musicals, who also stood to lose if large numbers of people preferred to stay at home and watch TV rather than go out. In the story, John hints at this trend, when he says that it is hard to sell tickets for a local operetta: "Unless they [people] know someone in it personally, they'd rather stay home with a good TV show." Indeed, during the 1950s many movie theaters did close as people turned their attention elsewhere for entertainment. But in the long term, fears of the

Mom came home in a new dress and shoes. (Serg Zastavkin / Shutterstock.com)

demise of the film industry proved unfounded, since television could not duplicate the experience of watching a full-length film on a large screen in a darkened theater.

Many of those in the 1950s who did not have a television relied on radio for their home entertainment. Hugh and his parents fall in that category. Hugh points out to John that although they do not have a TV they do "of course" have a radio. The phrase he uses suggests the universality of radio ownership during that period. Indeed, in 1945, 95 percent of U.S. households owned a radio. However, in the 1950s, the rise of television reduced the popularity of radio, and many radio stations switched programming from news and plays to music. The invention of the portable transistor radio in this decade, as well as the growth of rock and roll music that could be played over the radio, helped radio stations to stay in business.

CRITICAL OVERVIEW

McCullers's short stories have not garnered as much critical attention as her novels. However, some critics have commented on "The Haunted Boy." Margaret B. McDowell, in *Carson McCullers*, describes the story as an "extended and dynamic portrayal of a troubled child." She argues that the work shows "the psychic tension of a child torn between pity for—and anger against—a parent and also the tension between his need to appear mature and his need to express fear." For Robert S. Phillips, in "Freaking Out: The Short Stories of Carson McCullers," an essay published in *Southwest Review* in 1978 and quoted by Judith Giblin James in *Wunderkind: The Reputation of Carson McCullers, 1940–1990*, "the story is marred by a pat ending, but Hugh's fear is made extraordinarily real. One does not soon forget his terror at the simple act of opening the upstairs bathroom door." In *Understanding Carson McCullers*, Virginia Spencer Carr notes that the story contains one of the few positive father figures in McCullers's fiction and concludes, "Although the ending is mawkish and lacks conviction, the reader appreciates the boy's emergence from moral isolation into self-knowledge." When McCullers's short stories were reprinted in 1987 as *Collected Stories*, Michiko Kakutani reviewed them in the *New York Times*. Although Kakutani does not single out "The Haunted Boy" directly for comment, her remark about the structure of many of the stories might well be applied to it. After using an example from one of McCullers's novels, Kakutani writes, "This moment when everything suddenly changes recurs in almost every one of these stories, dividing time irrevocably into a now and then, a before and after." In "The Haunted Boy," that would be the moment when Hugh discovered his mother after her suicide attempt. Kakutani's conclusion that McCullers's stories are not as effective as her novels, standing "as interesting, though minor, additions to the writer's oeuvre," is a view that many writers on McCullers share.

CRITICISM

Bryan Aubrey

Aubrey holds a Ph.D. in English. In the following essay, he discusses some of the autobiographical elements in "The Haunted Boy" and assesses the success of the story as a literary work.

The works of Carson McCullers are generally credited with having much insight into the demands and complexities of love, and what it feels like for people who are outsiders or in some way unable to create the emotional connections with others that they desperately need. McCullers writes about the human heart and the pain it endures when it cannot find the fulfillment that it seeks. She understands loneliness and isolation. In "The Haunted Boy," she is able to imagine

> OFTEN, ONE APPARENTLY DESIRABLE EMOTION CARRIES WITH IT AS A KIND OF UNDERTOW ANOTHER EMOTION THAT IS ITS OPPOSITE, AND THESE TWO (OR MORE) CONFLICTING EMOTIONS MAY NEVER BE HAPPILY RESOLVED."

herself into the mind and heart of a fourteen-year-old boy who has been dealt a devastating blow when he sees the mother he loves lying in the bathroom covered in blood following a suicide attempt. After that, Hugh endures loss and loneliness as his mother is confined to a hospital for three months to be treated for depression. For Hugh, these are three long months "strained with dullness and want and dread." All a teenage boy's need for his mother is contained in that short phrase, as well as his fear of what the future may hold. Hugh's sense of abandonment must be great, as is his stoicism. In all that time he never gives way to tears. He holds his emotions at bay and cuts himself off from most of his friends at school. But stoicism, although it may mask deeper feelings, does not remove them. Eventually they flare up, but even then, despite the story's apparently positive ending, they are not fully resolved.

Some of the roots of the story can be traced to elements in McCullers's own life. In 1948, like Hugh's mother in the story, she had a bout with depression and slashed her left wrist in what appeared to be a half-hearted suicide attempt. As a result, she was hospitalized at a psychiatric clinic in New York City for three weeks. The following year, also like the mother in the story, she had to have a pregnancy terminated because her doctors decided that giving birth would be too risky for her delicate health. Although it is not known precisely when the story was written, it was published in 1955, just five months after the death of McCullers's mother. McCullers had been very dependent on her mother for much of her life, especially following the suicide of her husband, Reeves, in November 1953. McCullers, however, was not happy with her state of dependency, so the mother-daughter relationship was not a comfortable one for her. Her

WHAT DO I READ NEXT?

- McCullers's novella, *The Ballad of the Sad Café*, first published in 1951, is considered one of her best works. Set in a small town in Georgia, it features Miss Amelia, who owns a small store, and the love affair she has with a hunchback named Cousin Lymon, which does not end happily. Critics have admired the sympathy with which McCullers handles her eccentric characters, and the novella is regarded as an outstanding contribution to the literature of the grotesque. It is available in McCullers's *The Ballad of the Sad Café, and Other Stories* (2005).

- *The Complete Stories* by Flannery O'Connor (1971) contains thirty-one stories by one of McCullers's southern contemporaries. It gives an overall picture of O'Connor's contribution to twentieth-century literature. Like McCullers, O'Connor died young, at the age of thirty-nine, but not before she had created a niche for herself with her distinctive southern gothic tales.

- *The Collected Stories of Eudora Welty* (1982) contains forty-one stories by another of McCullers's contemporaries, Eudora Welty, who also hailed from the South and was one of the most distinguished American writers of the twentieth century. This volume also contains a preface written by the author.

- *Sixteen: Short Stories by Outstanding Writers for Young Adults* (1985), edited by Donald R. Gallo, contains sixteen stories by well-known writers for young adults on a range of themes that will be of interest to teenagers, including friendship, love, and families. The book includes a questions section that encourages readers to delve more deeply into some of the issues that the stories raise.

- *13: Thirteen Stories That Capture the Agony and Ecstasy of Being Thirteen* (2003), edited by James Howe, is a collection of stories about what it feels like to be thirteen and the kinds of situations that are likely to arise when one is that age.

- In *Best African American Fiction 2010*, the second volume of an annual edition, series editor Gerald Lyn Early and guest editor Nikki Giovanni select the best recent short stories and novel excerpts by African American authors. Writers represented include established and new authors, including Edwidge Danticat, Colson Whitehead, Amina Gautier, Jewell Parker Rhodes, and Desiree Cooper. There are historical and contemporary pieces in a wide variety of settings; of particular interest is the young-adult novel excerpt "Mary Jane," by Dorothy Sterling.

---

biographer, Virginia Spencer Carr, in her book *The Lonely Hunter: A Biography of Carson McCullers*, points out that in all of McCullers's fiction, she did not once create a happy, positive relationship between a mother and a daughter. Carr connects this to "The Haunted Boy," arguing that the seeds of the story "lay both in her feelings about Reeves's death by suicide and her worry and ambivalent attitude toward her mother." Carr highlights Hugh's sudden feeling of hatred for his friend John, quoting the phrase from the story, "as you hate people you have to need so badly." Carr

concludes by pointing out that all those who knew McCullers well realized that in this story she was "reacting to a severe love-hatred-and-guilt relationship which she tried, unsuccessfully, to suppress, while at the same time, to hide from her mother." There is, if this analysis is to be accepted, some creative disguise going on, since the gender of the main character in the story is male rather than female. Perhaps this was an attempt by the author to gain some perspective and distance from her immediate emotional entanglements so she could present the situation through a more objective eye.

Seeking elucidation of a literary work by examining biographical details is an interesting task, if only because it provides an excuse to engage in a kind of gossip about a famous person whom one did not actually know in person. But such piecing together of the origins of a story in the biography of the author says nothing about the quality of the final product: Is it a good story? Is it worth one's time reading it? With a few exceptions, McCullers's short fiction has not fared that well with critics, who regard her novels as her greater achievement. Richard M. Cook, for example, in his book *Carson McCullers*, comments that McCullers's best writing possesses a "rare sympathy for and insight into hidden suffering," but Cook finds this present only in the novels, compared to which all the short stories "seem trivial and thin."

Can "The Haunted Boy" escape such a charge of triviality? Certainly the story has some merit. Some might find it an example of exactly that "insight into hidden suffering" that Cook discovers only in the novels. In such a view, McCullers has painted a convincing portrait of the inner world of a boy who has endured a severe trauma in his life and who is slowly coming to an understanding that emotions can be very complex things. Often, one apparently desirable emotion carries with it as a kind of undertow another emotion that is its opposite, and these two (or more) conflicting emotions may never be happily resolved. Hugh is also beginning to learn that every individual lives alone with his or her deepest emotions, and it is not always easy or even possible to communicate them to others as part of an attempt to alleviate one's loneliness.

Elements of the structure of the story would surely also be admired by most readers. There is a very effective, slowly building sense of foreboding in this story: the, at first, unexplained terror of this boy who has had all his security taken from him; and his fear, also unexplained in the beginning, of being left alone in an empty house, as if he is afraid of ghosts. (He is, after all, "the haunted boy.") The tension builds for the reader just as it does for Hugh, and McCullers provides just enough information to keep the reader turning the page, such as the ominous way the "closed white bathroom door" is mentioned and how it revives in Hugh memories of "the other time," which is as yet unexplained. The climactic, tension-filled moments when Hugh actually climbs the stairs and enters the bathroom come about two-thirds of the way through the story, and only then does the reader learn exactly what it was that so traumatized Hugh in that "other time." After he discovers that no terrible thing awaits him there this time, the relief is such that all his repressed emotions suddenly start pouring out. The dramatic pacing of the story, and the authenticity of these climactic moments, are most effectively done.

On the other hand, the story has what some might see as a serious flaw. This concerns the ending, which has a tacked-on feeling. There is a sudden shift, marked on the printed page by a blank line, from the boy's interaction with his mother—so fraught with miscommunication—to a later interaction he has with his father, who up to this point has not appeared in the story. The scene the father has with his son is sentimental: everything is going to be all right now, they will all three go on summer picnics together, and Hugh really is becoming a man. It is as if the earlier issues exposed in the story are now no longer consequential, since at the end Hugh feels that he is, as a result of his talk with his dad, "no longer a haunted boy." But one cannot help but feel that this ending is unsatisfactory and contrary to the tenor of what precedes it. No drafts survive of McCullers's manuscript, so it is impossible to know how the story evolved in her mind, but it is almost as if for some reason she felt that the story needed a happy ending, although this could hardly be said to be true of any of her other work. If the reader simply ignores the final scene and imagines the story ending with Hugh's words "All afternoon I felt—odd" followed by perhaps a sentence or two of reflection on the significance of that comment, it might well be a more powerful story, more singular in its focus and more steadfast in what it conveys. After all, the point of the story, happy ending notwithstanding, is surely that the boy cannot communicate with his mother. Even when he overcomes his hostile outburst and is warm toward her, he has not removed the causes of his anger and resentment, of which his mother remains entirely oblivious. A few minutes of happy talk between father and son is not likely to assuage this deep-seated ambivalence in Hugh's feelings or their explosive power. Things may be patched up for now, but the lack of communication between mother and son suggests that it is only a matter of time before conflict breaks out again.

Hugh found her lying on the floor in a pool of blood. *(Edw / Shutterstock.com)*

Source: Bryan Aubrey, Critical Essay on "The Haunted Boy," in *Short Stories for Students*, Gale, Cengage Learning, 2011.

Cynthia Wu

In the following excerpt, Wu concludes that in McCullers's stories the author examines the subject of race relations by "introducing the possibility of ethnic difference among whites."

In Carson McCullers'... collection of short stories, *The Ballad of the Sad Café and Other Stories*, issues of ethnic difference, white racialization, and the negotiation of identities play a central role. This is not surprising, considering that the loosely imagined body of texts known as "the Southern Renaissance" has a strong preoccupation with these themes. Southern writers, both Anglo- and African American, have long foregrounded the "race question" in representing and imagining the New South following the Civil War, and McCullers is no exception. Her characters grapple with what it means to be white in the South, what it means *not* to be white, and what it means to challenge or comply with the standards of whiteness. However, what differentiates *The Ballad of the Sad Café and Other Stories* from most other pieces of southern literature is the relative absence of African American characters. If, as many theorists of race in the United States have pointed out, notions of "black" and notions of "white" are mutually constitutive and exist in a hierarchical binary, can whiteness ever be reconceptualized in a way that does not define it against and above blackness? In other words, can "white" exist apart from "black"?

I argue that McCullers attempts to answer "yes" to such questions by introducing European immigrant characters into southern fiction. This gesture interrogates white southern identity through means other than comparisons to black southern identity. It is important to note that the absence of African American characters in this collection of stories is not an oversight that resulted from presenting some new form of ethnic difference. Rather, this absence is functional. It serves to isolate and explore in some depth a new valance of race emerging in the New South without having to revert to the well-trodden path of imagining racialization within the black-white binary.

McCullers' conceptual replacement of the African American with the European immigrant in her examination of racial and ethnic difference has its counterpart in southern labor history. During the late-nineteenth and early-twentieth centuries, many southern states launched campaigns to attract European immigrants in response to the labor shortages caused by black migration to the West and Southwest immediately after the Civil War and to the North during the Great Migration. For a South struggling to rebuild itself both economically and ideologically, European immigrant labor seemed a viable and even more favorable replacement for black labor.

An avid recruiter of European immigrant labor in the years immediately following the Civil War, Richard Hathaway Edmonds founded a white-supremacist newsletter called the *Manufacturers' Record* to provide coverage on southern industry and capitalism. Edmonds launched the aggressive campaign to recruit laborers from Europe as a way to compensate for the declining black laborer population in the South. However, he intended for only immigrants of Anglo- and northern European stock to fulfill his goals. By the 1880s, the wave of immigrants from these areas gave way to those from eastern and southern Europe. This new influx of immigrants, Edmonds believed, did not assimilate properly and threatened the Anglo-European racial integrity of the South. By the 1920s, the *Manufacturers' Record* reversed its stance toward immigration, embracing nativist sentiments along with the rest of the United States and becoming one of the most vocal anti-immigrant publications.

Even if the South's desire for white immigrant labor had not been conflicted from the start, the region's attractiveness to European newcomers paled in comparison to that of the North. Southern historian Martha G. Synott argues that the South's attempt to lure and retain immigrants was doomed from the beginning because it lacked the high wages and inexpensive land that could be found in the North. And from the point of view of the employers, southern landowners were more willing to exploit black labor because of their impression that Jim Crow laws regulated the autonomy of blacks, making them more docile and reliable than immigrants. Moreover, the European immigrants were seen as being both lax about racial segregation and racially different in themselves. This impression only caused more problems for a South that still held on to ideals of maintaining Anglo-American supremacy.

This contentious dynamic between black labor and European immigrant labor was not isolated to the South nor was it new to the post-Civil War period. The northern economies and the southern economies were interdependent; labor and economic developments in the North had a bearing on the South and vice versa. The already sizable European immigrant presence in the northern states by the end of the nineteenth century affected the demographics of the laborer population in the southern states. Two separate articles by historian Jay R. Mandle, who takes a qualitative approach, and economist William J. Collins, who relies on empirical data, assert that European immigration to the North discouraged the entry of southern blacks and delayed the Great Migration. Historian Noel Ignatiev claims that during the nineteenth century, capitalism pitted the economic interests of Irish immigrants against those of slaves and free blacks. This maneuver, which met the North's labor demands, prolonged slavery in the South and the economic exploitation of free blacks on a national scale.

Both the conceptual and actual replacement of the black southerner with the European immigrant in the economy of the South finds its literary analog in McCullers' short fiction. Just as the one could not easily be replaced by the other in the southern economy without reaping certain ideological repercussions, this substitution in McCullers' literature creates a similar shockwave in the fabric of southern whiteness. Whereas African American characters had traditionally performed the function—or, the labor—of signifying ethno-racial difference in white southern literature, McCullers replaces them with European immigrants who perform the same task, albeit with different results. As I mentioned earlier, the absence of African American characters in this collection of McCullers' short fiction does not result from neglect: as she demonstrates in other texts, McCullers creates complex African American characters and interrogates the black-white racial divide in intricate ways. *The Member of the Wedding* (1946) is one example, and *The Heart is a Lonely Hunter* (1940) contains both African American and European immigrant characters. However, at this stage of the Southern Renaissance, the absence of African Americans characters in *The*

Ballad of the Sad Café and Other Stories is an enabling device. It becomes a strategic way of isolating white ethnic difference in reconceptualizing white identities in the New South....

Source: Cynthia Wu, "Expanding Southern Whiteness: Reconceptualizing Ethnic Difference in the Short Fiction of Carson McCullers," in *Southern Literary Journal*, Vol. 34, No. 1, Fall 2001, pp. 44–55.

Virginia Spencer Carr

In the following excerpt, Carr discusses McCullers's short fiction, placing it in the larger context of her overall artistic output.

McCullers was a much-acclaimed author and playwright both in America and abroad when her omnibus edition, *The Ballad of the Sad Café: The Novels and Short Stories of Carson McCullers*, appeared a few weeks after *The Member of the Wedding* closed its long and successful run on Broadway. Although all of the stories (with the exception of "A Domestic Dilemma") had appeared in such magazines as the *New Yorker*, *Mademoiselle*, and *Harper's Bazaar*, they had never before been brought together in a single volume. Thus, with her three novels, a novella, and six short stories published in a single volume, McCullers was able to reach new readers. Reviewers and scholars alike praised her mastery of the short story and continued to commend her skill as a novelist. Pleased by the book's critical reception, Houghton Mifflin brought out a year later (1952) still another collected edition of McCullers's work, *The Ballad of the Sad Café and Collected Short Stories*, which included the novella and the same short stories that had appeared in the original volume, but excluded the novels since they had become readily available in paperback. A reprint edition, published in 1955, included a new story, "The Haunted Boy."

McCullers's posthumous collection, *The Mortgaged Heart* (1971), contained three stories that had not been collected previously ("Correspondence," "Art and Mr. Mahoney," and "Who Has Seen the Wind?") and a handful of apprentice stories that had never been published. It also included many of McCullers's nonfiction pieces and a half dozen poems. Nothing else was published of McCullers except reprint editions and foreign translations of individual works until a much needed new volume, *Collected Stories of Carson McCullers: Including The Member of the Wedding and The Ballad of the Sad Café*, appeared in 1987.

THROUGHOUT MCCULLERS'S CANON, IT IS NOTEWORTHY THAT THE CHILDREN SHE DEPICTS HAVE NO STRONG EMOTIONAL TIES WITH THEIR MOTHERS."

In tale after tale, regardless of its date of composition, the conflicts depicted by McCullers are intensified by the "immense complexity of love," a phrase that the author coined for one of her most successful short stories, "A Domestic Dilemma." Such love may be between a husband and his wife, an adolescent piano pupil and her teacher, a simple boy and a male cousin he idolizes, a "haunted" youth and his suicidal mother, a seemingly indifferent mother and her tubercular daughter, a jockey and his injured friend, a young girl "in love with a wedding" (or enamored of a Brazilian pen pal who never writes back), an Amazonian woman and a hunchback dwarf, and countless other fictional potential conjoinings that never quite materialize. Most of the latent love relationships in McCullers's short fiction never reach maturity, and for good reason. As her narrator expressed it in *The Ballad of the Sad Café* (and evident, as well, throughout her writings), "The value and quality of any love is determined solely by the lover himself," and such myopic vision by its very nature destines one's love to go unnoticed or bitterly unrequited.

To McCullers, a lover was always vulnerable unless he loved someone—or some thing—from whom he expected nothing in return. In "A Tree. A Rock. A Cloud.," a beery tramp confides to a pink-eared newspaper boy, a stranger to him, his "science of love," which he conceived after being abandoned by his wife. The tramp's sterile formula has led him to love things that cannot love back—first, a goldfish, then a tree, a rock, a cloud. But he invites the catcalls of mill workers in the all-night café in which he accosts the child and tells him: "Son! Hey Son!... I love you." Despite his declaration, the tramp knows that he can walk out alone into the predawn silence and never see his so-called "beloved" again. Loving a woman is the "last step" to his science, he tells the boy. "I go cautious. And I am not quite ready yet." The reader feels intuitively that the dissolute tramp will never be ready for the final step. He will not risk again his vulnerability to *eros*.

Whereas all of McCullers's novels are set in the South, only six of her short stories—"A Tree. A Rock. A Cloud.," "Art and Mr. Mahoney," "The Haunted Boy," "The March," and two apprentice pieces, "Breath from the Sky" and "The Aliens"—make such a setting explicit. At least ten of her stories have obvious settings in the North, and three of her earliest stories ("Sucker," "Like That," and "The Orphanage") have settings that could be anywhere (although the characters, dialogue, and events offer a kind of southern authenticity to the setting, which could well be McCullers's hometown in Georgia or the fictional towns in which *The Heart Is a Lonely Hunter* and *The Member of the Wedding* are set). Her characters who do, in fact, live in the North are often transplanted southerners whose home region remains a memory of pain and anguish.

Despite the acclaim of McCullers's short fiction over the years, little criticism was devoted to the work as a whole until 1978, when Robert Phillips's excellent critical discussion, "Freaking Out: The Short Stories of Carson McCullers" added a new dimension to McCullers scholarship. Phillips demonstrated that most of the characters in her short stories behave quite normally on the surface, yet suffer an "inner freaking-out." Though they exhibit none of the vagaries or physical grotesqueries common to the characters in her longer works, they are immobilized as "spiritual isolates of circumstance."

Another significant characteristic unique to the short stories is the way in which McCullers transformed her personal reality into fiction. Whereas readers who know something of McCullers's girlhood in Georgia (or who knew the author personally) can recognize readily the autobiographical elements in the novels—especially in her depiction of Mick Kelly, Frankie Addams, and Jester Clane—the self-portraits in her short fiction are more cleverly disguised. On the other hand, McCullers's husband appears almost full cloth in three of the short stories: "Instant of the Hour After," "Who Has Seen the Wind?" and "A Domestic Dilemma." In the novels, Reeves McCullers can be recognized only in the characterization of Jake Blount.

... Throughout McCullers's canon, it is noteworthy that the children she depicts have no strong emotional ties with their mothers. Lamar Smith believed that his sister "did not want to strip herself 'that bare' and reveal her utter dependency" on their mother. "Sister was too vulnerable," he continued. "She was our mother's favorite child, and somehow my sister Rita and I understood this. We were convinced that Sister was a genius, and that our mother was, also, for letting that genius flower." McCullers's fictional mothers—if they are mentioned at all—either die in childbirth, as does Frankie's in *The Member of the Wedding*; are too preoccupied with helping to support the family when the father cannot, as does Mick's in *The Heart Is a Lonely Hunter*; drink too much, as does Emily Meadows in "A Domestic Dilemma"; or attempt suicide, as does Hugh's in "The Haunted Boy." On the other hand, the fathers in her fiction are treated rather compassionately. Like Mick's and Frankie's fathers, they suffer because they fail to communicate with their daughters, who are only vaguely aware of their sense of loss and appear reticent to deal with them directly.

... In "The Haunted Boy," another story of wounded adolescence and rejection set in Georgia, Hugh is haunted by the fear that he will return from school one day and discover his mother lying in a pool of blood on the bathroom floor, just as he had discovered her a few months earlier after a failed suicide attempt that resulted in her being sent to the state mental hospital in Milledgeville. Although the boy's mother has recovered and is back home when the story opens, Hugh cannot forgive his mother for what he sees as her attempt to abandon him. The boy's hostility and sense of guilt drive him to his friend John for succor, but John is insensitive to Hugh's unspoken needs, and, thus, cannot share his burden. Hugh recognizes in his distress, finally, that he hates John, reasoning that "you hate people you have to need so badly!"

Young Hugh's admission reflects the ambivalence of McCullers's own feelings toward her mother, with whom she felt increasingly uncomfortable (in direct proportion to her dependency upon her) after her husband's suicide. Yet in making her protagonist an adolescent boy (a gender disguise that the author employed in much of her fiction), McCullers successfully objectified her ambivalent love-hate-guilt feelings, feelings that she tried repeatedly to suppress in her life and to conceal from her mother. Friends of McCullers who knew her mother may have viewed the tale as a thinly disguised fiction of a "haunted girl." McCullers probably began work on the story in 1954, but the exact date of composition is unknown. Her mother died of a bleeding ulcer in 1955, five months before "The Haunted Boy"—ultimately yet another version of the author's thesis on love presented in *The Ballad of the Sad Café*—was published.

McCullers ends this tale, too, in strange fashion compared to her usual final resolutions. It is Hugh's father who now partially redeems him. Whereas he had distanced himself from his son during his wife's crisis, he now praises Hugh for his courage in accepting the experience and treats him like a grown-up for the first time. "The Haunted Boy" provides one of the few father figures in McCullers's fiction who make any positive impression upon a son or daughter. Although the ending is mawkish and lacks conviction, the reader appreciates the boy's emergence from moral isolation into self-knowledge.

Source: Virginia Spencer Carr, "The Short Fiction," in *Understanding Carson McCullers*, University of South Carolina Press, 1990, pp. 127–63.

Patricia P. Kelly

In the following essay, Kelly discusses how much of McCullers's short fiction reveals a sense of the pain and loneliness associated with adolescence.

From the publication of *The Heart Is a Lonely Hunter* (Boston: Houghton Mifflin, 1940) at twenty-three-years-old to *Clock Without Hands* (Boston: Houghton Mifflin, 1961), her last novel, Carson McCullers received wide literary acclaim. Unfortunately, her work has rarely appeared in high school anthologies even though much of it reveals a special sense of adolescence and the loneliness and pain associated with the growing awareness of self and others.

The Mortgaged Heart (Boston: Houghton Mifflin, 1971), published after McCullers' death, collects some of her little known and formerly unpublished work. Some of the early stories develop youthful characters who reappear briefly in later novels. In "Sucker," written when McCullers herself was a teenager, Pete's current desire for Maybelle's attention takes precedence over Sucker's needs. Sucker, an orphaned cousin,

> THE FANTASTIC AND GROTESQUE TALES, OFTEN RELATED BY BLACK SERVANTS, ARE A WAY OF TAKING US OUTSIDE THE WORLD OF THE CHARACTERS INTO THE LARGER CULTURE."

worships the older boy and tried to gain Pete's approval in much the way that Pete longs for Maybelle's attention. When Maybelle rejects Pete, he verbally attacks Sucker, who decides to be a "sucker" no more. He hardens with hate, and changes radically. The relationship is damaged beyond repair. An awareness of what it means to be female is the focus of "Like That," also an early short story. The younger sister rejects the notion of wearing lipstick and stockings, coping with bodily changes, and crying over boys. She doesn't want to grow up "if it's like that." In "Breath from the Sky," Constance, a teenager set apart from her family because of tuberculosis, grapples with the loneliness they cannot enter, and her illness consumes the longings of emerging womanhood. Two other adolescents in McCullers' short stories realize the tenuousness of their dependence on others. When the youthful Hugh in "The Haunted Boy" finds his mother with slashed wrists, his protected childhood comes to an end. The horror of the incident and the fear that it will happen again, although his mother has apparently recovered from her breakdown, haunts him. Even though life for him has taken on its former warmth and order, he no longer innocently trusts that it will continue. In a different way, Frances in "Wunderkind" finds her life in disarray. Mister Bilderbach, her piano teacher, has treated her as a daughter but chooses to reject her totally when her talent does not develop as it should. Frances returns to a family she has long before mentally abandoned, stripped of dreams for the future.

Three of McCullers' novels contain distinctive, fully characterized teenagers. In the fourteen months covered by *The Heart Is a Lonely Hunter*, Mick Kelly goes from a tomboyish childhood to responsible womanhood, from unlimited possibilities to the restraints of a ten-hour-a-day job, suppressing her own needs for those of her family. Leaving the grubby clothes of childhood behind, she attempts to gain social success, only to have her prom party erupt into a brawl. Mick's first sexual experience with Harry leaves her convinced there are better things in life but devastates Harry, whose moral convictions will not allow him to forgive himself. They part, both the worse for the encounter. An intelligent, potentially gifted musician but a victim of the Depression, Mick quits school to work in a five-and-dime store. When toward the end she can no longer hear the music in her head, we despair because she has joined the town's living dead; her dreams are gone and daily survival has replaced them. The novel's four other characters: John Singer, the deaf mute; Jake Flount, the union organizer; Dr. Copeland, the black physician; and Biff Brannon, the restaurant owner, are interwoven with Mick's story, but hers is the most powerful because it touches our own experiences. We can distance ourselves from the bizarre events in the others' lives, for that is the rest of the world, but Mick is the youth in each of us.

Frankie Addams in *The Member of the Wedding* (Boston: Houghton Mifflin, 1946) typified that period between childhood and adolescence. Her name changes trace that development. *Frankie* is the too large twelve-year-old with grimy, calloused feet, crusty elbows, and cropped hair. *F. Jasmine*, a name she chooses to match her new image, wears an organdy dress and patent leather shoes but still has crusty elbows. *Frances*, the adolescent with scrubbed elbows, emerges with more self-control and awareness of others. For Frankie, her brother's wedding becomes a symbol of belonging: "they are the we of me." If they accept her into the wedding and into their lives, she imagines her own existence will gain meaning. She, of course, has no understanding of the magnitude of her expectations. After her public embarrassment of throwing herself into the street behind the couple's departing car, crying, "Take me with you," *Frankie* must come to terms with the rejection. As *Frances* she begins the struggle to shape her own life.

Jester Clane, an older adolescent in *Clock Without Hands*, rejects his grandfather's views of justice and the South and struggles to assert a human rights position in a community tied to the past. The generations clash, the new order

replaces the old, and Judge Clane with others like him count time on a clock without hands. Events are inevitable, but their time is not clearly marked. Jester is able to maintain his position because the larger society supports it, whereas his father had committed suicide, unable to sustain his stand for social justice against stronger forces.

The motivating forces of loneliness, however, are not confined to adolescent characters who define themselves in relation to others. Like Frankie, who seeks a "we of me," the characters in *The Heart Is a Lonely Hunter* turn to the deaf mute Singer as a tie-line, a person somehow different who can keep loneliness from washing them away. Singer turns to an equally ineffectual source, Antonapoulos, a huge, insensitive moron, totally incapable of responding to Singer's needs. Antonapoulos' death breaks Singer's lifeline and he commits suicide. Protagonists in *The Ballad of the Sad Cafe and Collected Short Stories* (Boston: Houghton Mifflin, 1952) come to terms with their loneliness in different ways. When John Ferris in "The Sojourner" visits his former wife, the emptiness of his own life surfaces as he watches her with a child. He resolves to alter the course of his life, but we sense that any changes will not last. In "A Domestic Dilemma," Martin knows his wife's alcoholism will destroy their lives, but he realizes his need for her will keep him in the miserable, lonely existence.

This need for somebody, anybody, to help push back the dark loneliness drives Miss Amelia, in *The Ballad of the Sad Cafe*, to battle for Cousin Lymon's love. Miss Amelia, a man-sized woman, does not want to face life without Cousin Lymon, a hunch-back, who has made the cafe the center of social activity for the town and brought her back into the community. The return of her former husband Marvin Macy threatens to end the order of her life because Cousin Lymon becomes infatuated with Marvin. In a culminating battle in which love, hate, and retribution are inextricably interwoven, Miss Amelia loses. This novel is perhaps the most macabre of McCullers' fiction because no ordinary characters intervene to stop the madness.

From a teaching perspective, several of McCullers' short stories are excellent for classroom instruction, particularly "Sucker" and "Like That." Of her longer works *The Member of the Wedding* appears in both dramatic and novel form, giving it adaptability to various reading and interest levels or to comparative study. The work also focuses on a preteen; Frankie's problems are complex while those of the characters around her are never expanded. Another useful source in planning teaching approaches for McCullers' fiction is the "Author's Outline of The Mute," (later developed as *The Heart Is a Lonely Hunter* and found in *The Mortgaged Heart*). Looking at an author's plans for theme, character, and plot development and matching these against the final text can reveal a great deal about the writer's craft. Changes are evident, and the motivations for some of them are explored in Virginia Spencer Carr's biography, *The Lonely Hunter* (New York: Doubleday, 1975), a comprehensive source of background material.

Writing generally in the Southern milieu, McCullers often intermingles bizarre and ordinary characters and events. The fantastic and grotesque tales, often related by black servants, are a way of taking us outside the world of the characters into the larger culture. Some tales tantalize—begun but never finished—making us feel much like Frankie Addams and Jester Clane, who "despise... half a story." But they and we keep coming back for more.

Source: Patricia P. Kelly, "Recommended: Carson McCullers," in *English Journal*, Vol. 71, No. 6, October 1982, pp. 67–68.

SOURCES

Boyd, Lydia, "Brief History of the Television Industry," in *Duke Universities Digital Collections*, http://library.duke.edu/digitalcollections/adaccess/radio-tv.html (accessed June 1, 2010).

———, "Brief History of the Radio Industry," in *Duke Universities Digital Collections*, http://library.duke.edu/digitalcollections/adaccess/radio-tv.html (accessed June 1, 2010).

"A Brief History of Depression," in *emental-health.com*, http://www.emental-health.com/depr_history.htm#1950s, (accessed June 1, 2010).

Carr, Virginia Spencer, *The Lonely Hunter: A Biography of Carson McCullers*, Doubleday, 1975, pp. 417–18.

———, *Understanding Carson McCullers*, University of South Carolina Press, 1990, p. 152.

Cook, Richard M., *Carson McCullers*, Frederick Ungar, 1975, pp. 123, 126.

James, Judith Giblin, *Wunderkind: The Reputation of Carson McCullers, 1940–1990*, Camden House, 1995, p. 183.

Kakutani, Michiko, Review of *Collected Stories*, in *New York Times*, July 14, 1987.

Lagadeg, Hakim, "The History and Evolution of Television," in *Helium*, http://www.helium.com/items/567178-the-history-and-evolution-of-television-the-1940s-and-1950s (accessed June 1, 2010).

McCullers, Carson, "The Haunted Boy," in *Collected Short Stories and the Novel: The Ballad of the Sad Café*, Houghton Mifflin, 1955, pp. 106–17.

McDowell, Margaret B., *Carson McCullers*, Twayne's United States Author Series, No. 354, Twayne Publishers, 1980, p. 119.

Rabkin, Judith, "Public Attitudes Toward Mental Illness: A Review of the Literature," in *Schizophrenia Bulletin*, No. 10, Fall 1974, http://schizophreniabulletin.oxfordjournals.org/cgi/reprint/1/10/9.pdf (accessed June 3, 2010).

FURTHER READING

Bloom, Harold, ed., *Carson McCullers*, Modern Critical Views, Chelsea House, 2009.
> This is a collection of critical essays that cover a range of McCullers's fiction and its place in American literature. It includes a chronology and a bibliography, as well as an introduction by Bloom.

Savigneau, Josyane, *Carson McCullers: A Life*, translated by Joan E. Howard, Houghton Mifflin, 2001.
> This biography is sympathetic to McCullers, whom Savigneau regards as a great writer. The biographer discusses many unpublished manuscripts and letters by McCullers, although she does not include any detailed analysis of the works. This is a useful book although it does not replace the earlier biography by Virginia Spencer Carr.

Tippins, Sherrill, *February House: The Story of W. H. Auden, Carson McCullers, Jane and Paul Bowles, Benjamin Britten, and Gypsy Rose Lee, Under One Roof in Brooklyn*, Mariner Books, 2006.
> This is an entertaining account of the bohemian group of writers, theater people, composers, and intellectuals who shared a house in Brooklyn, New York, in 1940.

Westling, Louise, *Sacred Groves and Ravaged Gardens: The Fiction of Eudora Welty, Carson McCullers, and Flannery O'Connor*, University of Georgia Press, 1985.
> In this study, Westling examines the impact of the culture of the South on the work of

Eudora Welty, Carson McCullers, and Flannery O'Connor. She places particular emphasis on the role of women.

SUGGESTED SEARCH TERMS

Carson McCullers

Carson McCullers AND The Haunted Boy

mental illness AND 1950s

Carson McCullers AND short fiction

depression AND suicide

McCullers AND coming-of-age

southern women writers

Reeves McCullers

Carson McCullers AND southern literature

point of view in fiction writing

The House of Asterion

JORGE LUIS BORGES

1947

The Argentine writer Jorge Luis Borges was veritably raised in his father's library and proceeded to spend his life making profound contributions to libraries around the world as the preeminent Latin American author of his era and a patriarch of postmodernism. The stories of his two most famous collections, *Ficciones* (1944) and *El Aleph* (1949), present the characteristic Borgesian blend of metaphysical quandaries, intricate plotlines, mortal circumstances, and startled revelations on the part of both characters and reader. For "La casa de Asterión" ("The House of Asterion"), Borges drew on Greek mythology and the ancient version of one of his favorite symbols, the labyrinth, to fashion a cryptic story to fill a few blank pages for the literary magazine *Los Anales de Buenos Aires* as it was going to press in the spring of 1947. The story was subsequently published in *El Aleph*.

Advancing through the story, the reader gleans from the first-person account that the narrator is a seclusive and increasingly peculiar aristocrat, only to find at the end that the Minotaur—with the body of a man and the head of a bull—has told of his life in the labyrinth. The Minotaur was slain by Theseus, whose casual aside on the beast's fairly indifferent death explicitly reveals the creature's identity to the reader to close the story. Borges was inspired to write this story in part by an 1896 painting by G. K. Watts, *The Minotaur*, which depicts the muscular torso and taurine (bull-like)

Jorge Luis Borges (*The Library of Congress*)

head of a pensive and subtly pathetic Minotaur looking out to sea, with a bird crushed under his left hand. "The House of Asterion" has appeared in Borges's English-language volumes *Labyrinths* (1962) and *Collected Fictions* (1998).

AUTHOR BIOGRAPHY

Borges was born in Buenos Aires, Argentina, on August 24, 1899, into an upper-class family of Spanish, Portuguese, and English heritage. Both of his grandfathers were Argentine military officers of high rank, while his father was a lawyer and a modestly accomplished man of letters, having published a novel as well as the premier Spanish translation of the Persian poetry of Omar Khayyám. As a boy who showed signs of frailness at a young age, including a congenital

eye defect from his father's side, Borges led a sheltered childhood. Because of his father's distrust of the nation's educational system, he did not attend school until he was nine years old. In the meantime, he was enthralled by his father's library—a place he would reminiscence fondly about as an adult—and read voraciously, showing early interest in the English-language work of authors such as Robert Louis Stevenson, Rudyard Kipling, Charles Dickens, Oscar Wilde, Edgar Allan Poe, and Mark Twain. He would later remark, once he became a phenomenally successful author, that he almost felt as though he had never left his father's library. He published a translation of a Wilde story into Spanish at age nine. Through boyhood, he read the popular gaucho novels—South American Westerns—of Eduardo Gutiérrez and lamented being bookish rather than inclined to action.

Borges's family traveled to Europe in 1914 and were unable to return to Argentina because of the outbreak of World War I. Borges finished high school in Geneva, Switzerland. He began his literary career as a poet in Spain in the early 1920s, as part of the avant-garde *ultraísmo* movement, inspired in part by expressionism, Dadaism, and cubism. Borges returned to Buenos Aires and frequently contributed poems and essays to literary journals, including two he founded. He drew on his expansive knowledge of classic texts in various languages and of theories from various movements in writing essays on Argentine culture, on his beliefs about the art of literature, and on an array of obscure topics. Experimenting with a longer form, in 1930 he wrote *Evaristo Carriego*, a biography of a poet friend of the family, which became dominated by Borges's fascination with old-time Buenos Aires and its guitar-playing, knife-fighting hoodlums. In 1935 he published *A Universal History of Infamy*, humorously relating the lives of eclectic villains in a parody of respectful biography. On Christmas Eve in 1938, he struck his head against a window that had been recently painted and left open and developed blood poisoning, leaving him on the brink of death. After he recovered, he feared failing in a familiar genre and instead tried writing a short story—and that would be the literary form in which he would most excel. His first effort was "Pierre Menard, Author of the Quixote," which describes the efforts of Menard to conceive a text, utterly of his own volition, that happens to be identical to Miguel de Cervantes's masterpiece *Don Quixote*.

Borges produced two collections of short stories, *Ficciones* (1944) and *El Aleph* (1949), that in certain senses transcended the genre as it was then known. Borges's stories tend to be heavily philosophical, to manipulate the boundaries between author and story and between story and reader, and to subjugate the characters to the plot; they are often referred to, using the term of the 1944 title, as "fictions." Publishing various further works of short fiction and nonfiction while teaching and lecturing extensively, Borges gradually gained renown in the Spanish-speaking world, especially after the dictatorship of Juan Perón, to which Borges was vocally opposed, was brought down in 1955. He and the Irish playwright Samuel Beckett were co-awarded the prestigious International Publishers' Formentor Prize in 1961, and English language translations of his work began appearing in 1962. Though he eventually went blind because of his eye defect, Borges lived out his life as one of the world's most accomplished writers, writing, teaching, and lecturing throughout the Americas and beyond. *The Book of Sand* (1975) was his last substantial short-story collection. Borges returned to Geneva, Switzerland, where he died of liver cancer on June 14, 1986.

PLOT SUMMARY

"The House of Asterion" opens with an epigraph from the *Library*, or *Bibliotheca*, attributed to Apollodorus, although the ancient Greek scholar Apollodorus of Athens (circa 180–120 BCE) is understood by modern scholars to have predated the *Library*; the work must have been completed by another (or others). The epigraph indicates that Asterion is a prince. Only a reader extremely well versed in Greek mythology would recognize the obscure original name of the Minotaur. It has been noted that this supposed quotation is not identical to the source text—a misquotation that can be seen as legitimate in the context of a fictional story.

The narrator opens by admitting the negative qualities his detractors accuse him of. This admission suggests that the narrator is honest, but the qualities he mentions—arrogance, misanthropy, and madness—suggest that even if he is honest, he may be either delusional or unintentionally deceitful. When the narrator states that he will punish the accusations "in due time," the reader may wonder whether the narrator actually has the power to do so—especially since he professes not to leave his house. The footnote regarding Asterion's use of "fourteen" as meaning "infinite" can be understood as coming from a scholar or historian who has analyzed this text. The statement about the indefinite number of doors to the house being always open, to both men and animals, offers the first indication of the strangeness of the house itself and of the animalistic nature of the narrator.

With the comments on the absence of "womanly splendors," gaudy decor, and even furniture, the narrator seems a monk of the highest order. The narrator claims that there is no other house like his—but the scholar Gene Bell-Villada, in *Borges and His Fiction*, notes that other ancient Greeks did write of a labyrinth in Egypt, built by Amenemhe III around 2300 BCE. The reader's suspicion that Asterion, named in the title and the epigraph, must be narrating this first-person account is confirmed halfway through the first paragraph, where Asterion names himself in asserting that he is not a prisoner.

In his account of an afternoon of going out into the streets, Asterion gives the impression that his royal lineage was the cause for the people's worshipful behavior. Used to his own taurine face, Asterion notes the "colorless faces, flat as the palm of one's hand" of the people, where his own human hands would indeed match those faces. Of course, seeing the Minotaur at dusk, the people presumably feel and act on feelings of great terror, and the reader may glean from textual clues that the people are frightened of, not reverent toward, Asterion. A *stylobate* is a Greek architectural feature, a flat part supporting columns. The reference to a "temple of the Axes" may or may not be intended to refer to a specific Greek temple; a root of the word *labyrinth* is *labrys*, a double-edged axe, and Borges may have been offering a clue with the name of this temple.

In the brief second paragraph, Asterion claims to be uninterested in written works, even asserting his belief that "nothing can be communicated by the art of writing." He refers to writing and the differences between letters as trivial matters, unfit for the attention of one of such greatness. How this text came into being, then, goes unaddressed—and reasonably so, since in addressing that concern Borges would have perhaps unveiled his sleight of hand regarding Asterion's identity. The description of Asterion's impatience as being generous almost makes it seem a positive quality. Nonetheless, he is clearly wistful over his illiteracy, especially given his solitude.

Asterion comes across as even more psychologically curious through the third paragraph, in which he describes his habitual means of passing the time. Where he runs "like a charging ram" through the halls, the sentence only alludes to his crashing headfirst into the walls, leaving him to "tumble dizzily to the ground." Since he also tosses himself from rooftops, he seems both extremely indifferent to his own health and extremely durable. His games of sleeping and pretending to sleep, along with his other games, suggest that his loneliness has driven him to all this bizarre behavior. His game of imagining another self, another Asterion, is the most telling clue to the extent of his isolation. Meanwhile, throughout the paragraph the house itself likewise grows more curious, marked as it is by "halls of stone" and several rooftops. Asterion's comments to his imagined other self reveal the house's various intersections, multiple courtyards, neglected cisterns (typically used for storing water) filled with sand, and forking halls.

The house is the focus of the fourth paragraph— and given the story's title, the reader may assume all along that the house merits as much interest as Asterion himself, if not more. Asterion's perspective on his own house is quite baffling, especially since the reader cannot be sure whether to take his comments literally or figuratively. He states that "each part of the house occurs many times" and "any particular place is another place," but this may mean either that parts of the house look similar, that parts of the house are identical, or that Asterion is simply incapable of distinguishing parts of the house from each other (as he is incapable of distinguishing the designs of letters). For Asterion, whose world is essentially limited to his home, the house is not merely "as big as the world" but "*is* the world." Asterion does not profess to get lost in his house, but it seems that he only finds his way to the street and a view of the sea with great difficulty, passing through "every single courtyard" and "every single dusty gallery." If he has reached the view of the sea and the temple more than once, he perhaps cannot discern whether they are the same sea and the same temple that he last saw, so he must conclude that there are "fourteen [an infinite number of] seas and temples." Critics liken the equivalency

of fourteen and infinity to a young child's manner of counting, where beyond the highest known number (perhaps this would be ten for the Minotaur—the number of his fingers or toes), the numbers reach an incomprehensible amount, which might be called "a lot" or might be marked by an arbitrary high number—for the Minotaur, fourteen. Indeed, he believes that there are fourteen of everything, except for the sun above and himself below. Asterion even wonders whether he himself created the sun, the stars, and his house and does not remember doing so—suggesting that he truly does not recall how he came to live there.

The fifth paragraph reveals incidents in Asterion's existence that may strike the reader as not only extraordinary but even absurd; the mystery must be revealed for the story to finally make sense. With nine men arriving every nine years, where Asterion says his task is to "free them from all evil," the reader will understand from their fallen bodies that Asterion somehow, without using his hands, kills them. The reader may imagine Asterion as too powerful to greet these delicate humans, whom he is overjoyed to see, without crushing the life out of them; their bodies become mere landmarks in the expansive house. Of the uncertain number of men who have come, one spoke of a redeemer who would someday arrive, and this prophecy brought peace to Asterion's mind in his solitude. His words here—"I know that my redeemer lives, and in the end he will rise and stand above the dust"— are understood to deliberately echo a biblical passage spoken by the long-suffering Job, who remarks, "For I know that my Redeemer liveth, and that he shall stand at the latter day upon the earth" (Job 19:25). Asterion hints at his true feelings toward his house and heightens the reader's sympathy when he expresses the hope that his redeemer will take him "to a place with fewer galleries and fewer doors." When Asterion wonders what sort of shape his redeemer will take— whether a bull or a man or a bull with a man's face—the reader will naturally consider the unspoken alternative of a man with a bull's face, and this, of course, is the nature of the Minotaur.

The closing lines leave no doubt about Asterion's identity. The hero Theseus, speaking to Ariadne, wonders about how "the Minotaur scarcely defended itself," and the reader understands that Asterion's redeemer has at last come and slain him.

CHARACTERS

Ariadne

Ariadne exists only in name in this story, where at the end, Theseus, who has killed the Minotaur, tells her of the creature's acceptance of its fate. The story ends before she responds. Thus, the reader learns nothing of her background in the context of Greek mythology; she is actually Asterion's half-sister, and she assisted Theseus in his task of killing the Minotaur.

Asterion

Borges focuses virtually all of the attention in this story on Asterion, who at the end turns out to be the Minotaur, a character from Greek mythology with whom most readers will be familiar. Theseus and Ariadne are only as present as is necessary for Asterion's identity as the Minotaur to be revealed. While the story makes a fine puzzle, what is even more impressive is the extent to which Borges convincingly inhabits the mind of this creature with a man's body and a bull's head. Critics have noted that few, if any, significant predecessors exist in which the author has inverted the typical literary relationship between the hero and the evil creature to present the creature as the first-person protagonist. As cited by Maurice Bennett in "Borges's 'The House of Asterion,'" Borges noted in an interview that the significance of "The House of Asterion" lies in the narrator's identity as a "monster." Borges remarked,

> I felt there might be something true in the idea of a monster wanting to be killed, needing to be killed. Knowing itself masterless . . . he knew all the time there was something awful about him, so he must have felt thankful to the hero who killed him.

Although the Minotaur is indeed a monster, in attributing a high degree of self-consciousness and even intellect to him, Borges renders Asterion very human.

Depending on the reader's perspective, then, the story can be seen either as highlighting the monstrous in this being who is passed off by the author as human, or as highlighting the human in this creature who is actually a monster. The hints at Asterion's monstrosity are in a sense geared toward providing the reader with clues as to his identity, though not enough to reveal the story's secret, while the evidence of his humanity serves to inspire sympathy in the reader. The tension between these two facets of Asterion's identity is sustained throughout, so

that the reader alternately views him as an appalling monster or as sentimental and pathetic— that is, as human.

The townspeople's reactions to Asterion are likely understood as fearful even in a first reading and as terror-stricken in a second. In response, the Minotaur appears to use, perhaps subconsciously, a sort of psychological defense mechanism in interpreting the people's reactions as "crude supplications" performed in worship, rather than confronting the truth of their extreme antipathy toward him. Later in the story, Asterion's discussion of his illiteracy implies that he could not learn to read even if he wanted to, and his identity as a beast explains this. Yet in an unbeastlike way, he laments this inability of his, since "the nights and the days are long." The first of the solitary games he describes are savage and gruesome, and few readers will understand the mindset of one who bruises and batters his own body for entertainment. But the last game he describes, of imagining another Asterion, is reminiscent of a lonely child inventing an imaginary friend, and though he speaks of having "a good laugh" with himself, the sadness of the conceit is unmistakable. Asterion's final paragraph tells of his excitement over the visitors he receives every nine years, and most readers will understand at this point that, to joyously kill these visitors without bloodying his hands, Asterion must be some sort of savage beast or creature. Indeed, like a beast, he can consider these fallen bodies as little more than temporary installations in the galleries; but he closes his narrative by expressing the very human wish that he might be delivered by some redeemer "to a place with fewer galleries and fewer doors"—as if he has a conception, as no beast does, of an afterlife.

Different critics have seen Borges's Asterion as symbolic of different ideas. Indeed, given that the story draws on Greek mythology, which is itself symbolically rich, and that Borges has commented elsewhere on both the Minotaur and the concept of the labyrinth, various symbolic readings of his representation of the myth are possible. Bennett, focusing on the Minotaur's self-appointed fate of wandering the labyrinth, finds that the maze's "monstrous inhabitant is an analog for that human creature who produces fictive labyrinths while calling a bewilderingly complex universe home: the artist." Bennett further compares the Minotaur to the mystic and the philosopher. In other words, the Minotaur "becomes a symbol of man and his aspirations mediated through the imagination." Mark Frisch, focusing on Borges's conception of the labyrinth as symbolic of the universe in "'El Aleph' (The Aleph) and 'La casa de Asterión' (The House of Asterion): Between Monism and Chaos," finds that Asterion "represents the unitary center that those seek who attempt singularly to define and understand the universe or the self." From this perspective, the Minotaur's activities and state of mind "underscore that, often, we are deluded in the understanding of ourselves and of our relationship to the world. We are both the frightened and the frightening center of this labyrinth." Stuart Davis, in "Rereading and Rewriting Traditions: The Case of Borges's 'La casa de Asterión,'" identifies the Minotaur with his mother, since Asterion defines himself by his royal lineage, and with Ariadne, his half-sister, who is obliged to help Theseus slay her half-brother and who is given no voice in the story. Asterion thus represents the marginalization of women in society as well as general threats to patriarchal law and order. There may be many other interpretations of what Asterion signifies in this story.

Theseus

In the Greek myth, Theseus kills the Minotaur as one of many tasks he undertakes in building up his heroic stature. While ordinarily portrayed, then, as an epitome of masculinity and grandeur, Borges gives him a casual, colloquial line that renders him quite ordinary. As Theseus notes, he met little resistance from Asterion, who would have immediately recognized the sword-bearing hero as his redeemer, since all the other men who came had been sacrifices sent into the labyrinth unarmed. The reader understands, then, that in this story, Theseus's defeat of the Minotaur was no awe-inspiring deed.

THEMES

Labyrinth

The labyrinth is a favorite idea and literary device of Borges's, appearing in different forms—from physical to metaphorical to metaphysical—in a great number of his stories. While they appear scattered throughout his original Spanish editions, in English translation these stories were grouped together in the collection *Labyrinths*. In terms of the literary tradition, the

TOPICS FOR FURTHER STUDY

- Pick any other story from Borges's collection *Labyrinths*, and write an essay that compares the use of the motif of the labyrinth in that story with its use in "The House of Asterion."

- In the style of "The House of Asterion," write a short story narrated in the first person by a unique creature from mythology (such as Greek or Norse), classic literature, or modern popular literature whose perspective is not provided in the original work. Use StoryJumper or another online story creator to help you write and illustrate your story.

- Imagine the solitary Minotaur attempting to socialize online in the twenty-first century. Create a multi-page personal Web site for Asterion, including separate sections or pages on his house and the surroundings, using pictures gathered from the Internet; on his hobbies, explaining those described in Borges's story as well as some you imagine for him; and on his philosophical interests, as presented in a first-person essay. Use a graphic scheme that seems appropriate in light of Asterion's personality. Also invent other personal information to be presented, such as favorite songs, movies, or artists.

- Read "The Fall of the House of Usher," a short story by Edgar Allan Poe that has been published as part of the "Classic Frights" series for young adults. Write an essay comparing and contrasting the relationships between the houses and their inhabitants, especially regarding how the houses affect the psyches of those who live there, in this story and in "The House of Asterion."

- Create a written or oral presentation on the history of bullfighting, with a focus on what the practice of bullfighting has signified regarding humans' attitudes toward animals in general in various cultures.

labyrinth inhabited by the mythological Minotaur, as found on the Greek island of Crete, can be understood as the original labyrinth, with the common term derived from the original proper name. (A labyrinth indeed exists on Crete.) The name *Labyrinth* refers not to the mazelike structure itself but, from the root *labrys*, to the double-headed axe, which, as Robert Graves notes in *The Greek Myths*, was a "familiar emblem of Cretan sovereignty." As some scholars believe, the Cretan king Minos's palace was originally called the Labyrinth, but the name was transferred to the maze that the Minotaur—meaning "bull of Minos"—came to inhabit.

The significance and possible symbolism of the labyrinth in "The House of Asterion" is linked with that of the Minotaur himself. Borges makes this connection explicit in remarks found in *The Book of Imaginary Beings*, a prose work of his, written with Margarita Guerrero. He remarks,

> The idea of a house built so that people could become lost in it is perhaps more unusual than that of a man with a bull's head, but both ideas go well together and the image of the labyrinth fits with the image of the Minotaur. It is equally fitting that in the center of a monstrous house there be a monstrous inhabitant.

Aside from their both being monstrous, the ideas of the labyrinth and the Minotaur "go well together" because, for example, the bull-headed creature, who would be characteristically stubborn, is placed in a maze where only the most stubborn of beings would be able to find its way out; because this appalling creature is deliberately hidden away from the sight of humankind, as civilized society casts out those considered untouchable; and because this instinctive beast is thus effectively prevented from affecting society, just as an individual internally represses his own beastly instincts.

In the work of Borges, the labyrinth is often understood as a symbol with cosmological implications. Although from an outside perspective, a labyrinth may be known to be finite, from the inside, its confines can seem infinite, as they do to Asterion; one may never cease wandering about such a maze if it is large enough. This paradox of perspective can relate to conceptions of the universe, which many believe to be infinite in expanse, but which may, perhaps, be finite from the perspective of a creator god. A related cosmological question is whether or not there is order to the universe and to the workings of mankind. Has a creator god imparted some

labyrinthine design on the universe, or is it rationally self-ordering, or is the world nothing but chaos?

Further words from Borges, from an interview with Roberto Alifano in *Twenty-four Conversations with Borges, Including a Selection of Poems*, offer essential insight into his conception of the cosmological significance of the labyrinth, which he considered "a symbol of bewilderment, a symbol of being lost in life." Alifano asked Borges whether the image of someone lost in a labyrinth suggests a certain pessimism about the destiny of humankind, and Borges responded:

> No, I don't. I believe that in the idea of the labyrinth there is also hope, or salvation; if we were positively sure the universe is a labyrinth, we would feel secure. But it may not be a labyrinth. In the labyrinth there is a center: that terrible center is the minotaur. However, we don't know if the universe has a center; perhaps it doesn't. Consequently, it is probable that the universe is not a labyrinth but simply chaos, and if that is so, we are indeed lost.

Borges, however, stated that the visibly ordered nature of the universe—as with planetary rotation, seasons, and life cycles of all kinds—does lead one to believe that "there is an order" and "a secret center of the universe" as well as "a great architect who conceived it." Still, since the mind of this architect—or, perhaps, the divine laws that govern the universe—may be beyond human understanding, one may conclude that the cosmos "may be irrational, that logic cannot be applied to it, that the universe is unexplainable to us, to mankind—and *that* in itself is a terrifying idea." Thus, the labyrinth may convey either a hopeful sense of design and order or a dreadful sense of unmitigated chaos.

Different critics, then, in considering various aspects of the Minotaur myth and of Borges's remarks on the subject, have concocted various theories about the symbolic value of the labyrinth in "The House of Asterion." Bennett, drawing a collective impression from Borges's comments, finds that "the labyrinth becomes a symbol that unites the universe, time and space, and literature in a single trope." And just as the labyrinth defines Asterion's life, "man's life, too, composes a labyrinth of fear, pretension, conjecture, and above all, *hope*." Frisch expands on Borges's cosmological comments to understand the labyrinth as representing the universe as well as the self. Since the Minotaur, the life of the labyrinth, is slain within it, the story is thus seen as

The house had empty rooms and open doorways. *(Zastol'skiy Victor Leonidovich / Shutterstock.com)*

highlighting "the impossibility of understanding ourselves and thus the world." Davis notes that since King Minos ordered Daedalus to construct the labyrinth to contain the Minotaur, the labyrinth symbolizes the patriarchal order's containment of that which is considered beastly and abject within a nonlinear "feminine space."

Isolation

Beyond the implications of the Greek myth, Borges's story says much about the effects of solitude on the psyche. Asterion can be considered as both *isolated*, in that he is cut off from society owing to others' actions and his circumstances, and as *solitary*, in that he chooses to remain alone in the labyrinth despite evidently being able to come and go at will. The primary reason for Asterion's isolation, of course, is his bestial nature. Regardless of how willing he might be to intermingle with humanity, he will forever be an outcast owing to his appearance, which inspires terror in the people who see him

when he does leave the confines of the labyrinth. In turn, he is filled with dread at the sight of the unfamiliar human faces; even if he has no mirror, he would presumably see his own reflection in pools of water from time to time. Furthermore, although his thoughts indicate that he is quite intelligent, Asterion's actions indicate that he does not operate like an ordinary human, which would also make assimilation difficult. Had the labyrinth not been constructed to contain him, one may imagine that the Minotaur still would not have found a niche within society but, rather, would have sought out some other isolated locale, such as a cave deep in the woods or a mountaintop refuge.

Asterion's patterns of thought and action are nonetheless very human in being shaped by his solitude. His characterization of the people's behavior upon seeing him as worshipful seems a psychic defense mechanism that shields him from the detrimental effects of fully understanding the people's repulsion. To justify his isolation, he asserts that he is unique and "formed for greatness," and he claims to be philosophically uninterested in communicating with others through writing—a perspective that handily evades the fact that he has no one to correspond with anyway, and that also justifies his failure to learn to read. Perhaps narratives of normal people's interactions with each other, quotidian and extraordinary alike, would only leave him lamenting his inability to himself benefit from such interactions. Asterion goes so far as to essentially classify all literature as "vexatious and trivial." The games Asterion plays are primarily bestial ones, exciting his senses, toughening his body, and simulating the intensity of the hunt. His game of pretending to sleep may conjure in the reader's mind images of prisoners kept in solitary confinement for overly long periods. Above all, his game of imagining another self—as who else could he imagine successfully interacting with—must inspire sympathy in the reader, who may now think of a child who conceives an imaginary friend, perhaps to account for an absence of siblings, friends, or attentive parents. Asterion might have solved the problem of his loneliness by attempting to befriend one or more of the visiting men, who are sent in as sacrifices. But perhaps because he has been so thoroughly conditioned to embrace his loneliness, companionship has become inconceivable to him. He allows his taurine mind and self to reign over what humanity he possesses through his body, so that at the sounds of the footsteps and voices, he can only obey his instincts and slaughter them—an act he justifies again through the lens of his loneliness, considering himself a sort of savior, if not a god, who must "free them from all evil." That is, in his extreme loneliness, he becomes the god of his own world, the only world he knows.

STYLE

First-Person Narrative

Borges's story takes the cryptic—and not entirely explicable—form of a first-person narrative record. In presenting the circumstances from the perspective of Asterion, the Minotaur, the author adeptly allows the reader to view life in the labyrinth as the Minotaur might have viewed it, a perspective absent from the original Greek myth. The reader may be surprised and

even somewhat enlightened to find at the end that he has been inhabiting the mind of a creature with a man's body and a bull's head. With this in mind, the story's brevity seems appropriate, since however profound his thoughts may be, the Minotaur's existence is extremely limited by his circumstances, and a longer story might have too quickly exhausted the narrative possibilities.

What is curious about this first-person perspective is that it cannot be easily explained as legitimate. In particular, the footnote regarding Asterion's numerical understanding is quite deceitful on the part of Borges. The commenting editor would have to be considered a scholar who has analyzed this surviving historical text; but later the narrator confesses to be illiterate, and the story never reveals who else could have recorded his thoughts on his behalf. Of course, only after the narrator's identity as the Minotaur is revealed can the reader realize that the writing of this text may never have been possible—who would have taken the dictation? It seems unlikely that Asterion, with his bull's mouth, could even speak a human language. Borges is known for stretching the boundaries of reality, especially where the reader may not expect the author to do so, even in a work of fiction. With this story, based as it is on Greek mythology, the reader could perhaps imagine that a scribe god, such as Hermes, descended to listen to and interpret the Minotaur's story, which he recorded for the benefit of the ages.

Cryptic Puzzle

Borges quite deliberately fashioned this story as a puzzle, although the reader may not realize that this is so until the narrative becomes so extraordinary, even absurd, as to defy any rational explanation. Although certain educated readers will recognize Apollodorus's *Library* as being a record of Greek mythology, the typical reader is likely to expect the story to be taking place in a realizable world; and in the context of the real world, this story is effectively impossible. Only Asterion's identity as not a human in a house but a bull-headed man in a labyrinth can explain the utterly bizarre circumstances. Borges does leave clues to Asterion's bestial nature throughout—from the people's terror to his bloody games—and toward the end of the story, he introduces hints that might allow even the reader with only the faintest familiarity with the Minotaur to guess that this is his story. With

Asterion's conjectures as to the physical form his redeemer will take, defined as they are by degree of bullness or humanness, Borges effectively lays his cards on the table. Throughout a second reading, then, the story is certain to be understood from an entirely different perspective from that of the first reading, with the reader now knowing that Asterion is the Minotaur.

Postmodernism

Borges is widely acclaimed in part for the role he played in shifting the global movement in literature away from modernism, which was shaped by realistic visions and examinations of the progress of mankind, into a new movement characterized in part by the breakdown of such visions and a new focus on the dimensions, boundaries, and meanings of fiction. This new movement has been dubbed postmodernism—which is widely acknowledged to be a nebulous term—and Douwe Fokkema, in *Literary History, Modernism, and Postmodernism*, suggests that "the writer who contributed more than anyone else to the invention and acceptance of the new code is Jorge Luis Borges."

Helping to explain this code, the scholar Martin Stabb, in *Borges Revisited*, presents a number of features of Borges's work that are characteristic of postmodernism, and several of these features are represented in "The House of Asterion." One signal trait is circularity and reliance upon repetition, narrative strategies that serve to negate the idea of progress. In this story, Asterion's entire life is marked by circularity, repetition, and a lack of progress, as he is destined to wander the labyrinth endlessly until the end of his days. Borges thus characterizes the mind of one who must devise strategies to cope with this extreme circularity; many human minds would surely be frustrated to the point of insanity in such circumstances. Another postmodern trait is the presentation of stories through fragments rather than as an integrated whole, as with a traditional novel with central characters who undergo dramatic experiences in linear progression through time. Borges, in fact, never wrote such a traditional novel, partly out of the belief that the novel form was not suited to his energies or to the themes and ideas he wanted to present. Asterion's story, is, of course, quite a brief story, and it is a fragment in that the story is not made more whole either by the complete telling of the Minotaur myth or by the addition of another perspective aside from Asterion's.

The reader is given only a portion of the greater story. Yet another hallmark of postmodernism is the merging, stretching, or twisting of genres, with texts often defying—and thus effacing—the reader's expectations as far as the unwritten rules of literature are concerned. Here, the footnote is a sly means of leading the reader to approach the story, perhaps subconsciously, as a version of truth—even in the context of a collection of fictional stories—and to thus inhabit the perspective of Asterion more completely; and the story is made more effective. Thus, Borges has taken a tale from the mythological genre and transformed it into a sort of confessional memoir or autobiographical essay. A final postmodern trait evident in this story is a focus on perceptions and interpretations of the self. The story indeed consists entirely of Asterion's explaining and justifying himself, with regard to all his thoughts and behaviors alike, for an unspecified audience.

HISTORICAL CONTEXT

Greek Mythology

In reimagining the myth of the Minotaur from the creature's perspective, Borges may be expanding upon, responding to, or countering the meanings inherent in the original myth. Although the myth is so complex that it may be impossible to surmise Borges's precise intentions in adapting it, a fuller understanding of that myth lends added depth to "The House of Asterion." The *Library* of Apollodorus, cited by Borges, is one of the earliest written records of Greek mythology. In *The Greek Myths*, Robert Graves has collected many different versions of the stories and offers interpretation with regard to their historical significance. In the mythology, Minos, a son of Zeus, claimed the Cretan throne upon the death of his adoptive father, Asterius, and to prove his right to rule asserted that the gods would answer any prayer he made. He then dedicated an altar to Poseidon in preparation for a sacrifice, and he prayed that a bull would be sent up from the sea. A splendid white bull swam ashore, but Minos found the bull too beautiful to be sacrificed, and so he slaughtered another instead. Minos married Pasiphaë—the queen referred to in Borges's epigraph—a daughter of Helios, the sun god, and a nymph. Poseidon, affronted by Minos's failure to slaughter the white bull, made Pasiphaë fall in love with the

COMPARE & CONTRAST

- **1500 BCE:** According to Greek mythology, a creature with the body of a man and the head of a bull occupies the Labyrinth at Knossos on the island of Crete.

  1940s: Beginning in 1941, the stubbornly anti-humanitarian German Nazis occupy the island of Crete.

  Today: The minds of most Greeks are occupied with concerns over the nation's debt crisis and austerity measures, with little hope for the return of a bull (rising) market.

- **1500 BCE:** As recorded in Greek mythology, Crete wages war with Athens, which becomes obliged to send sacrifices to the Minotaur.

  1940s: From 1946 to 1949, Greece is engulfed in civil war between the Greek National Army, based in Athens, and the military wing of the Greek Communist Party, which operates out of bases in Yugoslavia, to the north.

  Today: In 2008, riots flare after a youth is shot by a police officer, reflecting anger among the younger population over high unemployment and government corruption; in 2010, strikes and demonstrations are staged in response to austerity measures passed to solve Greece's debt problem, with over 100,000 people marching through Athens.

- **1500 BCE:** In Crete's Minoan civilization, known as the earliest European civilization, the island is ruled by a king, believed by some historians to bear the title of "Minos."

  1940s: Having joined the nation of Greece in 1913, Crete is ruled by the Greek monarchy, in the person of King George II until 1947 and then King Paul.

  Today: Greece became a parliamentary democracy in 1975 following the 1973 abolition of the monarchy, and today Crete is governed by the Greek president and prime minister, who in 2010 are Karolos Papoulias and George Papandreou, respectively.

---

bull. She spoke with Daedalus, a renowned craftsman, who constructed a hollow wooden cow that allowed Pasiphaë to act on her affection for the bull. She then conceived a son with the body of a man and the head of a bull. This son was named Asterion, meaning "of the sun," but he came to be known as the Minotaur, meaning "bull of Minos."

King Minos, disgraced by his wife's actions and hoping to avoid scandal, consulted an oracle and was told to have Daedalus construct him a retreat at Knossos that would include a great maze. Minos placed the Minotaur within this maze, called the Labyrinth. Later, Minos held sway over the Athenians, and he demanded that the Athenians sacrifice seven young men and seven young women to the Minotaur every nine years—or, more accurately, "at the end of every Great Year of one hundred lunations," or cycles of the moon. (Borges is understood to have used the figure of nine young men not with any specific intent but only in misrecalling the myth.) The burgeoning hero Theseus, whether by chance or by design, ended up among the third group of Athenian sacrifices, and he intended to kill the Minotaur. (Coincidentally, Theseus, a son of Poseidon, had just killed the Minotaur's father, the white bull sent by Poseidon, which had come to terrorize the region around Athens.) Ariadne, a daughter of Minos, fell in love with Theseus and promised to help him slay the Minotaur. She gave him a magical ball of thread, given to her by Daedalus, that would unwind itself through the Labyrinth and lead straight to the Minotaur. Theseus unspooled the thread, slew the Minotaur, and followed the thread to find his way back out again.

In exploring the origins of the Minotaur myth, Graves notes that "Minos" was evidently

He was a Minotaur—part man, part bull. *(janprchal/ Shutterstock.com)*

a royal title for a dynasty that ruled Crete in the early second millennium BCE and that had a sky-bull for an emblem, while "Pasiphaë" was a title of the moon. Thus, the story of the Minotaur's conception "points to a ritual marriage under an oak between the Moon-priestess, wearing cow's horns, and the Minos-king, wearing a bull's mask," and further, "the marriage seems to have been understood as one between Sun and Moon." Thus, the Minotaur can be understood as representing the product of the union of the sun and the moon. In the myth, where the Minotaur's mother is a child of Helios, the sun god, while the white bull was sent from the sea by Poseidon, the Minotaur can accordingly be understood as part god, part man, and part divine beast.

Borges perhaps alludes to the Minotaur's divine lineage when he has Asterion compare himself to the "intricate sun" and wonder whether he might have "created the stars and the sun and this huge house, and no longer remember it." In *The Book of Imaginary Beings*, Borges notes in his entry on the Minotaur that bull worship was "typical of pre-Hellenic regions, which held sacred bullfights." Otherwise, critics have suggested that, for example, Borges intended to diminish Theseus's stature by making his slaying of the Minotaur unimpressive and his comment fairly unheroic, or that Borges's framing the story with references to the unvoiced Pasiphaë and to Ariadne represents a comment on the oppression of patriarchy. But Borges has noted that his primary intention was to explore the psyche of the curious character of the Minotaur, and beyond that, any statements regarding his intentions vis-à-vis the myth must be purely conjectural.

CRITICAL OVERVIEW

Borges has almost universally earned high praise from critics for the stories in his two most famous collections, *Ficciones* and *El Aleph*, with the latter containing "La casa de Asterión." While Spanish-language critics have produced dozens of essays on this story, far fewer English-language scholars have weighed in on "The House of Asterion," which is brief and simple compared to many of Borges's other stories. Gene H. Bell-Villada, in *Borges and His Fiction: A Guide to His Mind and Art*, calls the story an "ingenious literary puzzle" that is "quite clever, Borges the puzzle maker at his best," but he classes it among "skilled but lightweight" stories by the author. In *Jorge Luis Borges*, George R. McMurray notes that Borges's variation on the myth of the Minotaur is "both playful and original." In his essay "Borges and American Fiction, 1950–1970," Tony Tanner calls "The House of Asterion" a "touching little story" about the labyrinths of the world that humans build and live in.

Among those who have delved more deeply into the story, Stuart Davis, in "Rereading and Rewriting Traditions: The Case of Borges's 'La case de Asterión,'" confirms that "relatively little critical attention" has been paid to this story. That attention has been "marked by existential and symbolic readings of the labyrinth and the ways in which the character's understanding of his world reflects our own attempts to understand reality." Davis himself examines Borges's story as challenging mythical archetypes, to conclude that "the abjected monstrous Minotaur and the unvoiced women with whom he is so intimately connected become a symbol of marginality against, and within, the patriarchal symbolic order." Maurice J. Bennett, in his essay "Borges's 'The House of Asterion,'" asserts that, as with many of the author's stories, "the issues raised transcend the immediate fictional occasion to address human experience in general. The ancient myth is transformed into an ironic fantasy on the antics of man comically—tragically—lost or imprisoned in existence." Mark Frisch, in "'El Aleph' (The Aleph) and 'La case de Asterión' (The House of Asterion): Between Monism and Chaos," examining Borges as a precursor or paradigm of postmodernity, stresses how the author has departed from modernity in his "rejection of singular, totalizing visions" through the presentation of stories in which truths are multifaceted, unattainable, or unknowable. The portrayal of the Minotaur indefinitely wandering his labyrinth is suggestive of the futility of man's search for the ultimate truths of the universe.

CRITICISM

Michael Allen Holmes

Holmes is a writer and editor. In the following essay, he considers how Asterion's territorial instincts can be understood to have affected his perspective on his labyrinthine house in Borges's "The House of Asterion."

"The House of Asterion" offers the first-time reader many chances to wonder at the bizarre thoughts, experiences, and habits of Asterion. His existence seems stranger by the paragraph, until at last Borges reveals his game: Asterion is the Minotaur. His identity as a creature with the body of a man and the head of a bull explains much of what has been told, such as regarding Asterion's frightful encounter with the people outside his house and the men who visit every nine years. The paragraph in which Asterion considers the unique structure of his house, using his ad hoc counting system, might yet be read as mostly nonsense; the Minotaur is a bull-headed creature who cannot read or count very high and so cannot understand a place as complex as the labyrinth, and so his view of it is simply erroneous. A close reading of this passage, however, reveals a particular territorial logic behind his conception of his house.

The thought processes of animals, to be sure, can at best be understood only schematically by

> ONE MIGHT GUESS THAT ASTERION'S
> FATE WOULD HAVE ACTUALLY BEEN LESS
> TOLERABLE IF HIS REFUGE FROM HUMANITY WAS
> NOT A LABYRINTH BUT A SINGLE GREAT ROOM."

humans. Regardless of how many studies might be conducted regarding animals' short-term memory, capacity for logic, ability to communicate, problem-solving skills, and so forth, the resulting scientific understanding is secondhand; no human will ever *be* an animal of any sort, and so to precisely understand an animal's sense of being is impossible. One can certainly pretend to be an animal, as children do at play, perhaps by limiting one's thought processes and actions to those perceived as important to the animal. If pretending to be a dog, one might scratch at the door to ask for a walk, seek to play with another dog or person, or pace out a circle several times before lying down for a nap. Many animals, of course, whether domesticated or wild, are territorial. Such an animal will mark out territory considered its own, often with bodily fluids such as urine or saliva, and in the event of an incursion by a stranger, defend it. One can imagine that, especially in the wild but also in domesticity, once an animal has demarcated a territory, it is likely to spend many hours meandering through that territory; this behavior serves not only to broadly establish the animal's scent and presence but also to familiarize the animal with every square inch of its territory.

The mind may be understood as constantly collecting images, which the brain then processes as either important and worth retaining or unimportant and disposable. In pacing its territory, then, an animal's mind will store a continuous stream of images of that territory, with each locale progressively being seen from an ever-increasing number of perspectives. As various images of a particular locale are collected, the brain can subconsciously fine-tune its three-dimensional conception of that locale; and in time, the animal develops a near-perfect sense of the proportions of its territory. Evolutionary biology would suggest that the animal mind at

WHAT DO I READ NEXT?

- *Ficciones* (1944) was the collection of short fiction that catapulted Borges to international fame. One of its most famous stories is "The Garden of Forking Paths," in which the labyrinth is a prominent motif.

- A notable classic novel that humanizes a character perceived as a monster is Mary Shelley's *Frankenstein* (1818), available in a 2007 Penguin edition. Contrary to modern images of Frankenstein's monster as a witless giant, the monster acts rationally and philosophizes extensively.

- In *Steppenwolf* (1927), by the German author and Nobel Prize–winner Hermann Hesse, Harry Haller leaves a record of his struggles to reconcile himself with his animal nature. The novel is available in a 2002 English translation from Picador.

- A recent novel styled along similar lines to "The House of Asterion" is John Gardner's *Grendel* (1971), which presents the perspective of the infamous beast in the Anglo-Saxon epic poem *Beowulf*, written sometime between 700 and 1000 CE.

- The French author Alain Robbe-Grillet is, along with Borges, typically classified as a postmodernist. His *In the Labyrinth* (1959) is a challenging read, featuring circular repetition and the deconstruction of time and space. Grove Press published an English translation in 1994.

- A classic postmodern collection of short stories is John Barth's *Lost in the Funhouse* (1968), addressing the nature of fiction through the mazelike connections among the stories.

- Gloria Bird's short story "History," included in *Stories for a Winter's Night: Short Fiction by Native Americans* (2000), ends with an old man named Colón living an isolated life on a ship with only his dog to keep him company.

- *The Lost Books of the Odyssey* (2007) is a novel by Zachary Mason featuring reconstructions and revisions of the myth of Odysseus as recorded by Homer in *The Odyssey*.

- Borges once noted that he disliked the work of Ernest Hemingway because of the author's tendency to condone the violence he portrayed. *Death in the Afternoon* (1932) is Hemingway's nonfiction paean to bullfighting in Spain.

- Robert Louis Stevenson was one of Borges's favorite authors; his novella *Strange Case of Dr. Jekyll and Mr. Hyde* (1886), which is appropriate for young adults, relates the experiences of a man who concocts a potion that causes him to develop a split personality. The novella is available in a 2008 edition from Oxford.

least subconsciously, if not consciously, engages in this process because, in the event of a sudden invasion of its territory, the animal, to ensure its survival, needs to have a perfect sense of what its best choice of action will be. If the invader is a larger predator, the animal will need to know the best means of hiding within or escaping from its territory. If the invader is a competitor of the same species, the animal will likely defend its territory, and having a near-perfect subconscious or conscious understanding of its space will allow it to best take strategic advantage of the surroundings while aggressively engaged.

Behavior of this sort can easily be seen in domesticated animals, whose territory would be defined by the houses or yards to which they are confined. House cats may repeatedly pace the perimeters of rooms, from where they can take in the activity of the room by looking to one side only. If furniture is moved or new objects are introduced to the space, some cats may be compelled to carefully explore the new arrangements at length before again feeling settled, as if familiarizing themselves with the reconfigured territory is of the utmost importance. These cats may be excited to jump up and down from novel heights or gather new perspectives in walking around new corners. Other cats, whether lazier, less agile, or confined indoors for too long, may lose their territorial instincts and be uninterested in such concerns as the feng shui of the house.

Having a bull's head, Asterion would presumably be blessed with the territorial instincts of a bull. As such, he is challenged as no ordinary animal ever is in being placed in the devious corridors of the labyrinth, which was designed to make escape practically impossible. In *The Greek Myths*, Graves refers to the labyrinth as an "inextricable maze." The fact that Theseus needs to make use of a "magic ball of thread" to find his way in and out indicates that the labyrinth is so confounding that a human might not be able to escape soon enough to avoid dying of starvation within. Asterion, on the other hand, can be assumed to survive by using his beast's hunting instincts and killing and eating small animals. Meanwhile, as any creature in such circumstances would, he repeatedly paces its corridors, with his mind certainly seeking to devise a comprehensive map of his location. But an animal's mind is not adapted to developing or following complex directions. An animal might be able to intuitively memorize a brief enough technical route (as do mice in laboratories), especially with help from the scent of food at the end of the maze. In the wilderness, of course, animals are extremely adept at using the arrays of clues provided by nature to determine and understand their physical location over great distances. But in a man-made expanse such as the labyrinth, expressly designed to confuse the one within, with no natural clues to be found, the process of traveling from the entrance to the middle and back would perhaps be so complex as to defy an animal's understanding. The identical, or nearly identical, corridors, intersections, galleries, and cisterns would perhaps be just as incomprehensible to an animal as a forest full of trees is to the average domesticated human.

While Asterion's instincts would compel him to seek to map out the territory he understands to be his own, he reveals that a comprehensive understanding of the labyrinth has indeed eluded him:

when speaking with his imagined other self, he sometimes makes mistakes in narrating their tours through the halls. And thus, since certain parts of the labyrinth are identical to other parts, his animal brain cannot form a definitive map of his territory and would perhaps continue processing images collected by the eyes as being new locales to memorize. Yet another gallery will resemble one from before—or is it the same gallery?—and, unable to distinguish new from old, the instinctively territorial animal mind will have no choice but to process images and locales as new. The result would be an unending stream of images processed by the brain as new locales to be mapped and memorized.

Asterion's commentary on his labyrinthine house seems to confirm this conception of his territorial instincts at work. Where he notes that "each part of the house occurs many times," it is conceivable that Daedalus did indeed design the labyrinth so that any locale within the maze is perceptibly identical to at least one other locale. Thus, "any particular place is another place." If his mind were to continuously process images as new, Asterion could indeed count the wellheads, courtyards, and drinking troughs indefinitely; and thus, even if there are only several of each, he would eventually conclude that there are an uncountable or infinite number of them. And then, if it is a territory with a seemingly infinite expanse—even within a finite space—it would be appropriate to state that not only is it "as big as the world" but "it *is* the world," which could likewise be infinite. Upon at last escaping the maze to reach the sight of the temple and the sea, he failed to understand that sight perhaps because it seemed to negate his conception of the labyrinth as internally infinite; the singular view would have indicated that the labyrinth had definite limits. Thus, to reconcile his conception of the labyrinth as infinite with the singular sight of the sea and temple, a "night vision" led him to conclude that there are also an infinite number of seas and temples. Whenever he might again happen upon the sight of the temple and sea, his mind, having now settled upon the belief that everything about the labyrinth is infinite, could conclude that this is a different temple and a different sea than he last saw—and so with recursion, one temple and one sea indeed become an infinite number of temples and seas.

It is interesting that, though Borges's Asterion laments that time in the uneventful labyrinth passes slowly, and though he expresses the wish to be transported somewhere with fewer galleries and doors, he does not seem to despair over his circumstances. He professes to find ample distraction in testing himself physically and playing imaginative games. If his mind, unable to anticipate how the terrain will unfold, is continuously processing his whereabouts as novel, his senses would be heightened accordingly; this would facilitate his pretending to hunt or be hunted as he ever rounds new corners. One might guess that Asterion's fate would have actually been less tolerable if his refuge from humanity was not a labyrinth but a single great room. In such a room, his mind would have taken little time and energy to map the territory, and his senses would have soon dulled; apathy and atrophy would have likely ensued. Borges has noted, in the chapter "Nightmares" in *Seven Nights*, that he was originally beset by "the nightmare of the labyrinth"—one of two recurring features of his nightmares, the other being the mirror—after seeing an engraving of the labyrinth of Crete, a great, "ominously closed," amphitheater-sized structure with cracks on the outside, in a book as a child. He remarks that he then believed "that if one had a magnifying glass powerful enough, one could look through the cracks and see the Minotaur in the terrible center of the labyrinth." In writing "The House of Asterion," he perhaps reconciled himself to that nightmarish thought of the labyrinth by allowing Asterion a tolerable life inside it; and in reading the story, one can gather that what would be a nightmarish residence for any human turns out to be a source of endless stimulation for the territorial Minotaur.

Source: Michael Allen Holmes, Critical Essay on "The House of Asterion," in *Short Stories for Students*, Gale, Cengage Learning, 2011.

Mark Frisch

In the following excerpt, Frisch discusses Borges as an early postmodernist through an examination of "La Casa de Asterion."

Writers, critics, and scholars have regularly mentioned Jorge Luis Borges as a precursor or as one of the first of the postmoderns. The association has become fairly automatic. Yet, at this point in the discussion of the postmodern, that relationship raises more questions than it resolves. What is the nature and what are the parameters of postmodern culture, and how does that relate to the vision and the ideas that Borges projects in his writing? Current

> WHILE THE NOTION OF THE UNIVERSE AS A LABYRINTH IS A PROMINENT AND DOMINANT IMAGE IN BORGES'S THINKING AND WRITING, IT DOES NOT NECESSARILY SUGGEST THE DESPERATION AND CHAOS THAT MANY ASSOCIATE WITH IT."

postmodernist discussion often focuses on the dissolution of the concept of the self. What approach does Borges take toward the subject and subjectivity? Many have linked feminism and postmodernity. How does Borges portray women and love in his writing? What actual connection exists between Borges and feminism? With Jean François Lyotard's definition of postmodernity as a loss of faith in the "Great Narratives," the battle lines over the historical and political implications of the postmodern quickly formed. Those with monistic, utopian visions found their visions threatened by the postmodern turn. What do Borges's attitudes toward history have to do with postmodern studies? To what extent do Borges's writings and ideas have political implications? What are those implications for Latin America, whose writers Borges has influenced?

An attempt at answering these questions not only provides some different perspectives on both Borges and the postmodern debate, but also calls attention to an aspect of Borges's vision that poststructuralist and postmodern critics have largely overlooked or ignored. The critical readings of Borges have often focused on his challenge to the "One." His metaphor of the universe as an indecipherable, pluralistic labyrinth and his philosophical support for that vision found widespread acceptance among critics, writers, and scholars. They have read his writings as a literary and cultural challenge to the monistic vision of modernism, and have regularly referred to his repeated rejection of singular, totalizing visions. Over and over again, his stories and other prose and poetic pieces question, parody, and ironically undermine a number of the totalizing qualities of the modernist vision. We may think we have finally found the exit from the labyrinth only to discover that we have entered yet another.

However, because of Borges's role as a precursor or an early postmodernist, these same critics have often overlooked the way in which he not only challenges the "One" but also affirms the "Many." He depends on the concept of a singular, totalizing vision, while acknowledging that we shall never attain such an understanding. His agnosticism does not become monistic in its negation. Neither is it an affirmation of chaos. Ultimately, the dichotomy between the "One" and the "Many" merge into irresolution in this labyrinth that expresses man's and woman's limitations. His vision continues to express and affirm certain values and urges us to define positive knowledge. Borges is a skeptical pluralist, but he avoids an absolute relativism. For Borges, the idea of the labyrinth does not automatically imply pessimism, chaos, and despair, but may suggest hope and affirmation. If the universe is a labyrinth, it has a center. For Borges, that suggests a coherent cosmos, although an inexplicable one. While such a pluralistic, labyrinthine universe may be indecipherable, certain journeys within the labyrinth or between labyrinths may still be possible. That is, we still might be able to get there from here, depending on where and how far we are attempting to go.

Reading Borges with an eye to the current debate over postmodernity and postmodern issues provides insights into aspects of his writings that have not been fully explored. It also helps introduce and clarify some of the defining themes and contentions of postmodernity. It provides the more thoroughly versed student of the postmodern with a perspective on that movement as seen from one of its early founders or precursors, and it highlights how that cultural discussion is caught in a similar debate between the "One" and the "Many," between a radical relativism and an expression of the limits of pluralism, between viewing the universe as ordered but inexplicable and viewing it as chaotic, between affirming the possibility of positive knowledge and accepting a rather nihilistic attitude. In so doing, it underscores essential similarities and definitive differences between some present-day proponents of the postmodern turn and one of its founders.

"EL ALEPH": BORGES'S METAPHOR FOR MODERNIST AND POSTMODERNIST SENSIBILITIES

Two well-known Borges stories, "El Aleph" ("The Aleph") and "La casa de Asterión" ("The

House of Asterion"), raise a number of issues around which the postmodern discussion turns. Two critical symbols, the Aleph and the labyrinth, help define his pluralistic vision. His skeptical, agnostic intellectual position challenges totalities and argues for multiple perspectives but at the same time suggests that a delicate balance exists between monism and pluralism. "El Aleph" defines certain postmodern and modern sensibilities; at the same time, it raises a number of issues crucial to the postmodern debate, such as the nature of the self, of love, and of history. They illustrate how Borges defines a pluralistic vision that challenges and subverts some of the perceptions and values of aesthetic modernism, and yet how he avoids a radical relativism that argues for chaos rather than a cosmos....

THE LABYRINTH, "LA CASA DE ASTERIÓN," AND PLURALITY

While "El Aleph" helps distinguish Borges's writings, vision, and view of the world from those writers usually grouped as "modernists," his use of the labyrinth as a symbol defines an important line of debate among writers, critics, and scholars of the postmodern. Critics have rightly pointed to the labyrinth as a dominant symbol in Borges's fiction. Again and again Borges employs the image to suggest that there are limits to our knowledge and understanding, and that differences and alternative points of view may be limitless. Some have found such attitudes disheartening and despairing. Borges challenges that pessimistic association with the labyrinth. An examination of the short story, "La casa de Asterión" ("The House of Asterion"), from Borges's collection of stories *El Aleph* (1949), and a look at some of his comments on the subject illustrate why he sees the labyrinth as a symbol of hope rather than despair.

In the story "La casa de Asterión" ("The House of Asterion"), Borges gives the Minotaur a voice. The story is based on the myth of the Minotaur and the labyrinth from Ovid's *Metamorphoses* and from Apollodorus's *Bibliotheca*. Embarrassed by the birth of the half-bull and half-man Minotaur to his adulterous wife, Minos commissions Daedalus to construct the labyrinth to house the Minotaur. Regularly, Athenian youths are sacrificed to him. In his imprisonment in a labyrinth, the Minotaur becomes the creator of a labyrinth and the hunter. Eventually, Theseus decides to rid the world of the monster. Using the thread that his lover, Ariadne, gives him, he enters the labyrinth, slays the Minotaur and succeeds in exiting.

As the beast at the center of the labyrinth, this creature represents the unitary center that those seek who attempt singularly to define and understand the universe or the self. Fundamentally, this half-man half-bull comprehends neither himself nor his circumstances. His labyrinthine house that imprisons him symbolizes the world and his ultimate failure and frustration in comprehending it. He rejects that he is the labyrinth's prisoner. "¿Repetiré que no hay una puerta cerrada, añadiré que no hay una cerradura?" (1974) [Must I repeat that this house has no doors? Need I add that there are no locks and no keys?] (1981) Its size, structure, and complexity mirror the labyrinthine universe:

> ... [Each part of the house occurs many times; any particular place is another place. There is not one wellhead, one courtyard, one drinking trough, or one manger; there are fourteen [an infinite number of] mangers, drinking troughs, courtyards, wellheads. The house is as big as the world—or rather, it *is* the world.]

(1998)

As the Minotaur fails to grasp the nature of his labyrinth, so he misunderstands his actions and interactions. He always comes up short. He deceives, deludes, and misrepresents his world so that ultimately it costs him his life. He dismisses accusations of pride, misanthropy, and madness, and asserts that his house remains open to anyone who wishes to enter. However, his slaughter of those who do enter belies those claims. He asserts he is not imprisoned, nor the keeper of a prison, as people can come and go as they please. Yet, he seems to be both. He plays at being hunted, but is himself a hunter. He feigns sleeping and realizes from the changing light that at times he actually does sleep, suggesting a blur between waking and sleep, between "reality" and fiction. He runs happily after the nine men who enter every nine years "para que yo les libere de todo mal" (1974). [So that I can free them from all evil] (1998). He is not aware of his role in their deaths, his hand in evil. He asserts his uniqueness: "El hecho es que soy único" (1974). [The fact is, I am unique] (1998). Yet, in his solitude and isolation, he dreams that another Asterión will come to visit him. Because he has a queen for a mother, he feels superior to the masses. He considers himself to have godlike powers.

"Quizá yo he creado las estrellas y el sol y la enorme casa, pero ya no me acuerdo" (1974). [Perhaps I have created the stars and the sun and this huge house, and no longer remember it] (1998). As a half-bull and half-man, however, he is a monster. He misinterprets Teseo's (Theseus's) purpose and role. He views him as a redeemer and offers almost no resistance as the last lines of the story suggests: "¿Lo creerás, Ariadna?"—dijo Teseo—. "El minotauro apenas se defendió" (1974). [Can you believe it, Ariadne? said Theseus. The Minotaur scarcely defended itself.] (1998, 221). In short, the actions and thoughts of the Minotaur underscore that, often, we are deluded in the understanding of ourselves and of our relationship to the world. We are both the frightened and the frightening center of this labyrinth with the power of life and death. We are also Teseo doing battle with and attempting to subdue the Minotaur within us by entering the labyrinth. The story highlights a common Borges theme: the impossibility of understanding ourselves and thus the world.

While the notion of the universe as a labyrinth is a prominent and dominant image in Borges's thinking and writing, it does not necessarily suggest the desperation and chaos that many associate with it. In an interview with Roberto Alifano, Borges speaks of the labyrinth as a "magical" symbol. Alifano then asks whether he considers the image of losing ourselves in a labyrinth as a pessimistic view for the future of mankind. Borges's response provides telling insight into the dynamic at work within his writings and has implications for contemporary postmodern discourse:

> ... [*B*: No, I don't. I believe that in the idea of the labyrinth there is also hope, or salvation; if we were positively sure that the universe is a labyrinth, we would feel secure. But it may not be a labyrinth. In the labyrinth there is a center: that terrible center is the Minotaur. However, we don't know if the universe has a center; perhaps it doesn't. Consequently, it is probable that the universe is not a labyrinth but simply chaos, and if that is so, we are indeed lost.]

(Borges 1984b)

When Alifano asks if Borges thinks that the world may not be chaotic, but rather a cosmos and that there may be a secret center to the world, Borges replies that to think of a cosmos is to think of a labyrinth, either demonic or divine. He asserts that if the world has a center, then life is coherent, and we believe we somehow are saved.

He suggests that there are facts that lead us to think that the Universe has a coherent form:

> ... [*B*. Think, for example, of the rotation of the planets, the seasons of the year, the different stages in our lives. All that leads us to believe there is a labyrinth, that there is an order, that there is a secret center of the universe, as you have suggested, that there is a great architect who conceived it. But it also leads us think that it may be irrational, that logic cannot be applied to it, that the universe is unexplainable to us, to mankind—and that in itself is a terrifying idea.]

(Borges 1984b)

Borges highlights here the meaning and the significance of the labyrinth, the powerful, dominant image that permeates his work. Ever the skeptic intellectually, he admits that the world may not be labyrinthine, but rather chaotic, and that we cannot know for certain. However, the symbol of the labyrinth serves as the foreground or background for many of his best writings, as critics have frequently asserted. These comments and his repeated use of that symbol suggest his predilection toward a sense of order, but an inexplicable and possibly frightening one. That image suggests an ordered universe, but one whose understanding is beyond our reach.

This dynamic between the One and the Many permeates Borges's works. His view throughout is not simply to negate the One. He seems quite sensitive to the interdependence of the One and the Many. His best-known stories from *Ficciones* and *El Aleph*, as well as those in other collections, his poetry and his prose in books such as *Otras inquisiciones (Other Inquisitions)* suggest this symbiotic relationship. Most of his main characters do not deny the existence of the One, but rather question whether man/woman can ever grasp its totality with our limited human resources. His concepts of subjectivity and the self, of love, of history and universal history, express a similar interdependence between pluralistic and totalizing visions as well. They have implications for gender issues, historical, and political questions as well, as chapters 5, 6, and 7 illustrate. Borges captures this dynamic relationship between the One and the Many when he states in "El idioma analítico de John Wilkins" ("The Analytic Language of John Wilkins"):

> ... [Obviously there is no classification of the universe that is not arbitrary and conjectural. The reason is very simple: we do not know what the universe is... .

> But the impossibility of penetrating the divine scheme of the universe cannot dissuade us from outlining human schemes, even though we are aware that they are provisional.]

(1981)

Postmodern critic, Matei Calinescu, has a related notion in mind when he states in discussing the relationship between the One and the Many:

> Incidentally, the near certainty that the effort to unify multiplicity will fail and will eventually be confronted by irreducible "facts" or "fictions" or "worlds" does not mean that such effort should not be undertaken. On the contrary, monistic or reductionist assumptions should be constantly tested and retested against an irreducibility that in the process of being assailed from all sides, is as open to change, revision, and enrichment as are the hypotheses that challenge it.

(Calinescu [*Zeitgeist in Babel*] 1991, 163)

Source: Mark Frisch, introduction, "'El Aleph' ('The Aleph') and 'La Casa de Asterion' (The House of Asterion): Between Monism and Chaos," in *You Might Be Able to Get There from Here: Reconsidering Borges and the Postmodern*, Farleigh Dickinson University Press, 2004, pp. 15–29.

Roberto Alifano

In the following interview, Roberto Alifano asks Borges about personal memories as well as his use of labyrinths and tigers in his writing.

These conversations are part of a series of dialogues from recorded interviews done by Roberto Alifano, an Argentine writer and intimate friend of Borges, in the period 1981 to 1983. The overall series will be published by Altamira/Lascaux Publishers in 1984.

SOME PERSONAL MEMORIES

ALIFANO: What was your first literary reading?

BORGES: I believe that my first reading was *Grimm's Fairy Tales* in an English version. I was very young, I don't know exactly.

ALIFANO: How old were you?

BORGES: I don't know. But I can't remember a time in my childhood in which I didn't know how to read or write. I was educated by my father's library, perhaps more than by high school or the university. Much of that formation I owe to my grandmother, who was English and knew the Bible by heart. So I could say that I came upon literature via the Holy Ghost and by the verses I used to hear at home. My mother, for example, knew by heart *El Fausto* by Estanislao del Campo.

> " I BELIEVE THAT ALL OF US, AT ONE TIME OR ANOTHER, HAVE FELT THAT WE ARE LOST, AND I SAW IN THE LABYRINTH THE SYMBOL OF THAT CONDITION. SINCE THEN I HAVE HELD THAT VISION OF THE LABYRINTH."

ALIFANO: Your education was also bilingual, wasn't it?

BORGES: Yes, at home my English grandmother spoke her native language; the rest of the family spoke Spanish. I was very young, but knew that with my maternal grandmother, Leonor Acevedo de Suárez, I had to speak Spanish and that with my paternal grandmother, Frances Haslam Arnett, I had to speak English. As to my readings, those I remember, were first in English, since my father's library had mainly English books. Also, around that time, I read some books together with my sister Norah; I believe they were stories by Poe and novels by Hugo, Dumas and Walter Scott.

ALIFANO: Didn't you finish high school in Switzerland?

BORGES: Yes. And that was fortunate for me, for I was a good student of Latin and I wrote verse in Latin with the help of the *Gradus at Parnassum* by Guicherat. My favorite readings in Latin were Seneca and Tacitus.

ALIFANO: What year did your family move to Switzerland?

BORGES: In 1914. We lived there throughout the time of the First World War. I remember that I saw in a week the mobilization of about three hundred thousand men to defend the border. The Swiss Armed Forces had only three colonels and it was proposed that one of them be promoted to the rank of General for the duration of the war. Colonel Odeou, who was our neighbor, was chosen for the post. And he accepted on the condition that his salary not be increased. How odd, isn't it! In Argentina the complete opposite happens; there are more generals than tanks or more admirals than ships. And they spend their lives giving themselves raises.

ALIFANO: During those years you taught yourself German, didn't you?

BORGES: Yes. It was during the last or next-to-last year of the war. I was seventeen. I owe my love for German culture to Carlyle, but I decided to teach myself German to read Schopenhauer's *The World as Will and Idea* in the original, and also Heine and Goethe.

ALIFANO: You have said on past occasions that one of the persons who encouraged you most to become a writer was your father. What was Doctor Jorge Guillermo Borges like?

BORGES: My father was an admirable man in every way. And he was a professor of psychology and modern languages. I remember him as a brilliant man, although perhaps somewhat shy. I believe that I inherited my shyness from him. My father taught three courses a week and earned a fairly respectable salary, enough to support his family. Any money left over he spent on books to enrich his library and to give as presents to his students. I believe that in some way he foresaw that I could be a writer, that I had a literary destiny, and he encouraged me to fulfill it. I remember that my father always advised me to write a great deal, never to abandon writing, but to do it only when I felt the need to and, essentially, not to hurry into print, that there was always time enough for that.

ALIFANO: When did you decide to publish your first book?

BORGES: Well, following my father's advice, I decided to do it after I had written my third or fourth book. That first book was titled (*is* titled) *Fervor de Buenos Aires* (*Fervor of Buenos Aires*) and was published in 1923. My father paid for the edition; he gave me three hundred pesos for its printing and I ran full of enthusiasm to a press. I remember we were about to go to Europe and were compelled to finish its production in six days. Then copies were given away among my friends in Buenos Aires. In Spain the distinguished writer, Gómez de la Serna, praised it in a review; undoubtedly it was undeserving of such praise.

ALIFANO: In 1926 you were already a well-known poet and César Tiempo and Juan Pedro Vignale included your poetry in an anthology of Argentine poetry they edited. A year later, you published your second volume of poetry: Luna de enfrente *(Moon Across the Way).*

BORGES: That anthology was entitled *Exposición de la actual poesia argentina* (*Showcase of Recent Argentine Poetry*) and it took two years to appear. There, in a prologue to my poems, I stated that I was writing another book on the theme of Buenos Aires or, more precisely, on the theme of Palermo, the neighborhood of Buenos Aires where I lived. It was to be entitled simply, *Cuaderno San Martin* (*San Martin Notebook*). It came out in 1929 and I never imagined that that book of poetry was to earn several prizes; among them the second Municipal Prize for Literature. But if you allow me a brief digression, I will tell you something funny.

ALIFANO: Please do.

BORGES: Well, in 1930 I received a pleasant surprise: in that year, twenty-seven copies of my book had been sold. I was so moved that I wanted to know the name of each one of my readers so I could thank them personally for having bought my book. I told this to my mother and she was very moved. "Twenty-seven books is an incredible amount," she said to me. And added: "You are becoming a famous man, Georgie."

ALIFANO: You just mentioned your mother— someone I met personally and for whom I had great affection. I propose that we speak of doña Leonor.

BORGES: My mother was an extraordinary person. I should speak, above all, of her kindness toward me. I'll tell you a secret of mine: I feel somewhat guilty for not having been a happy man and so to have given her a deserved happiness. I feel that guilt; perhaps I should have been more understanding of her. But I don't know, I suppose that all children, when our mother dies, feel that we have taken her for granted as we do with the moon or the sun or the seasons, and feel we have taken advantage of her. Before her death it doesn't dawn on us. My mother was an intelligent and gracious woman who, I believe, had no enemies. She was a friend to all kinds of people. Sometimes very old black women came to our home to visit her; those women were descendants of slaves who had belonged to my family. One of those black women bore the same name as my mother: Leonor Acevedo. During the nineteenth century some slaves took the name of their masters; that is why that woman had the same name as my mother. I remember that during the harsh years of Perón's dictatorship, when I was expelled from the presidency of the Society of Writers for refusing to hang Perón's portrait in my office, we were threatened by a thug. The fellow called late at night and my mother answered the door: "I am going to kill you and your son," said a voice, appropriately uncouth and professionally malevolent. "Why?" asked my mother. "Because I am a Peronist," added the unknown man. Then my mother answered him: "Well, if you want to kill my son it's very easy. He leaves home for his office every morning at eight; all you have to do is wait for him. As to myself, señor, I have turned eighty and I advise you to hurry up if you want to kill me because I might very well die on you beforehand."

ALIFANO: An admirably courageous attitude, worthy of doña Leonor.

BORGES: How lovely, besides, that "Yo-me-le-muero-antes" (I might very well die on you beforehand)! It is something said in a delightful colloquial manner. Now, what a stupid threat! Well, really, all death threats are stupid and ridiculous. In what other way can one be threatened except with death? What would be truly clever, original, would be to threaten someone with immortality!

ALIFANO: The threat was never carried out, obviously.

BORGES: No, it never was. I am telling you that anecdote and my mother died of natural causes nearing her one-hundredth birthday. Poor mother! She complained that God had kept her alive too long. I remember that when she turned ninety-five, she said to me: "Goodness me, Georgie, I think I overdid it." Every night she would ask God for her not to wake up the following morning. And then she would wake up and cry; but she didn't complain. There came a night in which God surely heard her and she died at four in the morning.

ALIFANO: Is it true that your mother didn't admire the compadritos *(local toughs) nor the* guapos *(the machos), that as time went on you included in your work beginning with your essay on the poet Evaristo Carriego?*

BORGES: No, she didn't admire them. Once she said to me: "Let it be the last time you write about those ill-bred men. I am fed up with your hoodlums. You describe them as though they were brave men but the *guapos* are nothing but a bunch of bums." My mother didn't like that theme in the least and blamed poor

Carriego, who was also fascinated by the cult of courage, for having corrupted me.

ALIFANO: Carriego, who was from your neighborhood, rubbed elbows with the guapos, *didn't he?*

BORGES: Yes, he personally met almost all the criminals of his time. I, on the other hand, also met them, but when they were somewhat on the sidelines, when they had already retired. I met the *guapo* Nicolás Paredes, for example, when he was very old, and I became a friend of his. The last time I visited him at his house, he gave me a present, an orange. He lived in abject misery and before I left he said: "No one leaves my house empty-handed, Borges." And as he couldn't find anything else to give me, he gave me an orange which I would have liked to preserve forever.

ALIFANO: What did your mother think of Evaristo Carriego who was a friend of your family?

BORGES: She thought he was a good young man, but without any talent. Carriego died in 1912 and in 1930 I published that book-length essay on him. My mother asked me then: "Why did you write a book about that boy?" I explained to her, searching for an excuse, that it was because he had been a neighbor of ours. "But, son," she answered, "If you are going to write a book about each of our neighbors, we are finished."

ALIFANO: You frequently mention the Andalusian writer Rafael Cansinos-Asséns, whom you considered to be your mentor. What memories do you have of him?

BORGES: Ah, truly great memories. He was one of the last persons I saw before I returned from Europe in the 1920's and it was as though at one time I had come upon all the libraries of the West and of the East. Cansinos-Asséns boasted that he could greet the stars in fourteen classical and modern languages. He was a man who had read all the books of the world; at least that was the impression I had of him whenever we spoke. He translated Barbusse from French, Secuence from English, *The Thousand and One Nights* from Arabic. He translated Latin writers and translated an excellent selection of the Talmud directly from Hebrew.

ALIFANO: Did you see Cansinos-Asséns frequently?

BORGES: Yes, quite frequently. I used to attend a *tertulia* (a coterie) which he directed in a coffee house of Madrid. During those years there were several *tertulias* in Spain; another one was the one of Ramón Gómez de la Serna, in the famous Café de Pombo. The painter Gutiérrez Solana, who painted a great painting of all the members, used to attend that *tertulia*. I went to it once and didn't care for it; I preferred the *tertulia* of Cansinos-Asséns.

ALIFANO: Cansinos-Asséns was a man of very modest means, wasn't he?

BORGES: Yes. He lived very frugally and earned his living as a translator. He was a man who hardly ever left his library. I remember he had written a very lovely poem on the theme of the sea. And I congratulated him and he, with his Andalusian accent, answered me: "Yes, yes, the sea surely must be very beautiful. I hope to see it sometime."

ALIFANO: So he had never been to the sea?

BORGES: No, he had never seen the sea. Like Coleridge he held the archetype in his imagination and had thus solved the whole thing in an admirable way.

ALIFANO: Borges, you said that Gómez de la Serna had praised your first book, Fervor de Buenos Aires, *but a moment ago you said you didn't like the* tertulia *of the Café de Pombo that he led, together with Gutiérrez Solana. Why didn't you like it?*

BORGES: I didn't care for it because Gómez de la Serna was a sort of dictator, who spoke badly of everybody else; the *tertulia* of Cansinos-Asséns was quite the opposite. There no one was allowed to speak ill about others. When I attended the *tertulia* of Gómez de la Serna, invited by him, I was bothered, above all, by a poor wretch who was there, a sort of professional buffoon who came every Saturday wearing on his wrist a bracelet with rattles. Gómez de la Serna had him shake hands, and then he would ask: "Rattle, rattle where is the serpent?" And all those attending would laugh at that idiocy. That seemed to me very sad. I thought that Gómez de la Serna had no right to use that wretch to play such a cruel joke, which is better forgotten. When I left (convinced, moreover, that I would never return), Gómez de la Serna said to me: "I am sure that you've never seen anything like this in Buenos Aires." "No, luckily I've never seen anything like it," I answered.

ALIFANO: And yet, what a great writer Gómez de la Serna was! Did you at any time see him as a man of genius?

BORGES: Yes. I have no doubt that he was a man of genius. A great writer with a poetic sense of life, but I believe that he regrettably went astray with those brief utterances or images that he called *Greguerías*, and which were like thinking in bubbles. I am sure that he could have accomplished better work if he had thought in a wider scheme. He had crafted a remarkable prose; next to Alfonso Reyes he was one of the great prose writers in the history of the Spanish language. Few have mastered the language like Gómez de la Serna, but I insist, that he went astray by that obsession with thinking fragmentarily. Unfortunately, he had read a book by Jules Renard titled *Regard*, and which is written in small statements. Gómez de la Serna gave his bubbles the name of *Greguerías* and began inventing those atoms of thought. I now remember that Baldomero Fernandez Moreno defined the *Greguerías* as "ingenious and ephemeral fancies." And it is true. They are exactly that. One of those *Greguerías* states, for example, "The fish most difficult to catch in the water is the soap." I see it as an appealing witticism that can surprise, but which is nothing more than a passing fancy. A metaphor, as I understand it, must gather deeper affinities.

ALIFANO: Yes.

BORGES: But if one uses a metaphor such as: "No man can step twice in the same river," we find that the content is more profound. The comparison between river and time makes it a true and inevitable metaphor, not something used for its mere shock effect and that is foreign to poetic thinking.

ALIFANO: Was the review of your book Fervor de Buenos Aires *published in a journal from Madrid?*

BORGES: No. It was published in a famous magazine: la *Revista de Occidente* (*The Magazine of* [the] *West*).

ALIFANO: That was the magazine that Ortega y Gasset founded and directed, wasn't it?

BORGES: Yes, the very same one.

ALIFANO: And what is your opinion of the Spanish poet Oliverio Girondo?

BORGES: Girondo was a willfully extravagant man. I think he strove very hard to imitate Gómez de la Serna. I never liked what he wrote. Recently Mujica Lainez reminded me of some lines that Girondo wrote about Venice and which read: "Beneath the bridges, the gondoliers make love to the night . . ." What wretchedness! Those lines seem so awful to me.

ALIFANO: Borges, what was Buenos Aires like during the 1920's when you came back from Europe?

BORGES: It was very exciting. There was a great cultural life, much like in any European country; I was much surprised by it. Culture, during those years, was a living thing. I remember that in all the cafés there were interesting characters who created excitement and interest. People also played ingenious practical jokes on each other. Great pranks took place in Buenos Aires. I also met the writer and sociologist, José Ingenieros, who had his coterie and was famous at the time. He and the novelist Macedonio Fernández played memorable pranks; they had a great sense of humor. I regret to hear that all that is not done anymore; it's too bad, don't you think so, Alifano?

ALIFANO: Yes. I agree with you. Particularly the coteries have disappeared in Buenos Aires. . . . Can we speak a little about your friends? Who were your friends during those years?

BORGES: Well, the friends that I remember most—almost all are now dead—but I can name to you Enrique Amorim, Francisco Luis Bernárdez, Ernesto Palacio, from whom I later grew apart because he became a follower of Perón, Carlos Mastronardi, Ulyses Petit de Murat, Eduardo Gonzáles Lanuza, Ricardo Molinari, Xul Solar . . . Dear God, there are so many! I would not want to forget any of them!

ALIFANO: When did you meet Adolfo Bioy Casares?

BORGES: Many years ago, but Adolfito is younger than I am by a few years. I can't remember how I came to meet him; even less, the date we met, since my dates are always vague. Later I met Silvina Ocampo, and when she married Adolfito at a farm he had in the Buenos Aires province, I was a witness at the wedding, I and the foreman of the farm.

ALIFANO: Your mutual friendship has benefited literature since you have collaborated in the writing of the famous Bustos Domecq stories, that strange character who for more than forty years inhabits the rather small territory of Argentine writing. Besides, you and Bioy founded and directed for many years the El Séptimo Circulo editions which published in Spanish the most remarkable short stories from around the world.

BORGES: How strange, isn't it! Silvina Ocampo disliked the Bustos Domecq stories. When Adolfito and I would read them aloud to some of our friends, she would say they were a string of silly things and she would leave. The truth is we used to make up those stories to have some fun; now I am taken aback by the baroque style in which we wrote them.

ALIFANO: And yet Silvina and Bioy together wrote an excellent detective novel, Los que aman, odian *(Those Who Love, Hate), a good contribution to the genre, in a style not identical with that of the Bustos Domecq stories but yet rather similar. Do you remember that novel?*

BORGES: Yes. It is very good. It's a shame that Adolfito and Silvina have not written other works together! Silvina is a woman of genius. I would say that she is the best Argentine short story writer . . . .

ALIFANO: I completely agree with you. And what is your opinion of Bioy?

BORGES: Bioy Casares is the only classical man that I have known. I owe him so many things. . . . Adolfito is the least superstitious reader I know, he is immune to all types of fanaticisms; he is a person who professes, perhaps to the outrage of everyone, the cult of Doctor Johnson, of Voltaire and of Confucius. He has written one of the more timeless novels in Argentine letters, a fantastical novel which I was honored to exalt and did not hesitate to label as perfect: I am referring to *La invención de Morel* (*Morel's Invention*). I'll tell you something about Adolfito. Sometimes, in his home, he picks up a book and without revealing who the author is he reads aloud a few paragraphs to make his guests laugh. Then it comes out he was reading from one of his first books, *Mariá Merluza la planchadora* (*Mariá Merluza the Laundry Woman*) or *La estatua casera* (*The Domestic Statue*). Isn't that funny?

THE LABYRINTH AND THE TIGER

ALIFANO: Borges, I would like to talk with you about two themes which seem to obsess you and which you repeat throughout your work. I am referring to labyrinths and to the figure of the tiger. How did labyrinths enter your literary work; what fascinates you about them?

BORGES: I discovered the labyrinth in a book published in France by Garnier that my father had in his library. The book had a very odd engraving that took a whole page and represented a building which resembled an amphitheater. I remember that it had cracks and seemed tall, taller than the cypresses and the men that stood around it. My eyesight was not perfect—I was very myopic—but I thought that if I used a magnifying glass I would be able to see a minotaur within the building. That labyrinth was, besides a symbol of bewilderment, a symbol of being lost in life. I believe that all of us, at one time or another, have felt that we are lost, and I saw in the labyrinth the symbol of that condition. Since then I have held that vision of the labyrinth.

ALIFANO: What has always intrigued me about labyrinths is not that people get lost within them, but rather that they are constructions intentionally made to confound us. Don't you think this concept is odd?

BORGES: Yes, the idea of an architect of labyrinths is indeed odd. It is the idea of the father of Icarus, Daedalus, who was the first builder of a labyrinth: the labyrinth of Crete. Then we find Joyce's conception, if we are looking for a more literary figure. I have always been puzzled by the labyrinth. It is a very strange idea which has never left me.

ALIFANO: In your stories, various forms of labyrinths appear. Labyrinths placed in time, like the one of "The Garden of the Forking Paths," where you tell about a lost labyrinth . . . .

BORGES: Ah, yes, in it I do speak of a lost labyrinth. . . . Now, a lost labyrinth seems to me to be something magical, and it is because a labyrinth is a place where one loses oneself, a place (in my story) which in turn is lost in time. The idea of a labyrinth which disappears, of a lost labyrinth, is twice as magical. That story is a tale which I imagined to be multiplied or forked in various directions. In that story the reader is presented with all the events leading to the execution of a crime whose intention the reader does not understand. I dedicated that story to Victoria Ocampo . . . .

ALIFANO: Do you conceive the image of losing ourselves in a labyrinth as a pessimistic view of the future of mankind?

BORGES: No, I don't. I believe that in the idea of the labyrinth there is also hope, or salvation, since if we were positively sure the universe is a labyrinth, we would feel secure. But it may not be a labyrinth. In the labyrinth there is a center; that terrible center is the minotaur. However, we don't know if the universe has a center; perhaps it doesn't. Consequently, it is probable that the universe is not a labyrinth but simply chaos, and if that is so we are indeed lost.

ALIFANO: Do you believe that the universe may have a secret center?

BORGES: I don't see why not. It is easy to conceive that it has a center, one that can be terrible, or demonic or divine. I believe that if we think in those terms unconsciously we are thinking of the labyrinth. That is, if we believe there is a center, somehow we are saved. If that center exists, life is coherent. There are events which surely lead us to think that the universe is a coherent structure. Think for example on the rotation of the planets, the seasons of the year, the different stages in our lives.... All that leads us to believe that there is a labyrinth, that there is an order, that there is a secret center of the universe, as you have suggested, that there is a great architect who conceived it. But it also leads us to think that it may be irrational, that logic cannot be applied to it, that the universe is unexplainable to us, to mankind—and *that* in itself is a terrifying idea.

ALIFANO: All those aspects of the labyrinth fascinated you then?

BORGES: Yes, all of them. But I have also been attracted by the very word *labyrinth*, which is a beautiful word. It derives from the Greek *labyrinthos*, which initially denoted the shafts and corridors of a mine and that now denotes that strange construction especially built so that people would get lost in it. Now, the English word *maze* is not as enchanting or as powerful as the Spanish word *laberinto*. *Maze* also denotes a dance, in which the dancers weave a sort of labyrinth in space and time. Then we find *amazement*, to be amazed, to be unamazed, but I believe that *labyrinth* is the essential word, and it is the one I am drawn to.

ALIFANO: I propose that we go on to the other image: the image of the tiger. Why do you, in choosing an animal, usually choose the image of the tiger?

BORGES: Chesterton said that the tiger was a symbol of terrible elegance. What a lovely phrase, don't you think so? The tiger's terrible elegance.... Well, when I was a child and was taken to the zoo, I used to stop for a long time in front of the tiger's cage to see him pacing back and forth. I liked his natural beauty, his black stripes and his golden stripes. And now that I am blind, one single color remains for me, and it is precisely the color of the tiger, the color yellow. For me, things can be red, they can be blue; the blues can be green, etc., but the yellow is the only color that I see. That is why, since it is the color I see most clearly, I have used it many times and I have associated it with the tiger.

ALIFANO: You must have derived from that the title of one of your books of poems, The Gold of the Tigers, *am I right?*

BORGES: Yes, that is right. And in the last poem of that book which has the same title as the book, I speak of the tiger and the color yellow.

Until the hour of yellow dusk
How often I looked
At the mighty tiger of Bengal
Coming and going in his set path
Behind the iron bars,
Unsuspecting they were his jail.
Later, other tigers came to me,
Blake's burning tyger;
Then, other golds came to me,
Zeus' golden and loving metal,
The ring that after nine nights
Gives birth to nine new rings and these, to nine more,
In endless repetition.
As the years passed
The other colors left me
And now I am left with
The faint light, the inextricable shadow
And the gold of my beginnings.
Oh dusks, tigers, radiance
Out of myths and epics.
Oh, and even a more desired gold, your hair
That my hands long to hold.

ALIFANO: It is a great poem, Borges! I feel that through it you express, in a "light, winged and sacred" way (forgive me for using Plato's words), your fascination with tigers and the color yellow....

BORGES: In the poem I also mention sunsets, which are another frequent theme of my writings, and which I see as yellow; in any case they seem to me to be yellow. Because of that for many years I also used yellow ties that startled my friends. Some considered them too bright, but to me they were not that bright. They were barely visible. I remember now Oscar Wilde's joke when he said to a friend—if the metaphor be allowed—"Look here, only a deaf man can wear such a bright tie so shamelessly." And what is even more odd is that when I told this anecdote to a lady, she said: "And why don't you listen to what people say about your tie?" She proved to be much more extravagant than Wilde, don't you think?

Source: Roberto Alifano, "Jorge Luis Borges: Interview," in *Massachusetts Review*, translated by Nicomedes Suárez-Aráuz and William Barnstone, Vol. 24, No. 3, Autumn 1983, pp. 501–15.

SOURCES

Alifano, Roberto, *Twenty-four Conversations with Borges, Including a Selection of Poems*, translated by Nicomedes Suárez Araúz, et al., Lascaux Publishers, 1984, pp. 23–26.

Barranechea, Ana María, *Borges: The Labyrinth Maker*, New York University Press, 1965.

Bell-Villada, Gene H., *Borges and His Fiction: A Guide to His Mind and Art*, University of North Carolina Press, 1981, pp. 136–45.

Bennett, Maurice J., "Borges's 'The House of Asterion,'" in *Explicator*, Vol. 50, No. 3, Spring 1992, pp. 166–70.

Borges, Jorge Luis, *The Book of Imaginary Beings*, with Margarita Guerrero, translated by Norman Thomas di Giovanni, E. P. Dutton, 1969, pp. 158–59.

———, "The House of Asterion," in *Collected Fictions*, translated by Andrew Hurley, Penguin, 1998, pp. 220–22.

———, "Nightmares," in *Seven Nights*, translated by Eliot Weinberger, New Directions, 1984, pp. 26–41.

Costa, René de, "Fun in *Fictions* and *The Aleph*," in *Humor in Borges*, Wayne State University Press, 2000, pp. 77–97.

Davis, Stuart, "Rereading and Rewriting Traditions: The Case of Borges's 'La casa de Asterión,'" in *Romance Studies*, Vol. 22, No. 2, July 2004, pp. 139–48.

Fokkema, Douwe W., *Literary History, Modernism, and Postmodernism*, John Benjamins, 1984, pp. 37–56.

Frisch, Mark, "Introduction: 'El Aleph' (The Aleph) and 'La casa de Asterión' (The House of Asterion): Between Monism and Chaos," in *You Might Be Able to Get There from Here: Reconsidering Borges and the Postmodern*, Fairleigh Dickinson University Press, 2004, pp. 15–29.

Graves, Robert, *The Greek Myths*, Vol. 1, George Braziller, 1955, pp. 292–98, 308–11, 336–48.

Griffin, Donald R., *Animal Minds: Beyond Cognition to Consciousness*, University of Chicago Press, 2001.

Kristeva, Julia, *Powers of Horror: An Essay on Abjection*, translated by Leon S. Roudiez, Columbia University Press, 1982, pp. 1–18, 23–25.

McMurray, George R., *Jorge Luis Borges*, Ungar, 1980, p. 23.

Molloy, Sylvia, *Signs of Borges*, translated by Oscar Montero, Duke University Press, 1994, pp. 1–4.

Pérez, Alberto Julián, "Jorge Luis Borges," in *Dictionary of Literary Biography*, Vol. 113, *Modern Latin-American Fiction Writers, First Series*, edited by William Luis, Gale Research, 1992, pp. 67–81.

Stabb, Martin S., *Borges Revisited*, Twayne Publishers, 1991, pp. 124–26.

Sturrock, John, *Paper Tigers: The Ideal Fictions of Jorge Luis Borges*, Clarendon Press, 1977, p. 188.

Tanner, Tony, "Borges and American Fiction, 1950–1970," in *Critical Essays on Jorge Luis Borges*, edited by Jaime Alazraki, G. K. Hall, 1987, pp. 165–73.

FURTHER READING

Alter, Robert, *Partial Magic: The Novel as a Self-Conscious Genre*, University of California Press, 1975.
    Alter discusses Borges at length in this volume on the nature of fiction through the close of the modernist period. The title comes from an essay by Borges called "Partial Magic in the Quixote."

Cervantes, Miguel de, *Don Quixote*, translated by Charles Jarvis, Oxford University Press, 1999.
    Originally published in 1605, *Don Quixote*, one of the most significant Spanish works in history, is an epic of self-deception, relating the travels and tribulations of Quixote, an inept country gentleman who fancies himself a noble knight, and his companion Sancho Panza. The Spanish-speaking Borges first read this influential work in English translation.

Márquez, Garbíel Garcia, *One Hundred Years of Solitude*, translated by Gregory Rabassa, Harper & Row, 1970.
    Following Borges's influential use of a style ultimately dubbed postmodernism, the Colombian author Márquez, who won the Nobel Prize in 1982, wrote in a related style labeled magical realism. This novel, first published in Spanish in 1967, tells of a century filled with solitary experiences in the lives of the ill-fated Buendia family.

Ovid, *Metamorphoses*, translated by A. D. Melville, Oxford University Press, 1986.
    This renowned classic narrative poem, finished in the year 8 by the Roman poet Ovid, focuses on instances of change and transformation in relating Greek mythology from the creation to the historical rise of Julius Caesar.

SUGGESTED SEARCH TERMS

Jorge Luis Borges

The House of Asterion

labyrinths

Minotaur

Minotaur AND Jorge Luis Borges

Jorge Luis Borges AND postmodernism

Minotaur AND Crete

Asterion AND Greek mythology

Crete AND Labyrinth AND Greek mythology

labyrinth AND Jorge Luis Borges

If You Eat, You Never Die

TONY ROMANO

2009

Tony Romano's short story "If You Eat, You Never Die" is the title story of the twenty-four tales included in the 2009 collection *If You Eat, You Never Die: Chicago Tales*. Read together, the closely related stories depict three generations of the Comingo family, Italian immigrants living on the outskirts of Chicago during an unspecified era.

In the five pages of "If You Eat, You Never Die," Romano brings to life the struggles and values of the Comingo family through themes of love, cultural conflict, and assimilation. By telling this particular story through the eyes of Lucia, matriarch of the Comingo clan, he uses authentic dialect and speech patterns to underscore the importance of control for Lucia—over her son in particular and her family in general. In an unfamiliar culture where daily life is a test of survival skills, Lucia worries that her boys—in this story, Jim—are being set adrift in a sea of values and morals she cannot understand and does not share.

In addition to the 2009 collection, "If You Eat, You Never Die" has been published in the *Chicago Tribune* and featured on National Public Radio's *Sound of Writing*.

AUTHOR BIOGRAPHY

Romano was born June 30, 1957, and grew up in Chicago, Illinois. He earned his bachelor of arts degree at Chicago's DePaul University before

Mama made steaks, and Jimmy fought with her over the smallest piece. (William Berry | Shutterstock.com)

graduating with a master of arts degree from Northeastern Illinois University, also in Chicago. Now married with three daughters, Romano has taught high school English and psychology in Illinois for more than twenty-five years.

Although Romano has written two nonfiction books—*Psychology and You* with Frank and Judith McMahon and *Expository Composition: Discovering Your Voice* with Gary Anderson—he did not become known for his writing until the publication of his first novel, *When the World Was Young*, in 2007. Also about a family of Italian Americans living in Chicago's Little Italy, the novel explores the immigrant experience in 1950s America.

Romano chose to stay with what he knew when he wrote his short story "If You Eat, You Never Die" and the compilation that shares its title, published in 2009. Rather than a novel, he wrote the book as a series of interrelated short stories that are best understood as one piece of literature, yet each brief story stands on its own. In a sense, the book is an exploration of family dynamics, and those dynamics are what Romano has cited as his main inspiration. The title is actually a quote from Romano's father. "It's something my father used to say and still says. If you look back at the ordinary moments of your life, you find these sublime lines, these artistic lines," he explained in an interview on *Chicagoist.com*.

According to Robert Duffer of the *Time Out Chicago* Web site, the short story collection came about as the result of another project. Romano needed a topic for his master's thesis in the early 1990s and found that he could choose to write fiction. What he wrote for that assignment eventually became *If You Eat, You Never Die*. Duffer calls the book "a novel-in-stories."

Romano has received numerous awards for his writing. In addition to twice winning the PEN Syndicated Fiction Project award and receiving two Pushcart Prize nominations, he earned the Midland Authors Finalist Prize and a spot on *Chicago Tribune* Best Books list in 2007 for *When the World Was Young*. He earned the same two honors in 2008 for *If You Eat, You Never Die*.

Although his books and their subsequent awards honor Romano, he finds great reward elsewhere. Each year, he organizes Writer's Week at his high school in Illinois. Writers come in from across the nation to make presentations and speak to the students. "It sends the message to kids that writing is not just some 5-paragraph essay you are going to write for an SAT exam," Romano said in *Chicagoist.com*, "Writing is written by living, breathing people."

PLOT SUMMARY

"If You Eat, You Never Die" is told in the first person by Lucia, matriarch of the Cummings family. As the story opens, her son Jim's wrestling coach is sitting at her kitchen table while seventeen-year-old Jim stands by the refrigerator. Lucia points out that Jim is too skinny, that she can see his bones through his too-small t-shirt.

As Coach begins to talk to Lucia about the importance of Jim making weight and thus needing to eat less at home, Lucia burns herself on a hot tray of cream puffs. She is only half-listening to him as she bakes, and the fact that the food she is baking is specifically the type of food Coach wants Jim to stop eating is reflective of the values and attitudes of both Coach and Lucia. She wants to feed her son. Food is love. Coach wants Jim to make his weight goal so that he can wrestle and feel successful as he becomes a valued member of a team in his new country.

Coach asks Lucia to sit down and give him her attention for five minutes and so she does. He proceeds to explain that Jim was disqualified from a wrestling match that day because he was one pound overweight. Lucia's mind is wandering as he talks because she believes he thinks she is stupid. She tells readers that she taught herself English by listening to others at the supermarket. She admits her English is not perfect and that she is a source of shame to her two sons, but she also says they do not understand that her sole reason for uprooting herself and her family is so that her boys can have a chance for a better life.

Lucia is bored with Coach and his talking. When he tells her Jim worked hard for three weeks and his efforts were for nothing, she misunderstands him and thinks he is talking about the work Jim does for Coach at his liquor store. Jim does not get paid for the labor he provides but Coach believes he is giving Jim a chance to develop a work ethic. Coach tells Lucia that wrestling is another opportunity for Jim to learn in practice and then put those skills he has learned to use during matches. Lucia thinks this talk is nonsense because once he graduates, Jim will no longer wrestle but will need to find a job and make money.

At that, Jim and Coach look at one another and smile as if they pity Lucia. She notices the exchange of glances. While Coach tells her she needs to give her son a chance to succeed, Lucia sees it more as an issue of eating or not eating. She sees her son's sunken cheeks and pale complexion, the pants that now hang too low on his waist, and she remembers when he nearly died from malnutrition as a baby. His cries are burned into her memory, and she responds to everything Coach says with a suggestion of food for Jim. Coach loses his temper and yells, causing Lucia to jump up and begin making a new tray of cream puffs.

At this, Jim loses his temper as well and yells at his mother to listen. Coach continues talking, but realizes his efforts are useless and leaves, frustrated. Lucia grabs her rosary beads and prays that Coach never come back to her kitchen again. She hates living in America, where she does not understand the values and social norms, the attitudes and choices people make.

Dinner that night consists of steak, salad, artichoke, and pasta. Lucia tries to get Jim to eat one of the biggest pieces of steak. Jim mortifies his mother by pulling the piece in half with his fork and eating it. A dismayed Lucia considers the size of the piece of steak suitable only for a bird, and she is reminded again of when Jim was a baby and almost died. She whispers "Eat" but no one hears her.

CHARACTERS

Coach

In Lucia's eyes, Coach is a man who talks too much and says too little. He tries to explain to her the importance of feeding Jim less so that he can lose weight for the next high school wrestling match. Lucia does not completely trust Coach because he has "hired" Jim to help out at his liquor store, but he does not pay him for his time, saying instead that he is helping the boy learn skills he can one day use to his benefit, possibly to run his own business.

Coach is not necessarily an intelligent man; Romano depicts him as a bit of a slob who is passionate about his wrestlers and somewhat impatient when dealing with someone who frustrates him, as Lucia clearly does. Before his visit is over, Lucia has tuned him out.

Coach seems to have taken a personal interest in Jim, and that is why he visits Lucia. He wants her to understand that in order to do well as a wrestler, Jim needs to keep his weight down. When Lucia cannot, or refuses to, see the logic behind Coach's stance, she blows up and all communication ceases. Coach leaves having made no progress in getting Lucia to understand what he believes Jim needs.

Giacomo Comingo
See Jim Cummings

Lucia Comingo
See Lucia Cummings

Jim Cummings
Giacomo's Americanized name is Jim, and he is Lucia's seventeen-year-old son. A wrestler with promise, he was disqualified from his most recent match for being one pound overweight. Jim respects his mother and understands that her experiences in Italy with him as a child—where he nearly died of malnutrition—influence her response to Coach's request that she not feed him so much, so often. Yet he wants to succeed as a wrestler, to make Coach proud, and to help the team win. Feeling pulled in two directions, he struggles to remain respectful and loyal to his mother and still maintain his self-identity.

Lucia remembers the crisis when her baby refused to nurse: "I give my milk three month, but I no have nough. My chest, they get hard. So I give bottle. Giacomo no take. He cry eh cry." Jim has heard this story so often that to him, it is just a story. It has lost its meaning in the retelling.

Lucia Cummings
Lucia Cummings is the narrator of the story and the matriarch of the Cummings family. Lucia learned English in the marketplace, picking up words she needed to know and understand but not grasping grammar, tense, or anything beyond the most rudimentary sounds and meanings. Yet it is enough for her to get by, and, through the kitchen scene depicted in "If You Eat, You Never

Die," it is clear Lucia is respected by both her son Jim and Coach.

Lucia is not an educated woman. She left school very early to work full time in a factory in Italy, a fact she keeps secret from her two sons. She knows they are ashamed of her at times, in public, but she takes comfort in knowing that she sacrificed her own desire to remain in Italy—the only home she had ever known—to make a better life for her boys.

Having lived her entire life in Italy, Lucia's values and cultural norms clash with those of the Americans among whom she now lives. From her perspective as a mother, life is simple: Survival is key. Her job is to see that her children survive. The most basic means of survival is food. Hence, Lucia loves her children by feeding them. Providing them with food is the one constant in her life, whether she lives in Italy or America. When Coach requests that she withhold food from her beloved son—even though he has a good reason—Lucia explodes in anger. To her "Old World" traditional values, his request is an affront to Jim's human rights and to her duty as a loving mother. His request underscores her wish that she had never come to America, to a society that holds no meaning or comfort for her.

THEMES

Familial Love
The most obvious theme in "If You Eat, You Never Die" is familial love. It is what drives Lucia's every decision as well as her reaction to Coach's request that she not feed Jim. Familial love drove Lucia to leave behind family and the only friends she had ever known in Italy. She states: "They no understand. I come to this country to make better for my two son."

Family is a mainstay in the traditional Italian culture. Everything revolves around family, and this is true for Lucia. It is even true, to an extent, for Jim, who is trying to assimilate into American culture without leaving behind his mother. The value he places on familial love is evident in the way he restrains himself from looking at Lucia while Coach tries to convince her to stop overfeeding him. Coach repeatedly asks Lucia to ask Jim why he wants to lose weight, but Jim cannot even meet her eyes, because he knows how she feels about the

TOPICS FOR FURTHER STUDY

- Imagine the conversation Jim and Lucia have later that night after dinner. What do they say to one another? How do they talk? Write a one-page dialogue between these two characters.

- Using a computer illustration program, illustrate the scene described in this short story. You can make one picture or create a strip of panels, like in a comic book, of the scene.

- Jim's brother Michael is mentioned once in this story. Write a character sketch of what you think Michael might be like. Is he younger or older than Jim? What does he look like? Provide enough detail so that he becomes a full-fledged character in the story.

- Retell this story from Jim's point of view. Be sure to use authentic language and mannerisms appropriate for a seventeen-year-old Italian immigrant. Post your story to a Wiki page and allow your classmates to add detail to the story.

- During World War II, Japanese immigrants living in America were forced into internment camps under the auspices of protecting the country from possible traitors and spies. *Japanese American Internment Camps* provides a detailed look at life in those camps. Read through this brief book and compare what you learn there to the life Romano depicts for Italian immigrants in Chicago. What are the similarities and differences? Develop a PowerPoint or Keynote presentation for the class.

- Together with two or more people, research the Italian immigrant experience in Chicago in the 1950s. Using what you have learned, write your own one-act play using three or more fictional characters. Consider the following: What were the common hardships faced by this immigrant population? What cultural habits set them apart from their American peers? How were their speech and mannerisms different than those commonly found in American society? Incorporate some of these considerations into your play and act it out for the class or have a friend record it and post it on YouTube.

---

subject, about him. He loves her; he does not want to hurt her, even as he strives to build a life of his own. Only when Lucia passes down the edict that if Jim does not eat, he does not wrestle does her son lose his temper. As she describes it: "Giacomo hit table. He scream, 'You're not even listening.'"

Assimilation

The theme of assimilation is most evident in the way Romano presents Lucia's efforts to learn English. "I understand most everything. I no stupid. When I come to this country, I say, 'Lucia learn English. Nobody cheat Lucia.' So I go to market eh watch. I listen," Lucia says of her language skills. Lucia's broken English—she uses "eh" for "and" and leaves the second syllable off words like "pocket" and "kitchen"—keeps her separated from the very society into which she tries to assimilate. Perhaps that is the point: She will learn English, but she will not master it. She will use it, but she will not embrace it.

Assimilation is also addressed in more subtle ways. The family name was originally Comingo. Like millions of immigrants, Lucia and her family changed their name to Cummings to sound more American and fit into the culture. Giacomo goes by Jim, and he tries to assimilate by joining the wrestling team and learning skills in Coach's liquor store that will help him in the future. Romano uses Jim as an example of a character who is trying to assimilate, while Lucia is a character who refuses to completely assimilate and remains dedicated to her roots. In

Jimmy stood with his hands in his pockets while the coach talked. (Monkey Business Images / Shutterstock.com)

the story, she uses Italian words when she is particularly angry or emotional. She refuses to call her son by his Americanized name, and she absolutely will not entertain the idea that feeding him smaller portions might actually help him attain his short-term goal of being allowed to participate in a wrestling match.

Cultural Conflict

Along with assimilation, Romano also incorporates the theme of cultural conflict. This is especially depicted in Lucia's character. For her, the world is basically black and white, good and bad, right and wrong. Feeding her son is right; not feeding him is wrong. But even within the realm of eating, there is a right and wrong.

Coach eats, and Lucia suspects that he enjoys eating because he is fat. But she criticizes what he eats—how Americans in general eat—when she says, "He have big stomach, soft like dough. But he have face like flour. He no eat good. Maybe French fry every day. Americano, they eat like dirty animale." This is a result of her Italian culture and values. But her focus on

eating beyond reason creates conflict for herself and for Jim.

When Coach tries to explain to Lucia that to let Jim meet his weight goal is to let him have a chance at success, she cannot see the logic. For her, the issue is eating versus not eating. The discussion ends in an argument, and Coach leaves frustrated. Lucia feels defeated as well and says: "I wish I no come to this country. I wish I stay by *paese*, by farm. Everybody work togeth. Everybody eat. I no understand America. Is crazy." The cultural conflict is never-ending for Lucia.

STYLE

First-Person Narrative

Lucia tells the story in first person, meaning she tells it from her point of view, using the word "I" and sharing her opinions and interpretations of the kitchen scene. By using first person, Romano makes the story come alive, as the reader is invited to observe while the characters interact.

First-person narrative also provides insight into the narrator that the reader would not otherwise understand. For example, Lucia explains that her son Giacomo almost died as an infant because he would not eat. Although she is not emotional or dramatic in her retelling the event, it is her very lack of emotional response that permits the reader to realize how great an impact that event had on her life. If a narrator had told her story from an uninvolved, emotionally detached point of view, it would have been hard to grasp the deep meaning of that brief but powerful experience.

Dialect

Lucia speaks in broken English throughout the story, giving it an air of authenticity. Her grammar is poor, and she says things like, "Giacomo, he no move. Hands in pock" and "The tray make hot eh I drop." Her narration is provided in short, choppy sentences. In many instances, the words are not even complete sentences, but simple groupings like "Is too small" and "Is crazy language." Lucia's apparent struggle with her command of English is a constant reminder to the reader that the narrator, though the most powerful character in the story, is also the one with the least competence or desire to assimilate into the culture.

The use of dialect also implies that Lucia will never sever her ties to the Old World lifestyle in which she grew up. The values she held in Italy are the same ones she will cling to in America, even at the expense of herself and her sons, which is ironic given that she moved to America to give her sons a chance for a better life.

Linked Short Stories

"If You Eat, You Never Die" is just one story in a collection of related short stories. Although each story stands alone and can be appreciated for its own merit, read together, the collection provides a more detailed, intimate look into the lives of the Comingo family.

The collection of stories is told from the points of view of seven different narrators and allows the reader to see the Comingo family as both a cohesive unit and as a group of individuals, each in his or her own stage of settling in or preparing to move on. In her *Chicagoist.com* Web site article, Betsy MiKel describes the entire book as a "patchwork story" that "speaks of each character's relationship with heritage and capacity for unconditional love, grief, and strength."

By reading the stories leading up to "If You Eat, You Never Die," for example, the reader learns from a chapter narrated by Jim that food is akin to religion in the Comingo household. He explains that he is twenty-one pounds under his normal weight and that Lucia responds to his refusal to eat with anger. Readers also come to understand that Lucia came to America alone, six months before the rest of the family arrived. Pregnant with Jim at the time, she found a job, an apartment for her family, and a storefront for her husband to set up shop as a barber. She changed the family name to Cummings to appear more American and began her new life enthusiastically, though she regretted leaving behind her family more than she would ever say.

Each story feeds off the others, and yet Romano crafted each one in such a way that it captures a moment, a scene, a day in the life of one or more of the Comingo family. The book in its entirety is similar to a photo album. Each page is interesting on its own, but when understood in the context of surrounding pages, it makes even more sense.

HISTORICAL CONTEXT

Immigrant Experience

By 1903, there were approximately 1.2 million Italian immigrants in the United States. Most of them—over ninety percent—lived in metropolitan regions, including New York City, Cleveland, and Chicago. When Congress passed the first Quota Act in 1921, thereby limiting the number of immigrants allowed into the United States, Italians had surpassed the Irish as the second largest immigrant population. The largest group remained German Americans.

As the number of immigrants increased, so did the unease of native-born Americans. In fact, other immigrant populations developed a dislike of Italian immigrants, primarily because they were seen as violent criminals, a stereotype perpetuated by the fact that, especially in Chicago, organized crime—the Mafia—was led by high-profile first-generation men like Al Capone. Thanks to media saturation, the Mafia became, in the public's mind, representative of the entire Italian immigrant population.

The overwhelming majority of immigrants who came from Italy in the late nineteenth and early twentieth centuries were from southern Italy, a region known for its intense poverty. Most of these newcomers had few if any skills and sought work as laborers, which is why they settled in cities. Industries of all kinds relied upon cheap labor to profit.

Immigrant life was fraught with hardship. Unsanitary, overcrowded living conditions led to rampant disease, and this situation did nothing to alleviate the stereotype of the Italian immigrant as dirty and desperate. During World War II, hundreds of thousands of Italians who had managed to settle without receiving American citizenship were forced to carry identification cards that categorized them as resident aliens.

Assimilation—the ability to adapt to one's surroundings—was easier for younger immigrants, and the cultural and social obstacles faced by the Italian population were similar to those experienced by other immigrant groups. At the turn of the twenty-first century, immigration and how it was handled in the United States was an issue rife with conflict and criticism.

The topic of immigration was a major cause for debate in politics, media, and American culture in general in the early years of the twenty-first

Jimmy was on the school wrestling team. *(Jin Young Lee / Shutterstock.com)*

century. Conflict over who should be allowed to emigrate to America and their rights and responsibilities once they arrived divided the nation into opposing camps. With its emphasis on the immigrant experience, "If You Eat, You Never Die" provides readers with an opportunity to observe—from their perspective—the challenges and hardships faced by immigrants.

Popularity of the Short Story

Short stories are often praised if they are judged to have qualities similar to novels—in-depth character development, flow of thought, unique or effective style. Such a comparison inherently values the novel form over the short story.

Toward the end of the first decade of the twenty-first century, the short story form grew in popularity, not only in its availability on the market, but also among readers. Long valued as an easier way for new writers to break into print, publishers have historically hesitated to buy short story collections because they do not sell as well as novels. But at the time Romano published *If You Eat, You Never Die*, other reputable

writers were also releasing new short story collections.

Alice Munro published *Too Much Happiness*—and won the Man Booker Prize for it—while Ha Jin gave readers *A Good Fall*. Romano was in good company, and in 2009 literary agent Susan Golomb told Alexandra Alter of the *Wall Street Journal* that "there's this myth of negativity around the popularity of the short story; there have been some breakouts this year."

CRITICAL OVERVIEW

Because "If You Eat, You Never Die" is part of a collection of interwoven stories, critics did not review the story by itself. Their analysis of the collection, *If You Eat, You Never Die*, however, was overwhelmingly positive.

A *Kirkus Reviews* contributor praises the story for its depiction of the Chicago immigrant experience, stating, "[Romano] effectively evokes the city's ethnic life and the culture clashes it produces, both at the dinner table and out in the neighborhoods." Other critics recognized the universal reach within the stories of one particular culture. Donna Seaman of *Booklist* says, "Romano has a penetrating eye, respect for life, poise, and deep understanding of how helpless we are when emotions and actions betray reason." Megan Hodge of *Library Journal* calls each individual story "a pearl by its own merit" and credits Romano's ability to effectively balance the mundane with the remarkable for a complete account of both characters and the culture in which they live. She acknowledges that "Romano deftly and sensitively guides readers through lives that are both pedestrian and profound."

A contributor to *Publishers Weekly* deems the collection "haunting" and warns readers that finishing the book does not necessarily mean they are done with it: "Dreams, and the failure to reach those dreams, choices, risks and settling ([or] not settling) permeate this moving collection of tales that will stay with the reader long after the book is shut."

CRITICISM

Rebecca Valentine

Valentine is a writer and editor whose focus includes American history and the humanities. In the following essay, she explores the "food is love" motif in "If You Eat, You Never Die."

A motif is a literary device used by writers to say more than what appears on the surface of the story. It is symbolic in that it literally means one thing, but within the context of the story, represents something else. What gives a motif power is the frequency—and deftness—with which a writer uses it.

In traditional Italian culture, food is almost a religion. Important decisions are made at the kitchen table, around food, while family members laugh and squabble. Most major events, such as weddings and funerals, births and celebrations, revolve around food. Food is sustenance. Food is love. Italian culture is steeped in food, and food preparation is conducted with the same passion and attention as is given to its consumption. Hand-in-hand with the idea of food as a cornerstone of the traditional Italian culture is the concept of family as the foundation of society. Everything revolves around family, and family comes before anything else.

Food feeds the family, keeping it strong and nourished.

This is the primary value Lucia brings with her to America when she emigrates from her beloved homeland. She agrees to assimilate, but only to a certain degree. For example, she learns English, but not in its proper form—and she will not learn more than she absolutely has to. When angry or emotional, she still reverts to using Italian. It is her compromise. But food? There can be no compromise there. Her life is consumed by food preparation, and it is always done with an eye on nurturing her son, Giacomo, who uses the American name Jim. In the opening scene of the story, Lucia is baking cream puffs. Coach sits at her kitchen table, and she cannot help but point out to the reader that he is fat, with a big stomach, but a face like flour. Her use of the word "but" indicates that in Lucia's eyes, fat is preferable. It indicates health and vitality, possibly even hints at a higher standing in the social hierarchy, since traditionally, only the wealthy have had the luxury to overeat.

But Coach is saying things to Lucia that she does not want to hear, and she burns herself and ultimately drops the baking tray. The cream puffs are ruined. She cannot serve them to (read that as "love") her family.

The fact that Lucia taught herself a new language by listening to others in the supermarket is another example of the "food is love" motif. Where else in her new Chicago neighborhood would a woman like Lucia spend so much time? Because the supermarket is her home away from home, she is comfortable there, able to fit in and eavesdrop on other customers.

When Coach tries to make Lucia understand that feeding Jim too much only hinders his ability to achieve success, she insists she does no such thing. For her, she is not taking away his chance for happiness, but giving him a chance to eat. Jim, who is younger and thus able to adapt to his new culture with greater ease and speed, says, "This is not about eating, Mama." Angry because she believes Coach is bullying her son, Lucia again refers to Coach's size and calls him a "Big fatso." Her mind immediately recalls helplessly watching Giacomo starve nearly to death when her body was unable to produce enough milk to sustain him. He refused the baby bottle, and she knew he was dying. It was an experience that served only to underscore her belief in the idea that food is love.

WHAT DO I READ NEXT?

- Dominic Candeloro's *Chicago's Italians: Immigrants, Ethnics, Americans*, part of the "Making of America" series, is a 2003 exploration of the Italian American presence in Chicago from 1850 through the post-World War II era. Historian Candeloro offers discussion of the population's influence as well as the unique challenges it faces into the twenty-first century.

- Romano's debut novel, *When the World Was Young* (2007), follows the Peccatori family, residents of Chicago's "Little Italy" in 1957. Through the lives of Agostino and Angela Rosa and their five children, themes of cultural identity, heritage, and family bonds are explored.

- *Mexican White Boy* is Matt de la Pena's 2008 young-adult novel featuring teenager Danny Lopez. Danny is an outsider in his wealthy private school in California but feels nothing but shame when he visits his relatives across the border in Mexico. Written in a style that mixes Spanish with street vernacular, the novel touches on themes of cultural awareness and self-identity.

- Editor Donald Gallo's *First Crossing: Stories About Teen Immigrants* features eleven stories about contemporary teenage immigrants from all walks of life. Published in 2007, this collection of stories holds nothing back as it shares teens' attitudes, angst, and anger as well as their hopes and happiness.

- Author An Na won the American Library Association's Printz Award for Teenage Literature for her 2003 novel, *A Step from Heaven*. Four-year-old Ju leaves Korea and her beloved grandmother to move with her parents to America. As she matures, readers experience her joys as well as the many frustrations Ju and her parents endure in their new country.

- Gary Soto's 1992 collection *Living Up the Street* is the author's autobiographical account in the form of twenty-one stories—of growing up in the barrio.

- Gina Cascone's 2005 memoir, *Life Al Dente: Laughter and Love in an Italian-American Family*, is a spirited recollection of her tight-knit family of all daughters. The author's father wanted a boy so badly he decided to raise her as one, with hilarious results.

- *I Love You Like a Tomato* (2003) is Marie Giordano's coming-of-age story about Chi-Chi Maggiordino. She and her widowed mother and brother are Italian immigrants living in Minneapolis in the 1950s. ChiChi is clueless about how to bring happiness back into her family after her father is killed, but everything changes the day she meets two Italian dwarves.

As Coach and Lucia continue to argue, she rises from her seat at the table and begins banging around the kitchen as she prepares to start over and bake a new batch of cream puffs. She admits to ignoring him. "I no listen. I cook." By five o'clock that evening, Lucia has prepared a multicourse meal of salad, artichoke, pasta, and steak—an abundance of food, an abundance of love.

The entire last scene of the story focuses on the steak. It is no coincidence that the meat is the focal point, even though there are a lot of other food choices on that kitchen table, and possibly on Giacomo's plate. Historically, meat is a luxury food, available only to those who can afford it. Putting meat on the table is, for Lucia, a personal success.

When Lucia notices her son selecting the smallest portion of steak, she jumps from her chair and quickly stabs it with her own fork, claiming it as her own. Giacomo firmly tells her

Mama (Lucia) loves to cook and see her family eat. *(fcarucci | Shutterstock.com)*

to sit down, letting her know by the set of his mouth that he is not fooling around. Lucia is taken aback by the look on her son's face, but she obeys his command.

He tears apart that piece of meat and the blood flows out of it. Though seemingly an insignificant statement, Romano is letting the reader know here that Lucia, in her concern for Giacomo's health, is imagining the life blood flowing out of him. She is frightened as she inspects her small piece of steak and then her son's. Her mind cruelly returns her to the moments so long ago when she had to watch as his life ebbed. Her fear claims her bravado, and she cannot help but instruct her boy to eat, though it comes out only as a whisper.

Romano is an Italian American who grew up in Chicago. Knowledge of his heritage allowed him to incorporate the "food is love" motif throughout this brief story. It says more clearly through symbolism and implication what

direct address could not. Lucia will love her family with food despite what Americans and her new social norms expect of her. She will not let go of that value, even as it creates conflict within her family. She will not stop loving them.

Source: Rebecca Valentine, Critical Essay on "If You Eat, You Never Die," in *Short Stories for Students*, Gale, Cengage Learning, 2011.

Betsy Mikel

In the following interview, Mikel asks Romano what being a writer is all about.

Tony Romano's *If You Eat, You Never Die: Chicago Tales* tells the story of an Italian American family. Each family member approaches his or her Italian heritage and future in America differently. And so the story of the Italian Comingos turned American Cummings contains many stories. Teenage Giacomo, who is insistent on losing weight to compete in a wrestling match, tells the first chapter. Another is told in the broken English of Lucia, his strong-willed mother. The stories of older brother Michelino, who as an adult changes his family name back to Comingo, and father Fabio, a barber who lacks ambition, play out, too. The patchwork story that emerges from *If You Eat, You Never Die*, speaks of each character's relationship with heritage and capacity for unconditional love, grief, and strength. We spoke with Chicago-based author Tony Romano about *If You Eat, You Never Die* and what being a writer is all about.

C: In the book, the title signifies the words of the mother of the family, Lucia. Does the saying "If You Eat, You Never Die" come from something your mother said?

Tony Romano: It's something my father used to say and still says. If you look back at the ordinary moments of your life, you find these sublime lines, these artistic lines. I don't know if it makes any sense, but to his culture and to our culture it makes sense. To be able to show the cover to my dad ... he was thrilled and a little stunned. Just to get that recognition. Those are his words.

C: What about the subtitle, Chicago Tales? *Could this book have taken place anywhere else?*

TR: I've heard some people say that it could take place somewhere else. I grew up in Chicago and I think you need to be familiar with your setting. The thing about Chicago is that there are a lot of hard workers, and you don't get anything given to you. I think that comes through in the characters more than the place.

C: Does your work draw inspiration from Chicago? How are you tied to the city?

TR: I always looked at Chicago as being made up of all these small towns. Especially as a kid you have all these boundaries, and all you know is one or two streets. I knew everyone on my block and knew everyone's business. And growing up in a city of millions, I felt like I knew everyone. As a kid, it was a good place to grow up. I felt safe and watched over. We didn't need adults to organize our activities. It was part of our education.

C: What do you do when you aren't writing or teaching high school students?

TR: I organize this week at school called writer's week where I bring in writers from all around the country. The writers end up on the summer reading list and we do some of it in class. It sends the message to kids that writing is not just some 5-paragraph essay you are going to write for an SAT exam. Writing is written by living breathing people. It's the best week at school for the kids.

C: Do you have any advice for aspiring writers?

TR: Discipline. No matter how hard things are going, you need to write every day or nearly every day. I went through years of rejection. I took me five or six years to find an agent. During all that time, I was writing. And persistence. Once you do the writing, you have to be stupid about sending it out to be rejected. Regardless of how the world of publishing is changing, discipline and persistence are critical.

Source: Betsy Mikel, "Chicago Author Spotlight: Tony Romano," in *Chicagoist.com*, March 9, 2010.

Publishers Weekly

In the following review, the themes of Romano's work are outlined.

In this haunting collection of linked short stories, Romano (*When the World Was Young*) explores the Italian immigrant experience in Chicago. Primarily set in the 1950s, several stories are narrated by Michelino and Giacomo as boys. These stories expand to include tales told through the eyes of their mother, Lucia, and later their own wives and daughters. Romano

also examines the family from the outside in, such as the story "No Balls" in which Giacomo's coach vents his frustration when Lucia forces her son to eat so much that he's overweight for his wrestling match. In "Comic Books" Giacomo learns a difficult lesson when he sees how his friend Angelo "earns" a motorbike from a local merchant. The overwhelming themes of love, loss, grief, struggle and isolation are expressed in unsentimental and sometimes even desperate prose. Dreams, and the failure to reach those dreams, choices, risks and settling (or not settling) permeate this moving collection of tales that will stay with the reader long after the book is shut.

Source: "Fiction of Big Shoulders," in *Publishers Weekly*, Vol. 255, No. 42, October 20, 2008, p. 3.

Kirkus Reviews

In the following review, the author discusses Romano's obvious feeling for his characters and his ability to follow their subtle transformations through the decades.

Romano (*When the World Was Young*, 2007) focuses on the Comingo family, which arrives in Chicago shortly after World War II. Underachieving patriarch Fabio manages a barbershop with a dearth of customers. Headstrong mother Lucia offers heaping helpings of both food and no-nonsense wisdom, including the axiom that provides the book's title. Son Giacomo is eager to escape his heritage; older brother Michelino proudly embraces it. Each family member speaks in the first person, a decision that could have produced clichéd, stereotypical prose. A pair of stories told in Lucia's pidgin English do shade too far in that direction ("I no understand America. Is crazy"). But the author's depth of feeling for his characters, combined with his ability to follow their subtle transformations through the decades, is affecting. The best-drawn character is Giacomo, or Jim (Americanization of names is a running theme). We follow him from after-school jobs to revelations about his mother to adulthood as a father and counselor—a job that, ironically, doesn't let him escape his feelings of being smothered by Mom. At the center of the book are a series of bittersweet stories set during Lucia and Fabio's courtship in Italy, revealing that their union was clumsy and, to an extent, unwanted. The climactic ending, in which multiple voices weave together, feels earned instead of mawkish. By the book's close Romano has offered a wealth of details about jobs, heartbreak, religion and the business of making it in America. Though he doesn't get into as much nitty-gritty about the Windy City as one of his obvious inspirations, Stuart Dybek's *The Coast of Chicago* (1990), he effectively evokes the city's ethnic life and the culture clashes it produces, both at the dinner table and out in the neighborhoods.

A spirited evocation of a complex immigrant culture, willing to show the scars its characters bear.

Source: Review of *If You Eat, You Never Die*, in *Kirkus Reviews*, October 15, 2008.

Donna Seaman

In the following review, Seaman characterizes Romano's storytelling as having a "penetrating eye, respect for life, and deep understanding."

Italian-born Lucia struggles with English, her husband Fabio's lack of ambition, and the willfulness of her American sons, Giacomo (Jimmy) and Michelino (Michael), and channels all her love and fury into cooking. In masterfully distilled stories of the Comingos turned Cummings, Romano illuminates a Chicago neighborhood and an entire universe of dreams and disappointments. All the psychological luster of his debut novel, *When the World Was Young* (2007), is found here curiously amplified by the restraint of the shorter form. Romano narrates fluently from different points of view, juxtaposing Italy-set stories of Lucia's and Fabio's youths with dramatic coming-of-age episodes in the Chicago lives of their sons, spiraling back and forward in time to reveal secrets, shame, regret, and relief. In bruising encounters, husbands and wives struggle over money and responsibility, and children reject smothering parental concern, while everyone pays the price of outsiderness, assimilation, and thwarted love. Romano has a penetrating eye, respect for life, poise, and deep understanding of how helpless we are when emotions and actions betray reason.

Two books in two years. Seven narrators. Four pizzas. Tony Romano knows well the meaning of abundance. . . .

Source: Donna Seaman, Review of *If You Eat, You Never Die: Chicago Tales*, in *Booklist*, Vol. 105, No. 8, December 15, 2008, p. 23.

Joshua Cohen

In the following review, Cohen examines the loss of innocence in Romano's first novel.

The world was young in 1957 when the Peccatoris, an Italian family in Chicago, suffer the loss of two-year-old Benito. This death precipitates dramatic change, as family members begin revealing secrets or creating new ones to hide. When oldest brother Santo tries to keep his sister, Victoria, from hanging around with local hood Eddie Milano, they spot an older Italian woman attacking their father, Agostino. After the death of Benito, Santo is determined to discover what precipitated the attack, and Victoria becomes even more determined to see Eddie. Agostino sees Benito's death as punishment for his philandering, and wife Angela Rosa believes she could have saved Benito; their guilty feelings lead to an iciness in their marriage affecting all the children. Eventually, Agostino confesses his sins to his brother Vincenzo, which enables Santo to find out the truth. Examining the loss of innocence, respected short story author Romano gracefully considers whether knowing the truth is always for the best while capturing the values and characters of a 1950s Italian neighborhood. Recommended.

Source: Joshua Cohen, Review of *When the World Was Young*, in *Library Journal*, Vol. 132, No. 9, May 15, 2007, p. 84.

Joanne Wilkinson

In the following review of When the World Was Young*, Wilkinson describes Romano's ability to write "heart-wrenching" passages.*

This tenderhearted novel about an immigrant family during the 1950s features Angela Rosa and Agostino Peccatori, who still long for the sight of the Apennine Hills ringing their Italian hometown. With five children, however, they have no time for self-indulgence. Angela Rosa is constantly cooking and cleaning, while Agostino puts in long hours running the family-owned corner tavern. Their oldest son, Santo, is longing for a girlfriend and a job that would give him some independence, while 16-year-old Victoria, feeling suffocated by her family's strict rules, has begun to smoke and flirt with bad-boy Eddie Milano. But when their baby brother, Benito, succumbs to a high fever, the entire family seems to come apart, each nurturing a private grief. Romano describes the mourning process in heart-wrenching passages even as he relays the love and the secrets—Agostino's infidelity, Victoria's pregnancy—that bind and separate family members. In addition, he offers a finely detailed depiction of the Peccatoris' West Side Chicago neighborhood, from its Italian beef stands to its majestic Catholic church.

Source: Joanne Wilkinson, Review of *When the World Was Young*, in *Booklist*, Vol. 103, No. 16, April 15, 2007, p. 35.

SOURCES

Alter, Alexandra, "When Brevity Is a Virtue," in *Wall Street Journal*, November 20, 2009, p. W11.

Duffer, Robert, "Tony Romano's New Story Collection Slices Off a Piece of West Side Life," in *Time Out Chicago*, January 1–7, 2009, http://chicago.timeout.com/articles/books/70122/if-you-eat-you-never-die-by-tony-romano-book-review (accessed June 18, 2010).

"Fiction of Big Shoulders: Pick of the Week," in *Publishers Weekly*, Vol. 255, No. 42, October 20, 2008, p. 3.

Hodge, Megan, Review of *If You Eat, You Never Die: Chicago Tales*, in *Library Journal*, Vol. 134, No. 1, January 1, 2009, p. 86.

Mikel, Betsy, "Chicago Author Spotlight: Tony Romano," in *Chicagoist.com*, March 9, 2010, http://chicagoist.com/2010/03/09/spotlight_tony_romano.php (accessed July 6, 2010).

Review of *If You Eat, You Never Die*, in *Kirkus Reviews*, October 15, 2008.

Romano, Tony, "If You Eat, You Never Die," in *If You Eat, You Never Die: Chicago Tales*, HarperCollins, 2009, pp. 15–20.

Seaman, Donna, Review of *If You Eat, You Never Die: Chicago Tales*, in *Booklist*, Vol. 105, No. 8, December 15, 2008, p. 23.

Veronesi, Gene P., "Italian-Americans & Their Communities of Cleveland," in *Cleveland Memory Project*, http://www.clevelandmemory.org/italians/partii.html (accessed July 20, 2010).

FURTHER READING

Bruchac, Joseph, *The Heart of a Chief*, Puffin, 2001.
    Written for young adults, this novel is told from the perspective of eleven-year-old Chris Nicola, a Penacook boy whose heritage provides him with stories and courage to rise to the challenges presented by a modern society. Chris, like those young characters in Romano's stories, tries to assimilate into a society without being fully aware of the expectations imposed upon him.

Catrambone, Kathy, and Ellen Shubart, *Taylor Street: Chicago's Little Italy*, Arcadia Publishing, 2007.
    Chicago's Near West Side is the city's most famous neighborhood, and readers are taken back to that setting in the late nineteenth century in this pictorial history volume of the "Images of America" series.

Jenkins, Wilbert L., *Climbing Up to Glory: A Short History of African Americans during the Civil War and Reconstruction*, SR Books, 2002.
    Just as Tony Romano depicts the struggles of a fictional Italian immigrant family in Chicago, Jenkins records the social struggles of real African Americans during this most transitional period in American History. He examines the obstacles and challenges faced by African Americans whose very freedom depended upon the Civil War and the country's ensuing laws and regulations.

Meyer, Jared, *Frequently Asked Questions about Being an Immigrant Teen*, Rosen Publishing Group, 2007.
    This sixty-four-page part of the "FAQ: Teen Life" series attempts to answer the most common questions related to teen immigrants in America.

Paterno, Joe, and Joe DiMaggio, *Italians in America—Our Contribution*, Alpha Home Entertainment, 2008.
    These two famous figures from the athletic world are joined by other famous Italians, including Frank Sinatra and Frank Capra, in a seventy-five-minute video exploration of famous and not-so-famous Italians who have left their mark on America.

SUGGESTED SEARCH TERMS

If You Eat You Never Die

Tony Romano

Tony Romano AND Italian American

Tony Romano AND short story

Italian American immigrants AND fiction

young adult literature AND Italian American immigrants

Italian immigrants AND Chicago

Italian American AND teens

teens AND immigrants

1950s AND Italian Americans

Leiningen Versus the Ants

CARL STEPHENSON

1938

"Leiningen Versus the Ants" is a short story by the twentieth-century German writer Carl Stephenson. It was first published in English in *Esquire* in December 1938 and has been reprinted many times since in short story anthologies. It is one of the most popular adventure stories ever written. It can be found in *Great Stories of Suspense and Adventure*, edited by Beth Johnson and Barbara Solot and published by Townsend Press in 2003; *Twenty-One Great Stories*, edited by Abraham H. Lass and Norma L. Tasman (Signet, 1969); *Classic Adventure Stories: Twenty-one Tales of People Pushed to the Limit*, edited by Stephen Vincent Brennan (Lyons Press, 2004), and *Fictional Ants*, published by Books LLC in 2010.

"Leiningen Versus the Ants" is an adventure story set on a large plantation in Brazil. The protagonist, Leiningen, is a German settler who learns that his plantation is threatened by an advancing army of millions of ants. The ant army stretches for ten miles and is two miles wide. The ants will destroy the plantation and kill Leiningen and all his men unless he can figure out a way to stop them. The story is a classic of its kind; the protagonist must battle the forces of nature in order to survive.

AUTHOR BIOGRAPHY

Not much is known about the life and work of Stephenson. He was born in Vienna, Austria, on November 3, 1893. He also published work under

The plantation was in a thick jungle. *(yFact | Shutterstock.com)*

the name of Stephen Sorel. He has even been confused with the American medieval historian Carl Stephenson (1886–1954). The date of his death is unknown, but is likely to have been in the late 1960s.

The best source in English for information about Stephenson's life is the introduction to "Leiningen Versus the Ants" written in 2010 by Dan Neyer, for the Web site *The Nostalgia League*. According to Neyer, Stephenson was the head of a publishing company based in Berlin, Germany, and Vienna, Austria, that published works of German literature as well as translations of English, American, and French writers. Stephenson translated some of these works himself. Under the name of Stephen Sorel, he published some works of literary criticism in the 1920s, and at least one work of fiction. None of these works have been translated into English. "Leiningen Versus the Ants," the story that was to preserve his name, was first published, according to Neyer, in the German magazine, *Die Neue Linie* (*The New Line*), in 1937, before being translated into

English (by whom it is not known but possibly by Stephenson himself) and appearing in *Esquire* in December 1938. The story was adapted for a radio play in 1948, and in 1954 it was made into a film, *The Naked Jungle*, starring Charlton Heston and Eleanor Parker.

Neyer consulted a German-language bibliography of Stephenson's works, and he comments that it lists three works that may be sequels to his famous story. These are, in English translation, *Riot in the Pampas*; *Emissaries of Hell: Leiningen's Fight with the Wilderness*, and *Marabunta: Amazon Adventure*, all published in the 1950s. (Marabunta is a name for army ants.) None of these works, however, have been translated into English.

Some sources list Stephenson's death as occurring in 1954, but this is incorrect, probably resulting from the confusion of identity between the author and the American historian of the same name. Many books by Stephenson or edited by him were published in German after that date, up to 1967.

PLOT SUMMARY

"Leiningen Versus the Ants" is set on a plantation in Brazil. When the story begins, the District Commissioner is warning Leiningen, the German settler who owns the plantation, that an army of ants is on its way and will reach the plantation within two days. The ant army is ten miles long and two miles wide and destroys everything in its path. The District Commissioner advises Leiningen to abandon the plantation while he has time, but Leiningen will not hear of it. He says he is ready for any challenge.

Leiningen has been a successful planter in Brazil for three years, and he is confident that he can prevail. He has triumphed over natural disasters many times before. That evening he addresses his four hundred workers, who trust him as their leader to defeat the ants.

The ants approach, all living creatures fleeing from their path. Leiningen prepares his first line of defense. This is a horseshoe-shaped ditch, twelve feet across, and bordered on the fourth side by a river. Leiningen releases a dam he has built, diverting water into the ditch to form a moat all around the plantation. He is confident this will deter the ants. There is also another ditch, this one concrete, within the outer one that extends around the ranch house and other buildings. He fills this inner ditch with gasoline. Then he rides his horse to the southern end of the ditch and observes the ants as they arrive and get closer and closer to the water ditch.

The ant army halts as it sees the ditch and sends out scouts to survey the situation. This takes over an hour. Then the ants advance again, pouring into the water, struggling to survive as they sink, with other ants clambering over them, using them as bridges. As they continue to swim and sink they gradually make their way across the ditch, far faster than Leiningen thought they could. He gives orders to increase the flow of water into the ditches. His men also throw clods of earth and sand at the ants and spray them with gasoline. The ants respond by extending the length of their assault, stretching Leiningen's limited manpower and resources. Some ants succeed in reaching the inner bank. One man who is trying to beat them back with a shovel gets attacked by the ants, and is stung mercilessly. Leiningen orders the panic-stricken man to put his arms in the gasoline, and Indian

MEDIA ADAPTATIONS

- "Leiningen Versus the Ants" was adapted into a thirty-minute radio play in 1948 and presented on the show *Escape*. The play is available at the Web site maintained by *The Nostalgia League*.

- The story was adapted for a film, *The Naked Jungle*, produced by Frank Freeman, Jr., and George Pal, directed by Byron Haskin, and starring Charlton Heston and Eleanor Parker. It was released by Paramount in 1954 and is available on DVD.

- The story was freely adapted, with a different setting, by an unknown author for a comic book, *Strange Suspense Stories*, in August 1954. This version was called "Von Mohl Vs. the Ants," and it was illustrated by Steve Ditko. The story can be read and seen at the Web site maintained by *The Nostalgia League*.

- *MacGyver* was an ABC-TV series about an adventure hero and secret agent named MacGyver, played by Richard Dean Anderson. In "Trumbo's World," episode six of the first season (1985–1986), MacGyver helps a man in the Amazon jungle defend his plantation against an attack by billions of ants. The episode can be found on *MacGyver*, Season One, released by Paramount on DVD in 2005.

medicine man gives him a drink to lessen the power of the ants' venom.

As Leiningen surveys the situation, he believes he is, at least for the moment, victorious. The extra water flooding into the ditch has made a difference. More ants are drowning and others are heading for safety on the far bank where they came from. Leiningen's men celebrate. It is now evening, and although the ants have retreated, Leiningen is not entirely confident that they will not make another attack before dawn. He orders the men to make night patrols to observe the situation.

At dawn, Leiningen rides out and surveys the ditch. The ants are motionless, and he believes they do not have a chance of getting across the ditch. But when he gets to the western section of the ditch, he notices many of the ants gnawing at the stalks of the leaves on the trees, causing the leaves to fall to the ground. At first Leiningen thinks the ants are merely getting food for the rest of the army, but then he watches the ants push the leaves to the edge of the ditch. He realizes they are building rafts for themselves. Indeed, the ants launch the leaves into the current, each leaf with several ants on it. They are crossing the ditch by the thousands, and Leiningen knows that the situation is very serious.

Leiningen watches as a stag runs down a hill and collapses. It is covered with ants and is in agony. Leiningen shoots it to put it out of its misery. The ants eat the stag in six minutes, leaving only the bones.

Soon the ants have almost completed a crossing a mile wide by means of the leaves. Leiningen gains a short respite by ordering the man who controls the dam to lower and then raise the level of the water in the ditch. When the water level falls, the leaves sink almost to the bed, and millions more ants start the crossing, only to be swept away and drowned when the water level suddenly rises. But this only works for a while, and in another area of the ditch, the ants succeed in making the crossing to the inner bank while the water is low. Many of the men run for their lives. Leiningen knows the plantation is lost, and he orders his men to retreat to within the second moat. The men assemble at one of the trenches, which is filled with gasoline, and Leiningen gives them a pep talk. They still have confidence in him. The ants begin eating the crops at the plantation, ignoring the gasoline barrier.

That evening Leiningen calculates his losses and decides it will not be difficult to recover from this disaster using intensive farming methods. He sleeps soundly and is up at dawn. All he can see is a vast expanse of ants. However, at first he thinks the gasoline trenches will hold them off. But then the ants gather twigs and leaves and lay them on the gasoline. Soon they step over the bridge they have created and are climbing up the other side of the trench. Leiningen orders that a match be put to the gasoline, and soon there is a wall of fire and smoke as the gasoline ignites. When it dies down, the ants, not totally destroyed, try again, only to meet another wall of flame. This happens three times in all, but the ants keep coming. Then, the gasoline stops

flowing into the trench. A temporary solution is quickly found by bringing up two old fire trucks and hosing the ants with gasoline.

However, this does not hold the ants at bay for long, and Leiningen's men begin to lose heart. Two of them panic and try to flee to the rafts at the river, but the ants soon cover them. In agony, they jump into the river but are soon killed by piranhas or crocodiles.

Leiningen realizes there is only one hope left: if he can manage to dam the entire river, the water from it would engulf not only the ditches but the entire plantation, leaving the ranch house and outbuildings, which sat on a hill, untouched. But to accomplish this he must run two ant-covered miles to reach the dam, and then get back. It seems like an almost impossible mission, but he believes he can do it, and he informs his men of his plan. He puts on boots, gloves, mosquito goggles, and puts rags soaked in gasoline in his clothing. He puts cotton wool in his ears and nose and then gets his men to soak him in gasoline. The Indian medicine man smears him with medicine, the odor of which, the man says, will repel the ants.

Leiningen runs to the dam and turns the wheel to start the flooding of the plantation. By now he is covered in ants, which are biting him. He starts the return journey, nearly blinded by ant bites. He is almost overwhelmed, but a vision of the dying stag he had seen earlier makes him redouble his efforts. He refuses to die like that. He leaps through the wall of burning gasoline, falls down and loses consciousness. His men rush to help him and carry him into the ranch house.

Leiningen's plan has worked. The plantation is entirely flooded, and a wall of gasoline flames has stopped the ants from climbing the hill up to the house. They are all swept away in the flood.

Leiningen lies in bed covered in bandages. The men are gathered around him, wondering if he will survive. One man gives him a powerful sleeping medicine. Leiningen says that he told them he would come back. Then he falls asleep. It is clear that he will live through his ordeal.

CHARACTERS

The Ants
The ants number in the millions or even billions. They form a highly disciplined army that collectively is able to determine the most efficient way

of reaching its goal. They are capable of killing any creature, including humans, that stands in their path. They first attack the eyes, making the victim blind. The District Commissioner tells Leiningen that the ants will "eat a full-grown buffalo to the bones." The ants are also presented as if they possess qualities that make them more than insects. It is almost as if they possess human attributes. Leiningen and his men "began to stir with the unpleasant suspicion that inside every single one of those insects dwelt a thought. And that thought was: Ditch or no ditch, we'll get to your flesh!" The ants gaze thoughtfully at the gasoline; not satisfied with occupying the plantation, they exhibit greed and are eager to get at the men and the horses.

The District Commissioner

The District Commissioner is a local Brazilian official. He appears only at the beginning of the story. He informs Leiningen of the approaching army of ants and the grave danger that this poses. He is frustrated by Leiningen's refusal to abandon the plantation and tells the German that he and all his workers will be killed.

Indian Medicine Man

The medicine man is an old Indian who has prepared a drink that will reduce the effects of the ants' venom. He gives some of it to one of the men who has been bitten. Later, he gives Leiningen some medicine to put on his face that will by its odor repel the ants, and it is partially successful for a while.

Leiningen

Leiningen is a German plantation owner in Brazil and the hero of the tale. He is a big, confident man who has run his plantation for three years and has lived in Brazil for much longer than that. He has overcome every obstacle he has faced in developing his plantation, and his farming methods, based on modern science, have produced remarkably high yields.

He is at least middle-aged and possibly older. He is described as follows: "With his bristling gray hair, bulky nose, and intelligent eyes, he had the look of an aging and shabby eagle." He is intelligent and resourceful, trusting in the power of his own intellect. He is not the sort of man to run away from a challenge. He is more successful than most of the other European settlers in the region, who have given up in the face of natural disasters such as drought and disease.

Leiningen's motto is "the human brain needs only to become fully aware of its powers to conquer even the elements."

Leiningen is also an excellent leader; his men follow his orders without question and have confidence in his abilities to deliver them from this great peril. Leiningen is also courageous. When he knows that the only chance he and his men have is to reach the dam, which is two miles away across ant-covered ground, it does not occur to him to send someone else to do the job. He does it himself, and through courage, perseverance, will power, and a refusal to be beaten, he succeeds in the face of great odds.

The Men

Leiningen's men are not individualized. None of them are given names, but they must be drawn from the local Brazilian population. There are four hundred of these men who work on the plantation. They follow Leiningen's orders and have great confidence in his abilities to get them out of their predicament. They trust him. However, when the tide turns against them they lose heart and start to pray for deliverance. Two of them die as they try to flee to the river. When Leiningen returns from his mission to flood the plantation weak but victorious, they take care of him, cleaning his wounds and giving him healing drugs. All they want is for their leader to recover.

THEMES

Man versus Nature

Almost all stories contain conflict in some form or another. The main conflict in this story is between man and nature, in the form of the battle between Leiningen and his men and the ants. It is a struggle for possession of the plantation, and also a life and death struggle. If Leiningen and his men lose, which they come close to doing, they will all die. In the situation that exists as the story begins, man has subdued nature, in the sense that Leiningen has farmed his plantation successfully for three years. He has faced conflicts with nature before, in the form of drought and disease, and he has always emerged victorious. Through the cultivation of his plantation, he has harnessed a sometimes hostile nature to serve his own ends. In the situation he faces with the ants, however, he confronts his biggest test as nature mounts a

TOPICS FOR FURTHER STUDY

- Write a short story based on the man versus nature theme. Try to follow the common structure of the adventure tale in which more and more difficulties pile up for the protagonist until the climax is reached. To get some ideas, try searching on Google News with the search term *man survives ordeal* for some real-life stories on which to base your story.

- Watch one of the screen adaptations of "Leiningen Versus the Ants," either *The Naked Jungle* or the "Trumbo's World" episode from the television series *MacGyver*. Write a review in which you compare the adaptation to the original short story. In what ways have the filmmakers altered the original story? What have they added and what have they left out? Is the film version true to the spirit of the original? Post your review on your blog and invite classmates to watch and comment as well.

- Using the Internet and your public or school library, research the topic of army ants. If you can, consult *Animals Attack: Fire Ants* (KidHaven Press, 2003), a book for young adults. People sometimes compare ant behavior to human behavior. In terms of army ants, is there any justification in such comparisons? Give a PowerPoint presentation to your class in which you explain why ants go to war against one another and what forms the battles take.

- Go to http://www.glogster.com (or other digital poster maker program) and create a glog (a kind of poster) that might serve to advertise a movie version of "Leiningen Versus the Ants." You can share your glog with friends on your Web page or social networking site.

formidable challenge to his power. The ants form a destructive force of nature that few can withstand, and Leiningen must focus all his energy on repelling it. Apart from the initial disagreement between the District Commissioner and Leiningen, which serves merely as exposition that sets the story up; one conflict makes up the entire story. Leiningen does not experience any conflict within himself, and there is no conflict between him and his men, or between the men themselves. Everything is focused on the external enemy that must be defeated.

Creativity

From the beginning, Leiningen shows great creativity in dealing with the crisis. After observing the destruction that ants were capable of, he planned his system of inner and outer ditches that could be turned into moats. Once his system gets tested, he shows continuing creativity by responding to individual crises as they arise. He shows he has the skill to adapt to what is needed at the time. For him it is a battle of wits, almost like a chess game or a sporting contest, between him and the ants, and he trusts in the power of his human brain to win. At one point the narrator comments that to an observer it might have appeared that Leiningen's chances of winning were only one in a thousand, but that assessment would be based solely on the way the situation looked to the eye, failing to take into account "the unseen activities that can go on in a man's brain." One example of Leiningen's creativity occurs when the battle is going against him, and he comes up with the idea of lowering and then quickly raising the levels of water in the moat. It should also be pointed out that creativity occurs on both sides, since the ants exhibit considerable ingenuity in figuring out various methods to get across the water.

Leadership

In order to win his battle with the ants, it is critical that Leiningen wxhibit leadership. He is the sole man in control; his workers simply do what he tells them. He shows himself up to the task, strategically directing his men like an army general. First, he believes in himself and is sure that he can defeat the ants, and he conveys this self-confidence to the men, who take heart from his example. They too become confident of winning. But the men do not possess Leiningen's presence of mind and creativity, and they are easily discouraged. Unlike him, they do not see the larger picture, and Leiningen knows he must work hard to keep their morale up. When one

Fires were set to stop the ants. (*Chad Littlejohn / Shutterstock.com*)

man is bitten by ants and panics, it is Leiningen who must intervene and tell the man to immerse his arm in gasoline. When the ants win the first round of battle, Leiningen rallies his men and inspires them again with his cheery and confident manner. Not a single man takes up Leiningen's offer to allow them to escape via the river while there is still time. This unanimous vote of confidence is testimony to the fact that Leiningen is a resilient and effective leader. Finally, when he only has one option left in the battle, Leiningen shows outstanding qualities of leadership when he runs two miles to the dam and back in order to flood the entire plantation and drown all the ants. He knows that this is a task that he must do himself rather than delegating it to one of the men. The fact that he is successful against great odds shows that he possesses one more quality of leadership: outstanding courage.

STYLE

Point of View

The story is told by an omniscient (all-seeing) third-person narrator. This means that the narrator has complete knowledge of the world of the story and can report all the details of the action and also get into the mind of all the characters to reveal what they are thinking and feeling. The omniscient narrator also knows the previous history of the characters, what they have done in the past. In this story, however, although the narrator is omniscient, the focus is almost

entirely on the mind and actions of Leiningen, the main character or protagonist. It is mainly through his eyes that the story is presented, since none of the other characters (the men, the Indian medicine man, the District Commissioner) are presented in any detail. Although this is an adventure story that emphasizes action rather than the inner world of the characters, the narrator does devote some space to Leiningen's thought processes, his view of himself, and his confidence in his ability to defeat the ant army.

Image and Metaphor

The story is told with the use of vivid imagery. An image is like a mental picture that readers can see in their minds as they read the story. This story has many memorable images. Perhaps one of the best is the extended image, covering three paragraphs about the stricken stag: "a strange creature, writhing rather than running, an animal-like blackened statue with shapeless head and four quivering feet that buckled under it almost constantly." Not only is this a vivid image in itself, it also serves as an ominous foreshadowing of what could happen to Leiningen and his men.

In the descriptions of the ants, the images sometimes become metaphors. A metaphor occurs when something is described by a term that would normally be used to describe something else. The purpose is to bring out an unexpected similarity between the two things. For example, in this story the ants are more than once referred to as "devils," and the District Commissioner says that "every single one of them [is] a fiend from hell." The ants are also referred to as "sons of hell," and Leiningen wonders, "Was there nothing on earth that could sweep this devil's spawn back into the hell from which it came?" The metaphor in which the ants are presented as devils adds a kind of supernatural, metaphysical element to the story, suggesting a contest between good and evil. Indeed, at one point the ants are referred to as an "evil black throng."

HISTORICAL CONTEXT

European Immigration to Brazil

"Leiningen Versus the Ants" has no specific date for its setting. Although published in the 1930s, the author may have had in mind a nineteenth-century setting or a more contemporary date. There is no way of knowing, since the only

COMPARE
&
CONTRAST

- **1930s:** Black fire ants, a type of stinging ant, from South America start to gain a foothold in the United States, having first found their way to the country via contaminated cargo ships arriving at the port of Mobile, Alabama, around 1918. In the late 1930s, the red fire ant makes its entry into the United States for the first time.

  Today: Red fire ants infest much of the southeastern United States and Puerto Rico, having replaced native species and the imported black fire ant.

- **1930s:** About one million German immigrants, or those of German descent, live in Brazil. They live mainly in the southern part of the country. German is the second most commonly used language in Brazil. German immigration to Brazil began in the early nineteenth century.

Today: Brazilians of German origin make up about 10 percent of the population of Brazil. Over sixteen million people in Brazil are German speakers.

- **1930s:** Commercial short fiction flourishes in the United States in popular magazines such as the *Saturday Evening Post* and *Scribner's*. Many weekly and monthly magazines regularly feature short stories, and demand for quality short fiction is high.

  Today: The market for short stories in major commercial magazines is much smaller than even a decade or two ago. Few popular magazines regularly publish short fiction. One notable exception is the *New Yorker*, which continues to publish short fiction every week.

---

clue the presence of a well-established German plantation owner in Brazil—could apply to the mid-nineteenth century as well as the twentieth century, since German immigration to Brazil began as early as 1824. It was part of widespread European immigration to that country that continued into the twentieth century.

In the nineteenth century, European immigrants to Brazil were mostly Portuguese, Italians, and Spaniards, but Germans also accounted for significant numbers of immigrants. By mid-century, nearly 13 percent of immigrants were German. In the late 1870s, over two thousand Germans per year immigrated to Brazil, settling mostly in Santa Catarina, Rio Grande do Sul, Sao Paulo, and Espirito Santo. German immigration increased after World War I. Between 1914 and 1923, there were 29,339 German immigrants. From 1924 to 1933, this figure rose to 61,728, but from 1934 to 1939, the five years immediately preceding the outbreak of World War II, the number fell to 16,243, although this was still the third-largest national contingent, behind the Italians and Japanese. In the period from 1884 to 1949, a total of 178,250 Germans immigrated to Brazil, amounting to 4.2 percent of total immigration in that period.

In her book, *Brazil: People and Institutions*, from which the above statistics are taken, T. Lynn Smith notes that a significant aspect of German immigration to Brazil was that they did not assimilate with the local population:

> By maintaining their native language and other cultural characteristics, an attachment for the mother country, and a feeling of racial superiority and by reproducing at a very rapid rate, a small number of immigrants have proved sufficient to blanket much of south Brazil with people of Teutonic stock and German culture.

Smith also quotes the comments of Michael G. Mulhall, an English editor of a magazine in Argentina, about how the German communities in Brazil managed to preserve their distinctive culture. Writing in 1871, Mulhall observed:

> Imagine to yourself, reader, a country nearly as large as Belgium or Holland cut out of these Brazilian forests, where the inhabitants are exclusively German, and speak no other

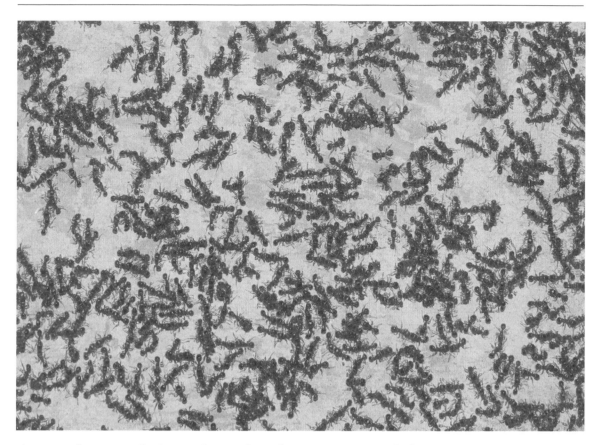

An army of ants ten miles long and two miles wide was coming towards them. (Anton Gvozdikov | Shutterstock.com)

language; where chapels and schools meet you at every opening in the wood; where the mountainsides have been in many cases cleared to make room for corn-fields; where women travel alone through the forests in perfect security; where agricultural and manufacturing industry flourish undisturbed; where crime is unknown and public instruction almost on a level with that of Prussia.

The German immigrants worked to preserve their language. Smith points out that the Germans' desire to preserve their cultural identity, as well as their high birthrate, made their impact on Brazil greater than might otherwise have been the case, given that immigrants from Germany numbered far fewer than those from Italy, Portugal, Spain, and, from the 1920s on, Japan.

CRITICAL OVERVIEW

In the nearly seventy-five years since its publication, "Leiningen Versus the Ants" has been much read by a wide variety of people but little commented upon by literary critics. This is not surprising, since it is the only work by the author that appeared in English, and it appeared simply as one story in a magazine, not a collection of stories in a book that might have attracted the attentions of reviewers and critics. In addition, as a good old-fashioned adventure story, "Leiningen Versus the Ants" does not require a great deal of literary analysis. Of the story's popularity there can be no doubt. A Google search on the title produces over 27,000 Web documents. The story is frequently part of high school reading lists, and since its first English-language publication in 1938, it has been reprinted in many anthologies.

One critic who commented on the story was Beth Johnson, editor with Barbara Solot of the anthology *Great Stories of Suspense and Adventure*, which includes "Leiningen Versus the Ants." In her "Afterword," Johnson notes that most adventure stories are about outer rather than inner conflicts, and those conflicts may be about "man versus man," "man versus fate," or—possibly the most common—"man versus nature." She notes that "Leiningen Versus the Ants" belongs to the last of these three categories, a type of adventure story that "involve[s] fierce contests between intelligent, skillful people...and the awesome natural world."

CRITICISM

Bryan Aubrey

Aubrey holds a Ph.D. in English. In the following essay, he discusses the structure of the plot in "Leiningen Versus the Ants" and the extent to which it is based on real-life ant behavior.

"Leiningen Versus the Ants" is a remarkable piece of work. Because of its swift action, gripping conflict, and vivid and horrifying imagery, once people have read it they are not likely to forget it. Indeed, there may be many a middle aged man or woman in the United States and elsewhere who remembers nothing of his or her high-school English class except "Leiningen Versus the Ants." It may well be the perfect adventure story in the category that depicts a desperate conflict between resourceful and intelligent man and relentless and overwhelming nature.

A quick look at the structure of the story gives a clue to one of the reasons it is so effective. The exposition is quick and clear, delivered mostly in dialogue. This is the section in a story that gives the reader the initial information about the situation and the characters and suggests what the conflict is going to be about. In a story that covers forty pages (as it appears in *Great Stories of Suspense and Adventure*), the exposition takes a mere two pages. After just two more pages in which some background information about Leiningen is given, the ants arrive. The author does not waste his time or the reader's: he gets straight to the action. The series of events that follow constitute what is sometimes called the rising action of the plot, in which there are twists and turns in the action, complications set in, and usually in an adventure story, the situation of the protagonist gets worse and worse until it seems hopeless. Often the complications make up a series of crises, which is certainly true for this story. The first crisis comes when the ants ingeniously try to create a bridge over the water ditch by clambering over the sinking, drowning bodies of their comrades. Leiningen overcomes the crisis by increasing the flow of water into the ditches. A second crisis

comes when the ants start to cross the water on rafts made of leaves. Leiningen meets this challenge by rapidly raising and lowering the level of water in the ditch, but that only works for a while, and the men are forced to retreat to the inner moat.

The next crisis comes when the ants figure out a way to cross the gasoline-covered trench. Leiningen responds by igniting the gasoline, but the ants keep coming. Yet another crisis occurs when one of the gasoline pumps is blocked, and Leiningen solves this one by using two old fire trucks to spray gasoline on the ants. This, too, only works for a while, and the story now reaches what is usually referred to as the climax. The climax is the do-or-die moment when the hero must either go down to defeat or rouse himself to a superhuman effort and emerge victorious. Leiningen of course accomplishes the latter, with the climax—when he rushes across ant-covered terrain to reach the dam and flood the plantation taking up about eight pages, or 20 percent of the story. It is followed by what is often called the falling action, or *dénouement* (a French term that literally means "unknotting"), in which the plot is resolved: the hero has succeeded or failed and any loose ends are tied up. The falling action in this story is the final defeat of the ants, which are swept away in the flood of water; the denouement shows Leiningen weak but alive, with the suggestion that with a little rest he will be well able to fight another day.

The story is not only an exciting one but its fictional world is completely coherent in the sense that no reader questions whether the action is plausible or not. These are killer ants, millions of them, and the reader partakes vicariously in the struggle of Leiningen and his men to fend off these rampaging insects. But when one thinks about the story afterwards, the question

WHAT DO I READ NEXT?

- Betsy Haynes is a popular author of grotesque and fantastic tales for young people, and her novel *Attack of the Killer Ants* (1996) is characteristic of her work. Two school bullies who like to stomp on ants, get their comeuppance when they are carried off by the ants who want to enslave them.

- *In the Amazon Jungle* by Algot Lange was first published in 1912. Lange was an European explorer who set out on an expedition to the Amazon jungle between Brazil and Peru. This is his true account of that expedition and the many dangers he encountered and survived, including wild animals, poisonous ants, and snakes. Left alone after his Indian guides died, and almost dead himself from fever, he was rescued by a local tribe and nursed back to health. This riveting tale is a good example of the man versus nature theme. It is available in a 2010 edition published by Book Jungle.

- *The Most Dangerous Game* by Richard Connell is a classic adventure story first published in 1924. Sanger Rainsford, an American big-game hunter, is stranded on a South American island until he is rescued by a General Zaroff. Rainsford soon finds out that Zaroff likes to hunt men, and he thinks of it as a game. In this "dangerous game," Rainsford is armed only with a knife, while the other man possesses a gun and hunting dogs. The story can be found in many anthologies and also in an edition published in 2006 by Filiquarian Publishing.

- *Yakabou Must Choose: An African Adventure for Boys and Girls* (2004) by Dennis Perry is an adventure story set in Africa. A fifteen-year-old boy named Yakabou, who needs to buy batteries for his radio, is accused of stealing them. As a punishment he is banished from the village by the chief, and he has to decide whether to run away or live like the "Old Africans." After a number of adventures, he is able to return to the village.

- Jack London (1876–1916) was an American writer who is known for his adventure novels and short stories. *The Best Short Stories of Jack London* (2008) is a collection of ten stories, including his most famous, "To Build a Fire," in which a man has to survive bitterly cold temperatures in the Klondike area in Canada after falling into a creek.

- *Hatchet* (1987), a survival tale by Gary Paulsen, is the story of thirteen-year-old Brian Robeson who is stranded alone in the Canadian wilderness following a plane crash. He must figure out what he has to do in order to survive. He manages to find food; deal with wild animals; make a bow, arrows, and a spear; and carve out a shelter from the underside of a rock.

---

may well present itself: how much of this is fact, or at least based on fact, and how much is fiction? Can ants really do all the things they do in this story? Can they really kill a stag and leave it just as white bones in six minutes, and, even more to the point, can they do such things to humans, as the District Commissioner warns Leiningen that they can?

The short answer is—fortunately—no, but that does not mean that the author, Stephenson, made it all up. Ants are indeed aggressive insects that are ruthless hunters and also go to war; they fight ferociously against each other in huge numbers, and they can inflict great devastation on an enemy. They can also exhibit actions that seem to express a remarkable intelligence.

In his book *The Ants*, Wilhelm Goetsch quotes a study by a man named Vosseler, who describes what happens when an ant army emerges from a hole in the earth and goes on the warpath:

Like a shoreless river they pour in all directions over the ground and the low shrubbery, covering the earth with their dense swarm. A mad scampering begins on all sides. Crickets, cockroaches, spiders, caterpillars, maggots—any creatures large or small, armed or unarmed . . . take aimless and headlong flight from the ruthless army.

Another authority, Julian Huxley, in his book, *Ants*, notes the ferocity of legionary or driver ants, a nomadic ant species that attacks large prey: "even horses and cattle are attacked and killed, when tethered."

A most fascinating account of the behavior of ant armies has been written by Dale R. Morris, who was part of a film crew sent to Costa Rica by the British Broadcasting Corporation (BBC) to prepare a documentary about killer ants. His article, originally titled "Massive Attack," was published in *BBC Wildlife* magazine in 2002, and has been reprinted on Morris's own Web site under the title "Ants in My Pants," along with another article by Morris, "In Search of Killer Ants," which provides more details of the expedition and also makes a number of allusions to "Leiningen Versus the Ants."

Morris observes the ant army on the move, "an insidious wave, flowing like oil across the forest floor" as small creatures flee from its path. He sees a scorpion and then a grasshopper fall victim to the ants, whose army measures twenty-five meters wide and five meters long—somewhat less formidable than the army in the story, which is ten miles long and two miles wide. Morris follows the trail of the army ants back to their bivouac, a kind of temporary nest. Dressed in a protective suit, he puts his hand inside the bivouac, but he gets more than he bargained for. Soon he is covered by stinging ants, and his protective suit does little to thwart them. Morris writes, "I tried to remain calm, but I couldn't. Instead, I ran away in the manner of a headless chicken, screaming in pain whilst flailing spasmodically." This description sounds rather like the plantation worker in the story who is similarly bitten: "Screaming, frantic with pain, the man danced and twirled like one possessed by evil spirits." With the help of an assistant, Morris manages to get free of the ants but comments on the damage they inflicted: "My neck had inflamed, my ears had turned purple and my arms looked like the surface of the moon." He notes that some of the ants clung on fiercely and were difficult to

The ants attacked the humans in droves. *(Garsya / Shutterstock.com)*

remove, which also reflects the incident in the story. Even after the man has doused his arm in gasoline, "the fierce jaws did not loosen; another man had to help him squash and remove each separate insect."

After their trip to Costa Rica, Morris and the other members of the BBC crew traveled to Tanzania, in East Africa, where they investigated the Siafu ant species, also called driver ants. A local tribesman informed them that the ants brought down and killed a tethered cow, and Morris also learned that the ants once killed a man who was drunk, had fallen and broken his leg, and therefore could not escape. A similar fate befalls a man in *The Naked Jungle*, the 1954 movie adaptation of "Leiningen Versus the Ants," in which a white settler, an enemy of Leiningen, is attacked and killed by the ants while he is drunk.

As far as the intelligence of ants is concerned, Huxley reports that there are reliable accounts of "driver ants bridging streams by each worker seizing a twig and then forming a living chain-bridge across the water, over which the rest of the army can cross." This of course is very close to what the ants in "Leiningen Versus the Ants" manage to accomplish when faced first with a water barrier and then a ditch full of gasoline. It would seem that author Carl Stephenson knew a lot about ants, and when he wrote his classic story he simply took known ant behavior and ramped it up a few notches. Killer ants in real life? Not if you are a human—but as Morris's account shows, they can certainly make you feel pretty uncomfortable if you are none too careful.

Source: Bryan Aubrey, Critical Essay on "Leiningen Versus the Ants," in *Short Stories for Students*, Gale, Cengage Learning, 2011.

CRITICISM

Catherine Dominic

Dominic is a novelist, freelance writer, and editor. In the following essay, she explores the way in which Carl Stephenson uses the characterization of Leiningen and of the ants themselves as means of creating and sustaining tension in "Leiningen Versus the Ants."

"Leiningen Versus the Ants" is a much anthologized short story that features stylistic and thematic extremes. It lends itself as a clear example of a short story relying heavily on exposition rather than dialogue, and it is a textbook representation of the commonly discussed theme of man versus nature. Despite long passages of uninterrupted narrative, and the initially incomprehensible nature of the danger posed by mere insects, Carl Stephenson's story quickly becomes a gripping tale of survival. While not an overly complex tale, "Leiningen Versus the Ants" draws readers in through its portrayal of an arrogant protagonist who initially warrants contempt, but who nevertheless proves to be a deeply engaging character. Stephenson establishes the framework for the story's conflict, revealing as gradually to the reader as to Leiningen the enormity of the danger faced by Leiningen's plantation. At the same time, the ants themselves are gradually recognized as having a startling array of very human qualities. All of this is achieved through a storytelling technique that aside from the opening and closing scenes is nearly devoid of dialogue.

Most of what little dialogue there is in "Leiningen Versus the Ants" appears at the beginning of the story. Leiningen is told by a Brazilian government official about the approaching army of voracious ants. The official is adamant about the danger in which Leiningen is placing himself and his workers, stating that the ants are "not creatures you can fight—they're an act of God! . . . And

> WHILE NOT AN OVERLY COMPLEX TALE, 'LEININGEN VERSUS THE ANTS' DRAWS READERS IN THROUGH ITS PORTRAYAL OF AN ARROGANT PROTAGONIST WHO INITIALLY WARRANTS CONTEMPT, BUT WHO NEVERTHELESS PROVES TO BE A DEEPLY ENGAGING CHARACTER."

every single one of them a fiend from hell." In contrast to the official's state of near panic, Leiningen remains calm, impassive, even lighthearted. Despite being informed that the ants can devour a buffalo clean to the bones, Leiningen assures the official that his own intelligence will prevail. Leiningen then privately recounts the number of other natural disasters he has weathered in the past three years as a planter in Brazil. He harshly judges people who flee unnecessarily from such dangers, or who are conquered easily by the elements, or who lazily do not bother to prepare themselves for disaster. He cites "cunning," "organization," and his marshalling of "the resources of modern science" as factors that have contributed to the profitability of his plantation. In the paragraphs that fall between Leiningen's conversation with the official and the visible approach of the ants, Leiningen is presented as smart but stubborn, and disdainful of individuals who fail to think themselves out of dangerous situations. "The ants," he thinks, "were indeed mighty, but the brain of man was mightier." The story thus far has progressed largely through Leiningen's own thoughts; Stephenson has established his protagonist as a man who regards himself as intellectually superior to most others, and one who arrogantly anticipates an opportunity to conquer the threatening element of nature that has emerged.

Throughout the next portion of the story, in which the ants' first efforts to attack the plantation are described, the narration remains uninterrupted by dialogue. The ants are increasingly depicted as possessing almost humanlike qualities, making them an even more impressive foe, in Leiningen's estimation. When Leiningen examines the approach of his enemy, viewing their sheer number, he wonders whether or not his own cunning and intelligence will be up to this challenge. Now the ants are seen as more organized than a human army. Leiningen observes the way the ants send out scouts and communicate with the rest of the army the results of their reconnaissance mission. They are further attributed with human qualities when it is noted that the ants "expected that at some point they would find a way to cross the water." To have expectations and to adjust ones plans based on those expectations is not a quality typically associated with the insect world. Indeed, Leiningen and his men begin to suspect the ants are thinking of how they will cross the ditch and feast upon them. As the ants are increasingly viewed not simply as vicious creatures, but thinking creatures, Leiningen and his men grow rapidly more fearful.

Almost as quickly as Leiningen acknowledges the extreme nature of the danger he and his fellows are in, he finds a new reserve of energy and confidence. As fear subsides, he begins to view his battle with the ants as a game of "Olympic" proportions, "a gigantic and thrilling game, from which he was determined to emerge victor." Although this overly confident attitude is a testament to Leiningen's arrogance, it nevertheless serves to calm the men and enables them to redouble their own efforts at keeping the ants at bay. Temporarily able to hold off the enemy, Leiningen grows increasingly sure of success. Such confidence is short lived, however. In disbelief, Leiningen watches the ants do what he previously believed impossible: make rafts to ford the ditch. They do so by chewing leaves and piling onto them like little boats. His previously buoyant spirit, deflated by the rafting ants, collapses completely when he watches the ants devour the stag.

Leiningen's actions continue to reveal much about his character. He begins to regard the ants with some level of sick admiration. After the ants cover the stag, Leiningen takes out his watch and times how long it takes them to devour the animal down to the bone. He does not run in fear and panic; he calmly admires the ants' efficiency before turning to his next plan. The ants' ingenuity and skill generate in Leiningen a "cold and violent purpose" that replaces mere optimism in his intelligence. With each new effort by Leiningen, the ants try a different tactic; Leiningen's success is always undercut by a new tactic by the ants. Repeatedly, Leiningen reflects on the ants' humanlike understanding, stating that they

seemed to "know their duty." Later, the ants are attributed with the human quality of "greed," even though their actions are more accurately described as instinctual, and geared toward self-preservation, rather than being motivated by selfish desires to gorge themselves on Leiningen's plantation. As the siege continues, Leiningen comments on the ants' "perseverance," another quality more human than insectlike.

Contemplating his final effort to save his own life and the lives of the remaining men, Leiningen hopes that the ants are not as "almighty" as he had believed. Although he steps back from this description, Leiningen for a moment considers the ants to be an all-powerful, godlike force. Their efforts have been so impressive that, in Leiningen's eyes, the ants have not only been compared to humans, but have transcended such an analogy. To Leiningen's credit, he continues to bolster the hopes of his men that survival is possible. He takes heroic measures, risking his life to dam the river and flood the whole plantation the ants are traversing, and sustaining great personal injury in the process. Unbelievably, Leiningen does not succumb to the direct assault of the ants, but remembering in a moment of terror the six minutes it took for the ants to devour the stag, Leiningen finds the strength to rise again and save himself. At the end of the story, the triumphant Leiningen jokes, grins, and sleeps. His arrogance as much as his intelligence saves him.

The few words that Leiningen speaks in the story are statements designed to encourage his men. Leiningen has, to this point, demonstrated no affection for the men, only an interest in preserving the wealth that the plantation represents. While it may be argued that as a character he is flawed in his disregard for the well-being of his men, he manages, through his brashness and cunning, to protect and save many of them. His motivations may be selfish—he protects the men because he needs them to protect the plantation—but the result is a positive one for most of the men. At the same time, Leiningen, in the end, loses his crops, suffers the nearly complete destruction of his plantation, and does lose some of the men who die either by ant attack or through their own efforts to escape by crossing the crocodile- and piranha-infested river. Had he fled when warned, he would still have lost the plantation, but his body would be whole and unharmed, and he would not have lost a single man.

Leiningen's actions rivet the reader to the story, and his swaggering, intelligent, risk-taking character contributes significantly to the story's tension. The tension further mounts as Leiningen becomes increasingly impressed with the human qualities the ants possess. Consequently, his understanding of the danger in which he has placed himself and his men is gradually solidified. This process also contributes to the swelling of the story's suspense. Despite being a man of few words, and as much because of his faults as well as his strengths, Leiningen serves as the focal point for the story's conflict and is the basis for the reader's sustained engagement with the narrative.

Source: Catherine Dominic, Critical Essay on "Leiningen Versus the Ants," in *Short Stories for Students*, Gale, Cengage Learning, 2011.

Joshua Blu Buhs

In the following excerpt, Buhs discusses ant sociology and the interaction of ants with humans as chronicled in literature.

THE MEANING OF ANTS

... By the time that *Solenopsis invicta* reached North America, ants had been a favorite object of moral lessons for millennia, "statements as to [their] intelligence, diligence, avarice, foresight and policy...a part of the common patrimony that we acquire in prepatory school," the Nobel Prize-winning playwright Maurice Maeterlinck said. "Go to the ant, you sluggard," advised the author of Proverbs (6:6), for instance. "Consider its way, and be wise! It has no commander, no overseer or ruler, yet it stores its provisions in summer and gathers its food at harvest." During the nineteenth century and into the twentieth, however, changing agricultural practices—especially in the U.S. Midwest—and a generation of self-consciously secular ant biologists combined to create a new image of the insects, one that did not replace the traditional notion, but grew along side and challenged it. Ants became less a paragon of virtue and more of a "monster," in the original sense of that word: an omen of bad things to come.

In the second half of the nineteenth century, agriculture in the American Midwest intensified. Railroads and canals connected markets, increasing demand for produce and the availability of capital. New agricultural machines became available and farm size grew. Crops were planted in dense, homogenous stands.

(The South would follow this same trajectory in later years, although prodded by the federal government's investment, not market forces.) These farms were bonanzas for insects, providing copious amounts of food in relatively restricted areas, and throughout the later years of the nineteenth century insect populations irrupted across the region: locusts, the chinch bug, and the Colorado potato beetle, for example, all devoured crops. Prior generations—although sometimes vociferously battling insects—often had looked indulgently upon insects. Nettlesome though they may have been, bugs were also seen as products of God's imagination, material proof of His being....

Cooperation, Wheeler acknowledged, is an awesome force for good—cooperation promised to counter the horrors of nationalism so graphically illustrated during World War I—but cooperation could be perverted, too, and lead to social disintegration. Ants were the most successful insect group on earth, a status that Wheeler attributed to their highly developed social organization: but they were also monsters, warnings of what could happen if humans subsumed too much of their individuality into society. As the poet W. H. Auden wrote decades later, what insects "mean to themselves or to God is a meaningless question: they to us are quite simply what we must never become."

Broadly understood as a rebuke to the religious understandings of ants, Wheeler's ideas leaped the fence surrounding the Ivory Tower, entered the popular culture, and merged with the increasing distaste of insects generally. His view found a place in Arpaud Ferenczy's 1924 novel *The Ants of Timothy Thümmel*, for example—in which a tribe of African ants suffered when politicians, soldiers, and clerics decided that they need not work, but should instead be served by others—and the popular accounts of Maeterlinck and the British scientist Julian Huxley. In these works, fear of communism's consequences mixed with admiration for the ant's cooperative lifestyle. By the mid to late 1930s, though, and continuing into the 1940s, writings about ants became increasingly pessimistic, dovetailing with critiques of Soviet communism and Nazi totalitarianism. "Is there anything subliminally foreboding about this fascination with the ant-hill?" the editors of *Christian Century* asked about the popularity of ant farms in postwar America. "Is it a dreadful future we see through this translucent plastic—regimented automatons, driven, dutiful in their prescribed pointless doing?" Sparked by the work of the psychologist T. C. Schnierla, the American press developed a taste for stories about army ants—South American insects that moved as a phalanx across the jungle, leaving a path of devastation. Swarming killers of the jungle, the *Saturday Evening Post* called them. "Their conduct seems often a grotesque parody of man at his worst," *Newsweek* reported. "The ants bivouac regularly, like Caesar's legions; as camp followers they have plump parasitic beetles; they can even claim a sort of airforce of flies and scavenger birds." The myrmecologist Caryl Haskins caught the mood in 1939 with *Of Ants and Men* (a selection of the month by the Scientific Book Club) and later in 1951 with *Of Societies and Men*, arguing that ants lived in totalitarian states, the insect equivalents of Nazis and communists.

This view of ants found its most refined expression in Carl Stephenson's 1938 story "Leiningen versus the Ants," and the story's popularity over the next two decades proves the degree to which ants were seen as dangerous: William Conrad voiced Leiningen in a 1948 radio play and Charlton Heston brought the character to the silver screen six years later. Originally published in *Esquire* magazine, then selling about half a million copies each month, the tale chronicled the battle between Leiningen, a white plantation owner in South America, and "twenty square miles of life destroying ants." An example of civilization, Leiningen had struggled to carve his plantation out of the oppressive Amazonian jungle and he stood his ground when army ants marched toward his property, telling a Brazilian official, "When I began this model farm and plantation three years ago, I took into account all that could conceivably happen to it. And now I'm ready for anything and everything—including your ants." The fight was epic: he filled a moat with water, but the ants crossed on rafts of leaves; he shoveled dirt on the advancing hordes, but they continued unimpeded; he built a wall of fire around his land, but it ran out of fuel. The ants devoured his crops and forced Leiningen and his servants to take refuge on a small disc of raised land. Finally, Leiningen wrapped himself in kerosene-soaked rags and dashed two miles across a sea of ants that could strip a buffalo to bones "before you can spit three times" to open a dam and drown the insects. The

ants ate through the rags and gobbled his flesh; he staggered and fell unconscious, but not before he flooded his plantation, destroying everything that he had built—and killing the ants. The story illustrated the mettle, ingenuity, and determination of humans in the face of adversity; it also emphasized the threat posed by ants. They did not deserve praise, but opprobrium—not emulation, but hatred. The proper response was not to observe and celebrate them, but to kill them. The ants were a people, as Proverbs 30:25 said, but a dangerous people, epitomizing the mindless savagery that Americans saw in Nazism, communism, and other forms of totalitarianism.

Source: Joshua Blu Buhs, "Grins a Prohibitive Fracture, 1945–1957," in *The Fire Ants War: Nature, Science, and Public Policy in Twentieth-century America*, University of Chicago Press, 2004, pp. 41–46.

William H. Gotwald, Jr.

In the following excerpt, Gotwald describes how ants are used as metaphors and mythology in literature.

ARMY ANTS AND THE MILITARY METAPHOR

. . . The behavior of army ants surely invites comparison to military maneuvers, strategy, and logistics. Even the earliest references to these ants (e.g., Swainson 1835) described how they move about in "armies." Frank M. Chapman (1929, p. 185), a distinguished ornithologist and former curator of birds at the American Museum of Natural History, recounted the movement of a "detachment" of army ants in Panama and noted of their attack on invertebrates of the forest floor: "One expects to hear the blare of trumpets and cries of agony." Perhaps the military metaphor as applied to army ants reached its pinnacle in the popular literature with the publication of William Beebe's article "The Home Town of the Army Ants" (1919). Beebe, an authority on tropical biology and popularizer of scientific research, used numerous military terms to describe the ants and their biology, including *legionaries, warriors, scouts, soldiers, guards, sappers, booty, battalions, scimitars*, (referring to their mandibles), *Spartan, squad, expedition, battle*, and even *court-martial*. "Army ants," he wrote (1919, p. 454), "have no insignia to lay aside, and their swords are too firmly hafted in their own beings to be hung up as post-bellum mural decorations, or—as is done only in poster-land—metamorphosed into pruning-hooks and ploughshares."

The military metaphor is fixed in place with the stubborn cement of time, and at least some of the terms are now incorporated into the scientific literature. The late T. C. Schneirla, prominent behaviorist at the American Museum of Natural History, did more than anyone else to ensure that such terms as *raid*, *booty*, and *bivouac* achieved a certain exclusivity in their use in describing army ant lifeways. Schneirla, who pioneered modern research into the behavior of army ants, especially in the New World tropics, promoted the military metaphor as a useful exercise in distinguishing army ants from the many other species of predatory ants.

ARMY ANTS MYTHOLOGIZED

No one account did more to immortalize army ants and their murderous exploits than Carl Stephenson's remarkable short story "Leiningen versus the Ants." In it, a Brazilian plantation is besieged by an advancing tide of ravenous army ants that indiscriminately devours every living thing in its path. Leiningen, the intractable owner of the plantation, is warned of the approaching horde: "The Brazilian official threw up lean and lanky arms and clawed the air with wildly distended fingers. 'Leiningen!' he shouted. 'You're insane! They're not creatures you can fight—they're an elemental—an act of God! Ten miles long, two miles wide—ants, nothing but ants! And every single one of them a fiend from hell; before you can spit three times they'll eat a full-grown buffalo to the bones. I tell you if you don't clear out at once there'll be nothing left of you but a skeleton picked as clean as your own plantation'" (Stephenson 1940).

As the frenzied mass of ants reaches the plantation, Leiningen mounts his horse and rides toward the oncoming swarm, ready to defend life, limb, and property: "It was a sight one could never forget. Over the range of hills, as far as eye could see, crept a darkening hem, ever longer and broader, until the shadow spread across the slope from east to west, then downwards, downwards, uncannily swift, and all the green herbage of that wide vista was being mown as by a giant sickle, leaving only the vast moving shadow, extending, deepening, and moving rapidly nearer."

Of course, this is the stuff of which movies are made. Indeed, Hollywood could not resist the temptation to commit to film this epic, primeval battle of man against nature. In 1954, Stephenson's tale was transformed into *The Naked Jungle*, a cinematic adventure starring Charlton Heston and Eleanor Parker. The ants rampage, stripping the flesh from men and horses unfortunate enough to stumble into the seething legion, leaving in their wake impeccably cleaned skeletons, grisly reminders of their insatiable appetite. Live ants abound in the film, scurrying about with convincing predatory authority, but under cursory examination they reveal themselves to be carpenter ants of the genus *Camponotus*.

On a more somber note, one cannot help but speculate that the red ants that suffuse the novel *One Hundred Years of Solitude*, the spectral masterpiece by Nobel Prize winner Gabriel Garcia Márquez, one of Latin America's most celebrated writers, are army ants. We are told, for instance, that the sleeping couple, Aureliano and Amaranta Ursula, "are awaked by a torrent of carnivorous ants who were ready to eat them alive." Later, the devastation of human tragedy descends on the reader as Amaranta dies producing a son, the last of the family line. Aureliano, absorbed in his grief and his nostalgia for lost friendships, forgets his newborn son in his reflective preoccupation. His dreaminess is soon shattered: "And then he saw the child. It was a dry and bloated bag of skin that all the ants in the world were dragging toward their holes along the stone path in the garden."

As excessive and embellished as some fictional accounts are, we may find at their core a kernel of truth. Du Chaillu (1861), recounting his explorations of central Africa, reported: "The negroes relate that criminals were in former times exposed in the path of the bashikouay ants, as the most cruel manner of putting to death." And when collecting stories about driver ants in Ghana, I was told of an infant who died in the onslaught of a foraging swarm of these ants. Although I could not confirm this story in any official way, it is not a tale that challenges credulity. Ghanaian women traditionally till their family gardens and when doing so are in the habit of depositing their babies on the ground in the shade of nearby trees.

Is it any wonder, then, given the mythology and the reality of army ants, that these insects are popularly regarded today as nature's consummate predators, warriors whose deeds would make the likes of Genghis Khan blush with envy?

Source: William H. Gotwald, Jr., "Army Ants and the Military Metaphor," in *Army Ants: The Biology of Social Predation*, Cornell University Press, 1995, pp. 250–52.

SOURCES

Dalton, Quinn, "*The Atlantic* and the Decline of the Short Story," in *mediabistro.com*, http://www.mediabistro.com/articles/cache/a4183.asp (accessed June 15, 2010).

"German Speaking Populations Outside Germany," in *BBGerman*, http://www.bbgerman.com/german-speaking-population-outisde-german.html (accessed June 15, 2010).

Goetsch, Wilhelm, *The Ants*, University of Michigan Press, 1969, p. 46.

Huxley, Julian, *Ants*, 1930, reprint, AMS Press, 1969, pp. 40, 64.

Johnson, Beth, "Afterword," in *Great Stories of Suspense and Adventure*, edited by Beth Johnson and Barbara Solot, Townsend Press, 2003, pp. 180–81.

Lockley, Timothy C., "Imported Fire Ants," in *Radcliffe's IPM World Textbook*, University of Minnesota, http://ipmworld.umn.edu/chapters/lockley.htm (accessed June 15, 2010).

Morris, Dale R., "Ants in My Pants," in *geckoeye.com*, http://www.geckoeye.com/writing.php?article=ants (accessed June 17, 2010).

———, "In Search of Killer Ants," in *geckoeye.com*, http://www.geckoeye.com/writing.php?article=killer (accessed June 17, 2010).

Neyer, Dan, "Introduction," in *The Library: "Leiningen Versus the Ants,"* The Nostalgia League, http://thenostalgialeague.com/olmag/stephenson-leiningen-versus-the-ants.html (accessed June 1, 2010).

Smith, T. Lynn, *Brazil: People and Institutions*, rev. ed., Louisiana State University Press, 1954, p. 236.

Stephenson, Carl, "Leiningen Versus the Ants," in *Great Stories of Suspense and Adventure*, edited by Beth Johnson and Barbara Solot, Townsend Press, 2003, pp. 51–92.

FURTHER READING

Gordon, Deborah M., *Ants at Work: How an Insect Society is Organized*, W. W. Norton, 2000.

Gordon is a scientist who spent seventeen summers studying colonies of harvester ants in the Arizona desert. The result is an engaging and sometimes humorous account, part science and part memoir, of how these ants go about their lives. The book is illustrated by many drawings.

Gordon, Nick, *In the Heart of the Amazon*, John Blake, 2002.

Gordon is an acclaimed photographer and filmmaker, and this book is a collection of nonfiction stories drawn from Gordon's many years of living and working in the Amazon jungle.

Moffett, Mark W., *Adventures among Ants: A Global Safari with a Cast of Trillions*, University of California Press, 2010.

Biologist and explorer Moffett recounts his travels to four different continents as he studied ant societies. The book includes not only accounts of how ant societies function but also Moffett's remarkable close up photographs of ants as they perform their different roles. Reviewers have commented on Moffett's accessible writing style and the interesting ways in which he presents his material.

Thoreau, Henry David, *Walden*, Beacon Press, 2004.

This is Thoreau's account of the two-and-a-half years he spent living on the edge of Walden Pond, near Concord, Massachusetts. Chapter 12, "Brute Neighbors," contains his description of a war he witnessed between two ant colonies.

SUGGESTED SEARCH TERMS

Carl Stephenson

Carl Stephenson AND Leiningen Versus the Ants

killer ants

ant behavior

army ants

Marabunta

man versus nature

adventure story genre

The Man Who Would Be King

RUDYARD KIPLING

1888

Rudyard Kipling's "The Man Who Would Be King" is acknowledged as a masterpiece of short fiction, yet controversy has continued for a century about Kipling's place in the canon of English literature. First known as a young genius from the British colony of India, he fascinated his readers with his fresh tales of Anglo-Indian life when he arrived in London in 1889. Kipling became known as an apologist for the British Empire, explicitly in such poems as "The White Man's Burden" and "Recessional." Even after winning the Nobel Prize for Literature in 1907, the first Englishman to receive this honor, Kipling was hated by liberal critics of colonialism. Though he continued to publish and be read until his death in 1936, he came to be viewed as part of history rather than as part of literature as the British Empire broke up. Slowly, critics have begun to revive Kipling's reputation as an artist, citing his genius with language, compression, and ironic narrators. He is now accepted as a pioneer of the English short story.

"The Man Who Would Be King" was written and first published in India as part of the collection called *The Phantom Rickshaw* (1888). The twenty-three-year-old author took it with him to London. Original readers read it for the adventure and did not consider it as fantasy, for explorers like Sir James Brooke, the white rajah of Sarawak, had actually carved out such native kingdoms for themselves. Today, the story is often seen as a parable on imperialism. Its

Rudyard Kipling

ambiguity allows it to be read both ways, as the justification of empire and as a criticism of it. A copy of the story can be found in *The Man Who Would Be King and Other Stories*, published by Oxford World Classics in 2008.

AUTHOR BIOGRAPHY

Kipling was born on December 30, 1865, in Bombay, India, to Alice MacDonald Kipling and John Lockwood Kipling, a sculptor, artist, writer, and professor at an architectural school in Bombay. As a child, Kipling spoke better Hindi than English, a fact that may have prompted his parents to send him at age five, and his sister Trix, age three, to England, while they remained in India. Anglo-Indians often sent their children away from the heat and disease of India and the influence of Indian servants. Kipling felt abandoned when he had to live with

Captain and Mrs. Holloway in Portsmouth, England. Kipling named their home "The House of Desolation." While there, he became nearsighted and suffered a nervous breakdown from cruel treatment. This left permanent emotional scars that colored his writing.

In 1878 Kipling entered United Services College at Westward Ho!, Devon, England, a school that prepared boys for the armed forces. He wrote of this time in *Stalky & Co.* (1899). Kipling's father, now curator of the Lahore Museum, secured him a position as assistant editor at a small local paper, the *Civil and Military Gazette*. At sixteen, he arrived back in India where, as a journalist, he wrote local news for other Anglo-Indians, and this gave him background material for the Indian stories. In 1886, he published his first collection of poetry, *Departmental Ditties*. He also published his short stories in the *Gazette* in 1886 and 1887, collected as *Plain Tales from the Hills* in 1888. In 1887, he was transferred to the *Pioneer* in Allahabad, India, where he published six more volumes of short stories in 1888: *Soldiers Three*, *The Story of the Gadsbys*, *In Black and White*, *Under the Deodars*, *The Phantom Rickshaw*, and *Wee Willie Winkie*. Taking his collected works, he arrived in London in 1889, becoming instantly famous at the age of twenty-three with his fascinating tales and poems of India.

He wrote his first novel, *The Light that Failed*, in 1890. With American publishing agent Wolcott Balestier, he collaborated on another novel, *The Naulahka* (1891). When Balestier died suddenly, Kipling married Balestier's sister Caroline in 1892. He moved to be near his new in-laws in Brattleboro, Vermont, where his daughter Josephine was born in 1892. In the United States, Kipling produced *Barrack-Room Ballads* (1892), *Jungle Book* (1894–1895), and *Captains Courageous* (1897). In 1896, a second daughter, Elsie, was born. The family then moved to Torquay, Devon, England, where Kipling's son, John, was born in 1897.

During this time Kipling began to be more strident in his defense of the British Empire, resulting in more and more critical attacks on his conservative politics. He published *Kim* in 1901, *Just So Stories* in 1902, and *Puck of Pook's Hill* in 1906, winning the Nobel Prize for Literature in 1907, the first English author to do so. Though he continued to write, his professional reputation declined during the first decades of the twentieth century. He died of a perforated duodenal ulcer at the age of seventy on January 18, 1936.

PLOT SUMMARY

The first-person narrator begins by saying he once almost knew a king and was even promised a part in the ruling of the kingdom, but the king is dead, and he will have to look for his own crown now. The incident begins in a train that travels between Ajmir and Mhow in India. The narrator usually travels first class but, low on funds, has to go intermediate class, which includes the poor and bums. Into the train carriage comes a black-browed man, with whom the narrator feels some rapport as a fellow wanderer to forgotten corners of the empire. They speak of their experiences with the seamier side of life in India.

The man wants to send a telegram but has no money, and neither does the narrator. The stranger persuades the narrator to come back early from his trip and go to Marwar Junction to find his red-haired friend and deliver the message, "He has gone south for the week." The narrator agrees but warns the man not to try his usual trick of posing as a newspaperman from the *Backwoodsman*. The real correspondent (the narrator himself) is around and will cause him trouble. The man says that he is going to try to blackmail the rajah of Degumber over killing his father's widow, threatening that he will put it in the newspaper unless he gets paid off.

The stranger gets off the train, and the narrator reflects on this type of scam he has heard of before. The imposters usually die suddenly. The native officials are so terrified of getting into the British papers that they can be easily blackmailed, but the narrator says that no one really cares about these petty rulers, for these are the evil places of the earth.

The narrator meets the train at Marwar Junction and finds the red-haired man and delivers the message. The narrator decides to report the black-browed man and the red-haired man to the authorities to get them deported before they get themselves into trouble with their extortion schemes. The narrator returns to his newspaper office, describing the colorful visitors in an Indian pressroom and the hectic schedule with half-naked natives printing the paper all night as he waits by the telegraph for late-breaking news

MEDIA ADAPTATIONS

- *The Man Who Would Be King* is a 1975 film adapted from Kipling's story and directed by John Huston, starring Sean Connery, Michael Caine, Saeed Jaffrey, and Christopher Plummer. It was produced by Columbia Pictures and Allied Artists Pictures Corporation.

- *The Man Who Would Be King and Other Stories* is read by Fred Williams for Blackstone Audio in 2009. It runs twelve hours in length on Encoded Windows Media.

from Europe. India is a dangerous place in the hot season with many deaths and plagues. In such a hot season, late at night, the two men walk into the narrator's office, demanding a drink. They know he is the one who got them deported from Degumber State and demand that he help them now.

Daniel Dravot, the red-haired man, introduces himself and Peachey Carnehan, the man with the eyebrows, as former soldiers who have tried every profession. Peachey announces that India is no longer big enough for them; they are going to Kafiristan in Afghanistan to become kings, and they want to look at books and maps. Peachey brings up their "Contrack," which says that they will not touch liquor or women while they are becoming kings and that they will be loyal to each other. The narrator warns them they will be killed as soon as they leave India. He tries to offer them a job. They insist they fought in the Second Afghan War with Roberts, so they know the land as far as Jagdallak. They spend time looking at the materials on Afghanistan, and the narrator agrees to see them off the next day.

The next day, the narrator finds the two at the Serai, the bazaar, but he does not recognize them at first. Dravot is disguised as a mad priest going to Kabul to sell toys to the emir, and Peachey is going as his servant. The caravan men are impressed, inviting the priest to come with them for good luck, because they believe the mad are protected by God. The narrator sees that underneath the toys they carry in their packs, the two adventurers have rifles and ammunition. They have invested all their money in camels and rifles and will be going through Khyber Pass with the caravan. Dravot asks for a good luck charm, and the narrator gives him a Masonic charm from his watch. Ten days later the narrator hears the duo made it to Peshawur and went with the caravan to Kabul.

Two years later, an old crippled man with gray hair walks into the newspaper office. He announces that he is Peachey Carnehan and insists that he and Dravot were once the kings of Kafiristan. The narrator gives him a drink, and Peachey, obviously crazed, tells their story. At this point the narrative shifts to the nested story that the newspaperman hears from Peachey, who describes the journey they had made. As he told it, when he and Dravot got to Kafiristan, they had to kill and eat the camels, who could go no farther; then they killed a man with a mule cart so they could take his cart to carry their guns. After a while, they had to kill and eat the mules. In the mountains, when they saw the Kafirs fighting among themselves in a feud, Peachey and Dravot interfered with their rifles, helping one side win.

Peachey explains how Dravot began to act like a King and ordered the men he helped win to carry the rifles. Dravot pretended he knew their idol god, Imbra, and the people began to worship him as a god as well. He negotiated between the warring villages and made peace. Dravot showed the villages how to start cultivating the land and set up a legal system to settle disputes. Then Peachey went to the next valley, found poor people starving, and brought them to the first valley. He gave them land, making them part of the kingdom in a ritual with goat's blood. The pair went to another valley and made friends with the chief of Bashkai, threatening him to make him join their union. Peachey began to drill the men and with this small army took over other villages, splitting from Dravot, who was doing the same. When they reunited after a few months, they had a large army, and Dravot began claiming he was the son of Alexander the Great. He bragged that they had gold and jewels in their land, and he made them each a gold crown.

Once they had their kingdom and crowns, Dravot decided to stop fighting and establish the kingdom through Freemasonry. They brought forward the chief at Bashkai whom they renamed Billy Fish, and Dravot told Peachey to give him the Masonic handshake. Peachey was surprised that Billy Fish knew the Fellow Craft grip. Dravot had discovered that this tribe knew Freemasonry to the second degree, so he claimed he was a Grand Master and that he would build a lodge for their higher initiation rites. Peachey objected that it is against the Masonic law to do this, but Dravot saw this as a way to conquer without using warfare. He made their temple of Imbra into a lodge room, and the women made their aprons. Dravot claimed that they were gods who were Grand Masters of the Craft who had come to make Kafiristan peaceful and prosperous.

One priest became suspicious and turned over the temple stone Dravot sat on only to find the same Master's Mark on it that was on Dravot's apron. The people were convinced, and Dravot said he would make a nation of them. He learned their language and made bridges over the ravines. Dravot was so good at being king that Peachey simply took his orders. Peachey began making deals to get more rifles, distributed them, and drilled the men, becoming a kind of commander-in-chief. Dravot claimed he would make these white natives into Englishmen and part of the British Empire and believed that Queen Victoria would give him a knighthood.

Dravot decided he must have a wife, but Peachey reminded him of the contract—no women. Dravot insisted, even though the people were uneasy because a woman cannot marry a god. Only Billy Fish and Peachey supported Dravot. When the bride was brought to Dravot, she bit him on the neck in terror, and he began to bleed. The natives realized he was human, not a god. When Dravot ran for his life with Billy Fish and Peachey, the natives pursued them. Finally, Dravot took the blame and asked Peachey's forgiveness, saying he would meet the natives alone to save Peachey's life. Peachey insisted on sticking with him to the end. The natives killed Billy Fish and forced Dravot to the middle of a rope bridge over a ravine and cut the cords, so that he fell to his death. They crucified Peachey with pegs, but he lived through the night, so they let him go.

Peachey, crippled and half mad, makes it back to India alone. He shows the narrator what he carried in his sack all the way to keep him company on the road: Dravot's shrunken head with his gold crown. Peachey is found the next day begging in the street until he gets sunstroke. The narrator takes him to a mission where he dies, but no trace of Daniel Dravot's head is ever found.

CHARACTERS

The Bride
Dravot decides to take a bride. When she is brought to Dravot, she bites him, and he begins to bleed, proving that he is not a god.

Peachey Taliaferro Carnehan
Peachey is the black-browed man whom the narrator meets in the intermediate-class carriage on the train. He is smaller than Dravot and has a taste for whiskey. He and Dravot are former military men trying to succeed in India by their wits. Peachey is the one who announces that the two friends are going away to be kings because India is not big enough for them. He says they are not little men, meaning, they know how to think big, like Brooke, the white rajah of Sarawak. Peachey is proud of the "Contrack" they have made and gives it as proof of their sincerity. While Peachey's weakness is drink, Dravot's is women.

Peachey, for all his talk, is a loyal sidekick. When they disguise themselves, he goes as the servant. Dravot always takes the lead. Peachey has the courage to back Dravot, but Dravot is the one with the charisma and authority to pull off their adventure. The people fear Peachey as the military man, but they love Dravot, their king. Though Dravot initially makes Peachey a king too, Peachey admits to the narrator that it was really Dravot who was king. Peachey is so full of admiration for Dravot's talent to pull off the hoax that he stands out of the way and decides to take orders. He becomes the commander-in-chief, training the army and trading for more guns and ammunition. He learns from Dravot, copying his methods of coercion.

Of the two, however, only Peachey seems to hang on to his common sense. He is a perfect companion and partner for Dravot, with enough caution to put on the brakes at the right time, because Dravot drives everything to extremes. Peachey is the shrewd counselor who advises

Dravot in key moments. He warns about the illegality of their Masonic impersonations or when they are about to lose the people's trust with the marriage. Even when Dravot hurts Peachey's feelings and ignores his advice, Peachey remains loyal. He is true to his own oath in the contract and remains at Dravot's side. Peachey wins some respect from the natives after he survives the crucifixion for a night. They let him go. When he returns to India mad and disfigured, there is a measure of sympathy for him from both reader and narrator. His loyalty and love for Dravot are proven by his holding on to the shrunken head of his partner. He truly seems to believe that Dravot is a king.

Daniel Dravot
Daniel Dravot is a big showy man who swaggers and tries to act like a gentleman. A former sergeant, he becomes a con man and adventurer with his partner Peachey Carnehan. He has been a soldier, sailor, pressman, preacher, and blackmailer. He has red hair and a red beard that he chews while thinking. Dravot is energetic, ambitious, and imaginative. As is seen in his performance as the mad priest, he has considerable dramatic skill. With his very first encounter with the Kafirs, he knows how to command and intimidate them, bowing to their god, Imbra, as though familiar with their ways. He becomes the leader over his partner, Peachey, because of his natural skill at bluffing and his knowledge of the native languages. His daring and optimism are infectious, drawing in the support of others through his persuasive charm and confidence. He is both a parody and an embodiment of the methods of imperialism, using military force and cultural manipulation to get control of the people.

Although Dravot's reforms of native life seem humane, with the stopping of feuds, cultivation of the land, and the brotherhood of the Masonic lodge, he rides roughshod over the native religion and customs, insisting on taking a bride without permission, an act that is his undoing and that breaks the contract the partners set up. He is more rogue than villain, however, and retains the reader's sympathy to some degree because of his loyalty to Peachey. Though readers are always aware of Dravot's delusions of grandeur and may disapprove his lack of morality, they are drawn into the adventure with the narrator, half wishing him to succeed and half hoping he will be put in his place.

Dravot sees the natives of Kafiristan as simple enough to bully into submission. Though he puffs up the natives as having white skin and being budding Englishmen with his training, he does not really intend to treat them as equals because that would diminish his own power. He invents a society that, like the British Empire, will seemingly improve the natives' lives while making them dependent. Dravot does not have enough self-discipline to maintain his role as king. He has presented himself to the people as a god and begins to believe in his own invincibility. He misunderstands kingship, thinking it means merely his own self-interest rather than responsibility. He breaks several laws, causing his luck to change. He also hurts Peachey's feelings, not giving him proper credit for being loyal.

Dravot regains sympathy, however, by the manner in which he dies. He dies like a king, taking full responsibility for his folly. He tries to save Peachey and Billy Fish, but when he cannot, he dies with dignity and courage.

Billy Fish

Billy Fish is the chief of the village of Bashkai, the second village Peachey subdues by copying Dravot's methods. Peachey leaves the chief in charge, telling him to hold the village until he comes again. The chief becomes a loyal supporter of the two adventurers. At the Masonic Lodge initiation, all the local men are renamed after soldiers Peachey and Dravot know in India. The chief is named Billy Fish after a man who drove a big tank-engine. Billy Fish gives Peachey the Fellow Craft grip, showing that the Kafirs are fellow Masons, and this is the key Dravot uses to further subdue the tribes without warfare.

Peachey consults Billy Fish, who explains that Dravot is making a mistake about the marriage. Billy confesses that no one thought the two men were gods until they showed the sign of the Grand Master in the temple. He knows trouble is coming and offers to be loyal to Dravot and Peachey, inviting them to come to his village of Bashkai until the storm blows over. He pays for his loyalty to them with his life but does not run off when given the chance, because he is a chief and has given his word.

Narrator

The story's narrator is an unnamed Anglo-Indian newspaperman in India, who works for the *Backwoodsman*, the paper that Peachey pretends to work for in his scams. Peachey does not know the real reporter is the person to whom he is talking. The narrator is cynical, thinking he has seen and heard everything in the newspaper business. Although he seems to go along with Peachey, discussing the seamy side of life with him as if he has been a loafer himself, he turns in the pair to the police and gets them evicted from Degumber state, supposedly to save them from danger.

The name of the newspaper indicates the kind of life the narrator leads. He lives on a forsaken spot of earth where the heat is so unbearable it kills people. His newspaper is run primitively with half-naked natives, yet he also has to deal with missionaries who want to run free stories for their causes and society ladies or generals who have their own pet stories to publish. He is frequently up late at night because he cannot put the paper to bed until he gets the latest news from Europe on the telegraph. Sometimes he gets to travel to cover stories but often with no budget to travel first class.

The narrator tries to talk Carnehan and Dravot out of their projected adventure by offering them jobs. He becomes an accomplice to their schemes, however, bullied by Dravot's insistence that he owes them a favor. He has a certain amount of sympathy for the two, though he knows they are out of their depth in their plan to be kings. He is also the sympathetic listener to Peachey's tale when he returns, the one who takes him to the missionary for help when he is dying in the street. After all, the narrator is a Brother Mason who remains the sole witness to their venture.

The Priest

The priest doubts that Dravot is a god but, upon turning over the temple stone where Dravot sits, finds a Freemason's mark that convinces everyone Dravot is telling the truth.

THEMES

Imperialism

Kipling expresses the classical view of empire in his poem "The White Man's Burden," including the moral justification for colonizing natives of backward or uncivilized countries. Although European countries used force to subdue and rule their colonies, and the basic motive was obviously to increase their own power and

TOPICS FOR FURTHER STUDY

- Read the young-adult classic *The Coral Island* (1857) by Scottish author R. M. Ballantyne, about teen boys marooned on a Polynesian island. Compare and contrast the attitudes of the young Scottish boys towards the natives with the attitudes of Carnehan and Dravot towards the natives of Afghanistan. Is fifteen-year-old Ralph Rover a colonialist in training in the way he and the other boys view their adventures? Explain your conclusions in a report to class, using significant passages from the book that verify your opinions.

- Compare the American independence movement with the Indian independence movement. What arguments for colonization made by Great Britain were refuted by the writings of Thomas Paine and Mohandas Gandhi in their respective countries and time periods? In what ways were the circumstances surrounding each colony's desire for freedom very different? Write a paper with your conclusions and document your sources.

- Read Kipling's poem "The White Man's Burden" aloud in class and discuss the implications of what the poem is saying and under what circumstances he wrote the poem. How have attitudes towards race changed since Kipling's day? To conclude, discuss the role of film, Internet, and television in changing the public perception of race in society, providing video and audio examples from today as support for your presentation.

- In a group, using Sitemark or another bookmarking tool, organize the most useful Web sites you can find on Victorian history and the British Empire that would shed light on the historical background of "The Man Who Would Be King." Share these with the class in a presentation, pointing out features that illuminate details of Kipling's story, such as the conditions in India and Afghanistan at the time, the Great Game between the English and Russian Empires, and how Britain benefited from India as a colony.

- Write a paper focusing on some aspect of the history of the Western presence in Afghanistan, from the nineteenth century to the present day. How has lack of understanding of the culture, the people, and the land, contributed to problems for Western invaders, peacemakers, and adventurers? As part of your research, participate in a current reputable blog about the situation in Afghanistan today and incorporate the discussion there into your conclusions, along with your other research.

---

wealth, many like Kipling believed this to be a necessary evil serving a more universal good: white Europeans, they believed, had a superior culture which they were spreading to ignorant people through their imperial dominance. It was not only their technology such as railroads, bridges, dams, and telegraphs that they could give to these primitive places, but also their supposedly superior morality.

"The Man Who Would Be King" explores the complexity of empire building and is often read today as a parable of colonial history. The narrator of "The Man Who Would Be King," for instance, describes the small warring kingdoms of India as the dark places of the earth. The motives of Dravot and Peachey are blatantly self-serving. They want power and wealth, and following the example of the British Empire, which they have served as soldiers, and the example of other adventurers who won approval for their private empire building, such as Sir James Brooke in Borneo, they go forth with complete moral confidence that the means they use will justify the ends. Kafiristan represents an even wilder place than India, and though the natives are white, they are treated as though they are stupid and must be controlled. If they obey, they will be made over in the image of Englishmen. Dravot and Peachey thus display both the good and the bad of empire building. They attempt to bring peace and justice to the land, so the people stop feuding and cooperate. The price, however, is subservience.

Law and Order

The story opens with a statement about the law. One of Kipling's favorite themes is the law that must be obeyed. In *Jungle Book*, it is spoken of as the Law of the Jungle, or the law of nature. The law spoken of in this story refers to the laws of Freemasonry that bind not only Dravot and Peachey but also the Kafirs. The two friends begin their venture with a written contract, stating their mission and intentions to each other. When the contract is broken, their luck changes. Dravot and Peachey enter Kafiristan as the embodiment of a certain kind of British law and order. When they enforce their rule by shooting people at random to set an example, they rationalize that such an act is necessary to get the attention of a people they consider primitive and violent. They use their superior military knowledge to set up a system of order, and Dravot institutes a court system for grievances. On the other hand, Dravot breaks the laws of Freemasonry by setting up a Master Lodge without permission or the knowledge of how to administer it properly. He breaks the law of the contract and the marriage laws of the Kafirs. Too many laws are broken by the kings, and they must pay in the end, for a king cannot be a king without upholding the law.

Brotherhood

One of the ideals of Freemasonry is brotherhood. The theme of brotherhood is demonstrated in an unlikely way when Dravot finds out the Kafirs he has been exploiting are also Freemasons. This makes them all Brothers, technically. Dravot, however, ignores the real meaning of brotherhood as a sharing of common humanity. He once again exploits the situation by making it seem that he will raise up the Kafirs, but instead, he takes advantage of them. Only after his fall does Dravot try to act in the spirit of brotherhood by taking all of the blame so that Peachey

Sean Connery as Danny Dravot in the 1975 film version of the story. (© Trinity Mirror | Mirrorpix | Alamy)

can escape. Peachey and Billy Fish, however, demonstrate brotherhood by staying with Dravot to the end.

Pride

Hubris is the Greek word for the sin of the tragic hero, roughly translated as pride or overreaching. In some ways Dravot is a tragic hero, full of grand schemes, some of which might produce some good and some of which actually succeed, despite all odds. Instead of being content and moderate, however, he gets inflated and out of balance, going beyond what he can handle or deserves. In Greek tragedy, the hero often falls, like Creon in Sophocles' play *Antigone* because he puts himself at odds with the religious tradition of the people. He believes he is superior to the gods and promptly gets punished. Dravot tries to convince both the people and himself that he was a god and therefore above the law but finds out otherwise.

STYLE

Short Story

Kipling has the distinction of popularizing the short story genre in England. Though the short story had been developed in other countries like France and the United States, the British in the 1890s were still addicted to long Victorian novels. Kipling was forced into developing his short story techniques when he was an Indian journalist, given a short space in his newspaper for brief stories of local interest. His background in journalism taught him to compress information and to appeal to his readers. When his stories first came out in London, he was constantly compared to Bret Harte, who wrote about the American frontier, as in "The Outcasts of Poker Flat" (1869). Kipling's stories about the frontier of the empire in India contained their own local color and a narrative tone, sometimes humorous or ironic, using colloquial dialogue for characters, inspired by the work of Mark Twain. Kipling made famous the knowing, cynical narrator who could be an observer of the strange ways of his own community.

Colonial Fiction

Colonial fiction was written by Europeans who lived in or traveled to the British colonies, depicting life that was exotic to the readers back home. Besides Kipling, whose *Kim* (1901) and short stories about his life in India were devoured in Britain and America, H. Rider Haggard was another colonial writer who wrote adventure stories about whites and blacks in South Africa where he lived for a time. His novel *She* (1889) tells of a mysterious white queen in black Africa, and *King Solomon's Mines* (1885) romanticizes white adventurers in Africa looking for lost worlds and jewels. Joseph Conrad, who visited many colonial spots of the world in the British Merchant Navy, wrote of the Malaysian islands in *Lord Jim* (1899), based on the story of Sir James Brooke. Conrad's novella *Heart of Darkness* (1899) tells of the atrocities in the African Congo that Conrad had witnessed. It is often compared to "The Man Who Would Be King" in its theme of the corrupted white king. Robert Louis Stevenson settled in Samoa and wrote *South Sea Tales* in 1893, and R. M. Ballantyne was a Scottish author who had been to Canada with the Hudson Bay Company and wrote *Hudson's Bay, or Life in the Wilds of North America* in 1847. This kind of fiction not only depicted life in the European colonies to white readers but also assumed a validating point of view for colonialism.

Adventure Story

"The Man Who Would Be King" is, above all else, a thrilling adventure story about two drifters who invade Afghanistan to carve out a kingdom for themselves with a few rifles and plenty of confidence. The adventure story, in both long and short fiction, was an accepted genre of nineteenth-century storytelling. Like the dime novels about the cowboys of the Old West fighting Indians and outlaws, the story focuses on action and bravado. Sir Walter Scott had whetted the appetite for such stories in novels like *Rob Roy* (1817), in which the Highlanders of Scotland were compared with American Indians in their primitive lifestyle. Herman Melville's *Typee* (1846), about cannibalism in the Polynesian islands, was published in London and became an instant hit. Robert Louis Stevenson's *Treasure Island* (1883) tells of piracy in the South Sea Islands. Mark Twain's *Huckleberry Finn* (1885), about a runaway boy and slave on the Mississippi River, uses vernacular dialogue and local color. In an age where many never traveled, adventure fiction satisfied the urge to see other lands and to escape from the humdrum industrial life in cities.

HISTORICAL CONTEXT

The British Empire

In the late-sixteenth and early-seventeenth centuries, European governments began voyages of exploration and conquest, creating overseas colonies for trade and monopolies on resources (slaves, lumber, cotton, spices, metals, gems, tea, and land). Portugal, Spain, France, The Netherlands, Russia, and England had large empires, but England became the most powerful empire in world history. At one time it controlled the British Isles, American colonies, India, Canada, Australia, New Zealand, Singapore, Suez and parts of the Middle East, Malaysia, Borneo, Samoa, Caribbean islands, and parts of Africa. Britain's superior navy and technological and industrial advances gave it the advantage over other countries.

India, where Kipling was born, was a major colonial source of wealth for England. The

COMPARE
&
CONTRAST

- **1888:** India is under the rule of the British Empire.

  Today: India is partitioned into the two modern independent nations of India and Pakistan.

- **1888:** Afghanistan is ruled by Muslim emirs overseen by a British presence.

  Today: Afghanistan is in a state of civil war. American troops are stationed there to help curb native terrorist groups connected to the attacks of September 11, 2001, on New York City and Washington, DC.

- **1888:** Kafiristan is a province in the Hindu Kush region of Afghanistan, populated by fierce tribes who rebel against Muslim rule.

  Today: After Muslim subjugation, Kafiristan is renamed Nuristan. Only the Kalasha tribe escape Muslim rule and keep their ancient culture alive.

- **1888:** The Kalasha fight to avoid being converted or taken as slaves by Muslims.

  Today: The Kalasha fight to preserve their endangered culture through tourism and Internet documentaries on YouTube.

British East India Company was given permission by a Mughal emperor in 1617 to trade in India. In protecting its trading interests, Britain used more and more military force, until it took over large areas of India and its administration, with the cooperation of local rulers. In 1857, after the Indian Mutiny, the English crown took over the whole country, adding India to its empire.

In Afghanistan, the primary setting "The Man Who Would Be King," England fought two wars in the nineteenth century as part of the Great Game between the Russian and British Empires for control of Asian trade routes. The first war (1839–1842) destroyed the British army as the Afghans fought fiercely to resist foreign rulers. The Second Anglo-Afghan War (1878–1880) was fought by the British under Field Marshal Roberts. It ended in the boundaries of Afghanistan being decided by Russia and England and with the British installation of a ruler whose foreign policies they could control, Amir Abdur Rahman (who ruled from 1880 to 1901). In Kipling's story, Dravot and Peachey fought under Roberts, and so they are familiar with the Afghan territory. When Dravot and Peachey enter Afghanistan, the country is under British supervision but ruled by Afghan Muslims.

Kafiristan

Located in the northeastern part of Afghanistan, Kafiristan (modern Nuristan), at the time of the narrative, was inhabited by tribes that resisted Muslim rule and religion. These pagan tribes are targeted by Dravot and Peachey as their future subjects because of their remote location, because of the intertribal warfare that will make it easy to enter and control, and because the tribes are mysteriously white-skinned rather than dark. The Kafirs claimed to be the descendents of Alexander the Great's army, which invaded Afghanistan in the fourth century BCE.

White Adventurer Kings

Dravot and Peachey take as their role model the historical Sir James Brooke (1803–1868), who became the white rajah, or king, of Sarawak in Borneo. Once a soldier in the Bengal army in India, he sailed to Borneo in 1838, offered help to the Sultan of Brunei in putting down a rebellion, and then threatened the Sultan with force until he was offered the position of rajah of Sarawak in 1842, a title that he handed down in his family. He was knighted in England for his expansion of the empire.

Kipling's story is also based partly on the story of American adventurer Josiah Harlan

He rode on a camel, like a king. (*Svetlana Privezentseva /*
Shutterstock.com)

and Grand Master). They perform symbolic rituals that support such moral ideals as brotherhood, belief in a supreme being, self-mastery, order, and restraint. Secret signs, handshakes, words, and phrases help them identify one another, as when Peachey appeals to the narrator on the train to take a message to Dravot, sprinkling his request with Masonic references. "On the square," for instance, refers to one of the stonemasons' tools, the square, and the allusion to his mother means the Mother Lodge. When Dravot leaves for Afghanistan, he asks the narrator for a good luck charm, and the narrator provides him with a Mason's compass from his watch chain.

Dravot and Peachey use their Masonic connections in India and Afghanistan where Lodges, like Kipling's in Lahore, could provide a common connection to men of all religions and ethnic backgrounds. The epigraph of the story about being brother to a prince is a Masonic reference. Masonic lore also makes statements about what constitutes kingship. Biblical figuers like Solomon, Noah, and Moses are models of wisdom. Obligations are the part of the ritual where the member swears to abide by the rules, as when Dravot and Peachey made their contract.

(1799–1871), who went to Afghanistan with the intention of becoming a king and ultimately became the Prince of Ghor by winning local conflicts and training natives to fight. Thinking of himself as Alexander the Great, he set off with his troops over the Hindu Kush (the valleys that Dravot and Peachey exploit in Kipling's story).

Freemasonry

Freemasonry is a symbolic framework in "The Man Who Would Be King." The Freemasons are a fraternal organization, known throughout the world, which Kipling joined in India three years before he wrote the story. They derive their name from the profession of stonemasons and use the symbols of their work (the square, the hammer, the compass, and the apron) and embrace the allegorical story of building King Solomon's Temple. Freemasons meet in groups called Grand Lodges whose members are ranked in the Craft (Entered Apprentice, Fellow Craft,

CRITICAL OVERVIEW

When Kipling arrived in London from India in 1889, he had with him six volumes of published short stories, one of which included "The Man Who Would Be King." He not only brought fresh material from colonial India, but he also made popular the short story as a genre in English literature. He was hailed immediately as the new man on the literary horizon. Andrew Lang, in an unsigned review for the *Daily News* in November 1889, claims that Kipling takes the reader captive with fascinating tales of Anglo-Indian life and that one could learn more of India from them than from Blue Books. He likens Kipling to Guy de Maupassant without the pessimism. W. E. Henley, in an anonymous review for the *Scots Observer* in 1890, deplores the slang in the stories but praises Kipling for his use of dialect. J. M. Barrie, in the *Contemporary Review* in 1891, called "The Man Who Would Be King" "the most audacious thing in fiction" and compares Kipling with Bret Harte. Oscar Wilde, on the other hand, complains in "The True

Function and Value of Criticism" in *The Nineteenth Century* that Kipling "knows vulgarity better than anyone has ever known it." J. H. Millar, in *Blackwood's* magazine in 1898, praises Kipling as reviving imperial sentiment in the British, but by 1899, the criticism of Kipling's jingoism (aggressive foreign policy of imperialism motivated by extreme and biased patriotism) begins to appear, as in "The Voice of the Hooligan" by Robert Buchanan in the *Contemporary Review*, in which he wonders what happened to the humanitarian values in literature.

After many years of critics neglecting Kipling as a serious writer, Bonamy Dobrée, in the *Monthly Criterion* in 1927, was the first modern critic to reevaluate Kipling's contribution, citing his art as superior to his moralizing. Edmund Wilson's famous essay "The Kipling that Nobody Read" begins the psychological interpretation of Kipling's work, while at the same time praising Kipling for mastering his craft. In 1943, Lionel Trilling, in a review reprinted in his famous *The Liberal Imagination* in 1951, is unable to dissociate Kipling from imperialism and declares that "Kipling belongs irrevocably to our past." Phillip Mallett's biography *Rudyard Kipling: A Literary Life* (2003) represents the argument made more and more often by critics today that Kipling's political ideas as expressed in his writing have been oversimplified and that in any case, Kipling deserves to be considered the greatest short story writer in English history.

CRITICISM

Susan Andersen

Andersen is a writer and teacher with a Ph.D. in English literature. In the following essay, she compares Kipling's methods as a writer to Dravot's methods as a conqueror in "The Man Who Would Be King." Both the author and his character insist on being a law unto themselves.

Although Kipling is an author who has always been enjoyed by readers, his official place in literature has been contended. Can anyone who was called the "prophet of the British Empire" still be relevant or condemned for his colonial politics? Kipling was quite aware of what people found offensive, and yet he could say, in his autobiography, *Something of Myself: For My Friends Known and Unknown*, "I would

DESPITE HIS NOBEL PRIZE, KIPLING WAS NOT ACCORDED THE NAME OF ARTIST UNTIL LONG AFTER HIS DEATH."

not to-day recommend any writer to concern himself overly with reviews." The critics could not influence what he wrote. Like Daniel Dravot in "The Man Who Would Be King," Kipling understood the power of his own voice and continued to use it as he saw fit to create his fictional kingdom, knowing there were plenty of readers willing to share the adventure.

In "The Man Who Would Be King," having succeeded in subduing the Kafirs by force, Dravot declares that he and Peachey are "Gods and sons of Alexander, and Past Grand-Masters in the Craft." Kipling also felt like a god in relation to his characters. In " The Last of the Stories," Kipling imagines meeting his own characters in the Limbo of Lost Endeavor where they talk back to him and criticize what he has done with their lives. He is surprised that created characters have independent life. In the essay "Literature," Kipling describes the primal author as so powerful he had to be killed by the tribe for creating "words that may become alive and walk up and down in the hearts of the hearers." The tribe is afraid of what stories the artist may tell posterity about them. This primal storyteller is described as a "masterless man" who is "afflicted . . . with the magic of the necessary word," yet says Kipling, "The magic of Literature lies in the words, and not in any man." Somehow, like a shaman, the author is one who can call up these words endowed with their own life. He is not in control.

In his autobiography, Kipling describes how he wrote at the dictate of his "Daemon"—a source of inspiration he felt from outside his own personality. If he followed what he was told to do, the words did the rest. As he mentions in "Literature," "All it demands is that the magic of every word shall be tried out to the uttermost by every means, fair or foul, that the mind of man can suggest." Like Dravot, the author must be bold and follow the design to the end, even if the tribe kills him for it.

WHAT DO I READ NEXT?

- *Things Fall Apart* by Chinua Achebe (1958, Anchor, 1999) is a world classic showing the impact of British imperialism on the Ibo tribe in Nigeria. The first part of the novel pictures the traditional life of the Ibo before the British invaded from the point of view of the warrior Okonkwo. He is the tragic protagonist, baffled by the incomprehensible values of the missionaries, who arrive to destroy the Ibo way of life.

- *Robinson Crusoe* by Daniel Defoe (1719, Oxford World Classic Paperback, 2009) is a tale of pioneering and colonial spirit. Crusoe loses his Brazilian plantation but makes another from scratch as a castaway on a Caribbean island with his servant Friday, returning to England a rich man.

- Kiran Desai's best-selling *Hullabaloo in the Guava Orchard* (2000) is a story for young adults set in a village in India in postcolonial days, showing the modern aftermath of the British occupation of India for three hundred years. It humorously describes the clash of Indian customs with modern Indian civil service policies copied from the British Raj. Young Sampath Chawla escapes the contradictory demands of this mixed culture by trying to live alone in a guava orchard with his friends, the monkeys, only to be sought out as a wise holy man.

- Mary Kingsley's *Travels in West Africa* (1897, National Geographic Adventure Classics, 2002) was a best-selling book in England, despite the fact that the *Times* refused to review it because Kingsley's experience traveling alone as a white woman among black tribes countered the notions of propriety of the British Empire. She denied that African natives were inferior peoples and criticized the missionaries for destroying their way of life.

- *The Collected Poems of Rudyard Kipling* (Wordsworth Editions, 1999) includes the poems of the definitive 1940 edition. Kipling was thought of as the unofficial poet laureate of England. His poems and ballads use colloquial speech and rhythms, which account for their continued popularity. The book reprints George Orwell's important 1942 critical discussion of the poems.

- *Josiah the Great: The True Story of the Man Who Would Be King* by Ben Macintyre (HarperCollins, 2004) tells the historical tale of one of the models for Kipling's story. American Josiah Harlan in 1838, with his native Afghan troops, raised an American flag on the Hindu Kush, declaring that he was the Prince of Ghor and heir to Alexander the Great. A year later he was ousted by the British army and died in obscurity in San Francisco.

This view of literature as a primal force with a life of its own gets around the moral issues that have so exercised critics who wish to dismiss Kipling on the grounds of his politics. Whether one interprets "The Man Who Would Be King" as glorifying empires or as a fable criticizing imperialism, one must at least accept it as a masterpiece of storytelling. Randall Jarrell, in "On Preparing to Read Kipling," calls Kipling "one of the writers who have used English best" and claims it does not matter what he thought

about imperialism because "the stories themselves are literature.... Good writing will take care of itself." Does this mean that Kipling thinks the artist is above the law, that he is a god who can make up his own rules, and, like Dravot, claim when reproached for his conduct that he answers to no one?

One of the themes of Kipling's fiction is the notion of the law as a force to be reckoned with. Whether one calls it the Law of the Jungle, a law of nature, Mosaic law, or in the case of this particular story, Masonic law, it is law that holds life together and saves humans from chaos and their own worst tendencies. "The Man Who Would Be King" begins with the sentence, "The Law . . . lays down a fair conduct of life, and one not easy to follow." This refers to Freemasonry, which stands for the lawfulness of life in general to which both Peachey and Dravot have agreed to abide by as Masons. In this story the question raised is whether kings make the law, as Dravot seems to think, or whether they represent the law. In this story, the law as an external force appears to win, because Dravot has broken faith with it, yet Dravot's deed of creating a kingdom outside the norms of the law remains an awesome achievement and fascination to the narrator and the reader alike. Kipling says in "Literature," "Literature has always stood a little outside the law as the one calling that is absolutely free." While a man's social conduct is subject to the law, his imagination is free. The storyteller is like a god. However, Kipling, like Dravot, paid the price, in terms of his historical reputation, for following his Daemon's design wherever it led him. Despite his Nobel Prize, Kipling was not accorded the name of artist until long after his death.

The tension between what the law demands and what the imagination demands is the same tension of opposites found in empire building. Edward Said says in *Culture and Imperialism* that "the colonial territories are realms of possibility" for the imperial imagination. Dravot, as well as Kipling's real life friend Cecil Rhodes, who carved out a country of diamond mines for himself in South Africa, are in Edward Said's terms, true imperialists who see "a protracted, almost metaphysical obligation to rule subordinate, inferior, or less advanced peoples." There is a certain romance in such adventures as Dravot's, that despite modern anti-colonial feeling, begs to be told as a story of the tribe, like the sagas of winning the American West. In westerns, the American Indians, like the natives in Kipling's fiction, are often pictured as ignorant and uncivilized. Said sees as equally important to empire building itself the stories that make empires possible: "The power to narrate, or to block other narratives from forming and emerging, is very important to culture and imperialism." Writers like Kipling, Conrad, H. Rider Haggard, Robert Louis Stevenson, and even Jane Austen perpetuate the values of British domination in their stories. This is why Kipling, on the one hand, cannot be forgiven for his blatant statements condoning imperialism, yet the power of his stories still draws in readers like Dravot's bluff draws in the natives.

Several critics speak of Kipling's narrative power as coercive. J. I. M. Stewart, in "The Mature Craftsman," mentions that Kipling's stories could appear as "bullying performances" if the reader does not manage to feel "radical sympathy." John Bayley, in "The False Structure," claims a "hypnotic actuality, in which lies and truth form a seamless whole" in Kipling's stories, "sometimes gently and persuasively, sometimes with sarcasm and force." Kipling uses his language without restraint: "it was necessary that every word should tell, carry, weigh, taste and, if need were, smell," he says in *Something of Myself*. At the same time, Elliot L. Gilbert contends in "Silence and Survival in Kipling's Life and Art" that a rhetorical technique in the stories is to "withhold some final revelation" so that the mystery remains.

In his preface to *The Phantom Rickshaw* in which "The Man Who Would Be King " first appeared, Kipling says the stories are "a collection of facts that never quite explained themselves." He appears not to know what the facts mean, as though he is just a reporter and not responsible. Likewise, as an author, he does not judge the story of Dravot as right or wrong; he merely lays the facts before us. This ambiguity of Dravot's failure (are we meant to admire his attempt or condemn it?) is part of Kipling's appeal to contemporary readers who appreciate open-endedness in fiction.

Kipling's narrators definitely play a part in keeping the meaning layered and ambiguous. The narrative frame distances the story, so that, for instance, in "The Man Who Would Be King," the newspaperman narrator represents a more cynical and realistic check on the fantastic actions of Dravot and Peachey. He is the sole recipient of the tale and sees the shrunken head of Dravot as evidence, and yet Peachey dies and the head disappears, leaving the story told but without proof. The double narration of the newspaperman repeating Peachey's tale allows for even more distance, since we are not obliged to accept the mad Peachey's ramblings. Kipling can have it both ways and revel in Dravot's adventure without explicitly condemning or

Danny fell to his death from a rope bridge above the water. (Joe Gough | Shutterstock.com)

verifying it, yet because of Dravot's extremist folly, the story also serves as a cautionary tale against empire building.

The significance of Dravot's head suggests the Celtic stories of King Bran the Blessed, whose severed head could speak and magically protect his people. Likewise, Dravot's head protects Peachey for a year after his death, as Peachey makes his way back to India carrying the head in a bag and talking to it. In mythical terms, at least, this shows that Dravot is a true king. From this perspective, Dravot's self-creation as king magically happens through his speech. He says, "By virtue of the authority vested in me by my own right hand . . . I declare myself . . . King of Kafiristan." Like the primal author in Kipling's fable, he is killed by the tribe for his power to create with words.

Kipling thus confirms Edward Said's thesis in *Culture and Imperialism* that the power behind empire is not an army but words themselves. More than celebrating empire, Kipling celebrates his own imagination in his stories. In *Something of Myself*, Kipling identifies with Browning's artist,

Fra Lippo Lippi, the Renaissance monk criticized by his superiors for enjoying his own painted characters in his frescoes too much, for giving them too much life. As Zoreh T. Sullivan points out in "Kipling the Nightwalker," the narrator in "The Man Who Would Be King" "sits in his office, distant, ironic, and judgmental, while he cheerfully creates doubles—Dravot and Peachey—to act out his most fearsome fantasies." Kipling honors the power of the law to contain human excesses, while at the same time, he honors literature as a law unto itself. In *Something of Myself*, he claims, "Every man must be his own law in his own work," a very Dravot-like statement.

Source: Susan K. Andersen, Critical Essay on "The Man Who Would Be King," in *Short Stories for Students*, Gale, Cengage Learning, 2011.

Monthly Review

In the following essay, the editors of Monthly Review *note renewed interest in "The White Man's Burden," and explain the poem's significance for early twenty-first-century American neoconservatives who support imperialism, a recurring theme in Kipling's stories.*

> THE U.S. IMPERIAL ROLE IN THE
> PHILIPPINES, THE SUBJECT OF KIPLING'S 'WHITE
> MAN'S BURDEN,' IS THUS BEING PRESENTED AS
> A MODEL FOR THE KIND OF IMPERIAL ROLE
> THAT BOOT AND OTHER NEOCONSERVATIVES
> ARE NOW URGING ON THE UNITED STATES."

We are living in a period in which the rhetoric of empire knows few bounds. In a special report on "America and Empire" in August, the London-based *Economist* magazine asked whether the United States would, in the event of "regime changes...effected peacefully" in Iran and Syria, "really be prepared to shoulder the white man's burden across the Middle East?" The answer it gave was that this was "unlikely"— the U.S. commitment to empire did not go so far. What is significant, however, is that the question was asked at all.

Current U.S. wars in Afghanistan and Iraq have led observers to wonder whether there aren't similarities and historical linkages between the "new" imperialism of the twenty-first century and the imperialism of the nineteenth and early twentieth centuries. As Jonathan Marcus, the BBC's defense correspondent, commented a few months back:

> It should be remembered that more than one hundred years ago, the British poet Rudyard Kipling wrote his famous poem about what he styled as "the white man's burden"—a warning about the responsibilities of empire that was directed not at London but at Washington and its new-found imperial responsibilities in the Philippines. It is not clear if President George W. Bush is a reader of poetry or of Kipling. But Kipling's sentiments are as relevant today as they were when the poem was written in the aftermath of the Spanish-American War.

(July 17, 2003)

A number of other modern-day proponents of imperialism have also drawn connections with Kipling's poem, which begins with the lines:

> Take up the White Man's burden—
> Send forth the best ye breed—

Before discussing the reasons for this sudden renewed interest in Kipling's "White Man's Burden," it is necessary to provide some background on the history of U.S. imperialism in order to put the poem in context.

FROM THE SPANISH-AMERICAN WAR TO THE PHILIPPINE-AMERICAN WAR

In the Spanish-American War of 1898 the United States seized the Spanish colonies in the Carribean and the Pacific, emerging for the first time as a world power. As in Cuba, Spanish colonial rule in the Philippines had given rise to a national liberation struggle. Immediately after the U.S. naval bombardment of Manila on May 1, 1898, in which the Spanish fleet was destroyed, Admiral Dewey sent a gunboat to fetch the exiled Filipino revolutionary leader Emilio Aguinaldo from Hong Kong. The United States wanted Aguinaldo to lead a renewed revolt against Spain to prosecute the war before U.S. troops could arrive. The Filipinos were so successful that in less than two months they had all but defeated the Spanish on the main island of Luzon, bottling up the remaining Spanish troops in the capital city of Manila, while almost all of the archipelago fell into Filipino hands. In June, Filipino leaders issued their own Declaration of Independence based on the U.S. model. When U.S. forces finally arrived at the end of June the 15,000 Spanish troops holed up in Manila were surrounded by the Filipino army entrenched around the city—so that U.S. forces had to request permission to cross Filipino lines to engage these remaining Spanish troops. The Spanish army surrendered Manila to U.S. forces after only a few hours of fighting on August 13, 1898. In an agreement between the United States and Spain, Filipino forces were kept out of the city and were allowed no part in the surrender. This was the final battle of the war. John Hay, U.S. ambassador to Britain, captured the imperialist spirit of the time when he wrote of the Spanish-American War as a whole that it was "a splendid little war."

With the fighting with Spain over, however, the United States refused to acknowledge the existence of the new Philippine Republic. In October 1898 the McKinley administration publicly revealed for the first time that it intended to annex the entire Philippines. In arriving at this decision President McKinley is reported to have said that "God Almighty" had ordered him to make the Philippines a U.S. colony. Within days of this announcement the New England Anti-Imperialist League was established in Boston. Its membership was to include such luminaries as Mark Twain, William James, Charles Francis Adams and Andrew Carnegie. Nevertheless, the administration went ahead and concluded the Treaty of Paris in December, in which Spain agreed to cede the Philippines to the new imperial power, along with its other possessions seized by the United States in the war.

This was followed by a fierce debate in the Senate on the ratification of the treaty, centering on the status of the Philippines, which, except for the city of Manila, was under the control of the nascent Philippine Republic. On February 4, 1899, U.S. troops under orders to provoke a conflict with the Filipino forces ringing Manila were moved into disputed ground lying between U.S. and Filipino lines on the outskirts of the city. When they encountered Filipino soldiers the U.S. soldiers called "Halt" and then opened fire, killing three. The U.S. forces immediately began a general offensive with their full firepower in what amounted to a surprise attack (the top Filipino officers were then away attending a lavish celebratory ball), inflicting enormous casualties on the Filipino troops. The *San Francisco Call* reported on February 5 that the moment the news reached Washington McKinley told "an intimate friend . . . that the Manila engagement would, in his opinion, insure the ratification of the treaty tomorrow."

These calculations proved correct and on the following day the Senate ratified the Treaty of Paris officially ending the Spanish-American War—ceding Guam, Puerto Rico, and the Philippines to the United States, and putting Cuba under U.S. control. It stipulated that the United States would pay Spain twenty million dollars for the territories that it gained through the war. But this did little to disguise the fact that the Spanish-American War was an outright seizure of an overseas colonial empire by the United States, in response to the perceived need of U.S. business, just recovering from an economic downturn, for new global markets.

The United States immediately pushed forward in the Philippine-American War that it had begun two days before—in what was to prove to be one of history's more barbaric wars of imperial conquest. The U.S. goal in this period was to expand not only into the Caribbean but also far into the Pacific—and by colonizing the Philippine Islands to gain a doorway into the huge Chinese market. (In 1900 the United States sent troops from the Philippines to China to join with the other imperial powers in putting down the Boxer Rebellion.)

Kipling's "White Man's Burden," subtitled "The United States and the Philippine Islands," was published in *McClure's Magazine* in February 1899. It was written when the debate over ratification of the Treaty of Paris was still taking place, and while the anti-imperialist movement in the United States was loudly decrying the plan to annex the Philippines. Kipling urged the United States, with special reference to the Philippines, to join Britain in the pursuit of the racial responsibilities of empire:

> Your new-caught sullen peoples,
> Half devil and half child.

Many in the United States, including President McKinley and Theodore Roosevelt, welcomed Kipling's rousing call for the United States to engage in "savage wars," beginning in the Philippines. Senator Albert J. Beveridge of Indiana declared: "God has not been preparing the English-speaking and Teutonic peoples for a thousand years for nothing but vain and idle self-contemplation and self-admiration. . . . He has made us adept in government that we may administer government among savage and senile peoples." In the end more than 126,000 officers and men were sent to the Philippines to put down the Filipino resistance during a war that lasted officially from 1899 to 1902 but actually continued much longer, with sporadic resistance for most of a decade. U.S. troops logged 2,800 engagements with the Filipino resistance. At least a quarter of a million Filipinos, most of them civilians, were killed along with 4,200 U.S. soldiers (more than ten times the number of U.S. fatalities in the Spanish-American War).

From the beginning it was clear that the Filipino forces were unable to match the United States in conventional warfare. They therefore quickly switched to guerrilla warfare. U.S. troops at war with the Filipinos boasted in a popular marching song that they would "civilize them with the Krag" (referring to the Norwegian-designed gun with which the U.S. forces were outfitted). Yet they found themselves facing interminable small attacks and ambushes by Filipinos, who often carried long knives known as bolos. These guerrilla attacks resulted in combat deaths of U.S. soldiers in small numbers on a regular basis. As in all prolonged guerrilla wars, the strength of the Filipino resistance was due to the fact that it had the support of the Filipino population in general. As General Arthur Mac-Arthur (the father of Douglas MacArthur), who became military governor of the Philippines in 1900, confided to a reporter in 1899:

> When I first started in against these rebels, I believed that Aguinaldo's troops represented only a faction. I did not like to believe that the whole population of Luzon—the native population that is—was opposed to us and our offers of aid and good government. But after having come this far, after having occupied several towns and cities in succession...I have been reluctantly compelled to believe that the Filipino masses are loyal to Aguinaldo and the government which he heads.

Faced with a guerrilla struggle supported by the vast majority of the population, the U.S. military responded by rounding populations in concentration camps, burning down villages (Filipinos were sometimes forced to carry the petrol used in burning down their own homes), mass hangings and bayonetings of suspects, systematic raping of women and girls, and torture. The most infamous torture technique, used repeatedly in the war, was the so-called "water cure." Vast quantities of water were forced down the throats of prisoners. Their stomachs were then stepped on so that the water shot out three feet in the air "like an artesian well." Most victims died not long afterwards. General Frederick Funston did not hesitate to announce that he had personally strung up a group of thirty-five Filipino civilians suspected of supporting the Filipino revolutionaries. Major Edwin Glenn saw no reason to deny the charge that he had made a group of forty-seven Filipino prisoners kneel and "repent of their sins" before bayoneting and clubbing them to death. General Jacob Smith ordered his troops to "kill and burn," to target "everything over ten," and to turn the island of Samar into "a howling wilderness." General William Shafter in California declared that it might be necessary to kill half the Filipino population in order to bring "perfect justice" to the other half. During the Philippine War the United States reversed the normal casualty statistics of war—usually many more are wounded than killed. According to official statistics (discussed in Congressional hearings on the war) U.S. troops killed fifteen times as many Filipinos as they wounded. This fit with frequent reports by U.S. soldiers that wounded and captured

Filipino combatants were summarily executed on the spot.

The war continued after the capture of Aguinaldo in March 1901 but was declared officially over by President Theodore Roosevelt on July 4, 1902—in an attempt to quell criticism of U.S. atrocities. At that time, the northern islands had been mostly "pacified" but the conquest of the southern islands was still ongoing and the struggle continued for years—though the United States from then on characterized the rebels as mere bandits.

In the southern Philippines the U.S. colonial army was at war with Muslim Filipinos, known as Moros. In 1906 what came to be known as the Moro Massacre was carried out by U.S. troops when at least nine hundred Filipinos, including women and children, were trapped in a volcanic crater on the island of Jolo and shot at and bombarded for days. All of the Filipinos were killed while the U.S. troops suffered only a handful of casualties. Mark Twain responded to early reports (which indicated that those massacred totaled six hundred rather than nine hundred men, women and children as later determined) with bitter satire: "With six hundred engaged on each side, we lost fifteen men killed outright, and we had thirty-two wounded—counting that nose and that elbow. The enemy numbered six hundred—including women and children—and we abolished them utterly, leaving not even a baby alive to cry for its dead mother. *This is incomparably the greatest victory that was ever achieved by the Christian soldiers of the United States.*" Viewing a widely distributed photo that showed U.S. soldiers overlooking piles of Filipino dead in the crater, W. E. B. Du Bois declared in a letter to Moorfield Storey, president of the Anti-Imperialist League (and later first president of the NAACP), that it was "the most illuminating thing I have ever seen. I want especially to have it framed and put upon the walls of my recitation room to impress upon the students what wars and especially Wars of Conquest really mean."

President Theodore Roosevelt immediately commended his good friend General Leonard Wood, who had carried out the Moro Massacre, writing: "I congratulate you and the officers and men of your command upon the brilliant feat of arms wherein you and they so well upheld the honor of the American flag." Like Kipling, Roosevelt seldom hesitated to promote the imperialist cause or to forward doctrines of racial superiority. Yet Kipling's novels, stories and verses were distinguished by the fact that they seemed to many individuals in the white world to evoke a transcendent and noble cause. At the same time they did not fail to reach out and acknowledge the hatred that the colonized had for the colonizer. In presenting the Nobel Prize in Literature to Kipling in 1907 the Nobel Committee proclaimed, "his imperialism is not of the uncompromising type that pays no regard to the sentiments of others." It was precisely this that made Kipling's "White Man's Burden" and other outpourings from his pen so effective as ideological veils for a barbaric reality.

The year Kipling's poem appeared, 1899, marked not only the end of the Spanish-American War (through the ratification of the Treaty of Paris) and the beginning of the Philippine-American War, but also the beginning of the Boer War in South Africa. These were classic imperialist wars and they generated anti-imperialist movements and radical critiques in response. It was the Boer War that gave rise to John A. Hobson's *Imperialism, A Study* (1902), which argued "Nowhere under such conditions"—referring specifically to British imperialism in South Africa—"is the theory of white government as a trust for civilization made valid." The opening sentence of Lenin's *Imperialism, the Highest Stage of Capitalism*, written in 1915, stated that "especially since the Spanish-American War (1898), and the Anglo-Boer War (1899–1902), the economic and also the political literature of the two hemispheres has more and more often adopted the term 'imperialism' in order to define the present era."

KIPLING'S MESSAGE TO IMPERIALISTS AFTER ONE HUNDRED YEARS

Although imperialism has remained a reality over the last century, the term itself was branded as beyond the pale within polite establishment circles for most of the twentieth century—so great was the anti-imperialist outrage arising out of the Philippine-American War and the Boer War, and so effective was the Marxist theory of imperialism in stripping the veil away from global capitalist relations. In the last few years, however, "imperialism" has once again become a rallying cry—for neoconservatives and neoliberals alike. As Alan Murray, Washington Bureau Chief of CNBC recently acknowledged in a statement directed principally at the

elites: "We are all, it seems, imperialists now" (*Wall Street Journal*, July 15, 2003).

If one were to doubt for a moment that the current expansion of U.S. empire is but the continuation of a century-long history of U.S. overseas imperialism, Michael Ignatieff (Professor of Human Rights Policy at Harvard's Kennedy School of Government) has made it as clear as day:

> The Iraq operation most resembles the conquest of the Philippines between 1898 and 1902. Both were wars of conquest, both were urged by an ideological elite on a divided country and both cost much more than anyone had bargained for. Just as in Iraq, winning the war was the easy part. . . . More than 120,000 American troops were sent to the Philippines to put down the guerrilla resistance, and 4,000 never came home. It remains to be seen whether Iraq will cost thousands of American lives—and whether the American public will accept such a heavy toll as the price of success in Iraq.

(*New York Times Magazine*, September 7, 2003).

With representatives of the establishment openly espousing imperialist ambitions, we shouldn't be surprised at the repeated attempts to bring back the "white man's burden" argument in one form or another. In the closing pages of his prize-winning book, *The Savage Wars of Peace* Max Boot quotes Kipling's poem:

> Take up the White Man's burden—
> And reap his old reward:
> The blame of those ye better,
> The hate of those ye guard—

Boot insists that Kipling was right, that "colonists everywhere, usually received scant thanks afterward." Nevertheless, we should be encouraged, he tells us, by the fact that "the bulk of the people did not resist American occupation, as they surely would have done if it had been nasty and brutal. Many Cubans, Haitians, Dominicans, and others may secretly have welcomed U.S. rule." Boot's main implication seems clear enough—the United States should again "Take up the White Man's burden." His book, published in 2002, ends by arguing that the United States should have deposed Saddam Hussein and occupied Iraq at the time of the 1991 Gulf War. That task, he implied, remained to be accomplished.

Boot is former editorial features editor of the *Wall Street Journal*, now Olin Senior Fellow in National Security Studies with the Council on

Foreign Relations. The title of *The Savage Wars of Peace* was taken straight from a line in Kipling's "White Man's Burden." Boot's 428-page glorification of U.S. imperialist wars received the Best Book of 2002 Award from the *Washington Post, Christian Science Monitor*, and the *Los Angeles Times* and won the 2003 General Wallace M. Greene Jr. Award for the best non-fiction book pertaining to Marine Corps history. Boot contends that the Philippine War was "one of the most successful counterinsurgencies waged by a Western army in modern times" and declares that, "by the standards of the day, the conduct of U.S. soldiers was better than average for colonial wars." The U.S. imperial role in the Philippines, the subject of Kipling's "White Man's Burden," is thus being presented as a model for the kind of imperial role that Boot and other neoconservatives are now urging on the United States. Even before the war in Iraq, Ignatieff remarked: "imperialism used to be the white man's burden. This gave it a bad reputation. But imperialism doesn't stop being necessary because it is politically incorrect"—a point that might well be read as extending to the "white man's burden" itself (*New York Times Magazine*, July 28, 2002).

The Philippine-American War is now being rediscovered as the closest approximation in U.S. history to the problems the United States is encountering in Iraq. Further, the United States has taken advantage of the September 11, 2001 attacks to intervene militarily not just in the Middle East but also around the globe— including the Philippines where it has deployed thousands of troops to aid the Philippine army in fighting Moro insurgents in the southern islands. In this new imperialist climate Niall Ferguson, Herzog Professor of History at the Stern School of Business, New York University, and one of the principal advocates of the new imperialism, has addressed Kipling's poem "The White Man's Burden" in his book *Empire* (2002). "No one," Ferguson tells us,

> would dare use such politically incorrect language today. The reality is nevertheless that the United States has—whether it admits it or not—taken up some kind of global burden, just as Kipling urged. It considers itself responsible not just for waging a war against terrorism and rogue states, but also for spreading the benefits of capitalism and democracy overseas. And just like the British Empire before it, the American Empire unfailingly acts in the name

of liberty, even when its own self-interest is manifestly uppermost.

Despite Ferguson's claim that "no one would dare" to call this "the white man's burden" today since it is "politically incorrect," sympathetic references to this term keep on cropping up—and in the most privileged circles. Boot— hardly a marginal figure since affiliated with the influential Council on Foreign Relations—is a good example. Like Ferguson himself, he tries to incorporate the "white man's burden" into a long history of idealistic intervention, downplaying the realities of racism and imperialism: "In the early twentieth century," he writes in the final chapter of his book (entitled *In Defense of the Pax Americana*), "Americans talked of spreading Anglo-Saxon civilization and taking up the 'white man's burden'; today they talk of spreading democracy and defending human rights. Whatever you call it, this represents an idealistic impulse that has always been a big part in America's impetus for going to war."

Today's imperialists see Kipling's poem mainly as an attempt to stiffen the spine of the U.S. ruling class of his day in preparation for what he called "the savage wars of peace." And it is precisely in this way that they now allude to the "white man's burden" in relation to the twenty-first century. Thus for the *Economist* magazine the question is simply whether the United States is "prepared to shoulder the white man's burden across the Middle East."

As an analyst of as well as a spokesman for imperialism Kipling was head and shoulders above this in the sense that he accurately perceived the looming contradictions of his own time. He knew that the British Empire was overstretched and doomed—even as he struggled to redeem it and to inspire the rising United States to enter the imperial stage alongside it. Only two years before writing "The White Man's Burden" he wrote his celebrated verse, "Recessional":

> Far-called, our navies melt away;
> On dune and headland sinks the fire;
> Lo, all our pomp of yesterday
> Is one with Nineveh and Tyre!
> Judge of Nations, spare us yet,
> Lest we forget—lest we forget!

The United States is now leading the way into a new phase of imperialism. This will be marked not only by increased conflict between center and periphery—rationalized in the West by veiled and not-so-veiled racism—but also by increased intercapitalist rivalry. This will likely speed up the long-run decline of the American Empire, rather than the reverse. And in this situation a call for a closing of the ranks between those of European extraction (Samuel Huntington's "clash of civilizations" argument or some substitute) is likely to become more appealing among U.S. and British elites. It should be remembered that Kipling's "White Man's Burden" was a call for the joint exploitation of the globe by what Du Bois was later to call "the white masters of the world" in the face of the ebbing of British fortunes. At no time, then, should we underestimate the three-fold threat of militarism, imperialism, and racism—or forget that capitalist societies have historically been identified with all three.

Source: "Kipling, the 'White Man's Burden' and U.S. Imperialism," in *Monthly Review*, Vol. 55, No. 6, November 2003, pp. 1–11.

Thomas A. Shippey and Michael Short

In the following essay, Shippey and Short seek to show how Kipling used setting, "frames," and linguistic tactics to convey theme in "The Man Who Would Be King."

In H. G. Well's *The New Machiavelli* (Bk. 1, ch.4: 6) the narrator (a Liberal politician of the early twentieth century) chronicles his rejection of the fashionable Kiplingism of his generation. Yet in spite of his dislike and even hatred of all that Kipling stood for, he cannot help feeling that in some misunderstood essentials the man was right. In particular he cites a few lines of verse as the expression of 'quintessential wisdom':

> The 'eathen in 'is blindness bows down to wood and
> stone;
> 'E don't obey no orders unless they is 'is own;
> 'E keeps 'is side-arms awful: 'e leaves 'em all about,
> An' then comes up the regiment an' pokes the
> 'eathen out.
> All along o' dirtiness, all along o' mess,
> All along o' doin' things rather-more-or-less. . . .

Wells saw the last two lines as having not only a military meaning but also an economic and a cultural one, reflecting on the 'condition of England' question itself. In this he was certainly right; post-war criticism of Kipling has been especially successful in pointing out the originality and depth of Kipling's pseudo-naive statements of the traditional value of order and discipline. What Wells might have added was that to Kipling order and discipline were also

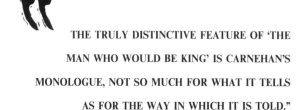

THE TRULY DISTINCTIVE FEATURE OF 'THE MAN WHO WOULD BE KING' IS CARNEHAN'S MONOLOGUE, NOT SO MUCH FOR WHAT IT TELLS AS FOR THE WAY IN WHICH IT IS TOLD."

artistic absolutes. No other English author (not even Jane Austen) has been so exclusively preoccupied with finish, with perfection of structure in little space; and as a concomitant to that, we can now see that none of his contemporaries (not even his close family friend, Henry James) was as fascinated by narrative technique for its own sake, by the process of appearing to let stories tell themselves, often through the mouths of unskilled and inarticulate speakers. This paper seeks to show how in one story, "The Man Who Would Be King" (1888), Kipling used two devices to make narrative mode convey his story's theme: the setting up of an individualized language for the story's central narrator, and the use, around the centre, of a series of multiple "frames" acting as ironic commentary on events and also (with as much importance) as a deliberately uncertain "legitimization" of the story that is told.

Kipling's use of the "framed" story has indeed already attracted a certain amount of critical attention. It is obvious that all his life he was interested in the many possible variants of "stories within stories" and that he tried out many types successfully: for instance, the story told by one man to his friends, but reported by an omniscient narrator (the "closed" frame, *e.g.*, "On Greenhow Hill" [1891]); the story told by someone to an "I" narrator who then retells it to the reader with some commentary of his own (the "open" frame, *e.g.*, "Love-o'-Women" [1893]); the four-party conversation reported by one of the four, where a story emerges slowly from the separate information of the various speakers, but in which the climax need never be directly expressed (*e.g.*, "Mrs. Bathurst" [1904], but see also "Sea Constables" [1926]). The variety of interrelationships possible between speakers and audiences in the end almost defies analysis; there is some evidence that this aspect of Kipling's stories affected Bertolt Brecht, and helped in the creation of his ideas of "epic theatre." But more important than the technical variety of the "frames" is their variety of purpose. Obviously they could be used ironically, or else (through a sense of the passage of time) pathetically. But in Kipling their purpose is increasingly to force some new slant on the reader's apprehension, often reminding him very aggressively that his sense of truth is limited by his own experience, and that this is an unreliable guide. "Of course you don't believe it," the narrator remarks at the end of "The Broken-Link Handicap" (1888). "You would credit anything about Russia's designs on India, or the recommendations of the Currency Commission; but a little bit of sober fact is more than you can stand." In less truculent mood the narrator turns to another listener after hearing a particularly unlikely story in *My Lord the Elephant* (1893), but gets a thoroughly flat and indisputable reply:

> "Is it true, Jock?"
> "Ay; true as t'owd bitch has getten t'mange. Orth'-
> ris, yo' maun't let
> t'dawgs hev owt to do wi' her."

It would be a mistake to regard such endings as these as merely comic justifications of fantasy; as Wells also saw, the makings of fantasy were much more prominent in Victorian and Edwardian times than most readers, or writers, were prepared to accept.

With this curious intention in mind it is much more possible to appreciate the *finesse* of "The Man Who Would Be King"—"one of the best stories in the world," as Wells's "Sleeper" remarks in the year 2100. In this the central story can only be approached through a multiple, six-part "frame," whose main function is to prevent the reader from exercising his normal powers of judgment. The six parts run as follows.

In the first scene (A) we are introduced to the 'I' narrator, a journalist travelling across India, for once in an Intermediate railway-carriage, *i.e.*, one not normally used by Europeans of official status. In the carriage he meets a strange and unnamed Englishman, who asks him to pass on a message; though unwilling at first, he agrees on hearing the "Loafer" use code-phrases that prove he is a Freemason, and indeed succeeds in passing on the message (in scene B) some eight days later. One should note, though, that the message has no significance at all for the story. The two scenes are introduced *only* to

show the narrator's descent into a world unfamiliar to him but in some strange way perfectly predictable to his "Loafer" companion. The "Loafer" (later named as Peachey Taliaferro Carnehan) shows an astonishing grasp of the inner workings of the Indian transport system, and seems also to be quite certain of the likely movements and reactions of his friend; he plots the narrator's itinerary for him and arranges interconnections with confident ease. His success in these practical matters gives a retrospective verisimilitude to his bizarre and scandalous story, told also in a confident and matter-of-fact way, about the Degumber Rajah's father's widow, a story which the narrator does not know whether to believe:

> "I wanted to get hold of the Degumber Rajah down
>   here about his father's widow, and give him a
>   jump."
> "What did he do to his father's widow then?"
> "Filled her up with red pepper and slippered her to
>   death as she hung from a beam . . ."
> He got out at a little roadside station, and
>   I reflected . . .

The results of the reflection never become clear. Certainly the narrator (although a journalist) does not even consider following up the case of the Degumber Rajah; its macabre details make it unbelievable in a world of "the Railway and the Telegraph." On the other hand, he shows no sign of disbelieving it, still less when the appearance of Carnehan's friend exactly on time proves that the man was not simply mad. In the end he merely suspends judgment, obliging the reader to do likewise—"If the man with the beard had given me a rupee I should have kept it as a memento of a rather curious affair." Later on he uses his official status to keep the two "Loafers" away from the Degumber Rajah, so that the issue is never put to test. The affair fizzles out; but for the reader a wedge has been driven between truth and credibility.

Doubt is reinforced (with Kipling's characteristic indirection) at the start of the next scene (C), which the narrator begins by describing his normal, respectable job—that of editing a newspaper. For though he does not say so, the editor's duty as he tells it is simply that of acting as a screen between the many confused worlds of his contributors and the casual expectations of his audience. He is a filter, a censor, on occasion a liar, and he is well aware of it. It is under these circumstances that he meets the "Loafers" again. They march uproariously into his office, bearing him no malice for the affair of Degumber State, and with no prompting disclose to him their project of becoming "Kings of Kafiristan," a territory outside the borders of Empire. Of course the narrator thinks them mad, drunk, or sunstruck, but once more does not interfere while they borrow his maps and books. This scene is linked immediately to that of the "Loafers'" departure [the] next day (D), Carnehan disguised as a servant and his friend, Daniel Dravot, as a mad priest, with twenty rifles and ammunition hidden away in their baggage. For a moment the success of their disguises, like the appearance of Dravot in scene B, breaks through the narrator's scepticism, and he admits that "There was just the chance, therefore, that Carnehan and Dravot would be able to wander through Afghanistan without detection. But, beyond, they would find death—certain and awful death." The incident is closed by a letter from Peshawar describing the two as comic madmen; they have, therefore, covered some distance, but are still not taken seriously.

For three years they are forgotten, and indeed Daniel Dravot never returns alive; but then a scarred and broken man, just recognisable as Peachey Carnehan, reappears to tell the fantastic story of their kingship and downfall in Kafiristan, bringing with him as confirmation the head of Dravot and a golden crown. It is this narrative of Carnehan's that forms the story's kernel, "framed" here by the scenes of his reappearance to the narrator (E) and his death next day (F). At this point one might expect some assertion as to whether Carnehan is reliable or not, an issue left in doubt at least twice before. But, in fact, Kipling goes to great lengths to leave the matter uncertain. At the very end of the story, indeed, Peachey's central narrative appears to be confirmed by the golden crown, seen by the narrator and inexplicable in any other way. But the next day it has disappeared; and when the narrator asks the Superintendent of the Asylum to which Carnehan has been committed, "'do you happen to know if he had anything upon him by any chance when he died?'" the Superintendent answers "'Not to my knowledge.'" The proof has vanished, though the cautious indirection of both speakers in the last dialogue prevents even a firm disbelief from being formed. So, for the third time, the narrator's scepticism is broken, but, as in scenes B and D, re-established by the return to familiar and official surroundings. Men's

awareness of truth, it is suggested, is something relative, dependent on the conventions of the worlds in which they move.

This point is of course of some importance in itself, as a philosophical matter. Yet one might wonder whether the whole elaborate apparatus of "framing" is not after all a complicated side-issue, an excuse for allowing Kipling to tell, through the mouth of Peachey Carnehan, the sort of adventure-story which one might have expected from Rider Haggard. If this were so, one would have to admit that the arrangement, though cunning, was unnecessarily long drawn-out. But, in fact, the "frames" have a narrative purpose as well as an instructive one. The truly distinctive feature of "The Man Who Would Be King" is Carnehan's monologue, not so much for what it tells as for the way in which it is told. Unlike the, at times, laboriously realistic "fantastic journeys" of Wells or Verne or Haggard, Carnehan's story is presented in a style itself fantastic. The "frames," however, have prepared the reader for glimpses of a truly alien world which may not be explicable or even expressible in official and European terms; as a result the very incongruity of much of what Carnehan says carries a certain conviction, confirming that his story is true as he sees it, mysterious though this may be to others. The mixed nature of his world is reinforced also by the elements, parodic but not entirely to be dismissed, of Masonic ritual and reference to the Bible—though they do not see it themselves, the "Contrack" which Dravot and Carnehan draw up with each other is reminiscent of the Covenant that Israel made with God, while in the end Carnehan expiates his partner's sin through crucifixion; on his last appearance he sings a perverted hymn, almost blasphemously applicable to himself and Dravot.

All these strands help one to recognize, if not to define, what it is to be a King; and yet the centre of the story is not irony, nor instruction, but the delineation of a strange world and a stranger viewpoint through the medium of a single speaking voice. Whatever he thinks of adventure-stories, no reader should be indifferent to the inarticulate rhetoric of Carnehan, which colors the events he describes in a way never precisely recaptured by Kipling or anybody else. The technical question of greatest interest must be: "how can Kipling create and maintain an idiosyncratic style which has to convey impressions of a near-incredible world without at the same time alienating his readers?" The answers are, for 1888, unexpectedly subtle linguistically. They can be reached most easily by comparing Carnehan's speech with the skilful, reasonable, but no longer entirely self-confident style of the 'I' narrator explaining what happens in the "frames."

One obvious point must be made first. Carnehan—who has after all been crucified—is clearly mad. At the start of his narrative he asks the "I" narrator to keep looking him in the eyes "'or maybe my words will all go to pieces.'" Five times after this the current of his speech is broken by some digression or interjection, as he has to be called back to his subject; nevertheless, these reminders of insanity gradually become less obtrusive, and the story gathers pace and clarity. However, as he reaches the climax—Dravot's death and his own crucifixion—Carnehan begins to wander again. He goes back to speaking of himself in the third person; he reverts to a beggar's servility; he confuses himself and Dravot:

> "But Peachey, Peachey Taliaferro, I tell you,
> Sir, in confidence as betwixt two friends, he lost
> his head, Sir. No, he didn't, neither. The King
> lost his head, so he did, all along o' one of those
> cunning rope-bridges. Kindly let me have the
> paper-cutter, Sir. It tilted this way...."

In a way, this flight from reality only confirms that some traumatic event has in fact occurred; but certainty as to what would be inappropriate. It is at this blend of madness and sense, realism and mystery, that Kipling is aiming.

Probably the first distinguishing mark of the monologue is its lack of normal temporal or causative sequence. After the narrator's second interruption, as Carnehan starts to tell of the entry into Kafiristan, we are given a sample of his wandering mind:

> "And then these camels were no use, and
> Peachey said to Dravot—'For the Lord's sake
> let's get out of this before our heads are
> chopped off,' and with that they killed the cam-
> els all among the mountains, not having any-
> thing in particular to eat, but first they took off
> the boxes with the guns and ammunition, till
> two men came along driving four mules."

In this sentence the last conjunction "till" is not accompanied by the usual lexical items of duration (*c.f.* "they sat there till..."? "they waited till..."?); killing the camels and taking off their loads are given in the wrong order; "all

among the mountains" is pleonastic; and the threat of decapitation seems to come from nowhere and lead to nothing. Yet the outline of a desperate situation is dimly visible, while the quotation, the extra details, and the backtracking suggest also a struggle for exactness on Peachey's part. His lame and abrupt conjunctions "and then... and... and with that... but first" further imply events too powerful and immediate for the speaker to control them. Similar vagaries appear repeatedly near this place. A few lines before Carnehan has explained that the country was too mountainous for camels, with curious redundancy: "'That was in a most mountaineous country, and our camels couldn't go along any more because of the mountains.'" A little later he repeats himself more rhetorically: "'The country was mountaineous and the mules were most contrary and the inhabitants was dispersed and solitary.'" Partly the effect is comic, as "high-style" vocabulary ("most contrary... inhabitants... solitary") clashes with "low-style" grammar ("inhabitants was"); but also the repetitiousness, the drift of irrelevance, and the very positive nature of Peachey's assertions, give a sense of curious, almost monotonous immediacy to the journey. It is as if the narrator can remember what has happened, but has little idea of which events are more important than others; we are made aware of the process of recall as much as its results.

That this sensation was produced deliberately is proved by Kipling's highlighting of Peachey's syntactic meanderings through contrast with the very careful and lucid interjections of the editor-narrator.

> "Take some more whisky," I said very slowly,
> "What did you and Daniel Dravot do *when* the
> camels could go no farther *because* of the rough
> roads *that* led into Kafiristan?"... He paused
> for a moment, *while* I asked him *if* he could
> remember the nature of the country *through
> which* he had journeyed. [The words which
> mark the relations between grammatical units,
> conjunctions and relative pronouns, have been
> italicized.]

The contrast points out Peachey's madness; but it shows also that his manner of speech is consistent even in its abnormality. The opposition of official and "Loafer," present from the first scene of the "frames," is mirrored here by different linguistic habits, the one controlled, organizing, "editing," the other seeming to present raw experience in a manner unacceptable to many, but nevertheless not to be summarily dismissed as mere imagination.

This comparative lack of connections does not deny a certain rhetorical and even poetic impulse in Peachey. We have seen this already in his near recitative "all among the mountains." There are flashes of wit, often, in the conversations he reports, as when Dravot kills a man for his mules:

> "Dravot up and dances in front of them, singing— 'Sell me four mules.' Says the first man—'If you are rich enough to buy you are rich enough to rob'; but before ever he could put his hand to his knife, Dravot breaks his neck over his knee . . . "

There is a certain rhythmic heightening in the alliterative parallels of "hand . . . knife . . . neck . . . knee," and also in the neat concealed antithesis of "rich enough to buy . . . rich enough to rob," where the first infinitive is of course active in sense ("to buy from us"), the second passive ("to be robbed by us"). A certain power of this kind—not often present in the narrator's drier style—helps to make the monologue more impressive in a disorderly way; with another device (rather rare in modern standard English) Kipling manages to make such impressiveness more prominent, and also to connect it increasingly with the dominant but unlucky figure of Dravot.

This device is known to linguists as the use of "marked theme." Most English declarative sentences, in a language now uninflected, follow very strictly the order Subject—Verb—Object, with only limited freedom as to where to put adverbial and connective elements. Repeatedly Peachey breaks these rules of normal word-order, from his first appearance in the narrator's office in scene E: "'I've come back,' he repeated; "and I was the King of Kafiristan—me and Dravot—*crowned Kings* we was! *In this office* we settled it . . . '" (In this quotation, and subsequently, "marked theme" has been italicized; it is worth noting that on all but two occasions of those cited, it is the Object or Complement of the sentence which has been moved to the front—the most unusual and hence most marked form of "marked theme.") At this point, the breaches of normal word-order perhaps seem only a slightly vulgar form of emphasis, connected with Peachey's false concords ("we was"). But as the monologue continues these breaches occur in increasingly grave contexts, and begin to take on an alternative range of suggestions—not vulgar and colloquial,

but archaic and, especially, Biblical. In these circumstances "marked theme" is associated in particular with Dravot, who as the story continues becomes more and more the king and the rash, ruling spirit, with Peachey acting as his restraint and acolyte. Early on, Peachey distinguishes between them: "'I wasn't King,'" said Carnehan. "'Dravot he was the King and *a handsome man* he looked with the gold crown on his head and all.'" Later, as Dravot returns from his first triumphal expedition, he boasts to Peachey of the riches of their dominion: "'*Gold* I've seen, and *turquoise* I've kicked out of the cliffs, and there's garnets in the sands of the river . . . .'" He explains also that the Kafirs have a rudimentary Masonic organization, and that this is to be their means of control: "'*A God and a Grand-Master of the Craft* am I, and *a Lodge in the Third Degree* I will open . . . .'" Peachey protests that this is illegal, but is overborne: "'I've forty chiefs at my heel, and *passed and raised according to their merits* they shall be.'" This imperative and overbearing streak reappears in Dravot, to be expressed in similar fashion every time he makes a major error. Meddling with the Masonic organization is one. Breaking the "Contrack" by taking a wife is the next, again over Peachey's appeals: "'These women are whiter than you or me, and *a Queen* I will have for the winter months.'" And when the "Queen" exposes Dravot's humanity (by biting him) and the Kafirs rebel, we see the megalomania persisting in Dravot in spite of his failure: "'*An Emperor* am I,'" says Daniel, "'and *next year* I shall be a Knight of the Queen.'"

These instances are of course dispersed through a fairly long story (which however contains other examples). But the sensitivity of any native speaker to such abnormalities is very high; they contribute a tone, even if they are never analyzed grammatically or consciously. The utility of "marked theme" for Kipling lies largely in its potential ambiguity. The device often suggests will-power and imperiousness in Dravot; it can also be just faintly comic. As he ruminates on his Kingdom's potential, Dravot considers bringing in other Englishmen as deputies: "'There's Mackray, Sergeant-pensioner at Segowli—*many's the good dinner* he's given me, and his wife a pair of trousers.'" The second-hand trousers co-exist with the golden crown, and Dravot notices no incongruity. Moreover, the incongruity which the reader notices does not entirely detract from the narrative. Like Peachey's rambling style, it even contains a hint of verisimilitude; for just as the "Loafer" in Dravot emerges in the middle of his Kingship, so even in their most obvious scenes of "Loaferdom" Carnehan and Dravot show flashes of regal self-assurance—as we have seen, just enough to shake the "I" narrator's scepticism at two or three moments. The linguistic habits associated with Dravot continue the work of the "frames"; they give strong suggestions of discrepant worlds co-existing, but forbid any final resolution.

There should be no doubt that Kipling, with his notorious sensitivity to language, knew in these cases exactly what he was doing. Other devices are less interesting, or may be more accidental. In the first category we may include Carnehan and Dravot's continual mistakes of number, "we starts...we goes...they fires," which serve to remind us of their humble origin even in the most exalted moments; or else their use of thematized "gloss-tags" for the same purpose, as at the end: "'The mountains *they* danced at night and the mountains *they* tried to fall on Peachey's head, but Dan *he* held up his hand, and Peachey came along bent double.'" In the second category is the curious fact that several climaxes in the monologue centre on passivity (or impassivity) and are marked by double negatives. Peachey's first complaint about Dravot is that he "'would *never* take advice, *not though* I begged of him!'" This same self-assurance of Dravot's becomes a virtue, however, in the centre of the story, when Dravot allows the priest to discover the Master's Mark without showing any sign of concern, and "'*never* winked an eye, *not when* ten priests took and tilted over the Grand-Master's chair.'" At the end the same construction, though, marks failure. It is the Kafirs who close determinedly on the white men, not breaking the silence that shows their purpose "'*not though* the King knocked down the first man...*not though* old Peachey fired his last cartridge....'" The repetition of this construction might allow one to see an inversion of silent assurance from Dravot to the Kafirs, and may be intentional. But though the examples are prominent, they are too few for absolute certainty as to Kipling's degree of control.

Only one device deserves equal consideration with the use of "marked theme," and it is one which makes no ironic point and no point about the characters, having rather a pronounced and pervasive effect on how the reader *visualizes* the narrative. It is a matter of sentence-structure. Carnehan is reluctant to use subordinate clauses; he is fairly slow, also, to use pronouns anaphorically, *i.e.*, as substitutes for people or objects already named. Instead, everything has to be detailed and repeated, while most of his sentences become strings of loosely-connected or independent main clauses. Almost any passage of his speech shows this, apart from dialogue, but one might take this passage describing the establishment of the Kingdom. The two white men are living in a Kafir village:

> "Then a lot of men came into the valley, and Carnehan and Dravot picks them off with the rifles before they knew where they was, and runs down into the valley and up again the other side and finds another village, same as the first one, and the people all falls down flat on their faces, and Dravot says—'Now what is the trouble between you two villages?' and the people point to a woman, as fair as you or me, that was carried off, and Dravot takes her back to the first village and counts up the dead—eight there was."

In this sentence grammatical subjects of clauses alternate six times. "A lot of men" come into the valley; Carnehan and Dravot shoot at and pursue them; "the people" submit; Dravot asks why they have attacked; they tell him; he does something about it. The clumsiness of this narration is increased by the very obvious gaps in the story, filled only by repeated "ands." How do Carnehan and Dravot know that the "lot of men" are enemies? Why do the others decide to worship them? What makes them run down the valley and up the other side? The reader has to supply his own answers, if he cares to. But the effect of this mode of narrative is obviously a calculated one on Kipling's part. Its main feature is suddenness and surprise, events taking place without preparation or explanation, and often being abandoned for something else before they have been understood; there is considerable vagueness also in the subjects ("a lot of men... the people") which prevents a reader from ever quite catching up. Yet at the same time there is evidence of a desire for total clarity on Peachey's part. He tells the narrator how many dead men there were; he notes the captured woman's complexion; he observes obscurely that the second village was "same as the first one"; the very way in which he alternates from one side to the next in the sentence quoted suggests a close visualization of the scene he is describing. Probably the best way to characterize the style is to say that it suggests difficulties of *focus*. Constantly peering at details and trying to describe an entire scene, Peachey forgets larger matters and leaves human motives especially in the dark. As a result, the style persuades one that there is truth (somewhere) in what Peachey says, but still gives even the plainest and most realistic matters a touch of the inexplicable.

In places this style becomes an intensely powerful one, worthy of comparison even with Shakespeare's "wise fools." It can be used comically, in keeping with one side of the adventurers' characters: "'The Chief comes along first, and Carnehan shakes hands with him and whirls his arms about, same as Dravot used, and very much surprised that Chief was, and strokes my eyebrows.'" Here the "marked theme" ("very much surprised"), the changes of tense, and the shift from third to first person ("Carnehan . . . my") co-operate with the shifts of subject and the general unpredictability of what happens to suggest something of the staggering effect that the "Loafers" have on the Kafirs. Elsewhere a similar style can be horrific, the capture of Dravot and Carnehan being given with a strange mixture of detail and detachment:

> "They took them without any sound. Not a little whisper all along the snow, not though the King knocked down the first man that set hands on him—not though old Peachey fired his last cartridge into the brown of 'em. Not a single solitary sound did those swines make. They just closed up tight, and I tell you their furs stunk. There was a man called Billy Fish, a good friend of us all, and they cut his throat, Sir, then and there, like a pig; and the King kicks up the bloody snow and says: 'We've had a dashed fine run for our money. What's coming next?'"

The interweaving of past and present tenses, of first and third persons, is disturbing enough in its testimony to Peachey's state of mind. These are capped, though, by the rhetorical, repetitive start ("without any sound . . . not a little whisper . . . not a single, solitary sound") and even more by the alternation of grammatical subjects, "they . . . those swines . . . they . . . they" set against "the King . . . old Peachey . . . a man called Billy Fish." Perhaps the most gruesome touch is the sudden vividness of "'I tell you their furs stunk,'" where for the only time Peachey speaks in the first person as if close to his experience, but where he picks on a peripheral and trivial detail, fixed in his mind (one assumes) by the trauma of fear surrounding it. In moments like this Peachey's

monologue reaches the heights of art, but without sacrificing either the "low style" that reminds us of what he is (in the eyes of the world) or the abnormalities that tell us he is mad.

This blending, of course, is Kipling's aim and achievement, central to the ironic consideration of whether Carnehan and Dravot are kings in fact or only in potential (as hinted at in the opposition of the title, "The *Man* Who Would Be *King*"), and to the uncertain reliability of both Carnehan and the "I" narrator, as expressed through the monologue's "frames." What is most surprising (in a 19th century writer) is the deliberation with which Kipling has deployed his considerable linguistic knowledge; in our own day perhaps only William Golding has made a comparable attempt to convey abnormal states of mind through unusual syntax. But one can see similar preoccupations elsewhere in Kipling, for instance in the opium-smoker's monologue of "The Gate of the Hundred Sorrows" (1888), or, in "The Man Who Would Be King," in the easily detachable linguistic parodies of the newspaper report, the native correspondent's letter, the "Contrack," or Dravot's "mad priest monologue." All these in their way cast sidelights on the central action, and serve also as examples of language variety echoing different habits of mind.

Perhaps the last point, though, should be this. Unlike some other novelists, Kipling does not seem to have conceived his central monologue with its distinctive forms as a device for developing *character*. We never learn anything but the most obvious facts about Dravot and Carnehan, and as so often in Kipling's stories, pay more attention to what they represent than what they are. The real purpose of the monologue is to provide a different mode of narrative for events which (if related simply) would seem more at home in a boy's adventure-book, and would receive easy dismissal. But in the way they *are* told, the events seem increasingly far-off and irrecoverable, in a world quite separate from that of the "I" narrator or his readers, a world which might genuinely have a logic (as it has a syntax) of its own. The issue of truth versus credibility is suspended with all the skill in Kipling's power, so that one's main response is in the end one of pity—for a Kingdom and a Kingship that can never be entirely grasped, but which, we must believe, existed in full power at least in one man's mind. One's feelings are well expressed by Hippolyta in *A Mid-summer Night's Dream*, as she defends the fantastic (and stylistically confused) stories of lovers and actors from the sceptic Theseus. It is true, she admits, that the imagination can create forms on its own:

> But all the story of the night told over,
> And all their minds transfigured so together,
> More witnesseth than fancy's images,
> And grows to something of great constancy;
> But howsoever, strange and admirable.

Source: Thomas A. Shippey and Michael Short, "Framing and Distancing in Kipling's 'The Man Who Would Be King,'" in *Journal of Narrative Technique*, Vol. 2, No. 2, May 1972, pp. 75–87.

SOURCES

Barrie, J. M., "Mr. Kipling's Stories," in *Kipling: The Critical Heritage*, edited by Roger Lancelyn Green, Barnes & Noble, 1971, p. 81; originally published in *Contemporary Review*, Vol. 59, March 1891, pp. 364–72.

Bauer, Helen Pike, *Rudyard Kipling: A Study of the Short Fiction*, Twayne's Studies in Short Fiction, No. 58, Twayne Publishers, 1994, pp. 28, 31–33, 40.

Bayley, John, "The False Structure," in *Critical Essays on Rudyard Kipling*, edited by Harold Orel, G. K. Hall, 1989, p. 145.

Buchanan, Robert, "The Voice of the Hooligan," in *Kipling: The Critical Heritage*, edited by Roger Lancelyn Green, Barnes & Noble, 1971, p. 233; originally published in *Contemporary Review*, Vol. 86, December 1899, pp. 774–89.

Dobrée, Bonamy, "Rudyard Kipling," in *Kipling: The Critical Heritage*, edited by Roger Lancelyn Green, Barnes & Noble, 1971, p. 350; originally published in *Monthly Criterion*, Vol. 6, December 1927, pp. 499–515.

Fussell, Paul, "Freemasonry and Humane Ethics in Kipling's 'The Man Who Would Be King,'" in *English Literary History*, Vol. 25, No. 3, September 1958, pp. 216–33.

Gilbert, Elliot L., "Silence and Survival in Kipling's Art and Life," in *Rudyard Kipling: Modern Critical Views*, edited with an introduction by Harold Bloom, Chelsea House, 1987, p. 105.

Harrison, James, *Rudyard Kipling*, Twayne's English Author Series, No. 339, Twayne Publishers, 1982, pp. 5, 10, 154.

Henley, W. E., Review of *Soldiers Three, Plain Tales from the Hills*, and *Departmental Ditties*, in *Kipling: The Critical Heritage*, edited by Roger Lancelyn Green, Barnes & Noble, 1971, p 55; originally published in *Scots Observer*, May 3, 1890.

Jarrell, Randall, "On Preparing to Read Kipling," in *Rudyard Kipling: Modern Critical Views*, edited with an introduction by Harold Bloom, Chelsea House, 1987, pp. 12, 22.

Kipling, Rudyard, "The Last of the Stories," in *Writings on Writing*, edited by Sandra Kemp and Lisa Lewis, Cambridge University Press, 1996, pp. 11–24; originally published in *Week's News*, September 15, 1889.

———, "Literature," in *Writings on Writing*, edited by Sandra Kemp and Lisa Lewis, Cambridge University Press, 1996, pp. 49–52; originally a speech given at the Anniversary Banquet of the Royal Academy, May 5, 1906.

———, "The Man Who Would Be King," in *The Man Who Would Be King and Other Stories*, edited by Louis L. Cornell, Oxford's World Classics, 2008, pp. 244–79.

———, Preface to *The Phantom Rickshaw and Other Eerie Tales*, in *Writings on Writing*, edited by Sandra Kemp and Lisa Lewis, Cambridge University Press, 1996, p. 9.

———, *Something of Myself: For My Friends Known and Unknown*, Doubleday, Doran, 1937, pp. 221, 228.

Lang, Andrew, Review of *Plain Tales from the Hills*, in *Kipling: The Critical Heritage*, edited by Roger Lancelyn Green, Barnes & Noble, 1971, p. 47; originally published in *Daily News*, November 2, 1899.

Mallett, Phillip, *Rudyard Kipling: A Literary Life*, Palgrave Macmillan, 2003, pp. 24, 100, 208.

Marx, Edward, "How We Lost Kafiristan," in *Representations*, Vol. 67, Summer 1999, pp. 44–66.

Millar, J. H., "The Works of Mr. Kipling," in *Kipling: The Critical Heritage*, edited by Roger Lancelyn Green, Barnes & Noble, 1971, p. 200; originally published in *Blackwood's Magazine*, Vol. 164, October 1898, pp. 470–82.

Said, Edward, *Culture and Imperialism*, Vintage Books, 1994, pp. xiii, 10, 64.

Stewart, J. I. M., "The Mature Craftsman," in *Critical Essays on Rudyard Kipling*, edited by Harold Orel, G. K. Hall, 1989, p. 129.

Sullivan, Zoreh T., "Kipling the Nightwalker," in *Rudyard Kipling: Modern Critical Views*, edited with an introduction by Harold Bloom, Chelsea House, 1987, p. 74.

Trilling, Lionel, "Kipling," in *Kipling's Mind and Art*, edited by Andrew Rutherford, Oliver and Boyd, 1964, p. 85; originally published in 1943 and reprinted in *The Liberal Imagination*, 1951.

Wilde, Oscar, "The True Function and Value of Criticism," in *Kipling: The Critical Heritage*, edited by Roger Lancelyn Green, Barnes & Noble, 1971, p. 104; originally published in *Nineteenth Century*, Vol. 28, July–September 1890.

Wilson, Edmund, "The Kipling Nobody Read," in *Kipling's Mind and Art*, edited by Andrew Rutherford, Oliver and Boyd, 1964, p. 17; originally published in *Atlantic Monthly*, Vol. 167, 1941, pp. 201–14; reprinted from *The Wound and the Bow*, 1952.

FURTHER READING

Cross, John, ed., *The Age of Kipling* , Simon and Schuster, 1972.

> With photographs of Kipling and his times, the book collects articles by twenty eminent scholars on such topics as Kipling's father, his boyhood writings, the friendship with Wolcott Balestier, the Boer War, Kipling and H. Rider Haggard, the influence of the Hill Stations and Music Halls, Kipling's imperialism, his reputation, and interpretation of his work in films.

Fox, Ralph, *The Colonial Policy of British Imperialism*, introduction by Ian Talbot, Oxford University Press, 2008.

> This classic text on empire by socialist writer Fox argues that the British working class suffers from capitalism based on imperial monopolies. Written during the depression of the 1930s, Fox lays bare the costly politics and economics of imperialist policies.

Gandhi, Mohandas, *An Autobiography: The Story of My Experiments With Truth*, translated by Mahadev H. Desai with a new preface and foreword by Sissela Bok, Beacon, 1993.

> This is Gandhi's account of how he used the principle of nonviolent resistance to fight British colonialism. As an inspiration for Indian independence, he was considered an outlaw by the British, but a hero and holy man by Indians.

Gilmour, David, *The Long Recessional: The Imperial Life of Rudyard Kipling*, Farrar, Straus, and Giroux, 2002.

> Gilmour's outstanding biography explains Kipling's paradoxical devotion to the British Empire that continued even when he was acutely aware of its collapse. The title refers to Kipling's poem "Recessional" written for Queen Victoria's Diamond Jubilee, which warns Britain not to be blinded by its own power.

Kipling, Rudyard, *Jungle Book*, Sterling, 2007.

> The collection of tales includes the favorites about Mowgli, a boy brought up by wolves who teach him the Law of the Jungle. These are delightful fables that illustrate the behavior of individuals and society.

SUGGESTED SEARCH TERMS

Rudyard Kipling

The Man Who Would Be King

The Man Who Would Be King AND Kipling

Kafiristan

Freemasonry

Kipling AND imperialism

British Empire

Kipling AND short story

Kipling AND colonial fiction

Kipling AND colonial India

My Lucy Friend Who Smells Like Corn

SANDRA CISNEROS

1991

Sandra Cisneros's short story "My Lucy Friend Who Smells Like Corn," is only three pages long and is told through the eyes of a very young girl, possibly between the ages of eight and ten. The language of the story is very distinctive and, at times, very funny. Readers might imagine sitting down in some hidden place where no other adults are around and listening to the unrestrained thoughts of a loving—but somewhat insecure girl commenting on her limited but whole-heartedly-felt view of friendship.

While working toward her master's degree in creative writing, Cisneros was challenged by the typical writing style of her peers, and this short story is a prime example of how Cisneros battled against the standards of mainstream writing by creating her own unique way of voicing a story. She does not worry about sentence structure or proper grammar. Rather she recreates characters as she has seen and heard them in real life—her life, which does not fit the mainstream model. The main character of "My Lucy Friend Who Smells Like Corn" is never named, but there is no need to do so. The young girl is present on the page through her observations of her friend Lucy, the emotions she feels for Lucy, and through her dreams.

"My Lucy Friend Who Smells Like Corn" was published in 1991 in the short story collection *Woman Hollering Creek*, which won the 1991 Lannan Foundation Literary Award. This

Sandra Cisneros *(AP / Wide World Photos. Reproduced by permission)*

short story is the first in the collection and helps define the first section, which contains stories with young protagonists.

AUTHOR BIOGRAPHY

Cisneros was born in Chicago, Illinois, on December 20, 1954. Her father, Alfredo Cisneros de Moral, was born in Mexico but immigrated to Chicago, Illinois, where he met and married Elvira Cordero Angulano. Cisneros is the third of seven children and the only girl. As she grew up, her family moved back and forth between Mexico City and different places in the United States. The constant difficulties of readjusting to new neighborhoods and schools led her to reading and the more interior world of writing. Her parents finally settled in a Mexican American neighborhood in Chicago. The house was old and the outbuildings around the house were falling apart. It was this house and the years she spent living there that inspired Cisneros's first novel, *The House on Mango Street*, published in 1984.

Cisneros began writing poetry in high school and became the editor of the school's literary magazine. In 1976, she graduated from Loyola University in Chicago, earning a bachelor's degree in English. Afterward, she attended the University of Iowa Writers Workshop, where she graduated in 1978 with a master of fine arts. Though she earned a degree, Cisneros was disappointed with her experience at Iowa. Her experiences and background were very different from those of the teachers and students around her. This realization eventually helped her discover her own voice, her unique topics of interest, and her manner of telling a story.

Cisneros returned to Illinois after the Iowa experience and counseled high school dropouts in an alternative school system in Chicago. In 1984, following the success of *The House on Mango Street*, which won the American Book Award in 1985, Cisneros was offered teaching positions as a visiting professor at the University of California at Berkeley, the University of Michigan, and Our Lady of the Lake University in San Antonio, Texas.

Cisneros continued to receive accolades from critics for her work. Her collection of short stories *Woman Hollering Creek* (1991), which contains "My Lucy Friend Who Smells Like Corn," was named a noteworthy book of the year by the *New York Times* and by the *American Library Journal*. In 1995 she was honored with a MacArthur Fellowship, also known as the "Genius" Award. Cisneros wrote a second novel, *Caramelo*, in 2002. Like *The House on Mango Street*, *Caramelo* contains many details that reflect Cisneros's life, such as the protagonist being the only girl in the midst of six brothers and the frequent moving of the family between Mexico and the United States.

Cisneros is often credited with being one of the first authors to open the publishing business to Hispanic literature. She was one of the first Hispanic writers to land a contract with a major publisher. Her influence extends beyond literature to running the Macondo Foundation, a group of writers who use their skills to help promote socially-engaged activities in their communities.

PLOT SUMMARY

"My Lucy Friend Who Smells Like Corn" is told through the voice of a young, unnamed narrator. The focus of the story is the narrator's

MEDIA ADAPTATIONS

- Published in 2005 by Random House, *Loose Woman, and Woman Hollering Creek and Other Stories* is available in audio format read by Cisneros. The compilation contains samples of Cisneros's poetry and short fiction, including the short story "My Lucy Friend Who Smells Like Corn."

admiration for her friend Lucy, whom the narrator wants to be like in almost every way. The narrator begins with the unusual description of Lucy, who, as is revealed in the title of this story, smells like corn. Rather than the buttery smell of corn-on-the-cob or popcorn, Lucy smells like tortillas or *nixtamal* (a specially processed form of corn, or maize, used in making Mexican tamales, tortillas, and corn chips). This description alerts the reader that either the narrator or Lucy, or maybe both, are either a part of or familiar with Mexican culture. Cisneros never states directly that this story is about two Mexican American girls. She merely hints at this through the details that she does provide, like the food and aromas of corn.

Cisneros also never reveals the ages of the narrator and Lucy. She does, however, mention the activities that they share, such as playing with paper cutout dolls. This activity suits elementary school-aged children—girls old enough to use scissors but young enough to be enthralled by the simplicity of cutting out dolls and their wardrobes and acting out make-believe scenarios for them. The girls also play games that use marbles. When the narrator describes the marbles that she and Lucy are trading, she says one is "like the yellow blood of butterflies." Who but a child would conjure up a description of a butterfly against the windshield of a car to describe the color of an item?

Both these activities, playing with paper dolls and with marbles, suggest not only uncomplicated pastimes of youth, they also hint at the economic status of the girls' families. There is no mention of a large collection of expensive dolls, dollhouses, and doll clothes. Paper dolls and marbles provide cheap, old-fashioned entertainment. So once again, Cisneros leaves it to the reader's imagination to fill in the missing information. She paints the picture and lets the reader interpret who these girls are and what kind of lives they lead.

The second paragraph of the story begins with a quote that apparently comes from Lucy, though again, Cisneros is vague about the attribution. "*Have you ever eated dog food?*" someone asks, speaking in non-traditional English grammar. Cisneros does not correct the child's language, realizing that children do not always form verb tenses correctly. Here again, Cisneros says a lot through implication. Through this question, Lucy is further described. She is a tough little girl who is not pretentious about the type of food she consumes. Readers might ask why she is eating dog food, however. Is it because her family is too poor to afford higher costing food? Or is Lucy merely trying to prove to the girls how tough she is? Also in this paragraph, Cisneros subtly points out that another little girl, Janey, insists that Lucy prove she eats dog food. Whereas the narrator takes Lucy at her word, Janey demands that Lucy open her mouth and show her the dog food. In contrast, the narrator states, she likes Lucy not for the wild things she does but for the way she smells and because Lucy has "aqua flip-flops" that match hers, which the pair bought while shopping together. Through these words, Cisneros demonstrates that the narrator and Lucy are close friends, closer to one another than to Janey.

By the third paragraph, the narrator exposes not just her longing to be Lucy's friend but also her desire to be just like Lucy. The narrator says that even if she has to submit herself to the torture of staying in the sun, even if it is "a million trillion degrees outside," she wants her skin to darken to the same tone as Lucy's skin. Lucy's family members—eight sisters that the narrator names—are all dark-skinned and the narrator wants to fit in with them.

In the fourth paragraph, the narrator describes a house that is likely Lucy's, though this is never directly stated. This house has a screen door with no screen in it. There is a small black dog biting at fleas. The windows are painted in different colors. The missing screen may mean negligence or poverty. The same could be said about the flea-bitten dog. As for the windows, the narrator comes to her own conclusions. Either Lucy's father "got tired" the day he was painting or he just forgot to finish the job. Meanwhile, Lucy's mother washes clothes in an old-fashioned washing machine, the type that has a double-roller, hand-cranked wringer. This type of washing machine was obsolete after the 1950s. So either this story is set in the 1950s or the family could not afford a more modern machine. Lucy, at one time, had the chore of using this washing machine and in the process her hand got pulled into the wringer rollers where it became stuck. Her mother had to reverse the rollers to free her daughter's hand. The narrator wonders if Lucy's arm flattened out and had to be pumped up with air to go back to normal. Amazement comes when the narrator discovers that after this trauma, even though Lucy's fingernail turned black and eventually fell off, she never cried.

In the next paragraph, the narrator provides details of Lucy's family's laundry and describes how they hang the clothes on the line so they do not stretch or wrinkle the fabric. Hanging the clothes on the line is like an art. It is through the depiction of the clothes hanging outside that the narrator acknowledges that there are no males around. Lucy's siblings are all girls. The father is seldom home, and the mother is tired from taking care of all the children. And these children, the narrator states, all share one another's clothes, except for Olivia, and that, in the narrator's mind, makes Olivia stingy.

In the sixth paragraph, the story begins to conclude. The narrator is sitting in the sun, as she mentioned earlier, trying to tan her skin. This section is peppered with poetic language that a child might use. The narrator states that it is that time of day when the sun "makes the streets dizzy" and makes the narrator feel like she has a hat on top of her head. The narrator also returns to the detail of smells, as the heat of the day makes everything smell like corn. The narrator takes herself deeper into her dream of being like Lucy. She wishes she slept in a bed with a bunch of sisters tucked all around her feet and head. She would even like it if she had siblings she could yell at "one at a time or all together." This would be so much better than her situation, where she sleeps alone on a chair-bed.

The narrator's life is so different from Lucy's, and Lucy's life, in the narrator's mind, is so much more exciting and full. As she describes in the seventh paragraph, the narrator will go home to the admonishment of her grandmother (the Spanish word *abuelita* is an informal way to refer to a grandmother, like "grandma" or "grammy"). Her grandmother will scold her because she has dirtied her dress. This same dress, her grandmother will remind her, needs to be worn again the next day.

In the last paragraph, the narrator laughs all her cares away, disregarding her grandmother's disappointment as well as her own. Instead, she will laugh with Lucy as they jump on an old mattress that has been thrown outside. They will play silly games, such as wearing their shoes on their hands. They will also join forces and confront Janey, whom neither of them likes, and they will tell her they are never going to be friends with her. They are going to do kid things, like running backwards and waving to people they do not know. They will dare one another to do scary things like facing rats and walking on top of the porch railing. And then they will return to normal activities, like cutting out paper dolls. They will even create their own dolls and color them and the clothes they make for them.

Most importantly, the narrator reveals her ultimate dream. She and Lucy would be sisters, or at least pretend they are. They are so close to one another, with their arms wrapped around one another's neck and their teeth falling out at the same time, whispering secrets into one another's ears. The narrator ends her story as it began, with a reminder that Lucy, her friend, smells like corn.

CHARACTERS

Abuelita

Abuelita is an affectionate Spanish-language term for grandmother. The narrator refers to Abuelita, or granny, as a person who greets her at her house, and scolds her for dirtying her dress. Readers can assume that the grandmother is one of the authority figures at the narrator's house, possibly taking care of the narrator while the mother and father are at work. It is also possible that the narrator's grandmother lives with them, making this a multi-generational home. This might also suggest that there is not enough money in the family for the grandmother, or the parents, to afford a home for themselves.

Amber Sue Anguiano

Lucy Anguiano, the focus of this story, has many sisters. Amber Sue is her youngest sister.

Cheli Anguiano

Cheli Anguiano is another of Lucy's sisters. Her name is mentioned when the narrator lists Lucy's siblings, but nothing special is mentioned about this particular sister.

Herminia Anguiano

Herminia is another of Lucy Anguiano's sisters. There is no further information given about Herminia.

Lucy Anguiano

Lucy Anguiano is the focus of this story. The narrator describes Lucy, as well as her affection for this young girl. Readers are given specific details about Lucy, but there is a lot of missing information. For example, readers know that Lucy smells like corn, but they do not know how old she is or what she looks like. Her skin is dark, but readers do not know the color of Lucy's hair. Readers also know that she is a friend of the narrator and that she sleeps in one bed with her eight sisters. They know she has no brothers and that her father is seldom at home.

Lucy works hard, helping her mother wash clothes. Readers also know that Lucy is tough. She does not cry when her fingers are accidentally crushed in the wringer part of the clothes washer. The accident is harsh enough for Lucy's finger to turn black and for her to lose a fingernail. But she does not complain. She is also tough enough to eat dog food. Lucy is methodical in hanging out the washed clothes on the outdoor clothesline. The line is only so long, and Lucy must make perfect use of the limited length. She also hangs the clothes in the best way so they have less wrinkles.

By using examples of what the narrator and Lucy do together, the author insinuates the closeness of the relationship between her and the narrator. Though readers are never told specifically how Lucy feels about the narrator, readers can assume the narrator's feelings are reciprocated. For instance, Lucy buys the same kind of flip flops as the narrator. They both love the same pastimes, like making cut-out paper dolls.

Margarita Anguiano

Margarita Anguiano is one of Lucy's sisters. Margarita is not singled out with any special characteristics or traits.

Nancy Anguiano

Nancy Anguiano is Lucy's sister. Nothing more than her name is given in this story.

Norma Anguiano

Norma Anguiano is another of Lucy's sisters. That is all that readers are told about her.

Ofelia Anguiano

Ofelia Anguiano is Lucy's sister. No other information is provided about her.

Olivia Anguiano

Olivia Anguiano is Lucy's sister. Though Lucy and her other sisters often borrow one another's clothes, Olivia does not. Because of Olivia's unwillingness to share, the narrator calls Olivia stingy.

Mama

In one part of the story, there is a reference to Mama. From the context of this reference, readers can infer that it is Lucy's mother. Lucy cries out to her when her hand becomes stuck in the washing machine. Mama is described as being tired and having so many children around her that she cannot think.

Narrator

The first-person narrator of this story is never named, nor is much information about her physical description offered. Readers know the narrator more through what she thinks and feels than through what she looks like. Readers can assume that the narrator and Lucy are about the same age. Though the narrator is adventuresome and creative, she does not have a strong sense of self.

The narrator wants to not only look like Lucy, she wants to be Lucy, or at least be one of Lucy's sisters. The narrator suffers in the heat so the sun will make her as dark-skinned as Lucy. She wants to wear the same kind of clothes as her friend and sleep in her bed, along with all eight of Lucy's sisters.

Like Lucy, the narrator is also adventurous, not worried about taking risks. She thinks nothing of balancing herself on the top of a porch railing or sticking her feet under the porch, tempting the rats that live there to bite her toes. Whether the narrator is doing this to impress Lucy or merely because she likes taking chances is not made clear. But she does not appear to show fear. Readers might assume that the narrator wants to seem as strong as Lucy, who is not squeamish when she eats dog food or terribly disturbed when she squashes her fingers in the wringer on the old-fashioned clothes washer.

Though the narrator wishes she had as many sisters as Lucy so she would not have to sleep alone, she appears to want Lucy to herself. The narrator plans to go with Lucy to tell Janey, another girl to who wants to hang around them, to stay away. The narrator seems to want to have Lucy's full attention.

Janey Ortiz

Janey Ortiz is a peer of both the narrator and Lucy. She is not as impressed with Lucy as the narrator is. When Lucy mentions that she is eating dog food, for example, Janey insists that Lucy open her mouth and prove it. The narrator contrasts herself with Janey, proving, at least in her mind, that she is a closer friend to Lucy than Janey is. Later in the story, the narrator plans to go with Lucy and tell Janey that Lucy and the narrator will never, ever be friends with her. Janey is a minor character, used only to demonstrate how close the narrator and Lucy are to one another.

THEMES

Friendship

One of the main themes in "My Lucy Friend Who Smells Like Corn" is the friendship of two young girls. Friendship dominates the content of this story more so than any other aspect of the narrator's life. There are hints at other relationships in this story, such as Lucy's connection to her eight sisters and the narrator's desire to have similar relationships with siblings. There is also the lack of friendship between the narrator and Lucy and their peer, Janey. But the narrator's attraction to and support for Lucy resonates throughout.

The narrator never directly states how much she likes Lucy, but almost every description of

what she and Lucy do or how the narrator imagines what Lucy is like is saturated with the emotions Lucy inspires in the narrator. That the narrator wants to look like Lucy, to have eight sisters like Lucy, to dress like Lucy, even to be as brave as Lucy, resonates with the deep admiration that the narrator has for this young girl.

Another aspect of this theme of friendship is that despite the poverty, extreme heat, lack of toys, and shortage of food and clothing, the young narrator remains a cheerful child because of her close relationship with Lucy. It is her friendship with Lucy that keeps the narrator's heart alive through all her challenges.

Family

Though parents and siblings are all but absent from this story, the author provides a sense of family. Not all aspects of family, in this story, are positive, but the child narrator and her friend Lucy appear well supported by family, given the indications of poverty the narrator describes.

The most prominent aspect of family is the large number of siblings that Lucy has. Though her eight sisters never appear in the story, they are each individually named. One of them, Olivia, is even given a personality trait, that of stinginess, a characteristic that the author, through omission, insinuates the other sisters do not possess. If Olivia stands out due to her stinginess, one can assume that the other sisters are generous, sharing their short supply of material objects.

Lucy's mother is also mentioned. Her mother is often tired out by the number of children she has given birth to and now must feed and take care of. In her fatigue, she has trained Lucy to help with chores, while still keeping an eye on her, and being there when Lucy is hurt. Lucy's father, in contrast, is there infrequently, coming and going as he pleases. He helps out but only partially. He half paints the house but forgets to finish it or to match the colors.

The narrator's family is represented only by her grandmother, who is at home when the narrator comes in from school. The grandmother acts as disciplinarian as she scolds the narrator for getting her school dress dirty. There is no mention of a mother or father. The narrator longs for family, though. She wants to have sisters gather all around her, even squeezed together in one bed, like Lucy and her sisters. A big family is a good thing, the narrator suggests.

TOPICS FOR FURTHER STUDY

- Read Virginia Brackett's young-adult biography *A Home in the Heart: The Story of Sandra Cisneros* (2004). Did you find Cisneros's youth to be more like the narrator of "My Lucy Friend Who Smells Like Corn" or more like Lucy? Write an essay describing what you think Cisneros was like as a child, as well as what you think the short story's narrator and Lucy were like. How are they different? What do they have in common? Which one do you most relate to?

- Write a description of your best friend from elementary school. Use "My Lucy Friend Who Smells Like Corn" as your model. Create descriptions of your friend to help readers form vivid images of what he or she looked, smelled, and sounded like. What were some of the games you played? How did your friend's family differ from yours? What were the best things about this friend that you wanted to imitate? Be creative with your descriptions. Think about how you felt when you were young and use the language of an elementary school student to voice your story. Read your story to your class or post it on your Web site.

- Choose Chicago (where Cisneros lived as a child) or San Antonio (where she lives as an adult) and research the Hispanic population living there or use both areas to compare. What percentage of the city's population is Hispanic? How did these numbers change from the 1960s (when Cisneros was in school) to the present day? How has the political environment (rules about immigration, voting rights, or political power) changed over the past five decades? Create a Web page that contains the data you have collected and provide links to other Web sites that might broaden understanding of the challenges that Hispanic immigrants have faced and continue to confront in these two cities. Give a brief description of your project to your class and direct them to your Web pages.

- Research various Mexican and Mexican American holidays and celebrations (such as Cinco de Mayo, Día de los Muertos, Guadalupe Day, or Día de los Niños). Choose several celebrations and provide historical backgrounds (how they originated), descriptions of what each holiday entails (food, costumes, music, etc), and when these celebrations occur. Use photographs to accompany your class presentation and provide Web links so your classmates can further explore these special holidays.

- Work with the employees at your school cafeteria and help them plan a meal of Mexican dishes. Research the components of three different meals and the ingredients that are needed to make them. Then offer three possible menus to the cafeteria staff to serve on the chosen day. Clear your project with your school principal (maybe ask one of your teachers to sponsor your project) and then advertise the event throughout your school, making colorful, Mexican inspired posters to capture the attention of your fellow students. You could tie this meal to a Mexican holiday.

Hispanic American Culture

There are several clues as to the culture of the characters in Cisneros's short story. First there is the mention of the foods that the narrator is familiar with, such as tortillas and a bread flour called *nixtamal*. There are Spanish words sprinkled through the story, such as *y la*, which means "and the." The author places these words in the text without translating them, as if to assume readers are also Hispanic or at least can understand the Spanish words.

Names can also provide hints as to the culture in a story. The name Margarita can imply a

Lucy's hair smelled so good—like warm corn tortillas. (Mike Flippo | Shutterstock.com)

Spanish-speaking culture, as can Cheli. Last names such as Ortiz and Anguiano also suggest a Hispanic background.

Childhood

The theme of childhood is presented in several different ways. First, there is the language of the narrator, who does not always use correct grammar. She sometimes omits words that normally would be present in a properly constructed adult sentence. This could signify a child who has not completed her language studies or could reflect a child who is bilingual and is mixing up the grammatical constructs of two different languages. The narrator also uses images that reflect a child's way of looking at the world and her lack of self-consciousness in expressing herself. She thinks Lucy's tongue resembles a worm, for example. And she speaks of doing somersaults, even though her *chones* (Spanish for underpants) might show.

Childhood is also expressed through the activities that the narrator mentions. She and Lucy play a game of marbles and cut out paper dolls—pastimes of young girls. The narrator also wants them to wear their shoes on their hands and race backwards. The narrator's dreams reflect desires of a child, such as preferring to sleep in a bed filled with siblings rather than sleeping alone.

Self-Identity

A theme that Cisneros often uses in her writing is that of self-identity. She concentrates on females who are either looking for a definition of self or are having trouble defining themselves. In "My Lucy Friend Who Smells Like Corn," the narrator spends most of her time describing Lucy and the fun she has playing with the girl. Underlying this activity, though, is the narrator's desire to be Lucy. Rather than appreciating her own identity, the narrator wants her skin to be darker like Lucy's. She wants to have eight sisters like Lucy has. She wants to dress like Lucy does.

If the narrator were more confident in herself, she could have a relationship with Lucy without wanting to change her own identity. She could compare Lucy's dark skin with her lighter skin, rather than sweating under the sun as she struggles to make her skin match Lucy's.

But this is not what she does. Though the narrator never states that she does not want to be who she is, she longs to be someone she is not. This signifies that either she has no strong self-identity, no definition of who she is, or that she does not like who she is and wants a different identity.

STYLE

Nonstandard English

In order to authentically portray the narrator of this story as a young girl, Cisneros employs nonstandard English in "My Lucy Friend Who Smells Like Corn." Rather than using crisp, grammatically correct sentence structure, she allows her narrator to speak as a child would, without the influence of adults who might correct her usage. This makes the reader hear the story as if a young girl were telling it or as if the reader were listening to the thoughts of a child.

Examples of this are the word "eated" rather than the grammatically correct form of "eaten." Another example is the phrase "corn smell hair," which in the proper form would be "corn-smelling hair" or more simply "hair that smells of corn." When talking about Lucy sleeping with a lot of sisters in the same bed, the narrator states she wants to do the same, with some of the siblings "at the top and some at the feets." A child might improperly add an *s* to a word to make it plural, not knowing the word's irregular plural form. The narrator also uses the sentence, "Her whole family like that." She is describing how dark-skinned Lucy's family is. But in so stating, Cisneros has the narrator omit the verb. In standard English, every sentence must contain a verb. But a young child might not know this. Her language is understandable, but it is constructed in the grammatically incorrect form of a child's speech.

Poetic Prose

Cisneros has been published both as a prose fiction writer and as a poet. Often her prose takes on poetic forms, which enhance the language of her writing. In this short story, Cisneros uses terms such as "grasshopper green" to describe a marble that the girls are playing with. Rather than using only the color green to describe the marble, the author uses a common object, in this case a grasshopper, to provide a more poetic rendering, thus giving the reader a more vivid image of the color.

The author also uses the poetic figure of speech called simile. When using a simile, a writer compares two dissimilar objects, accompanied with the word *like* or *as* in the comparison. For example, to provide a precise noise for the eating of dog food in this story, the narrator uses the phrase "crunching like ice." This simile helps the reader to imagine the sound more vividly.

Spanglish

Often without explaining or translating, Cisneros uses Spanish phrases mixed in with the overall English language of her story to emphasize the Hispanic background of her characters. In some ways, this mimics Spanglish, an intertwined use of Spanish and English phrases and words common among bilingual speakers.

Examples in Cisneros's short story are the words *nixtamal* (a type of corn flour), *y la* (which means "and the"), and *chones* (which means "underwear").

HISTORICAL CONTEXT

Chicano/a Literature

Chicano/a literature refers to the body of work written by both male and female writers of Mexican descent. This body of work includes both oral and written stories dating back to the early years before the Spanish conquest of Mexico. Though Chicano/a literature may have been popular with Spanish-speaking readers, much of this literature went unnoticed by the general U.S. population until the 1960s. Publishers did not believe there was an audience for literature written by Mexican Americans and therefore did not publish it. In the 1960s, however, this began to change.

The 1960s were highly influenced by the civil rights movement, which caused a general reflection on the topic of ethnicity and culture. Like other ethnic groups, with the emphasis on civil rights and the importance of cultural pride, Mexican Americans became more interested in telling their stories through their own voices and their own experiences, no matter how much their stories and expressions differed from the generally accepted white, European American literary styles.

COMPARE
&
CONTRAST

- **1990s:** In 1990, the U.S. Census Bureau calculates that 13,174,000 Mexican Americans live in the United States.

  2000s: In 2009, according to the U.S. Census Bureau, the estimated Mexican American population in the United States is 20,640,711.

- **1990s:** According to the U.S. Census of 1990, 22.4 million Hispanics live in the United States. Of the entire U.S. Hispanic population, 63 percent are of Mexican heritage. Of the Mexican American population in the United States, 73 percent live in either California or Texas.

2000s: In 2008, the U.S. Census Bureau counted 46.9 million Hispanic people living in the United States, which constitutes 15 percent of the total U.S. population. The largest Mexican American populations live in four different states, California, Texas, Illinois, and Arizona.

- **1990s:** According to the U.S. Census figures, 25.8 percent of Mexican American families live below the U. S. official poverty line, which is $19,157 per year for a family of four.

2000s: Though the poverty rate in general for U.S. citizens falls, Hispanic Americans continue to represent the second poorest ethnic group in the nation.

Though mainstream publishing houses were slow to appreciate the literature of these varied ethnic groups, Chicano/a publishers began to spring up in the late 1960s and early 1970s. One of the most notable was Quinto Sol, founded in Berkeley, California, by Octavio I. Romano in 1967. Quinto Sol not only promoted Chicano/a authors, it awarded prizes to help support rising stars. One of the earliest writers selected was Rudolfo Anaya, who wrote the popular novel *Bless Me, Ultima* (1972). This novel follows the development of a young Mexican American boy, who grows up with guidance from a beloved neighbor and *curandera*, a Mexican healer. Anaya became one of Quinto Sol's most successful authors. Arte Publico Press, which published Cisneros's *The House on Mango Street*, was another early publisher and promoter of Chicano/a literature.

With the help of these publishing houses, Chicano/a literature began to be read by more diverse audiences. As a result (and along with the influence of the civil rights movement and the less well-known Hispanic civil rights movement), colleges around the nation began to teach literature courses that included more than the traditional works written by English and American white male authors. In the late 1960s and early 1970s, novels and poetry written not only by Hispanics but by African Americans, Asian Americans, Native Americans, and women, began to appear on college syllabi.

Other Chicano/a authors who opened the doors in the publishing market during the 1960s and 1970s include Raymond Barrio, author of *The Plum Plum Pickers* (1969). Barrio's novel was political, helping to increase awareness about the life-threatening conditions under which Mexican immigrants worked in the fields. His book is considered a classic of Chicano early literature. Although she was not one of the earliest Chicana authors, Lorna Dee Cervantes is a Mexican American poet whose work is considered to have had a strong influence on other Chicano/a writers. Cervantes also leans toward the political and considers herself a feminist. Her collection of poetry *Emplumada* (1982) won an American Book Award.

Hispanic Civil Rights Movement
Spurred by the civil rights movement, which focused on the rights of African Americans, the

They used all available clothespins and space on the clothesline. (*Manuel Fernandes | Shutterstock.com*)

Hispanic civil rights movement (also called the Chicano civil rights movement) gained publicity in the 1960s. As a result of these civil rights movements, a heightened awareness of the importance of culture affected many ethnic groups, including Mexican Americans.

Reies Lopez Tijerina is often listed as one of the first prominent figures of the modern Hispanic civil rights movement. He led demonstrations to fight for the right of land ownership in the Southwest. Many Mexican Americans owned ancestral land in that area and were forced to abandon it after the Mexican War (1846–1848). Rudolfo Gonzales, a poet and political activist, was another figure who increased cultural awareness of Mexican Americans in the 1960s. Gonzales, whose poem "I am Joaquín" became very popular with Mexican Americans, worked with César Chávez in his struggle to help Mexican American farm workers in the United States. Chávez helped form the

United Farm Workers, which fought to give farm workers decent working conditions.

Mexican American students also became a part of the Hispanic civil rights movement when, in 1968, they protested the inequalities present in the school systems in southern California. Students living in east Los Angeles went to schools that were rundown and poorly equipped, especially in comparison to students in other parts of southern California. To bring attention to the poverty of their schools, Mexican American students, wearing brown berets and using the slogan "Brown Pride," walked out of classes en mass during the first week in March 1968.

One of the undercurrents of the Hispanic civil rights movement was changing the stereotypical and negative images of Mexican Americans that often appeared in the media. The movement brought Mexican American people together as they realized that they had a greater voice when they worked collectively. The Brown

Pride slogan of the student uprising helped people embrace their heritage, just as the Black Power slogan had helped empower African Americans. Political organizers and activists were not the only ones who promoted Brown Pride. Motivated by a new awareness and pride in their Mexican heritage, Mexican American artists (visual, performance, and literary) thrived during the late 1960s and 1970s. Their involvement in creating works that reflected their Mexican culture led to the development of a smaller branch of the Hispanic civil rights movement, which was called the Chicano art movement.

CRITICAL OVERVIEW

Though not as popular as *House on Mango Street*, Cisneros's short story collection *Woman Hollering Creek* met with critical success. It is in this collection that "My Lucy Friend Who Smells Like Corn" was published. In his review of the collection, Bill Oliver, writing for the *New England Review*, states that Cisneros's "words have the power to discomfit." This is a good thing, Oliver suggests, as Cisneros's stories make her readers think. And what Cisneros lacks in the art of storytelling, she makes up for by writing so strongly, Oliver concludes. As a matter of fact, one of Cisneros's outstanding qualities, Oliver believes, is her "fierceness." She tells stories of women who are strong and determined. In summing up the female characters in this collection, Oliver writes that they are women who "need to learn how to start over." Their challenges are based on the fact that they have so much "that holds them back."

Adria Bernardi of the *Chicago Tribune* writes that in her stories in this collection, Cisneros "echoes a widening chorus of the voices of Latino cultures." The characters and themes Cisneros has created in her stories come from "her heart" and "revolve around being a Latina living in the United States, a theme that is central to her work." Bernardi also quotes Cisneros, who has stated that she especially likes to share her stories of Hispanic people in the United States with readers who know very little about the culture. It is through her stories that Cisneros enjoys "dismantling stereotypes."

In a *Washington Post* review of *Woman Hollering Creek*, Susan Wood describes Cisneros as "a writer of power and eloquence and great lyrical beauty." Wood continues praising Cisneros's work by stating that "the Chicana experience could not have found a voice more suited to its telling." She concludes her review by saying, "Cisneros knows both that the heart can be broken and that it can rise and soar like a bird," and because of this, Cisneros's stories should be listened to "for a long time to come."

Writing for *Commonweal*, Ilan Stavans describes the stories in Cisneros's short story collection as "verbal photographs, memorabilia, reminiscences of growing up in a Hispanic milieu." Later in the same article, Stavans compares Cisneros's fiction to "delicate porcelain figures, fragile yet capable of carrying symbolic weight." Stavans states that Cisneros's style "is candid, engaging, rich in language." The only problem Stavans finds is that Cisneros "bases most of her cast on stereotype." Despite this, Stavans writes that readers will find in Cisneros's stories "a voice welcomely different and a prose both refreshing and often hypnotizing."

Kirsten Backstrom, in the publication *off our backs*, writes specifically about the short story "My Lucy Friend Who Smells Like Corn." Backstrom states that even though Cisneros tells this story in a childlike voice, she "addresses the adult reader who can see what the child is learning in spite of herself." Backstrom adds that "these aren't just a child's random thoughts, but also a mature writer's crafted subtle voice." Cisneros "speaks to the experiences of women and girls."

Writing for the *Harvard Review*, Sarah Kafatou describes this short story collection as Cisneros's "richest, most ambitious and most uneven so far." But Kafatou adds that the best of the stories in this book are like "little miracles, occasions for crying and laughing and praying and getting up and going on."

"Cisneros is the impassioned bard of the Mexican border," writes Matthew Gilbert in the *Boston Globe*. Through the stories in her collection *Woman Hollering Creek*, she "proves that she is a writer of deep sympathies." And as for the story "My Lucy Friend Who Smells Like Corn," Gilbert writes that it is so "rich" that it reads like a "prose poem."

Elise Gunst, writing for the *Houston Chronicle*, finds that this short story collection "offers a gift to the uninitiated, the chance to taste deeply of Hispanic culture while accompanied by a knowing and generous guide." *Newsday* reviewer

Sarah Kerr describes the stories in Cisneros's *Woman Hollering Creek* as having "fresh, finely tuned images and the kind of life-affirming optimism that seem to have dropped from sight in recent American fiction." Kerr adds that "the subject of these stories may be new for some, but the writer's talent shouldn't escape anyone who reads them."

From Cisneros's fellow novelist Barbara Kingsolver, writing for the *Los Angeles Times*, come these words to describe Cisneros's writing talents as demonstrated through her short story collection: "Nearly every sentence contains an explosive sensory image." Cisneros's fiction is like poetry, in Kingsolver's opinion, so she advises readers to "enjoy it, revel in it."

CRITICISM

Joyce Hart

Hart is a published writer and teacher of creative writing. In the following essay, she examines the author's presentation of the implications of being female in "My Lucy Friend Who Smells Like Corn."

Cisneros is referred to as a feminist writer because female characters and female issues often dominate her stories. Her narrators and protagonists are often female, and male characters play only minor roles. Because of this predominance of female characters, it is not difficult to discern Cisneros's image of women as she has created them in her fiction. This is true in stories such as "My Lucy Friend Who Smells Like Corn." In this very short story, the narrator is a young girl who is fascinated by her female friend Lucy. These girls are the main characters of this story; in addition, the only named characters in this short story are female. As a matter of fact, all mentioned characters are female except for a brief reference to Lucy's father, who, the narrator emphasizes, is seldom home and has only plays a marginal role. Readers do not have to read this story too deeply in order to explore how Cisneros portrays women, how she exposes women's thoughts and desires, and how she sees them looking at the world around them. Upon closer examination, readers can discern what Cisneros believes drives women, how she envisions female relationships, what she thinks are women's challenges and how women tend to confront them.

> IS THE AUTHOR SAYING THAT ALTHOUGH SOME PAIN IN LIFE MUST BE ENDURED, OTHER PAIN IS SELF-INFLICTED AND WOMEN CAN AND SHOULD AVOID IT?"

Evaluating what Cisneros implies about women can be done even though "My Lucy Friend Who Smells Like Corn" is told from the perspective of a child. After all, it is in childhood that a young girl begins to define herself and her future role in society. In order to write an authentic story, the author needed to look back at her own childhood or closely watch young girls, listen to their conversations, and ask them about their thoughts. She needed to tease out details of what childhood was like for her or is like for other female children. Then she had to think about how these experiences helped to form a mature woman. The author might have asked herself how childhood relationships affected who she became. How did her childhood fantasies form the woman that she turned out to be? Readers should not conclude that "My Lucy Friend Who Smells Like Corn" is merely a tale of childhood. This story should not be read just for the slice-of-life vignette that lies on the surface. Rather, the story should be pondered and reflected upon so that the author's underlying view of what these young girls might one day become is made clear. In the things these female children see, hear, think, and mimic there are clues to understand what Cisneros believes it means to be female.

One of the first impressions that Cisneros provides of the young female narrator is that the girl has a lot of spunk. She is bold not only in her actions but in her thoughts. She is not afraid to be challenged, but she also exhibits courage by being forthright about her thoughts. She is daring in admitting the truth of her interior world. She looks life straight in the eye and describes things as she sees them. An example of this trait is exhibited when the narrator shares her experience of riding in a car and seeing the crushed bodies of insects on the windshield. She does not look away from these scenes. She looks

WHAT DO I READ NEXT?

- *Woman Hollering Creek* (1991) is Cisneros's most popular short story collection. Some of the stories, such as "My Lucy Friend Who Smells Like Corn" are no more than two or three pages long. Others, such as the story that bears the same name as the title of this collection is much longer. The collection includes "Barbie-Q," "Mericans," and "Eyes of Zapata." The Spanish-language version, *El Arroyo De La Llorona Y Otros Cuentos* (1996), is also available.

- Cisneros is best known for her 1984 novel *The House on Mango Street*, a coming-of-age story about Esperanza, a young teen. The book covers a not-so-happy year in the life of Esperanza, beginning with her family's move to a new neighborhood. The story is told through the young girl's impressions of life as if recorded in a diary. Not all the entries are gloomy, though Esperanza faces many difficult challenges. Cisneros invites her readers to witness life in a poor Hispanic neighborhood in Chicago as experienced by a young girl who is sometimes hopeful and sometimes despairs about what she witnesses.

- A popular young-adult short story collection, Julia Alvarez's *How the García Girls Lost their Accents* (1991) centers on the lives of four sisters from the Dominican Republic. The sisters have moved to the United States, and the stories deal with their experiences during the transition. Their way of life in the Dominican Republic is also explained, including the harsh aspects of living under the dictatorship of Rafael Trujillo. These stories offer readers a glimpse into some of the challenges of immigration.

- N. Scott Momaday's novel *House Made of Dawn* (1968) is a Pulitzer Prize-winning story of a young Native American man who returns from World War II and has difficulty relating to life on a New Mexico Indian reservation. The old traditional ways of his family's tribe conflict with the young man's awareness of life in the modern world. This novel has been credited for the successful recognition of literature written by and about Native Americans. Momaday's work helped open doors for later publications by Native American writers such as Sherman Alexie, Louise Erdrich, and Leslie Marmon Silko.

- V. S. Naipaul's 1959 novel *Miguel Street*, winner of 1961 Somerset Maugham Award, tells the story of a young man and the people he meets in a poor section of Trinidad. The characters are eccentric, such as a carpenter and a poet who never finish anything they start and a mad man whom the citizens of this small island finally declare to be a prophet. Many of the stories are tragic, but they are told with a sense of humor that helps readers uncover many important truths about life. The unnamed narrator interweaves his own story in and out of the lives of those who live around him until the last few chapters, when the narrator finds a way to leave the island and start a new life for himself.

- *Enrique's Journey* (2007) by Sonia Nazario was originally told in a Pulitzer Prize-winning newspaper story in the *Los Angeles Times*. The book expands on the article, telling the true story of a young Honduran teen who came to the United States in search of his mother. During his journey, Enrique is robbed, beaten, jailed, and deported, but he finally reaches his mother, Lourdes. Nazario has been praised for her intensive research on this topic and for her talent for telling a gripping story about the horrors of illegal immigration.

so directly and so intensely that she knows the color of a butterfly's blood, which, in the her mind, is an undisputed yellow. In expressing this thought, Cisneros shows how the narrator understands that life is not just a fun ride through the countryside on a Sunday afternoon. As the narrator witnesses the squashed body of a butterfly, she grasps the concept that life is a mixture of pleasure and pain. The pleasure comes from the sight of the beauty in a butterfly's wing or in watching the butterfly flitter through the tall grasses of a field. But then there is also death. And when death happens, the narrator takes it in. She does not turn away from it. She not only looks at it, she later objectifies the experience, using the color of the butterfly's blood to explain how one of her marbles looks. This is one of this young female's strengths: transforming something frightening into something she can use. This is one of the powers that women have, the author implies. A woman can, despite her fear, look at life and death without flinching.

Cisneros explains the narrator's inner knowledge of the balance of pain and beauty in life through the young girl's attempts to darken her skin. Though the heat makes her dizzy, the child is willing to purposefully sit in the hot sunlight, exposing herself to the rays that pound down on the top of her head, pressing into her scalp like a heavy hat. She is willing to endure this discomfort because of her definition of beauty. She wants her skin to darken. She wants her complexion to take on a darker tone until it almost looks black. She wants to look like Lucy and is willing to endure the heat and its consequential headache so she might attain the beauty she perceives in her friend Lucy. In providing this glimpse into how the narrator thinks, Cisneros not only points out the strength of the narrator's convictions and her tolerance for pain, but also offers a glimpse into the girl's psychology. This young girl has something missing in her life. She has a deep longing or need to be something that she is not. There is a quality that she does not like about herself. The girl thinks it is merely the color of her skin, but what lies under this belief? What is Cisneros saying about women with this need? How do women want to change their appearances and why do they do this?

In the narrator's case, the young girl wants desperately to belong. She wants to look like Lucy so people will think she is a member of Lucy's family. She wants Lucy to know that she likes her so much she is willing to burn her skin so they will match. She not only wants skin as dark as Lucy's, she also wants to dress like Lucy. It is not good enough that emotion binds them together. She wants their outsides to match. So is Cisneros suggesting that women value physical appearance more than inner qualities such as emotions and intelligence? Is the author saying that although some pain in life must be endured, other pain is self-inflicted and women can and should avoid it? Cisneros presents these questions implicitly and leaves the reader to reflect on them. She neither commends nor condemns the narrator's actions. She just points them out and implies that what the narrator is doing may be motivated by something deeper than the color of her skin. Readers might sense that the narrator is misguided, but Cisneros does not play the role of judge. She only implies that readers might want to consider what the narrator is doing and then ask themselves if they see similar patterns in their own behavior.

There is another scene in this story that is worthy of deeper reflection. Lucy has the constant company of eight sisters. When she goes to bed, she has all those arms and legs to cuddle around her. She has all those heads to rub, all the sounds of contented sleeping to lull her into her dreams. In contrast, the narrator sleeps alone in a narrow, single bed-chair. She longs for a big bed crowded with siblings. Though Lucy's mother complains of all the work that she has to do in order to feed and take care of her nine daughters, the narrator pays little attention to this. Rather than using her powers of observation, as the narrator does in the beginning of this story in looking at death square in the face, she falls into the deception of fantasy. She is blinded by her desire to belong, her need to be like Lucy, and her fantasies of how much fun it would be to have so many sisters. What the narrator does not see is that having eight sisters also means a lot of extra work, especially when it comes to laundry. There are clotheslines full of pajamas, shirts, and dresses, not to mention Lucy's father's jeans. There are loads of heavy, wet clothes that must be pushed through the wringer. Although she recalls the danger in using the old-fashioned washing machine, the narrator continues to romanticize Lucy's life. Even if in the process of washing clothes, sometimes fingers get smashed and fingernails turn black and fall off, the narrator continues to believe that having all those children around is fun. The narrator also ignores the mother's sighs of fatigue and continues to wish for sisters. Having a large number of siblings is not a nuisance, the narrator believes, but rather a great comfort.

That a girl her own age is forced to do heavy labor or that a woman is exhausted from raising so many children without support does not register in the narrator's thoughts. Whereas before, the narrator's ability to see beauty in pain appeared to be a gift, Cisneros now presents the underside of that capability. The aptitude of turning something negative into something positive can be an asset, but it can also pull a woman into a role of servitude and passivity. To suffer in silence can be looked at as strength as it can build character and fortitude. But women, Cisneros implies, also need to speak up, to voice their opinions, to say when enough is enough. Though the narrator looks clear-mindedly at the death of the butterfly, she does not do the same with all aspects of her friend Lucy's life. She does not see the discomfort of sleeping with eight little bodies all scrunched up beside her in bed. She does not feel the toll that the drudgery of continual loads of laundry takes out of a young girl's life. Through the story of Lucy and the laundry, Cisneros once again appears to be offering a warning. The author seems to be telling women to not go blindly into marriage, to make sure the man you marry is willing to help you raise your family. She also seems to provide awareness of the effort it takes to raise one child, let alone nine of them. Protect yourself by consciously choosing your role and not creating a fantasy of marriage and motherhood. Be a child when you are playing children's games, but keep your eyes unclouded by childhood fantasies when you are defining yourself as a woman.

Sometimes with subtle implications and other times with very clear suggestions and warnings, Cisneros writes a story about two young girls who play innocent little girl games. Even though this three-page story at first appears to merely recount a childhood memory, Cisneros has a reason for revealing the hidden thoughts of female children. The author knows these girls will one day become wives and mothers. They will be the models for a new generation of women. The author implies that she wants her readers to think about this and to take that role seriously.

They were best friends, but she wished Lucy was her sister. (Beth Van Trees / Shutterstock.com)

Source: Joyce Hart, Critical Essay on "My Lucy Friend Who Smells Like Corn," in *Short Stories for Students*, Gale, Cengage Learning, 2011.

Alexandra Fitts

In the following excerpt, Fitts observes that in Woman Hollering Creek, *powerful female icons are modernized and provided nuances that add to their legends and legacies.*

Sandra Cisneros's collection of stories *Woman Hollering Creek* (1991) depicts the situation of the Mexican-American woman: typically caught between two cultures, she resides in a cultural borderland. The topics of the stories range from the confusions of a bicultural and bilingual childhood to the struggles of a dark-skinned woman to recognize her own beauty in the land of Barbie dolls and blond beauty queens. While Cisneros does not attempt to force easy resolutions on such complex subject matter, she does search for a "place" that will respect Spanish and Indian heritage along with Mexican tradition without resorting to a nostalgic

> IN THIS COLLECTION OF STORIES, CISNEROS TACKLES A NUMBER OF MEXICAN RELIGIOUS AND CULTURAL ICONS, PARTICULARLY THOSE FEMALE ARCHETYPES WHOSE IMAGES OFTEN STILL DEFINE THE ROLE OF CHICANAS."

longing for a distant motherland (a Mexico that, in some cases, the characters have never seen). Her characters engage in a continual process of cultural mediation, as they struggle to reconcile their Mexican past with their American present. Further complicating this struggle is the fact that most of her characters are young women who must sort through the competing stories that they hear about a woman's "place" until they find one where they can reside comfortably. Part of this negotiation is the incorporation of key feminine archetypes from the Mexican tradition and the reconsideration of these figures in a way that will reflect the realities of the modern Chicana experience. Cisneros reevaluates, and in a way revalues, the three most prevalent representations of Mexican womanhood: the passive virgin, the sinful seductress, and the traitorous mother, idolized in the figures of the Virgin of Guadalupe, La Malinche, and La Llorona. Along the lines of U.S. feminism, these female icons could be seen as promoting an image of women that is detrimental, but they may also serve as emblems of feminine power and pre-conquest Mexican beliefs. Sandra Cisneros tackles each of these feminine figures in *Woman Hollering Creek*. La Malinche in "Never Marry a Mexican," the Virgin of Guadalupe in "Little Miracles, Kept Promises," and La Llorona in "Woman Hollering Creek." Rather than merely casting aside these figures, Cisneros searches for a transformation of them that will allow for the past while opening up the future. However, her goal does not seem to be as uncomplicated as merely redeeming these figures as powerful female icons. Instead, she modernizes and adds nuance to their legends and their legacies.

It could be said that the place of the Mexican-American woman is by force of immigration always in the borderlands. Of course, many Chicanas physically inhabit the borderlands between

Mexico and the United States—that place that is neither entirely one country nor the other, but something else, a unique amalgamation of the two. The Mexican-American woman, however, is not marginalized by her physical location as much as she is by both her sex and her ethnicity. In the words of Chicana critic and activist Gloria Anzaldua, "this is her home / this thin edge of / barbwire." She must live on the fence because she can never occupy a full place in any of the cultures to which she nominally belongs. In the U.S., she is separated by her color, her language, and her history. In Mexican and Chicano societies, she is defined and limited by the traditions of machismo and the teachings of the Catholic Church. Anzaldua writes, "Alienated from her mother culture, 'alien' in the dominant culture, the woman of color does not feel safe within the inner life of her Self. Petrified, she can't respond, her face caught between los intersticios (the cracks), the spaces between the different worlds she inhabits." Much of this can be said for any person, male or female, who lives as a minority within a dominant culture. Anzaldua makes a special case for the Chicana, however. Dominated in both cultures, she is even less at home in either than is a male, be he white, Mexican, or Chicano. Furthermore, the Mexican and Chicana woman has repeatedly served as mediator between the two cultures. She is too often the sexual property that links white men and Mexican men in a system of exchange.

The historical representative of this sexualized position as cultural mediator is La Malinche. Malinche, dona Marina, Malinalli—she has many names and many incarnations. What we know of her is that she was an Indian woman who served as interpreter and lover to Hernan Cortes while he conquered her land and massacred her people. Infamous as a traitor and a whore, her legacy has been to serve as a representative of the victimization of the native people of Mexico at the hands of the whites, and as the shameful reminder of a woman's complicity.

... Sandra Cisneros tackles the legacy of La Malinche in the story "Never Marry a Mexican." In this story, a Chicana woman seeks revenge on the white lover who has rejected her by becoming the sexual tutor of his teenaged son. Though the first-person narrator does not say how the son will pay for the sins of the father, it is clear that he must pay, as she lulls him into false confidence waiting for the right moment or, as she puts it, the moment when she will snap her teeth. The reference to La Malinche and Cortes is made explicit from the start, as she recalls that her lover, Drew, used to call her his "Malinalli" (another name for Malinche) and that he looked like Cortes with his dark beard and white skin. Like the legendary Malinche, the narrator is an accomplice in her own domination and a traitor to the "sisterhood." She admits, "I've been accomplice, committed premeditated crimes. I'm guilty of having caused deliberate pain to other women. I'm vindictive and cruel, and I'm capable of anything." She also says that, though a painter, she must support herself in other ways. Sometimes she acts as a translator, though she also relies on the generosity of her lovers, which, she says, "is a form of prostitution." She translates the language (although Spanish is now the "native" language), as did La Malinche, but also serves as a cultural intermediary, a sort of ambassador to the white world in which she moves but which she does not fully inhabit.

Cisneros's Malinche is a complex, modern figure. She is at once victim and victimizer, as she turns her hurt and anger on others. She is certainly not the "abjectly passive" victim that Paz described, but she does allow herself to fall into relationship after relationship with unavailable men—always married, and always white. For the narrator, whose real name is Clemencia, the issues of race and gender are at odds, as she feels forced to choose her primary allegiance. Clemencia's parents are both Mexican, her father born in Mexico, her mother in the U.S. The title of the story, "Never Marry a Mexican," is her mother's often-repeated advice. Clemencia's mother felt inescapable discrimination from both cultures. As a lower-class Chicana, she was looked down on by her husband's upper-middle-class Mexican family, but she also suffered discrimination in mainstream U.S. society because of her dark skin. The answer, for her, was to marry out and supposedly up, and she instilled in her daughters the belief that the only appropriate future husbands for them were whites.

Clemencia buys into this prejudice against her own heritage to some extent, but her feelings about race are more complex than those expressed by her mother. She says that she never saw Mexican men, or Latin men of any sort, as potential lovers, yet she considers her mother to be the true traitor because she married a white

man almost immediately after the death of Clemencia's father. Clemencia and her sister move from their suburban neighborhood to the Mexican part of town in a romanticized quest for a cultural connection. At first, they think the neighborhood is quaint and charming, but soon they realize that the realities of life in the barrio are anything but charming. Not fully at home in either culture, she ultimately decides that she must define and situate herself as a Chicana, though this decision is perhaps a moot point, as her lovers clearly have also been taught to "never marry a Mexican." Though born in the U.S. to a mother who does not even speak Spanish, she is Mexican in the eyes of the world. To the white men with whom she has affairs, she is a sexual mystery, the exotic dark-skinned woman with whom they can have sex before going home to their pale, polished wives.

Though Clemencia struggles with the allegiance she feels, or is forced into, with others of her race, her lack of loyalty to other women is much clearer. Where La Malinche is considered primarily as a traitor to her race, we see in Clemencia the impact of a woman's betrayal of the "sisterhood" of other women. The problem is that Clemencia feels no such sisterhood with white women—already excluded from their society, she is well aware of the power differential between a white woman and a dark-skinned woman, and for her, this difference negates any kinship they might share. She says, thinking of her lover's son: "All I know is I was sleeping with your father the night you were born. In the same bed where you were conceived. I was sleeping with your father and didn't give a damn about that woman, your mother. If she was a brown woman like me, I might've had a harder time living with myself, but since she's not, I don't care."

Cisneros complicates La Malinche, as she is represented by Clemenda. She is neither entirely a victim, nor merely a self-serving woman who betrays her people for her own gain. Like La Malinche, she is defined by her race and her sex, and she struggles with these meanings that are imposed on her body. However, this story does not present an apology for La Malinche, nor an uncomplicated recuperation of the figure. While the reader may sympathize with Clemencia up to a point, she ultimately turns into a sort of obsessive stalker, who can find power only through sexuality and, perhaps, violence. The contradictions of her legacy remain intact, as

Cisneros lends some justification (and perhaps sympathy) to her actions, but falls short of a whole-hearted vindication of La Malinche.

... Cisneros's book also reflects the importance of the Virgin of Guadalupe in the Chicano psyche and cultural practice, as numerous stories in *Woman Hollering Creek* make mention of her. The most interesting of these in its treatment of the Virgin is "Little Miracles, Kept Promise." The story takes the form of a series of notes to the Virgin and other popular saints, left at a shrine somewhere in Texas. They ask for everything from overtime pay to a good man, and they give thanks for recovering a stolen truck or for graduating from high school. The authors of the notes reflect a wide variety of Chicano lifestyles—some write in Spanish, most in English, some display a traditional and unquestioning faith, others the petty complaints of disgruntled teenagers. The last note in the story is from a young woman, Chayo, who writes of the challenges of being a modern Chicana. She is nagged by her mother for cutting her hair, for spending too much time alone, for becoming a painter. She describes herself as "straddling both" worlds, but her mother accuses her of being a malinchista, a "white girl" who is betraying her Mexican heritage by attempting to break out of the role that it defines for women. This is not an uncommon epithet, and it is used to imply that a woman is a traitor for "consorting with Anglos or accepting Anglo cultural patterns."

Again, we see La Malinche as the betrayer of her culture, in this case because she is stepping outside the bounds of acceptable behavior for women and daring to express feminine power and sexuality. We learn that Chayo has left a note and a braid of her hair to give thanks to the Virgin because she has found out that she is not pregnant and she is not sure that she wants to be a mother. We also learn of Chayo's struggles with her race, her gender, and her religious beliefs. Her mother's Virgin is not one to whom Chayo can relate, just as she cannot imagine herself in her mother's abnegating role. She does not want a passionless Virgin who calmly forgives all, but rather: "I wanted you bare-breasted, snakes in your hands. I wanted you leaping and somersaulting the backs of bulls. I wanted you swallowing raw hearts and rattling volcanic ash. I wasn't going to be my mother or my grandma. All that self-sacrifice, all that silent suffering. Hell no. Not here. Not me."

Now, however, Chayo has come to terms with the Virgin, and the way that she has done this is by accepting a version of her that is neither exactly Malinche nor Virgen. Chayo recognizes the power of both, and rather than deny either of them, she sees their ability to help her negotiate her position in each of her two cultures. She is able to accept both the Virgin's pacifism and Malinche's sexuality through knowledge of her own Indian heritage. She learns of the goddess's transition from the Aztec serpent goddess, to Tonantsin, to Guadalupe, and, seeing "all of her facets," Chayo can recognize the strength of the image. She finds a goddess who has snakes in her hands, but who still allows for the beliefs of Catholicism: "that you could have the power to rally a people when a country was born, and again during civil war, and during a farmworkers' strike in California made me think that there is power in my mother's patience, strength in my grandmother's endurance." She ends the story saying, "I could love you, and finally learn to love me."

In an essay called "Guadalupe the Sex Goddess" in the collection *Goddess of the Americas*, Cisneros describes her own youthful discomfort with her body, and the reluctance to discuss sex or birth control: "What a culture of denial. Don't get pregnant! But no one tells you how not to. This is why I was angry for so many years every time I saw la Virgen de Guadalupe, my culture's role model for brown women like me. She was damn dangerous, an ideal so lofty and unrealistic it was laughable." Like Chayo in "Little Miracles, Kept Promises," Cisneros writes that she came to her own acceptance of the Virgin through a knowledge of her pre-Colombian past. Most importantly, she states, "My Virgen de Guadalupe is not the mother of God. She is God. She is a face for a god without a face, an indigena for a god without ethnicity, a female deity for a god who is genderless." This understanding of the Virgin, which seems to be the one at which Chayo eventually arrives, is a clear reflection of Anzaldua's claims for the Virgin of Guadalupe as a mediator of not just culture, but also gender, race, and history.

While La Malinche and the Virgin of Guadalupe are figures that appear again and again in modern Chicana writing, there is a third female figure that has left a lasting impact on the construction of Mexican and Chicana womanhood. The title figure of Cisneros's book is the "hollering woman," or La Llorona, of Mexican legend. According to Americo Paredes, La Llorona is "the wailing woman in white [seeking] her children who died in childbirth. Originally an Aztec goddess who sacrificed babies and disappeared shrieking into lakes or rivers, La Llorona usually appears near a well, stream, or washing place. The Hispanicized form has La Llorona murdering her own children born out of wedlock when her lover married a woman of his own station."

Again, we see an Aztec female goddess transformed into a guilty reminder of a woman's sin. Though there are various versions of the legend, La Llorona is guilty on a number of scores, all affronts to the accepted roles for women. She is a sexual transgressor, but even more importantly, she betrays all of the traditional notions of motherhood. When her children became a burden to her, she simply murdered them. Like La Malinche, La Llorona is a symbol of motherhood gone wrong. La Malinche's betrayal of her "children" was in her sinful collaboration with their oppressive "father," but La Llorona's betrayal of motherhood is even more perverse. For this sin she is doomed to an eternity of repentance with her continual wailing as a reminder to all of her crime, and of the repercussions of transgression.

Cisneros's first transformation of La Llorona is one from the "wailing woman" of legend to the "hollering woman" of the title story. *Woman Hollering Creek* is a real place, situated in Texas near San Antonio. Cleofilas, the protagonist of the story, wonders about the origin of this appellation, thinking: "La Gritona. Such a funny name for such a lovely arroyo. But that's what they call the creek that ran behind the house. Though no one could say whether the woman had hollered from anger or pain. The natives only knew the arroyo one crossed on the way to San Antonio, and then once again on the way back, was called Woman Hollering, a name no one from these parts questioned, little less understood."

... This is precisely Sandra Cisneros's accomplishment in *Woman Hollering Creek*. In this collection of stories, Cisneros tackles a number of Mexican religious and cultural icons, particularly those female archetypes whose images often still define the role of Chicanas. While all of these symbols are shown to have power in the construction of Chicano identity, some are questioned more than others. La Malinche did not

fare exceptionally well in Cisneros's retelling of her story. While she does modernize La Malinche and provide some shading to her villainy, ultimately, she is still a traitor. The reader can comprehend Clemencia's confusion and anger, but she is still an overtly sexualized figure who trades her body for power. In the end, Clemencia is not so terribly far from the La Malinche described by Paz.

However, the stories "Woman Hollering Creek" and "Little Miracles, Kept Promises" represent precisely the reconsideration of female archetypes that Anzaldua calls for. Cleofilas learns from her time in the U.S. that life is not a telenovela and that being a wife and mother may not be the only possibilities open for women. While remaining true to her beliefs, she rejects the passive abnegation of the Virgin. In "Little Miracles, Kept Promises," Chayo does not cast aside the legacy of her mythical and actual fore-mothers, but manages to find strength in certain parts of their images. She does not need to either entirely reject or entirely accept their proscribed roles. Instead, she can recognize the strength of the Virgin without emulating her passivity and aspire to the sexual freedom of La Malinche without betraying her culture. We see in this story that through a reconnection to both her Indian and her Mexican past, a young Chicana can negotiate the unstable ground of her own cultural borderland.

A number of feminist scholars have searched for a recuperation of the "goddess" as a representation of feminine power, and many Chicanas have found this matriarchal figure in Guadalupe and La Malinche, and in their fore-mothers, Tonantsin and Coatlicue. The revaluation of the passive Virgin or of the reviled Malinche and Llorona can be more than a image-boosting exercise. As Margaret Randall writes in "Guadalupe, Subversive Virgin": "A saint or secular being may be spawned by the orthodoxy, but claimed, or reclaimed by people in need. More impressive still is when groups of people gain self-knowledge and power enough to produce warriors of their own. Control of our history, of our stories, has traditionally been in the hands of those who hold power over our lives. Social change is largely about people retrieving their stories."

The fact that Cisneros does not offer an easy reconciliation with La Malinche does not weaken her reconsideration of these three figures. In fact, her refusal to valorize or validate all aspects of their legacies further elucidates the struggle to come to terms with such contradictory images. As Anzaldua points out in *Borderlands*, "[l]iving in a state of psychic unrest, in a Borderland, is what makes poets write and artists create." The borderland is not, and cannot be, a place of ease and security. It is precisely that unease, insecurity, and ambivalence that make the borderlands such a fertile zone.

Source: Alexandra Fitts, "Sandra Cisneros's Modern Malinche: A Reconsideration of Feminine Archetypes in *Woman Hollering Creek*," in *International Fiction Review*, Vol. 29, No. 1–2, January 2002, pp. 11–22.

Jeff Thomson

In the following excerpt, Thomson discusses the gender-based ideologies which are essential to the strong female characters of the stories in Woman Hollering Creek.

The wars begin here, in our hearts and in our beds" says Inés, witch woman and "sometime wife" to Emiliano Zapata in "Eyes of Zapata," the most ambitious story of Sandra Cisneros's second collection, *Woman Hollering Creek and Other Stories*. In Inés, Cisneros presents a narrator who is capable of seeing both at a distance and up close, who is able to encompass both the physically violent world of Zapata's revolution and the emotionally violent world of love. She is able to see both worlds and, more importantly, understands how the pain of both worlds is merely a manifestation of the same disease—a failure of love. Cisneros says in a voice that is Inés speaking to Zapata but also Cisneros speaking to the reader (the two are easily confused—even Cisneros claims to have woken from a dream believing she was Inés [Sagel 74]):

> We drag these bodies around with us, these bodies that have nothing at all to do with you, with me, with who we really are, these bodies that give us pleasure and pain. Though I've learned how to abandon mine at will, it seems to me we never free ourselves completely until we love, until we lose ourselves inside each other. Then we see a little of what is called heaven. When we can be that close we no longer are Inés and Emiliano, but something bigger than our lives. And we can forgive, finally.

When a writer claims to identify with a character to the extent that she wakes up unsure who is who, one can assume that that character is going to speak deeply and come as close to the truth as fiction can come to the truth of the human heart. This is true of Inés.

Inés is the fully aware feminine self, a woman who has seen her own reality—her people embroiled in a civil war and led by her deceitful, unfaithful husband—and does not flinch or look away. She takes the deepest pain inside herself and through it claims the power of her own identity. Ingesting the pain of her world by facing it head-on gives her strength and the will to persevere: "And I took to eating black things—*huitlacoche* the corn mushroom, coffee, dark chilies, the bruised part of the fruit, the darkest, blackest things to make me hard and strong." This is the power of Cisneros's women, to see and to remember, to master the pain of the past and understand the confluence of all things; women continue in a cycle of birth and blood; they become themselves through the honest acceptance of the world beyond the body. Cisneros believes women must overcome and change their worlds from the inside out. They must become the "authors" of their own fate.

Yet what sets Inés apart from most of the women in the collection is her acceptance of all pain, not just female pain. She sees the small boy inside Zapata, the boy thrust unprepared into leadership and war; she sees the bodies of the *federale* corpses hanging in the trees, drying like leather, dangling like earrings; she sees her father, who once turned his back on her, placed with his back against the wall, ready for the firing squad. What particularly defines this story is the acceptance of masculine suffering as well as feminine. "We are all widows," Inés says. "the men as well as the women, even the children. *All clinging to the tail of the horse of our jefe Zapata*. All of us scarred from these nine years of *aguantando*—enduring" (original italics). The image of every widow, male or female, clinging to the horse's tail doesn't absolve men from blame for beginning and continuing this war, but at the same time it doesn't exclude them from suffering.

The union of gender, and gender-based ideologies, is essential to the strong, feminine characters of the later stories of *Woman Hollering Creek*, because for Cisneros it is necessary to include masculine suffering to achieve a total synthesis. Each of the earlier pieces is independent of the others, yet as whole sections they define specific areas of adversity—specifically feminine adversity. The first section, "My Lucy Friend Who Smells like Corn," takes a form similar to that established by Cisneros in her earlier, applauded collection *The House on Mango Street*—childhood vignettes. The "Lucy Friend" story sets up the paradigm of the Cisneros's female world:

> There ain't no boys here. Only girls and one father who is never home hardly and one mother who says *Ay! I'm real tired* and so many sisters there's no time to count them.... I think it would be fun to sleep with sisters you could yell at one at a time or all together, instead of alone on the fold out chair in the living room.

This is a world without men, where the fathers are drunk or absent, the mothers are left to raise the children alone and the only possible salvation is a sisterhood that more often than not fails.

The stories continue in this vein, establishing aspects of an archetypal Chicana female identity. "Eleven" sets up a system of multiple selves like "little wooden dolls that fit one inside the other" and the difficulty of maintaining a unity of self in the face of authority. "Mexican Movies" and "Barbie-Q" are concerned with stereotypes and enforced identity. From her young girl's voice, Cisneros satirizes the portrayals of Mexicans in film by contrasting a Chicana family's daily life with the films of Pedro Infante (his name itself denotes a child-like, false identity) who "always sings riding a horse and wears a big sombrero and never tears the dresses off the ladies, and the ladies throw flowers from balconies and usually somebody dies, but not Pedro Infante because he has to sing the happy song at the end." Although the barrio life of Cisneros's families is usually far from wealthy, here at least she presents us with a world of safety and security, where the false happiness of women tossing flowers from balconies doesn't interfere with the games the sisters play in the aisles. And then

> The movie ends. The Lights go on. Somebody picks us up...carries us in the cold to the car that smells like ashtrays.... [B]y now we're awake but it's nice to go on pretending with our eyes shut because here's the best part. Mama and Papa carry us upstairs to the third-floor where we live, take off our shoes and cover us, so when we wake up it's Sunday already, and we're in our beds and happy.

The satire is so subtle that one is led to believe the girls and perhaps even her parents do not see the films as stereotypes that limit their ability to be accepted in the white world, but the reader is obviously meant to.

... The overall theme of these stories is the vulnerability of the mostly female narrators; their world is defined externally to them. The barrios and smalltowns are, as Barbara Harlow notes about *Mango Street*, filled with "stories which recount the histories of the neighborhood's inhabitants embedded in the longer history of Hispanic immigration, relocation, and political displacement in the United States." [*Criticism in the Borderlands*, 1991] The vignettes that Cisneros offers are not supposed to be read as isolated incidents, but rather emblematic of a social structure that allows little cultural movement and less possibility for the formation of an identity outside the boundaries of the barrio. Cisneros moves through a paradigm of feminine life—childhood, adolescence, adulthood—exploring avenues of possible escape, possible identity.

Source: Jeff Thomson, "What is Called Heaven: Identity in Sandra Cisneros's *Woman Hollering Creek*," in *Studies in Short Fiction*, Vol. 31, No. 3, Summer 1994, pp. 415–24.

Raúl Niño

In the following interview, Niño and Cisneros discuss her writing and how, having "made it," Cisneros is using her fame to help promote other minority writers.

Sandra Cisneros' reputation in the Latino writing community was established years before she was allowed to slip through the guarded gates of New York's publishing industry. Two small-press poetry books—*Bad Boys* and *My Wicked, Wicked Ways*—and one volume of short fiction, *House on Mango Street*, preceded her breakthrough book, *Woman Hollering Creek and Other Stories*, published by Random House in 1991. Cisneros supported herself during her lean financial years with two NEA awards and teaching positions at several universities around the country: "I lived the life of a migrant professor," she says. Her "migrant professor" years, however, are a nostalgic memory today. Though Cisneros has "made it" in the mainstream publishing world, she's not forgotten where she came from or how she got there, and she is determined to use her hard-earned fame to help bring recognition to other long-neglected writers.

BKL: Aside from the obvious gains of success—a truck, a house, and a washer and dryer ...

" A BAD REMARK ABOUT MY POEMS BY A CLOSE FRIEND OF MINE MADE ME HOLE UP AND START THROWING THE POEMS UNDER THE BED. FOR THREE YEARS I DIDN'T SHOW ANYONE MY POEMS."

CISNEROS: Love that washer! It's going right now.

BKL. What have been the other benefits?

CISNEROS: Aside from the physical accruements, I feel very blessed. I complain sometimes about the pain of the solitude that comes with writing and about how uneventful my life is when I'm closed up, my one-woman life sentence. But it's the kind of angst every writer dreams of having. The hard part is the solitude, especially since I live alone, and there's no one to catch me when I spiral off the deep end and come out of the writing late at night, between 12 and 3, what I call my "night madness hours." There isn't anyone there to reel me back, to say "ya, ya, ya . . . there, there, there" when I really need it. That's the hard part. But, on the other hand, there also isn't anyone there to get in my way. This may sound corny, but one of the big blessings is that I have a house of my own—my own space where there isn't anyone there to say "Mi hija, can you please water the front lawn?"

BKL: Are you a mama's girl or a papa's girl? Who played the bigger role in your life?

CISNEROS: I'm the product of a fierce woman who was brave enough to raise her daughter in a nontraditional way, who fought for my right to be a person of letters. And she did that in a household where she could have certainly trained me to be a housewife, but, instead, she let me go and study during times when perhaps I should have been helping her out. And she fought for my right to go to college and made sure I had a quiet space in the house when my six brothers were noisy. That was rare!

But I am a product of both my parents. As an only daughter, I am my father's favorite child. I think I benefited from these two amazing

people who loved us all fiercely and gave us a stable environment and had a great deal of faith in us. They never complained about our grades, and whatever we wanted we were encouraged to do. My father never interrupted my plans to go to college; he thought I would go and find a husband. My mother, on the other hand, wanted me to have an education to fall back on, a parachute; she wanted me to be independent. My parents believed in us, that we could rise above our circumstances, and they taught us to believe in ourselves even when the education system did not.

BKL: You made your mark in the literary world with your fiction, yet you're rooted in poetry. Are you writing poetry these days?

CISNEROS. Yeah! But I've always written poetry. It's a funny thing: I trained to be a poet, I studied as a poet, and I always wrote poems. Yet when I was writing poems I was also writing fiction. But in graduate school, I had to declare myself one or the other, and I said "poet" because I had been training with a poet. Had I been training with a fiction writer, perhaps the story would be different. What happened in 1987 when my book of poetry came out was that I was in a suicidal, depressed period in my life. I was very, very ill then—and very sensitive to any kind of criticism. A bad remark about my poems by a close friend of mine made me hole up and start throwing the poems under the bed. For three years I didn't show anyone my poems. I was writing them but just throwing them under the bed. And it was good to have that period of writing only for myself. It helped me break a lot of taboos. The poems changed. I think this newer manuscript is very different. They're looser poems. They're wilder, more ribald. They're coming from a very different place.

BKL: What about the new novel, how's that going?

CISNEROS: In the beginning, I despaired because there was so much about the book that was unknown to me, but I'm finding out a little more about my character and the story each day. The only thing that calms me is knowing I'm an intuitive person. In everything I've done in my life, including all the choices I've made as a writer, I've followed my gut and my heart. It's taken me where I've needed to go so far, and I hope that it's going to be true for this novel.

BKL: Your writing hasn't been overtly political. Do you see this changing in your new work?

CISNEROS: I disagree with the question completely. I think that my work is overtly political; in fact, I've had to tone back sometimes.

BKL: Even House on Mango Street?

CISNEROS: I think *House on Mango Street* is a very political work; it's really a book about a woman in her twenties coming to her political consciousness as a feminist woman of color. I definitely disagree with people who feel that my work is very subtle politically. I would take the opposite stance and say that it is fiercely political. Perhaps what is subtle is the way in which we define politics. My method is perhaps not traditional "revolutionary" Latino writing, but it's political all the same.

BKL: The literary landscape is still relatively devoid of Latinos. Is it xenophobia, is it racism, is it stubbornness on the part of the publishing establishment, or is it all of the above? What's been your experience as a Latina?

CISNEROS: I think it's ignorance.

BKL: Just ignorance?

CISNEROS: Yeah, but ignorance is racism, isn't it? I think what's happening right now is that publishers have found a couple of Latino writers and are continuing to request work from them. The other Latino writers out there are just not known. And unless we few who are in those positions where we are asked to speak, unless we mention the others, it's going to take a long, long time before they get discovered, too.

BKL: Do you think that in the last few years, with the success of Latino writers such as Gary Soto and yourself, for example, that the established publishing world has begun to listen? Are they getting the message?

CISNEROS: You know what I think will get the message through? When we have Latinos in all positions of publishing and journalism, when it is Latinos who are asking the questions and acting as editors down the line, making decisions about who and what gets published and about what books get reviewed. Recently I saw Luis Rodriguez on the front cover of the *L.A. Times* book review section reviewing two Latino books. I said, "Oh my God! On the front cover! A Latino writer!" I'm talking about a Chicano, from East L.A., in the *L.A. Times*! I nearly did a back flip. I did do a mental back flip. I saw this and said "Orale!" And that's how it should be. There should be working-class writers, people of color, making the decisions that

affect us all, whether it's determining funding in the arts or deciding what should be published or what is considered quality literature. It's very important that we make inroads at all the levels that affect us.

BKL: You've been anthologized considerably in recent years. Is there a danger in this?

CISNEROS: My agent and I have been very judicious about which anthologies I let my work appear in. While I'm in a position to say no to certain anthologies, I'm not always able to affect the anthology itself. That's why I've been careful about what my being in a particular anthology means, not just to me, but to the collective of Latino writers. If I get asked to be in an anthology, will I be the only Latina in it, and if so, will it be of any use? What's the lesser evil? Is it better to be in this anthology or better not to be in it as a political statement? These are choices that we can't just make across the board. Every time someone approaches us we have to think about it. Sometimes we can suggest to the editor, "Sandra doesn't want to be in this anthology because it's being labeled as 'Hispanic.'" Making that point just might change the subtitle of the anthology.

BKL: Do you consider Gary Soto, Ana Castillo, Pat Mora, Luis Rodriguez and yourself as a "school of writing" with a distinct voice?

CISNEROS: I guess I'd have to. Among ourselves we'd disagree, but, on the other hand, we'd all have to concede that we're part of a generation that has been university trained. Certainly we're a generation of writers who have had more time to focus on the craft of writing. We're living in a time in history when, as writers, we're not alone. We're very much affected by what the others are writing, and there's a community of Chicano writers that we're responding to. I think, as a generation, we are much more craft conscious than those before us, but we're just as political, though in a different way. We're all warriors, but we have different weapons.

BKL: How so?

CISNEROS: The generation before ours was an oral one; poetry was performed before an audience. We are a paper generation; we've learned the craft of poetry from and on the printed page. But we've also had to learn how to perform our work and not always under the best of circumstances. Denise Chavez and I have traded stories about who's had the worst reading situation. She had to once perform in the Texas heat, in the open air, before a beer-drinking, gordita-eating crowd. I once read at a variety function where I had to follow a group of feather dancers. But these experiences helped us learn how to perform our paper poems with the energy and rhythm we had learned from an earlier generation of Chicano writers. We gained something from that previous generation, but we added something by studying poetry in workshops. I have to add, though, that I've always been disgusted by the elitist workshop attitude that there is only one school of poetry, that it exist only on the page, and that all other kinds of poetry are half-ass.

BKL: You've always been a strong supporter of libraries. Now that libraries are suffering stiff cuts in government funding, do you see a role for writers as library advocates?

CISNEROS: You know I'm a different kind of revolucionaria, but I'm no less radical than the revolucionarias in the beginning of the Chicano movimiento. And I really do believe in a revolution, not with guns...but with books. That's the weapon I have, and I know it's power. I know how books changed my life. It's especially important for me to be an advocate for libraries because I come from a community, from a culture of the working class, where we couldn't afford to buy books. So I'm aware, as are many other Chicano writers, of how people can be saved by books. I think about who I was, a quiet person who was never asked to speak in class or never picked for anything, and how I am finding that with words I have the power to make people listen, to make them think in a new way, to make them cry, to make them laugh. It's a powerful thing to make people listen to you.

I feel that libraries are here for everybody, especially for people like us who had no books in the house. I'm never going to stop complaining about the cutbacks in library funding, or the lack of books available in the neighborhoods that need them the most, or the overspending on lavish new libraries instead of a balanced distribution of funds to all libraries. There are many inequities in the system, and those of us who are in positions to be listened to have to speak, have to make our voices heard. Libraries are a means of getting our books out there to people who can't afford to buy them. As Eduardo Galeano says, "I write for a public that can not afford to buy my books." It's an awful irony for a writer to say this, but the public library is the means of getting those stories out there. Schools are one way, but libraries are the best way.

Source: Raúl Niño, "An Interview with Sandra Cisneros," in *Booklist*, Vol. 90, No. 1, September 1, 1993, pp. 36–37.

SOURCES

Backstrom, Kirsten, Review of *Woman Hollering Creek*, in *off our backs*, Vol. 21, No. 11, December 31, 1991, p. 11.

Bernardi, Adria, "Latino Voice Vignettes of Varied Neighborhood Life Come Straight from the Heart," in *Chicago Tribune*, August 4, 1991, p. 12.

Campbell, Paul R., "U.S. Population Projections," in *U.S. Census Bureau*, http://www.census.gov/population/www/projections/ppl47.html (accessed June 13, 2010).

Cisneros, Sandra, "My Lucy Friend Who Smells Like Corn," in *Woman Hollering Creek*, Vintage Books, 1992, pp. 3–5.

———, "About Sandra Cisneros," in *Sandra Cisneros Home Page*, http://www.sandracisneros.com/bio.php (accessed June 13, 2010).

Dalaker, Joseph, "Poverty in the United States, 2000," in *U.S. Census Bureau*, http://www.census.gov/prod/2001pubs/p60-214.pdf (accessed June 13, 2010).

Gilbert, Matthew, "Cisneros Gives Voice to the Dispossessed," in *Boston Globe*, May 14, 1991.

Gunst, Elise, "Taste Deeply of Hispanic Culture with Sandra Cisneros as Guide," in *Houston Chronicle*, May 5, 1991, p. 23.

"The Hispanic Population," in *U.S. Census Bureau*, http://www.census.gov/prod/2001pubs/c2kbr01-3.pdf (accessed June 13, 2010).

Kafatou, Sarah, Review of *Woman Hollering Creek*, in *Harvard Review*, No. 3, Winter 1993, pp. 193–98.

Kerr, Sarah, "Latino Life in Strokes of Gritty Realism," in *Newsday*, April 14, 1991, p. 23.

Kingsolver, Barbara, "Poetic Fiction with a Tex-Mex Tilt," in *Los Angeles Times*, April 28, 1991, p. 3.

Oliver, Bill, "Tangents to Trespasses," in *New England Review*, Vol. 15, No. 3, Summer 1993, pp. 208–12.

Rosales, Francisco A., *Chicano!: The History of the Mexican American Civil Rights Movement*, Arte Publico Press, 1997.

Stavans, Ilan, "Una Nueva Voz," in *Commonweal*, Vol. 118, No. 15, September 13, 1991, p. 524–25.

Valdivieso, Rafael, "Demographic Trends of the Mexican-American Population: Implications for School," in *ERIC Clearinghouse on Rural Education and Small Schools*, http://www.ericdigests.org/pre-9217/trends.htm (accessed August 11, 2010).

Wood, Susan, "The Voice of Esperanza," in *Washington Post*, June 9, 1991, p. X3.

FURTHER READING

Alegre, Cesar, *Extraordinary Hispanic Americans*, Children's Press, 2007.

> In this young-adult selection, Alegre offers brief biographies of more than 200 people with varied backgrounds. The book features stories of Hispanic politicians, entertainers, and sports figures. Historical figures as well as present-day personalities are included.

Garcia, Alma M., *The Mexican Americans*, Greenwood, 2008.

> Garcia offers a look into the lives of Mexican immigrants in the United States. In the process, she examines Mexican history, relationships between the United States and Mexico, and current events both in Mexico and in the Mexican American communities in the States.

Grabman, Richard, *Gods, Gachupines and Gringos: A People's History of Mexico*, Editorial Mazatlan, 2009.

> Grabman begins with the Aztec and Mayan civilizations and continues through Spain's conquest, the wars with the United States, and modern times. His book is not a typical history book with an emphasis on dates and battles, but rather a look at the people and their history and culture.

López, Tiffany, *Growing up Chicana/o*, Harper Paperbacks, 1995.

> This book contains twenty personal essays and stories written by prominent Mexican American personalities about their experiences growing up. Authors include Patricia Preciado Martin, Alberto Alvaro Ríos, Marta Salina, David Nava Monreal, and Cisneros. Also included is a foreword written by award-winning novelist Rudolfo Anaya.

Merrell, Floyd, *The Mexicans: A Sense of Culture*, Westview Press, 2003.

> Merrell is a professor of Spanish American literature who specializes in Latin American culture and civilization. In this book, he provides a panorama of the diversity of Latin American society as well as an overview of Mexican history.

Sanna, Ellyn, *Latino Folklore and Culture: Stories of Family, Traditions of Pride*, Mason Crest Publishers, 2005.

> Sanna has written an introduction to Hispanic culture for young-adult readers. In this book, explanations of ghost stories, old sayings, and traditional celebrations are offered to further develop an understanding of people coming from Mexico and other Hispanic communities.

SUGGESTED SEARCH TERMS

Sandra Cisneros

Sandra Cisneros AND Hispanic literature

Sandra Cisneros AND poetry

Sandra Cisneros AND Yellow House

Sandra Cisneros AND short stories

Sandra Cisneros AND activism

Sandra Cisneros AND feminism

Woman Hollering Creek

Hispanic literature

Latina literature AND Cisneros

Sandra Cisneros interview

Woman Hollering Creek reviews

The Nose

NIKOLAI VASIL'EVICH GOGOL

1836

Lauded as the father of Russian prose realism, nineteenth-century Russian poet and fiction writer Nikolai Gogol also explored the fantastic and the absurd, embedding unlikely, bizarre elements into ostensibly realist stories. In the twentieth century, this genre became identified as magical realism, and it is into this category that stories such as "The Nose" are now placed. In "The Nose," Gogol inserts a strange and unexplained element into an otherwise realistic story about a barber and a civil servant. One man wakes to find a disembodied nose in his loaf of bread, while another arises to find his nose missing. When the civil servant with the missing nose hurries about town, attempting to find his nose, he sees it masquerading as a man. His nose is eventually returned to him, but the police officer who finds the nose confirms that it appeared in human form before he apprehended the nose (as an actual nose). Eventually the protagonist awakens to find his nose once again in place upon his face. At the end of the story, the narrator comments on the strangeness of the story. The only explanation he offers is that sometimes absurd things happen. While the story is occasionally read as though the loss of the nose happened in a dream and was intended to represent the man's fears of castration and loss of virility and power, the work is more commonly regarded as an example of Gogol's desire to experiment with prose forms and to challenge the literary and political status quo in nineteenth-century Russia.

Nikolai Vasil'evich Gogol (© Mary Evans Picture Library | Alamy)

Originally published as "Nos" in 1836 in the journal *Sovremennik*, "The Nose" was later included in the 1842 collection of his works, *Sochinennia* (Works). It is also available in volume 2 of *The Complete Tales of Nikolai Gogol*, edited, introduced, and annotated by Leonard J. Kent. The volume was published by Random House in 1964 and reprinted by the University of Chicago Press in 1985.

AUTHOR BIOGRAPHY

Born on March 20, 1809, in the village of Velikie Sorochintsy in the Ukrainian region of Russia, Gogol was the first of Maria Ivanovna and Vasilii Afanas'evich Gogol-Ianovsky's children to survive. Gogol's parents were small landowners, whose modest means were challenged by their ever-increasing family. Gogol's birth was followed by that of a sister in 1811, a brother in 1812, and three more sisters between 1821 and 1825. At the age of ten, Gogol left for school; his education paid for by a distant relative who became Gogol's benefactor. In 1821, Gogol began his career at the High School for Advanced Study in Nezhin in a rigorous nine-year course of study. Gogol's childhood was marred by the death of his brother in 1819 and by the death of his father in 1825. Assuming his role as the head of the household after his father's death, Gogol applied himself in school with a new vigor. He left for St. Petersburg in 1828 following his graduation.

While he sought to devote himself to writing—he self-published some of his poetry and stories—Gogol eventually took a position in a government department and in 1830 was transferred to a position in the ministry of the court. Continuing to publish short works in literary journals, Gogol published a series of short stories in 1831 and 1832 called *Vechera na khutore bliz Dikan'ki* (*Evenings on a Farm near Dikanka*). The stories combined a realistic account of peasant life in small villages with the supernatural elements often present in folk tales. His Ukrainian heritage was dear to him and is evoked in these stories. The works were popular, and upon this early success, Gogol built a readership for subsequent short story collections. His work, which often included thoroughly researched historical accounts of Russia's past, also impressed upon Gogol's literary peers the significance of his talent.

In 1831, Gogol secured a teaching position at the Patriotic Institute. In 1836, "The Nose" was accepted for publication in the journal *Sovremennik* (*The Contemporary*), published by another giant of Russian literature, Alexander Pushkin. With his eye on a career as a Russian historian, Gogol sought and was awarded an assistant professorship of history in 1834 at the University of St. Petersburg. The appointment was short-lived. In 1835, Gogol left his teaching position and began writing in earnest once again. Gogol left for Europe in 1836. He traveled extensively and wrote prolifically. He returned to Russia in 1839 to attend to financial and familial affairs. He completed the first volume of *Pokhozhdeniia Chichikova, ili Mertvye dushi* (*The Adventures of Chichikov, or Dead Souls*) in Rome in 1840. Gogol traveled again to Moscow to handle the work's publication in 1842. His interest in religion and spirituality became his focus in 1847 and 1848, an interest that took him to Jerusalem. For the next several years, Gogol explored the relationship between his writing and his spirituality. When a priest with whom Gogol had been in contact for many years condemned him and his works, he stopped writing, burned some of his work, and stopped eating. He died on February 21, 1852.

PLOT SUMMARY

Section I

"The Nose" is divided into three sections. The first opens with a barber named Ivan Yakovlevich awakening to the smell of freshly baked bread. After his wife, Praskovia Osipovna, removes the loaves from the oven, Ivan dons a jacket and proceeds to slice onions to eat with his bread. As he cuts into the loaf, he finds that something has been baked into the center of it. Further inspection reveals that the object is a nose. With horror, Yakovlevich realizes that the nose looks familiar to him. His wife is outraged and demands to know whose nose he has removed while shaving his customers. Yakovlevich recognizes the nose as that of Platon Kovaliov, a collegiate assessor who has regular shaving appointments twice a week.

While Yakovlevich's wife demands he remove the nose from the house at once, Yakovlevich attempts to figure out how the incident has occurred; he wonders if he came home drunk the previous night. Fearing being found out by the police, Yakovlevich wraps the nose up and tries to find a place to discard it. He settles on the Isakievsky Bridge over the river Neva. He flings the rag containing the nose into the river and sets off to find a drink. Not long after, he is questioned by a police inspector who has noticed Yakovlevich loitering on the bridge. Before the section ends, the reader is informed that "the incident is completely veiled in obscurity, and absolutely nothing is known of what happened next."

Section II

In the next section, Kovaliov, the collegiate assessor whom Yakovlevich suspects to be nose-less, in fact wakes up to find "a completely flat space where his nose should have been." Distraught, Kovaliov dresses quickly and decides to go to the police commissioner at once. Covering his face with his handkerchief, Kovaliov heads out on foot, as he cannot find a cab. Along the way, he stops and stares at a sight he is unable to believe. As a carriage stops in front of a house, a uniformed man steps out, a man Kovaliov recognizes as his own nose. He

MEDIA ADAPTATIONS

- *Le Nez* is a French animated short film produced in 1963, directed by Alexander Alexeieff and Claire Parker.

- *A Nose* is a 1966 animated short film based on "The Nose," adapted and directed by Mordicai Gerstein. It was produced by Pelican Films.

- *Nos* is a 1971 Polish short film for television adapted from "The Nose" and directed by Stanislaw Lenartowicz. It was produced by Zespol Filmowy "Iluzjon."

- *Nos* is a 1977 Russian television drama adapted from "The Nose" and directed by Rolan Bykov. It was produced in the former Soviet Union by the production company Ekran.

- *The Nose* is a 1991 short film based on "The Nose," written by Desmond Dim and Ekachai Uekrongtham, and directed by Uekrongtham.

- *Peterburgskie povesti* (*Petersburg Stories*) is a 2005 Russian language audio CD of a selection of Gogol's short stories, including "The Nose." The stories are read by V. Tsimbalov.

- *The Collected Tales of Nikolai Gogol*, translated from the Russian into English by Richard Pevear and Larissa Volokhonsky is available as an audio CD produced by Recording for the Blind and Dyslexic in 2007.

wonders how this turn of events is even possible and runs after the carriage.

Kovaliov follows his nose into a church, the Kazansky Cathedral, and spies him praying. Studying the nose's uniform, Kovaliov realizes that the nose is a civil councilor, a man apparently of some importance whom Kovaliov is unsure how to approach. Nevertheless, Kovaliov musters his courage and approaches the nose, attempting to explain the situation to the confused man. When Kovaliov comes to the point and states, "Why, you are my own nose!" the nose dismisses Kovaliov and his accusation, stating that he is an "independent individual." Kovaliov becomes momentarily distracted and finds that the nose has escaped the church. He locates a cab and instructs the driver to go to the police commissioner's residence.

When he arrives there, a porter informs him that the commissioner has just departed. Kovaliov decides to place an advertisement in the paper regarding his missing nose and scolds the cab driver into hurrying. A lengthy encounter with the newspaper clerk ensues, in which Kovaliov attempts to once again explain his rather unique situation. Eventually realizing that Kovaliov is talking about his actual nose impersonating a civil servant and running off, the clerk informs Kovaliov that he cannot place such an advertisement, for the newspaper might lose its reputation due to the absurd nature of the incident. Attempting to ease Kovaliov's distress, the clerk unthinkingly offers Kovaliov a bit of snuff (a powdered tobacco product that is inhaled through the nose). Kovaliov is obviously outraged and leaves the newspaper office, seeking now the police inspector, who rapidly dismisses Kovaliov and his outrageous claim. Arriving home, Kovaliov's anger is once again inflamed at the insolent nature of his servant, Ivan, who is lying about, "spitting on the ceiling."

Kovaliov racks his brain, trying to understand why such a misfortune has befallen him. He wonders if Madame Podtochina might in some way be responsible, as he has flirted endlessly with her daughter without seeking her hand in marriage. Kovaliov wonders if she has hired "peasant witches" to remove his nose. As he is contemplating this possibility, a police officer is admitted into Kovaliov's home; the reader is informed that this is the same officer who questioned Ivan Yakovlevich at the beginning of the story. The officer informs Kovaliov that his nose has been found. He states, "the strange thing is that I myself took him for a gentleman at first, but fortunately I had my spectacles with me and I soon saw that it was a nose."

The officer goes on to state that Ivan Yakovlevich is somehow involved in the crime and is in custody and that the nose is now once again a nose, not a gentleman. He then hands the nose to Kovaliov. Elation turns to horror when Kovaliov realizes he has no idea how to make the nose a part of his face once again. A doctor is summoned and declares the reattachment of the nose an impossibility. Kovaliov writes to Madam Podtochina to see if she could attend to the matter of reattachment, still supposing she had something to do with the nose's removal. Her response reveals that she is clearly bewildered by Kovaliov's accusation. Several days pass, and rumors abound about what has happened to Kovaliov. The reader is treated to a number of anecdotes about other absurd occurrences in this region.

Section III
In this section, Kovaliov wakes up about two weeks after his nose originally disappeared and finds that it is once again firmly in place. Ivan Yakovlevich arrives to shave Kovaliov as scheduled. He is surprised to find Kovaliov's nose back in place and very gingerly performs his duties. Kovaliov is clearly nervous as Yakovlevich shaves his beard. Satisfied that it is now permanently in place, Kovaliov goes about his business as before. As the story concludes, the narrator asserts that sometimes absurd things happen without explanation.

CHARACTERS

Cab Driver
The cab driver is the much-abused man who takes Kovaliov first to the police commissioner's house and then to the newspaper office. Kovaliov berates the man repeatedly and even hits him on the back with his fist.

Clerk
The clerk is an elderly gentleman who works at the newspaper in which Kovaliov seeks to place an ad about his missing nose. Kovaliov's exchange with the newspaper clerk takes several pages to relate, and in this exchange much of the story's humor is conveyed. Before he attends to Kovaliov, the clerk must count out money and dispense the various documents allotted to the other customers. As Kovaliov begins to describe the situation concerning his errant nose, the clerk misunderstands him, asking what "this Mr. Nosov" has robbed Kovaliov of. After finally comprehending Kovaliov's bizarre story, the clerk refuses to print such an advertisement in the newspaper, for fear of damaging the paper's reputation. When Kovaliov shows the clerk the flat space on his face where his nose had once been, the clerk grows sympathetic. Trying to cheer Kovaliov, the clerk offers

Kovaliov a pinch of snuff, which Kovaliov can obviously not inhale. Kovaliov leaves angry and disheartened.

Doctor

Kovaliov summons the doctor after his nose has been returned to him. Following an examination that oddly includes a couple of flicks to the empty space on Kovaliov's face, the doctor announces that while he could put the nose back on, it would be "much worse" for Kovaliov if he did. The doctor fails to elaborate on this point but does offer to buy it from Kovaliov, an offer Kovaliov refuses.

Ivan

Ivan is Kovaliov's valet, or personal servant.

Platon Kovaliov

Platon Kovaliov is a collegiate assessor who is proud of the authority he possesses and the respect he believes he commands in the community. His comments about his broad circle of notable acquaintances suggest his sense of superiority over such individuals as his barber, Ivan Yakovlevich. It is with utter disbelief and dismay that Kovaliov awakens to find his nose simply missing from his face. In contrast with the physical appearance of Ivan Yakovlevich, Kovaliov wears cleaned and pressed shirts and is well-groomed (by Ivan Yakovlevich). His horror at having his appearance so drastically altered cannot be overstated; he is in a state of panic as he departs to find the police commissioner. When Kovaliov spies his own nose, dressed in an impeccable uniform, parading about town, he is shocked but certain that this well-appointed figure is indeed his nose. He is humble and cautious when he approaches his nose; he treads carefully when speaking with the nose, as he recognizes him as an officer of rank. Envisioning his life without his nose, Kovaliov is dismayed by what others will think of him. His sense of self worth is utterly destroyed, and he admits that he would have rather lost an arm or leg. Kovaliov despairs, stating, "Without a nose a man is goodness knows what ... good for nothing but to be flung out of the window." For a short while, Kovaliov wonders if it is all a dream or an illusion. Like Yakovlevich, Kovaliov considers the role of alcohol in the course of events, suspecting that his servant Ivan left him the vodka he uses after shaving to drink instead of his customary water. Pinching himself he quickly dismisses the

notion that he is drunk and can only consider himself a blameless victim. Kovaliov's joy at the mysterious reappearance of his nose upon his face is boundless. He treats himself to a cup of chocolate and peers into the mirror at every opportunity to make sure his nose is still present. Triumphantly, after meeting with Madame Podtochina, Kovaliov pulls out his snuffbox and inhales a pinch of snuff into each nostril, thinking gleefully that he will never marry Madame Podtochina's daughter.

The Nose

Kovaliov's nose appears as a person, a uniformed civil councilor who intimidates Kovaliov with his apparent importance.

Praskovia Osipovna

Praskovia Osipovna is the wife of the barber, Ivan Yakovlevich. She is described as heavyset and fond of coffee-drinking. Yakovlevich appears to be wary about upsetting his wife. He opts to not have the coffee he desires with his bread and onions because "he knew that it was utterly impossible to ask for two things at once," for his wife "greatly disliked such caprices." She is happy to let Yakovlevich have the bread, for there will now be more coffee left for her. When Yakovlevich discovers the nose, Praskovia immediately begins to scold and accuse her husband of treachery, and she threatens to report him to the police. She vehemently insists that he dispose of the nose at once.

Aleksandra Podtochina

Madam Podtochina, as Kovaliov refers to her, is a woman whose daughter Kovaliov has been flirting with. Kovaliov suspects Madam Podtochina has paid witches to magically remove his nose, but when he actually confronts her, via letter, about this notion, she is clearly befuddled. She appears at the end of the story, when she runs into a jubilant Kovaliov, after his nose has returned to his face.

Police Commissioner

The police commissioner does not appear in the story, but Kovaliov does attempt to meet with him about his nose, only to find that the commissioner has gone out.

Police Inspector Number 1

First referred to as a police inspector, this gentleman appears in the story in the first section, when he questions Ivan Yakovlevich. He later appears at Kovaliov's home, and is in this instance referred to as a police officer. The narrator informs the reader that this is in fact the same officer who questioned Yakovlevich on the bridge. The inspector/officer brings the nose to Kovaliov and describes how he followed the nose, which he first took to be a man before realizing it was a nose. The officer additionally mentions that Yakovlevich is in police custody in connection with the case.

Police Inspector Number 2

In the second section of the story, this police inspector—not to be confused with the gentleman referred to as both inspector and officer and who has direct contact with Yakovlevich at the beginning of the story and the nose itself near the end of the story—receives Kovaliov in his home with some irritation, berating him for appearing after dinner and for having his nose removed in the first place.

Porter

The porter works for the police commissioner and informs Kovaliov that the commissioner is not home when Kovaliov arrives to speak with him.

Ivan Yakovlevich

Ivan Yakovlevich is a barber who finds a nose baked into his loaf of bread. Yakovlevich's wife suggests that he cut off someone's nose while shaving, and he wonders if this is true. He is uncertain, because he cannot remember if he had been drunk the night before or not. Interestingly, he never suspects his wife, who made the bread, of having anything to do with the disembodied nose finding its way into the loaf. A paragraph is devoted to the characterization of Yakovlevich as a Russian worker and a drunk. His physical appearance is shabby, his clothes stained and missing buttons. Frightened of police involvement, Yakovlevich initially wants to hide the nose, but at his wife's urging takes it out of the house and seeks to rid himself of the nose as quickly as possible. Yakovlevich ends up flinging the nose over the bridge into the river. Although the police inspector who questions him about his activities on the bridge later informs Kovaliov that Yakovlevich is in custody, Yakovlevich nevertheless appears at the story's end to shave Kovaliov. This act is performed with great care, and Yakovlevich marvels at the amazing, reattached nose.

THEMES

Class Conflict

Throughout "The Nose" runs an undercurrent of class conflict, lending the ostensibly humorous, absurd story a counterweight of serious social commentary. The contrast between the characters of Ivan Yakovlevich and Platon Kovaliov highlights the class issues in the story. Yakovlevich's appearance is depicted as slovenly, and he recalls the way Kovaliov always mentions the way his hands stink. By contrast, Kovaliov presents an impeccable figure, clean and tidy. Yakovlevich is portrayed as simpleminded and confused, whereas Kovaliov thinks very highly of himself and comes off as snobbish and rude. Neither character is treated with much sympathy by Gogol.

When Kovaliov is about to approach his nose in church, he first assesses its uniform, surmising that the nose is a civil councilor. His trepidation suggests that the nose is of higher rank than Kovaliov, yet when he speaks to the nose, despite his deferential attitude, Kovaliov remarks that the nose ought to know its "proper place." He goes on to say that as a major (which would be the equivalent military title for someone of Kovaliov's civil rank), it is quite improper for him to not have a nose, although an old woman selling oranges on the bridge could get along just fine without one. The degradation of not having a nose, according to Kovaliov, is acceptable for someone of a lower social class to endure, but it is unthinkable that someone of his rank should not have a nose.

The importance of his rank, and hence his social status, is emphasized again when the police inspector states "that a respectable man does not have his nose pulled off." Kovaliov is enraged by this insult to his respectability. In addition to these examples of the significance of class and rank in Russian society, Gogol highlights the attitude of social superiority to which Kovaliov subscribes by depicting the verbal and physical abuse to which he subjects those he considers beneath him. The cab driver is berated and beaten, the newspaper clerk is condescended to, Kovaliov's servant Ivan is scolded often, and when Yakovelich returns at the end of the story to shave Kovaliov, he is shouted at and accused of being unclean.

TOPICS FOR
FURTHER
STUDY

- Gogol's work and that of other magical realists bridge a gap between the fantastic and straightforward, realistic story-telling. Write your own short story in which elements of the fantastic, magical, supernatural, or absurd are carefully integrated into an otherwise realistic story. Keep in mind that even in the realistic portions of Gogol's story, the absurd elements are accepted with little more than curiosity; they become a part of the real world. Furthermore, the realism of Gogol's story is not without its own agenda. Gogol highlights, largely through characterization, aspects of Russian life and culture. Though absurd, the story has a point. Your story should be focused on a particular purpose or sentiment you would like to convey, and you should make an effort to marry the fantastic or absurd with the realistic as seamlessly as possible.

- The policies of Tsar Nicholas I shaped the lives of Russian citizens by creating a culture of fear and suspicion. Using print and Internet sources, research the reign of Nicholas I. Create an interactive Web site with links to other sources of information on nineteenth-century Russia and the reign of this tsar. Discuss how he came to power, the policies for which he is known, his attitudes regarding the Russian national identity, and the end of his reign.

- Living in imperial Russia, Gogol wrote during a time of government oppression and intense censorship. Many of his works allude to the dangers and pressures of living in such a society. Similarly, Lisa See in *Snow Flower and the Secret Fan* (published by Random House in 2006) explores the oppressiveness of the Chinese culture, particularly for women, in nineteenth-century imperial China. Read See's novel and consider the ways in which the political and social cultures of China during this time shape the lives of the characters in the novel. Do traditions and a distinct sense of national identity oppress individuals or improve their lives? Write an essay in which you explore such issues, and share it with the class in a print version, blog, or oral presentation.

- "The Nose" is an example of the nineteenth-century Russian magical realist style, a style that Gogol was pivotal in establishing and that influenced many other writers. Magical realism is also prevalent in the works of many twentieth- and twenty-first-century Latin American writers, and it is not limited to novels and short stories. With a book group, read one of the plays in young-adult collection *Nine Plays by José Cruz González: Magical Realism and Mature Themes in Theatre for Young Audiences*. (The collection of González's plays was edited by Coleman A. Jennings and published by the University of Texas Press in 2008.) As you discuss the play, compare González's use of magical realism with Gogol's. How do the authors employ elements of the supernatural or absurd in their works? Is the effect humorous or serious? How do the authors treat themes relevant to their respective societies and cultures? Prepare an oral presentation for the class, or set up an online blog discussion in which members of your group post their thoughts and opinions regarding the two works.

Absurdity

Elements of the absurd—the outrageously illogical or obviously fantastical—are apparent early on in "The Nose." The fifth paragraph opens with the revelation that the strange white mass that Ivan Yakovlevich finds in his freshly baked loaf of bread is, in fact, a nose. Furthermore, the nose seems familiar to Yakovlevich. Although

The barber found a nose in the rolls his wife made for breakfast. (cobalt88 | Shutterstock.com)

cannot all be dreaming or hallucinating. After the nose is somehow reunited with Kovaliov's face, another unexplained, bizarre twist, the narrator comments on the story's absurdity, admitting that "there is a great deal that is improbable in it." The narrator suggests that perhaps the most incomprehensible thing is "that authors can choose such subjects." The narrator concludes by asserting that absurd things do in fact happen, "not often, but they do happen."

Skaz *Narration*

The type of narration Gogol employs in "The Nose" is one in which the narrative voice conveys the sense that the story is being relayed personally and orally by a specific individual. This style features digressions by the narrator, as when the narrator of "The Nose" states, "I am afraid I am a little to blame for not having so far said more about Ivan Yakovlevich," before he begins a paragraph about Yakovlevich's appearance and habits. This style of narration is what is known as *skaz* narration.

As Donald Fanger states in *The Creation of Nikolai Gogol*, in "The Nose" the "narration is by Gogol's elusive *skaz* narrator—ostensibly omniscient, but full of gaps, irrelevancies and non-sequiturs." Such a gap in the relating of information by the narrator occurs, for example, at the end of the first section of the story, when the narrator states that "the incident is completely veiled in obscurity, and absolutely nothing is known of what happened next." The narrator also concludes the story with much conjecture about the nature of the absurd elements, and the possible motives of authors who utilize such elements in their works.

The narrator's tone is conversational: he seems to be wondering aloud in the same way a reader might as he or she reads the story. This type of narration suits a tale of magical realism in that it appears to be a story repeatedly retold through word-of-mouth, much like the other fantastic incidents the narrator mentions near the end of "The Nose." The absurd elements are perhaps more easily digested by readers when it appears as though they are being told by a gossiping neighbor rather than an authoritative, all-knowing (omniscient) narrator.

he is overcome by an initial feeling of horror, the subsequent reactions of the characters in the story to the nose are milder, and more along the lines of confusion rather than the shock and disgust readers might expect. Yakovlevich's wife does not question what it is her husband has found but immediately suspects that he has cut the nose off of someone.

Later, when Kovaliov realizes his nose is missing, the narrator explains that "an extremely absurd flat space" appears where Kovaliov's nose once resided. The nose appears to have been separated from its person by some other means than physical violence, another bizarre element. Perhaps the strangest aspect of the story is the way the nose appears to masquerade as a man in uniform. Readers at this point may begin to assume that Kovaliov is hallucinating or dreaming. When the police officer arrives and confirms the dual nature of the nose (it is an actual nose that has been dressed as a man), the story takes yet another absurd turn of events. Now, it is apparent that everyone can recognize the nose/man as both nose and man. They

Magical Realism

Magical realism is a literary style in which a realistic story is infused with elements of the absurd, elements that exist outside the realm of logic and reason. As a specific literary movement, magical realism developed in the mid-twentieth century, and the name was coined in reference to the works of Latin American authors. However, as poet and critic Dana Gioia observes in a 1998 essay published in *Sniper Logic* and reproduced on Gioia's Web site, the style known as magical realism "has been around since the early development of the novel and short story as modern literary forms." Gioia notes that "The Nose" "fulfills virtually every requirement of this purportedly contemporary style."

Likewise, James D. Hardy and Leonard Stanton, in a 2002 essay for the journal *Janus Head*, maintain that in Gogol's story, "magical realism takes the form of an abrupt abrogation of natural law, for no discernible reason and to no clear purpose." In "The Nose," Gogol integrates the absurd elements of the disembodied nose and the nose taking human form seamlessly into a story about St. Petersburg society.

HISTORICAL CONTEXT

Russian Literary Romanticism and Realism

Russian literature in the first half of the nineteenth century was influenced by the romantic movement in Europe. In particular, Russian writers favored the culture and philosophy of the German romantic movement, as David Offord points out in the 2001 *Routledge Companion to Russian Literature*. Romantic literature incorporated a sentimentalized view of the past and valued individualism and emotionalism over intellectualism and rationalism. Russian romanticism also included spiritual and nationalist ideals. Early Russian romantics sought universal truths in art, emotion, the human soul, and placed a high value on idealism.

Dmitrij Čiževskij, in the 1974 *History of Nineteenth-Century Russian Literature*, Vol. 1, *The Romantic Period*, describes the particular style of Russian romanticists and realists, observing that in general, romantics in their writing utilized such poetic stylistic devices as metaphor, hyperbole, and personification. By contrast, realists sought to portray the world in a less multidimensional or layered manner and featured more straightforward prose than the romantics. Gogol is regarded as one of the most accomplished romantic prose writers of the time period and is also considered a forerunner of Russian realism. His early stories, inspired by Russian folk tales, accurately depicted Russian life in small villages. The supernatural elements of the folk tales, along with their strong Russian flavor, provided the romantic elements to the stories, while the detailed descriptions of daily life reflected Gogol's growing interest in realism. His later works continued to bridge the gap between romanticism and realism. "The Nose," for example, incorporates the unbelievable or absurd in place of supernatural folk elements and integrates these features with an otherwise realist style in which the unpleasant aspects of Russian urban life are plainly related.

Tsarist Russia in the Early to Mid-Nineteenth Century

During Gogol's lifetime, Russia was an empire ruled by a supreme hereditary ruler called a tsar (also spelled czar). In tsarist Russia, all power was centralized with the tsar; he wielded the ultimate authority. Tsar Nicholas I ruled from 1825 to 1855. Nicholas was a repressive ruler. He came into power during a time of revolutionary activity in which radical individuals and movements sought to overthrow the tsarist government. In order to ensure his continued reign, Nicholas instituted measures designed to ferret out anyone suspected of possessing radical beliefs. Secret police spied on, captured, and imprisoned citizens who spoke out against the monarchy. In pursuit of a strong autocracy (a system of government in which power resides with one individual), Nicholas sought to prevent the influx of liberal, western European ideas and promoted the idea of a Russian national identity that excluded any foreign influences.

Intertwined with these political aims was the effort by Nicholas to promote the Russian Orthodox Church as the single religious authority in Russia. Censorship of literary materials by the police and clergy was strict, and punishment of liberalism was certain. "The Nose" faced some degree of censorship; it was considered vulgar for the nose—a humorous and absurd element of Gogol's story—to appear in the Kazansky Cathedral. Gogol was initially forced to change this location. A small group of educated nobles, the intellegentsia, began to drift away from a

COMPARE
&
CONTRAST

- **1830s:** Russia in the 1830s is an imperialist empire ruled by the autocratic Tsar Nicholas I.

  Today: Russia becomes an independent nation following the dissolution of the Soviet Union in 1991. The nation is governed by President Dmitriy Medvedev, who is elected in 2008; his appointed premier, former president Vladimir Putin; and cabinet officials, who are also appointed by the president.

- **1830s:** Russia is enjoying what will later be referred to as the golden age of Russian literature. Great writers during this time period shape the course of Russian literature for decades to come and include such notable authors as Gogol, Alexander Pushkin, Mikhail Lermontov, Ivan Turgenev, and Fyodor Dostoyevsky.

  Today: Contemporary Russian writers include the recent winners of the Russian Booker Prize, Mikhail Yelizarov, for *Librarian* (2008), and Yelena Chizhova, for *A Time of Women* (2009). Yelizarov's novel is described as mystical in nature, while Chizhova's focuses on the Soviet past.

- **1830s:** The city of St. Petersburg, once considered Russia's most "Western" city in terms of the influence of European ideas and philosophy, a designation encouraged by Peter the Great when the city was first founded, remains the center of power for Tsar Nicholas I, who is less tolerant of the Western influence than Peter. The city is also the setting of many great works of Russian literature, such as "The Nose," where many geographic features of the city, including the Neva river, Nevsky Prospekt, and Kazansky Cathedral, play an integral role in his story.

  Today: St. Petersburg is a popular tourist destination for travelers to Russia. The city's literary past draws visitors who seek the atmosphere that once inspired Russia's great authors. The city is also a favorite among tourists for its historical stature as the unofficial capital of the Russian Empire, as well as its European-inspired neoclassical architecture.

government it had previously supported as a result of the severe repression Nicholas instituted. Many of these individuals were writers who began to explore realism in fiction in an effort to depict life as it truly was.

CRITICAL OVERVIEW

Gogol's work received a variety of critical reactions during his lifetime. As Amy Singleton Adams points out in the chapter on Gogol in the *Dictionary of Literary Biography*, "The Nose" was rejected by the *Moskovskii nabliudatel* (Moscow Observer) before Alexander Pushkin published it in his journal. John M. Thompson contends in the 2009 *Russia and the Soviet Union*

that the work of the conservative Gogol "was praised by the radical critics among the intelligentsia, who urged that literature be used as a weapon against the evils of government and society."

Other critics have focused on Gogol's examination of Russian society in "The Nose." Fruma Gottschalk, in a 1972 introduction to "The Nose," states that Gogol "exposed the overbearing snobbish values of St. Petersburg's society." Echoing this assessment, David Magarshack contends that in the story, Gogol exploits the opportunity to pen "a bitingly satirical exposure of the stupidity of officialdom, and of the snobbery, self-complacency and indifference of the higher classes of Russian society."

While some critics identify sexual elements in the story and claim that the nose is symbolic

The barber acted as though nothing had happened. *(Khoo Eng Yow / Shutterstock.com)*

of another feature of the male anatomy, many find this type of analysis fruitless. Fanger, in the 1979 *The Creation of Nikolai Gogol*, asserts that such commentaries, and others that attempt to fashion the story "as an indictment of physicality" or a "sermon against godlessness," remain "unconvincing."

"The Nose" has also been evaluated as an early example of magical realism, with Gioia observing in a 1998 *Sniper Logic* essay that Gogol's story meets all the stylistic requirements to be considered a work of magical realism. Hardy and Stanton similarly study the magical realist elements of the story in their essay for a 2002 issue of *Janus Head*. Hardy and Leonard examine the way Gogol inverts the usual causal relationship between magical elements and plot developments.

CRITICISM

Catherine Dominic

Dominic is a novelist, freelance writer, and editor. In the following essay, she traces the development of Gogol's notion of fractured identity in his short

story "The Nose," arguing that the work reflects his views on the potential for conflict between one's personal identity and one's notion of national identity in nineteenth-century imperial Russia.

Although some scholars note that Gogol was politically conservative, he did live under an oppressive regime, and he had encounters with government censors who found potentially troublesome material in his works. Speaking through the narrator at the end of "The Nose," Gogol additionally makes mocking comments about the government. These features, combined with a method of characterization in "The Nose" through which individuals display a fragmented sense of self, suggest that through his story, Gogol is examining the way a government intent on preserving a national identity is actually playing a role in stripping its citizens of their own personal identity.

This view is supported by critics such as Edyta M. Bojanowska, who, in her 2007 *Nikolai Gogol: Between Ukrainian and Russian Nationalism*, maintains that Gogol's sense of his Ukrainian identity conflicted with his sense of his

WHAT DO I READ NEXT?

- Gogol's novel *Dead Souls* was originally published in 1842 and is regarded as a superbly realistic examination of Russian society that skillfully incorporates elements of the supernatural. A modern translation by Richard Pevear and Larissa Volokhonsky was published in 1997 by Vintage.

- Gogol's short story "The Overcoat" was originally published in 1842 and is counted among the writer's masterpieces. Like many of Gogol's other writings, "The Overcoat" combines elements of the fantastic with an otherwise realistically told story about a civil servant whose overcoat has been stolen. The harshest truths about the inequities of Russian society are presented as the man endeavors to recover the lost coat. A modern English translation is available in the collection *The Overcoat and Other Tales of Good and Evil*, translated by David Magarshack and published by W. W. Norton in 1965.

- Alexandr Sergeyevitch Pushkin, regarded as one of Russia's greatest poets, was also Gogol's contemporary and mentor. His works are noted for their simplicity as well as their lyrical nature. His short stories have been translated into English by Gillon R. Aitken and published as *The Complete Tales of Alexandr Sergeyevitch Pushkin* by W. W. Norton in 1996.

- Greta Bucher's *Daily Life in Imperial Russia*, published by Greenwood in 2008, surveys the history of Russia as a tsarist empire and offers an analysis of Russian culture among different classes during this time period.

- *One Hundred Years of Solitude*, by Colombian novelist Gabriel García Márquez, was first published in 1967. The highly acclaimed novel is one of the works that helped define the modern magical realist style. It was reprinted by Harper Perennial Modern Classics in 2006.

- Francesca Lia Block's young-adult novel *Echo* is written in the magical realist style. A coming-of-age story, it follows the Los Angeles adventures of a teenage girl named Echo who encounters a variety of supernatural creatures along her journey to find herself. It was published by HarperTeen in 2002.

Russianness. Bojanowska's analysis emphasizes the Ukrainian versus Russian component of Gogol's conflict and the presence of this conflict in his works; however, her analysis of "The Nose" is peripheral. Furthermore, the struggle between individual and national identity that pervades the story is present in a manner independent of Gogol's personal Ukrainian/Russian context. Gogol's treatment of the fractured nature of personal identity and its relation to Russian national identity is handled in a manner that makes evident the likelihood that many Russians suffered this sense of fragmentation and conflict. Throughout "The Nose," Gogol captures images of the fractured and divided self, primarily through the characterization of Ivan Yakovlevich and Planton Kovaliov. Such portraits emphasize the sense of personal conflict Gogol experienced and also highlight the role of the state in de-emphasizing individuality in favor of a unified national character.

The Russian Empire of the nineteenth century contained a number of culturally diverse regions. The regime feared revolts, such as the unsuccessful Polish revolt against tsarist Russia in 1830. Other regions that could be described as reluctant members of the Russian Empire included the Ukrainian and Kazahk regions. Not until the end of the twentieth century were such regions finally recognized as independent nations, when the Soviet Union was dismantled in 1991. (The Soviet Union came into being at

> THROUGHOUT 'THE NOSE,' GOGOL CAPTURES IMAGES OF THE FRACTURED AND DIVIDED SELF, PRIMARILY THROUGH THE CHARACTERIZATION OF IVAN YAKOVLEVICH AND PLANTON KOVALIOV. SUCH PORTRAITS EMPHASIZE THE SENSE OF PERSONAL CONFLICT GOGOL EXPERIENCED AND ALSO HIGHLIGHT THE ROLE OF THE STATE IN DE-EMPHASIZING INDIVIDUALITY IN FAVOR OF A UNIFIED NATIONAL CHARACTER."

the end of World War I, when communist revolutionaries overthrew the tsarist empire.) In these regions and throughout Russia, Tsar Nicholas I attempted to suppress ideas and influences that ran counter to his vision of a unified national Russian identity.

In this oppressive atmosphere, the Ukrainian-born St. Petersburg resident Gogol sought to advance his career as a writer, while steering clear of the Russian censors and any accusations of wrongdoing. He was not always successful. As Leonard J. Kent observes in his footnotes to "The Nose," the Russian censor evaluating the story found the presence of the nose in Kazansky Cathedral to be a violation of what the Church considers to be sacred. As Gogol's story begins, the conflict about the fragmented or lost nature of personal identity is immediately revealed. From the first description of Ivan Yakovlevich that Gogol provides, a sense of loss is injected into the story. Yakovlevich is a barber, and the signboard that draws the attention of passersby to his place of business is devoid of Yakovlevich's name; only a picture of a lathered gentleman waiting to be shaved (along with a notice that bloodletting is also available) remains on the sign. (Bloodletting was a practice by which blood was drawn from an individual as a means of preventing or curing illnesses.) Yakovlevich's name is lost, and the note that the text regarding bloodletting remains on the sign is also indicative of loss, the loss of blood symbolizing the loss of something intrinsic to one's self.

Yakovlevich's lack of personal identity is underscored when the narrator highlights his status as a "self-respecting Russian workman," who, like his peers, "was a terrible drunkard." Lumped into a large class of other workmen, Yakovlevich is characterized as an interchangeable drone devoid of a distinct personal identity. His reaction to the appearance of the nose in his daily bread is one of horror and confusion, a reaction that quickly dissolves and gives way to fear of what the authorities will do if he is caught in possession of a stray body part. He begins to tremble just thinking of the police uniform. Yakovlevich is later questioned and taken into custody. Significantly, Yakovlevich's fear of the symbol of Russian authority—the police—overwhelms him. His desires—to eat his bread and onions, to let his wife have the extra coffee—and his natural inclinations regarding the nose—to wrap it up and "put it in a corner"—dissolve the instant he thinks of the police. His personal identity and agency are subsumed, or overtaken, by his sense of the all-powerful Russian empire and the enforcer of its laws, the police. Yakovlevich's view of the national agenda thwarts his personal agenda.

Like Yakovlevich, Kovaliov is depicted as interchangeable with other members of his social class, despite the fact that he is the type of collegiate assessor who has been appointed rather than one who has earned the title through academic study. The narrator makes this distinction and proceeds to convey the sense of self-importance that all collegiate assessors have, despite the way in which they came about their title. He goes on to observe, "It is the same, of course, with all grades and titles." Gogol presents the reader with two characters from different classes, both of whom he judges harshly. In the narrator's estimation, all workmen are drunks, and all civil servants are pompous. Furthermore, the narrator explains, Kovaliov is in St. Petersburg to seek "a post befitting his rank" and perhaps "a bride with a fortune of two hundred thousand." His attention to rank, power, money, and social position are highlighted at every turn. Kovaliov seeks to insert himself as much as possible into his understanding of the Russian national identity, while Yakovlevich seeks to hide from it.

When Kovaliov loses his nose, he is most concerned about how the change in his appearance might hamper his respectability among his peers and among females. He is, quite literally, fractured or divided, and the respect and power

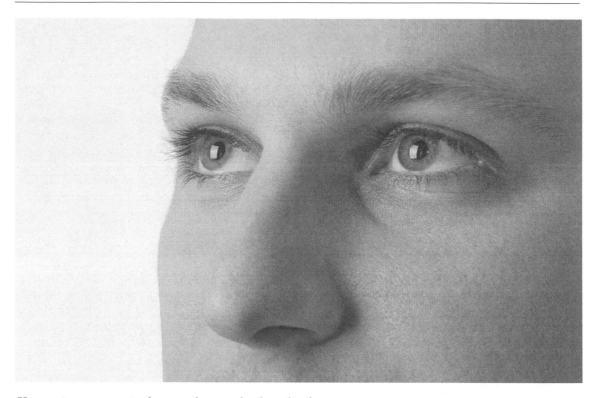

He was just as surprised to see the nose back on his face. (*Anna Sedneva | Shutterstock.com*)

he normally takes for granted is endangered, as is his sense of wholeness as an individual. Kovaliov's physical fragmentation is reflective of his psychological fragmentation, of his sense that he is divided. Because Kovaliov associates his potency as an official with the nose and because his occupational identity appears to comprise to a large degree his entire sense of self, the nose may be regarded as a symbol of Kovaliov's sense of his Russian identity. Without the power of his rank or the ability to show his face in public and thus wield whatever power he might have, Kovaliov loses all sense of self. His Russianness is tied to the position the government has bestowed upon him; he is, in effect, only who the state has told him to be. By making this connection, Gogol forces the reader to consider the relationship between one's sense of personal identity and one's sense of national identity. For Kovaliov, these identities are intertwined, so much so that he is frantic, panicked, and lost at the alteration of his physical appearance, which he associates with his position as a government representative. Kovaliov tells the nose, after it takes human form and appears all over St. Petersburg in uniform, "I am a major, by the way. For me to go

about without a nose, you must admit, is improper." The fact that the nose masquerades as a uniformed "civil councilor," a position of sufficient rank to apparently impress Kovaliov enough to pause before he approaches the nose, also emphasizes its status as a symbol of Russian national identity. It does not take the form of a peasant or a drunken workman, but of a respected individual employed in the service of its government.

As the separation from his nose intensifies Kovaliov's feeling of anxiety, his sense of fracture is heightened. A desperation fuels Kovaliov's efforts to reunite himself with his nose. When it finally, through no direct action on his part, reattaches itself to his face, Kovaliov's sense of wholeness returns. He is so completely restored to his former self that he behaves just as arrogantly and condescendingly to his "inferiors" as before, without being humbled by the experience. The reader is informed that "from that time forth Major Kovaliov promenaded about, as though nothing had happened."

At the story's end, the narrator questions why an author would write such a story, one that "is absolutely without profit to our country." In this statement, Gogol mocks works of literature designed to "profit" Russia, to enhance its sense of Kovaliov-like self-importance. The notion this statement suggests is that Gogol wrote the story in part to demonstrate the dangers of behaving only in ways that profit the nation, for in doing so, one's own identity becomes divided or lost altogether.

Source: Catherine Dominic, Critical Essay on "The Nose," in *Short Stories for Students*, Gale, Cengage Learning, 2011.

> YET GOGOL'S HERO IS AS REPRESENTATIVE OF HIS COUNTRY AND HIS AGE AS THE BENEVOLENT PICKWICK WHO STANDS FOR THE CHEERFUL MEDIOCRE TYPE, HALF-LOVINGLY CARICATURED BY THE ENEMIES OF ENGLAND."

Alice Birkhead

In the following essay, Birkhead compares Gogol's fictional characters to those of English novelist Charles Dickens.

The greater humorists have seldom been content to keep their imagination within very narrow bounds since even a trained psychologist would have difficulty in grasping national characteristics unless there were offered for his inspection a large number of types. Cervantes chose Don Quixote as his hero, a poor half-crazy knight, so eager to win glory that he wanders in quest of adventures all over the countryside. Dickens decided that the England he loved could be seen to the best advantage through the spectacles of Samuel Pickwick, a retired elderly merchant, travelling at leisure with a kind of club. Gogol, more nearly approaching the English satirist than the Spanish in his lack of bitterness, hit upon the strangest of excuses for the peregrinations of Tchitchikoff [*Dead Souls*].

Gogol, like Dickens, was a young man when he began to write. It is clear that he set before himself almost the same literary ideals—to draw certain of his country-people in such broad outline that the reader might laugh at their absurdities, yet forbear to imitate; to hold up to public notice some abuses that were accepted far too indifferently by his country. Dickens's brief experience in a lawyer's office had given him the opportunity of studying the legal system of the times. He had probably met sharp practitioners like Messrs. Dodson and Fogg, and seen them get victims into their clutches as harmless and benevolent as Mr. Samuel Pickwick, for he was familiar with every possible grade of lawyer's clerk. In the same way Gogol, who held a small clerical post in a Government office in St. Petersburg, found plenty of material for his studies of the corruption of the Russian bureaucracy. He may even have come across a rogue with a scheme to make his fortune easily by the purchase of dead "souls," or serfs, from owners who were only too glad to escape paying the taxes demanded by the Government. As Tchitchikoff explains to doubtful proprietors, "souls," set down in the Census lists, although they might have completed their earthly career, were, nevertheless, still taxed like the living ones.

Gogol came from the South, and understood the subtleties of bargaining, for his ancestors had been used to traffic in "souls." He wanted to describe the beauties of the Southern spring, the khorovods of the village maids and the gallants stepping forward to hold their white hands as they laughed and sang "Lords, show the bridegroom." He wanted also to urge Russia to advance from the lassitude and idleness that reduced many of the owners of fine estates to a condition little better than that of their ignorant peasants. Therefore he withdrew his hero from the Department of Justice, where he had made his way to a lucrative position through a comely appearance and a desire to please, and set him off on a tour through various corners of the Empire, with the idea that he might one day settle down on his own property with a fine complement of live serfs.

Tchitchikoff did not address himself at random to any owners of the land, but selected the men who were most to his taste, since he hoped, as far as possible, to acquire the "dead souls" from friendship. This prudence of his hero is enlarged upon by Gogol, who intended to present the miser, the spendthrift, and the futile dreamer as warnings to his countryfolk to strive against the natural tendencies most fatal in any age to the Russian. The dealers in serfs are all, in their way, quite as true to type as Messrs. Dodson and Fogg, Mr. Justice Stareleigh, and their myrmidons. It would be possible to find a modern equivalent for Nozdreff, the half-attractive wastrel who tries to bully Tchitchikoff into buying his dog, his chestnut mare, or an old hand-organ, and finally proposes to gamble for the "souls," having his full share of the national passion for the card-tables.

Gogol is not altogether hopeless when he draws Nozdreff, for the braggart has some energy at least, but he must have groaned over many a Maniloff in real life—that amiable procrastinator seems to cause him such intense exasperation. Maniloff is willing to give away his "souls," but Tchitchikoff, on the whole, prefers to do business with Sobakievitch, who gives him an excellent meal and drives a shrewder bargain. Yet his britchka rolls rather gaily from the model landlord's house in search of Pliushkin, "the ragged man with the patched clothes," as his own serfs describe him.

Tumbledown buildings and slovenly interiors were the correct background for a novel of manners in which Maniloff, Nozdreff, and Pliushkin moved—types so universally recognized that they are household words in Russia. Dickens, with equal truth, dwells on the snugness and prosperity of the English farms where jolly Mr. Wardle entertains Mr. Pickwick and his brethren. England, in 1837, was entering on an era of substantial peace that made the Victorian writers almost gloat over details of Victorian comfort. Russia had not taken the step that led to the formation of a middle class—the very idea of the emancipation of the serfs would have given Tchitchikoff cause to shudder! Yet Gogol's hero is as representative of his country and his age as the benevolent Pickwick who stands for the cheerful mediocre type, half-lovingly caricatured by the enemies of England.

Gogol was a true Russian in refusing a hero possessed of all the virtues for his greatest book. "Who is he? A knave, of course." The student of Russian literature knows very well that he must not shrink from meanness laid bare in a country where the poorest runs to give alms to "the unfortunate" when he passes through a town on his way to exile in Siberia. The satirist relents when the bold adventurer falls upon evil days, and reveals hidden feelings in his hero which had been stifled by the dreariness of his home life and the miserable isolation of his earliest surroundings. In the same way, Dickens brought the roguish Alfred Jingle low to discover certain fine qualities in the strolling player and his snivelling servant Job as soon as he had placed them in a debtors' prison. Although Gogol and Dickens knew how to apply the scourge, there is no trace of cynicism in their work nor indifference to the world around them. It was their generous humanity rather than their intellectual powers which placed them among the writers whose works are for all time. Everybody in Russia has a certain sympathy for that smooth-faced adventurer Tchitchikoff, as everybody in England has an affectionate regard for pompous, kind-hearted Mr. Samuel Pickwick.

One of the chief causes of Dickens's enormous popularity is the pleasant impression he gives of an England where the squalor of town life is but drawn in relief to the cheerful abundance of the country. He knew London and its debtors' prisons and mean streets from the sharp reality of a precocious childhood. He idealized the farmhouses he had seen as he rattled past them on a stage coach. He loved the old-fashioned inns where he fared on shoulders of mutton, caper sauce, mince pies, roast beef, and oysters. One need not be a thoroughgoing materialist to enjoy descriptions of an English dinner served in the solid English style, with all the heartiness suggested by Dickens's own enjoyment!

Dickens must have received hospitality from a family like the Wardles' some memorable Christmastide, and henceforth thought of the English farmhouse in terms of holly, carol-singing, and baked meats. He must have been welcomed at a provincial assembly as a distinguished stranger, and forthwith been inspired with the belief that the good people of the provinces invariably approved of any man with a decent coat and agreeable manners. Alfred Jingle's furious successes with "the ladies" find a very close parallel in the welcome given to Tchitchikoff at the governor's ball, where he was searching for landowners who seemed very suitable for his purpose. It is in dealing with "the emotions of a little town" that Gogol and Dickens tend to exceed ever so slightly in their satire. A Russian reader finds it hard to believe in the demonstrations of the governor "holding in one hand a bonbon motto and a Bolognese spaniel," both of which are flung to the four winds that he may extend a more cordial greeting to the hero. The aspirations of Mrs. Leo Hunter have shed abroad great mirth, but her name cannot be reckoned among the national types which Dickens found quite easily in London.

Gogol has a keen appreciation of the homely atmosphere suggested by bliny (pancakes), smoked sturgeon, kalatchi (meat patties), votrushka (pancakes with curd), and caviare. His inns are unattractive in comparison with the inns of Dickens, but the traveller in Russia need seldom hire a bed or pay for his own dinner. Maniloff, the slipshod landlord, offers "cabbage soup with a pure heart," and Madame Kobotchina turns most agreeably from a grasping, churlish woman into a perfect fairy godmother when she prepares butter-cakes and garlic tarts for her unexpected guest. "Evidently one of those women who own a small landed property and cry over bad crops and losses, who hold their heads on one side and accumulate money in motley little bags, stowed away in chests of drawers," she is a character Dickens would have drawn as well as Gogol. Both wrote their first great comedies before they had been touched by love. Pickwick has no heroine other than simpering Arabella Allen, who proves a mere excuse for placing the hero in ludicrous situations, and *Dead Souls* gives only a glimpse of the rare Ulinka dwelling in the peaceful valley where Tentyotnikoff passes days in futile dreaming. There are tantalizing moments when the young girl of the governor's ball seems to enter into the story, but she passes, as the sordid creatures pass encountered by Tchitchikoff on his journeyings.

Dickens glorified the old stagecoach, with its unsociable passengers relaxing on snowy nights when they are compelled to share the hospitality of some country inn, the stout, rubicund drivers, and the well-fed horses trotting at their well-regulated pace. The coach represents the Englishman and his slow, steady ideals of social progress, as the tröika, that dashing three-horse vehicle, is the symbol of the Russian, with his keen love of excitement and reckless desire for change. "Ah, the tröika—the bird-tröika! Who invented thee? Of course, thou couldst only have had thy birth among a dashing race—in that land which has extended smoothly, glidingly, over half the earth, and where one may count the verst-pillars till the eyes swim. The horses dash on like a whirlwind; the spokes of the wheels have become merged into one smooth circle; the road quakes and the foot-traveller cries out in alarm—while yet the tröika flies on, on, on." No wonder that Tchitchikoff smiled as he swung lightly on leather cushions, and his servant's cap blew off, while the honest

Petrushka himself jolted roughly against his master! Petrushka is a poor substitute for the incomparable Sam Weller, though his peculiar characteristics have endeared him to readers who believe in Gogol's text, "Love us when we are dirty, for everyone will love us when we are clean."

Source: Alice Birkhead, "The Russian Pickwick," in *Living Age*, Vol. 287, No. 3721, October 30, 1915, pp. 312–15.

G. R. Noyes

In the following essay, Noyes discusses elements of pathos and humor in some of Gogol's short stories.

Not many years ago a lecturer on literature, of more than local reputation, and of unusual talent for catching the attention of the typical summer school public, commented somewhat as follows on the gloomy, depressing tone of Russian authors: "Just think of even the titles of their works! *Dead Souls*! The very name is enough to send a shiver through one's frame!" Poor Gogol! This lecturer was not more ignorant of him than are most other professors of literature, but he ought to have read at least a few pages of a book that is a spiritual cousin of *Huckleberry Finn* and *The Gentle Grafter* before he indulged in reflections on its serio-comic title.

Turgenieff, Dostolevski, and Tolstoy have been well translated into English, and have won not only the enthusiastic admiration of discriminating judges, but genuine popularity. Gogol (1809–52), their predecessor, the great realist and satirist who, together with the poet Pushkin, laid the foundations for all modern Russian literature, has had no such good fortune. No collected edition of even his best work has ever been printed in English. Most translations of single works that have appeared are now out of print. There could be no more worthy enterprise for friends of Russia than to prepare a proper edition of Gogol, with an adequate account of his life and literary significance. An edition of this kind ought at least to pay its own way.

The Russophile enthusiasm awakened by the present war has as yet done little for Gogol. In particular, the reissue of an anonymous translation of his masterpiece, *Dead Souls*, apparently the version originally published by Vizetelly in 1887, cannot be regarded with satisfaction. The translator seems to have had a competent knowledge of Russian and English, but he capriciously omitted important paragraphs, and even whole pages, of the original. Such are the description of Sobakevich as a bear in chapter v, Gogol's moralizing on his own task in chapter vii, and his famous apostrophe to Russia in chapter xi. Furthermore, Gogol printed only eleven chapters of his projected comic epic, which, however, form a well-rounded whole. Of a sequel, hopelessly inferior in talent, he left only fragments, which were published after his death. The translation prints continuously Gogol's finished work and his fragments, with no hint of the gap between them, and then adds a continuation of the book by one Vaschenko-Zakharchenko that is forgotten and unregarded in Russia. The new introduction furnished by Stephen Graham is perfunctory and uninforming. Altogether, the volume does not command respect.

I.

Gogol is of all Russian writers the nearest akin to Mark Twain or O. Henry. He has the same command of the grotesque, the same blending of fantastic humor with occasional homely pathos, the same lack of any intellectual, philosophic insight into the depths of human character such as lends distinction to the work of his great successors. This very likeness to our American humorists has hindered Gogol from winning the wide fame that he deserves. He is no master of plot; the subjects of both *The Inspector* and *Dead Souls* were suggested to him by Pushkin. His whole narrative art lies in stringing together, around some central figure, a succession of amusing incidents. His genius is in the creation of clear, distinct characters. These characters, however, are not types of universal significance, like Don Quixote and his squire, but rather local, Russian oddities. His humor and pathos are expressed through an unfamiliar medium that in our eyes dims their brilliancy. His grafters are like our own, but, like O. Henry,

Gogol emphasizes not their souls but the tools of their trade, and those tools were emphatically made in Russia. Hence the humorous portraits that are so rich in suggestion to Gogol's countrymen may lose their savor in a translation. The difficulty is the same with other humorists, say, with Aristophanes. But no one attempts to read Aristophanes who has not a certain elementary knowledge of Athenian life, while a similar knowledge of Russian conditions is not yet a necessary part of even the most finished literary education.

Yet Gogol was too great a man of letters for us to sum up his genius by any such crude formulas and comparisons as have been suggested. He grew up in the romantic period of Russian literature, and paid toll to its spirit. *Taras Bulba* is a splendidly successful tale of the Cossack wars against Poland. Here we have the Cossack point of view of the conflict described by Sienkiewicz in *With Fire and Sword*. A small volume, *Taras Bulba* has a barbaric largeness of setting. This prose epic is full of a boyish delight in conflict that recalls hours spent with *Marmion*. The conventional love story is virtually absent; mere adventure and bloodshed are raised to the level of art by an Homeric vigor of style. So in the ghost story, "The Viy" (translated as "The King of the Gnomes"), Gogol succeeds in giving literary form to some of the grimmer elements of popular superstition. A gay young student, bethinking himself of the prayers appropriate to his plight, overcomes and beats to death a witch who has attacked him and ridden him over the fields by night. The witch revenges herself by having the student forced to read prayers for three successive nights over her dead body. For two nights he faces valiantly the evil spirits who crowd about his charmed circle; on the third, just before cock-crow, he dies from terror at the sight of the Viy, a subterranean goblin:

> Suddenly the church became quiet. The howling of wolves was heard in the distance, and soon heavy steps echoed through the church. Glancing sideways, Homa saw that they were leading forward a stout, squatty, bandy-legged being. He was all covered with black earth. His legs and arms, sprinkled with earth, resembled stout, sinewy roots. He stepped heavily and continually stumbled. His long eyelashes reached to the floor. With terror Homa remarked that his face was of iron. Supporting him under the arms, they led him up and placed him just opposite the place where Homa was standing.

"Lift up my eyelashes; I cannot see," said the Viy in a subterranean voice, and the whole throng rushed to raise his eyelashes.

"Do not look!" an inner voice whispered to the student. He could not refrain—he looked.

"That is he!" cried the Viy and levelled an iron finger at him. And all the spirits in the church rushed upon the student. Fainting, he crashed upon the floor, and there for very terror his spirit left him.

But *Taras Bulba* and "The Viy," however excellent in themselves, are subordinate incidents in Gogol's career. His genius was essentially realistic and satiric. It expressed itself best in a short story, "The Overcoat"; in a farce-comedy, *The Inspector*, and in *Dead Souls*.

Akaki Akakievich, the hero of "The Overcoat," is a copying-clerk of some fifty years, who by conscientious, unremitting toil barely earns enough to keep himself alive. His overcoat wears out and he suffers incredible privations in order to buy another:

> He thought and thought and decided that he would have to lessen his ordinary expenses, at least for a year; to give up drinking tea in the evening and not to light a candle in the evening, and if he had some work to do, to go into the landlady's room and work by her candle; when he walked the streets, to step over the stones and slabs as lightly and cautiously as he could, almost on tiptoe, in order not to wear out the soles of his boots too fast.... To tell the truth, at first it was somewhat hard for him to get accustomed to such privations, but later he got used to them and all went well—he even learned how to get along without eating anything at all in the evening. To make up for that, he nourished himself spiritually, cherishing in his thoughts the eternal idea of his future overcoat.

At last he procures the overcoat, only to have it stolen from him that same evening. He soon catches cold, takes to his bed, and dies, more from a broken heart than from the fever. Such is the slender plot of a tale that is rightly termed the germ of the Russian novel. Gogol loved to discourse on the invisible tears that lay hidden beneath the laughter of his writings. In this tale they are not hidden at all. Sympathy, compelling human sympathy, runs through this portrait of a man of no moment in the great world:

> The young clerks laughed and jested at Akaki Akakievich to the full measure of their office wit; they related in his presence various stories that they had made up about him; they told how his landlady, an old woman of seventy, used to beat him, and would ask when they were going to be married; they sprinkled bits of paper on his head and called it snow. But never a word would Akaki Akakievich reply to all this, behaving as though he were quite alone in the room. It did not even have any influence on his work; in the midst of all these annoyances he did not make a single mistake in his writing. Only when the joking became quite unbearable, when they joggled his elbow and kept him from attending to his business, he would say: "Let me alone! Why do you insult me?" And there was something strange in these words and in the voice with which they were uttered. In it could be heard something that moved one to pity, so that one young man, who had only recently entered the office, and who had permitted himself to follow the example of his comrades in making fun of Akaki Akakievich, suddenly stopped as though stricken with fear, and from that time on all seemed changed before his eyes and appeared to him in a different light. Some supernatural force repelled him from the comrades with whom he had become acquainted and whom he had taken for decent, cultivated fellows. And long after that, in his merriest moments, there would arise before him the figure of a short little clerk with a bald spot on his forehead, and with those piercing words of his: "Let me alone! Why do you insult me?" And in these piercing words there rang out other words: "I am thy brother." And the poor young man covered his face in his hands, and many times did he tremble in his later life when he saw how much inhumanity there is in man, how much fierce cruelty is hidden beneath refined, cultivated society manners, and, O God! even in many a man whom the world recognizes as noble and honorable.

Such tears it is difficult to discover beneath the ludicrous satire of *The Inspector*. A drunken scapegrace, detained at a provincial inn for want of cash to continue his travels, is mistaken by the mayor and other town functionaries for the inspector sent from St. Petersburg to examine their conduct of affairs. At first nonplussed at the situation in which he finds himself, he has just sense enough to enter into the part, "borrow" money from all whom he meets, and make his escape before the imposture forced upon him is discovered and before the real inspector appears. The comedy portrays a small world of petty graft and bribery. It has held the stage as part of the répertoire of almost every Russian theatre from Gogol's day to our own.

II.

The whole-souled laughter of the *The Inspector* (1836) made Gogol dear to the souls of Russian liberals. Here was a man, they argued, who dared to rebuke spiritual wickedness in high places. His fame as a reformer was increased by *Dead Souls* (1842). This book shows the same world of graft, ignorance, and stupidity, but of graft, ignorance, and stupidity that spread over all Russia.

In days before the emancipation of the serfs (1861) the wealth of a Russian country gentleman was estimated by the number of *souls* or serfs whom he possessed, and he was taxed so much per soul for his human property. A census of *souls* was made at irregular intervals. In 1842, nine years after the census of 1833, a serf-owner would still be paying taxes on certain serfs who had died since the official count was made. Furthermore, the Government, in order to encourage colonization, offered tracts of land in southern Russia to anyone who would settle there with enough serfs to till the soil. Here, then, are the elements of the bunco scheme that gives the title to Gogol's book. A swindler seeks to buy up *dead souls* by the hundred. With the papers representing his property he will go to the land office and claim a tract of land for colonization. Once possessed of this, he will mortgage serfs and land to the Government for hard cash.

In the portion of the book that he completed Gogol narrates the experiences of his swindler in one town and the surrounding country districts. There he meets different types of landowners: a silly, kindly dreamer, a loose-lived gambler, a wooden-headed old woman, a skinflint, and a miser. He purchases some souls and records the transaction at the proper office. He excites the curiosity and the gossip of the townspeople and drives off in search of further fields to exploit. The volume excels by its wonderfully concrete picture of the seamy side of Russian provincial life. Each satirical portrait is polished with perfect skill. Nothing great is exhibited, not even great villainy; murder, robbery, adultery, are not subjects that Gogol cares to treat. But no satire remains longer in the memory and grows less stale with repeated readings. Nozdrev and Sobakevich are types as familiar to the Russians as are Falstaff and Dogberry to ourselves. And a discerning reader finds tears rather than wrath beneath Gogol's ridicule. He has performed with perfect art his task of presenting a series of abhorrent types while preserving an attitude of human kindliness and charity. Even the base

Chichikov, the swindler, he hoped some time to bring to redemption.

Gogol was now the idol of all progressive Russians. We are in the time of Nicholas I, be it remembered, when the censorship was at its worst. No criticism of the Government, no open discussion of political, economic, or social problems, was possible in the press. Fiction and literary criticism were, however, a vehicle by means of which at least a point of view as to the state of Russia, and the measures needed to promote its progress, could be put forward. Hence the seriousness with which the Russian public scanned the works of its great artists for indications of their social theories. And, surely, no man had more bitingly shown the urgent need of reform than Gogol, with his vivid, sad, and true pictures of Russian corruption, ignorance, sloth, and coarse brutality. Suddenly Gogol issued, in 1846, a volume that effected a revolution in the public estimate of him, *Selections from my Correspondence with Friends*.

III.

As a matter of fact, when reflecting on public questions rather than picturing real conditions, Gogol had always been a conservative. He believed in personal honesty, decency, piety, and kindliness, morality of the sort that keeps families at peace. Of social philosophy he knew not a word; his ideal was the patriarchal old times, untouched by the money economics that were already creeping into Russia in his day. In serfdom, execrated by all Russians of the least progressive tendencies, he firmly believed as a divinely ordained institution. Into *Dead Souls* he wove lyric passages that breathe an unreflecting, boyish faith in the supreme excellence of Russia and its superiority to all other nations. Always a devoted member of the Russian Church, in his later years he became a religious fanatic. His new book breathes a devotional spirit and is aimed at the instruction of his fellow-countrymen. He adopts the tone of a prophet, proclaiming the virtues of autocracy and orthodoxy, and fulmining forth his scorn of western self-government and western education.

A state without an autocratic monarch is a mere automaton; it will do much, very much if it reaches the point that the United States have reached. And what are the United States? Carrion. Man in them is so withered that he is not worth a sucked egg-shell. A state without an autocratic monarch is like an orchestra without a leader: however good all the musicians may be, if there be not among them one who by the motion of his baton gives signals to the whole orchestra, the concert will amount to nothing.

Elsewhere he warns serf-owners from teaching their cattle to read, except for the purpose of perusing religious works. A village priest can give better instruction to hardworking peasants than "all the empty little books published for the common people by European philanthropists."

The *Selections* aroused the righteous wrath of the great critic Bielinski, the leader of Russian liberal thought, who addressed to Gogol a letter in which he hailed him as "preacher of the knout, apostle of ignorance, champion of obscurantism and insane bigotry, panegyrist of Tatar manners." Two or three sentences will show the tone of this famous document:

Russia sees its salvation not in mysticism, not in asceticism, not in pietism, but in the progress of civilization, culture, and humanity. It needs neither sermons nor prayers, but the awakening in the people of a feeling of human dignity, for so many ages lost in dirt and filth.... The most living, pressing national questions in Russia now are the abolishment of serfdom and of corporal punishment and the strictest possible execution of what laws we have ....

Remark one point. When a European, especially a Catholic, is seized by the religious spirit, he becomes a rebuker of unjust authority like the Hebrew prophets who rebuked the lawlessness of the mighty men of the earth. With us the contrary is the case. When a man (even a decent man) is seized by the disease known among psychiatrists as *religiosa mania*, he immediately begins to burn incense to the god on earth rather than to the God in heaven, and so exceeds all due measure that the very man who would like to reward him for his slavish zeal sees that he would thereby compromise himself in the eyes of society.

Bielinski has overstated the case. On the one hand, Gogol was not insincere or a renegade in his piety. On the other, though Bielinski's indictment still holds good against the powerful League of Russian People, Jew-baiters in the name of Christ and sanctimonious champions of despotism, it will not fit the Russian nation as a whole. Of this the most powerful witness is Leo Tolstoy.

Like Gogol, Tolstoy rejected the artistic works that had brought him fame, and in his later years assumed the tone of a prophet. Between the doctrines of the two men one can find now and then a chance resemblance: Gogol's advice to officials' wives that they economize on dress and so preserve their husbands from the temptation to take bribes, might seem a comic first hint of Tolstoy's doctrine of the simple life. But really a whole abyss separates the two men. Just as Gogol's "Overcoat" gave the hint for Dostoievski's *Poor Folk*, so Gogol's fanaticism was a more concrete, less mystical forerunner of Dostoievski's chauvinistic religiosity. In contrast to these two panegyrists of the established order, these slaves of a moribund tradition, Tolstoy is a free man and a rebel against government in the name of moral perfection for the individual. Whatever measure of truth there may be in his doctrine, in his character and temper he fulfils Bielinski's description of a religious leader in the free west.

IV.

Gogol died under a cloud, disliked by progressive Russians because of his *Selections*, and disliked by the authorities because of the negative tendencies of his artistic works. Turgenieff was punished for writing an article in which he termed him a great man. Bielinski pronounced *Dead Souls* a classic exclusively of Russia, and Korobka, one of the most recent critics of Gogol, chimes in with his opinion. But as time passes and Russian history and life become more familiar to outside nations, *Dead Souls* may after all prove to be a world classic. Rascality and meanness are independent of political barriers. A writer who can depict them as nothing but meanness and rascality, yet with a charity that does not refuse a handshake to the sneak and the rascal, with the light of humor that makes all men brothers, deserves a place among the great satirists and fun-makers of all ages.

Source: G. R. Noyes, "Gogol: A Precursor of Modern Realists in Russia," in *Nation*, Vol. 101, No. 2629, November 18, 1915, pp. 592–94.

Current Literature

In the following excerpt, an anonymous critic discusses Gogol's impact on modern literary realism on the occasion of the one-hundredth anniversary of his birth.

Gogol was the first Russian realistic novelist and dramatist. His position in Russian literature is unique. He is not only a great satirist—Russia has many satirists—but his works also display a lively sense of pure humor, which is an extremely rare quality in Russian authors. In his masterpieces, such as the novel *Dead Souls* and the comedy *Revizor*, he is unsparing in his exposition of Russian officialdom and Russian society. But in some of his smaller stories such "The Nose" and "The Diary of a Madman," he is a fun-maker pure and simple, with no more objective than our Mark Twain. His famous story, "The Cloak," however, combines all the characteristics of later Russian literature—grim humor, with a deep sense of pity for the lowly and oppressed, and a scrupulous realism. These are the qualities in Gogol which exerted the greatest influence on later Russian writers—Turgenev, Dostoyevsky, Goncharov and Grigorovich. "We are all descended from Gogol's cloak," said Turgenev.

"It is not humor," according to a critic in the *St. Petersburger Zeitung*, "that the Russian authors have learned from Gogol. Upon some of them, Turgenev, for example, this humorous element in Gogol exerted even an injurious influence. It is his strong realism that proved the best teacher of later Russian writers. For this is Gogol's peculiarity: he exaggerates and caricatures, yet his characters are real through and through, because the author has not merely tacked on certain funny features to them, after the fashion of some of our modern humorists, but the comic elements issue from their innermost being, from their profoundest depths. The whole of old Russia, not merely individual characters, live in Gogol's works. *Dead Souls* takes its title from the adventures of one who travels all over Russia in pursuance of a scheme of becoming an estate-holder by purchasing the dead serfs ('souls' of the dead), who are officially counted as living until the next census. This remarkable novel embraces types from every walk of Russian life. Gogol reproduced, so to speak, the collective physiognomy of Russian society. He is the first great master of mass and class psychology in his country. He achieved what Pushkin and Griboyedov only attempted. He exaggerates, but does not distort, so that his writings are never grotesque or uncanny. Gogol's laugh is quite unique. Sometimes it has all the bitterness and despair of Swift, sometimes it is as harmless and good-natured as Fritz Reuter's; but it cannot be compared to either the one or the other. Gogol comes nearest to the greatest idealist among the satirists, Cervantes, the author of *Don Quixote*. He himself calls Laughter the only honorable and noble personage among the numerous low, comic and trivial types of his creations."

The production of Gogol's comedy, the *Revizor*, in 1841 is a memorable event in the history of the Russian drama. The sensation it created in Russia was similar to the stir aroused in France in 1830 by Hugo's *Hernani*. It is so caustic, true, and clever a satire on the venality and stupidity of the Russian functionaries that it was only because of the favor it found with Nicholas I that it was finally permitted to be put on the boards under the Czar's own aegis. Turgenev calls Gogol's comedy "the most terrible satire ever produced on the stage." It created a storm of resentment in official circles, from which Gogol suffered exceedingly. The attacks upon him helped to accentuate the melancholy to which he was predisposed from early youth, and which drove him finally into a state of fanatical mysticism. He never recovered. In his change of mood he renounced his former liberal views and burnt as pernicious the manuscript of the last part of *Dead Souls*.

A rough draft of it found after his death was put into shape and published by his friends, but it is weak and ineffective, and clearly reflects his dwindling intellectual powers. Gogol died in Russia, after a pilgrimage to Jerusalem in 1848.

Source: "Gogol's Centenary Festival in Moscow," in *Current Literature*, Vol. 47, No. 2, August 1909, pp. 164–65.

Arthur Tilley

In the following essay, Tilley discusses how Gogol's supernatural elements and attention to detail shaped the writing of his successors.

At first sight the majority of [the tales collected in *Evenings at a Farm near Dikanka*] seem to be purely romantic in type, the supernatural element playing a large part in them. In "A Terrible Revenge," a Cossack story, it runs utterly riot. But in the others we find behind the naïve hocus-pocus of devils and witches a carefully drawn background of Little-Russian life; indeed the supernatural element itself is only an additional trait of national character. Very noticeable are the magnificent descriptions of scenery, true lyrical outbursts, which testify to the writer's passionate love for his native land. The most celebrated are that of the Dnieper in "A Terrible Revenge," that of the Ukraine night in "The May Night," and that of a hot summer's day at the beginning of "The Fair at Sorochintsi." One of the stories, "Ivan Feodorovitch Sponka and his Aunt," stands by itself. The supernatural element is entirely absent; it is a purely realistic picture of Russian country life, and though there is as little attempt at a plot as there is in its companions, the characters are drawn with great care and incision. Sponka is one of those negative, nondescript, unheroical heroes in whom Gogol delights, but the aunt is a notable woman, of marked energy and originality.

"Proprietors of the Olden Time" [from the collection entitled *Mirgorod*] is a masterpiece of its kind. It is a simple sketch of an old couple—a sort of Philemon and Baucis—who live in a country house far from the world, with no ideas beyond eating and drinking and loving one another, and showing hospitality to chance guests.

"The Story of how Ivan Nikiforovitch and Ivan Ivanovitch Quarrelled" is almost as admirable a picture of town life as the other is of country life. It has more movement than its companions, and there is some attempt at a story. Ivan Ivanovitch and Ivan Nikiforovitch were dear friends, till one day Ivan Nikiforovitch called Ivan Ivanovitch a gander, and they went to law, but there were many delays, and the case was never decided. This is all the story; but it is admirably told. The tone is more comic than in the country idyll, the irony is more pronounced, and, though it is perfectly good-natured, it has a spice of malice which reminds one of La Fontaine. The comic effect is often heightened by the grave, matter-of-fact air with which the most absurd things are said.

Most effective, too, is the adoption of an intimate button-holing tone which, by means of skillful little touches, helps to create the illusion that the narrator is telling something that he actually saw. Finally, it should be noticed that as well as the story last mentioned, it concludes in a somewhat melancholy key, and that the more laughable story is at bottom the sadder of the two; for the years roll on and the two old friends are never reconciled . . . .

[*Taras Bulba*] is Gogol's first attempt at something more ambitious than a short tale. The outcome of his grandfather's stories and of his own studies in Little-Russian history and folk-lore, it is a striking picture of the life of the Zaporozhian Cossacks in the sixteenth century. Readers of it have complained of its too-palpable imitations of Homer; but of Homer Gogol knew little or nothing, and the apparent Homeric reminiscences are due partly to the folk-songs which form the basis of much of his narrative, and

partly to the naïve freshness of his genius, with its natural capacity for vivid and soul-stirring narrative. Truly has the book been called the Little-Russian epic. Though in many respects it differs widely in manner from the works of our own great epic novelist, it recalls him in the vigor and color of the descriptions and the rapid movement of the narrative. Taras Bulba himself is cast in a heroic mould. His manners are barbarous, even to ferocity, but by his love for his country, his devotion to his comrades, and his heroic death, he compels our sympathy and admiration. A romantic love-story serves like a thread of gold to relieve the deep hues of the main texture.

[The volume *Arabesques* contains] amongst other miscellaneous pieces, four stories of no great merit. "Nevski Prospect" opens with a masterly description of the street from which it takes its name. "The Portrait" is a fantastic tale in the manner of Hoffmann, which promises well at the outset, but dies away to nothing. It is chiefly noticeable for the absence of the fun and kindly irony which had hitherto distinguished Gogol's humor. "The Memoirs of a Madman" has plenty of fun on the surface, but it is a gloomy tragedy at bottom, for it is the self diagnosis, in the shape of a diary, of the growing madness of a humble government clerk. There is something, no doubt, of personal recollection in the story, and, alas! something of prophecy. . . . [Two subsequent] short stories, "A Nose" and "The Calash," [are] both sharp satires in the guise of high comedy, the one of St. Petersburg, the other of provincial life. It is this vein of humor, this blending of laughter and irony, which appears fully developed in his well-known play, "The Inspector . . . ." The simplicity of the plot has provoked a smile from more than one countryman of Scribe and Sardou, but the plot is a mere peg on which to hang a scathing satire on the corruption of Russian official life. A rollicking farce on the surface, at the bottom it is bitter, serious truth.

Regard for humble or commonplace people, regard for apparently insignificant details—these are two of the leading features which the Russian realistic school has inherited from Gogol. The first feature is especially conspicuous in his story of "The Cloak."

"We all started from Gogol's story of 'The Cloak,'" said [Dostoïevsky]. . . . It is very true. That note of sublime pity is to be found alike in Turgéniev, and Dostoïevsky, and Tolstoy . . . .

The second feature, the careful observance of details, which at first sight appear trivial and insignificant, has been somewhat misunderstood both by imitators and critics. The thumb of the tailor in "The Cloak," which had "a deformed nail, thick and strong as a turtle's shell," has raised a contemptuous smile. But it should be noticed first that what Gogol asks his friend to send him are notes, not of every kind of detail, but of "incidents bearing upon human nature," and secondly, that he only uses for the purpose of his art those incidents and details that are really characteristic.... Another characteristic, not only of Gogol's, but more or less of the whole Russian school, is consciously affected by some would-be realists, as if it were an essential quality of realism. I mean the absence of a plot, or at best the barest pretence of a story as a framework upon which to construct studies of human character and society.... [However,] it is not the absence of plot which makes a story realistic, but the realism of a story, or rather the realistic handling of human character, which makes the absence of plot endurable. Further,... Gogol's execution is always lively, pregnant, and artistic.

Another conspicuous feature which Gogol has in common with his successors is his passionate love for his country. It is this very love which makes him so keenly alive to her faults. Like the Athenians and the French, the Russian writers combine with intense patriotism great frankness in their observations on national shortcomings. In Gogol this love of his country often...takes the form of magnificent descriptions of natural scenery.... .

Gogol was essentially a humorist; that is to say, he viewed the topsy-turvydom of life rather with sympathetic laughter than with savage indignation or scientific neutrality. But the quality of his humor underwent a considerable change during the ten years which separated "Dead Souls" from the "Evenings at the Farm near Dikanka." He began as an observer of the human comedy; he ended as a lasher of national vices. His earliest mood resembles the gentle malice of Jane Austen, his latest has the bitterness, though not the savageness, of Swift. Truly he said that after "The Inspector" he was no longer the same man. His self-imposed task of stemming the tide of national corruption proved, as well it might have done, too much for his strength. He had not that inexhaustible reserve of good humor, which enabled Molière, when he found the world crying out on him, to turn the laughter against himself and produce his masterpiece. He became himself not a misanthrope, for his pity for human nature saved him from that, but a melancholy recluse. And it is noteworthy that the more serious and bitter his criticisms of life became the more he laughed outwardly. "The Inspector" is on the surface a roaring farce; in "Dead Souls," if the laughter is not so loud, it is, so to speak, more out of place. Even Molière grows serious in the presence of a Tartuffe or a Don Juan, but Gogol in "Dead Souls" laughs at fools and villains alike.... It is, in fact, often a forced laughter, "Amidst laughter which is visible to the world I drop invisible tears," says Gogol, in words which are inscribed on his statue at Nyezhin; but in "Dead Souls" the tears are sometimes visible behind the laughter.

And if the laughter is somewhat forced the realism is also forced; it has become conscious and militant. Gogol contrasts in one place the happy lot of the idealist with the hard, ungrateful task of the realist, whose business it is to make a picture out of the sordid and contemptible elements of life. His realism does not consist in seeing only shadows. "Dead Souls" may be a true picture in the sense that it represents actual facts, but it cannot be a complete one. Even in Russia, under the Czar Nicholas, there must have been some public honesty, some domestic unselfishness. Thus, from the point of view of truth, and still more from that of art, the picture wants lights. Gogol, in short, has ceased to "see life steadily and see it whole." But, in spite of some elements of weakness, he is a great genius. The amount of his work, practically finished by the time he was one-and-thirty, is naturally not great; but take the best of it—take *"Taras Bulba,"* "The Inspector," "Dead Souls," and the best of the short stories, and you get a marked impression of strength and variety. There is truth, humor, imagination; he unites, in a rare degree, power with delicacy of observation; his touch is as light as it is firm.

Source: Arthur Tilley, "Gogol, the Father of Russian Realism," in *National Review*, Vol. 23, No. 137, July 1894, pp. 650–51.

SOURCES

Adams, Amy Singleton, "Nikolai Vasil'evich Gogol," in *Dictionary of Literary Biography*, Vol. 198, *Russian Literature in the Age of Pushkin and Gogol: Prose*, The Gale Group, 1999, pp. 137–66.

Bérard, Victor, "Czardom," in *The Russian Empire and Czarism*, David Nutt, 1905, pp. 214–99.

Bojanowska, Edyta M., Introduction to *Nikolai Gogol: Between Ukrainian and Russian Nationalism*, Harvard University Press, 2007, pp. 1–13.

Gi ževskij, Dmitrij, "Russian Literature in the Nineteenth Century," in *History of Nineteenth-Century Russian Literature*, Vol. 1, *The Romantic Period*, translated by Richard Noel Porter, edited by Serge A. Zenkovsky, Vanderbilt University Press, 1974, pp. 1–6.

DeMille, Alban Bertram, "Russia and the North," in *Literature in the Century*, W. & R. Chambers, 1903, pp. 480–521.

Fanger, Donald, "Beginnings: Fiction," in *The Creation of Nikolai Gogol*, Belknap Press, 1979, pp. 85–124.

Gioia, Dana, "Gabriel García Márquez and Magic Realism," in *Sniper Logic*, No. 6, 1998, reprint, 2009, http://www.danagioia.net/essays/emarquez.htm (accessed June 18, 2010).

Gogol, Nikolai, "The Nose," in *The Complete Tales of Nikolai Gogol*, Vol. 2, edited by Leonard J. Kent, Random House, 1964, reprint, University of Chicago Press, 1985, pp. 216–39.

Gottschalk, Fruma, Introduction to *The Nose*, Prideaux Press, 1972, pp. 1–10.

Hardy, James D., and Leonard Stanton, "Magical Realism in the Tales of Nikolai Gogol," in *Janus Head*, Vol. 2, No. 2, Fall 2002, http://www.janushead.org/5-2/hardystanton.pdf (accessed June 18, 2010).

Kent, Leonard J., ed., "Notes," in *The Complete Tales of Nikolai Gogol*, Vol. 2, Random House, 1964, reprint, University of Chicago Press, 1985, p. 222.

Lieven, Dominic, "The Russian Empire: Regions, Peoples, Geopolitics" and "Tsarist Empire: Power, Strategy, Decline," in *Empire: The Russian Empire and Its Rivals*, Yale University Press, 2000, pp. 201–30, 262–87.

Magarshack, David, "The Mature Artist," in *Gogol: A Life*, Faber and Faber, 1957, pp. 113–49.

Offord, Derek, "Nineteenth-Century Russian Thought and Literature," in *The Routledge Companion to Russian Literature*, edited by Neil Cornwell, Routledge, 2001, pp. 123–35.

"Peter I's Table of Ranks," in *Bucknell University: Russian History*, http://www.bucknell.edu/x20181.xml (accessed June 18, 2010).

"Russia," in *CIA: World Factbook*, https://www.cia.gov/library/publications/the-world-factbook/geos/rs.html (accessed June 18, 2010).

Thompson, John M., "Power, Backwardness, and Creativity, 1808–1855," in *Russia and the Soviet Union: A Historical Introduction from the Kievan State to the Present*, 6th ed., Westview Press, 2009, pp. 149–68.

"Timeline: Soviet Union," in *BBC News*, http://news.bbc.co.uk/2/hi/europe/1112551.stm (accessed June 17, 2010).

FURTHER READING

Frank, Joseph, *Between Religion and Rationality: Essays in Russian Literature and Culture*, Princeton University Press, 2010.

> Frank provides an examination of nineteenth- and twentieth-century Russian culture, thought, and history, analyzing the way the conflict between faith and reason pervades much of Russian literature and philosophy, as well as daily life.

Hart, Stephen M., and Wen-chin Ouyang, eds., *A Companion to Magical Realism*, Tamesis Books, 2010.

> The editors of this volume offer an in-depth study of magical realism as a movement born and bred in Germany that quickly spread to the rest of the world. The editors treat an array of writers including Gabriel García Marquez, Isabelle Allende, Salman Rushdie, W. B. Yeats, Nkagami Kenji, Ibrahim al-Kawani, and Ovid, many of whom have not previously been treated within the context of magical realism.

Nabokov, Vladimir, *Nikolai Gogol*, New Directions Books, 1944.

> Nabokov, one of Russia's greatest twentieth-century writers, offers a unique literary biography of Gogol. Nabokov discusses the centrality of the physical in Gogol's works and explores the way Gogol, like many Russian authors, focuses on the nose in particular in his writings. Nabokov begins the biography with Gogol's death and then proceeds to tell the story of his life.

Volkov, Solomon, *St. Petersburg: A Cultural History*, Free Press, 1995.

> Volkov investigates the cultural and historical development of the city of St. Petersburg. His assessment includes a section on nineteenth-century writers, including Gogol and Dostoyevsky, and their views on the city.

SUGGESTED SEARCH TERMS

Nikolai Gogol

Gogol AND The Nose

Gogol AND magical realism

Gogol AND Russian literature

Gogol AND censorship

Gogol AND tsarist Russia

Gogol AND Pushkin

Gogol AND Nicholas I

Gogol AND romanticism

On the Rainy River

TIM O'BRIEN

1990

"On the Rainy River" was first published as a short story in 1990, and later the same year as part of the longer work *The Things They Carried*. Critics and readers alike view author Tim O'Brien as one of the finest writers of the Vietnam era. O'Brien's novel *Going After Cacciato* won the National Book Award in 1979, and *The Things They Carried*, the collection containing "On the Rainy River," was a finalist for both the Pulitzer Prize and the National Book Critics Circle Award, and won the French Prix du Meilleur Livre Etranger (Award for the Best Foreign Book). Critic Robert R. Harris of the *New York Times* wrote on March 11, 1990 that this book was among the best fiction ever written about any war.

"On the Rainy River" at first seems simple; it is the story of a young man trying to make a good decision about whether he should obey the call of his country and go to war. On closer reading, it is a beautiful and complicated narrative of an older man recalling his youth, trying to forgive himself for what he views as a moral breakdown. O'Brien chose to name his fictional narrator Tim O'Brien, and gives the narrator biographical details that are the same as his own, leading readers to assume the narrator and the writer are one and the same. Such is not the case. However, the technique allows the story to comment on the nature of storytelling, on the way fiction can sometimes tell the truth, and on how memory reconstitutes and recomposes

Tim O'Brien (AP Images)

the events of the past. "On the Rainy River" can be read as a coming-of-age story, a story with historical significance, and a study of the nature of traumatic stress.

AUTHOR BIOGRAPHY

O'Brien was born on October 1, 1946, in Austin, Minnesota. The family moved to Worthington, Minnesota, in 1956. O'Brien's father was a veteran of World War II and sold insurance. His mother, also a veteran, was an elementary school teacher. O'Brien exhibited an early interest in magic, a motif that appears in a number of his books.

O'Brien graduated from Macalester College in St. Paul, Minnesota, in 1968. He served as student body president and achieved Phi Beta Kappa status while there, and he had plans to attend Harvard University for graduate study in the fall of the same year. However, these plans were dashed when he received his draft notice. Although he had been mildly opposed to the war, he saw no way to avoid the draft. Consequently, August 1968 saw him traveling not to Cambridge, Massachusetts, to begin graduate work, but to boot camp. From 1969 to 1970, he served as a foot soldier in the 46th Infantry in the Quang Ngai province of Vietnam.

His year in Vietnam changed his life. After returning to the United States, he began his delayed graduate studies at Harvard, majoring in political science. At the same time, he began his writing career, publishing articles in a variety of newspapers and magazines. In 1973, he published his first book, *If I Die in a Combat Zone, Box Me Up and Ship Me Home*. His first novel, *Northern Lights*, appeared two years later. With his growing interest and success in writing, he gave up working on his doctoral dissertation, and devoted himself to writing full time.

At the same time, he began writing the short stories that eventually became a part of his 1978 novel, *Going After Cacciato*. Two of these stories won O. Henry Memorial Awards, and in 1979, *Going After Cacciato* won the prestigious National Book Award.

After publishing his 1985 novel, *The Nuclear Age*, O'Brien concentrated on short fiction for the next four years. These stories were exquisite renderings of his time in Vietnam and include some of his very best short fiction. "How to Tell a True War Story" appeared in *Esquire* in 1987. O'Brien won the National Magazine Award in Fiction for his 1989 short story "The Things They Carried." "On the Rainy River" appeared in the January 1990 issue of *Playboy*. O'Brien then wrote additional stories as well as some connecting passages, and with these created the book *The Things They Carried* in 1990.

Critics praised the volume, although they were unsure how to classify it. While it appeared to be a collection of short stories, the same characters appeared throughout, and references to events reverberate throughout the entire book.

In addition, the work seemed highly autobiographical; yet O'Brien insisted it was a work of fiction. *The Things They Carried* received many impressive reviews and awards, including the *Chicago Tribune*'s Heartland Prize, the Melcher Award, and the French Prix du Meilleur Livre Etranger (award for the best foreign book). In addition, the book was a finalist for both the Pulitzer Prize and the National Book Critics Circle Award.

In 1994, O'Brien continued the theme of the Vietnam War in his darkly beautiful book *In the Lake of the Woods*, a novel set in northern Minnesota at a fish camp much like the one in "On the Rainy River." O'Brien has published numerous stories and articles in the years since, as well as the 1998 novel *Tomcat in Love* and the 2002 novel *July, July*. In 1999, O'Brien began teaching creative writing at Texas State University in San Marcos, Texas. Houghton Mifflin Harcourt publishers brought out the twentieth anniversary edition of *The Things They Carried*, including "On the Rainy River," in 2010.

MEDIA ADAPTATIONS

- "On the Rainy River" is included in the unabridged audiobook *The Things They Carried*, produced in 2005 by Recorded Books and narrated by Tom Stechschulte.
- The same recording of "On the Rainy River" from *The Things They Carried* is also available on CD in a six-disc set produced by Recorded Books in 2003.
- The American Palace Theatre adapted for stage five stories, including "On the Rainy River," from *The Things They Carried* in 2004 as part of their Literature to Life project. The play premiered at Playhouse Square in Cleveland, Ohio.

PLOT SUMMARY

"On the Rainy River" appears in the book *The Things They Carried* immediately after a very short story called "Spin." This short story closes with a reflection on the purpose of stories; O'Brien writes, "Stories are for those late hours in the night when you can't remember how you got from where you were to where you are. Stories are for eternity, when memory is erased, when there is nothing to remember except the story."

These words set up "On the Rainy River." The narrator, Tim O'Brien (not to be confused with the author Tim O'Brien), tells the reader that he is about to relate a story about something that happened twenty years earlier that he has never told anyone. He has been too embarrassed to share the story. He calls the story an "act of remembrance" and he contemplates the nature of courage.

The story begins in the present day, with a much older Tim O'Brien relating an event from the year when he was twenty-one. The entire story is told in flashback, so there are frequent references to not only the events of the story, but also to the narrator's life since the time of the event he relates.

O'Brien (the narrator) tells the reader that in June 1968, just after graduating from college, he received a draft notice. A draft notice informs the young man that he must report for duty in the army at a specified time and location or risk arrest and imprisonment. During the American involvement in the Vietnam War (from approximately 1963 to 1975), many American young people were drafted into the armed services to fight in Vietnam.

O'Brien relates that he believed the war was wrong, and that the facts of the war "were shrouded in uncertainty. " Many of the references Tim makes in this section might seem confusing to younger readers because they relate to people, events, and organizations from the 1960s. The USS *Maddox*, for example, was a ship involved in the Gulf of Tonkin incident, a brief naval battle that led to the active involvement of the United States in the Vietnam War in 1964. O'Brien also mentions Ho Chi Minh, the leader of North Vietnam; the Geneva Accords, an international set of agreements that divided Vietnam into a northern zone and a southern zone; SEATO, the Southeast Asia Treaty Organization; and the cold war, an unarmed conflict between the United States and the Soviet Union, lasting from the end of World War II until the breakup of the Soviet Union in 1991.

O'Brien reports that he was first in a rage about the draft notice and then paralyzed. He was in denial about the fact that soon he would have to report for active duty, sure that there must have been a mistake. When his father asked him what he was going to do, he replied, "Nothing. Wait."

O'Brien next explains that he spent the summer of 1968 working at a meat packing plant, removing blood clots from the necks of dead pigs with a high-power water spray. His description is graphic; the stench and constant spray of bloody water seems to permeate the whole scene. O'Brien relates that in the midst of this, he began to think about going to Canada to evade the draft. On the one hand, his conscience told him he should not fight in a war he did not believe in; on the other, he was afraid of what his parents and the people of Worthington would think about him if he ran away.

O'Brien reveals that he has talked about this event in his life before, but that it is not until he is writing this story now that he can tell the truth about what happened in 1968. One day while at the meat packing plant, Tim broke down. He went home, packed some clothes, left a short note for his parents, and began to drive north toward the Canadian border.

He finally arrived at the Rainy River, the boundary between Minnesota and Canada. He stopped at the Tip Top Lodge, and he met Elroy Berdahl, an eighty-one-year-old man who owned the camp. O'Brien states that he is now sure that Elroy knew immediately that Tim was a kid in trouble.

Tim stayed at the Tip Top Lodge for several days, helping Elroy take care of the property and having dinner with him. O'Brien writes that while he was at Elroy's he suffered from a conflict of conscience:

> My conscience told me to run, but some irrational and powerful force was resisting, like a weight pushing me toward the war. What it came down to, stupidly, was a sense of shame. Hot, stupid shame.

At one point, O'Brien relates, Elroy decided to settle up their accounts. He first calculated what Tim owed him for staying at the cottage and eating with him. And then, as if he had at first forgotten, he remembered the work Tim had done for him and tried to give Tim wages.

Tim refused, but later found the money tacked to his cottage door with a note that said, "EMERGENCY FUND."

O'Brien next looks back and describes himself as he must have appeared. He sees himself sitting in the cottage at the Tip Top Lodge, twenty years earlier, young and fit, writing letters to his parents, trying to muster the courage to go to Canada.

O'Brien then speaks of his last day with Elroy, when the old man took him fishing on the Rainy River. Elroy steers the boat directly across the river, nearly to the far shore in Canada. At this point, O'Brien shifts into second person, asking the reader to feel what it must have been like to have been twenty-one years old, trying to make this difficult decision, trying to imagine what life as an exile would be like.

Rather than get out of the boat, however, and swim to shore, all Tim could do was cry. He thought of all of his family and friends, what he would leave behind him, and what people would think of him. The thought of this overwhelmed and embarrassed him to such an extent, he knew that he could never run away.

O'Brien says that he does not remember saying good-bye to Elroy. He concludes his story by remembering briefly his life from the moment he drove away from Elroy's: the drive, the journey to Vietnam, the journey home again. "I survived," O'Brien writes, "but it's not a happy ending. I was a coward. I went to the war."

CHARACTERS

Elroy Berdahl

Elroy Berdahl is an eighty-one-year-old man who owns and operates the Tip Top Lodge, a northern Minnesota fishing camp where Tim lands after fleeing the meat packing plant and his worries about the draft. He is a skinny old man, balding, dressed in a flannel shirt and brown work pants. O'Brien portrays him as very smart and sharp:

> His eyes had the bluish gray color of a razor blade, the same polished shine, and as he peered up at me I felt a strange sharpness, almost painful, a cutting sensation, as if his gaze were somehow slicing me open.

Indeed, throughout the story, O'Brien uses images of sharpness to describe Elroy, returning to those "razor eyes." And yet, despite the sharpness, he treats Tim with extraordinary kindness. At the same time, he never pries or asks questions of Tim, never tries to find out why this twenty-one-year-old boy has come to this lodge near the Canadian border. O'Brien writes, "What I remember more than anything is the man's willful, almost ferocious silence. In all that time together, all those hours, he never asked the obvious questions." Instead, Elroy finds work for Tim to do around the lodge to keep him occupied during the day. In the evenings, Elroy makes dinner for Tim, after which the two play games or listen to music.

O'Brien believes that although Elroy never asks him why he is there, he already knows. Elroy is an educated, intelligent man, despite living in such isolation. He understands that many young men are leaving the United States to escape the draft and going to war in Vietnam. Although he is quiet, his ability to handle language is remarkable: "On those occasions when speech was necessary he had a way of compressing large thoughts into small, cryptic packets of language."

Ultimately, Elroy takes Tim across the Rainy River, giving him the opportunity to jump out of the boat and reach Canada. He has even given Tim money, on the pretense that he is paying the boy for his work. Although he has never spoken of Tim's difficult choice nor given him advice, he opens the door for Tim to make a decision on his own. Moreover, Elroy is completely nonjudgmental; although he provides the means through which Tim can evade the draft, he never reveals his thoughts about this act. Rather, he supports Tim in whatever he decides, without comment.

Elroy disappears from the story the next day, his role in the story finished. Tim never sees him again, yet he recalls with great detail the man who affected him so deeply.

Elroy is essential to "On the Rainy River." He is the mentor Tim needs and wants, without saying very much at all. In addition, Elroy helps Tim make the transition from being a boy to a man, simply by making it possible for him to reach a decision.

Tim O'Brien

The character of Tim O'Brien can be confusing for some readers, simply because the author of "On the Rainy River" is also named Tim

O'Brien. The author and the character share a number of biographical details: both the author and the character were raised in Worthington, Minnesota, they both went to Macalester College, they both received their draft notices in the summer of 1968. However, the writer fictionalizes his own life experience to address larger thematic concerns. That is, he adjusts, changes, and makes up events in the story to create something that is at once fiction, but also points to truth. Further, the character Tim O'Brien is pivotal in all of the stories of the larger collection, *The Things They Carried*.

Another difficulty presented by the character Tim is that there are really two Tims in the story: a forty-one-year-old man, who, twenty years after the events of the story, decides to write about his time on the Rainy River, and the younger Tim, who must choose to report for active military duty or cross the river to Canada. The setting of the story, then, shifts from the present day, when the older Tim decides to tell the reader something he has not shared before, to the past, when the twenty-one-year-old Tim must face the largest decision of his life.

The story emerges through the lens of an older, wiser man: Tim at forty-one has not only experienced the events of the Rainy River, he has also been to Vietnam and back, an experience that has indelibly changed his life. The older Tim is someone who possesses a sharp memory for detail and is able to recall with great clarity the thoughts and motivation of the younger Tim. Like the author of the story, the older Tim is a writer. There are hints throughout the story (and indeed, throughout all of the stories of *The Things They Carried*) that the Vietnam experience haunts him. He suffers from nightmares and from a guilty conscience, for things he did and for things he did not do. His decision to finally tell the story of how he ended up going to Vietnam was borne out of what sounds like post-traumatic stress: "[By] putting the facts down on paper, I'm hoping to relieve at least some of the pressure on my dreams."

The older Tim has sympathy for his younger self. He sees himself as a young kid, caught in an impossible, desperate situation: should he abandon his conscience and go to war in order to please the people he loves, or should he honor his conscience, thereby betraying his family and country? Because he writes in the aftermath of the war, at a time when some people have come to question the morality of the Vietnam War, the older Tim is able to situate the story of his experience on the Rainy River as a moral dilemma.

The younger Tim is less articulate than his older self. He is unable to express to his parents his feelings about the war or about his draft notice. He has few friends and no one to talk to in Worthington. Tim is a young man who has succeeded in school, been a leader at college, and has a bright future in front of him. But emotionally, he is shut down and lost. He moves through his initial disbelief that he will be drafted, to rage at what he sees as an injustice, to depression and an inability to act or make plans.

Young Tim is faced with questions about courage and shame. He is frightened by the prospect of war, and even more frightened by the thought of bringing shame on his family and friends. All of these emotions remain bottled up inside him. Even when he meets Elroy, he is unable to speak to him about why he is in northern Minnesota. Eventually, he tells Elroy about working in the slaughter house, at some length, although he still is unable to make the connection between the blood, smell, and horror and his fear of going to war. Tellingly, this is not a direct connection the older Tim ever makes, either, although this is a link that clearly the author of the story wants readers to make.

By the end of the story, the young Tim is unable to run away from what he sees as his obligation to his family and country. He weeps over his inability to make what he thinks is the moral choice. And finally, the older Tim passes harsh judgment on his younger self: "I was a coward. I went to the war."

Tim O'Brien's Father

The narrator's father is mentioned in the story during the time when Tim debates what to do about the draft notice.

Tim O'Brien's Mother

Tim's mother is not mentioned directly, but Tim worries about how dodging the draft will affect her and his father.

THEMES

Courage and Cowardice

Many war stories take as their theme the difference between courage and cowardice. The Civil War novella *The Red Badge of Courage* by Stephen Crane is one of the most famous stories to do so. In most cases, the protagonists of these stories work their way from initial cowardice to eventual courage. The journey from cowardice to courage is a kind of coming-of-age.

O'Brien, on the other hand, in "On the Rainy River" turns the notion of courage upside down. The protagonist, Tim, tells the story of a time some twenty years earlier when he received his draft notice to fight in the Vietnam War. The notice forced the young Tim to confront his ideas about courage. He says that he believed:

> If the stakes ever became high enough—if the evil were evil enough, if the good were good enough—I would simply tap a secret reservoir of courage that I had been accumulating inside me over the years.

The Vietnam War, however, did not fit these requirements. It was a murky war, and it was hard to know the difference between good and evil in such a war.

As the summer waned, however, and the day that he would have to leave for boot camp approached, Tim grew deeply afraid: "I sometimes felt the fear spreading inside me like weeds," the older Tim recalls. He began to think about running away to Canada, to escape the draft and the war. At the same time, he developed another fear: what would his family members and community friends think of him if he were to go to Canada? His fear of exile and of losing everything he had known up until that point grew at the same rate as did his fear of losing his life in war.

Ultimately, the young Tim chose not to go to Canada, and instead he went to Vietnam. While the conventional war story would see this as growth and as a turning away from cowardice toward courage, the older Tim sees it differently. "I would go to the war—I would kill and maybe die—because I was embarrassed not to." In the end, Tim believes that he exhibited cowardice, not courage, in going to Vietnam.

TOPICS FOR FURTHER STUDY

- Read O'Brien's memoir *If I Die in a Combat Zone, Box Me Up and Ship Me Home.* Write a character analysis of the author O'Brien that emerges in the memoir, and compare that character with the main character in "On the Rainy River." In what ways does O'Brien change and mold his fictional Tim O'Brien to serve the purposes of the story?

- Research the history of the military draft in the United States with three of your classmates, using books, journals, and the Internet. Imagine that it is 1968. Organize a debate with two of your group taking the affirmative stance and two the negative on the topic of a compulsory draft, from the perspective of students in 1968. Create a bookmarking site that records the Internet sources that would be valuable for researching this topic in the future.

- Read *The Sorrow of War* by Vietnamese author Bao Ninh, which was first published in 1991 and translated into English in 1993. What similarities do you find between this novel and the short story "On the Rainy River" in terms of images, metaphors, chronological sequencing, and the thematic treatment of memory? Write a book review of the novel that addresses these literary techniques. Post your review on your Web site and invite students to comment.

- Read the young-adult collection of short stories *Walking the Rez Road* (1993) by Jim Northrup. Set in Minnesota, the stories feature a Native American Vietnam War veteran, Luke Warmwater. These stories are often funny, but they point to darker truths. Write a short story in which the character of Luke Warmwater meets the older Tim O'Brien from "On the Rainy River."

- With the other members of your class, create a Web site about the short story "On the Rainy River." Include a biography of O'Brien, definitions of any unusual terms, a detailed explanation of historic references in the story, maps of Minnesota showing the Rainy River, pictures, videos, and reviews of the story. Use a program such as wikispaces.com to coordinate your class's efforts.

- Over 100,000 Americans left the United States rather than submit to being drafted. Those who opposed the war believed these young men were following their consciences; other Americans called them draft dodgers. Write a short story that follows the life of a young man who chose to leave the country because he was opposed to the war. If you prefer nonfiction, gather interviews and statements from those who dodged the draft. Create a Web page that compiles their recollections.

Moral Confusion

"On the Rainy River" is, at heart, a story of moral confusion. The main character, Tim, an older man relating the events of some twenty years earlier, tells the tale because he still is trying to come to terms with the decision he made as a twenty-one-year-old draftee to go to war rather than go to Canada. The moral confusion that gripped the young man two decades earlier continues to hound the older man, coming to him in nightmares.

Some people see the Vietnam War as a moral morass, a war that had neither purpose nor good end. O'Brien believed this to be the case before he went to the war; his time in Vietnam made him even less able to find any moral purpose in the conflict. Consequently, in this story, he writes about the moral dilemma faced by a younger, fictionalized version of himself.

The dilemma is simply this: if the young Tim chose to go to war, he would be forced to kill people for a cause he did not believe in. He

Rain on the river *(dutourdumonde | Shutterstock.com)*

viewed this as morally wrong. If, on the other hand, he chose not to go to war, but to go to Canada, he faced another moral wrong, that of betraying his country. At some level, he understood that he had a moral obligation to do what was expected of him. The problem, of course, was that he could not have it both ways. He could not live up to his obligations, nor please his family and community, if he were to go to Canada. At the same time, because of what the older Tim implies, the reader knows that this decision forced him into committing acts he considered immoral while in Vietnam.

"On the Rainy River" forces the reader to consider what can be done in the face of such an insolvable dilemma. Indeed, the narrator asks the reader to confront this problem directly:

> I want you to feel it.... You're twenty-one years old, you're scared.... What would you do? Would you jump?... Would you think about your family and your childhood and your dreams and all you're leaving behind?"

The only answer anyone can give is from his or her own heart. There is no moral choice, at least not in the world O'Brien depicts in "On the Rainy River."

STYLE

Narrator

The narrator of a story is the character who tells the story. In the case of "On the Rainy River," the narrator is an older man, telling of something that happened to him twenty years earlier, when he was drafted into the army.

One of the most interesting construction details of "On the Rainy River" is O'Brien's choice to name the narrator Tim O'Brien. Moreover, he gives his fictional narrator biographical details that coincide with his own: the narrator is from Worthington, Minnesota; he graduates from Macalester College in Minnesota; he has a scholarship to attend Harvard for graduate work; and, most importantly, he receives a draft notice in the summer of 1968. In fact, anyone who reads O'Brien's nonfiction memoir of his time in Vietnam, *If I Die in A Combat Zone,*

Box Me Up and Ship Me Home, will find even more similarities between O'Brien and his eponymous narrator.

For these reasons, when the narrator talks about his experience writing the story, it is easy for the reader to identify the narrator's experiences as identical to those of the author O'Brien. Such a reading, however, would be faulty. There are also many differences between the events of the story and O'Brien's life. Elroy, for example, is a completely fictional character, according to interviews with O'Brien. O'Brien never went to the Rainy River to try to escape to Canada.

Throughout the story, and the other stories of the collection, O'Brien plays with notions of truth and fiction. He seems to suggest that while all of the thoughts and feelings of the young Tim are true, they may never have happened. Likewise, his older narrator's analysis of his younger self may be true, but since the analysis is based on a fictional character, it may not be factual for the author.

This distinction troubles many readers who want the story to be either fact or fiction. However, just as the narrator tells the reader that the war in Vietnam is an ambiguous, murky proposition, he seems to be saying the same thing about fact and fiction: the two can be difficult to separate.

Imagery

One of the most striking features of "On the Rainy River" is the sharp, graphic, and gut-wrenching sensory imagery that O'Brien uses. It draws the reader in, enlisting all of the reader's senses. For example, his narrator's description of working in the meat packing plant is horrific: "After slaughter, the hogs were decapitated, split down the length of the belly, pried open, eviscerated, and strung up by the hind hocks on a high conveyer belt." The scene becomes even bloodier, and includes not only visual and tactile images but also olfactory ones:

> At night I'd go home smelling of pig.... Even after a hot bath, scrubbing hard, the stink was always there—like old bacon, or sausage, a dense greasy pig-stink that soaked deep into my skin and hair.

Likewise, his description of the Rainy River in October includes the smell of leaves and cleanness. When Elroy Berdahl opens the door of the Tip Top Lodge, the narrator uses imagery of a razor to describe him physically. This allows him to comment both on the man's physical appearance as well as on his mental acuity.

Like a poet, O'Brien does not waste words in simple description; rather, through the use of sensory imagery he manages to set the scene, build a mood, incorporate symbols, and make the story real for the reader.

HISTORICAL CONTEXT

The Vietnam War

"On the Rainy River" is set in 1968 at the height of the Vietnam War. Although the action of the story takes place entirely in northern Minnesota, the Vietnam War permeates the work. Indeed, O'Brien's experience as a foot soldier during the war deeply marks both his writing and his life.

The history of the Vietnam War has its roots in the French colonial period before World War II. In the aftermath of the war, a nationalist group called the Viet Minh, led by the communist leader Ho Chi Minh, won Vietnam's independence from France, according to Marilyn B. Young in her book *The Vietnam Wars 1945–1990*. After winning independence from the French in 1954, Vietnam was temporarily partitioned by the terms of the Geneva Conference into two nations, North Vietnam, which was supported by the communist bloc nations, and South Vietnam, a republic, until free elections could be held to reunify the nation. The United States became interested in the Vietnam as part of a larger effort to suppress communism throughout Asia. After failed elections, North Vietnam attempted to take over South Vietnam, aided by the Viet Cong, also known as the National Liberation Front (NLF), a guerrilla force of South Vietnamese communists. The United States involvement was initially limited to military advisors throughout the 1950s; however, by the 1960s, an increasing number of military personnel were being sent to Vietnam to help shore up the South Vietnamese government of Ngo Dinh Diem against attack from the communist North Vietnam and from the Viet Cong. Diem was not a popular leader, however, and Vietnamese Buddhists protested against his regime. Young reports that in 1963, Buddhist monks even began setting themselves on fire in protest to the Diem regime. The American presence grew rapidly after the 1963 assassination of Diem.

COMPARE & CONTRAST

- **1960s:** The United States becomes more deeply involved in the Vietnam War, with increasing numbers of troops being sent to Vietnam. In 1968 alone, over 500,000 men are serving there.

  1990: The United States becomes involved in the first Gulf War in 1990. About 500,000 American troops fight in Operation Desert Storm.

  Today: In 2010, about 90,000 military men and women are in Iraq. Some 60,000 troops are in Afghanistan.

- **1960s:** The United States is involved in a cold war with the Soviet Union in a fight against communism.

  1990: The Soviet Union begins to crumble, finally dissolving in 1991. The U.S. remains a superpower.

  Today: American military attention is focused on the Persian Gulf and Afghanistan in an action that begins with the terrorist attacks on the United States in 2001.

- **1960s:** A large scale bombing campaign is secretly waged by the United States inside Cambodian borders to prevent the passage of supplies and troops from North Vietnam to the south.

  1990: Vietnam invades Cambodia in 1978 and enters into a long and bloody war with its neighbor. Vietnamese troops occupy Cambodia until September 1989. A preliminary peace is reached in 1990, with a com-

  prehensive peace settlement reached at the Paris Conference in 1991.

  Today: Vietnam is no longer at war with either Cambodia or the United States, and diplomatic and economic relations have been reestablished. Many American Vietnam veterans and other American tourists visit Southeast Asia.

- **1960s:** Authors Tim O'Brien, Bruce Weigl, and Larry Heinemann, among many others, serve in the Vietnam War.

  1990: O'Brien, Weigl, and Heinemann, among other writers, publish creative work about their tours of duty in Vietnam.

  Today: Writing about the Vietnam War remains popular, O'Brien's *The Things They Carried*, including his story "On the Rainy River," is reissued in a twentieth anniversary edition.

- **1960s:** The United States has a system of selective service that drafts young men for duty in the armed services.

  1990: In 1973, the draft was abandoned, and the United States military becomes an all-volunteer force. In the 1990s, more than a half million volunteer troops serve in the first Gulf War.

  Today: The United States has an all-volunteer army, although young men are required to register with the Selective Service System on their eighteenth birthday.

By 1968, the year O'Brien was drafted to serve in the war, American troop strength was at its highest and the war was becoming increasingly unpopular at home in the United States. Young notes that a Gallup poll taken about this time showed that more people thought the war was wrong than supported it. The year opened with the North Vietnamese regular army and the NLF launching their biggest offensive to date, known as the Tet Offensive. (The Tet is the Vietnamese lunar New Year.) They were trying to force a collapse of the South Vietnamese government and bring to an end the stalemate in the war. The fighting took place in cities such as Hue and in isolated outposts such as Khe Sanh. There was even fighting in Saigon, the capital of South Vietnam.

The NLF suffered massive losses in the offensive, and most analysts view the Tet as a decisive American military victory. However, the American public, sickened by the growing lists of deaths and casualties and the brutality of the war depicted on television each night, became increasingly convinced that this was not a war Americans should be fighting. Civil unrest within the United States grew, leading to violence at the 1968 Democratic Convention in Chicago and across college campuses in all parts of the country. When the army leadership asked for an additional 206,000 troops, according to Young, President Lyndon B. Johnson refused, signaling a limit to the United States involvement.

When news of the March 1968 massacre of civilians at My Lai by an American platoon began to leak out about a year after the event, Americans were horrified. The conduct of American troops and the overall morality of the war were called into question. The moral dilemma O'Brien poignantly depicts in "On the Rainy River" was one many young men faced. O'Brien himself served in and around the villages surrounding My Lai during his tour of duty, just as the news of the massacre made headlines at home.

The year 1968 marked a turning point in the war. American leadership knew that the war was lost and began making plans for the eventual withdrawal of troops, although there were many more bloody battles and massive bombings of North Vietnam and neighboring Cambodia, as well as napalm deforestation in South Vietnam, before the last troops left in 1975. By the time the war was over, more than 59,000 Americans had died. While this was a terrible loss for the American people, it paled in comparison to the over three million Vietnamese killed, including both military and civilian casualties.

The Draft

Military conscription, or a draft, has been used in the United States since the Civil War, when both the Confederacy and the Union Armies instituted drafts to fill their ranks. During World War I and World War II, many young men in the United States were drafted into military service to fight on behalf of their country in the wars. The Selective Service System, the governmental agency that administered the draft, came into existence as it now exists in 1940.

He spent much time on the dock, fishing and thinking. *(Robert Ranson / Shutterstock.com)*

According to the Selective Service, "From 1948 until 1973, during both peacetime and periods of conflict, men were drafted to fill vacancies in the armed forces which could not be filled through voluntary means." Once drafted, a man was required to serve two years in service to his country.

During the Vietnam era, the most men drafted into the service was 382,010 in 1966, over 150,000 more men than had been drafted in the previous year. This was followed by 228,263 in 1967, and 296,406 in 1968, O'Brien's induction year, according to Selective Service records.

The draft was ended in 1973, and men were no longer required to register with the Selective Service System beginning in 1975. However, in 1980, the registration requirement was reinstated in case a draft was needed in the event of a serious crisis.

Throughout the 1960s, the draft was very unpopular, and a common sight during antiwar demonstrations was young men publicly burning their registration cards and draft notices. This was the context of O'Brien's story; his young protagonist was well aware that many of his peers were refusing service by choosing to go to Canada or opting to serve as conscientious objectors. At the same time, although it was not uncommon for some young men to refuse service in what they viewed as an immoral war, the vast majority of those called up reported for duty, just as O'Brien did, and made the journey to Vietnam.

CRITICAL OVERVIEW

When O'Brien won the National Book Award in 1979 for *Going After Cacciato*, readers and critics alike recognized the writer's talent. Eleven years later, with the publication of *The Things They Carried*, the collection that includes "On the Rainy River," O'Brien was universally recognized as one of the best writers of the Vietnam experience. He received nominations for such important awards as the Pulitzer Prize and the National Book Critics Circle Award and won the French Prize for Best Foreign Novel.

Robert R. Harris, for example, writing in the *New York Times Book Review* in 1990, calls the book "essential fiction." Harris argues that O'Brien's sensitive and insightful examination of courage, cowardice, imagination, and memory "places *The Things They Carried* high up on the list of best fiction about any war."

Likewise, Richard Eder wrote a very favorable review of *The Things They Carried* in the *Los Angeles Times Book Review* in 1990, stating:

[The] best of these stories—and none is written with less than the sharp edge of a honed vision—are memory as prophecy. They tell us not where we were but where we are; and perhaps where we will be.

Wade Fox, in *Whole Earth Review*, calls the book "one of the finest collections of stories I've read." Fox rightly identifies the primary themes of the book: "*The Things They Carried* is about guilt and responsibility, about courage and cowardice and the difficulty, sometimes, in distinguishing between them."

In addition to reviews, the book and individual stories such as "On the Rainy River" have been the subject of intense critical interest. Mark Taylor, in the *Centennial Review*, draws comparisons between Tim O'Brien's experiences with that of his character Tim O'Brien in stories such as "On the Rainy River": "*The Things They Carried* contains dazzling metafictional pyrotechnics... it offers, also, a moving and distinguished account of men fighting a war, which... bears some discernible relationship to Tim O'Brien's own war."

Many critics are interested in the metafictional quality of O'Brien's work. Metafiction is a term used for fiction that takes as its subject fiction itself. When O'Brien talks about his story as an "act of remembrance," or the role stories play in reconstituting a life, or the conflicting pressures of truth and fiction, he is engaging in metafictional techniques. Catherine Calloway's seminal article "'How to Tell a True War Story': Metafiction in *The Things They Carried*" was one of the first to address this quality in the novel. She writes, "O'Brien draws the reader into the text, calling the reader's attention to the process of invention and challenging him to determine which, if any, of the stories are true."

Kali Tal, in her book *Worlds of Hurt: Reading the Literatures of Trauma*, examines O'Brien's work through the lens of trauma theory, a theory that examines the effect trauma has on an individual writer or character.

Finally, Chris Daley, in the chapter "The 'Atrocious Privilege': Bearing Witness to War and Atrocity in O'Brien, Levi, and Remarque," argues that stories allow O'Brien to "explore different dimensions of his actual experience.":

The story "On the Rainy River," for example, achieves a truth about why both the quasi-fictional Tim O'Brien and the real Tim O'Brien went to war... that the memoir's version of this incident could not.

CRITICISM

Diane Andrews Henningfeld
Henningfeld holds the rank of professor emerita at Adrian College and publishes widely on literary topics. In the following essay, she uses trauma theory to analyze "On the Rainy River."

Mark A. Heberle, in his book *A Trauma Artist: Tim O'Brien and the Fiction of Vietnam*,

WHAT DO I READ NEXT?

- *Novel without a Name* (1995) by Duong Thu Huong is the story of Quan, an 18-year-old idealistic Vietnamese boy who joins the North Vietnamese army only to live through years of terrible hardship and disillusionment.

- *Mekong Diaries: Viet Cong Drawings and Stories, 1964–1975* (2008), by Sherry Buchanan with Nguyen Toan Thi, Tran Thi Huynh Nga, and Nam Nguyen, is a book of poetry, drawings, stories, artwork and photographs created by Viet Cong artists during the Vietnam War. Organized chronologically, the book provides beautifully reproduced visual documentation of the war from the perspective of the Vietnamese side.

- Newbery Award-winning writer Cynthia Kadahata offers a young-adult novel called *Cracker!: The Best Dog in Vietnam* (2007), the story of a seventeen-year-old American dog handler in the Vietnam War. The story shifts between Cracker's point of view and the dog handler's.

- *Going After Cacciato* (1978) won O'Brien the National Book Award for Fiction. The book is the story of Paul Berlin, a young soldier in Vietnam; Cacciato, a carefree deserter; and a magical journey from Vietnam to Paris.

- *South Wind Changing*, published in 1994, is a memoir by Jade Ngoc Quang Huynh, a young Vietnamese boy whose family is torn apart by the war. After serving time in a prison camp, he eventually escapes and finds his way to the United States.

- Michael Herr's 1968 classic *Dispatches* is an account of the Vietnam War from a news reporter embedded on the front lines.

- Stephen Crane asks readers to consider the nature of courage under fire in his famous book *The Red Badge of Courage*, written in 1895.

- *If I Die in a Combat Zone, Box Me Up and Ship Me Home* is O'Brien's first book, an autobiographical account of his own experiences in the Vietnam War. Many of O'Brien's fictional stories, including "On the Rainy River" have their basis in this book, published in 1973.

- Ron Kovic's *Born on the Fourth of July* is his 1976 autobiographical book detailing his decision to go to the Vietnam War and the aftermath of that decision. The book was made into a film starring Tom Cruise in 1989.

---

calls O'Brien "the most well-known and admired novelist of the war." At the same time, however, Heberle also calls O'Brien a "traumatized survivor of a war that will not end." Indeed, it is the trauma that O'Brien and his characters experience that not only forms the content of the stories of *The Things They Carried*, but also shapes the narrative itself.

To understand the effect of trauma on O'Brien's characters and narration, it would first be helpful to develop an understanding of trauma itself and how survivors of trauma

process the world around them. In the years after the Vietnam War, post-traumatic stress disorder, also known as PTSD, became an increasingly recognized psychological condition. People who suffer from PTSD have experienced a serious traumatic event in the past that continues to intrude in their daily lives. They often suffer from what is known as survivor guilt; that is, they question why they are still alive while their friends or family are dead. In addition, they often relive their traumatic experience in dreams or in flashbacks. Often, they report numbness and a lack of connection to reality,

> ALTHOUGH NOT SET IN VIETNAM, IT IS NONETHELESS THE FOUNDATIONAL STORY, THE MYTHIC POINT OF ORIGIN, THE PLACE WHERE THE TRAUMA BEGINS FOR O'BRIEN'S NARRATOR TIM."

while ongoing images of the traumatic event play out in their minds. Human relationships are difficult for those suffering from PTSD. As Cathy Caruth argues in *Unclaimed Experience: Trauma, Narrative, and History*, "Traumatic experience, beyond the psychological dimension of suffering it involves, suggests a certain paradox: that the most direct seeing of a violent event may occur as an absolute inability to know it." That is, although the survivor has seen the event with his eyes, he or she is unable to consciously understand or know what it is that he or she has seen. Instead, the images of the event intrude in both dreams and flashbacks where the event is reexperienced. Caruth continues:

> The repetitions of the traumatic event...thus suggest a larger relation to the event that extends beyond what can simply be seen or what can be known, and is inextricably tied up with the belatededness and incomprehensibility that remain at the heart of this repetitive seeing.

One of the key ways people attempt to cope with this incomprehensibility is to create narratives of the event. Kali Tal, in her book *Worlds of Hurt: Reading the Literatures of Trauma*, suggests that in war literature "narratives are generated in order to explain, rationalize, and define events. The symbols which these narratives create are born out of the traumatic events of wartime." As a result, trauma narrators share certain recognizable characteristics. First, they are repetitive. The storyteller returns to the traumatic event over and over, telling and retelling the story, trying to offer reasons, trying to define and explain what happened. Second, the storyteller attempts to recreate the event for the reader or listener. Third, as Tal argues, the retelling of the event in either fiction or memoir involves "the necessary rebuilding of shattered *personal* myths."

"On the Rainy River" illustrates all of these characteristics in both structure and content.

First and foremost, O'Brien structures the story as a flashback. His narrator is an older Tim, telling a story that took place some twenty years earlier, in 1968, rather than choosing to tell the story as it happens. Because of this, the narrator is able to "explain, rationalize, and define events." The story tells the reader that the narrator chose to go to war; thus, the implication is that the narrator has witnessed traumatic events as a result of his war service. It follows, then, that his retelling of the story of the Rainy River will be shaped by this later experience. He has had the time and the motivation to consider the previous events in light of the later events.

In addition, early in the story, it is clear that the narrator suffers from PTSD. He states:

> For more than twenty years I've had to live with it, feeling the shame, trying to push it away, and so by this act of remembrance, by putting the facts down on paper, I'm hoping to relieve at least some of the pressure on my dreams.

This sentence suggests that the events of which the narrator is about to speak haunt him. He is trying to recover the "facts" as if by writing them down on a piece of paper will tie them down, keep them from shifting in meaning, and keep them out of his dreams. In addition, throughout the story, the narrator portrays his younger self as numb and paralyzed as he attempts to process the facts of his draft notice. He also is unable to talk to anyone about what is bothering him or form connections with friends or family. While this might be an accurate description of the young Tim, it is also possible that the older Tim is superimposing his own difficulties with PTSD on the younger version of himself. That is, because he feels isolated, numb, and paralyzed in his life in 1988, he is transferring those same emotions and characteristics to his 1968 persona.

Further, although the narrator states that "this is one story I've never told before," a seeming contradiction of the assertion that one of the defining charactcristics of traumatic literature is that the stories are repeated and repeated, anyone familiar with O'Brien's work knows that while the *narrator* may not have told the story before, O'Brien surely has. The events of "On the Rainy River" are the reformulated and fictionalized account of O'Brien's own life, revealed in his memoir *If I Die in a Combat Zone, Box Me Up and Ship Me Home*. As Chris Daley argues in his chapter "The 'Atrocious Privilege': Bearing Witness to War and Atrocity in O'Brien, Levi and Remarque," "the story 'On the Rainy River'... achieves a truth about why both the quasi-fictional Tim O'Brien and the real Tim O'Brien went to war... that the memoir's version of this incident could not."

The second characteristic of a traumatic story, the attempt to recreate for the reader or listener the traumatic event, is obvious in "On the Rainy River." Not only does O'Brien offer excruciating sensory imagery (such as in his description of his job at the meat packing plant) to appeal to the reader's senses, he also tells the story directly to the reader. He even shifts from a first person point of view to second person:

> And I want you to feel it—the wind coming off the river, the waves, the silence, the wooded frontier. You're at the bow of a boat on the Rainy River. You're twenty-one years old, you're scared.... What would you do? Would you jump?

Finally, traumatic narration works to rebuild "shattered *personal* myths," to use Tal's words. The narrator's sense of self demands that he know the difference between right and wrong. He tells the reader early that he always believed that if the situation were evil enough, he could muster enough courage to do what needs to be done. In this way, he echoes Jonathan Shay, writing about PTSD in his book *Achilles in Vietnam: Combat Trauma and the Undoing of Character*, who argues that "our culture has raised us to believe that good character stands reliably between the good person and the possibility of horrible acts." The older Tim tries desperately to square these contradictory beliefs: I am a good person. A good person does not do horrible things. Participating in the Vietnam War is a horrible thing. The only logical conclusion this syllogism allows is that he is not a good person. The narrator accepts this, and in rebuilding his shattered sense of self, he substitutes the word coward for the word hero. Through the telling of this story, he is admitting to himself and the world he has suffered a moral breakdown. It is the only explanation that can fit the facts, according to the worldview he has set up for himself.

Yet even while he labels himself a coward, it seems as if "On the Rainy River" is an extended explanation of his cowardice. It is as if by telling the reader that he was only twenty-one, afraid,

already traumatized by working in the meat packing plant, alone, in a town where no one would understand his actions were he to choose to leave, he is offering a rationalization for his choice. Even his discussion of the immorality and ambiguity of the war serves to underscore the reasons why he labels himself a coward. Yet it is important to remember, again, that it is the older Tim telling the story. It is very difficult to sort out whether the younger Tim had these feelings at all, or whether his cowardice stemmed not from moral dilemma but from fear of death.

In a 2008 interview with Tobey C. Herzog, O'Brien continues to assert that he was guilty of a moral lapse in his choice to go to war:

> I didn't go to war as an innocent. I went to war knowing, at least convinced, that the Vietnam War was ill-conceived and morally wrong. That was my conviction. I didn't go to war an innocent. I went to war a "guilt...." I was not an innocent, I was a "guilt." I knew that the war was wrong.... My situation was different, and it separates me from a lot of veterans to this day. It doesn't make me better or worse, but different, in the sense that I believed that the war was wrong and I went to it anyway.

In asserting his difference from other war veterans, O'Brien is actively reconstituting his myth of self, casting himself as someone who failed morally, who knew better but went anyway. In so doing, he exerts some modicum of control on the situation. If it was his choice to go to Vietnam, no matter how wrongheaded that choice was, then the events that befell him there were not the result of randomness and chaos, but rather the result of his own decision. While it is difficult to assume responsibility for cowardice, it is less horrifying than acknowledging the complete absence of morality in the universe. In O'Brien's reconstruction, the logic goes something like this: I did something bad in going to war, ergo, I deserved the bad things that befell me as well as all of the suffering I have endured since that year. By casting himself in this way, he is able to hold out for himself the hope of forgiveness and redemption. In an amoral and chaotic universe, such hope is for fools.

While it would be a mistake to conflate the narrator's experience on the Rainy River with O'Brien's experience, since O'Brien did not go to a fishing camp in northern Minnesota to contemplate his escape to Canada, it is nonetheless possible to consider the role that "On the Rainy

The lodge on the hilltop (George Burba / Shutterstock.com)

River" serves in O'Brien's opus. Although not set in Vietnam, it is nonetheless the foundational story, the mythic point of origin, the place where the trauma begins for O'Brien's narrator Tim. All of the other stories in *The Things They Carried* can only unfold because of the choice Tim made in a boat on a choppy river. Likewise, all of O'Brien's writing, all of his work, has unfolded because of the choice he made long ago, to become a soldier.

Source: Diane Andrews Henningfeld, Critical Essay on "On the Rainy River," in *Short Stories for Students*, Gale, Cengage Learning, 2011.

Tina Chen

In the following excerpt, Chen asserts that "exile as a fluid and inescapable experience resulting from immersion in the moral ambiguity of the Vietnam War infects all aspects of the stories" in The Things They Carried.

Tim O'Brien is obsessed with telling a true war story. Truth, O'Brien's fiction about the Vietnam experience suggests, lies not in realistic depictions or definitive accounts. As O'Brien

argues, "[a]bsolute occurrence is irrelevant" because "a true war story does not depend upon that kind of truth" (*Things* [*The Things They Carried*]). Committed to examining the relationship between the concrete and the imagined, O'Brien dismantles binaristic notions of "happening-truth" and "story-truth": "A thing may happen and be a total lie; another thing may not happen and be truer than the truth." In order to assess whether he has written fiction that is "truer than the truth," O'Brien singles out the type of reaction his stories should provoke: "It comes down to gut instinct. A true war story, if truly told, makes the stomach believe." This emphasis on the body's visceral response to fiction aptly encapsulates O'Brien's investigation of the literal and metaphoric relationships between stories and bodies, particularly as such affiliations are forged by a psychology of exile and displacement. For O'Brien, the returning veteran's paradoxical desires—a yearning to reverse the unwilling transformations conjured by combat experience; the inexplicable sense of exile that troubles any possibility of an easy return or rest—are best expressed by how a

> **VIETNAM EXISTS AS BOTH PLACE OF ESTRANGEMENT AND IRONIC HOMELAND, A FICTIVE GEOGRAPHY ACTING SYNCHRONICALLY AS POINT OF RETURN AND ALIENATION. ALIENATION BECOMES A STATE OF DESIRE PRODUCING THE STORIES. RETURN IS FIGURED AS MOMENTARILY POSSIBLE, A JUNCTURE OF TIME, SPACE, AND DESIRE THAT NEVER OFFERS A DEFINITIVE RESTING PLACE.**

true war story "never seems to end" but can only be told and retold, different each time yet no less faithful to the truths it must convey.

O'Brien's compulsion to revisit his war experience through fiction is not unique. The moral ambiguity and unresolved conflicts characterizing U.S. involvement in Vietnam have made that war a compelling presence in the American literary and cultural imagination. Vietnam did more than redefine the *mythos* of war. According to John Hellmann, it provoked a crisis in the very narrative of nation:

> Americans entered Vietnam with certain expectations that a story, a distinctly American story, would unfold. When the story of America in Vietnam turned into something unexpected, the true nature of the larger story of America itself became the subject of intense cultural dispute. On the deepest level, the legacy of Vietnam is the disruption of our story, of our explanation of the past and vision of the future.

If the Vietnam War has been figured as a "disruption" of America's self-narration as nation, its rupturing of "our story" has none of the glamour or play that characterizes postmodernism. Rather, it has been cast as psychic trauma, a metaphysical fracture in the body politic that refuses to heal completely.

For O'Brien, the lingering hurts of the war are intimately linked to his stories, which, by virtue of their allegiance to the contradictory truths of war, resist closure. *The Things They Carried*, a collection of related short stories that appears grounded in O'Brien's own "real" combat experience even as it insists upon war as

an endless fiction, ponders the complexities of such connections. Written as a series of quasi-memoiristic episodes, the book questions the nature of truth and the possibility of ever having an unchallenged "sense of the definite." Directing readers beyond the stories to the narrative gaps within and between them, O'Brien renders the indescribable experiences of "Vietnam" as moments one may gesture to but never fully represent. After Vietnam, it becomes impossible to "tell where you are, or why you're there, and the only certainty is overwhelming ambiguity." O'Brien's war stories, which are ultimately "never about war," reflect the difficult choices forced upon those who have confronted the contradictions of combat: "There is no clarity. Everything swirls. The old rules are no longer binding, the old truths no longer true. Right spills over into wrong. Order blends into chaos, love into hate, ugliness into beauty, law into anarchy, civility into savagery."

The disorder of a world without rules underlies O'Brien's problematizing of the boundaries between personal memory and official history. O'Brien's vexed preoccupation with the disjunctures that make history unreliable and memory the condition for narrative is engendered by the impossibility of ever achieving an unproblematic return home—whether that return is to family, community, one's prewar subjectivity, or nation. As such, the stories in *The Things They Carried* reflect the rootless existence of an exile. Marked by a complex understanding of Vietnam and its indelible consequences, the stories demonstrate a preoccupation with the nature of displacement and alienation. While much critical attention has been directed to the idea of the Vietnam veteran who feels exiled from America, O'Brien's work demands a reconceptualization of exile: O'Brien is alienated from his nation, his friends, himself, and, however counterintuitively, Vietnam. Although O'Brien's fictive project centers on the impossibility of ascertaining any one "truth" from the experience of war, *Things* is guided nonetheless by an impulse to tell the truth, "though the truth is ugly." And the ugliness of the truth that Tim O'Brien tells, an ugliness paradoxically sublime in its "largeness" and "godliness," deals much more with perpetual unmooring than it does with any kind of resolution. Exile as a fluid and inescapable experience resulting from immersion in the moral ambiguity of the Vietnam War inflects all aspects of the stories in *Things*.

Exile in *The Things They Carried* is rendered as a multiply located mode of experience; it is a condition both singular and plural in its manifestations. What begins as a fear of exile from a centrally located home, a site firmly identified as the plains of Minnesota, proliferates into multiply situated points of exile upon returning from the war. As a careful reading of *Things* reveals, O'Brien's war stories are not about recovering from trauma or resolving the conflicts contributing to or created by the war in any permanent way; they are about accepting indeterminacy and learning to live not through Vietnam but with it. In a 1991 interview with Steven Kaplan, O'Brien admits: "My concerns as a human being and my concerns as an artist have at some point intersected in Vietnam—not just in the physical place, but in the spiritual and moral terrain of Vietnam.... There was an intersection of values, of what was and what was to come, that I'll always go back to," even though the stories "are almost all invented, even the Vietnam stuff." This conscious, deeply intentioned reconstruction of Vietnam invokes Salman Rushdie's concept of "homeland" as one which, for the exiled writer, is always already fictive in nature: "if we do look back, we must...do so in the knowledge—which gives rise to profound uncertainties—that our physical alienation...almost inevitably means that we will not be capable of reclaiming precisely the thing that was lost; that we will, in short, create fictions, not actual cities or villages, but invisible ones, imaginary homelands." Rushdie's eloquent articulation of an imaginary homeland recognizes the intimate relationship between an exilic longing and storytelling. O'Brien perceives such a connection occurring when "remembering is turned into a kind of rehappening." His contested "confession" to killing someone during the war in "Good Form" testifies to the curious relationship between the stories and the idea of return, where each sustains and makes possible the other:

> Here is the happening-truth. I was once a soldier. There were many bodies, real bodies with real faces, but I was young then and I was afraid to look. And now, twenty years later, I'm left with faceless responsibility and faceless grief.

> Here is the story-truth. He was a slim, dead, almost dainty young man of about twenty. He lay in the center of a red clay trail near the village of My Khe. His jaw was in his throat.

> His one eye was shut, the other eye was a star shaped hole. I killed him.

> What stories can do, I guess, is make things present.

> I can look at things I never looked at. I can attach faces to grief and love and pity and God. I can be brave. I can make myself feel again.

For O'Brien, the epistemology of displacement, mediated by the limitations and possibilities of his stories, registers on multiple levels: geographical, temporal, narrative, social, even moral. Although O'Brien's concept of displacement is predicated upon the impossibility of any permanent return, his work nonetheless insists upon multiple returns, however fleeting or unstable, to the imaginative landscape of Vietnam. These returns produce the stories, which in turn demand the acknowledgment of Vietnam as the central topos and creative core of the fiction. Vietnam exists as both place of estrangement and ironic homeland, a fictive geography acting synchronically as point of return and alienation. Alienation becomes a state of desire producing the stories. Return is figured as momentarily possible, a juncture of time, space, and desire that never offers a definitive resting place.

... *The Things They Carried* is a book that turns on a single realization: as part of imagining a return to Vietnam as home to engender a new way of reading and writing the world, distinctions disappear and the impossibility of separating experiences and stories, reality and the imaginary, into orderly categories transcends the desire for neatness and clarity. O'Brien's post-Vietnam world is a confusing, ambiguous place. No hard and fast rules exist; truth is always provisional, waiting to adapt itself to the next story, the next reality. *The Things They Carried* testifies to displacement as a complicated condition; the polyvalent and equivocal nature of its vision and its orientation transforms everything in its scope. As such, the careful detailing of metonymic and metaphoric relationships between the bodies, the stories, home, and Vietnam uncovers Tim O'Brien's own moral, which asserts:

> In a true war story, if there's a moral at all, it's like the thread that makes the cloth. You can't tease it out. You can't extract the meaning without unraveling the deeper meaning. And in the end, really, there's nothing much to say about a true war story, except maybe "Oh."

The figural relationships in the text make it unimaginable to talk about anything in isolation.

The metonymic act of substitution does more than replace one term with another; in the semiotic space between the two signs, meaning explodes beyond the signifying capacities of either figure, revealing the futility of talking about one figure without constantly referring to the other. And it is precisely that movement between tropes—a movement reinforced by the structure of the text as a collection of stories which talk to each other—that produces a more complicated vision of the world. In O'Brien's war stories, the figurations of home/body/Vietnam/stories coalesce to produce an awareness of how no single idea can be unraveled from the cloth woven by the connections between each of them. It is a profound realization, leaving us to say, with wonder and a little awe, "Oh."

Source: Tina Chen, "'Unraveling the Deeper Meaning': Exile and the Embodied Poetics of Displacement in Tim O'Brien's *The Things They Carried*," in *Contemporary Literature*, Vol. 39, No. 1, Spring 1998, pp. 77–97.

Martin Naparsteck

In the following excerpted interview, Naparsteck asks O'Brien about integrating fiction with his personal experiences while writing about the Vietnam War.

Tim O'Brien is widely considered the best of a talented group of Vietnam veterans who have devoted much of their writing to their war experiences. Sections of his most recent book, *The Things They Carried* (Houghton Mifflin/Seymour Lawrence, 1990), have won a National Magazine Award and an O. Henry Prize and have been included in *Best American Short Stories*. It follows by twelve years his National Book Award-winning *Going After Cacciato* (Delacorte Press/Seymour Lawrence, 1978), which until recently was often called the best work of fiction to come out of the war; the critical reaction to *The Things They Carried*, however, now makes it a prime candidate for that accolade. The latest book resists easy categorization: it is part novel, part collection of stories, part essays, part journalism; it is, more significantly, all at the same time. As O'Brien indicates below, he may have created a new literary form. His other books are *If I Die in a Combat Zone* (Delacorte Press/Seymour Lawrence, 1973), a memoir of his year in Vietnam; *Northern Lights* (Delacorte Press/Seymour Lawrence, 1975), an out-of-print novel about two brothers who become lost on a cross-country skiing trip in Minnesota; and *The Nuclear Age* (Knopf, 1985), about a man who,

> THE POINT BEING, AMONG OTHERS, THAT IN FICTION WE NOT ONLY TRANSFORM REALITY, WE SORT OF INVENT OUR OWN LIVES, INVENT OUR HISTORIES, OUR AUTOBIOGRAPHIES."

while building a bomb shelter in 1995, recalls his life as a radical.

This interview took place at O'Brien's home in Boxford, Massachusetts, about twenty-five miles north of Boston, on April 20, 1989. O'Brien had completed writing *The Things They Carried* and was working on some final revisions. . . .

Q. Do you ever feel that you've written so much about Vietnam that you've been typecast, like the town drunk?

A. Yeah, I do. I can't deny it's part of my material, my life, things I care about. Even if I don't write often, specifically, about Vietnam, a lot of the stuff, for example in *The Nuclear Age* and in *Northern Lights*—courage and obligation and so on—flows from that experience. Beyond that, I think all writers get typecast. I think Melville is typecast as a sea writer. And Conrad certainly is. Updike is a suburban-hyphen-domestic affairs writer. Shakespeare is a king writer. That has to happen, because an author like any other human being naturally gravitates toward a center of concerns that are particularly his or hers. Being typecast still irritates me at times, but not enough to make me say I'm not going to write about Vietnam, because I am, and I'm sure I will in the future.

Q. Your characters spend a great deal of time thinking about courage, which is a fairly common subject for Vietnam stories, but you handle it differently. One symbol that comes up a lot in other writers is John Wayne; Ron Kovic, for example, implicitly rejects that symbolism. You never mention John Wayne, and you do not write of courage as something that drew you to Vietnam. You handle courage in a more realistic way.

A. It's such a complicated subject, it's hard to know what to say. It's easy to break down courage into categories. There's moral courage versus physical courage and so on. Even that seems oversimplifying it. To break it down into categories of John Wayne and Socrates, for instance, seems to me to be really artificial. Like everything else, courage interpenetrates the whole fabric of a life. To take a strand out and say this is courage and this is something else violates a central humanness. In my own particular case, I hated the war in Vietnam and didn't want to go. I had no desire to test my capacity to charge a bunker; I had no desire to do that. Some guys did. And I never really understood it, from the moment of basic training. Why would guys want to die? Take the chance of dying? I just didn't get it. So I think my perspective on the issue probably varies a lot from that of a guy like Kovic who wanted to test himself. My concerns aren't those of other people, and the writing probably echoes that.

Q. It seems that your characters are very much concerned about courage, but they typically don't reach conclusions about it. You're not really making a statement about one type of courage being better than another.

A. The best literature is always explorative. It's searching for answers and never finding them. It's almost like Platonic dialogue. If you knew what courage is, if you had a really wonderful, philosophical explication of courage, you would do it as philosophy, as explication; you wouldn't write fiction. Fiction is a way of testing possibilities and testing hypotheses, and not defining, and so I think that more than anything the work is a way of me saying, yes, courage is clearly important in this character's life; he thinks about its importance in circumstances; the work is a way of searching for courage, finding out what it is. That's especially true in *Cacciato*, I think, where it's both a search for courage for him to walk away from that war and also a kind of search for what courage is, what the courageous thing to do is.

Q. Your first three books differ from the fourth in the treatment of courage. Courage doesn't seem to be a major theme in Nuclear Age, *which is more about figuring out what sanity is and is not. Do you think it was inevitable that in moving away from Vietnam you would move away from courage as a dominating topic?*

A. It's the same issue. It's like the other side of the coin in that this guy in *The Nuclear Age* had the courage to do what I didn't and a lot of other people didn't, which is to risk embarrassment and censure and endure humiliation about walking away from the war. If there's a courageous character in that book, it's that William character, who despite his service in a kind of Waspism and his wimpy attitude toward the war manages to do for the most part what he thinks is right. So I think it's not a departure from the earlier work but a looking at it from another angle. To me, he's the only hero I've written.

Q. It seems to me that in your first three books you were dealing with philosophical issues, such as courage, while The Nuclear Age *is more political. Do you feel that way?*

A. Not really. I see all four books as political in that they all deal with the impact of global forces on individual lives. In my own life and in *If I Die*, this huge thing—global politics—pushed me into the war, and similarly in *The Nuclear Age*, William Cowling is pushed into hiding and pushed away from his own life by global politics. I think anything I've ever written has that as its center theme, even more than issues of courage— how individual human lives are influenced by global forces beyond the horizon.

Q. I sensed in reading The Nuclear Age *that you were coming close to making a statement there, saying we should do something about this nuclear madness.*

A. I don't think I was making a statement; I certainly wasn't trying to. I was trying to write a comedy, basically, and a book that was funny, and I think the real difference between *The Nuclear Age* and the earlier works is tone. It had a more comedic tone to it. I'm not sure people cared for that. But my intent was to be different—like Shakespeare saying, "My subject may be life and death, but I want to have a comedic perspective on it."

Q. The reviewers were not always kind to The Nuclear Age. *Do you think a lot of them missed the comedic intent?*

A. That's probably it. I was trying to write a funny book. I think it is funny. But it's up to the ages. *Cacciato* may, a hundred years from now, not be read at all, while *The Nuclear Age* could be. The best road for most writers is to turn them out at the time. *Moby Dick*, for example, was trashed, worse than *Nuclear Age*. It was "the most hideous piece of garbage ever written," and what happens is that over time, I think, these things straighten themselves out. You can't as a writer defend your work or knock it. You have to say, "Let time take care of it." So I don't get too excited about bad reviews or good ones. I feel happy if they're good, feel sad if they're bad, but the feelings disappear pretty quickly, because ultimately I'm not writing for my contemporaries but for the ages, like every good writer should be. You're writing for history, in the hope that your book—out of the thousands that are published each year—might be the last to be read a hundred years from now and enjoyed.

Q. Was the story "Speaking of Courage" originally intended to be part of Cacciato?

A. Yes. It was a piece I took out. It's kind of an orphan. I've since rewritten it for *The Things They Carried*—pretty substantially rewritten it, in fact, changing everything except the lake, driving around the lake, but all the war stuff has been completely changed, and now I'm really fond of the story. I didn't care for it at all when it was originally written.

Q. Is that why it was left out of Cacciato?

A. Partly that and partly because it just didn't fit. It's a postwar story; *Cacciato* was a war story, and it just didn't have a proper home in that book.

Q. In rewriting it, you changed the character from Paul Berlin to Tim O'Brien.

A. The character becomes Tim, even though the Tim character is made up entirely, and then the Tim is transformed again into another guy, another character in *The Things They Carried* named Norman Bowker.

Q. Is the Tim character Tim O'Brien? In "The Lives of the Dead" there's a Timmy O'Brien.

A. Yeah, it is, in part. It's made up, but I use my own name. *The Things They Carried* is sort of half novel, half group of stories. It's part non-fiction, too: some of the stuff is commentary on the stories, talking about where a particular one came from. "Speaking of Courage," for example, came from a letter I received from a guy named Norman Bowker, a real guy, who committed suicide after I received his letter. He was talking to me in his letter about how he just couldn't adjust to coming home. It wasn't bad memories; it was that he couldn't talk to anybody about it. He didn't know what to say; he felt inarticulate. All he could do was drive around and around in his hometown in Iowa, around this lake. In the letter he asked me to write a story about it, and I did. This was after I published *If I Die.*

Q. Was this somebody you knew?

A. Yeah, in Vietnam. I sent him the story after it was published, and he said he liked it. Then I didn't hear from him for a long time. His mother finally wrote me. I wrote her and she wrote back saying he committed suicide by hanging himself in the locker room of a YMCA. So that's the terrible-happening anecdote that I include after the story in *The Things They Carried.* The commentary is partly about writing sources and partly about the writing itself.

The Things They Carried is my best book. There's no doubt in my mind about it. When I was writing *Cacciato* I had that feeling; I have that feeling now. I can tell by the strangeness of it. It's a new form, I think. I blended my own personality with the stories, and I'm writing about the stories, and yet everything is made up, including the commentary. The story about Norman Bowker is made up. There was no Norman Bowker. The point being, among others, that in fiction we not only transform reality, we sort of invent our own lives, invent our histories, our autobiographies. When Melville wrote *Moby Dick*, he was inventing himself, for posterity.

Q. Have you ever been approached about doing movies?

A.Cacciato and *The Nuclear Age* have both been taken by the movies. I've seen a few scripts. I've seen three on *Cacciato*, none of which are any good. There are some good parts in them, but by and large they tend to take all the dream-like, fantastic, surrealistic elements of the book out and tell a pretty straightforward, realistic story, which to me violates the whole aboutness of the book. The book is about the interweaving of memory on the one hand and the imagination, how one frees the other and back again, and that's gone. To me you don't have *Cacciato* anymore; you've got some new thing. I was asked to write a screenplay of the book, and I said "No," because you end up having to do what they did. You have to, the way movies are made. You have to screw up your own work, and if it's going to be screwed up, I would prefer that somebody else do it, not me.

Q. I've seen the term "magical realism" used in connection with your writing. Do you think Cacciato *fits into that grouping?*

A. I don't know. I think the term is a short-hand way of saying something that's much more complicated than that. No writer wants to be grouped in any category. Writing is being an individual; it's a creative enterprise, and a writer wants to make an individual, creative statement that's unrelated to anything that's been said before or afterward yet is simultaneously totally related not just to one thing but to everything. "Magical realism" is shorthand for imagination and memory and how they interlock, for what realism is, for what's real and not real.

Q. "How to Tell a True War Story" in The Things They Carried *seems to me to be very directly about the interlocking of memory and what actually happened. It also strikes me that this story is as much an essay as it is a story. Did you have that sense in writing it?*

A. It's a mixture, yes. It's like the rest of the book, in that it's part story, just raw story—six guys go up to the listening post in the mountains—and also a discussion about the making of the story, not a discussion by me as much as by the guys themselves. In a way it's part essay and part fiction, but in a way it's neither. I think that when you're reading the thing you have a total effect. To me, it has a singleness or unity to it. Rather than being part this and part that, it's all those things together. That story is the genesis for the idea for the whole book. When I'm talking about a happening, it seems essayish, but that stuff is invented and imagined; it isn't true in a literal sense. I don't, for example, believe that war is beautiful in any aesthetic way whatsoever. Even though the character sounds like me and says pretty pointblankly that war is beautiful, the harmonies and shapes and proportions, it's not me saying that. The guy who's narrating this story has my name and a lot of my characteristics, but it isn't really me. I never felt or thought that war's pretty, even though I can see how people such as Bill Broyles have said that. My personal feeling is that it's pretty ugly. I was in danger, and my perception never let me see any beauty. All I felt was fear. What I'm saying is that even with that nonfiction-sounding element in the story, everything in the story is fiction, beginning to end. To try to classify different elements of the story as fact or fiction seems to me artificial. Literature should be looked at not for its literal truths but for its emotional qualities. What matters in literature, I think, are pretty simple things—whether it moves me or not, whether it feels true. The actual literal truth should be superfluous. For example, here's a story: four guys go on a trail, a grenade sails out, one guy jumps on it, takes the blast,

and saves his buddies. Is it true? Well, yeah, it may have happened, but it doesn't feel true, because it feels stereotypical, hackneyed; it feels like Hollywood. But here's another story: four guys go on a trail, a grenade sails out, one guy jumps on it, takes the blast, and dies; before he dies, though, one of the guys says, "What the fuck you do that for?" and the dead guy says, "The story of my life, man," and starts to smile. He's dead. That didn't happen. Clearly, ever, and yet there's something about the absurdity of it and the horror of it—"What the fuck you do that for?"—which seems truer to me than something which might literally have happened. A story's truth shouldn't be measured by happening but by an entirely different standard, a standard of emotion, feeling "Does it ring true?" as opposed to "Is it true?"

Q. The narrator of "How to Tell a True War Story" comes to a different understanding of what happens at the end of the story than he had at the beginning. At the end he climbs into the tree to pick out parts of his friend, who's died in an explosion, giving the impression that he didn't quite understand the truth at the beginning, maybe because it was too difficult to remember, too hard on him. It's the exercising of his imagination that gets him at the truth.

A. Yes, I think it is. I think exercising the imagination is the main way of finding truth, that if you take almost any experience of your own life that means something to you, that really hits you, let's say the death of your mother, over the course of time your imagination is going to do things with that experience to render it into something that you can deal with and that has meaning to it. You're going to select some details and forget others: she's lying in bed dying for five weeks; you're not going to remember every detail of that; you're going to pick out of your memory, pluck out, certain conspicuous elements, and then you're going to reorder them. The experience that you remember is going to have a power to it that the total experience didn't have. You went to fix breakfast while she was dying, the phone rang, you had to deal with it— all that random stuff that you've forgotten will be rearranged by your imagination into a new kind of experience. I think in war we tend to block out the long, hard moments of boredom, standing around, sitting around, waiting, which is a lot of what war is. It's ninety-nine percent monotony, and what the imagination does is to push that away and take what's left and reorder it into patterns that give meaning to it.

Q. In Cacciato *you have the observation post scenes, which seem to be almost directly essays, and in one of them you talk about how to use imagination. There are a lot of dream sequences in literature, but Berlin is not really dreaming; he's wide awake, and he's controlling what he's thinking about, and what he thinks about makes up half the novel.*

A. Dreams are dangerous. I don't think I've ever used a real dream. Berlin is awake the same way you and I are now, only alone, and he's staring at the beach and thinking; he's imagining in a way we all do at times. It's a kind of daydream, but it's not an *Alice in Wonderland* or Hobbity sort of thing where events happen at random that come only from the subconscious. It's a mixture of the subconscious and the directed, the same way stories are written. What Berlin is doing is what I do with a typewriter: I'm half living in a rational world and half living in a kind of trance, imagining. Berlin's process in the observation post was meant, at least in part, to echo my own process of imagining that book—not dreaming it and not just controlling it, but a trancelike, half-awake, half-alert imagining.

Q. A lot of guys from Vietnam go to the Breadloaf writers conference in Vermont because they know you teach there every summer.

A. There are always some, which is good.

Q. They usually try to select you as their teacher.

A. They try to. They don't always get me. I think of myself not as a soldier anymore. That's all over. I think of myself as someone who now and then writes about the war, but my daily concerns are just the same as yours. When you're writing a book about Vietnam you don't think of yourself as a soldier; you think of yourself as a writer. The subject matter is war, and you're trying to make a sentence that's graceful, you're trying to make a character come alive, you're trying to make a scene shake with meaning and also with a dramatic feel; your attention is on writing that matters. I feel bad when I meet a vet who thinks that because we both shared this soldiering thing we can also share the other thing, writing, without work, and to me writing is really hard work. Anybody who's done it knows that just making a simple sentence is work. My chief asset as a human being, as a writer, is that I'm tenacious; I work just constantly, stubbornly, and like it. I mean I really like it—I get angry, I feel rotten, if somebody calls me in the middle of work and says, "Let's go play golf," because I like writing that much. If you want to be a writer, you've got to learn to be an eagle soaring up above and a mule who keeps climbing and climbing and climbing.

Source: Martin Naparsteck, "An Interview with Tim O'Brien," in *Contemporary Literature*, Vol. 32, No. 1, Spring 1991, pp. 1–11.

SOURCES

"Background Note: Cambodia," in *U.S. Department of State: Diplomacy in Action*, http://www.state.gov/r/pa/ei/bgn/2732.htm (accessed August 24, 2010).

Calloway, Catherine, "'How to Tell a True War Story': Metafiction in *The Things They Carried*," in *Critique: Studies in Contemporary Fiction*, Vol. 36, No. 4, Summer 1995, p. 249.

Caruth, Cathy, *Unclaimed Experience: Trauma, Narrative, and History*, Johns Hopkins University Press, 1996, pp. 5, 90–91.

Eder, Richard, Review of *The Things They Carried*, in *Los Angeles Times Book Review*, April 1, 1990, p. 3.

Daley, Chris, "The 'Atrocious Privilege': Bearing Witness to War and Atrocity in O'Brien, Levi, and Remarque," in *Arms and the Self: War, the Military, and Autobiographical Writing*, edited by Alex Vernon, Kent State University Press, 2005, p. 184.

Fox, Wade, Review of *The Things They Carried*, in *Whole Earth Review*, No. 86, Fall 1995, p. 58.

Harris, Robert R., Review of *The Things They Carried*, in *New York Times Book Review*, March 11, 1990, p. 8.

Heberle, Mark A., *A Trauma Artist: Tim O'Brien and the Fiction of Vietnam*, University of Iowa Press, 2001, pp. 1–2.

Herzog, Tobey C., "Conversation with Tim O'Brien," in *Writing Vietnam, Writing Life: Caputo, Heinemann, O'Brien, Butler*, University of Iowa Press, 2008, pp. 88–133.

"History and Records," in *Selective Service System*, April 30, 2002, http://www.sss.gov/backgr.htm (accessed June 1, 2010).

"International Visitors to Vietnam in July and 7 Months of 2010," in *Vietnam National Administration of Tourism*, http://www.vietnamtourism.gov.vn/english/index.php?cat=012035&itemid=3464 (accessed August 24, 2010).

O'Brien, Tim, "On the Rainy River," in *The Things They Carried*, Penguin Books, 1990, pp. 41–63.

"On This Day—1950–2005: 31 May," in *BBC*, http://news.bbc.co.uk/onthisday/hi/dates/stories/may/31/newsid_2481000/2481543.stm (accessed August 24, 2010).

Shay, Jonathan, *Achilles in Vietnam: Combat Trauma and the Undoing of Character*, Simon and Schuster, 1994, p. 31.

Tal, Kali, *Worlds of Hurt: Reading the Literatures of Trauma*, Cambridge University Press, 1996, pp. 76, 121.

Taylor, Mark, "Tim O'Brien's War," in *Centennial Review*, Vol. 39, No. 2, Spring 1995, p. 213.

Young, Marilyn B., *The Vietnam Wars 1945–1990*, Harper Perennial, 1991, pp. 2, 210–42.

FURTHER READING

Gettleman, Marvin E., June Franklin, Marilyn B. Young, and H. Bruce Franklin, eds., *Vietnam and America: The Most Comprehensive Documented History of the Vietnam War*, 2nd ed., Grove Press, 1995.
> A necessary book for any student of the Vietnam War, this work contains a comprehensive collection of primary sources regarding the history of the war.

Gitlin, Todd, *The Sixties: Years of Hope, Days of Rage*, rev. ed., Bantam, 1993.
> The story of the tumultuous decade, told by the man elected as president of the Students for a Democratic Society in 1963, this book is a standard social history of the era.

Mason, Bobbie Ann, *In Country*, Harper & Row, 1985.
> Sam Hughes is a young girl whose father was killed in the Vietnam War before her birth. *In Country* tells the story of her coming-of-age and learning about her father.

O'Brien, Tim, *In the Lake of the Woods*, Penguin, 1994.
> O'Brien's next book after *The Things They Carried* is a darker rendering of the horrific experience of war that features a politician named John Wade.

Terry, Wallace, *Bloods: An Oral History of the Vietnam War by Black Veterans*, Random House, 1984.
> This book is a collection of first-person accounts by African American soldiers about experiences in Vietnam

Van Devanter, Lynda, *Home before Morning: The True Story of an Army Nurse in Vietnam*, Beaufort Books, 1983.
> This book is an autobiographical account of one woman's experience serving as an Army nurse in Vietnam.

Weigl, Bruce, *Song of Napalm*, Atlantic Monthly Press, 1988.
> Weigl represents his tour of duty in Vietnam in poetic form in this influential book.

SUGGESTED SEARCH TERMS

Tim O'Brien

The Things They Carried

Vietnam War AND Tim O'Brien

Tim O'Brien AND courage

war AND O'Brien

Vietnam War

If I Die in a Combat Zone AND Tim O'Brien

military draft

On the Rainy River AND O'Brien

war literature AND Tim O'Brien

O Yes

TILLIE OLSEN

1957

Tillie Olsen's short story "O Yes" was first published in 1957 as "Baptism" in the University of
Nebraska literary journal, *Prairie Schooner*.
This short story was later titled "O Yes" and
included in Olsen's short-story collection *Tell
Me a Riddle*, published in 1961. The title of the
story refers to the responsive chant that the
members of a church make to the words they
hear in the sermon. "O Yes" includes characters
who appeared in two of Olsen's other short stories, "Hey Sailor What Ship" and "Tell Me a
Riddle." Olsen's thoughts about race, public
education, and motherhood are revealed in "O
Yes." "O Yes" is a story clearly situated in the
1950s and in Olsen's own experiences. She occasionally attended a Baptist church located in a
predominately black neighborhood, and she
once saw a white visitor faint at the intensity of
that church experience. She incorporates these
experiences in the first part of "O Yes." Olsen
also witnessed the separation and exclusion that
occurs when children transition into junior high
school, when cultural and social pressures mag-
nify differences in race and economics. These
experiences are expressed in the second part of
"O Yes."

Although "O Yes" is not as well known or
anthologized as frequently as the short stories "I
Stand Here Ironing" and "Tell Me a Riddle,"
both of which were also included in *Tell Me a
Riddle*, it has been reprinted in at least two literary anthologies: the *Oxford Book of Women's*

Tillie Olsen (© Christopher Felver / Corbis)

Writing in the United States (1995) and *Discoveries: Fifty Stories of the Quest* (1992).

AUTHOR BIOGRAPHY

Tybile (nicknamed Tillie) Olsen was born January 14, 1912, in Omaha, Nebraska. Her parents, Samuel and Ira Learner, were Russian Jewish immigrants who fled Russia in 1905 for political reasons. The second oldest of six children, Olsen grew up in Omaha, where her father supported the family as a painter and paperhanger. She attended Omaha Central High School but left school after the eleventh grade without graduating. For the next several years she worked in a series of poor-paying jobs such as hotel maid, waitress, laundry worker, factory worker, and packing plant worker. Olsen's parents were active in the socialist movement, and Olsen grew up heavily influenced by her their activities. She joined the Young Communist League and was jailed in 1930 after attempting to organize meat-packing workers in Kansas City, Kansas. Whether from her work in the packing plants or her time in jail, Olsen contracted pleurisy and

incipient tuberculosis. While recovering in Minnesota, she began writing a novel, *Yonnondio: From the Thirties*. She became pregnant shortly after she started writing and gave birth to a daughter, Karla, in 1932.

Olsen moved to California, where she began working to help organize longshoremen and was again jailed in 1934. While involved in union organizing, Olsen wrote essays for the *Nation* and the *New Republic*. In 1934, part of the first chapter of *Yonnondio* was published in *Partisan Review* as "The Iron Throat," which resulted in a book contract from Random House. However, Olsen was occupied with union activities and busy raising her daughter, and she set the novel aside unfinished. The following year, she began living with Jack Olsen, a union organizer and fellow member of the Young Communist League, whom she married in 1936. Together, they had three daughters, Julie, Kathie, and Laurie. Because the family needed her income, Olsen continued to work, once again performing a series of low-paying jobs as a secretary and waitress. Olsen did, however, continue with her activism. During the McCarthy era of the early 1950s, both Olsen and her husband were investigated because of their labor organizing activities.

In 1954, with her children in school, Olsen took a creative writing class at San Francisco State College. She was awarded a Wallace Stegner Fellowship in Creative Writing at Stanford University in 1955. The following year she published her first short story, "I Stand Here Ironing," in the *Pacific Spectator*. Olsen quickly followed with three more short stories, "Sailor, What Ship" (1957), "O Yes" (1957), and "Tell Me a Riddle" (1961), which won the O. Henry Award for Best American Short Story. The success of these short stories led to a number of fellowships, including a Ford Foundation Grant (1959), a Radcliffe Institute for Independent Study Fellowship (1962–64), and a National Endowment for the Arts Fellowship (1968). These fellowships allowed Olsen to quit her other jobs and devote herself to writing and teaching.

In 1970, Olsen helped to establish the Feminist Press, which focuses on publishing texts written by lesser known American women writers. During the next few years, she taught creative writing classes at several universities, including Stanford University, the Massachusetts Institute of Technology, the University of Massachusetts, and Amherst College. In 1974, she revised and completed her early novel *Yonnondio: From the Thirties*. The following year, she was honored with an award from the American Academy and National Institute of Arts and Letters. In 1978, a collection of Olsen's articles and speeches, *Silences*, was published. She served as editor of *Mother to Daughter, Daughter to Mother: A Daybook and Reader* in 1984 and wrote a series of essays for *Mothers and Daughters: That Special Quality: An Exploration in Photographs* (1987). In 1994, Olsen received a Rea Award for the Short Story, for her collection of short stories published in *Tell Me a Riddle*. Olsen died on January 1, 2007, in Oakland, California.

PLOT SUMMARY

1

"O Yes" begins at a baptism in a storefront church. Twelve-year-old Carol and her mother are at New Strangers Baptist Church to attend the baptism of Carol's best friend, Parry. Carol and her mother, Helen, are the only white people in the church. Carol's nervousness shows in the tight grip that she keeps on her mother's hand. The church is awash in vivid colors. On the ceiling above the baptism tank is a painting of a "blue-painted River of Jordan." The two choirs wear robes "of wine, of blue, of red." When the choirs begin to sing, Parry begins tapping and clapping to the music; Carol is initially ready to join in when she suddenly recognizes Eddie from school. Parry tells Carol that there are other students from their school at the church as well. Carol, now anxious, "scans the faces to see who else she might know, who else might know her."

As the service continues, Carol worries that Eddie might see her the next day and speak to her "right in front of somebody at school." When Carol feels Parry's arm next to hers, she begins to play a game they played when they were young. Carol taps a rhythm on Parry's arm, asking her friend to guess the title of a song, but Parry is staring fixedly at the baptismal tank at the front of the church. When Carol asks Parry if she is scared, Parry says no in the jive language she has recently adopted. The preacher begins to speak about the nature of God, and Carol grows drowsy in the heat of the church. The touch of Parry's arm next to her own causes Carol to begin daydreaming. She remembers

MEDIA ADAPTATIONS

- Although there are no video or audio recordings of "O Yes," a story from the same collection has been adapted for film. *Tell Me a Riddle*, directed by Lee Grant, and starring Melvyn Douglas and Lila Kedrova, was filmed in 1980 and is available from Warner Brothers in VHS and DVD formats.

- A film about Olsen's life, *Tillie Olsen—A Heart in Action*, filmed over a period of seven years, was completed in 2007. The film, directed by Annie Hershey, includes an overview of Olsen's life as writer, activist, and feminist. This film includes several interviews with Olsen, who also reads from many of her works.

- *Tillie Olsen: A Profile* (1980) is a National Public Radio audio recording focusing on Olsen's life.

when she and Parry sat together in elementary school and recalls the sound of chalk on the blackboard and the "rustle of books." Carol also recalls the secret game she and Parry played, the "drumming tattoo of fingers on her arm." As the minister's voice continues, Carol is lost in the memories of elementary school, playing volleyball and jump rope with Parry. These happy memories are interrupted by a scream, which draws Carol back into the church and the service. The congregants are holding their hands in the air and moaning "O yes." The response acknowledges what the preacher has said, but the sounds of these moans and the congregants' obvious emotions are alien to Carol.

The preacher's sermon is punctuated by responses from the congregants. For a moment, Carol forgets Eddie and joins in the responses, but then there is another scream and more noises, "like feet and hands thrashing around." The woman who screamed is crying and shaking, which makes Carol shake. When Carol turns to Parry to ask why the woman has screamed, Parry ignores the question. Her attention is still fixed on the baptismal tank. Carol turns to her mother, but her eyes are closed and she appears to be asleep. In response to the commotion going on around her, Carol focuses on the fan she is holding. There is an illustration of Jesus walking on water and Carol stares at it, hoping that if she stares at it deeply enough, it will create a protective wall around her. Carol tries to make the noises that surround her smaller and farther away. She imagines turning the noises into a phonograph record but without the screaming. When Carol asks her mother if they can leave, her mother only holds her tightly. Parry's mother is also moaning, and Carol tries not to look at those who sit around her. Carol's eyes are closed, but when she hears a new voice, she opens her eyes and sees a different classmate. The thrashing of bodies seems greater, as does the work of the ushers, who rush around the church "with the look of grave and loving support on their faces." All of the sounds and images from within the small church swirl together, overwhelming Carol. As she faints, Carol remembers the Hostess Foods plant, where Parry's mother, Alva, works and where she took the girls one day. Now, though, the plant seems to be under water. Carol imagines herself swimming in the plant, where it is cool and quiet.

In the next moment, Carol's mother is holding a cup of water to Carol's mouth and urging her to drink. Carol is now in her mother's car, with Helen and Alva bending over her. Parry is there, too, but she makes no move to touch Carol. Instead, she addresses her with her new jive talk, and Carol automatically responds using the same language. Carol wants to go home, and Parry says that it was their mothers' idea for Carol to be at the baptism and that it is better if Carol goes home. Alva accepts the blame for Carol's collapse, saying that she should have warned Carol about the intensity of the church service. Alva tries to explain that the emotional intensity of the church service allows people to put aside the troubles of the week, but Carol tries not to listen. The church is a spiritual home for the congregants and they feel safe letting their emotions come out, but Carol can still hear the screaming in her head and begs her mother to take her home.

The final brief paragraph of this first part of "O Yes" is set aside in italics. It is a surreal memory, a dream vision of Alva's, whose emotional ties to her congregation and church inhabit her memories. Alva recalls being pregnant with Parry and in a clinic waiting to give birth. Alva was only fifteen years old, all alone, and far from home. In her dream vision, Alva is comforted by a voice that reassures her that she is loved and protected. In the vision, a small child appears, holding a stick with a bright star on the end. The child is Jesus, who will guide Alva in her moment of need. Alva dreams that she was lost but is now saved, and she sees the bodies of sinners who were not saved. As Alva struggles from the darkness, the small child Jesus brings Alva to the light. As she gives birth to her daughter, Alva is comforted by her religious faith. Although she had felt alone and friendless, her deep faith offered an escape into a dream vision in which she was not alone. Alva has tried to explain the intensity of black religious experience, which takes participants out of the troubles of the world and brings them comfort. This dream vision illustrates for readers what Carol could not and did not wish to understand.

2

The second section of "O Yes" takes place in Carol's home. Helen is telling her husband, Len, about what happened in the church. He points out that Helen and Alva should have known to warn Carol. Helen instinctively understands that something significant happened to Carol, but that she did not "realize" that she and Alva should have prepared Carol for the emotional intensity of the experience. Jeannie, Carol's sister, thinks that her mother does not "realize a lot of things." Helen worries that Carol and Parry seem to have grown apart in the past few months. Jeannie impatiently tells her mother to "grow up" and reminds her parents that Parry now spends time with "her own crowd." She likes jive and jazz. Moreover, the teachers at the junior high treat Parry "like a dummy," while the white kids "treat her like dirt." Helen worries that this separate treatment is hurting Parry. Jeannie worries that it will hurt Carol. The friendship between Carol and Parry is over, and although Helen protests, she also knows that Jeannie has been speaking the truth. Jeannie insists that the world is "sorting" Carol and Parry into different directions.

Jeannie continues telling her parents about the reality of junior high, where racial differences do matter. What also matters is dressing correctly and sitting with the right people at lunch. Other things that matter, according to Jeannie, include "how much homework you do and how you act to the teacher and what you laugh at." When Helen and Len protest that Carol and Parry do not have to be part of this sorting process, Jeannie becomes upset and almost shouts that the pressures in school do not allow for changes to the rules. Helen suddenly recalls the welcoming ceremony when Carol first entered Franklin Junior High and the girls were told how to dress. Helen recalls other conversations with Carol, when she said that a girl who rebelled and refused to conform should be expelled. Helen suddenly remembers that the homework is more complex in junior high and wonders how students who have no parental help at home can finish their work. Parry has no one to help her with her homework. Helen also recalls the time when Carol said that her friends from school would not go to an event with Carol if Parry was also attending. At this point Jeannie is very angry and practically screams at her parents to ask why they do not move to another town if it is so important to them that race not matter at their school. Len finally interrupts, complaining that the subject is too much to discuss in one day. He pulls both Jeannie and Helen to the window, where they can watch Carol and Parry playing together on the street in front of their home. For a brief moment it seems as if the girls are not divided any longer.

Several months pass, and occasionally Carol asks her mother if she recalls the day that Carol fainted at Parry's church. Carol and Parry do not spend much time together and most days Carol is given a ride to school by Melanie's mother. When Helen suggests that the girls might want to give Parry a ride, Carol explains that she spends time after school with other friends, and Parry goes home to babysit her younger siblings. Carol and Parry no longer do their homework together, and the girls never call one another to discuss what they will wear to school or to make plans to see one another. Time passes and "the sorting goes on."

Carol is sick with mumps and Parry is asked to bring Carol's homework to her. Parry tells Carol that the teachers each wrote down the assignments, since they did not trust Parry to tell Carol her assignments. What Parry does

not say is that one teacher asked if Parry's mother worked for Carol's mother. The teacher sent a hall monitor to watch Parry take Carol's books from the locker and to make sure that Parry did not steal anything. The teacher made Parry swear that she would go straight to Carol's house after school and not stop anywhere else and not lose anything. Parry says nothing of this insult to Carol but instead asks if she will really do all the homework she has missed. Parry claims that she never opens her books. Parry entertains Carol, filling the time the two girls are together with gossip from school and talk about new clothes. Parry draws lipstick faces on Carol's book covers and straightens Carol's bedcovers and then suddenly, she is gone.

Carol is still sick the next day when she hears the sound of gospel music pouring from her mother's radio. Carol flees her bedroom, "shrieking and shrieking" for her mother to turn off the radio. The music recalls the morning in the church. Carol tells her mother that she hears the screaming at the church "all the time" and asks why the people screamed. Helen thinks of several responses but discards all of them. She might tell Carol that the screaming is the emotion of an oppressed people or that the church is their home or that their history must be endured and screaming helps the people endure. Helen thinks about all these things but says none of them to Carol. Carol admits that the teachers and her friends do not like Parry, whom they do not even know. Carol is ashamed to admit that she is no longer Parry's friend. Carol mentions Vicky, who had been at the church that day and who is often in trouble at school. She refuses to follow the rules. Now when Carol sees Vicky, she identifies with her, as if they had shared a common experience at the church that day when she fainted. Carol sobs in her mother's arms and begs to forget what happened. She wants to be like Melanie and not care about Parry or the people from the church. Helen thinks about how difficult it is to grow up but how necessary it is to feel the emotions that Carol is feeling. Helen thinks of this as "*a long baptism into the seas of humankind*" and wishes that she, too, could scream and find the helping hands of fellow congregants to hold her and offer support.

At the conclusion of the story, Olsen has included a dedication. The dedication is to a former English teacher, Margaret Heaton, who was a close friend of Olsen's. In an interview with Joanne

Frye, Olsen describes taking Heaton to a service at a black church. The intensity of the service caused Heaton to faint. Heaton had recently died at the time that Olsen was writing "O Yes."

CHARACTERS

Carol

Carol is the protagonist in "O Yes." She and her mother are identified as the only white people at New Strangers Baptist Church, where a Sunday morning service opens the story. Carol has been best friends with Parry almost their entire life, but that changes in junior high school. Because the friendship appears to be drifting apart, their mothers have agreed that Carol should attend Parry's baptism. Parry is comfortable at her church, but the experience is a new one for Carol, who is overwhelmed with the emotional intensity of the service. Carol tries at the church service to reestablish the closeness of friendship with Parry by playing a game from their childhood.

The church service creates demands on Carol that she is not willing to accept. Among those present are black students from her school who are not part of Carol's white group of friends. Carol worries that one of the black students will use this visit to the church as an opening to speak to her at school.

When Carol becomes ill with mumps, Parry visits and for a brief moment the girls have a connection, but at the same time, it is clear that they are no longer friends. The school itself is demanding different things from each girl. At the conclusion of the story, Carol hears a gospel song, and the trauma of that day of the church causes her to break down in tears, during which she laments the end of her friendship with Parry and all that she has lost because white and black students are categorized into different paths and different friendships.

Chairback Evans

Evans gives the sermon at New Strangers Baptist Church and is referred to as a preacher. The sermon provides the background for the events that occur in the church. Evans's sermon on the nature of God is met with periodic responses from the congregation. His sermon is rousing and punctuated by grand and expansive gestures, all of which are matched by the congregation. This sermon proves to be the catalyst for Carol's fainting.

Eddie Garlin

Eddie is a classmate of Carol's and is present at New Strangers Baptist Church for Parry's baptism. When Carol sees Eddie, she is concerned that he might choose to speak with her at school. Eddie is black and is not part of Carol's group at school. For Carol to be seen speaking with Eddie would be a transgression of the "sorting" process at Franklin Junior High School.

Helen

Helen is Carol's mother. She is very naive about the realities of junior high school. Helen worries that the events at the church have traumatized Carol. Helen is so naive about the pressures at school that her older daughter, Jeannie, yells at her to "grow up." Helen awakens to the changes in her daughter's life when she recalls what Carol said about the school assembly the first day at Franklin Junior High, when students were told about acceptable clothing and about how to avoid getting a bad reputation. Helen also remembers the story about a girl being punished for wearing lipstick and Carol's wish that the girl be expelled before she gives the school a bad reputation. Helen notes that Parry and Carol do not spend much time together any more. All of these observations help Helen finally comprehend that it is junior high itself that is separating Carol from her childhood friend. At the conclusion of the story Helen tries to comfort Carol, who finally acknowledges that she and Parry are no longer friends. Helen silently thinks that it is better for Carol to feel the pain of loss than to live untouched by heartache.

Jeannie

Jeannie is Carol's sixteen-year-old sister. She has already gone through the transformation that happens in junior high school. Jeannie has no patience with her parents' ignorance about the reality of junior high school life. She practically yells at them, as she tries to make her parents understand the transformation that junior high school makes in a child's life. Jeannie knows that race does matter at school. She also asks her parents why they choose to live in a place where race is important. Unlike her parents, Jeannie understands that the innocence of childhood ends when the reality of the world intrudes.

Len

Len is Carol's father. Although he is not as naive as his wife, Helen, Len appears to be even less willing to address the changes in Carol since she started junior high school. When confronted by Jeannie, Len says the problems at the school are too much to talk about in one day. He then distracts Jeannie and Helen by telling them to look out the window at Carol and Parry playing. He finds it easy to pretend that nothing has changed and that the turmoil of that day was only a brief interlude.

Melanie

Melanie is Carol's new friend at Franklin Junior High. Although she never actually appears in the story, Carol mentions that Melanie does not want Parry to be included in any activities.

Alva Phillips

Alva is Parry's mother. She is the only woman at New Strangers Baptist Church who is asked to give the invocation at the service, although there are several men who alternate in providing the call for the sermon. Alva accepts responsibility for Carol's collapse at the church and tries to explain to Carol why the people in the church responded with such emotional intensity to the preacher's words. Alva also has a dream vision that illustrates what she has tried to explain to Carol about the importance of the church in her life. The dream vision is about the birth of her own child. When alone and frightened and only fifteen years old, Alva felt that Jesus spoke to her and made the birth of her child easier for her to endure. Alva is a deeply religious woman who finds much comfort in her church experiences.

Lucinda Phillips

Lucinda is Parry's younger sister. In the church, she fiddles with her many petticoats and talks to Eddie, which helps to distract Carol from the emotional intensity of the minister's sermon.

Parialee Phillips

See Parry Phillips

Parry Phillips

It is Parry's baptism that opens "O Yes." She is twelve years old and attends Franklin Junior High School with Carol. At the church service, Parry is comfortable joining in the service because she has attended services at this church all her life. Parry's world is divided into two distinct periods of time. Before junior high, she and Carol were best friends. After the girls enter junior high, where the races are separate and mingling is not accepted, Parry and Carol can no longer be friends. Parry understands this change and responds by changing the way she speaks to signal her acceptance. She tries to create a new identity for herself by adopting the jive talk of jazz musicians to make her separation from Carol more distinct.

Because she is black, Parry has been categorized at school and sorted into a group, which is identifies her as an underachiever. Parialee's very name suggests the word "pariah," which is her role in her school. When the teachers give Parry homework to take to Carol, they treat her as if she is ignorant and cannot understand simple directions. The teachers also tell Parry they do not think she is responsible enough to take Carol her books and assign a hall monitor to watch Parry get Carol's books from her locker because they think she will steal if given an opportunity to do so. However, Parry normally goes home each day to watch her younger siblings while her mother works. Parry is very responsible and honest but she is defined by her race, which the teachers see as a reason to demean her.

Vicky

Vicky is referred to as Eddie's girlfriend. She was present at the church although she is not identified as having been there until much later in the story. It was Vicky's voice that drew Carol from her efforts to imagine herself absent from the intensity of the service. When she heard Vicky's cry of "O Help me, Jesus," Carol opened her eyes and fainted. Vicky is a rebel. She refuses to follow the rules at Franklin Junior High School, insists on wearing lipstick, and is punished almost every day. At the conclusion of "O Yes," Carol identifies with Vicky because it was "Vicky who got that way when I fainted." Carol would like to be a rebel, too, but she lacks the courage to break free of the sorting process at her school.

THEMES

Betrayal

At the conclusion of "O Yes," it is clear that Carol feels that she has betrayed her long-time friend Parry. When Carol hears gospel music on the radio, she becomes hysterical. The music

TOPICS FOR FURTHER STUDY

- Watch *Flirting*, a film about racism and interracial friendship, and write an essay in which you discuss the themes that you noticed in both the film and "O Yes." In your essay, consider the differences that you have noticed in the different story-telling techniques. For instance, how does Olsen's use of consciousness and inner thought in a story compare to the nuances of character expression and movement in film?

- Olsen uses people from her life and intertwines them with historical events to create characters and plots in her stories. Choose two or three people from your own past and merge them into a character whom you will make the center of your own short story. Like Olsen, you should change the factual details to suit your plot and theme. Read your story to your class and explain the choices you made in changing facts to fiction and why you made those choices. Alternatively, post it to your Web page, and blog about your choices.

- Olsen describes the unspoken rules that govern school friendships and separate people into categories. With three or four of your classmates, research segregation in schools in the mid-1950s. You could begin with a search of Internet newspaper archives found in your school library's databases. Once you have accumulated sufficient information, prepare an oral presentation of your material, using multimedia to augment your presentation. You might consider using PowerPoint slides of photos and old newspaper clippings or scenes of school segregation from documentaries or news reports. Be sure that every member of your group participates in this oral presentation.

- Read one of Roald Dahl's short stories and compare it to "O Yes." One source for Dahl's short stories is *The Collected Short Stories of Roald Dahl*, published in 1991 by Penguin. Write an essay in which you compare the two writers' stories, focusing on the differences and similarities in voice and theme. Consider whether there is are differences between the male author and the female author and whether each author approaches the life of a teenager differently.

- A story should evoke images and pictures in the reader's mind. Draw or illustrate in some way one of the images that Olsen's story created in your mind as you were reading. You can also use photography if you choose. Then write an essay that explains how you chose your image and what you think your image adds to your understanding of "O Yes."

---

recalls the day at the church when she fainted and had to leave. However, it was not only the emotional intensity of the experience at the church that caused Carol to collapse. Certainly the music, the heat, and the unfamiliar noises from the congregants all contributed, but Carol also felt isolated from everyone sitting near her, including Parry. Carol's mother was wrapped up in her own experience and was not responding to Carol, which is only one part of the betrayal experienced that day. More important, Parry was distracted as she waited for the moment of baptism. There was a distance between the girls, but it was not a new distance. Carol and Parry were already not as close as they had been in the past. Franklin Junior High had already separated them, which is what accounts for Carol's reaction to the gospel music many months later. The gospel music reminds Carol that she has betrayed her friendship with Parry. Carol tells her mother that "a lot of the teachers and kids don't like Parry." Carol cannot finish the sentence, but what she cannot voice is that Parry is not liked because she is black. Carol also admits,

Carol couldn't understand why she felt so guilty. *(Galina Barskaya / Shutterstock.com)*

"I'm not really her friend any more." This admission clarifies the betrayal that Carol remembers when she hears gospel music.

Race Relations

At the heart of "O Yes" is racism and the pain that racism creates. The episode at the church highlights the differences between the two races. Parry is comfortable in her church and is not disturbed by the emotionalism of the service. She has grown up in this church and is accustomed to the intensity of experience that surrounds her. For Carol, however, the experience at the church is different and even frightening. Alva explains that for black people, the church is a home, where they go to forget the oppression they experience. The church is also where black people go for community and protection and to escape their history and where they can allow their emotions to surface. The music at the church service helps the congregants to express what they have kept hidden inside. Alva says

that the preaching in the church finds a home in the people's hearts. Carol has no personal knowledge of oppression, has not experienced racism, and thus cannot relate to the emotional intensity of the church service.

The second issue about race in "O Yes" is revealed in the deteriorating friendship between Carol and Parry. Race was never an issue for Carol and Parry when they were younger. The two mothers were unconcerned about the differences between black and white, and thus, Carol and Parry were unconcerned. Then the girls entered junior high, where people are categorized based on race, clothing, academics, and demeanor. At their junior high, race matters and it is not acceptable for Carol and Parry to be friends. Carol's friends at school do not like Parry. Carol admits that the teachers do not like Parry either. Carol tells her mother that her friends or the teachers who dislike Parry "don't even know what she's like." They dislike Parry because she is black.

STYLE

Autobiographical Fiction

Sometimes the characters and events in a fictional piece are based on real life or on the experiences of the author, but their ultimate form and the way these characters respond to events are the creation of the author. While there is an element of autobiography, the story is fictional. In a series of interviews published in *Tillie Olsen: A Study of Her Short Fiction*, Olsen told Joanne Frye about two experiences that were similar to Carol's experience in "O Yes." In the first experience, Olsen took a close friend to a service at a black church. Olsen had been to the church many times and was familiar with both the sermons and the music. It did not occur to her that her guest had never before experienced that kind of intensity at a church service. Olsen's friend fainted. Olsen also told the story of her third daughter, who, although she did not faint, became frightened at a similar service when she attended a black church. Olsen combined the two experiences in her story, making the guest a child, Carol, but giving her the same experiences as Olsen's friend and daughter. In "O Yes," the characters are fictional, but they are based on people or character types from Olsen's own life. The people did exist, just not exactly as they are depicted in her story.

Dream Vision

The dream vision was a form of narrative that was frequently used in the Middle Ages. The narrator is asleep and dreams a story, which is actually told within the dream. Dream visions are usually allegories, as is the case in Olsen's short story. Allegories are a kind of metaphor in which persons or objects have a meaning outside of the narrative. The story being told actually means something else. In Alva's dream vision at the end of the first section of "O Yes," the story recounts an experience in which a frightened Alva is saved by a small child carrying a stick with a star at the end. The small child is Jesus, who saves Alva from her fears. She is fifteen years old, giving birth to her child, far from home, and very frightened. Her belief in God comforts her. This dream vision reinforces Alva's explanation of the importance of religion in black people's lives. In the Middles Ages, dream visions were almost always associated with religious fervor, as is true in Olsen's short story. Alva's dream vision occurs after she has tried unsuccessfully to explain to Carol the reasons for the emotional intensity and religious fervor that occur during services at New Strangers Baptist Church.

Jive

Jive is a form of slang spoken most often in the 1950s by black jazz musicians. Parry adopts this form of language because she is working on establishing her own identity, which is aligned to black culture. She understands that she cannot be part of Carol's white world, and using jive serves as a way to separate herself from Carol through language, just as they are separated by race and cultural taboos.

Narrative Voice

In a short story or novel, the narrator is the person who tells the story. When the narrator is a single person, the story is limited to only that person's point of view. One person tells the story and interprets it for the reader, including only the details experienced by or told to the narrator. In contrast, the third-person narrator provides an omniscient view of the action. In some cases, authors use multiple narrators, in which several characters tell their stories. This gives the reader the opportunity to see the characters from multiple perspectives. In "O Yes," Olsen uses narrative voice in a very different way than many readers might find typical. The story opens with an omniscient narrator, who describes the scene in the church. As part 1 continues, though, the narration begins to focus more on Carol's fragmented consciousness. There is an abrupt change in narration at the end of part 1, when the narrative voice shifts to Alva's dream vision. Her dream vision defines her response to the church service, which is vastly different from Carol's, and thus, very necessary for the reader to understand. In part 2, the narrative voice includes dialogue as family conversation, Parry's unspoken thoughts, and Helen's thoughts, which are sometimes structured as a stream of consciousness. This multifaceted narration adds complexity and depth to "O Yes."

Water Imagery and Symbolism

When originally published, the title of "O Yes" was "Baptism." The story begins with Parry's baptism, which will take place in the large water tank at the front of the church. This baptismal tank is one of the first things that Carol notices in the church. Parry's vision is also fixated on the water tank, and although she denies being frightened at the sight of the tank, there are two separate times in "O Yes" when Parry is depicted as staring at the tank. The first time is near the beginning of the service, when Carol asks "Parry, are you scared?" and Parry responds with a "No." Then when Carol hears a woman screaming, she turns to Parry to ask what is happening, but "Parry still ponders the platform" where the tank rests. The baptism tank is not the only water imagery in the church, though. Carol's fan contains an image of Jesus walking on water, and on the ceiling is a painting of the Jordan River.

Another important water image occurs when Carol faints and imagines she is under water. Carol remembers when Alva took Carol and Parry to the Hostess Foods factory where she works, but when she faints, the whole factory is under water and Carol and Parry must swim from room to room, as does Alva, who services the machines in the factory as she swims. The coolness of the water erases the heat of the church and cools down the emotional intensity of the service. Water also serves as an escape for Carol, who sinks into the water of her faint in grateful release. Thus water is not only needed for baptism and for religious iconography, it is also the means of escape and rescue from an intense experience. It is, after all, a glass of water that Carol is offered to bring her back to consciousness.

Symbolism is the use of one object to represent another object. Olsen uses symbolism in "O Yes" to create complexity of meaning. For instance, water symbolizes rebirth, which occurs in this story through baptism. The water tank at the front of the church is to be used for Parry's baptism. The splitting of the friendship symbolizes another kind of baptism—Carol's baptism into the "seas of humankind." There too, the use of "seas" refers to water, although no water is present. The bright colors and the sun shining so intensely that it nearly blinds Carol also symbolize the emotional intensity of the church service. The service also provides a form of emotional release for the congregants, who use the service as a way to cleanse themselves from the turmoil in their lives, essentially being baptized each week in the cleansing power of prayer.

HISTORICAL CONTEXT

Racism
In the 1950s blacks and whites often attended different schools and lived in different neighborhoods. Before the advent of forced busing in the 1960s, many black children attended schools in poorer neighborhoods. Because schools are supported by a complicated system of bonds supported by taxes, schools in black neighborhoods received less funding, and thus, had less money to pay salaries, maintain buildings, or buy new equipment. The result was that students at predominately black schools received a substandard level of education. In the early 1950s, the National Association for the Advancement of Colored People (NAACP) collected sufficient data to file several lawsuits arguing against segregation in schools. The lawsuits contended that black schools were underfunded, overcrowded, and understaffed and that black students were deprived of opportunities provided to white students. In a 1954 ruling, *Brown v. Board of Education of Topeka*, the U.S. Supreme Court declared that separate educational facilities for black and white children were unequal and unconstitutional. However, in many areas of the United States, local city, county, and state governments vowed to ignore the Supreme Court ruling.

African Americans also suffered discrimination in other areas of life. Many could not read the contracts they signed or were too intimidated to protest. A lack of knowledge about their legal rights meant that African Americans often languished in jail. In some cases, they were lynched by unruly mobs that were sometimes sanctioned by law enforcement organizations that looked the other way. In the southern states, nearly all public facilities were segregated to keep black and white people apart. Public restaurants, theaters, drinking fountains, and bathrooms all contained restrictions against white and black mingling together. Segregation also included housing and neighborhoods, where blacks and whites lived separately. After World War II, southern blacks moved to northern cities where there was less segregation than in the South, but discrimination also occurred in the northern states. When black families moved into northern cities, white neighbors moved to the suburbs, in what became known as "white flight," often leaving behind poverty-stricken urban ghetto neighborhoods. Thanks to television news, African American viewers witnessed blacks in several African countries win equality and independence from their colonial oppressors. Black southerners began actively protesting segregation and demanding equality. One significant confrontation took place at Central High School in Little Rock, Arkansas, in 1957. When

COMPARE & CONTRAST

- **1950s:** In 1950 the South African government establishes a policy of apartheid with the Population Registration Act.

  Today: Apartheid ends in South Africa in 1990. Continued opposition, international sanctions, and a diminishing white minority are all factors that influence the change.

- **1950s:** In December 1955, African American civil rights activist Rosa Parks is arrested in Montgomery, Alabama for refusing to give up her seat on a city bus to a white person. The action sparks a bus boycott that signifies the beginning of the civil rights movement.

  Today: In January 2010, a New York judge rules that the New York City Fire Department has been intentionally discriminating against African American applicants by continuing to use an exam that the department had been told put minority applicants at a disadvantage.

- **1950s:** On September 9, 1957, Congress passes the Civil Rights Act, the first such bill to be passed since Reconstruction. The act provides some preliminary attempts to secure voting rights for African Americans and creates the Civil Rights Commission to investigate claims of discrimination and segregation.

  Today: During the 2008 presidential election just over 65 percent of eligible African American citizens choose to vote.

- **1950s:** Many women begin to work outside the home but discover that childcare costs are eroding their salaries. Older siblings are recruited to watch younger children, just as Parry must do in Olsen's story.

  Today: Many women work outside the home, and childcare costs continue to be an important issue for most working mothers.

---

nine black students were enrolled in the all-white school, white protesters were met by Arkansas National Guardsmen who had been sent by governor Orval Faubus to "guarantee" the peace. President Dwight D. Eisenhower had to send in federal army troops to protect the nine black students. The entire confrontation was seen on television. Many white Americans were sympathetic to the black population and were willing to help black citizens fight against segregation. The televising of the fight for equal rights helped to galvanize white support by the mid-1960s.

Religion

Religion, religious belief, and church attendance had a revival in the 1950s. World War II resulted in the massive devastation of European cities and an estimated sixty million casualties. The atomic bomb that ended World War II in the Pacific, the subsequent testing of thermonuclear bombs and the cold war increased fear of even greater destruction. As a result, by the early 1950s, church attendance increased across the United States. Sixty percent of Americans claimed that they belonged to an organized religion and almost 50 percent of people claimed to attend church weekly. Religion was also associated with patriotism and community. Congress added the phrase "under God" to the Pledge of Allegiance in 1954. The words "In God We Trust," which had been placed on coins since the time of the Civil War, was adopted as the national motto in 1956. As if to prove the necessity of religion as part of American life, a series of religious films were released by Hollywood studios, including *The Ten Commandments* and *The Robe*. There were also a variety of religious offerings attracting worshippers. For example, L. Ron Hubbard's Church of Scientology in Los Angeles gained thousands of followers after he published his book *Dianetics: The Modern Science of Mental Health*. Billy Graham's traveling

The church had an African American congregation. *(bikeriderlondon | Shutterstock.com)*

religious crusades drew massive crowds. Although there were plenty of Americans attending traditional church services, whether at predominately white churches or at black churches like the church in "O Yes," the 1950s offered a variety of opportunities for religious expression and worship.

CRITICAL OVERVIEW

Olsen's legacy is primarily as an activist and a feminist writer who illuminated the lives of the invisible members of society. Her short story collection *Tell Me a Riddle* was reviewed by William Peden in the *New York Times*. Peden notes the strength of Olsen's work in creating complex characters with "feeling and understanding." According to Peden, Olsen's stories have an "almost miraculous rendering of the interrupted rhythms of thought and speech

patterns, with expert economy." Peden also writes that although this book is small, the achievements of the author are large. The stories in *Tell Me a Riddle* are "moving and eloquent," in Peden's opinion. In a review that focuses on each of the stories and many of the characters, Peden suggests that Olsen has emerged as "a significant and thoroughly adult literary talent." The many fellowships and grants that Olsen received after publishing these stories affirm Peden's praise and also attest to the strengths of this collection of stories.

By the time *Silences* was published in 1978, Olsen's reputation as a writer was well established. *Silences* was reviewed by novelist Margaret Atwood in the *New York Times*. In writing about Olsen, Atwood notes that there are few writers who "have gained such wide respect based on such a small body of published work." Atwood labels Olsen's voice "unique" and "powerful" and claims that women writers in the United States regard Olsen with "reverence." Atwood maintains that the reason for this reverence is that women writers understand the difficulties Olsen had to overcome to be a writer. She was a mother, wife, and wage-earner whose days were filled with the kind of obligations that left little time for artistic creativity.

By the time Olsen died in January 2007, her legacy as a writer had become clear. Olsen did not publish much, as Jess Row notes in the obituary that he wrote for the online magazine *Slate*, but she "deserves to be remembered." Row singles out *Tell Me a Riddle* in particular for acclaim. The stories in this collection are, according to Row, "some of the most powerfully compressed story writing of our time, written, it seems, without a minute or a word to spare." Row spends some time describing the hardships of Olsen's life—the abject poverty, the menial jobs, the years spent raising her children—and her activism on behalf of other writers who struggle to write while also struggling to earn a living.

Olsen's willingness to help other women writers was also noted in the obituary written by Mark Krupnick for the London *Guardian*. Krupnick mentions that two of the short stories in *Tell Me a Riddle*—the title story and "I Stand Here Ironing"—have been reprinted in nearly 200 anthologies, yet Olsen's writing is not Krupnick's focus. He reminds his readers that, although Olsen won many fellowships and grants, she did not use the money to fund her writing. Instead of writing, she used the freedom provided by the grants to "engage in a heroic campaign of consciousness-raising among younger women." What mattered to Olsen was helping new writers, reading and critiquing their work, and encouraging them to write. Although her books are certainly a fitting legacy, as Krupnick makes clear, it is Olsen's work in establishing women's studies courses and helping to publish less well-known feminist texts that remains an important part of her legacy.

CRITICISM

Sheri Metzger Karmiol

Karmiol teaches literature and drama at the University of New Mexico, where she is a lecturer in the University Honors Program. In the following essay, she discusses the importance of community in "O Yes."

There are several communities vying for attention in "O Yes." For example, her familial community helps Carol understand and deal with the challenges in her life. Another kind of community is the one created at the New Strangers Baptist Church, in which the community of congregants affirms Parry and Alva's sense of being part of a welcoming and safe refuge. However, the most important community in "O Yes" is the one that destroys friendships and separates Carol and Parry—the community created by their school. The racism and the prejudice that divide Carol' and Parry's lives at Franklin Junior High reveal a severed adolescent community in which some students are marginalized and labeled as failures. At the heart of "O Yes" is Olsen's commitment to and concern about community and whether communities are meeting people's needs. This story illustrates both the successes and the failures of communities and the difficulties inherent in seeking the ideal community.

In the opening paragraphs of "O Yes," Parry is at church to be baptized into her religious community. While the baptism at New Strangers Baptist Church is meant to integrate Parry into formal membership in the church, immersion into the baptismal tank is not required to become part of the community. The congregants' responsive "O Yes" also secures membership. By being present, Carol becomes a member of this community, but she also fears that by

WHAT DO I READ NEXT?

- Olsen's nonfiction book *Silences* (1978) is a collection of notes, letters, and essays in which the author writes about her struggle to balance work, childcare, and writing.

- Mildred Taylor's young-adult novel *Roll of Thunder, Hear My Cry* (1976, reissued in 2001) focuses on the issues of "sorting" that are so important in "O Yes."

- Graham Lorenz's novel *South Town* (1958, reissued in 2003) provides a good companion to Olsen's story. Written at about the same time, Graham's novel looks at racism and prejudice with believable characters and real situations common to adolescent life.

- Grace Paley's short stories are often compared to Olsen's, since both women were Jewish feminists who shared similar histories of social activism and wrote at the same time. *The Little Disturbances of Man: Stories of Women and Men at Love* (1959, reissued in 1973) was Paley's first collection of short stories. These first stories established Paley as a regional author whose characters were the people of her native New York City.

- *No Easy Answers* (1997), a collection of short stories edited by Donald R. Gallo, includes stories about teenagers from different ethnic, racial, and sociological backgrounds. Many of the subjects are from blue-collar families with modest incomes, and many are facing difficult choices in their lives. Some of the different cultures depicted in these stories include the lives of Korean, Chinese, Hispanic, and African American teenagers.

- *The Oxford Book of American Short Stories* (1992), edited by Joyce Carol Oates, is a collection of stories by some well-known American writers. What makes this collection interesting is that the editor includes a selection of stories that are less familiar to readers.

"

AT THE HEART OF 'O YES' IS OLSEN'S
COMMITMENT TO AND CONCERN ABOUT
COMMUNITY AND WHETHER COMMUNITIES ARE
MEETING PEOPLE'S NEEDS."

being present, she might be sacrificing the safety of the community of her white classmates. This explains her fear of being recognized by a black classmate and the even more threatening concern that a black classmate would speak to her at school, thus moving Carol from the accepted community of white students into the less desirable community to which the black students belong. To escape further immersion into Parry's community, which might result in a loss of white privilege, Carol collapses and thus ensures her escape.

The black church presents an intensity of communal experience that is frightening to Carol, who prefers to remain on the sidelines as an observer. In her book *Tillie Olsen: A Study of the Short Fiction*, Joanne S. Frye suggests that Carol's previous religious experiences "have not prepared her for this intensity or this expectation of involvement," and as a result, she is not prepared to meet the expectations of Parry's church, where congregants actively participate in the service, rather than simply observe the service. Alva tries to explain the importance of the church in her community, but Carol is unwilling to listen. For Alva, the church is her community. It releases the pain of being part of the oppressed black community and it creates hope for a better future. As Alva says, "Church is home." In that sense, the church is also the community of family, where joy is celebrated and painful lives are mended. The church gives Alva what Carol's family gives her—emotional support and love. As Alva's dream vision relates, the black church assuages loneliness, offers comfort, and facilitates the creation of a community. In functioning so well, Alva's church community comes close to being an ideal community.

Not all communities in "O Yes" function as well as the church community. For instance,

Olsen exposes the destructiveness of the junior high community that sorts Carol and Parry into separate and distinct racially-based communities. Readers learn of this destructiveness through Helen's unspoken thoughts. After Jeannie's emotional outburst, Helen is suddenly aware of all that has changed since Carol entered junior high. Helen realizes that she often helps Carol with her homework but recognizes that there are other children who receive no such help. Parry is one of the children receiving no help because she does not do homework. Parry does not bring books home because her teachers have already assigned her to a group of students, those whose future does not include college. Carol's world is different from Parry's. Carol does not have to babysit after school. She is free to go skating with her school club or study in the library or visit a friend. Upon entry into junior high school, Carol and Parry were sorted into separate lives and separate futures. This sorting reflects the world of the 1950s, when race and economic status determined whether students were directed toward college preparation in school. Frye suggests that it is important to understand the "social context that enacts the sorting," since this context is, according to Frye, "an essential dimension of the narrative richness" of Olsen's text. This sorting is a function of the differences in community and the desire to fit into a community. Frye reminds readers that

> the pressure to conform rises along class lines: clothing and behavior patterns and homework choices and the need for *your own* crowd all converge in the name of avoiding a "bad reputation for your school."

All of these choices experienced in school lead students toward a community that is based on an artificial and largely pre-determined sorting that occurs among school cohorts.

Prior to junior high, Carol and Parry had been a part of each other's families. The family is the natural community of childhood, but with the move into junior high, Carol and Parry no longer share a family community. Frye claims that "the family is in many ways a traditional source of human community, a place of comfort and companionship, especially when the 'larger' world seems fraught with divisiveness and hostility: racism, class divisions, political repressions." The importance of the family as community is revealed in the opening sequence of "O Yes." Readers see the family communities at the black church when both girls are accompanied by their mothers and later when Jeannie tries to tell her parents about how the junior high community functions.

With few exceptions, the junior high community is much stronger than the family community. This is largely because of the adolescent desire to conform. When students do not conform, as is the case with Carol's classmate, Vicky, who insists on wearing lipstick to class, the perfection of the community is threatened. When Carol tells her mother about Vicky's digression from acceptable behavior, Carol also says, "I hope they expel her; she's the kind that gives Franklin Jr. a bad rep." Carol's comment appears extreme for such a small violation, and her passion about the need to punish even small digressions is never in doubt. Vicky's behavior is a threat to the junior high community. Frye reminds readers that conformity is especially important for adolescents. This desire for conformity, says Frye, is "often reinforced by the threat of being or seeming to be a 'juvenile delinquent,' this thrust toward conformity was then (as now) especially potent in the years of early adolescence." Conforming is a necessary step toward creating the ideal community, but of course, the junior high school is not an ideal community, as Parry certainly realizes.

The transformative change in Carol and Parry's relationship becomes obvious when Parry visits Carol when she has the mumps. Parry bounds up the stairs and tosses the books and homework on Carol's bed. The words spill from Parry's mouth in quick succession and all the while Parry does not sit down. In fact, she moves around the bedroom restlessly, touching the old children's books on the bookshelf in Carol's room, staring out the window looking for a childhood tree that no longer exists, showing off her clothes to Carol, tightening the belt at her waist, directing a question to the old Rembrandt copy on the wall, drawing lipstick faces on the book covers, fluffing Carol's quilt, tossing their eighth grade graduation picture in the air, hitting the wind bell hanging from the ceiling, and finally fleeing down the stairs. Parry's visit is a whirlwind of hyperactivity that reveals how uncomfortable Parry feels in Carol's bedroom. The girls played together in this room on countless occasions as children, but now Parry knows she no longer belongs in Carol's room. This episode mirrors the opening when Carol is just as uncomfortable in Parry's church. Each girl finds a way to escape—Carol faints and Parry lets loose with a torrent of activity and words, as each seeks the safety of her own community.

There are a few moments in "O Yes," when Parry and Carol's communities overlap and the girls revert to the past. One time is in the church, when Carol instinctively begins playing an old familiar game on Parry's arm. Another example occurs later that same day when the two girls play outside with their pogo sticks, just as they have so many times in the past. In these few moments, the boundary dissolves and the two girls are again part of the same community. When the day ends, Carol and Parry return to their new communities, divided by race into black and white. When Carol faints at Parry's baptism, she is trying to withdraw from the church community, but at the same time, she is made a member of that community. Baptism is an immersion into a community, and Carol's experience suggests that her baptism into the human community cannot be resisted. A lifetime of friendship with Parry cannot be completely severed, as Carol's grief at the end of the story makes clear. At this point in Olsen's story, Carol has undergone her own baptism into the community of human suffering, or as her mother suggests, *the seas of humankind.*

In an interview with Frye, "Roots, Sources, and Circumstances: Tillie Olsen in Conversation with Joanna Frye," Olsen states that she wanted to write about the human need for community, but she also wanted to write about racism and the selection process that separates young people into different communities. "O Yes" succeeds in revealing the destructiveness of racial selection, but at the same time, Olsen also demonstrates that the familial community can offer healing. At the end of "O Yes" it is a mother who tries to comfort her daughter. Although Helen cannot solve the problems that have led to the loss of friendship, the comfort that Helen is able to share with Carol does reinforce the importance of the family community in her daughter's life. Olsen also suggests in this final scene that perhaps the divisive junior high community will not triumph.

Source: Sheri Metzger Karmiol, Critical Essay on "O Yes," in *Short Stories for Students*, Gale, Cengage Learning, 2011.

Carol saw the light coming through the window.
(vesilvio | Shutterstock.com)

Bonnie Lyons

In the following excerpt, Lyons argues that while Judaism shapes Olsen's work, her writing is most influenced by her experiences as a woman.

That Tillie Olsen's work is radically perfectibilistic in spirit and vision is obvious to most of her readers. Less obvious is that the two principal sources of that vision derive directly from her experience as a Jew and as a woman.

What is most deeply Jewish in Olsen is the secular messianic utopianism she inherited from her immigrant parents. That is, her political and social ideology directly reflects the radical Jewish background in which she grew up. But while her Jewish background provides a foundation for Olsen's basic political vision, it would be a mistake to view Jewishness itself as the living core, either in theme or imagery, of her work. Her experience as a woman is much more central, and is especially noticeable in her patterns of imagery. From the weak propagandistic early poetry to the great "Tell Me a Riddle," Olsen repeatedly emphasizes the human body and the mother/child relationship, aspects of human experience strongly identified with the female.

This is not to suggest that Olsen's explicit "femaleness" makes her work restricted in scope or marginal. Her habitual focus on the body does not suggest, for example, that the human is *merely* a body. On the contrary she grounds the spiritual *in* the body in very concrete and physical terms, emphatically insisting on the wholeness of the human. For Olsen the physical body makes the spiritual condition manifest: disfigurement, mutilation, and especially starvation are body images or ideas employed repeatedly to reflect both self-estrangement and estrangement from the world. Generally, hunger, eating, and feeding (nurturing) are the pivotal experiences that directly link the mother/child relationship on the one hand to the Jewish radical political vision on the other.

Olsen's vision lies between the Realist emphasis on victimization and the puniness of the individual, and the over-optimistic emphasis on the sheer human potentiality of some of the Romantics. In Olsen, human beings experience ravening hungers of all kinds: physical, emotional, intellectual, spiritual. But when these hungers are fed, the individuals develop their potential and give to others and to the world at large: fulfilled people are productive and nurturing in turn. In Olsen's view the deepest human hunger is to be fruitful, so human beings satisfy their own needs best by giving. The negative conclusions of this Rousseauvian view are likewise drawn: those who are prevented by circumstances from developing their productive and nurturing natures will be inclined in turn to become victimizers and stultifiers of others.

The Rousseauvian dimension of Olsen's work is most obviously demonstrated by the fact that in each of her fictions there is a child at or near the center of the story. The child poetically embodies mankind's two dominant characteristics: potential and hunger. Moreover, since she sees each individual human life and all human life in general as parallel journeys toward greater consciousness, what happens to the child is emblematic of the condition and fate of humankind.

Since for Olsen the deepest human hunger is to be fruitful, mothering, in its ideal form, is an example of intense fulfillment. It is also a source of knowledge. Through the experience, the mother discovers human potential and all the forces that operate to limit it; she comes to see human beings as born with enormous possibilities for joy, growth, and productivity which are unnaturally thwarted through class, age, sex and race prejudice.

What is implicit about nurturing and motherhood in her fiction is made explicit in *Silences*, where she insists on the "comprehensions possible out of motherhood" and specifies that these comprehensions include "*the very nature, needs, illimitable potentiality of the human being—and the everyday means by which these are distorted, discouraged, limited, extinguished.*" Moreover, Olsen asserts that because motherhood is a neglected theme in literature (neglected because mothers are not usually able to become writers), these comprehensions have not yet "come to powerful, undeniable, useful expression." Thus there are "aspects and understandings of human life as yet largely absent in literature." Olsen's own fiction is itself an attempt to redeem that "loss in literature."

... Olsen's exploration of the dirge and song of human life reflects her experience as a Jew and as a woman. Her ideology recapitulates the radical Jewish socialist background in which she grew up; her analysis in terms of the body and the mother/child relationship reflect her deeply felt experiences as a woman. Song and dirge alike emerge from the one radical (in the sense of root, fundamental) condition: the single individual in all his vulnerability, hunger, and yearning potentialities. The uncanny bittersweet harmonies Olsen has created by interweaving dirge and song, by vividly depicting the sheltering of or preying upon vulnerabilities, the nurturing or starving of hungers, the fulfillment or blighting of potentials—these give her own music its intense emotional resonance, as the song and dirge merge into a luminous, all encompassing chord: "the poem of itself."

Source: Bonnie Lyons, "Tillie Olsen: The Writer as a Jewish Woman," in *Studies in American Jewish Literature*, No. 5, 1986, pp. 89–102.

Marilyn Yalom

In the following excerpt, based on a public dialogue between Yalom and Olsen at the Stanford Center for Research on Women in 1980, Yalom provides an overview of Olsen's background, writing process, and major themes.

> HER VOICE SWEEPS ACROSS AN AUDIENCE LIKE THE WAVES OF AN OCEAN, SOMETIMES REPETITIOUS BUT NEVER MONOTONOUS, CARRYING HER LISTENERS ALONG INTO AN EXPLORATION OF LIFE, LITERATURE, AND, ABOVE ALL, THE NECESSITY OF HUMAN SOLIDARITY AND RESISTANCE IN THE FACE OF SOCIAL INJUSTICE."

... Olsen writes about people whose lives are circumscribed by their class and their sex. Yet she cannot be narrowly categorized as a "working class" or a "feminist" writer, since her work presses upon such broad social and existential issues as the interrelationship of self, family, and community, and the brute fact of death.

... Olsen's return to the publishing of fiction after an interval of more than twenty years was occasioned by the receipt of a Stegner Fellowship in Creative Writing at Stanford University in 1956. In the fifties, she wrote the four *Tell Me a Riddle* stories which appeared collectively in 1962. Then, with the unexpected discovery of the manuscript of her first novel, considered lost for many years, Olsen published in 1974 a still-unfinished version of *Yonnondio: From the Thirties*, a work that recalls the naturalism of Zola and the style of Elizabeth Madox Robert's *Time of Man* without losing its distinctly personal mode of literary expressionism. Her long-awaited last book, *Silences*, 1978, originally conceived as a talk to the Radcliffe Institute where she was a fellow from 1962–1964, received enthusiastic critical acclaim from reviewers who signaled its exhaustive scholarship and original style. In it, Olsen explodes the myth that genius "will out" whether it resides in a garret room or a manor house. Instead, she presents a convincing case for the influence of external circumstances on human achievement, most notably on the achievement of women whose literary productivity has traditionally been curtailed not only by material conditions but also by the demands of motherhood and the role of social nurturer.

To a large extent, Olsen understands her own success and limitations as a writer within this same conceptual framework. She sees herself as having been inhibited from writing by the general circumstances shared by most women whose lives are consumed by paid work and family responsibilities. As she writes in *Silences*: "substantial creative work demands time," and time was the least available commodity for Olsen when she "raised children without household help" and "worked on everyday jobs as well." If she was able to publish her first book at fifty, it was partially because at that time of life her hands were "lightened" by the exodus of children from the home.

Olsen insists that whenever a person achieves public recognition as a creator, "it is not by virtue of great innate capacity, which is far more common than has been assumed . . . but by virtue of special, freaky luck." She traces her own luck to the historical accident of having come to politics and publishing in the thirties when American literature began to concern itself seriously with the experience of people from the working class, and when there was a place to be published in many new little magazines. Olsen sees a parallel between the intellectual climate of the thirties, which encouraged her writing, and the civil rights and women's movements of the sixties and seventies, which created an audience for the writing of blacks and women.

She is, nonetheless, wary of such labels as "women's" literature, "black" literature, and "working class" literature. Such terms tend to be patronizing and exclusionary, and deny the universality of experience rooted in class, race and gender. Olsen says of herself that she writes about "people who must work for a living—that is, most of humanity. 'Working class' sounds limited, alien, 'them out there.'"

Class, gender and race are the three major factors which, according to Olsen, influence a person's sense of self. In 1978, in a Stanford course called "Sense of Identity in Modern Women Writers" where Olsen spoke as a guest lecturer, she surprised the students by asserting that for most human beings, sex, class and color create one's sense of identity. Two years later in a public speech at Stanford, she elaborated upon this point: "When I grew up . . . quest for identity was something only privileged people could concern themselves with." She believes that our core sense of identity is generally so "largely circumstanced by our sex, class and color" that the influence of other personal and cultural factors is of secondary importance.

Here as elsewhere Olsen chooses to veer away from strictly psychological issues, although her writing reveals a fine attention to the nuances of interpersonal process and an ability to create psychologically credible characters. Rather than focus on the "self" as a sui-generis entity, she conceptualizes quest for identity as a profound freedom issue with a societal base. Her convictions seem to spring both from a Marxist and feminist understanding of the material conditions that shape people's lives, and from her personal experience as a woman who stood there ironing, listening, nursing, fully immersed in the elemental issues of life.

Despite the generally insurmountable difficulties creative women face—and these are eloquently outlined in *Silences*—being a woman has not been for Tillie Olsen, as it was for Sylvia Plath, an "awful tragedy." [Plath, *Journals*.] The twenty years spent bearing and rearing her children, when "the simplest circumstances for creation did not exist," did not succeed in destroying Olsen's spirit or extinguishing her hope to write. She carried literature with her from home to the workplace, a poem tacked to the refrigerator door, a book held open in one hand while the other hung onto a bus strap. She kept her writing alive "after the kids were in bed, after the household tasks were done." And as she nurtured her children, so her life as a woman/mother/housekeeper nurtured her literary output. Much of her writing is anchored in the recognizably female experience of sustaining human life, from the basic physical care of babies and dying people to the encouragement of adolescents and young adults seeking their autonomy.

Olsen attends to subjects which male authors would usually ignore or find trivial: ironing, vacuuming, "bacon and eggs in the icebox." Her works are written from a distinctly female, often feminist, point of view, which underscores women's disadvantaged position in a society based on male values and privileges, without losing compassion for the victimized male as well as the victimized female. She was one of the first in the past quarter century to bring a consciously gendered voice to literature. That voice did not go unnoticed by members of the women's movement who recognized in Olsen a precursor and role model for their own literary endeavors. Olsen would be the first to attribute her publication success and literary renown in the seventies to the "luck" of having found a responsive audience in the feminist community. As she writes in *Silences*: "fortunate... are those born into the better climates, when a movement has created a special interest in one's sex, or in one's special subject."

It is largely her style, however, which accounts for her prestige in literary circles. Her style has evolved from the dense richness of *Yonnondio* to the compact lyricism of *Tell Me a Riddle* to the almost elliptical prose of *Silences*, retaining throughout a distinctive poetic quality. For example, in *Yonnondio* the description of work in a Chicago packinghouse during the summer months rises rhythmically with the heat to an unbearable crescendo, fusing the inhuman and the human—factory and workers—into a massive, suffering organic whole.

> And now the dog days are here, the white fierce heat throbbing, when breathing is the drawing in of a scorching flame and the pavement on the bare feet of the children is a sear; when the very young and the very old sicken and die, and the stench cooking down into the pavements and the oven houses throbs like a great wave of vomit in the air.
>
> There in the packing houses the men and women somehow toil through. Standing there, the one motion all day, their clothes salty with sweat, or walking in and out of the cooler till the cold is a fever and the heat a chill, and the stink bellying up from the blood house and casings forces the beginning of a vomit, even on those who boasted they hadn't a smeller any more.
>
> Oh yes, the heavy air clamps down like a coffin lid over the throbbing streets, on the thin cries of babies and the querulous voices of the old, and a sound of breathing hoarse and strained, of breathing feeble and labored goes up; and from beneath the glisten of sweat on a thousand brows, a mocking bitterness in old old words: is it hot enough for you? in a dozen dialects, is it hot enough, hot enough, hot enough for you?

Although the world depicted by Olsen in most of her writing is a world of material marginality and social conflict, and sometimes—as in *Yonnondio*—the bleakness rises to a level of almost malevolent intensity, still the characters in her fiction do not fall into despair. When asked what redeems her characters and keeps them from permanently despairing, Olsen articulates her belief in the power of human resiliency, as illustrated both in personal efforts at change and in the various liberation movements throughout history.

The human baby is one of her favorite examples of the potential for boundless possibility born within each person, which becomes undermined all too soon by the "color of our skin, the sex of our body, our walk of life," and other social and historical factors. Baby Bess in *Yonnondio*:

> Bess who has been fingering a fruit jar lid absently, heedlessly drops it, aimlessly groping across the table, reclaims it again. Lightning in her brain. She releases, grabs, releases, grabs. I can do. Bang! I did that. I can do I! A look of a neanderthal concentration is on her face. That noise! In triumphant, astounded joy she clashes the lid down. Bang, slam, whack. Release, grab, slam, bang, bang. Centuries of human drive work in her; human ecstacy of achievement; satisfaction deeper and more fundamental than sex. I can do, I use my powers; I!

At the other end of the life cycle are those who have been maimed and deformed—the aged and the dying—as portrayed in Olsen's masterpiece "Tell Me a Riddle." Nowhere is her art more evident than in this fifty-four page novella, the story of a poor, elderly, querulous Jewish couple, married for forty-seven trying years, and ultimately faced with the wife's cancerous death. In its compassionate evocation of one woman's encounter with death, "Tell Me a Riddle" has been compared to Tolstoy's classic story, "The Death of Ivan Ilych." What distinguishes "Tell Me a Riddle" from most other works on this subject is its focus on the couple as a unit experiencing death together. Even such a couple as this one, with its bitter history of antagonistic personalities and desires, can, when death becomes imminent, rise to a level of silent understanding that gives dignity to their final moments together. The story's special poignancy derives largely from the character of husband and wife. They are not conventional tragic figures from the world of a Hemingway or a Malraux, going to their deaths gravely with a sense of accomplishment. They are simply two people from the everyday world, undistinguished, even comical; two people who have known hardship, poverty, unpleasantness, the hourly grind of work and family life. They come from Olsen's world and represent not only its modest economic level and social class, but also the ability of its members to care for one another through a lifetime accumulation of mutually inflicted scars.

... When Olsen speaks in public, despite her occasional stuttering and a tendency to amplify a central theme almost to the point of digression, she has a remarkable ability to capture and hold an audience. She knows how to speak directly to an individual in the crowd and, at the same time, to create a sense of human community within the group. This is due, in part, to her compelling voice, but perhaps even more to the intensity of her emotions, her convictions, and her sense of authority, as she circles back, incessantly, to the interlocking themes of human endurance, resistance, and beneficent action.

She is fond of reading aloud from "I Stand Here Ironing" passages that embody these themes. The story, drawn from the experiences of her eldest child, suggests the affectionate interplay between a mother and daughter for whom life has not been easy, as well as the more hostile interplay between family and outside world. "I Stand Here Ironing" begins and ends with the image of mother at the ironing board (like Whistler's mother forever in a rocker) fretfully hoping that her nineteen year old will somehow find the strength to resist those oppressive forces which would roll over her, like an iron over a dress.

> She starts up the stairs to bed. "Don't get *me* up with the rest in the morning." "But I thought you were having midterms." "Oh, those," she comes back in, kisses me, and says quite lightly, "in a couple of years when we'll all be atomdead they won't matter a bit."
>
> She has said it before. She *believes* it. But because I have been dredging the past, and all that compounds a human being is so heavy and meaningful in me, I cannot endure it tonight.. ..She has much to her and probably little will come of it. She is a child of her age, of depression, of war, of fear.
>
> Let her be. So all that is in her will not bloom—but in how many does it? There is still enough left to live by. Only help her to know—help make it so there is a cause for her to know—that she is more than this dress on the ironing board, helpless before the iron.

Wherever Olsen goes, her impact on the public is tremendous. Her voice sweeps across an audience like the waves of an ocean, sometimes repetitious but never monotonous, carrying her listeners along into an exploration of life, literature, and, above all, the necessity of human solidarity and resistance in the face of social injustice. Often in her talks and readings, she herself is brought to tears by a passionate sense of responsibility to her formerly silenced self and

> HER PRODUCTIVITY HAS BEEN SMALL, BUT SHE WOULD NOT HAVE TO WRITE A GREAT DEAL MORE THAN SHE HAS TO EARN A PLACE AMONG THE EMINENT WRITERS OF SHORT STORIES."

to all the silenced people for whom she bears witness. Unsolicited letters attest to her sway. They speak of feelings "too deep for words," of "tears that come unexpectedly." One of the most telling statements was found in a single sentence: "Tillie has given us back to ourselves."

Source: Marilyn Yalom, "Tillie Olsen," in *Women Writers of the West Coast: Speaking of Their Lives and Careers*, edited by Marilyn Yalom, Capra Press, 1983, pp. 57–66.

William Van O'Connor

In the following essay, O'Connor praises Olsen's short stories for the power of their scenes of everyday life.

Tillie Olsen writes about anguish. One character thinks: "It is a long baptism into the seas of humankind, my daughter. Better immersion and in pain than to live untouched. Yet how will you sustain?"

In one story a soft-hearted sailor has lived a boisterous, rowdy, hard-drinking life. His world is empty, meaningless and in an eerie flux of days and nights at sea, transient acquaintanceships at bars and brothels when he is very drunk. His only refuge is a man whose life he had once saved, and the man's family. He has given the wife and children presents and much needed money. They have all loved him, and welcomed his visits. But now that he can tolerate his anguish only by constant drinking, during which he uses foul language and is an embarrassment before their friends, they are torn between devotion to him, or to what he once was, and their own respectability. Not being able to tolerate their disapproval, he leaves. Drunken, he looks back from a hill at their house, an island of light and warmth. The image blurs, and the house becomes impersonal and anonymous. One knows the sailor will find release from his pain only in the bottle, and finally in death.

An early scene in a second story presents a white girl in her early teens at a Negro church meeting. The singing, shouting, and strange rhythmic movements terrify her, and she faints. She has been very friendly with a colored girl her own age, having shared dolls, parties, and secrets. But white girls, in white society, eventually go their own paths, and, reluctantly, the girls give each other up. The white girl discovers she is filled with shame and guilt, and wants her mother to explain why there is so much misery and unhappiness. The mother embraces her, at the same time wondering where she herself would find that "place of strength" and "the gloved and loving hands" waiting "to support and understand."

In a third story, a mother, standing over her ironing board, ponders the life of her nineteen year old daughter. Someone, presumably a principal or counselor, has asked the mother "to come in and talk with me about your daughter." As she irons, she thinks back over the girl's life. The daughter was born in the depression. The father, unable to endure their poverty, leaves them. The mother works, puts the child in a nursery, then sends her to live with her husband's family. The mother remarries. There is never enough money, and they move frequently. The girl is not good in school, even though she tries hard. She has no close friends. She is small and dark, and not at all out-going. She does have one talent—she can be a sad-eyed clown, able to hold an audience enthralled; but a lack of money prevents the mother from helping her develop the talent. Eventually, the girl gives up in despair. The bomb becomes her symbol of frustration, and she justifies her passive opposition to society on the grounds that "we'll all be atom-dead" soon and nothing will matter. The mother believes that despite poverty and suffering there is "still enough to live by." But she does not know how to convince her daughter.

The story about the sailor is "Hey Sailor, What Ship?" The story about the white and colored children is "O Yes," and the one about the mother and daughter is "I Stand Here Ironing." The three stories have anguish and despair as the antagonists. The protagonists hope, but with no real confidence. There appears to be no margin on the far side of despair for the sailor to reach. The children in "O Yes" find that friendship dissolves under economic, racial and social pressures. And the mother merely hopes that she can communicate her own sense of the value of life, even of lives lived in desperate circumstances.

A fourth story, "Tell Me a Riddle," is about a Jewish couple who have been married for forty-seven years. The husband wants to retire to his lodge's Haven. He longs to be near other people, and to be free from economic worry. His wife wants to remain in her own house and to be free from all entanglements except the basic quarrel she has with her husband. Her quarrel with him has roots in the dim past. They have had many children, and were always poor. She resented his going out at night to visit with his cronies. She also had literary interests, but the pressure of work made it impossible for her to pursue them. Instead of reading, she sewed and scrubbed. Now in their old age they fight. Sometimes he cajoles her, hoping to win a victory; but she ridicules him, and soon he is calling her unpleasant names. Each gets a perverse joy out of their struggle, although he would be agreeable to a truce. Their children find all this distressing and unavailingly introduce many rational arguments about why it is foolish for their parents to quarrel.

She becomes ill, and after repeated refusals to visit a doctor she is examined. An operation follows, and the family learns she has cancer. She has about one year to live. A round of visits with their children follows. The grandchildren are noisy, and she is constantly tired. One child says, "Tell me a riddle, Grammy"; and she replies, "I know no riddles, child." In pain, she watches the activities of her children changing diapers; grandchildren climbing trees, hiding in closets; observes people in the streets, listens to sounds, and remembers. She relives her life, as a child in Europe, the birth of her children, the quarreling with her husband, and much else. Sometimes she sweats, sometimes she retches.

In California, they sit together on benches at the beach, watching other people playing, and looking out to sea. A grandchild who is a nurse lovingly attends her. He, the husband, feels death pursuing them, and refuses to take his wife home. These are the last two paragraphs:

> That last day the agony was perpetual. Time after time it lifted her almost off the bed, so they had to fight to hold her down. He could not endure and left the room; wept as if there never would be tears enough.

> Jeannie came to comfort him. In her light voice she said: Granddaddy, Granddaddy, don't cry. She is not there, she promised me. On the last day, she said she would go back to when she

first heard music, a little girl on the road of the village where she was born. She promised me. It is a wedding and they dance, while the flutes so joyous and vibrant tremble in the air. Leave her there, Granddaddy, it is all right. She promised me. Come back, come back and help her poor body to die.

"Tell Me a Riddle" is as full of anguish as "The Death of Ivan Ilytch." It is also as serene, with the distance and calm of tragedy. Miss Olsen shows the human being's capacity to endure his own suffering, his own irrationality, and his own despair. Only creatures capable of a great and transforming idealism could turn such suffering into peaceful acceptance. They are defeated, but they are not routed. Subjected to enormous indignities, they remain dignified. "Tell Me a Riddle" exhibits once again the classic tragic stance, and does it magnificently.

Miss Olsen's stories are quite skillfully put together. On occasion, San Francisco seems to be the locale of a story, but generally the setting is not specifically identified. There is a city, the ocean, or a poor neighborhood, and it could be any city, either ocean, and almost any poor neighborhood. The stories push away from the individual and the unique, toward the world of Everyman.

The sailor is any lonesome human being who hopes against hope that he can be free from his wretchedness. The white child is any child discovering ineradicable evil. The mother is any mother who has failed, or believes she has failed, in rearing her child. The Jewish couple are a man and a woman facing death.

Miss Olsen's method is reminiscent of [Thorton] Wilder's in *Our Town*, [Dylan] Thomas' in *Under Milk Wood*, and [Thomas] Hardy's in *The Dynasts*. She names characters, but usually one finds out very little about them. Sometimes they are only a voice. Conversations are universal rather than particularized. The voice of the Jewish husband—"You have important business, Mrs. Inahurry? The President wants to consult with you?"—is other Jewish voices one has heard, first generation immigrant, mocking, with ages of patience and suffering back of them. The sailor's language is any sailor's language: "She don't hafta be jealous. I got money for her." The young colored girl adopts jive talk: "Couple cats from Franklin Jr. chirp in the choir. No harm or alarm." The lonely child in the convalescent home writes an anguished

letter: "I am fine. How is the baby. If I write my letter nicely I will have a star." And "There never was a star."

Characters are rendered only as much as is necessary to place them in a certain kind of environment. The homes of the children in "Tell Me a Riddle" are not described. One does not know much about their husbands or wives. The voices come in over one another. One is married to a doctor, whom she quotes. Another can't bear to see her mother suffer. A third needs more money. They are people. They breathe, suffer, wonder.

The chronology or sequence of events in the stories is ordered not as these occurred, but as they impinge on a character's memory. As in [William] Faulkner's *Absalom, Absalom!* or *The Sound and the Fury*, Miss Olsen's stories seem gradually to "discover" themselves for the reader. She does, however, give the reader more assistance than Faulkner does. She does not immerse him so deeply in the dark recesses where events are happening but have not as yet been explained. She sets a scene quickly, usually, with a few sentences. Then the characters take over, talking, remembering, laughing or crying. Occasionally the author intrudes with a refrain, such as "*Hey Sailor, what ship?*" or a rhetorical commentary, such as "*So it is that she sits in the wind of the singing, among the thousand various faces of age.*" But mostly the action belongs to the characters.

When Miss Olsen is at her best, as in "Tell Me a Riddle," she is a writer of tremendous skill and power. Her productivity has been small, but she would not have to write a great deal more than she has to earn a place among the eminent writers of short stories.

Source: William Van O'Connor, "The Stories of Tillie Olsen," in *Studies in Short Fiction*, Vol. 1, No. 1, Fall 1963, pp. 21–25.

SOURCES

"Access to Child Care for Low Income Working Families," in *Child Care & Early Education Research Connections*, http://www.childcareresearch.org/childcare/resources/180? q = Access + to + Child + Care + for + Low + Income + Working + Families (accessed June 6, 2010).

Atwood, Margaret, "Obstacle Course," Review of *Silences*, in *New York Times*, July 30, 1978, p. BR1.

Baker, Al, "Judge Cites Discrimination in N.Y. Fire Dept.," in *New York Times*, January 13, 2010, http://www.nytimes.com/2010/01/14/nyregion/14fire.html (accessed June 10, 2010).

Coiner, Constance, "Tillie Olsen: Biographical Sketch and Thirties Publications," in *Better Red: The Writing and Resistance of Tillie Olsen and Meridel Le Sueur*, Oxford University Press, 1995, pp. 141–73.

"Congressional Reports: Joint Inquiry into Intelligence Community Activities before and after the Terrorist Attacks of September 11, 2001," in *GPO Access*, http://www.gpoaccess.gov/serialset/creports/911.html (accessed June 10, 2010).

Courtenay-Thompson, Fiona, and Kate Phelps, eds., *The 20th Century Year by Year: The People and Events That Shaped the Last Hundred Years*, Barnes & Noble, 1998, pp. 179–203.

Frye, Joanne, "O Yes," in *Tillie Olsen: A Study of Her Short Fiction*, Twayne Publishers, 1995, pp. 55–74.

———, "Roots, Sources, and Circumstances: Tillie Olsen in Conversation with Joanna Frye," in *Tillie Olsen: A Study of Her Short Fiction*, Twayne Publishers, 1995, pp. 156–64.

Glennon, Lorraine, ed., *The 20th Century: An Illustrated History of Our Lives and Times*, JG Press, 1999, pp. 377–406.

Harmon, William, William Flint Thrall, Addison Hibbard, and Clarence Hugh Holman, *A Handbook to Literature*, 11th ed., Pearson Prentice Hall, 2008, pp. 14, 51, 180, 361, 511–12, 540.

Jennings, Peter, and Todd Brewster, eds., *The Century*, Doubleday, 1998, pp. 332–36.

Krupnick, Mark, "Tillie Olsen: Feminist Author Famous for Helping Aspiring Women Writers to Find a Voice," in *Guardian* (London, England), January 4, 2007, p. 30.

Lopez, Mark Hugo, "Dissecting the 2008 Electorate: Most Diverse in U.S. History," in *Pew Research Center Publications*, http://pewresearch.org/pubs/1209/racial-ethnic-voters-presidential-election (accessed June 13, 2010).

Olsen, Tillie, "O Yes," in *Tell me a Riddle*, Dell, 1961, pp. 39–62.

Peden, William, "Dilemmas of Day-to-Day Living," Review of *Tell Me a Riddle*, in *New York Times*, November 12, 1961, p. BR 54.

Reid, Panthea, *Tillie Olsen: One Woman, Many Riddles*, Rutgers University Press, 2010, pp. 6–110.

Row, Jess, "Her Silences Spoke Volumes," in *Slate*, http://www.slate.com/id/2157161 (accessed June 13, 2010).

"Tillie Olsen," in *Tillie Olsen Home Page*, http://www.tillieolsen.net/obituary.php (accessed April 14, 2010).

FURTHER READING

Bauchner, Elizabeth, *Teen Minorities in Rural North America: Growing Up Different*, Mason Crest, 2007.
This book for adolescent readers focuses on the lives of rural teenagers who face racism and prejudice in their communities. The author explores some of the barriers that these adolescents face, including access to education, healthcare, and employment opportunities.

Davis, Thomas J., *Race Relations in the United States, 1940–1960*, Greenwood, 2008.
This young-adult book focuses on racism and anti-Semitism in the United States. The author provides essays about biographical figures and important events, as well as a timeline of the period.

Desetta, Al, ed., *The Courage to Be Yourself: True Stories by Teens about Cliques, Conflicts, and Overcoming Peer Pressure*, Free Spirit Publishing, 2005.
This book for teenage readers includes twenty-six short essays written by young people who describe segregation, exclusion, and intolerance based on physical appearance, race, ethnicity, or other differences.

Golden, Marita, and Susan Shreve, eds., *Skin Deep: Black Women & White Women Write about Race*, Anchor, 1996.
This books includes both fiction and nonfiction selections from a number of important authors, including Joyce Carol Oates, Alice Walker, bell hooks, Naomi Wolff, and Eudora Welty. Each story or essay probes issues of racial difference between white and black women.

Lucke, Margaret, *Schaum's Quick Guide to Writing Great Short Stories*, McGraw-Hill, 1999.
This text provides an easy-to-follow guide for writing stories. There are many tips for finding story ideas, developing a plot, and creating memorable characters.

Reddy, Maureen, ed., *Everyday Acts against Racism: Raising Children in a Multiracial World*, Seal, 1996.
This collection of twenty-one essays provides practical advice about ending racism.

SUGGESTED SEARCH TERMS

O Yes AND short story

O Yes AND Olsen

Olsen AND Tell Me a Riddle

Tillie Olsen AND short story

O Yes AND racism

Tillie Olsen AND racism

Tillie Olsen AND religion

Tillie Olsen AND autobiography

Tillie Olsen AND activism

Popular Mechanics

RAYMOND CARVER

1981

Raymond Carver's short story "Popular Mechanics" is less than 500 words long, but it offers readers several elements that are common to Carver's fiction from the 1970s and 1980s. It takes place in an indeterminate time and place: there are signs of contemporary society, but Carver's distinctive way with language makes the story feel as if it is taking place in a dream. The focus of the story is a couple inflicting violence on each other, verbally at first, but eventually the violence escalates to the verge of a physical brawl. A horrific event is implied in the end, but Carver does not explicitly describe it, instead trusting readers to draw the conclusions he has in mind from the facts they are given. In the 1980s, Raymond Carver became one of the most recognized and imitated voices in American fiction, and readers can see in this story the unique power of his prose.

"Popular Mechanics" was originally published in Carver's collection *Furious Seasons*, published by Capra Press in 1977, as "Mine." It was given the name "Popular Mechanics" in the 1981 collection *What We Talk About When We Talk About Love*, published by Alfred A. Knopf. In 1988, the year Carver died, it was included in the collection *Where I'm Calling From: New and Selected Stories* as "Little Things."

Raymond Carver (© Sophie Bassouls / Sygma / Corbis)

AUTHOR BIOGRAPHY

Carver was born on May 25, 1938, in Clatskanie, Oregon. His father, who had moved to the Pacific Northwest from Arkansas, was a sawmill worker, and his mother was a waitress. Carver grew up in Yakima, Washington. After graduating from high school, he went to work in a sawmill with his father. At age nineteen he was married to his first wife, Maryann Burk, who was sixteen years old and pregnant. Their first child, a daughter, was born in 1958, and a year later a son was born.

In 1958 the family moved to California, where both Carver and his wife worked several menial jobs at a time and Carver attended Chico State College (later renamed Chico State University). He did not complete his degree there, but transferred to Humboldt State College. With the support of the novelist John Gardner, under whom Carver studied at Chico State, he started submitting his short stories and fiction to magazines. His first story, "The Furious Seasons," was published in 1960 in *Selection*, and his first poem, "The Brass Ring," was published soon after in the magazine *Targets*. Throughout the 1960s he published in various small literary magazines, building his reputation.

After his story "Will You Please be Quiet, Please?" was selected for inclusion in *The Best American Short Stories, 1967* and Sacramento State College published his first book of poetry, *Near Klamath*, the same year, Carver was able to leave menial jobs and make a living teaching creative writing. He took visiting teaching positions at several universities, but a growing problem with alcoholism made it difficult for him to keep a job. His drinking became so bad that he was hospitalized several times in 1976 and 1977, on June 2, 1977, he quit drinking completely. Even during the years of his heaviest drinking, however, his stories and poems were published in magazines, and his reputation flourished.

In 1976, his first short-story collection, *Will You Please Be Quiet, Please?*, was published to great acclaim. In 1977, Carver met and fell in love with the poet Tess Gallagher. The two were together for the rest of his life. He and Maryann, who had helped him with his writing, were separated, though they did not formally divorce until 1982.

Carver published ten books of poetry and prose between 1977 and 1988 and received the most prestigious awards given to writers, including a Guggenheim Fellowship, a National Book Circle Critics Award, the Mildred and Harold Strauss Living Award, American Academy and Institute of Arts and Letters, nominations for the Pulitzer Prize for *Cathedral* in 1984 and the posthumous *Where I'm Calling From* in 1989, six O. Henry Awards, and an honorary doctorate of letters from Hartford University.

In 1987, Carver was diagnosed with lung cancer. He underwent surgery, but the cancer recurred. He and Tess Gallagher were married on June 17, 1988, and on August 2 he died at his home in Port Angeles, Washington.

PLOT SUMMARY

"Popular Mechanics" starts with an ominous image that prepares readers for the sordid tragedy that unfolds. It is snowing as the story

MEDIA
ADAPTATIONS

- Although there are no commercial recordings of Carver reading this particular story, American Audio Prose Library has released a CD of the author reading three other short stories: "Nobody Said Anything," "A Serious Talk," and "Fat." This 1983 release is available from the American Audio Prose Library Web site.

- Nine of Carver's stories were woven together to make the film *Short Cuts*, directed by Robert Altman and released in 1993. The Criterion Collection DVD includes the documentary "Luck, Trust, and Ketchup: Robert Altman in Carver Country," about the director's quest to personally understand the characters Carver wrote about.

- Carver was the subject of a BBC documentary, part of the "Great Writers of the Twentieth Century" series. A CD of this program is available from Films for the Arts and Humanities, released in 2006.

---

begins. Snow can be beautiful, but the rest of the first sentence paints a dreary picture: the snow is not sparkling and pristine, and it does not melt into clear rivulets in brilliant sunshine but turns to "dirty water." Readers are thus prepared for the ugly scene to come. This effect is amplified in the rest of the paragraph, as the dimming of the light outside affects the illumination inside the living room and kitchen, which are lit by nothing but the light coming through the small, high window.

When the story introduces its central characters, they are at the end of a bitter argument. The man has apparently decided that he has nothing else to say and has decided to simply leave. The violence with which he throws his clothes into the suitcase, "pushing" them in, might indicate his urgency to get out, but it could also be a sign that he is acting out for dramatic effect in an emotional battle. The first

words of dialogue in the story support this, as the woman shouts out how glad she is to see him leave, rather than accepting her good luck at being rid of her opponent. Readers do not know who these people are, what their relationship is, or what the issue is in this fight, but they can tell that these two people are accustomed to fighting, and when they do fight, they labor to say and do things that will hurt the other person.

As they are fighting, the woman picks up an item that the man is planning to take with him, a picture of their child. She may just take it to deny him something, choosing randomly from his suitcase. Taking the picture changes the situation, though. It draws the man's attention to the child, and from that moment on, the man determines that the picture will not be enough. He wants to take the actual child with him when he goes.

The woman holds the baby, bundled up in a blanket, in her arms. Even before the man makes a move toward her, the baby begins to cry, indicating that the mother might be trembling, fidgeting, or in some other way agitated. When the man actually moves to take the child, after three times announcing his intention to take him, she is shocked, as if their arguments are often filled with empty threats, and she never expected him to actually try to take the baby.

As she backs away, the man moves toward her. She becomes increasingly panicked. Eventually she moves into a small space behind the stove, holding tightly to the crying baby. The dangerous location, with the possibility of flame and lethal gas, increases the story's tension. The tension increases even more when a flowerpot falls to the floor. The couple are too engrossed in their struggle to notice it.

In trying to wrest the baby from its mother, the man pushes against the woman. The baby is between them, so there is a good possibility that he could be crushed, especially since they are both struggling so intensely. Before the action reaches its climax, Carver returns to the image of light, drawing attention to the fact that the sun has set outside and there is no more light coming through the window, plunging the room into near darkness.

The man pries the woman's fingers off the baby, whose screams add to the frenzy of the situation. When her grip loosens, the man pulls the baby away. The woman reacts with fury, refusing to lose the baby. She manages one last grab at the baby, catching it by the arm the man is not holding, and she pulls. The man, feeling the baby come out of his grasp, pulls in the opposite direction.

At the end of the story, Carver does not state what happened, but the conclusion is unavoidable. At the least, the baby must have had one or both arms broken, although it is very likely that he suffered an even worse injury. The story's title, "Popular Mechanics," gives readers some indication of the baby's fate. The destruction that is certain to occur following the story's last line is a matter of physics and mechanics, as opposed to the elevated emotions of the argument.

CHARACTERS

The Baby

The baby in this story is treated like an object that the man and the woman each want to control in order to hurt the other. The gender of the baby is mentioned only twice, when the father says "Let go of him"; otherwise, he is referred to as "the baby" by both the narrator and the people in the story. As the struggle between the characters progresses, the baby cries more and more fiercely, adding to the tension of the situation.

The Man

The man is leaving at the beginning of this story. He has his suitcase out and he is packing it, taking, in addition to his clothes, a picture of the child, who is presumably his son. The man appears to be a terrible father, judging from the woman's reaction when she hears that he wants to take the boy with him: she is so horrified by the suggestion that she seems to think that the man himself should be able to see how ridiculous it is. Her reaction, though, only serves to make the man more determined, so that his spontaneous decision to take the boy becomes an obsession. As he chases her, he doggedly proclaims "I want the baby" three times, ignoring her threats and pleas.

Although the man's determination to take the baby from the woman is irrational, he does pursue it with some logic. When he has her worked into a corner, he peels her fingers away from the child methodically, rather than assaulting her with overt violence. In his mind, this is a reasonable course of action to pursue, and it is the woman who is being unreasonable by refusing to give in to him.

The Woman

The woman is in a frenzy from the beginning of the story, apparently from an argument that has already been in progress. While the man silently packs his suitcase, she shouts at him and curses at him, trying to elicit some response. She goads the man about his refusal to look at her during their argument, trying to initiate more interaction and extend the argument further. When he still won't look at her, she takes a photograph of the baby from his suitcase. This does get the man's attention, as she intended, but it sets into motion the series of events that will lead to the story's tragic end.

When the man announces his intention to take the baby, the woman is horrified. No matter how bitter and personal their argument has been up to that point, she can see the danger inherent in putting the child in his hands. Her statements to him as he tries to take the baby are not as personally cruel as her earlier statements: she is amazed and horrified, but no longer angry, as she tries to protect the baby's life.

In the end, though, the competitive spirit overtakes the woman as well. When the man wrests the baby from her, her main thought is no longer about protecting the child. Carver writes a line that shows that she has forgotten to think of the baby as a human being, referring to "it": "She would have it, this baby." It is when the woman abandons any recognition of her child's humanity that the damage occurs.

THEMES

Husband-Wife Relationships

Carver never reveals to his readers whether the man and woman in "Popular Mechanics" are married, or whether one or both is the child's parent. They are living together and raising the child together, though, so for the purposes of this short story, they are functioning as a married couple.

In a well-functioning marriage, husbands and wives are bound to have some disagreements. Usually, they find some way, through patience and compromise, to accept each other's values. When children are involved, there is an even greater need to find common ground and settle differences. The man and woman in this story cannot be considered to be in a healthy relationship.

TOPICS FOR FURTHER STUDY

- It is clear that the characters in this story are deficient in the problem-solving skills they need to live decent lives. You can help them. Chose either the mother or the father and make a mind map for them at Mondomo.com or a similar Web site. While doing this, you may need to make up information about your character, what writers call the "back story." Your character's map should be complex enough to show them how they can take control of their problems before trouble occurs.

- Many of the angry, violent relationships in Carver's early stories are thought to have stemmed from his difficult first marriage and becoming a father at a young age. Read Angela Johnson's young-adult novel *The First Part Last*, about a contemporary teen named Bobby who is successful in raising his son and finishing his education. Chart the traits that Bobby possesses that enable him to succeed and then chart the traits exhibited by the father in "Popular Mechanics," using a Venn diagram. Identify which character you more closely resemble in each trait by highlighting them on the diagram.

- Dramatize a meeting between this couple and a marriage counselor. The students playing the man and the woman should be able to explain in detail what is bothering them, while the student playing the counselor should be prepared to offer sound advice. Conduct interviews with counselors, pastors, and other adults about what advice should be given to the couple to make the dramatization more realistic.

- Create a panel to argue the question of whether this story is a specifically American story or whether the attitudes and behaviors in it are common to all cultures. Offer examples from experience or from research to support your side.

- Raymond Carver's style has brought comparisons to the Russian writer Anton Chekhov, often considered the greatest short-story writer ever. Read Chekhov's story "Gooseberries," and write an essay in which you examine the similarities in style, even though the subjects of the stories could not be more different.

The story gives no clear indication of the cause of their fight, but it is clear that they are at a breaking point in their relationship at the outset of the story. At first, when the woman sees the man leaving, she fights against it. She does not ask him to stay, but she does goad him to look at her, trying to remain the focus of his attention just a little longer. When he tells her that he wants to take the baby with him, she laughs, knowing that he could never succeed as a caregiver for a baby. He becomes violent, though, when he cannot get what he wants, turning into a macho stereotype in a way that she does not anticipate. He lunges at the baby and intimidates the woman with his strength. She matches his force with equal force. This might work to equalize their respective power in a

relationship based on force, but the child ends up in the middle of their terrible semblance of a relationship, with tragic results.

Anger

This story is a study in the ways anger can escalate in a relationship, taking a domestic argument to lethal extremes. It starts with open hostility, as the man plans to break up their relationship and the woman shouts that she is happy to see him leave. Soon, however, their open hostility becomes subverted into a more understated competition. They use the child's presence as a weapon against each other. The woman begins by refusing to let the man take so much as a picture of the child with him, and the man responds by insisting that he wants to take the actual child. The man is so blinded by anger that he puts the child in danger, and the woman responds with her own increased anger, to the extent that she tries to wrest the child by the arm from the man's grip. By the end of the story, they both know that their emotions are wrong and dangerous, but they also know that their actions can hurt their enemy, and, fueled by anger, that is what matters most to each of them.

Weakness

As the battle that ensues between the man and the woman becomes increasingly primitive, the man has an advantage because he has more physical strength. Strength is not usually a significant factor in a contemporary personal relationship, but rage turns their relationship into something much more primitive until it reaches a point where strength alone matters. The woman runs from the man, knowing that he will be able to overpower her. When she is literally cornered, the man pushes with all of his might against her, and she still resists him. He is able to pry the baby loose from her desperate grip, but she reaches out and grabs onto the child's wrist.

In their fury, both of the adults are powerful, and the only weak element in this struggle, the only thing that can cede when two forces pull against each other, is the body of the infant.

Absurdity

Absurdity is the absence of logic or reason. Though the actions of this story follow a direct path to its end, the severity of its end and the deadpan title that Carver has given this story are comments on how flaring tempers can make a situation quickly turn absurd.

Most people know better than to allow a situation to escalate to pulling on the limbs of a baby. Still, terrible events do occur. The reason that the conclusion of this story is absurd is that Carver shows readers the perspectives of each of the parents and, while the emotions and actions are excessive, readers can see how each parent arrives at this point. The man is willing to end the bad situation at the start, until the woman confiscates the child's picture, driving him toward retaliation. The woman taunts him in a way that seems to be standard in their relationship, and she is surprised that the man would actually think that taking the child with him is a reasonable idea. They each have an idea of what should

She held the baby tightly. (*Monkey Business Images / Shutterstock.com*)

happen, but their inability to handle the situation causes it to spin out of control.

Their struggle results in the maiming or death of their child, an unavoidable effect that Carver coldly characterizes in the title as "mechanics." When the word "popular" is added to it, the title of the story refers to the title of a magazine that deals with science, physics, and technology, but not with the extremes of psyche that would lead parents to abuse their own child. The absurdity lies in the fact that the baby's fate in the story is not, by any means, popular.

STYLE

Tone

Raymond Carver often used a detached, almost otherworldly tone in his short stories. This tone is achieved through several techniques, one of which is the avoidance of the use of proper names, instead referring to people by their social positions: in this story the characters are "the man," "the woman," and "the baby," while other stories dub characters "the doctor," "the kid," "the bartender," and so on. Carver's writing was also notable for its lack of adornment. He used adjectives and adverbs very sparingly, often relying on nouns and verbs to convey the bare essence of his stories. Another technique that is noticeable in "Popular Mechanics" is the absence of quotation marks around lines of dialogue, giving spoken words no more narrative significance than anything else in the worlds his characters inhabit.

The result of these techniques is a sense of reality that is dry and predictable. Readers are not encouraged to step into the lives of Carver's characters, but instead to examine them as if they are living their lives behind glass. The aloof tone used in stories like "Popular Mechanics" does not promote empathy, but it does make readers approach the story with heightened attention, as every word or punctuation mark may be important.

Allusion

An allusion is an unstated reference to another literary work, often with action that resembles the action in that work. In "Popular Mechanics," there is a biblical allusion to the story of the judgment of Solomon, which is told in the First Book of Kings in the Old Testament.

In the biblical story, two women come before King Solomon, each claiming to be the true mother of a baby boy. One woman's infant son died, and she switched her dead child with the infant of the other woman. With no way to determine the child's parentage, Solomon decrees that the only fair thing to do would be to cut the child in half and give half to each mother. The lying mother accepts this verdict, but the child's true mother is aghast, and declares that she would rather lose her son than let him be harmed this way. Solomon can tell by this woman's reaction that she is the actual mother, and he then awards the baby to her.

The judgment of Solomon has come to represent any occasion where a judge might issue a flawed decree in order to see how the opposing parties react. When Carver refers to a baby being split in two as the matter being decided, he draws attention to the fact that there is a distinct lack of

wisdom in the actions of this battling couple, as well as a lack of compassion.

HISTORICAL CONTEXT

Minimalism

Carver was considered to be one of the leaders of the minimalist literary movement that flourished in the 1980s. Minimalism began in the 1950s as an experimental style and blossomed slowly until it became the prevailing literary style, popularized by writers such as Carver, Frederick Barthelme, and Ann Beattie. Though the minimalist style has always been present in literature, as in the writings of Johann Wolfgang von Goethe in the late 1700s, Edgar Allan Poe in the 1800s, and particularly to the writings of Ernest Hemingway in the early 1900s, it was controversial when it became overwhelmingly popular in the 1980s owing in particular to Carver and, even more particularly, to the impact of his collection *What We Talk About When We Talk About Love.*

Definitions of this style differ, depending on who is asked. In general, minimalist writing is characterized by a conspicuous lack of detail. Emotions are generally omitted, as the writers trust that readers will know what a character is feeling if the situation they find themselves in is described clearly enough. Adjectives and adverbs are often eliminated as well, leaving objects and actions to speak for themselves. In some extreme cases, as in "Popular Mechanics," characters are not even given names or descriptions. Leaving out so much detail involves the reader in a partnership with the author, forcing the reader to participate in putting the action together instead of passively accepting what is told. As Cynthia J. Hallett explained in her article "Minimalism and the Short Story," there is more to a minimalist story than the information given on the page. She quotes the writer Amy Hampell as saying,

> A lot of times what's not reported in your work is more important than what actually appears on the page. Frequently the emotional focus of the story is some underlying event that may not be described or even referred to in the story.

Hampell, Carver, and others whose works were branded with the minimalist label did not accept it willingly. The word was often used negatively, implying that a writer was jumping

COMPARE
&
CONTRAST

- **1981:** The publication of Carver's collection *What We Talk About When We Talk About Love* changes the literary world, as writers all over begin copying his minimalist style of short, direct sentences and his characteristic lack of description or character names.

  Today: Minimalist writing is generally considered to have been a fad that most of its practitioners never did as well as Carver.

- **1981:** Awareness of child abuse grows after the first federal legislation against it is passed in 1974, but it is still often considered a matter of family concern.

  Today: Doctors, hospitals, child-care providers, and educators are required to investigate any suspicion that a child under their care has been abused. Failure of medical personnel and educators to report suspected child abuse is a crime in most states.

- **1981:** The rate of divorce in the United States reaches its all-time high, with 5.3 divorces per 1,000 people in the population.

  Today: According to *DivorceMagazine.com*, the rate of divorce has dropped off steadily since the early 1980s, from an all-time high of 5.3 divorces per 1,000 people in 1981 to 3.6 in 2005. One key reason for this, however, is that fewer couples enter into marriage in the first place.

- **1981.** Writers using the minimalist approach, such as Carver, Ann Beattie, Amy Hempell, and Richard Ford, take an amoral, nonjudgmental tone in their writing. A reference to a biblical story stands out as odd in a work of fiction that is grounded in the middle-class values of Carver's America.

  Today: Since the attacks on the Pentagon and the World Trade Center in 2001, American literary writers like Cormac McCarthy and Elizabeth Strout have been successful with works that recognize the strength of the human spirit.

---

on a trend and purposely writing in an affected, conspicuous style. When Carver's third mainstream story collection, *Cathedral*, was published in 1984, the stories were more expressive and fleshed out, which critics took to be a sign that even the leader of the minimalist movement had lost interest in writing cryptic stories that emphasized the harshness of life. By the end of the 1980s, minimalist writing was viewed as dated and old-fashioned.

Dirty Realism

Carver is also identified by literary critics as one of the leading proponents of a style of writing, popular in the 1970s and 1980s, that focused on the lives of Americans in the lower middle class. This movement was dubbed "dirty realism," a name coined in the July 1983 edition of *Granta* magazine to describe stories whose characters tried to understand the complexities of their lives as they struggled at low-paying jobs or out of work, spending their time on menial, recognizable pursuits such as watching television and shopping. The writing in these works usually took on a flat, unimpressed tone, signaling a world-weariness in the characters. Other writers included in that same *Granta* issue were Richard Ford and Tobias Wolff; eventually the title came to apply to a generation of writers, including Jayne Ann Phillips, Charles Bukowski, and Bobbie Ann Mason, whose subjects were people who would be very unlikely to read literary works such as theirs. In addition to "dirty realism," names that were applied to this literary movement included "K-Mart realism," "TV realism," "white trash fiction," and "postalcoholic blue-collar minimalist hyperrealism."

They argued about the baby. *(Kurhan | Shutterstock.com)*

CRITICAL OVERVIEW

This story is notable because it appeared in three different collections of Carver's fiction under three different titles. Carver was famous for rewriting stories and publishing substantially altered versions, but this story remained the same throughout three phases of his career. It was published in *Furious Seasons*, a small-press publication, before Carver became famous, and was included in *Where I'm Calling From*, the volume of new and selected stories he was preparing when he died. As "Popular Mechanics" it was included in Carver's breakout collection *What We Talk About When We Talk About Love.*

His first collection with a major publisher, *Will You Please Be Quiet, Please?* earned Carver a nomination for the National Book Award, winning him some attention among literary insiders, but it was his second major collection, the 1981 *What We Talk About When We Talk About Love*, the one that carried "Popular Mechanics," that established him as a world-class artist. That collection had a distinctive mood that "Popular Mechanics" fit into well.

In *Understanding Raymond Carver*, Arthur M. Saltzman discusses *What We Talk About When We Talk About Love* as "Carver at his most astringent. The prose style displays the subtle ravages it recounts and runs almost to formula: gelid, skeletal sentences, stifled descriptions, pedestrian diction...." At the time of the collection's publication, there were many reviewers who saw its significance. Kirk Nesset, for instance, in *The Stories of Raymond Carver: A Critical Study*, cites Robert Stone, who called Carver "the greatest short story writer since Hemingway" and short story writer Robert Coover, who referred to Carver as the "godfather" of the minimalist school. As Robert Houston remarks in his review "A Stunning Inarticulateness" in the *Nation*, "Is there a better contemporary writer of short stories than Raymond Carver? Perhaps a handful as good, but none better." Still, there were those who looked at his stories for their content, as did Judith Chettle in *National Review*, who felt that "Carver's litany of the ills of Middle America is so unremitting that the reader becomes increasingly incredulous. His spare style... only heightens this impression of a human wasteland."

Carver's next collection of stories, *Cathedral*, in 1984, showed a broader and more humanistic view of the world. Critics who had disliked his work were won over, convinced that he was not just an author who delivered a distinctive style with no substance. Kathleen Westfall Shute, quoted by Ewing Campbell in *Raymond Carver: A Study of the Short Fiction*, said that Carver's later works

> afford his characters the gift he has always granted the reader: some light by which to navigate, the chance for insight, a greater range of freedom and personal choice and, by implication, the moral responsibility which such an unfettering demands.

CRITICISM

David Kelly

Kelly is a teacher of creative writing in Illinois. In the following essay, he explains why it is necessary for readers to be aware of the author when reading Carver's fiction.

The relationship between Raymond Carver's story "Popular Mechanics" and the story of the judgment of Solomon, told in the Old Testament in the First Book of Kings, is obscure but obvious, simple yet complicated. Carver's story ends with a baby being torn in two directions by its parents, while the biblical tale concerns two women, both prostitutes, laying claim to the same infant, with the true mother only giving up her claim when Solomon orders that the baby be cut into equal parts, half for each claimant. A telling difference, one that might not seem obvious at first, is one of proportion. In one case, the child is to be equally divided, while in the other case readers do not know his fate, but he is sure to be mutilated, with tendons ripped and joints dislocated; he may even lose a hand or a whole arm. This unevenness, the asymmetry of it, is indicative of Carver's fictional world, a world where nothing is evenly divided. Without the guidance of a ruler, without any power in charge, things happen without balance.

In the biblical story, Solomon can declare that equal division of the child is a just way to address the equal claims made by the women of

> THE DARKENING OF THE SKY IS SUCH A BLATANT METAPHOR FOR THE DESTRUCTION THESE CHARACTERS ARE HEADED TOWARD THAT IT DRAWS READERS' ATTENTION TOWARD THE AUTHOR, WHICH, IN THE STORY'S VOID OF ETHICS, IS EXACTLY WHAT IS NEEDED."

equal standing. One woman sees that this is not justice at all. She rejects Solomon's wisdom, pointing out that his dispassionate logic will kill the child, thereby making the whole dispute irrelevant. In "Popular Mechanics," the two parties, the man and the woman, never have any logical proposal to argue against. They are enraged with each other, and their rage leaves them with a sense of justice that is based on principles that are no more just than those behind the division of a wishbone: the winner will be the one left holding the largest piece. They have nothing but their limited wits and their emotions to guide them.

Like the women in the Bible, the characters in "Popular Mechanics" each think they deserve the baby. In the Solomon story, there is one legitimate claim and one false claim. The biblical story shows the inverse logic of love, as the true mother is the one who is willing to forego her claim to her actual child, which she believes will be awarded to the imposter. In Carver's story, readers do not get any context to tell which parent would be a better custodian of the boy. The story is set in the middle of a domestic dispute that began before the first line of the story. Readers do not know what made the man pack his suitcase this particular day. What is important to the story is the way the fury of both parents turns to competition. They each want the baby for their own selfish purposes: like the false mother in the Solomon story, they are each, in the climactic moment, so filled with fury that they are willing to accept the baby's death. Throughout the story, until her anger drives her past the stopping point, the woman in Carver's story tries to protect the baby and shelter him, while the man initially plans on leaving with just a picture

WHAT DO I READ NEXT?

- Carver was recognized as a master of his style and setting. Many stories in *What We Talk About When We Talk About Love* (1981) are reminiscent of one another, but the last one, "One More Thing," has characters and a situation that will particularly remind readers of "Popular Mechanics," with a father leaving his family in the middle of an argument.

- Carver's distinctive style was shaped by his editor, Gordon Lish. In 2009, twenty years after Carver's death, Jonathan Cape published a book called *Beginners*, which is a collection of the versions of the stories in *What We Talk About When We Talk About Love* as Carver originally submitted them, before Lish's sometimes massive edits. Though "Popular Mechanics," called "Mine" in this version, is not changed, some of the stories were cut by 50 percent or more.

- Readers can see an echo of Carver's terse style and his characters in the young-adult novel *You Don't Know Me*, written by David Klass and published by HarperTeen in 2002. Though Klass injects more grim humor into his work, the sense of alienation will be familiar to Carver's readers.

- In 1992, filmmaker Michael Cimino asked Carver to write a screenplay about the life of Russian novelist Fyodor Dostoyevsky. He and Tess Gallagher wrote a script that was never produced but was published as a book. *Dostoyevsky: A Screenplay* was published by Capra Press in 1985.

- Thrity Umrigar's 2009 novel *The Weight of Heaven* features a couple that is damaged, like the one in "Popular Mechanics," but in a contemporary context and style. It concerns Frank and Ellie Benton, who, for business

reasons, move from Michigan to India after the death of their son, and the cultural and economic complexities that put pressure on their already-strained marriage. It was published by Harper Perennial.

- Susan Straight's story "El Ojo de Agua," published in the Spring 2006 issue of *All-Story* magazine, won the O. Henry Award for Best Short Story in 2007. Like many of Straight's stories, it concerns the lives of poor Latinos in California, but her fluid use of modern culture marks her as a descendant of Carver's style of realism.

- Carver talked about his influences, his writing habits, and his view of the contemporary literary scene in a 1987 interview with Francesco Durante for the Italian publication *Il Mattino*. It can be found under the title "De Minimis: Raymond Carver and His World" in *Conversations with Raymond Carver*, published in 1990 by the University Press of Mississippi.

- At the time this story was published, many critics likened Carver's writing to that of his contemporary Ann Beattie. Though Beattie wrote about different social circumstances, her prose style was similar. "The Burning House," from the 1982 collection of the same name, will remind readers of Carver's sensibilities applied to other walks of life.

- In 1990, Scribner published *Carver Country: The World of Raymond Carver*, a book of artistic photographs introducing readers to places in Carver's life and works, including excerpts from his letters and interviews. The photos and supplementary text are by Bob Adelman; the introduction is by Tess Gallagher.

---

of him, a token of affection. If there were a moderator in the Carver story, a King Solomon figure, the horrific moment could most likely be made to pass without lasting consequences.

Carver's collection *What We Talk About When We Talk About Love*, a seminal work of fiction that imitators in the 1980s, is, after all, a book about living in a place and time with no

He packed his bag to leave her. *(Dmitry Rukhlenko | Shutterstock.com)*

presiding intelligence, no authority figure to make sense of life for its stubbornly unhappy characters. The couple in "The Bath," for instance, fear for their son, hit by a car on his way to school, but they cannot express their fears in any real way, even when the specter of death manifests itself in haunting telephone calls from a baker who cannot find the words to tell them he's calling for payment. In "A Serious Talk," Bert comes to his ex-wife's house on the day after Christmas intending to make her see past his alcoholism and to pretend that there is some semblance of normality to their life, but he ends up making a fool of himself and stealing her ashtray. In "Everything Stuck to Him," a man's grown daughter visits him in Italy and asks him to recall a story from her childhood, when he lived with the family, and he remembers one warm, happy humorous moment he and his wife shared—but that moment is tens of years and thousands of miles away. In these and other stories, the characters cannot figure life out for themselves, and they have no one to help them understand it. As the title of the collection implies, they know how to talk but they do not understand the meaning behind their words. They lack context.

Because there is no place in "Popular Mechanics" for a King Solomon-like character who can give the man and woman direction in their lives, the author presents himself. Readers are given hints of Carver's hand controlling the situation in the beginning, when the snow turns to rain, and in the end, when the narration draws attention to the sky growing darker and darker. There is not much subtlety to the symbolism—in fact, it is nearly clumsy, which is particularly notable in a story told in an otherwise clear tone. There are few objects in this story, and none of them, such as the potted plant or the baby's photograph, has the obvious symbolic value that the darkening sky has. The gathering dusk is an omen more appropriate for a Victorian gothic novel than for a minimalist short story. The darkening of the sky is such a blatant metaphor for the destruction these characters are headed toward that it draws readers' attention toward the author, which, in the story's void of ethics, is exactly what is needed.

Without the heavy symbolism, the characters in this story would be adrift and on their own. When the author makes his presence known, if only in the periphery of the reader's consciousness, the focus shifts from the sequence of events to the unspoken question of why this story is being told. Its semblance to ordinary life is not enough. "Popular Mechanics" looks like life, if only life at its worst, with angry people trying to hurt each other and lovers turned to opponents turned to competitors. Without the unstated awareness that someone is telling this story, the message is merely that life can be true. With the added awareness of the author, the message becomes that these characters have made their lives cruel, but that there can be order, too.

Carver's use of heavy-handed literary conceits, like melting snow at the end of a relationship and sundown portending doom, are important to the telling to this story. And it is important that the story is presented in Carver's distinct, conspicuous style, with the names and descriptions all but washed out, with all dialogue so dispirited that there are not even quotation marks to distinguish human voices from the physical world they speak to. Without a wise king like Solomon to rely on in late twentieth-century America, the best a reader of Carver's type of realism can hope to do is to fall into the hands of the author.

This is why the story's final line works, even though it breaks the point of view established in the lines that precede it. Carver breaks the fourth wall, to use a phrase from theater, speaking directly to his audience. The characters in the story have no sense of "the issue" that he speaks of, and they do not know that it has been "decided," nor would they have used such a word to describe what happened to their baby if the story carried on to the moment after they pulled the baby's arms in different directions. And they certainly would not appreciate an allusion to the story of King Solomon, if they understood the reference at all. For Carver to step in at this point in the story and raise philosophical questions is inconsistent, but it is also necessary. The world of this work is a place where clueless people act without awareness of themselves or the consequences of their actions. Somebody has to show readers that there is a reason for what happens here.

Source: David Kelly, Critical Essay on "Popular Mechanics," in *Short Stories for Students*, Gale, Cengage Learning, 2011.

Myles Weber

In the following excerpt, Weber explores Carver's minimalist fiction as a response to the chaos of modern society and as an affirmation of the inexhaustibility of literature.

One rarely hears talk of current literary movements these days, which is something of a pity since it can make discussing literature both fun and easy. A bit too easy, which I suppose is the point. We all know that categories serving a convenient purpose are based on suspect criteria, because Michel Foucault told us so. Still, if one risks making false observations by accepting convenient categories, one also risks disregarding valid observations by pretending not to.

So it is useful to remember that partisans of literary movements not long ago battled for critical favor and dominance of the marketplace. During the decade and a half that passed between the publication of Raymond Carver's first major story collection, *Will You Please Be Quiet, Please?*, and his death in 1989, the literary movement closely associated with his work, Minimalism, withstood harsh assault from critics, theorists, and writers aligned with another literary movement, Postmodernism. Reading through pieces that illuminate the period—essays by Christopher Lasch, Todd Gitlin, Hartwig Isernhagen, and a number of cranky Postmodernist authors—one sees that the underpinnings of a spirited Minimalist response were there, but none was forthcoming. This was because few authors identified themselves with the movement under attack even if critics placed them in it, and none at all warmed to the label Minimalist (who would?). This essay is intended as a revisiting of the social and intellectual currents that gave rise to Minimalism, not as a belated defense of the maligned, but I will not lament if, by attempting the former, I succeed at the latter.

* * *

Has time marched on so efficiently that I need to define Minimalism? Let me instead cite an exemplary work, a ten-page story by Ann Beattie called "Times." In it, a young couple spend Christmas at the woman's parents' home, the house she grew up in. In her bedroom, she finds photographs of a high school flame which touch off memories, none of which is all that jarring. That afternoon, her husband goes running in the park and drops his scarf. About two-thirds of the way through the story, we are told by the

> AS FOR CARVER, HIS SHORT WORKS WERE SIMILARLY DISMISSED, BY SOME ANYWAY, AS TOO SIMPLE, FOR HAVING NO PLOTS OR, AT BEST, PLOTS THAT WERE EASY TO FOLLOW AND REQUIRED NO EXPLICATION, AND FOR PRESENTING DRAMATIC CRISES WHICH WERE TOO EASILY SOLVED."

third-person narrator that, two months prior, the young man, Peter, confessed to his wife Cammy that he had been having an affair. Peter cried as he told her this, and the next morning Cammy bought expensive flowers to cheer herself up. Back in the story's present, Cammy's mother shows them an elaborate chocolate dessert she has made in the shape of a Yule log. The story ends with Cammy poking the dessert and licking the frosting off her finger.

A story such as this, with its domestic setting, its fading crisis (a past affair), and an ending that neither moves forward whatever plot there might be nor clearly elucidates the story's theme, illustrates what Minimalist fiction is. Or was. Already I am facing the dilemma of tenses. Does Minimalism still exist? Raymond Carver's death is significant to the answer, but most other authors herded into the Minimalist fold continue to produce. I will perhaps be forgiven if I slip into past tense, since the zenith of Minimalist influence and the discharge of criticism against it have passed.

* * *

More harshly than any other, William H. Gass issued broadsides against what he called "that major social and artistic malaise called minimalism." In a 1987 essay in the *New York Times Book Review*, he expressed distaste for the thinness of Minimalist works and the verbal reticence of their characters. He also admitted a vague amusement at "R. Carver," "T. Wolff," and "J. McInerney" that he did not explain. He had tired of reading works by "authors named Ann (or Anne)," he said; he wanted Proust, he wanted Literature.

What he wanted, to be sure, was male writing, notwithstanding his amusement at Carver, Wolff, and McInerney—three authors who dared not speak their gendered first names. He emphasized in particular the correlation between female authors and his pet peeve: first-person, present-tense narration. In his distaste for women writers, Gass was seconded by another Postmodernist author, John Barth, who categorized most of the work by contemporary American women as *Pre*modernist—and he didn't mean that in the good way. Though Barth credited Minimalism with being the force behind a short-story renaissance at the time, he echoed Gass's general critique. For example, he made jeering reference to what he called the phenomenon of the "three-eighth inch novel," a crack at both the presumed thinness of Minimalist writing and the manner of publication—the original trade paperback—that many writers, especially the youngest, used to break into print.

In his 1986 essay "A Few Words about Minimalism," Barth suggested that Minimalist authors used simple sentences because they were not well educated. He also blamed the shortened forms of Minimalist pieces on the authors' shrinking attention spans. Add to this Raymond Federman's criticism that Minimalism reflected "the conservative (and even reactionary) mood one feels in all parts of our culture and our sociopolitical life," and Bruce Bawer's observation that Minimalist works were the unwelcome result of a proliferation in university writing workshops and you get a pretty complete picture of the reaction against Minimalism among critics and Postmodernist writers. By far the most pervasive negative sentiment was that Minimalism was permeated by modesty, nonstridency, and unambitiousness. The phenomenon Gerald Graff calls "the vogue of alienation," which was present in Modernist and Postmodernist texts, was carried over in altered form: instead of wise-ass narrators or characters in 600- or 800-page novels like *Gravity's Rainbow* and *Giles Goat-Boy*, we had the passive narrators and characters of ten-page stories, sometimes by authors named Ann (or Anne).

Peter Cameron's "Not the Point" is illustrative. Cameron's female narrator has lost one of her twin sons to suicide and is in the process of selling her household possessions before relocating with her husband to the Philippines. But she is an ineffectual saleswoman. In a pivotal scene, a customer has come to her door to peruse the merchandise, but rather than show the woman around the house the narrator retreats into her bedroom and lies down on the bed. She pets the dog. If she is thinking about the major crises in her life—her son's suicide, her surviving son's non-cooperative manner, her strained marriage, her impending move to Asia—she does not relate those thoughts to the reader. Instead, she says: "I can hear the lady walking around the living room. She could be stealing everything, for all I know. That would be nice. That would be the easiest way to get rid of it."

In Raymond Carver's famous early story, "Neighbors," a husband and wife feed the cat and water plants for a vacationing couple across the hall. The husband, alone in the neighbors' apartment, snoops and commits small acts of thievery that play like important steps toward personal liberation (he eats from their refrigerator, lies down on their bed, tries on their clothes). His wife, taking her turn feeding the cat, uncovers photographs (of the neighbors? naked? engaging in sexual acts?). Though these characters, through their mischief, modestly challenge the Minimalist reputation for passivity, they pay for it in the end: the wife locks the neighbors' keys in the apartment, casting herself and her husband out of this vicarious Eden of sunburst clocks and Hawaiian shirts.

The disdain that critics directed at Minimalist works may have been professionally interested, but it was not off the mark. The modest, contracting self of Minimalist fiction was a symptom of the larger social crises out of which the authors worked. They faced the problems of the past century now in inflated and accelerated form (murkier rivers and beaches, more brutally mechanized street crime, more lethal sexually transmitted diseases). Postmodernists, reacting to the industrial and military realities of their times, were in some ways invigorated by the new conditions they had been forced to cope with. In contrast, the Minimalists grew up in a world that already had a postmodern sensibility. John Gardner once suggested that a Postmodernist writer's literary tantrums reflected the mind of someone raised in the church who loses his faith and, moreover, is embarrassed that he ever believed. I would suggest that Minimalists never made it to Sunday school. For them, everyday life was filtered through an inherited rhetoric of crisis, until the effect was numbing. Apathy and disengagement became techniques

of emotional self-management in a world where the typically masculine hero not only would fail to conquer, but usually was the first to be obliterated by the system.

Of course apathy and disengagement may not sound like ingredients for exciting or durable literature. But then, neither does obsessive epistemological self-reflexivity. Texts have always been criticized for the faults of the age in which they are written and for the limitations of their own literary movement's characterizing elements. Realist texts are dismissed for being doggedly middlebrow, Modernist texts for their self-importance, their elitism, and their early signs of slippage toward intentional obscurity of style, and Postmodernist texts for a multitude of sins against the reader: gratuitous obscurity, solipsism, impenetrability, verbosity and, at their very worst, nauseating cuteness. (A character in an Ann Beattie story might be named Ed, but never Oedipa.) Minimalist fiction is no exception: it, too, is vulnerable to the inherent weaknesses of its defining characteristics and the not altogether untroubled times in which it developed.

Raymond Carver recounts that when he first started writing in the 1960s he sensed that he would have to limit his scope to poetry and the short story.

> To write a novel, it seemed to me, a writer should be living in a world that makes sense, a world that a writer can believe in, draw a bead on, and then write about accurately. A world that will, for a time anyway, stay fixed in one place. Along with this there has to be a belief in the essential correctness of that world. A belief that the known world has reasons for existing, and is worth writing about, is not likely to go up in smoke in the process.

This is not to suggest that Minimalists have never written novels. Most have. But it does underscore the notion of a contracting self functioning as a defensive core in the face of a destabilized world, and suggests that to expect otherwise from these authors is to search for an anachronism, what Christopher Lasch calls "the imperial self of yesteryear."

* * *

Almost exactly concurrent with the rise of Minimalist fiction in American literature was the partial legitimization in the scientific communities of a new field called chaos, which explored the complexity of what were once considered simple systems and random patterns (those of snowflakes, oil spills, cigarette smoke). Chaos theory addressed the universe as we see and touch it on a human scale, not on the grand scale of the galaxies or the hypothetical realm of sub-atomic particles.

Without forcing the issue too badly, I believe meaningful comparisons can be made between Minimalist writers and the scientists who study chaos. On a superficial level, both have been held in contempt by professional rivals for being trendy, ephemeral attachments to their fields or, worse, creations of their own public relations efforts. More importantly, both Minimalist authors and those who study chaos grew up in a post-war world in which grand scientific theories and mammoth literary works were the order of the day, and both chose to seek explanations not in overscaled undertakings but within the common observations and everyday details of their lives.

According to James Gleick, whose introductory work *Chaos: Making a New Science* made the ideas of chaos theory accessible to a mass audience in 1987, the meteorologist Edward Lorenz used computers in the early 1960s to simulate weather patterns, constructing a set of very simple equations for heat convection which proved solvable as an unpredictable pattern that never repeats itself—what some would call no solution at all. With mathematical equations containing a total of only three variables, and using what would now be considered a primitive computer, Lorenz demonstrated that one could generate an infinitely varied pattern of convection possibilities from relatively simple origins, signaling complex and pure disorder in one of the most basic and presumably well-understood physical phenomena, heat convection. Or if not signaling disorder, then signaling some new kind of order that allows for unpredictability and for the "solution" to a problem to be acceptance that there is no conventional solution.

It may seem tenuous at first to draw parallels between the work of a meteorologist and the work of fiction writers, but my task is made easier by the fact that the reception to Lorenz's work by colleagues within his own field was in many ways similar to the reaction from some quarters of the literary establishment to Raymond Carver's stories. Not only did physicists incorrectly assume that Lorenz's variables were easily solvable, but once their complexity was convincingly demonstrated many scientists still insisted it would be trivial to run a computer program of such equations. Lorenz's work seemed to consume an inordinate amount of computer time, to no apparent purpose, which did not win him support from colleagues who saw themselves in competition for limited institutional resources.

As for Carver, his short works were similarly dismissed, by some anyway, as too simple, for having no plots or, at best, plots that were easy to follow and required no explication, and for presenting dramatic crises which were too easily solved. One critic responded to Carver's story "Preservation," in which a man's refrigerator breaks down, by offering what he considered the obvious solution: this unemployed, working-class man should buy a new refrigerator. Some critics, even when they allowed that Carver's individual stories were compelling, still dismissed them *in toto* as a repetitive string of dull trivialities—a fair enough reaction, I suppose, if such stories are simply not to one's tastes. Less fair, I believe, was the insistence that Carver had no concerns larger than spoiled food in a fictional refrigerator—just as it was premature to dismiss Edward Lorenz's work on heat convection as going nowhere. (It led meteorologists to a better understanding of the extent to which climatic patterns can be predicted.)

To continue the analogy, I believe one could say the stories in Carver's 1982 collection *What We Talk about When We Talk about Love* are without exception generated by only three central elements or variables: alcoholism, failed or failing marriages, and mortality. And yet, by my estimation at least, these three variables do not exhaust their dramatic possibilities in these seventeen stories. On the contrary, the collection seems to promise that the most fundamental elements of human drama will never lose their strength as ingredients for tragedy, for storytelling, for significant fiction, and were Carver to write a few dozen more stories with the same concerns (as, in fact, he did) he would not find himself in a quandary of depletion. Rather, he would create a larger body of work that suggested there are answers to be arrived at even by such simple means as his. Approached in this manner, Minimalist fiction is more than the domain of passive resignation. To the extent that passivity and resignation are elements of Minimalist fiction, they serve more broadly to establish Minimalism as a reservoir of literary confidence in what we might call fiction's ultimate stamina, as a sanctuary of hope in the ability of literature and people to survive.

* * *

Mitchell Feigenbaum's universal theory of chaos posits that the world is not primarily predictable and fixed with a few puzzling exceptions but, rather, that the phenomena of the natural world are fundamentally random, chaotic, and unpredictable, and that science has long concerned itself with the relatively few stable exceptions. In a literary world developing parallel to and in some ways informed by this kind of scientific work, small, seemingly purposeless elements in a story (a dropped scarf, a petted dog) and more important story elements together illustrate the mystery and beauty found in the world's disorderly and chaotic patterns. Ann Beattie's 1986 short story collection *Where You'll Find Me* opens with the story "In the White Night" which itself opens, happily for this essay, with a winter scene in which "an icy snow had been falling for hours, frozen granules mixed in with lighter stuff." The swirls of snow pelt against the skin of the main character, Carol, and remind her—"an odd thing to remember on a night like this"—of the way sand blows up at the beach, stinging the face. Immediately after making the mental connection, Carol glances above her parked car. "In the small, bright area under the streetlights," she notices, "there seemed for a second to be some logic to all the swirling snow." Later, she asserts that what happens in life does so at random, but that even the most horrible things, like her daughter developing leukemia, receive an "instant acceptance" of the kind one gives to a snowfall or to other phenomena against which one is powerless.

I think it useful to mention this scene here, not to strangle Minimalism and chaos with a rope of similarities, but to cite evidence that Minimalist writers did not merely recount the surface details of contemporary life using an appropriate post-Postmodernist literary style. They were aware of the wider intellectual concerns of their time, and helped to shape them. If, for the Postmodernists, the unpredictability of contemporary existence and the fragmentation of the post-war sensibility were too disorienting to permit the use of conventional literary techniques—were, in fact, a clarion call for non-

mimetic fiction, for fighting disorder with further disorder—for the Minimalists the incoherence of the world they inherited suggested a different tack, a way out of sorts. Minimalists investigated the "small" events or less explosive moments in people's lives, hoping that, by cumulative force, the chronicling of the turbulence would reveal some method in God's madness, some new world view, not necessarily one that rejoiced in disorder but one that at least stopped being so surprised by it all. Long after God's death was proclaimed far and wide, long after the moral neutrality of the universe was asserted, long after it became generally accepted that acts of creation lead inevitably to acts of destruction, the Postmodernists continued to express shock at these developments in our social history, and insisted that others respond in precisely the same way—insisted so adamantly, in fact, that they began to flirt with the domains of fanaticism and irrationality.

There is, after all, something fundamentally irrational about being angry at God for not existing. And though people are clearly capable of holding irrational views, it would be unreasonable to expect generation after generation of artists to maintain the same intensity of anger over this and other elements of Western disillusionment, the shock of which is bound to wear off eventually and become merely the sad droning of reality. The generation responsible for Postmodernist fiction may insist that a less manic literary style suggests passivity, but from another point of view it is a sign of maturity or wisdom. Or, at the very least, it points toward the inevitable passing of generations.

But—at least in literature—generations can repeat or revive themselves. Who would have guessed at the height of Minimalism's popularity that more than a decade later novels by Thomas Pynchon, Don DeLillo, and their admirer David Foster Wallace would be generating so much attention and praise? We still hear grumbling when such novels lose literary awards to short story collections or a good yarn, but for the most part these are times when divergent works coexist peacefully on bookstore shelves and important authors go uncategorized. I suggested at the opening of this essay that in some ways I lament the absence of talk about literary movements, but perhaps it's best this way, for all concerned. Perhaps we can extend this truce and all just get along. Perhaps Minimalist authors will enjoy a similar revival, and no one will much complain this time.

Source: Myles Weber, "Revisiting Minimalism," in *Northwest Review*, Vol. 37, No. 3, 1999, pp. 117–25.

John Muckle

In the following review, Muckle discusses Kirk Nesset's critical study on Carver and his body of work.

Raymond Carver's literary career has an unlikely but irresistible flavour of that most banal of American myths, the one usually associated with Horatio Alger. "Inauspicious beginnings" followed by grim determinations; hard work and dedication rewarded by "a meteoric rise to international acclaim, widespread appeal, and a continuing influence on American letters." Kirk Nesset's critical study, with its modest aims of "preliminary exploration and assessment," of "tying together Carver's achievement as a unifiable corpus" and a desire to "pave the way for Carver studies of the future," has a considerable stake in this triumphalist view of its subject—perhaps inevitably, since Carver's life is a true story.

He begins with a useful survey of Carver's reception and the contexts in which the writer has so far been placed. First, a political context in which Carver's stories were, on the left, taken as revealing "the waste and destructiveness that lurk beneath American life" or, in Carver's own words, "the dark side of Reagan's America," whilst attacked by critics of the right for failing to pull behind the aggressively patriotic economic optimism of the Reagan administration. Second, various literary "traditions" are invoked: a modernist one of Joyce, Hemingway and Kafka, an American "realist" one descending through Sherwood Anderson, John O'Hara, and Carver's immediate predecessor in the domestic story of (in his case) middle-class disillusionment, John Cheever. A previous generation of "postmodernists"—he names Barthelme, Pynchon, Coover, Gaddis and Gass (the emptily "reflexive" later novels of Gilbert Sorrentino would have made a good target)—are briefly characterised as that which Carver, or the amorphously-defined phenomenon of "minimalist" fiction, is said to be reacting against in a "post-post-modern modernism."

But just as Nesset invokes the label of "minimalism," distances himself from it (Carver detested the description), but continues to employ the term in order to characterise the

work of a similarly invoked-but-denied "school of Carver," he does not really explore the ways in which this fiction may be a revival of modernism. We are offered instead an account of his place in the five to ten year cycles of literary fashion—useful raw material for a study of the relations between cultural punditry and the book trade—but we never get to the bottom of what Carver's work might have to do with any of these writers or isms.

What really interests Nesset is Raymond Carver's stories, their technique and what they mean. His method is avowedly "formalist, New Critical in a postmodern-modernist, if old-fashioned way," though "recent literary theory, feminist and Marxist critiques" are said to inhabit his subtextual shadows. What emerges from the readings is a straightforwardly thematic approach. Stories are examined through the sexual politics of marriage, and through oppositions like "Insularity and Self-Enlargement" and "Communication and Control." Fair enough. Unfortunately, most of the "readings" turn out to be pedestrian explication. Palimpsests of quotation from previous critics and reviewers leave a dismaying impression that these stark, bone-like creations, so trenchantly bringing news from "outside" consensual culture, their spaces echoing with the unsaid, have already been so thoroughly filled in, written over, completed—and commodified—that readers are required only to murmur assent and pass on to the next thing. Relieved students of the future will be able to pull this book from the shelves, spared an encounter with Carver himself. At least Kirk Nesset has a sense of humour. He even cracks the odd apologetic joke at the expense of his subject's obstinate miserablism.

Carver said that good writings brings news of one world to another. But having brought the bad news, found it strangely welcomed, and in the process became a citizen of a new country, his later stories find him in vaguely affirmative mood with nothing particularly to affirm. Am I alone in finding these moments of supposed interchange, transformation, acceptance, possibility etc.... somewhat lame? "If you hang on the past you die a little every day," says the teenage girl at the end of Martin Scorsese's remake of *Cape Fear*. Carver seems to want to do both and somehow make that all right, perhaps because he cannot bear the terms of his success, or the guilt it seems to entail. It is the kind of longing for some impossible reconciliation that might haunt any of his characters, or anyone.

Perhaps the news brought from one world to another was too fragile, or just too terrible to survive retelling. It had to he blunted, transmuted into humanist gold, into "Carver country"—to satisfy liberal America, and to make his own success at the expense of all that unhappiness palatable to its author—to justify his own escape. And having arrived in "literature" (obligingly learning to speak its language) he finds the place not quite as advertised. Carver squirms a little at the accusations of the successful writer's first wife in *Intimacy*, that he is a twisted bastard who has become famous by publicly humiliating her, that his "work" is a worthless pretence, but he lets them stand. Carver asked some hard questions about human relationships and about the prerogatives of the writer in depicting them, particularly after the accolades start coming in. He seems to suggest that his readers should ask equally difficult questions of him.

Source: John Muckle, Review of *The Stories of Raymond Carver: A Critical Study*, in *Journal of American Studies*, Vol. 29, No. 3, December 1995, pp. 481–83.

John Powell

In the following excerpt, Powell discusses Carver's methods of leaving out details in the course of his narratives, creating a sense of menace and tension of something imminent.

The tracing of changes in Raymond Carver's short story style is one of the most persistent topics of Carver criticism. Unfortunately, by focusing on change, critics have overlooked one of the most consistent aspects of Carver's short stories, their sense of menace. In *Fires*, Carver explains: "I like it when there is some sense of menace in short stories.... There has to be tension, a sense that something is imminent ..." (17). William Stull notes that one of Carver's early stories, "Pastoral" (1963), is shaped "as an 'iceberg,' its marital conflict seven-eighths submerged" ("Raymond" 466).

Throughout his career, Carver achieved a sense of menace by leaving out, or by providing only clues to, crucial aspects of the story. Both character and reader sense that something dangerous or menacing is "imminent" or "submerged," but both character and reader, unable to find the meaning of the given clues, must battle between readings of those clues. Menace develops as meaning itself becomes elusive. A second part of the method by which Carver achieves his unique sense of menace is his basing existential matters on the story's clues instead of on clearly stated facts.

In "What Is It?" the used-car salesman eyes Leo and "watches for sudden movement" (*Will You Please*), watches for clues, and this watching highlights both characters' uncertainty about what the other sees or believes. This state of menacing uncertainty is equally evident in "What We Talk About When We Talk About Love" when the quiet conversation suddenly becomes much, much quieter. "'Just shut up for once in your life,' Mel said very quietly. 'Will you do me a favor and do that for a minute?'" (*What We Talk About*) These sentences seem out of place in a conversation investigating love, so Mel's relationship to Terri is made ambiguous just when he is attempting to clarify it. Here, the first sentence is a harsh command, but the next is a request for a favor in the form of a question. The incongruity of tone confuses, contradicts, and, therefore, menaces.

However, again, this sense that language is confusing rather than clarifying and that unanswerable but crucial questions are being asked does not simply impart menace within Carver's stories. In stories taken from throughout his career, Carver's menace affects the reader as he or she struggles with the language that seems to be stating something quite simple, but that is in reality hiding something, something important, and something that, once it seems clear, still isn't an answer.

... In *What We Talk About When We Talk About Love*, Carver continues to combine his polysemic technique with existential uncertainty to convey menace. In "Popular Mechanics," Carver certainly uses ambiguity and existentialism to this end. The last line of the story, "In this manner, the issue was decided," as Norman German and Jack Bedell point out, contains "a gruesome pun [on 'issue'] implying that the argument as well as the fate of the parents' offspring was decided."

Carver, however, combines the dual meaning of "the issue" with more disturbing, more menacing, existential questions concerning both the nature of the parents' relationship to the baby whom they physically fight over and with the state of the baby himself.

Ironically, the parents adore the icon of their baby but are careless with the baby itself. Early in the story, the husband is about to pack the baby's picture in his suitcase when the wife sees it and takes it to the living room. The argument over the baby's image turns into a struggle over the real baby, who, though identified as a boy, is usually referred to as "the baby," "this baby," or "it" ("She would have it, this baby"), thus disturbingly impersonalizing the child as an object to fight over—to the parents, a victory symbol and little else. (German and Bedell 259)

This icon of the child, a fiction within a fiction, makes the baby seem much more real, and once the reader recognizes that "issue" refers not only to the argument but also, possibly, to the child, the reader also recognizes the trap of having the completely dehumanized term "issue" refer to that more-real baby. Only then does the reader realize that the very state of, and, therefore, also the fate of, the baby are forever uncertain. "Issue" has not even been defined well enough to be decided.

The dehumanization of the baby in "Popular Mechanics" parallels the dehumanization of "the birthday boy," Scotty, in both "The Bath" and its revision, "A Small, Good Thing." The similarities between these two stories highlight the very fact that from *What We Talk About When We Talk About Love* through *Cathedral*, Carver continued to convey menace through polysemy and existential uncertainty. Nonetheless, there are critics who overlook or deny the similar elements in "The Bath" and "A Small, Good Thing" and search for differences. These critics overlook the precise manner in which Carver achieves his sense of menace.

Source: John Powell, "The Stories of Raymond Carver: The Menace of Perpetual Uncertainty," in *Studies in Short Fiction*, Vol. 31, No. 4, Fall 1994, p. 647.

William L. Stull

In the following excerpted interview, Stull and Carver discuss how Carver's poetry and stories intersect, the common denominators in his stories, and his writing style.

[The Bloomsbury Review:] In a good many instances, you've approached what seems to be a single incident from two angles, treating it in both poetry and prose. Are there limits on a writer's experience?

[Raymond Carver:] I don't feel I'm short on things to write about. But some things, I'm thinking of "Distress Sale" now, that poem, or the story "Why Don't You Dance?"—the yard sale situation—the idea, the image of the yard sale made such a strong impression on me that I dealt with it first in a poem and then in a story.

WORK BEGINS TO ACCUMULATE. IT GIVES YOU HEART TO GO ON. I COULDN'T BE WRITING THE STORIES I'M WRITING NOW IF I HADN'T WRITTEN THE ONES I HAVE WRITTEN."

The same thing is true with regard to the poem "Late Night with Fog and Horses" and the story "Blackbird Pie." In each instance I wrote the poem first and then wrote the story, I suppose, because I apparently felt a need to elaborate on the same theme.

Is narrative, the storytelling element, what links the genres for you?

Yes. And just as I'm more interested in representational art as opposed to abstract art, I'm more interested in poems with a narrative or story line to them than in free-associating poems that don't have any grounding in the real world.

Your new poetry openly celebrates intimacy, and in some poems the walls between life and art seem very thin. Is there a risk of sentimentality or embarrassment in that?

Any right-thinking reader or writer abjures sentimentality. But there's a difference between sentiment and sentimentality. I'm all for sentiment. I'm interested in the personal, intimate relationships in life, so why not deal with these relationships in literature? What about intimate experiences like those recounted in "A Haircut" or "The Gift"? Why can't such experiences be turned into poetry? These little experiences are important underpinnings in our daily lives, and I don't see any problem in turning them into poems. They are, after all, something that we all share—as readers, writers, and human beings.

You're not inclined to treat mundane matters ironically, then?

No. I can't imagine treating them ironically or denigrating them in any way. I don't think there should be any barriers, artificial or otherwise, between life as it's lived and life as it's written about. It's only natural to write about these things. The things that count are often intimate things. I'm embarrassed for the people who are embarrassed by the idea of someone writing about things such as haircuts and slippers and ashtrays and hominy and so on.

Still, for a long time, and even to an extent today, the facts of everyday living, things like getting haircuts and picking up the mail, were thought by some to be subjects beneath the poet's dignity.

But see where that's gotten us. So much of our poetry has become like something you see in a museum. You walk around and politely look at it and then go away and discuss it. It's been given over to teachers and students. And it also seems to me that of all the art forms, poetry is probably the one with the worst press, if you know what I mean. It's got the largest number of hanging judges involved on the peripheries. So many people who don't even read poetry often make pronouncements about it. These people feel that standards have been thrown out the window, the barbarians are at the gate, and nothing is sacred any longer. I don't have sympathy for guardians, so-called, of sacred flames.

You don't hold with the modernist notion that poetry needs to be difficult?

Of course not. I'm saying just the opposite. My friend Richard Ford recently passed along a remark he'd heard from Joyce Carol Oates. She told him, "Ray's poems are arousing resentment in some quarters because he's writing poetry that people can understand." I take that as a compliment. I don't have a whole lot of patience with obscurity or rhetoric, in life or in literature.

Do you ever write poems and stories concurrently?

I never have, not yet, anyway. When I was writing poems, that's all I wrote. No fiction, anyway. The only thing I could do outside of writing poems, in the way of literary work, was, very rarely, an essay or book review. And I did that, wrote the prose, in the evenings after I had written poetry all day. I wrote the poems during the daylight hours. And now that I'm writing stories again, I'm only writing stories and nothing else. I'd be hard put right now to sit down and write a poem.

You carried verbal economy to new extremes in revising the stories for What We Talk About When We Talk About Love *from their magazine versions. You told the* Paris Review *that you cut your work to the marrow, not just to the bone. Later, when you published alternate versions of the stories in* Fires, *you restored many of the*

excisions. What led you to perform such radical surgery in the first place?

It had to do with the theory of omission. If you can take anything out, take it out, as doing so will make the work stronger. Pare, pare, and pare some more. Maybe it also had something to do with whatever I was reading during that period. But maybe not. It got to where I wanted to pare everything down and maybe pare too much. Then I guess I must have reacted against that. I didn't write anything for about six months. Then I wrote "Cathedral" and all the other stories in that book in a fairly concentrated period of time. I've said that if I had gone any further in the direction I was going, the direction of the earlier stories, I would have been writing stories that I wouldn't have wanted to read myself . . . .

Recently, Neo-Realist fiction, yours included, has been faulted from the left. Some critics urge a return to the literary experimentalism of the late sixties and early seventies. How do you react?

It's strange, because a number of right-wing neoconservative critics say I'm painting too dark a picture of American life. I'm not putting a happy face on America. That's the stick they swing at me. As for the experimental fiction of the sixties and seventies, much of that work I have a hard time with. I think that literary experiment failed. In trying out different ways of expressing themselves, the experimental writers failed to communicate in the most fundamental and essential way. They got farther and farther away from their audience. But maybe this is what they wanted. Still, I think when people look back on that period fifty years from now it's going to be looked on as an odd time in the literary history of the country, an interruption, somehow . . . .

What makes your writing uniquely your own?

Well, certainly, the tone in the work, I suppose. Geoffrey Wolff said in a review of my first book of stories that he felt he could pick out a story of mine without seeing my name attached to it. I took that as a compliment. If you can find an author's fingerprints on the work, you can tell it's his and no other's.

Where do those fingerprints lie? In subject? In style?

Both. Subject and style, the two are pretty much inseparable, right? John Updike once said that when he thinks of writing a story only certain areas of writing and experience are open to him. Certain areas, and lives, are completely closed. So, the story chooses him. And I feel that's true of myself. Speaking as a poet and story writer, I think that my stories and poems have chosen me. I haven't had to go out looking for material. These things come. You're called to write them.

You're sometimes discussed as a social realist who focuses on the downside of working-class life. But, if your people are beat, they're seldom beaten. In fact, Kim Herzinger has suggested that your abiding subject is human endurance. Would you agree?

That's a preoccupation, yes, and a writer could do worse. I'm saying he could set his sights lower. Most things that we care for pass away or pass by in such a rush that we can scarcely get a fix on them. So it's really a question of enduring and abiding.

Endurance seemed about the most one could hope for in What We Talk About When We Talk About Love. *But in* Cathedral *things began to change. In that book some of your characters seemed to prosper in spirit, if not in hard cash.*

Yes, and as writer and a very interested bystander, I'm pleased to see this happening. A writer doesn't want to go on repeating himself, using the same characters in the same circumstances, time and again. It's not only desirable, it's healthy to move on. I'm not working any kind of conscious program in my stories, no, of course not. But it seems like every time I've finished a book there's been a clear line of demarcation. There's always been a time after I finished putting together a book manuscript when I haven't worked for a while on stories. After I finished *What We Talk About When We Talk About Love* I didn't write stories for a good long while. Six months or so. Then the first story that I wrote was "Cathedral." It happened again after *Cathedral*. I didn't write a story for nearly two years. It's true. I wrote poems. The first story that I wrote and published after *Cathedral* was "Boxes," which appeared in the *New Yorker*. Then five or six stories came very close together. And I feel these new stories are different from the earlier ones in kind and degree. There's something about the voice, yes. Again, speaking just as an outsider or bystander, I'm glad to see these changes at work.

What common denominators do you see in the new stories?

Well, for one thing, they've all been written in the first person. It's nothing I planned on. It's just the voice I heard and began to go with.

Let's turn to your early work, the stories collected in Will You Please Be Quiet, Please? *and* Furious Seasons. *Like your recent stories "Intimacy" and "Blackbird Pie," the very first two stories you ever published seem stylistically at opposite poles. Your first, "The Furious Seasons" (1960), is a long, complex narrative told in flashbacks. Your next is your shortest story ever, a Kafkaesque vignette called "The Father" (1961).*

I'd be more likely to write something like "The Father" today than to write "The Furious Seasons" again. I haven't reread that story in years, but in retrospect it feels gothic to me. I have a profound lack of interest in that story now. When I'm writing a story, it's the most important thing in the world to me. When I'm through with it, and it's published, I have very little interest in it.

If every story is a fresh start, is a writer's development really cumulative?

I feel it's cumulative in that you know you have written other stories and poems. Work begins to accumulate. It gives you heart to go on. I couldn't be writing the stories I'm writing now if I hadn't written the ones I have written. But there's no way in the world I could go back now and write another "Gazebo" or another "Where I'm Calling From" or for that matter anything else I've written.

You wrote many of the stories in Will You Please Be Quiet, Please? *during 1970–1971, when you were on your first NEA Fellowship. What did you learn about writing during that year of concentrated work?*

Well, to put it simply, I discovered that I could do it. I had been doing it in such a hit-or-miss fashion for so long, since the early sixties. But I discovered that if I went to my desk every day and applied myself I could seriously and steadily write stories. That was probably the biggest discovery I made. Somehow, I suppose at some deeper level, I was tapping into some things that were important to me, things I'd wanted to write about and finally was able to, without a sense of grief or shame or confusion. I was able to confront some things in the work head on. Call it subject matter. And I suppose during that time I fastened on or discovered a way of writing about these things. Something happened during that time in the writing, *to* the writing. It went underground and then it came up again, and it was bathed in a new light for me. I was starting to chip away, down to the image, then the figure itself. And it happened during that period.

What's next for Raymond Carver, once the current hubbub dies down?

I have a contract for the new book of stories, and I'm in a story-writing mood. I can't wait until I can get back to my desk and stay there. I have a lot of stories I want to write. I'm wild to get settled in here and be still.

Source: William L. Stull, "Matters of Life & Death: An Interview with Raymond Carver," in *Bloomsbury Review*, Vol. 8, No. 1, January/February 1988, pp. 14–17.

SOURCES

Carver, Raymond, "Popular Mechanics," in *What We Talk About When We Talk About Love*, Alfred A. Knopf, 1981, p. 123–25.

Chettle, Judith, Review of *What We Talk About When We Talk About Love* in *National Review*, Vol. 33, No. 24, December 11, 1981, p. 1503.

Hallett, Cynthia J., "Minimalism and the Short Story," in *Studies in Short Fiction*, Fall 1996, http://findarticles .com/p/articles/mi_m2455/is_n4_v33/ai_20906634/ ?tag=content;col1 (accessed July 22, 2010).

Houston, Robert, "A Stunning Inarticulateness," in *Nation*, Vol. 233, No. 1, July 4, 1981, pp. 23–25.

"Marriage and Divorce: Latest Statistics Available," in *divorcemag.com*, http://www.divorcemag.com/statistics/ statsUS.shtml (accessed July 23, 2010).

Nesset, Kirk, *The Stories of Raymond Carver: A Critical Study*, Ohio University Press, 1995, p. 29.

Saltzman, Arthur M., *Understanding Raymond Carver*, University of South Carolina Press, 1988, p. 100.

Campbell, Ewing, ed., *Raymond Carver: A Study of the Short Fiction*, Twayne Publishers, 1992, p. 120.

FURTHER READING

German, Norman, and Jack Bedell, "Physical and Social Laws in Ray Carver's 'Popular Mechanics,'" in *Critique: Studies in Contemporary Fiction*, Vol. 29, No. 4, Summer 1988, pp. 257–60.

One of the few scholarly examinations of the story, this essay breaks down elements such as setting and sound to find the story's deeper meaning.

Hall, Vanessa, "'It All Fell in on Him': Masculinities in Raymond Carver's Short Stories and American Culture during the 1970s and 1980s," in *Journal of Men's Studies*, Vol. 17, No. 2, Spring 2009, pp. 173–88.

Hall looks at Carver's work as a historical document with which to view American culture during his lifetime.

Just, Daniel, "Is Less More? A Reinvention of Realism in Raymond Carver's Minimalist Short Story," in *Critique: Studies in Contemporary Fiction*, Vol. 49, No. 3, Spring 2008, p. 203.

This essay starts with a famous criticism of Carver's work by the novelist John Barth and uses it to question the legitimacy of Carver's fiction.

Lainsbury, G. P., "The Function of Family in the Carver Chronotope," in *The Carver Chronotope: Inside the Life-World of Raymond Carver's Fiction*, Routledge, 2004, pp. 95–143.

The author looks at familial relations across the range of Carver's works and the consistencies that emerge in the portrayal of family.

Sklenicka, Carol, *Raymond Carver: A Writer's Life*, Scribner, 2009.

Published more than twenty years after Carver's death, this exhaustive scholarly work has been hailed as the definitive biography of the writer.

SUGGESTED SEARCH TERMS

Raymond Carver

Popular Mechanics AND Carver

Mine AND Furious Seasons

Carver AND minimalism

Carver AND What We Talk About When We Talk About Love

Carver AND realism

Carver AND 1980s fiction

Raymond Carver AND literary influence

Raymond Carver AND King Solomon

postminimalism AND literature

Saboteur

HA JIN

2000

Chinese American émigré Ha Jin is a poetry and fiction writer who has accomplished a transition executed masterfully by very few authors: that of writing not in his native language but in English as an adopted language. Jin lived in China for the first twenty-nine years of his life. His father was an army officer, so the family moved frequently in his youth, leaving him with a diminished sense of home. He enlisted in the Chinese army at the age of fourteen and served for five years, and he later pursued undergraduate and graduate degrees in literature. He came to the United States to seek a doctoral degree with the expectation that he would return to China, but the Tiananmen Square massacre of 1989 led him to reconsider. He has lived in the United States ever since.

Much of Jin's early work is striking in that incidents taking place in China were originally written in English, not translated from Chinese. The short story "Saboteur," which appears in the collection *The Bridegroom* (2000), takes place in the fictional Muji City in northeast China. A university lecturer and Communist Party member named Mr. Chiu is framed by two police officers, for unclear reasons, for causing a public disturbance. His detention and manipulation by the police while experiencing an attack of hepatitis stir great resentment in him, with tragic results.

Ha Jin *(AP Images)*

AUTHOR BIOGRAPHY

Xuefei Jin, who writes as Ha Jin, was born on February 21, 1956, in Jinzhou, China, where his father, a People's Liberation Army officer, was stationed at the time. The name *Xuefei* means "Snow Flying," as Jin was born at the time of a great snowstorm. He attended boarding school at age seven, but two years later he returned home because of the mass closure of schools during Mao Tse-tung's Cultural Revolution. This political program was intended to reinvigorate the nation's Communist ideology, and it which ultimately entailed the persecution of the bourgeoisie (the materialist middle class) and intellectuals. Jin's family was targeted because his grandfather had been a landowner, and most of his father's books were burned in a bonfire on the street. Jin joined the Little Red Guard, the youth faction of the student-led nationalist group, and spent several years "wearing red armbands, waving flags and singing revolutionary songs," as he told Dwight Garner of the *New York Times Magazine.*

Jin lied about his age to enlist in the Chinese army at only fourteen, out of both fear of a nuclear attack from the Soviet Union and a desire to be a hero. As he bided his time at a frigid northern outpost, he happened upon a translation of Leo Tolstoy's epic *War and Peace* and was surprised to feel a kinship with the Russians. He was discharged from the army at nineteen and, with schools still closed, became a telegraph operator, learning English from a radio program in his spare time. When colleges were reopened in 1977, Jin gained admission to Heilongjiang University, in the city of Harbin (the first part of which, *Ha*, would become his pen name), to major in English. The drills in English speech proved daunting, leading Jin and his classmates to seek painkillers to ease their aching facial muscles. After graduating with a bachelor's degree in 1981, Jin studied American literature at Shandong University, studying the likes of William Faulkner and Ernest Hemingway. He married Lisha Bian in 1982, and their son, Wen, was born the following year. In 1984 Jin earned a master's degree, and the following year he traveled overseas to Brandeis University in Massachusetts to pursue a doctorate; his wife joined him in 1987. After the horrific massacre of students and protesters by the Chinese army in Tiananmen Square in 1989, Jin determined to remain in the United States; luckily, Wen was able to soon leave China and join his parents.

Ensconced in the American literary scene, Jin resolved to forsake Chinese and write in English, beginning with the poetry collection *Between Silences: A Voice from China* (1990), addressing the impact of the Cultural Revolution from the perspective of a disillusioned former soldier and expatriate. He wrote about modern poetry for his doctoral dissertation, and he enrolled in creative writing classes at Boston University. His first and second short-story collections, *Ocean of Words: Army Stories* (1996) and *Under the Red Flag* (1997), both portraying life in China, won significant short-fiction awards, and his novel *Waiting* (1999) won the National Book Award. "Saboteur" appears in *The Bridegroom* (2000). In his more recent work, including the novel *A Free Life*, Jin has turned to writing about immigrant experiences in America. After teaching at Emory University in Atlanta, Georgia, Jin moved on to a professorship at Boston University, which he held as of 2010.

PLOT SUMMARY

"Saboteur" opens with Mr. Chiu and his new wife—who is referred to almost exclusively as "his bride" and is never named—eating a peaceful meal at a café outside the train station in the fictional Muji City. At an adjacent table, two policeman, one a "stout, middle-aged man," the other a younger man who is "tall and of athletic build," are laughing over tea. Mentions of the air smelling of rotten fruit and vendors calling out lazily suggest that it may be a very warm day. The mention of the statue of "Chairman Mao" in the square is a reference to Mao Tse-tung, the Communist leader of China from 1949 to 1976. Mr. Chiu is glad that his two-week honeymoon has come to an end, especially because only three months earlier he had suffered a bout of hepatitis, affecting his liver, and he remains anxious about possibly suffering a relapse. Hepatitis is most frequently a viral infection. The Chius are returning to their hometown of Harbin, an actual city located in the region known as Manchuria, in the far northeast corner of China (east of Mongolia and north of North Korea), in Heilongjiang Province.

Mr. Chiu's bride mentions that she has a headache; he suggests taking an aspirin, but she declines. At this point, the stout policeman splashes tea on them, dousing their sandals. After the bride curses the policeman, Mr. Chiu expresses his indignation, nonetheless respectfully addressing the officer as "Comrade Policeman." The policeman acts as though he has done nothing, but Mr. Chiu presses the matter, accusing the officer of having "tortured" them and violating the law. A large crowd has by now gathered round, and the policemen elect to take Mr. Chiu into custody, quickly handcuffing him. Mr. Chiu objects, but the stout officer brandishes his pistol, while the young officer labels him a "saboteur." The bride can only mumble insignificantly as Mr. Chiu resists, citing the train they need to catch, earning himself a punch in the chest and a rap on the hand with the pistol. As he is dragged away, Mr. Chiu instructs his bride to take the train and send someone back if he fails to follow.

Later, Mr. Chiu is found inhabiting a cell at the Railroad Police Station, with a single barred window overlooking a yard. Exhausted, he lies down to reflect on his circumstances. The fact that the Cultural Revolution has ended (setting the story sometime after 1976) allows Mr. Chiu to be unafraid of what might befall him. The Cultural Revolution was a time of political upheaval and social chaos, as Mao Tse-tung inspired youth to form militant revolutionary groups across the nation with the goal of purging capitalist interests from the nation. Mao Tse-tung died in 1976, and reforms associated with the revolution were discontinued within the next couple of years. Recently, Mr. Chiu notes, the Communist Party has been "propagating the idea" of legal equality among all citizens. He accordingly expects the institution of law enforcement to be "a law-abiding model for common people."

He is taken to an interrogation room, and on the way, the stout policeman crosses his path and fires an imaginary pistol at him. Mr. Chiu curses, and the burp he produces upon sitting is perhaps the first physiological indication that he may be in danger of a hepatitis relapse. He is surprised to see that the police there have a large file on him. The bureau chief asks Mr. Chiu some basic questions and then informs him that his crime is sabotage and he will be punished, especially because he has failed to act as a decent Communist. Mr. Chiu insists that the police officers in fact accosted him, and he delivers a lengthy lecture on the propriety of the actions of the police. The chief makes clear, though, that the official version of the event has already been determined in the officers' favor, as witnesses confirmed that he caused a public disturbance and disobeyed the officers. Beginning to feel pain in his stomach, Mr. Chiu still objects and refuses to confess and repent as instructed. The police confidently refuse to offer him any apology. As he is escorted out, Mr. Chiu vows to report the police to the Provincial Administration and likens them to the Japanese military police, who occupied swaths of China through the second Sino-Japanese War, which began in 1937, and World War II, which ended in 1945.

Back in the cell, Mr. Chiu is fed a light, simple meal. After eating, he feels further indications that a relapse is imminent, including a fever and chills, but his medicine is with his bride. Meanwhile, he has no television to watch and nothing to read. Still not frightened, he laments the work he will have to do to catch up after this delay. He tells a guard of his illness and potential death, but the guard tells him nothing will be done until Monday (today is Saturday). That night, Mr. Chiu sleeps well despite the fleas in the bed, as for some reason fleas decline to bite him, and in his fatigue he even appreciates his bride's absence. The next day, Sunday, proves uneventful, with Mr. Chiu devoting his attention to maintaining peace of mind, despite his fever, so as to avoid incurring a full relapse. However, his mind is drawn to "his paper on the nature of contradictions," and his anger at the police at times overwhelms him. He still believes that he will prove able to force the police to extend him an apology.

Mr. Chiu wakes on Monday morning to the sound of a man moaning; he soon discovers that a former student of his, Fenjin, is tied to a tree in the backyard, with his arms around the trunk behind him and cuffed together. Mr. Chiu realizes that his bride, whom he curses as "a stupid woman," must have sent this insignificant lawyer rather than an official from Harbin University, where he works. Mr. Chiu feels obligated to help but realizes that at present he can do nothing. A guard informs Mr. Chiu that Fenjin earned his punishment by insulting the bureau chief. Outside, the tall young policeman slaps Fenjin and pours water over his head, which he will do hourly to fend off sunstroke, before glancing

up defiantly at Mr. Chiu with his pistol glittering. Taken to speak with the chief again, Mr. Chiu remains confrontational, telling the chief that his detainment of Fenjin is illegal. The chief remains confident that Mr. Chiu has no leverage, not even with the news media.

The chief insists again that Mr. Chiu must admit his crime; if he does not, he must watch Fenjin be tortured in the sun. Beginning to suffer another acute attack of hepatitis, Mr. Chiu can hardly contain his anger as he reads a "self-criticism"—a confession and humble apology—that has been written on his behalf. Being assured of his and Fenjin's imminent release, he reluctantly signs the document. Ailing physically to such a degree that he has difficulty walking, Mr. Chiu harbors murderous thoughts as he exits the building, beltless, to meet Fenjin.

Mr. Chiu apologizes to Fenjin, whose fingers are trembling and whose clothes are wet and dirty, and the two depart the station. Mr. Chiu insists on buying Fenjin a couple of bowls of black tea, and before they go to the train station he proceeds to buy his former student soup at a second food stand and then four dishes at a series of four different restaurants in the vicinity of the police station. While eating, he repeatedly mutters his desire to kill all the policemen. Fenjin finds that Mr. Chiu, whose skin is yellowed and puckered as a result of the hepatitis attack, appears to him, for the first time, to be "an ugly man." The closing lines of the story note that some eight hundred people in Muji subsequently suffered acute attacks of hepatitis, with six, including two children, dying of the illness.

CHARACTERS

The Bride
The bride of Mr. Chiu seems to be a very timid character. She sparks Mr. Chiu's indignant response to their soaked sandals by calling the policeman a "hooligan," but once he is being arrested, she is "petrified" and can only mutter, "Oh, please, please!" Mr. Chiu, in fact, professes to be relieved at her absence after the honeymoon, and when she unwisely sends the ineffectual lawyer Fenjin to assist her husband, Mr. Chiu calls her "stupid" and "a bookworm, who only knew how to read foreign novels." The fact that Mr. Chiu's bride is never named is an indication of her secondary importance

both to Mr. Chiu, who seems more emotionally committed to his profession, and to the story.

Chiu Maguang

Mr. Chiu, the protagonist of the story, experiences the steady deterioration of his circumstances, his physical condition, and his psyche over the course of the story. As is often considered typical of highly educated professors, Mr. Chiu has a great deal of dignity, which is grounded in his sense of moral clarity. When his sandals are doused, he believes that the police have committed an injustice, and he is determined to right the wrong by lecturing the officer about his duty with regard to the law. He evidently believes in and trusts the institutions of his country, to the extent that he does not consider that there might be repercussions to his publicly accusing the officers of violating the law. When he comes to realize during his first interrogation that he cannot trust the police to operate according to the truth, he shifts his trust to other institutions, namely the news media as represented by the *Northeastern Daily* newspaper, the judiciary as represented by the People's Court in Beijing, and the government at large in the form of the Provincial Administration.

However, the police chief's confidence that he can do what he likes without consequences shakes Mr. Chiu's confidence in these institutions, and while alone in his cell, he cannot subdue his unresolved anger at the police. Although he appreciates the solitude and the break provided by the detention—an indication of the high level of stress he must ordinarily experience in his life as a university lecturer—his increasing physical discomfort and his concern over the threat of an acute hepatitis relapse heighten his stress about his immediate circumstances. As he inches toward realizing the hopelessness of his self-appointed quest to bring the truth of his unjust arrest to light, he recalls the adage, "When a scholar runs into soldiers, the more he argues, the muddier his point becomes"; this recollection foreshadows his abandoning his pursuit of the truth and relenting to the police chief's demands in the end. However, the mental costs of this defeat are too high: Mr. Chiu's moral order has been compromised. Enraged almost to madness, he proceeds to feverishly wander from restaurant to restaurant, spreading his hepatitis. There can be little doubt that Mr. Chiu spread his viral illness consciously, since "he made up his mind to do something" after signing the false confession. The reader may imagine that, as an ordinary man, Mr. Chiu could not have committed murder in a violent fashion, even in his extreme anger; but a certain psychological distance is allowed when he simply spreads a disease he is infected with, never knowing who might be infected and how seriously ill they might become. Nonetheless, his premeditated actions bring about the deaths of six people, including two children.

Fenjin

Fenjin's role in the story is significant, but his character is not. As a lawyer who does little but domestic detective work, he holds no sway with the police, who use him as leverage against Mr. Chiu by leaving him in a compromised position, secured to a tree in the yard in the blazing sunshine. Fenjin afterward calls the police "savages." He can only wonder why Mr. Chiu, his former teacher, insists on buying small servings of food at so many different restaurants.

Guards

A number of guards conduct Mr. Chiu from place to place and provide him with information when he is imprisoned.

Police Chief

The police chief, in whom power is centralized at the station, is portrayed more fully than any of the other police officers, mostly through his attitude toward Mr. Chiu. He appears only in the two interrogation scenes. He is confidently dismissive of all of Mr. Chiu's threats as to being held accountable for his officers' and his own actions, and this is surely part of his game: to leave the detainee with the impression that the police are in complete control and have no need to fear retaliation from any given citizen, even a respectable lecturer like Mr. Chiu. Indeed, the police chief seems to rightly believe that no newspaper or television station would run the risk of criticizing police actions with regard to such an insignificant matter, especially since the witness statements support the police. The chief smokes cigarettes, even blowing smoke in Mr. Chiu's face at the close of the first interview.

Scribe

A scribe ostensibly records what is said when Mr. Chiu is first interrogated. When Mr. Chiu is taken to speak with the chief the second time, the scribe is "empty-handed."

Second Interrogator

A man described only as "donkey-faced" assists the chief in the interrogations, supplying the witness's statements the first time and the prepared confession the second time.

Stout Policeman

The stout, middle-aged policeman is the one who douses Mr. Chiu's and his bride's sandals with tea, which he denies, and then orders Mr. Chiu's arrest, subduing him with blows. When the stout policeman sees Mr. Chiu in the police station hall, he fires an imaginary pistol at the detainee. The stout policeman's motivation for soaking the couple's shoes is never indicated. One conjecture would be that the police officers benefit somehow by making arrests that lead to convictions or confessions; they may be rewarded for their zeal, or they may even have quotas such as a certain number of arrests per week. Thus, the stout officer may have anticipated, based on Mr. Chiu's appearance and demeanor, that he would be angry enough at the indignity of this strange attack to respond aggressively, giving the officers grounds to arrest him.

Tall Policeman

The young, tall policeman assists the stout one in arresting Mr. Chiu. Later, he slaps Fenjin and dumps water on his head in the police station yard. After glancing up at Mr. Chiu, he spits a cigarette butt into the dust.

THEMES

Political Power

Jin's story vividly illustrates the skewed power dynamic between the police officers, exemplified by the bureau chief, and the captive citizen, Mr. Chiu. China's status as a Communist nation renders this situation inherently different from the case in a democratic country. In a democracy, police chiefs are often elected, and an outcry against a police chief, such as might be raised in a simple letter to the editor of a town newspaper, could very well cost the chief his job. In a Communist society, a police chief is more likely to be appointed and thus to have a working relationship with the superior who assigned him to the post. In turn, this superior may have a similar relationship with his superior, and on up through the levels of government; the linked

TOPICS FOR FURTHER STUDY

- Write a short story that is a fictionalized account of a time when you were frustrated by the unfair actions of people in authority. Write your story from a third-person perspective, in a style similar to Jin's in "Saboteur," and create a protagonist who is someone other than yourself. Share your short story on a blog and invite comments from your classmates.

- Research the social and economic consequences of the spread of severe acute respiratory syndrome (SARS) in China in late 2002 and early 2003. Create a multimedia presentation that includes statistics, medical evidence, and personal stories. Post the presentation and links to information on SARS on your Web site.

- Imagine that you are Mr. Chiu. After your trouble with the police described in "Saboteur," you are scheduled to give a lecture at your university "on the nature of contradictions," and so you decide to seize the opportunity to demonstrate your innocence. Devise a PowerPoint presentation that uses persuasive illustrations and graphics to make your case against the police.

- Read *The Communist Manifesto* (1848) by Karl Marx and Friedrich Engels (significant excerpts or summaries if not the whole work) and write an essay summarizing the Communist approach to government. For extra credit, create a Venn diagram (overlapping circles) that contrasts the communist philosophy with the capitalist philosophy as expressed by Adam Smith in *The Wealth of Nations*.

- Pick a story or essay by a Chinese American from *American Dragons: Twenty-five Asian American Voices* (1995), edited by Laurence Yep and aimed at young adults. Then, write a reflective paper in which you compare periods of time, events, experiences, or ideas in your own life that relate to those from the story or essay you choose.

officials likely have overlapping interests and priorities. Thus, these officials are unlikely to carry out or allow actions that reflect poorly on their fellow officials, even if their fellow officials are acting incompetently or illegally. This is a form of corruption that is, to be sure, by no means limited to Communist or nondemocratic nations. Throughout American history, elected officials have demonstrated a willingness to bend and break laws for the sake of fellow officials, friends, or themselves. In any nation, police officers may have more opportunities than other government employees to abuse their power, such as by planting evidence or by misreporting or concealing crimes.

In this story, Mr. Chiu assumes from the beginning of his ordeal that "the police ought to be a law-abiding model for the common people." But as soon as he puts the police officers in a compromised position by publicly accusing them of breaking the law, they simply arrest him. Even if other people had witnessed the police officer soaking Mr. Chiu's and his bride's sandals, they would clearly not benefit from reporting this information; the police might just label them accomplices and detain them as well, or the police could simply discard the reports provided by these honest witnesses, to show Mr. Chiu only the reports faulting him alone for the public disruption.

Once the material evidence of Mr. Chiu's guilt has been established, the police chief seems convinced that no action taken by Mr. Chiu could possibly threaten his livelihood. The regional newspaper may be unlikely to report such a minor incident of purported corruption because of censorship (the report would be deleted before publication) or because the newspaper depends on government licenses in order to operate, and political allies of the police chief might have the leverage to revoke the newspaper's license if any of its reports are deemed libel against the government. The People's Court in Beijing, in turn, would likely base its findings on the evidence provided by the police, which faults Mr. Chiu. Even if the police chief does not have allies in the Provincial Administration, that level of government would certainly not benefit from the publication of reports that the railroad police in Muji are corrupt, since it would reflect poorly on the province. Thus, although Mr. Chiu cites various ideals of honest governance in demanding an apology from the police, these ideals matter little in the practical functioning of the government that Jin depicts. In the end, in this dynamic, the police have all the power, and Mr. Chiu has none.

Truth

The police and Mr. Chiu prove to have greatly differing conceptions about the nature of truth. The police chief makes clear that the police are in a position to officially determine the truth of past circumstances, as based on the evidence they provide. In the first interrogation, the chief acts as though there is no reason to doubt the account provided by his officers, faulting Mr. Chiu. When Mr. Chiu tries to assert that the truth is otherwise, the chief deflects his pleas by "matter-of-factly" remarking, "That statement is groundless. You have no witness. Why should I believe you?" Even the marks on Mr. Chiu's hand fail to convince the chief that the police officer was the one who injured him. In the second interview, the chief goes further to enlighten Mr. Chiu, directly informing him, "We are not afraid of any story you make up. We call it fiction." Thus, the police operate not according to reality but according to the perception of reality that they provide, and it is this that Mr. Chiu finds impossible to accept. Indeed, as a "scholar" and "philosopher," pursuit of the truth and respect for the truth are part of his job description. His anger first flares when he blurts out, "But I am telling the truth!" Later, when shown the "self-criticism" that he is directed to sign, his conscience sings out, "Lie, lie!" He realizes by now, though, that he has little choice if he wishes to be able to leave the station to get treatment for his hepatitis. Stricken with pain and nausea, Mr. Chiu feverishly disregards his conscience upon signing the false confession; an inner voice tells him the confession is a lie—"but he shook his head and forced the voice away." Thus, having sacrificed the truth and unbalanced his psyche, Mr. Chiu spirals into a narcissistic rage that allows him to carry out his horrific revenge.

Sabotage

As the title indicates, the idea of sabotage is especially significant to the story. Mr. Chiu is accused by the young policeman of being a saboteur for "disrupting public order." That is, he is accused of sabotaging the ordinary functioning of society by disrupting people's daily life. This charge may strike the American reader as ridiculous, but in a Communist nation such as China—and China under Deng Xiaoping, who effectively ruled from 1978 through the early

The newlyweds had their breakfast in the outdoor café outside the train station. *(Vagabond / Shutterstock.com)*

1990s, has been characterized as a dictatorship—the politics of the matter can be everything, and even a false charge can bring severe consequences for the accused. Mr. Chiu attempts to reverse the charge by declaring that the police themselves "are the saboteurs of our social order" for having doused his and his wife's sandals with tea. When the police demonstrate their indifference to the truth, Mr. Chiu fulfills the charge against him: he indeed becomes a saboteur, causing several deaths by spreading his hepatitis infection at restaurants.

Another act of sabotage, one that is not directly characterized as such by the narrator, is the fact that the police sabotage Mr. Chiu's psyche. Up to this point in his life, he has trusted that those with authority will operate morally and will honor, even revere, the truth, values he upholds as well. Arguably, the functioning of civilized society substantially depends on people's faith in state institutions and their principled operation. Thus, in showing Mr. Chiu

that his trust in his nation's law enforcement is misplaced, the chief destroys a pillar of Mr. Chiu's implicit civic agreement to contribute positively to society. Considering the minimal extent of the consequences of Mr. Chiu's unjust detention—he lost a couple days of productivity and suffered a relapse that would presumably be treatable—his reaction seems absurd and extreme; he might even be classified as an agent of biological terrorism. Jin's point, though, may be that when the social contract between those who make the rules and those who follow the rules is sabotaged by the rule makers, in the minds of some, the whole rulebook gets thrown out the window.

STYLE

Realism

Jin's prose style, which is relatively spare as far as details and narrative insight are concerned, has been compared with that of renowned Russian authors Nikolai Gogol and Anton Chekhov, two authors for whom Jin has expressed admiration. Like Gogol and Chekhov, Jin often addresses the oppression of the common person in a setting dominated by agents of Communism or tyranny who are often cruelly indifferent to the fates of citizens. These sorts of circumstances seem to lend themselves to a stark portrayal of the reality under consideration. The absurdity of that reality is so powerful in and of itself that to exaggerate, distort, or remold the absurdity would be to diminish it in the eyes of the readers, but the author's intent is understood to be to give the reader the clearest and truest possible sense of that absurdity. Accordingly, "Saboteur" is written in what could be characterized as a realist style, laying out the circumstances succinctly, with sensory details but little metaphorical embellishment, and allowing the characters' thoughts and dialogue to convey the nuance of the scene. The result is a straightforward story that leaves the reader duly contemptuous of the police and sympathetic with Mr. Chiu but ultimately appalled by his action, seeing him, as Fenjin does, as "an ugly man."

Second-Language Literature

Jin is associated with very select literary company in that he writes in English as an adopted language. Joseph Conrad, who was born in modern-day

Ukraine but earned his early living as a seaman on voyages all over the world, actually learned English as a third language, after Polish and French. He became one of the most respected authors in the Western canon, and his style can be characterized as unique because of the singular way he has of expressing his thoughts, molded by having learned to express himself in other languages prior to English. Vladimir Nabokov began his career writing in Russian but likewise became a famous English-language novelist, inclined to clever descriptions and wordplay. In an interview with Te-hsing Shan in *Tamkang Review*, Jin refers to Conrad and Nabokov as "these two giants," and he affirms that "they established a tradition for later comers" and are part of his "literary heritage."

Jin's style should not necessarily be compared with the styles of his two predecessors, however, who also differ markedly from each other. Furthermore, in stories such as "Saboteur," it is not clear whether any particular aspect of his style should be attributed to his writing in an adopted language, owing to his evident mastery of English. At times, though, the reader may feel the prose has a singular rhythm or sense to it, as if the author is describing the circumstances from a shifted linguistic perspective. An example of this is the use by Mr. Chiu and his bride of the word "hoodlum" to describe the police officers, a word that is more likely to connote street-tough youths among American readers. Different readers may find that other particular terms and instances of syntax convey to them the author's unique sense of the English language. The conversations especially may strike the reader as reflecting a non-native grasp of English; this is explained by Jin's admission in an interview that while he originally writes his narratives in English, for conversation among Chinese characters, he conceives the lines in Chinese and then translates them into English. Although the fluent narration largely disguises the author's linguistic identity, the dialogue hints at the discrepancies between the rhythms of the author's two languages.

HISTORICAL CONTEXT

Chinese Cultural Revolution
"Saboteur," along with other stories from *The Bridegroom*, is understood to have taken place sometime between the end of the Cultural Revolution in 1976 and the Tiananmen Square massacre of 1989. The ten-year Cultural Revolution, begun in 1966, proved a turning point in Chinese history, but not quite in the manner that its instigator, Mao Tse-tung, intended. As chairman of various political entities, including the Communist Party and the nation itself, Mao led the People's Republic of China upon its inception through a protracted revolution referred to as the Chinese Civil War in 1949. Devoted to Marxist principles intended to benefit the proletariat (or working class), Mao feared by 1966 that capitalist-minded intellectuals and representatives of the bourgeoisie (or middle class) had infiltrated the nation's political machinery. He thus oversaw the promotion of a "Cultural Revolution" that would return the nation to its revolutionary Marxist roots, flushing the bourgeois—including his own political enemies—out of positions of control.

When students began to form "Red Guard" groups devoted to Mao's revolutionary principles, he encouraged and applauded them, and they soon blanketed the nation. Jin, as a preadolescent, was a member of the Little Red Guard, and in 1970, he joined the People's Liberation Army. In interviews he has positioned himself as sympathetic with Mao's ideals in support of the common people. Some Red Guard factions, however, defying Mao's more peaceful directives in their quest to eradicate the customs of the exploitative upper classes, turned violent in persecuting landholders, intellectuals, and anyone deemed insufficiently socialist. Ultimately, schools were closed, and the nation's government was paralyzed by contested authority and the voids left by purges of suspicious elements. The Cultural Revolution, which Mao had originally planned to last three months, continued for ten years, with Mao functioning as a dictator during that time. Over time, his influence and authority eroded because of the social chaos, and the Cultural Revolution drew to a close in 1976, the year of Mao's death.

A handful of powerful political figures maneuvered to fill the void left by Mao, and Deng, whose authority stemmed from his impressive record as a military commander during the Chinese Civil War—and from his twice being purged and then reinstated under Mao—emerged as the dominant persona. He signaled early on an intent to lead the nation through democratic reforms, launching a campaign to change the concept of

COMPARE & CONTRAST

- **1980s:** As capitalist values and morals are welcomed in China in the aftermath of Mao Tse-tung's Cultural Revolution, Chinese citizens, particularly farmers, find that the system allows more opportunities for making money.

  2000: In a system that allows for drastically lower wages than in Western markets, Chinese industry thrives, exporting heavily to the United States and European nations.

  Today: In the wake of the 2008 Olympics in Beijing, China is seen as a rapidly modernizing nation that could possibly become the world's foremost economic force later in the century.

- **1980s:** Deng Xiaoping, as general secretary of the Communist Party and chairman of the Central Military Commission, ends China's official antipathy to non-Communist nations and ideals, establishing international relationships with democracies and introducing capitalist-style reforms.

  2000: Jiang Zemin, leading China as president, chairman of the Central Military Commission, and general secretary of the

Communist Party, accelerates economic growth at home through further capitalist-style initiatives at a pace that surpasses global expectations while aggressively befriending powerful nations such as Russia.

  Today: With the Chinese economy soaring, Hu Jintao, leading China in the roles held by Jiang Zemin, is known for his domestic program of the "Harmonious Society" and for peaceful international relations.

- **1980s:** In 1985, China institutes a policy of nine years of mandatory education and develops and expands educational opportunities as a means of modernizing the nation.

  2000: Higher education is highly competitive, with about half of secondary-school graduates gaining admission to postsecondary institutions.

  Today: Signifying China's advances in science and technology, an area focused on throughout the education system over the preceding decades for the sake of national development, a lunar probe is scheduled for launch in late 2010.

---

truth from a subjective one, as it became under Mao's dictatorship and the Red Guard's persecutions, to an objective one, as determined by the practices of science and social reform. Ruan Ming, in *Deng Xiaoping: Chronicle of an Empire*, states that this approach "thoroughly negated dogmatism and theoretical despotism and laid the ideological foundation for China to move forward to reform and opening up to the outside world." By 1979, the Communist leadership and the Chinese people were optimistic about the nation's direction and potential for reform. However, Deng would not take advantage of the circumstances; as Ruan notes, he was "a pragmatic politician without profound insight," and when pressured by an influential antireform clique, he found himself "discarding political reform and

maintaining despotism." Deng went from democratically praising the rule of law as written, rather than as determined by the whims of the present leadership, to following Mao's example and requiring adherence to a theoretical groundwork laid for his own particular brand of authoritarianism.

Despite his despotic methods, Deng oversaw a remarkable degree of economic growth in China, especially because he welcomed capitalist practices and influences within the socialist system and developed productive relationships with important trading partners such as the United States. Jin signals a negative influence of capitalism in "Saboteur" when he tellingly notes that one of the witnesses faulting Mr. Chiu for the public disturbance was "a purchasing agent from

He waited impatiently for his release from his jail cell. *(Steve Snowden / Shutterstock.com)*

a shipyard in Shanghai" (that is, engaged in capitalist trade); the reader may gather that this agent's word matters more to those in power than the word of a university lecturer.

The peak of Deng's abandonment of and opposition to democratic reform was his disastrous suppression of the demonstrations at Tiananmen Square in June 1989. Tens of thousands of student protesters favoring democratic principles gathered in the politically significant Tiananmen Square, in Beijing, for several weeks following the death of a pro-democracy official in April 1989. Deng eventually dispatched tens of thousands of troops to the city; the protestors blocked them at the outskirts for more than two weeks. Having alienated the social democratic movement long ago, Deng was by now allied with totalitarian-minded dogmatists and militarists, who supported his inclination to "encircle and annihilate the trouble" as he had in defeating Chang Kai-shek's Nationalist forces in 1949. He classified the peaceful student protesters as a military enemy, and he assured his soldiers that they would be executed if they failed to carry out the order to attack with lethal force. As a result, thousands of protesters were massacred. This event,

which Jin and his wife watched unfold on television from their home in Boston, was the critical factor in his decision not to return to China. As Jin told Garner of the *New York Times Magazine*, "I was not mentally prepared for what happened. I had always thought that the Chinese Army was there to serve and protect the people." The massacre signaled the waning of Deng's power, and he stepped down from his highest offices beginning later that year, to be retired from politics by 1992, though he would continue to wield influence behind the scenes. In "Saboteur," Jin's views of the abuses of those in authority in the Deng Xiaoping era can be seen as represented in the attitudes and actions of the corrupt police officers.

CRITICAL OVERVIEW

In light of the various awards won by his works of fiction over the last two decades, Jin has gained steadily increasing attention in the United States. Most critics who review *The Bridegroom* take note of "Saboteur," the opening story. In the *New York Times*, Claire Messud observes that the stories in this collection "lay bare the ironies of tyranny in all its forms," with "Saboteur" constructed like a fable, with a clear lesson. Assessing this and another story, she states, "Laced with black humor, they refrain from entering fully into the human complexities of their characters: unjust power structures, rather than the individual experiences of the protagonists, are the focus of these tales." Messud notes that Jin's voice is "resonant" but he is not "particularly accessible" to Americans; rather, "he is a Chinese writer, writing about China, who happens to live in the United States." Considering the limitations of his style, such as his use of cliché and unambitious syntax, Messud concludes, "It is impossible to escape the impression that for Ha Jin, the English language—potentially so pliable, so complex—is ultimately an unwieldy tool that merely suffices for his purposes." She nonetheless affirms that "his eye for detail, his great storytelling talent—these universal gifts suffuse his work and make *The Bridegroom* a genuine pleasure."

A contributor to *Publishers Weekly* declares that "it's difficult to think of another writer who has captured the conflicting attitudes and desires, and the still-changing conditions of daily life, of post-Cultural Revolution China as well as Ha Jin does" in *The Bridegroom*. The stories are said to "attain their significant cumulative effect through spare prose penetrated by wit, insight and a fine sense of irony." The reviewer concludes that Jin "has a rare empathy for people striving to balance the past and the future while caught on the cusp of change." In *Booklist*, Nancy Pearl gives a similar characterization of "the author's deliberately flat writing style, with simple sentences, few metaphors or similes, and no play on language." She highlights how Mr. Chiu turns into a "killer" in "Saboteur," before concluding, "Altogether, this is a fine collection, sure to be in demand by fans of literary fiction." Writing for *Library Journal*, Shirley Quan affirms that "Jin uses this collection to exhibit his strong writing and storytelling skills with his laconic use of words."

CRITICISM

Michael Allen Holmes

Holmes is a writer and editor. In the following essay, he considers how the incidental details in "Saboteur" track the gradual erosion of the quintessentially logical Mr. Chiu's psyche.

WHAT DO I READ NEXT?

- Ha Jin's short-story collection, *Under the Red Flag* (1997), includes twelve tales set during Mao Tse-tung's Cultural Revolution.

- Jin was greatly influenced by the great Russian authors, especially Anton Chekhov, whose play *The Cherry Orchard* (1904) addresses the shifting societal positions of the aristocracy and the bourgeoisie in prerevolutionary Russia.

- Nikolai Gogol's short story "The Overcoat" (1842) is one of the foundational works of the Russian literary tradition, telling of an impoverished Russian government clerk and his tattered overcoat.

- Vladimir Pushkin, who first wrote in Russian but turned to writing in an impressively playful English, published *Pnin* in 1957. This novel is about a Russian professor who has moved to the United States.

- Joseph Conrad, who wrote in English as a third language, depicts a heroic response to government tyranny in *Nostromo*. Written in 1904, it is available in several modern editions.

- The renowned Chinese intellectual Lin Yutang's *My Country and My People* (1935) depicts life in China before the rise of Communism.

- The Chinese American author Amy Tan focuses more on relationships than does Jin. Her novel *The Joy Luck Club* (1989) revolves around the mothers and daughters of families that immigrated to America from China.

- *In the Year of the Boar and Jackie Robinson* (1984), a young-adult book by Bette Bao Lord, tells the story of a girl who moves away from China to join her father in America—as Jin's son joined him—and must adjust to life growing up in Brooklyn.

Jin's style in the stories of *The Bridegroom* (2000) is generally recognized by reviewers in similar terms, as perhaps spare, minimal, terse, or sparse. His prose is straightforward, introducing few rhetorical or theoretical conceptions and rarely using metaphors to convey physical details. What verbal flourishes can be found tend to be idioms or clichés, such as the observation, in "Saboteur," that the day "was going to be a scorcher." Some critics may be inclined to fault Jin for failing to delve further into the expressive possibilities of the English language. He moved to the United States in 1985, meaning that he had been immersed in American culture for fifteen years when this collection was published; and he began studying English via radio programming in 1976, prior to majoring in English as an undergraduate and then earning a master's degree in American literature. Thus, Jin's familiarity with the forms and possibilities of the English language should not be underestimated. Rather, it seems he has made conscious choices to emulate the understated style of certain American authors, perhaps in particular the 1954 Nobel Prize–winner Ernest Hemingway.

In an interview with Chris GoGwilt in *Guernica* magazine, Jin affirmed, "I love Hemingway," and he noted the "clear, very lucid" language used by the author in his masterpiece novella *The Old Man and the Sea*, which served to introduce Jin and many of his classmates to a certain "American mentality" of independent perseverance in the face of adversity and even impending failure. In terms of style, Hemingway is renowned for his concealment or suppression of essential facts about his characters' circumstances, which may be obscurely revealed through dialogue but never made explicit. For example, the brief story "Hills like White Elephants" is understood to portray a couple's emotionally strained discussion about having an abortion, but the text itself never even makes clear that the woman is pregnant. Jin is not

nearly so cryptic in his presentation of the circumstances in "Saboteur," which has the feel of a fable in that it is didactic, aimed at teaching. However, his carefully rationed descriptions and details provide a collective impression that bolsters the tangible sense of the story, and this collective impression is arguably enhanced by the smoothness of the gracefully unadorned language.

One of the first significant details in the story is the fact of Mr. Chiu's hepatitis, a disease involving inflammation of the liver. Mr. Chiu is certainly not portrayed as an alcoholic, which is one cause of hepatitis, so his infection would be understood as viral. The liver is associated with essential functions related to digestion and detoxification, and so in this story, the physical dysfunction of Mr. Chiu's liver may be understood to signify, in his mentality, a difficulty in digesting certain information or coming to terms with something. Such a trait becomes apparent when he is unable to accept the dousing of his and his bride's sandals—that is, he is unable to digest the blatant falsity of the police's claim that he wet his sandals himself. After the police tell him, "You're lying," he rejoins with what he perceives to be a truthful description of the situation, namely, that the police are violating the law, earning him his arrest and detention.

Mr. Chiu's belt is taken from him before he is locked in the cell, a detail that might not be significant except that he later leaves the police station without retrieving it. Through his confrontation with the police, Mr. Chiu has demonstrated his devotion to truthfulness and order, and the belt can be understood as the centerpiece of the male academic's standard outfit of dress shirt, dress pants, tie, and coat. Mr. Chiu refers to himself as a "lecturer," and the reader might conclude that Jin actually intends Mr. Chiu to be understood as a professor; but Jin is undoubtedly aware of the distinction between the two in American connotations, namely, that the professor likely has a stable contract, if not tenure, whereas a lecturer is likely to be more precariously employed, with lower pay, less academic standing, and a demanding schedule. This is a significant detail because, though he comes across as fairly levelheaded, Mr. Chiu's actions indicate that he perhaps experiences a high level of stress in his daily life. In protesting to the police chief, he stresses the importance of his being "late for a conference in the provincial capital," and he is later described, despite his illness, as "more upset than frightened, because he would have to catch up with his work once he was back home," which includes a paper to complete and two dozen books to start reading.

Jin provides a few clues about the precise nature of Mr. Chiu's academic work. Once beyond the formulaic context of the interrogation, Mr. Chiu asserts that he is "a scholar, a philosopher, and an expert in dialectical materialism." Although a precise definition of the term *dialectical materialism* is a discussion in and of itself, it can be understood as a philosophy formulated by Karl Marx and Friedrich Engels, authors of *The Communist Manifesto*, as the theoretical underpinning for their socialist system. The term refers to a materialist, or physically based, conception of the interactive forces that dictate the evolution of society through history. Thus, Mr. Chiu has expert knowledge of the foundations of the Communist government that China adopted in 1949. Mr. Chiu later notes that he taught Fenjin in "a course in Marxist materialism," which can likewise be understood as relating to the pure foundations of Communism. Notably, Jin has positioned himself in interviews as sympathetic with the Communist ideals that were proclaimed during Mao Tse-tung's Cultural Revolution. In this story, Mr. Chiu recalls a relevant saying of Chairman Mao's, indicating his familiarity with the Communist leader's quotations. Thus, Jin would seem to be sympathetic with the interests of his protagonist in this story. Mao Tse-tung's ideals were in some senses diluted during the subsequent reign of Deng Xiaoping, who through the 1980s gradually introduced capitalist, market-based concepts into China's socialist system.

As befits such a philosopher, Mr. Chiu seems especially concerned with logic, order, and truth throughout the story. He sees fit to inform the policemen that their "duty is to keep order," and he even asks them what their motivation was for violating the law. Although open-ended questions may be rhetorically effective in his work as a university lecturer, this one only incites the police to respond by arresting him, which he protests as "utterly unreasonable." In his cell, he figures that if he "reasoned with them," the outcome should be favorable. In his interrogation, he asserts that, "logically speaking," the chief should criticize and punish the officers who arrested him. The chief demurs, but, holding truthful ideals as an imperative,

Mr. Chiu insists, "You must compensate me for the damage and losses." However, the police will not cooperate with Mr. Chiu, and the smoke that the chief blows in his face signifies the smoke screen of falsehood that is enveloping him. Later, when he gets a good night's sleep despite the circumstances, "it seemed illogical." When he must spend the whole day lying in bed, his mind obsesses over "his paper on the nature of contradictions" and the injustice of the circumstances. Gradually, his sense of order is being unbalanced. Notably, when he was first taken to the jail cell, the sensory images were tranquil: the paired swings, like husband and wife, were swaying in the breeze, while "a cleaver was chopping rhythmically," that is, in a steady, patterned way. Later, when he is back in his cell, the rhythmic chopping has been replaced by an accordion that "kept coughing"—surely a dissonant, disorderly sound.

Although he is mentally focused on logic and order, Mr. Chiu demonstrates curious interactions with his visceral (that is, gut-level), sensory reality. In the beginning, "the air smelled of rotten melon." This might spoil some people's appetites, but he has no trouble ingesting his lunch. Especially curious is the tale of Mr. Chiu's going untouched by fleas during a countryside trip when his colleagues "were all afflicted with hundreds of bites." In a humorous but significant characterization, his colleagues suppose that he "must have tasted nonhuman to fleas." Thus, Jin portrays Mr. Chiu as atypical in being so intellectually attuned to reality that he is viscerally disconnected from it. He does not feel afraid during his detention, though one might expect him to, and has no trouble sleeping, despite the constant orange light and although many others would be too disturbed by the fleas. Even the physical presence of his wife seems unimportant to him, in that, "more amazing now, he didn't miss his bride a lot." The smell of meat does not rouse his appetite but only provokes him to think of enduring his detention calmly. He does become angry, but the outlet he conceives for his anger is nonphysical: he intends to "write an article about this experience."

It is at the midpoint of the story that Jin introduces the concept that will figure in the resolution of the plot, in a line understood to reflect a thought of Mr. Chiu's: "Damn those hoodlums, they had ordered more than they could eat!" In addition to foreshadowing the conclusion, this figure of speech itself merits examination, as the concept of ordering more than one can eat speaks of capitalist excess. In a Communist nation, food should be rationed for the benefit of all; in contrast, under capitalism, food may be "ordered" by paying customers, who may take more than they can eat while others go hungry. Here, Mr. Chiu plays the role of the food, as he intends to prove too much for the police to digest; on a literal level, he will cause food poisoning, spreading his hepatitis at nearby restaurants after his release.

Mr. Chiu's waking up to the noise of Fenjin's moaning marks the beginning of the end of the deterioration of his psyche. What ultimately does him in is his acute sense of morality; when he considers that however his lawyer might have earned it, Fenjin's capture "could never have occurred if Fenjin hadn't come to his rescue. So no matter what, Mr. Chiu had to do something." That is, he feels morally bound to help. He is not yet so disturbed, however, as to be unable to eat his "corn glue" and celery. Watching Fenjin get slapped and humiliated, however, he seems at last stirred by a visceral sense of the reality around him, "gripping the steel bars with both hands, his fingers white." At this point Mr. Chiu has been feverish since the night before; coincidentally, as the hepatitis attacks his body, he becomes more physically attuned to what is occurring around him. In turn, his anger grows more and more overwhelming. When he is at last forced to either sign the false self-criticism or watch Fenjin suffer in the sun, he chooses to assuage his guilt and sacrifice the truth, signing the document. At this point, in his feverish state, the visceral sense of his illness and his moral outrage coalesce. He feels "as though there were a bomb" in his chest, and his thoughts turn to terrorism and mass murder. He concedes that "he knew he could do nothing like that," but because of his illness and his overturned morality, he has been thrust into a visceral sense of outrage that overwhelms his common sense. An additional sign of the backwardness of the moment comes when Mr. Chiu's first consultation with his lawyer—which by law in America would be allowed to come before any conversations with the police—occurs only after he has signed the false confession and been released. In the end, poor Mr. Chiu, who has become a symbol of truth, moral order, academic integrity, and Communist idealism, is undone by his inability to cope with the corruption of the

He was interrogated by the police. (*Phase4Photography* / *Shutterstock.com*)

nation's system of authority. As the subtler details of the story reveal, Mr. Chiu collapses from his ordinary purely intellectual state into a purely visceral state of nausea, pain, and anger, transforming from a respectable citizen to a plague to society.

Source: Michael Allen Holmes, Critical Essay on "Saboteur," in *Short Stories for Students*, Gale, Cengage Learning, 2011.

Valerie Sayers

In the following review, Sayers contrasts Jin's newest novel, The Crazed, *with his first novel,* Waiting.

Ha Jin, who immigrated to the United States from China in 1985, has already published an impressive body of fiction and poetry in English. His short stories, which often appear in annual prize volumes, are odd and arresting compressions of Chinese life: a gay man takes an unattractive bride but is revealed and punished; the American Cowboy Chicken franchise opens a branch in a provincial city, and its workers become consumed with capitalist envy; a little girl observes her miserable kindergarten teacher and learns her first lessons in deceit. Ha Jin's first novel, *Waiting*, which won the National Book Award, is a beautiful and mysterious meditation on the meaning of inaction as well as an allegory of post-Cultural Revolution China. The fiction is realistic—the settings are rendered meticulously—but the plots seesaw between political absurdity on a grand scale and individual suffering in its smallest detail. In an age when so many critics have declared the death of literary realism, Ha Jin's depiction of real absurdity and absurd reality is a good argument against realism's premature burial.

The Crazed, his new novel, is also a compelling read, more directly political than *Waiting*, more focused on an inevitable plot march that will end in Tiananmen Square. The narrator, Jian Wan, is a graduate student studying for his Ph.D. entrance exams, which he hopes will propel him to Beijing University and marriage to his beloved professor's daughter. As the novel opens, however, his professor has suffered a stroke and is hospitalized, slipping in and out of hallucinations and fantasies. Jian Wan and another student are assigned to care for him while his wife makes her way back from a veterinary mission to Tibet and the hospital nurses busy themselves with their embroidery. The wife's presence in Tibet and the nurses' leisurely approach to medical crisis are typical of the novel's opening, with its matter-of-fact portrayal of a China populated by cynics and fanatics, "a paradise for idiots."

The straightforward narrative gives way to the dramatic—at times, to the operatic—as Jian's professor rants. His speeches recreate his sufferings during the Cultural Revolution, when he was declared a Demon Monster and made to wear signs and carry buckets of water designed to bend his body and his spirit. He recalls visualizing *The Inferno* during his torture sessions: "I'd imagine that the crazed people below and around me were like the blustering evil-doers, devils, and monsters cast into hell.... While reciting *The Divine Comedy* in my heart, I felt that my suffering was meant to help me enter purgatory. I had hope. Suffering can refine the soul." Jian wonders, naturally, if this means his professor sees himself in Christian terms, but the older man denies that he is religious. He intersperses memories of his sexual liaisons and his own ambitions with his talk of the spirit, and Jian is alternately revolted and moved to pity. Many of the professor's monologues and spoken dreams, which are designed to unveil his biography as well as to move the plot along, are ridiculously contrived in dramatic terms, yet their language is so direct that they remain strangely compelling. The patient is in a death struggle and declares that he must save his soul but admits,

"I'm afraid I'm not worthy of my suffering." Jian is most perplexed by his professor's disavowal of the scholar's life, which he declares has reduced him to the role of a clerk.

Gradually, however, Jian begins to believe his professor's warnings about the scorn heaped on true intellectuals, and decides to abandon his exams and to seek instead a position in the Policy Office. The irony is typical Ha Jin and would be delicious if the novel were not already moving so relentlessly toward the massacre in Beijing. Thwarted by a Communist Party official, Jian ultimately joins the student demonstrations—not because of his political beliefs but, as he says, for personal reasons. His professor is dead, his fiancée has abandoned him, and he is now a young man without a career. His journey to Beijing grants him a classical moment of epiphany. As the army attacks the gathering students, he aids a wounded woman but then abandons her. Horrified by his own cowardice, he undertakes the rescue of a little boy, as if he is redeeming his own youthful mistakes. The novel's climax is utterly realistic and utterly involving—its movement out of the sickroom and into the streets of Beijing provides just the right change of perception and scale.

Before this busy action takes the novel off into the satisfying territory of plot consummation, the pages of *The Crazed* are also filled with satisfying meditations on language itself, on the connections or lack of connections between language and action. Jian and his professor quote Rilke, Pound, Li Po. Jian sees language as romantic (and in a funny aside says that women who study foreign languages are more romantic than their peers). His own language is direct and often emotional in a nineteenth-century way: "My heart was shaking, filled with pity, dismay, and disgust." Overwrought adverbs such as "desperately" make frequent appearances—and why not? This is a novel about finding one's soul, about wanting to live, as Jian finally says, "actively and meaningfully."

The direct expression of emotion complements the subtle wit and irony that inform the narrative. The crazed themselves are a graceful motif woven through the minds of the characters. Stark images—a boy stung by a scorpion cries for hours on the hillside—alternate with Jian's straightforward interior monologue. He, too, is crazed as he watches his country come to crisis. He, too, struggles to find purpose in his life. And his very particular crisis, in the midst of his country's very particular crisis, becomes universal by virtue of its precise and passionate telling. Like all of us, Jian must act or lose his soul.

Source: Valerie Sayers, "The Road to Tiananmen," in *Commonweal*, Vol. 130, No. 3, February 14, 2003, pp. 17–18.

Helene Wong

In the following review, Wong discusses how Jin's everyday stories demonstrate a shrewd and compassionate observation of the resulting confusion of cultural change.

At first, the stories in this collection seem small, domestic, of petty concerns. Only as you progress do the writer's purpose and meaning become clear, and although it's not quite a case of the whole being greater than the sum of its parts, the small and domestic is revealed to be a microcosm of wider social change.

In his acclaimed novel *Waiting*, Ha Jin examined in subtle and painstaking detail a couple's conflict arising from cultural change in China. Again, only this time in a dozen different ways, he captures how individuals respond when values and traditions are in a state of flux.

His characters are middle-class academics, factory supervisors and shop assistants—perhaps because their education and new-found wealth render them more susceptible to Western influences than the peasant or the sophisticated and/or conservative elite.

At the heart of many of their stories is the classic struggle between East and West, the dilemma of whether to be an individual or part of a community.

Individualism takes different forms. In "The Woman from New York," it signifies independence: a happily married teacher decides to go to New York to explore a new way of life. But it also refers to difference, when her family and community are so suspicious of her unconventional decision that they effectively write her off.

In "A Tiger-Fighter is Hard to Find," individualism is about competition and when the quest for fame leads to loss of judgment. The ways in which characters cope with uniqueness, either in themselves or others, creates a palette of behaviour ranging from funny to tragic, with acts of defiance, irrationality, gossip, envy and revenge, often with damaging consequences.

A more direct clash between East and West is found in "After Cowboy Chicken Came to Town." Employees of a fast food outlet are puzzled and fascinated at the capitalist ways of their American owner, but when they try a little democratic behaviour of their own, they are out of their depth. As with most of the characters in this book, their attempt to integrate value systems ends in loss.

The psychological effects of the rapid uptake of Western culture in China are becoming a recurrent theme among its writers and filmmakers.

The picture they present is almost invariably of people adrift. Ha Jin's everyday stories demonstrate a shrewd and compassionate observation of the resulting confusion and unease and how this manifests itself.

He doesn't always spell out his characters' motivations; he leaves that for the reader to reflect upon. The reward for doing so is a feeling of poignancy and a deeper understanding of the small tragedies of life.

Source: Helene Wong, "Ha Jin: *The Bridegroom*," in *New Zealand Herald*, November 10, 2001.

Charmaine Chan

In the following review, Chan surmises that Jin's short stories in The Bridegroom *collection are easy to read, but that his seemingly uncomplicated and endearing protagonists can be ultimately repugnant.*

Ha Jin's short stories are as easy to read as TV soaps are to watch. But while his storylines may be uncomplicated and his writing unaffected, his work is far more thought-provoking and satisfying because of the complex characters conjured. Skilfully drawn and easy to relate to, many of his protagonists are initially endearing but ultimately repugnant.

Take Old Cheng in the title story, "The Bridegroom." A caring parent of an ugly girl, he is elated when he discovers she has somehow hooked Baowen, the most eligible bachelor in town.

Life continues happily for the couple until Baowen fails to return home one night. Cheng, fearing he has been unfaithful, soon discovers an even more unpalatable truth: his son-in-law has been arrested in "a case of homosexuality." In learning what the word means, Cheng doesn't know whether to believe an officer who describes it as "a mental, moral disease" or a maverick doctor who declares it to be something that cannot be cured.

Regardless, he gives his daughter an ultimatum: divorce (which would relieve the family of the stigma) or banishment. "If you want to wait for him," Cheng tells his lovesick daughter, "don't come to see me again."

This tale, like many of Ha Jin's stories, is about Everyman and Everywoman. It speaks of the search for happiness and the suffering many endure in the hope of something better.

And like much of the author's work set in post-Cultural Revolution China, it sketches a mucky picture of a society rushing to catch up but hobbled by ignorance and tradition.

Ha Jin's disenchantment with his native country is clear. Many stories are trenchant indictments of China's authoritarianism and social conventions—issues that also informed his last novel, *Waiting*, a distressing tale of unconsummated love. A U.S. resident for 15 years, Ha Jin scrutinises Chinese society with a detached but critical eye, picking on its more loathsome qualities and quirky habits.

"An Entrepreneur's Story" is one that prickles because it speaks so succinctly of the way in which money can make a difference. "The same children who were often told to avoid me will call me Uncle now," says the entrepreneur in question, adding, "Some girls keep throwing glances into my office when they pass by."

Instead of pleasing him, however, their change in behaviour has the opposite effect. Nevertheless he, too, succumbs to the predictable consequences of new-found wealth: He uses it to humiliate others and to buy love.

Direct and largely devoid of literary devices except for several delightful similes—a character waits "like a patient donkey" while another has a fleshy face that resembles a blowfish—Ha Jin's prose collars you from the off.

In galloping towards the denouements, however, the stories give the impression that they are going to finish with a bang, and often this is not the case.

Except for "Saboteur," the conclusion to which will make you shudder, they tend to close limply. Among the most flaccid endings is that of "The Woman From New York," about a math teacher who returns to Muji City (where most of the stories are set) to find friends and family suspicious of her new ways and envious of her experience.

Since leaving China in 1985, Ha Jin, professor of English and creative writing at Emory University, Atlanta, has published two books of poetry and two previous collections of stories, *Ocean Of Words*, which won the the PEN/Hemingway Award, and *Under The Red Flag*, which won the Flannery O'Connor Award for Short Fiction.

In addition to *Waiting*, which last year won the U.S. National Book Award for Fiction, he has also written the novel *In The Pond*.

What Ha Jin has to say on Chinese mores and motivations can smart. But while he pokes fun at his homeland, he also pillories the crassness of modern Western culture.

In "After Cowboy Chicken Came To Town," he explores the effects of capitalism on a people hungry for change. The story revolves around an American fast-food joint that is giving the people of Muji a taste for more than just fried chicken.

Capturing the absurdity of life in a disoriented China, one of the characters reveals a consequence of half a century of hardship: "Cowboy Chicken is so delicious," the man declares. "If I could eat it and drink Coke every day, I'd have no need for socialism."

Source: Charmaine Chan, "Prickly Look at Life in China," in *South China Morning Post*, September 30, 2000, p. 4.

SOURCES

Clark, Paul, *The Chinese Cultural Revolution: A History*, Cambridge University Press, 2008, p. 1.

Evans, Richard, *Deng Xiaoping and the Making of Modern China*, Viking, 1994, pp. 244–71, 310–15.

Garner, Dwight, "Ha Jin's Cultural Revolution," in *New York Times Magazine*, February 6, 2000.

Geyh, Paula E., "Ha Jin," in *Dictionary of Literary Biography*, Vol. 244: *American Short-Story Writers since World War II, Fourth Series*, edited by Patrick Meanor, The Gale Group, 2001, pp. 192–201.

GoGwilt, Chris, "Writing without Borders," in *Guernica*, January 2007, http://www.guernicamag.com/interviews/258/post/ (accessed August 19, 2010).

Jin, Ha, "Individualism Arrives in China," in *New Perspectives Quarterly*, Vol. 20, No. 1, January 2003, pp. 13–21.

———, "Saboteur," in *The Bridegroom*, Pantheon, 2000, pp. 3–16.

Messud, Claire, "Tiger-Fighter Meets Cowboy Chicken," in *New York Times Book Review*, October 22, 2000.

Ming, Ruan, *Deng Xiaoping: Chronicle of an Empire*, translated and edited by Nancy Liu, Peter Rand, and Lawrence R. Sullivan, Westview Press, 1994, pp. 15–17, 39–50, 61–64, 211–42.

Mitter, Rana, *Modern China*, Sterling Publishing, 2008.

Ni, Ting, "China," in *World Education Encyclopedia*, Vol. 1, 2nd ed., edited by Rebecca Marlow-Ferguson, The Gale Group, 2001, pp. 236–55.

Pearl, Nancy, Review of *The Bridegroom*, in *Booklist*, Vol. 97, No. 2, September 15, 2000, p. 216.

Quan, Shirley N., Review of *The Bridegroom*, in *Library Journal*, Vol. 125, No. 14, September 1, 2000, p. 254.

Review of *The Bridegroom*, in *Publishers Weekly*, Vol. 247, No. 36, September 4, 2000, p. 81.

Shan, Te-hsing, "In the Ocean of Words: An Interview with Ha Jin," in *Tamkang Review*, Vol. 38, No. 2, June 2008, pp. 135–57.

Smith, Wendy, "Coming to America," in *Publishers Weekly*, Vol. 254, No. 37, September 17, 2007, pp. 29–30.

Spirkin, Alexander, *Dialectical Materialism*, Progress Publishers, 1983.

Wang, Shaoguang, "Between Destruction and Construction: The First Year of the Cultural Revolution," in *The Chinese Cultural Revolution Reconsidered: Beyond Purge and Holocaust*, edited by Kam-yee Law, Palgrave Macmillan, 2003, pp. 25–57.

FURTHER READING

Ching, Frank, *China: The Truth about Its Human Rights Record*, Rider Books, 2008.

> This short, accessible work, published around the time of the Beijing Olympics, gives a knowledgeable accounting of China's recent record with regard to human rights.

Dostoevsky, Fyodor, *Crime and Punishment*, translated by Richard Pevear and Larissa Volokhonsky, Vintage Books, 1992.

> This influential Russian masterpiece zeroes in on the psychology of its protagonist, Raskolnikov, who morally rationalizes a murder but cannot escape the consequences.

Kafka, Franz, *The Castle*, translated by Mark Harman, Schocken Books, 1998.

> Known for sympathizing with the common person victimized by the system, Kafka presents here the challenging, surrealist story of K., who is thwarted at every turn in his attempts merely to gain entrance to the headquarters of the local supreme authority, the Castle.

Yung, Judy, Gordon H. Chang, and Him Mark Lai, eds., *Chinese American Voices: From the Gold Rush to the Present*, University of California Press, 2006.

> This collection of essays provides Chinese American perspectives from 1852 through the turn of the twenty-first century.

SUGGESTED SEARCH TERMS

Ha Jin

Saboteur

The Bridegroom AND Ha Jin

Saboteur AND The Bridegroom

Ha Jin AND Muji City

Ha Jin AND Chinese literature

Ha Jin AND China

Chinese American AND literature

immigrant AND literature

The Sisters

JAMES JOYCE

1914

Best known as a novelist and modernist icon, James Joyce wrote only one collection of short stories, *Dubliners*. The volume was first published in England in 1914 and in the United States in 1916. "The Sisters," the story that opens the collection, first appeared in rough draft form in the *Irish Homestead* on August 13, 1904. It was Joyce's first published work of fiction. In fact, the early version took less than a month to write, as it was composed upon a request made by *Irish Homestead* editor George Russell in July 1904. The final version of "The Sisters" is a brief but poignant story about a boy whose mentor, Catholic priest Father James Flynn, has died. The ordinariness of the events surrounding the death come as a shock to the boy, as do the rumors hinting at a scandal in his mentor's past. The events and the social decorum required for the wake must be observed and endured, but beneath these constraints, the boy feels a baffling sense of freedom. The tale, like Joyce's famed novel *Portrait of the Artist as a Young Man*, can be read as a coming-of-age story, but it is also a tale of grief and a critique of the Catholic Church. The story is a pivotal and formative work of fiction from a prominent modernist author. *Dubliners* has remained in print for nearly a century, and a 2006 Norton edition is readily available.

James Joyce (The Library of Congress)

AUTHOR BIOGRAPHY

Joyce was born February 2, 1882, in Dublin Ireland, the son of tax collector John Stanislaus and pianist Mary Jane Murray. The eldest of ten surviving children, Joyce was raised in a middle-class family that began to decline in both wealth and power over the course of his childhood. Joyce began writing at an early age, composing a poem critical of the Catholic Church when he was only nine years old. Catholicism and religion were highly influential in Joyce's life; he was educated as a boy by Jesuits (a Catholic order of priests and monks), attending first Clogowes Wood College and then Belvedere College. Joyce later attended University College Dublin, graduating with a degree in modern languages in 1902.

After graduating, Joyce immediately traveled to Paris, but he came home a year later when his mother was dying. He stayed in Dublin for another year; there he met Nora Barnacle in 1904. The pair fell in love, lived together, traveled together, and had two children (Georgio and Lucia), but they did not marry until much later, on July 4, 1931. The same year that Joyce met

Barnacle, he published his first short story, "The Sisters," in draft form in the *Irish Homestead*. He also moved with Barnacle to Pola, Austria-Hungary (now Pula, Croatia), in 1904 to teach English at the Berlitz School. The emigration marked the beginning of Joyce's life as an expatriate. Six months later, Joyce and Barnacle moved to Trieste, Austria-Hungary (now Trieste, Italy). They stayed for ten years, and Joyce continued his affiliation with the Berlitz School for much of this time. Although he was writing and publishing poetry and critical essays during this period, Joyce's first major work, *Dubliners*, was not published until 1914, although the stories within in it had all been written between 1904 and 1907. Also in 1914, Joyce began publishing *Portrait of the Artist as a Young Man* in serial form. It was released as a novel in 1916.

Joyce, Barnacle, and their children left Trieste for Zurich, Switzerland, during World War I. The period that ensued was marred by poverty, and Joyce relied on money from friends and family for support. At the time, Joyce was preoccupied with the composition of his masterwork, *Ulysses*. After World War I ended, Joyce and his family moved to Paris, where they stayed for the next twenty years. His play, *Exile*, was produced in Munich in 1919. *Ulysses* was published three years later, but the book's graphic scenes and language were highly controversial. The volume was banned throughout much of Europe and the United States.

During the 1930s, Joyce focused his efforts on the highly experimental novel *Finnegan's Wake*, and the book was ultimately published in 1939. The next year, in an effort to avoid the impending Nazi invasion, Joyce traveled to the south of France, and then back to Zurich. Joyce died following surgery for a perforated ulcer in Zurich on January 13, 1941. His remains are buried in Zurich's Fluntern cemetery.

PLOT SUMMARY

"The Sisters" is narrated by an unnamed boy of an indeterminate age. It is likely that he is in his early teens, as he resents being referred to as a child, is free to walk about Dublin unaccompanied, and is deemed old enough to drink a glass of sherry with his elders. No specific time period is assigned to the story, but it is likely that poem

MEDIA ADAPTATIONS

- Numerous audiobook adaptations of *Dubliners* have been recorded. The 2005 unabridged CD version, narrated by Frank McCourt, Ciarán Hinds, Donal Donnelly, Colm Meaney, Stephen Rea, and others, and produced by Caedmon, is widely available.

is set either in 1904 or little more than ten to twenty years prior.

The story begins as the boy describes a man who has died after a third stroke. The boy knew that the man was dying, and he walked to the man's window each night to see whether the candles had been lit, as was the custom when someone passed away. However, the boy did not go visit with the dying man. Earlier, the man had told the boy that he would die soon, but the boy did not believe him. The boy thinks about how the man was paralyzed by the strokes, and he is filled with morbid curiosity.

The boy goes downstairs for supper, where his aunt is serving stirabout (a type of porridge). A visitor named Mr. Cotter is also in the kitchen; he is smoking by the fire, and talking about a man who was "queer" and "uncanny." The boy is annoyed. He used to like Cotter, but now he thinks the man is self-important and boring. Cotter continues to speculate about a scandal connected to the odd man. The boy's uncle, Jack, tells him that Father James Flynn is dead. It seems that this is the man that both the boy and Cotter are referring to. The boy is aware that everyone is staring at him, so he does not react to the news and instead sits and eats.

The narrator's uncle explains that the boy and the priest were friends and that the priest was the boy's mentor. The boy's aunt prays for Father Flynn's soul. Cotter says he would not want his own children spending so much time with the priest, again hinting at a scandal of some sort. The boy questions Cotter (as does his aunt), but the man merely explains that

children should be outside playing with other children. Uncle Jack agrees, stating that exercise and cold baths are more valuable than learning. The boy continues to eat in an attempt to hide his rising anger. He thinks Cotter is stupid and wants to say so.

The scene changes abruptly; it is now evening. The narrator is presumably in bed, still angry at Cotter but wondering at the scandal the man was hinting at. The boy dreams of Father Flynn. His face follows the boy and tries to confess something, and the boy tries to forgive him. The next morning, the boy walks alone to the priest's house. The building has been shuttered, and a telegram announcing Father Flynn's death is posted on the door. Suddenly, the reality of the priest's death begins to sink in. The boy thinks about how he would go in if the priest were still alive and of how the priest would be dressed in his stained robes. He would greet the boy and bring out his snuffbox (a container to hold ground tobacco).

The boy wants to go in and see the body, but he walks away instead. He marvels at the sunny weather and all the lively people on the street. They seem strange to him in his grief. "I felt even annoyed at discovering in myself a sensation of freedom as if I had been freed from something by his death," the boy notes, surprising himself with the realization. Father Flynn has taught him so much; Latin, French history, and little-known aspects of Catholicism that deepened his understanding of religion. The boy and the priest discussed the mysteries inherent in communion and confession. He was put off by the priest's strange smile at first, but this feeling disappeared as he grew to know the man. The boy thinks of the dream he had last night and of Cotter's hints.

That evening, the boy and his aunt return to Father Flynn's home for the wake. Nannie, one of Father Flynn's sisters, lets them in; it seems that she is deaf or mute, as she communicates with basic hand gestures. Nannie leads them to the "dead-room," where Father Flynn's body is laid out. The boy's aunt goes in, but the boy hesitates, finally entering "on tiptoe" after Nannie insists. Aside from the candles, the room glows in the sunset. Nannie, the narrator, and his aunt kneel at the coffin, but the boy is unable to pray. Instead he looks at Nannie's thin dress and worn shoes. He imagines that the corpse is smiling, but when he stands and sees the body, he finds that the priest looks peaceful. The corpse is dressed in priest's robes and is holding a chalice (ceremonial cup). The room smells of flowers.

The group crosses themselves and goes downstairs. The boy sits in his usual chair and Nannie serves the sherry. Eliza, Father Flynn's other sister, is seated in the priest's chair. All sit silently and stare at the empty fireplace. The boy's aunt comments: "Ah, well, he's gone to a better world." Eliza sighs. The aunt inquires whether the death was peaceful, and Eliza replies that it was: "He had a beautiful death, God be praised." The women continue in this vein. Eliza says that Father O'Rourke gave her brother his last rites. Father O'Rourke also brought them the flowers and the candles and took care of the funeral arrangements.

Nannie nearly dozes off, tired from the excitement. Eliza reports that they had a woman come over to bathe and dress the body. "No one would think he'd make such a beautiful corpse," Eliza says. The women continue to exchange the reassuring clichés that tend to arise in the face of death. Eliza tells the group that she knew that Father Flynn was ailing. He had been planning on borrowing a car, a "new-fangled carriage," to drive her and Nannie out to their childhood home. The boy's aunt blesses the priest's soul once more. Eliza explains that her brother took being a priest too seriously. She says "his life was … crossed." The boy's aunt replies: "He was a disappointed man. You could see that." Eliza notes that Father Flynn once accidentally broke a communion chalice, and although it was empty, he was very upset by the incident. She indicates that this event is at the heart of the scandalous rumors.

The boy's aunt seems surprised that the event that sparked a scandal is so innocent, but Eliza explains that it "affected his mind." The priest began isolating himself and was found one night, alone in the confessional, laughing. Eliza pauses and it seems as if the group is listening for the priest, but the house, of course, remains silent. The boy again pictures Father Flynn's corpse. Eliza adds that when the priest was found laughing like that, it made people "think that there was something gone wrong with him …."

CHARACTERS

Aunt

The unnamed narrator's aunt houses and feeds her nephew and sends him to study with Father Flynn. The aunt is a fairly conventional person.

As a sign of her hospitality, she lays out mutton for Cotter, though she serves her nephew a plain dish of porridge. The boy's aunt defends Father Flynn despite the rumors that Cotter mentions, and she focuses mainly on all the good that the priest has done for her nephew. She even challenges Cotter's assertions that it is not good for children to be inside learning all day, defending the lessons. However, she does not ask the boy how he feels about the death of his friend, nor does she express any sympathy for the grief that the boy must certainly feel.

The boy's aunt goes with her nephew to the priest's wake, and she views the corpse, prays over it, and then goes to sit with his sisters (again without showing any strong emotions). She blesses the priest's soul on more than one occasion and exchanges small pleasantries with Eliza and Nannie. She says the typical condolences and soothing clichés that tend to accompany death, such as: "Ah, well, he's gone to a better world." The aunt is surprised to learn that the scandal surrounding Father Flynn was so innocent, but she is silent as Eliza explains how the priest's broken chalice began to affect his mind.

Boy

The unnamed narrator and protagonist is a boy, likely a teenager. He lives with his aunt and uncle, and no mention is made of his parents or where they might be. The boy was being mentored by Father Flynn, who was teaching him Latin and history and also about their religion. The boy knows that his thoughts about Catholicism were simple, but Father Flynn always listened to him and encouraged him. The boy is obviously affected by Father Flynn's death. He refuses to believe the priest when he tells him that he is dying. The narrator also goes to the priest's window every night to see if he is still alive. This vigil is a sign of the boy's love for the priest; but it is also notable that the boy was too afraid to go inside and visit with his dying mentor.

When the boy's uncle tells him that the priest is dead, he does not show any reaction, nor does he admit to his prior knowledge. He sits silently as Cotter angers him and is careful again not to show any emotion. Later that night, though, the boy worries and wonders about the rumors that Cotter had referred to. He also has a strange dream about Father Flynn. On the surface, the boy seems unaffected by his mentor's death, but it is clear to the reader that the boy is deeply troubled by it. This is evident when the narrator again goes to the priest's house without going inside. When he sees the death announcement on the door, Father Flynn's passing finally becomes a reality. The boy's grief is also obvious when he wonders at how the sunny day can go on without any acknowledgment of his friend's death. At the same time, though, the boy also feels a surprising sense of freedom in the wake of Father Flynn's demise.

The boy's dread of and preoccupation with his mentor's death is again evident when he and his aunt attend Father Flynn's wake. The boy is at first afraid to go into the room where the priest's body lies. He is also unable to pray while kneeling beside the body. He imagines that the priest is smiling, but when he dares to look, he sees that he bears a peaceful expression. The boy's feelings trail off at this point in the story. When he goes downstairs and the women begin to converse, he becomes a detached observer.

Cotter

Cotter, usually called "old Cotter" in the narrator's interior voice, is a friend of the boy and his aunt and uncle, but no specific relationship or connection is explained. After thinking about his mentor's death, the boy finds Cotter downstairs wondering about a "queer" man. The boy is annoyed to find Cotter there; when he was a child he used to like him, but now the narrator thinks he is self-important and boring. Cotter does little to change the boy's opinion. He continues to reference rumors about an unknown man, though it later becomes clear that he is talking about Father Flynn. Cotter seems insensitive, as it is the boy's uncle, Jack, who finally tells his nephew of the priest's death. Despite the sad news, Cotter continues to ramble on about the strange priest and how children are better off exercising than staying indoors with suspicious clergy members. He persists in this lecture even though both the boy and his aunt question Cotter's beliefs. Although the boy is angry at Cotter, he does not show it. Unaware of this animosity, Cotter helps himself to the plate of mutton set out by the boy's aunt.

Eliza

Eliza is Father Flynn's sister. No mention is made of her by the boy or his relatives, but her presence is revealed when the boy and his aunt go downstairs for sherry after viewing the priest's body. Eliza appears to be childless and unmarried. She lived with her brother and took care of him, and she knew he was ailing because she often found him in a strange state toward the end of his life. Eliza talks about her brother fondly but without any strong emotion. She says he wanted to take her and their sister, Nannie, to see their childhood home once more, but he died before he could do so. Eliza also says that Father Flynn "had a beautiful death," and she praises Father O'Rourke for performing the last rites and bringing them candles and flowers. It is clear that her own household was unable to afford these items.

Eliza's main narrative function is to reveal the scandal hinted at throughout the story. Even the boy, who did not know about the rumors, was at first uncomfortable with the strange priest. Eliza tells the boy's aunt that the priest broke a communion chalice, and although it was empty, the incident upset him so much that it began to affect his mental health. Eliza says that eventually Father Flynn was found laughing alone in the confessional, and people then began to see him as unstable. Eliza recounts these events without any noticeable emotion. The boy and his aunt do not react to this news, either; in fact, the boy does not seem to register it at all. Nevertheless, Nannie, Eliza, the boy, and his aunt all pause and listen to the silent house.

Father James Flynn

Although Father James Flynn is dead when the narrative begins, the story centers on his life, his death, and the other characters' reactions to his death. Father Flynn is called "queer" by Cotter, who says he would never allow his own children to spend time with the man. The boy, however, has grown fond of the priest, despite being put off by him at first. The boy recalls the strange way Father Flynn smiled at him, but he also recalls the way his mentor encouraged him to develop his own religious ideas. The boy thinks of the priest's stained robes and dreams a strange dream about him. In the dream, he begs for forgiveness for an unknown reason.

Eliza also recalls her brother fondly, and she notes that he had wanted to take his sisters to see their old home before he died. Although she does not say that her brother was mentally unstable, she does admit that he took his duties as a priest too seriously. Notably, all that the reader can know of the dead man is what the other character's think about him, say about him, and feel about him. Still, despite the scandal that surrounds him, Father Flynn died peacefully, and his corpse bears a serene expression.

Uncle Jack

The boy lives with Uncle Jack and his wife. Uncle Jack appears only in the opening scene, when the boy comes downstairs after thinking about his mentor's death. Like his wife, Jack does not show overt sympathy for the boy's loss or ask about his feelings. As Cotter rambles on about a strange man, Jack stops to inform his nephew: "Well, so your old friend is gone, you'll be sorry to hear." The uncle's halting delivery of the news may indicate the presence of at least some empathy. Nevertheless, he goes on to agree with Cotter's disparaging remarks about Father Flynn's relationship with the boy. He also does not attend the wake with his wife and nephew.

Nannie

Nannie is the sister of Father Flynn and Eliza. She lets the boy and his aunt in during the wake and takes them upstairs to view the corpse. She does not speak and apparently has difficulty hearing or understanding, as the boy's aunt would have had to shout to talk with her. She refrains from doing so out of respect for the dead, and instead, they communicate through basic hand gestures. Eliza takes the boy and his aunt upstairs to view the corpse and urges the boy to go into the "dead-room" when he hesitates. She kneels and prays with them over the corpse. As she does so, the boy notices her shabby dress and worn-out shoes. Nannie serves the boy and his aunt sherry downstairs, and she nods off through much of the ensuing conversation.

Father O'Rourke

Father O'Rourke is the priest who delivers the last rites to Father Flynn. He also brings Eliza and Nannie flowers and candles for the dead-room and makes the burial arrangements. Eliza calls Father O'Rourke a good friend, and she indicates that they would not have been able to afford the candles and flowers without Father O'Rourke's assistance.

THEMES

Grief

Because "The Sisters" is almost entirely about death and its effect on the surviving characters, it is important to acknowledge the role that grief plays in the story. The boy at first does not wish to believe or understand that his mentor is dying,

TOPICS FOR FURTHER STUDY

- Use Google Maps or Google Earth to study Dublin's geography and topography. Access additional atlases and maps as well (either in print or on the Internet). Can you find any maps that portray Dublin in the early 1900s? After conducting your research, create a map of Dublin, either with mapping or graphics software or by hand.

- Sherwood Anderson's short story collection *Winesburg, Ohio* is not only appropriate for young-adult readers but remarkably similar to *Dubliners*. Both collections are filled entirely with stories set in their title cities that capture a sense of place and explore the way a place shapes the people who live in it. After reading stories from both collections, write an essay comparing and contrasting their themes and structure.

- Another young-adult collection of linked short stories that captures a sense of place (and its effect) is *White Bread Competition*, by Jo Ann Yolanda Hernandez. The stories are set in San Antonio, Texas, and they portray Luz and her Mexican American family. They also explore how community and place shape character. After reading the collection, write a short story about your hometown and the influence that is has had on the people who live in it. Post the story on a Web page and invite your classmates to comment on how their hometowns have influenced them.

- Although Joyce's story is about a boy and the death of his mentor, it is titled "The Sisters." This would seem to suggest that the story is really about Eliza and Nannie. Why do you think Joyce used this title? What more can you learn about the story because of it? Stage a roundtable discussion or build a Wikispace page on the topic.

although he has been warned of the inevitable event by Father Flynn. Still, the boy keeps a secret vigil for his mentor, going to the man's

The two sisters *(dundanim | Shutterstock.com)*

window every night to see if the candles for the dead have been laid out, yet he never goes in to visit. He repeats this behavior after the candles have been lit, going up to the shuttered house, reading the death notice posted to the door, and turning back without going in. The boy also attempts to hide his grief from Cotter and his aunt and uncle, but it is clear to the reader when he expresses his disbelief at the sunny day and the lively street that persist in the face of his personal tragedy. At the same time, the boy also feels free, and he is shocked at the feeling. The boy knows he will no longer have to study with his mentor or maintain the friendship that once made him so uneasy.

The boy's grief can also be seen in his general sense of discomfort in the face of death. He has a strange dream about Father Flynn and is afraid to look at his body. When he finally does so, he is unable to pray and instead imagines that Father Flynn's corpse is smiling.

Although the boy's aunt does not exhibit much feeling upon Father Flynn's passing, she does acknowledge all that he has done for her

nephew and indicates that he was a kind and good man. She says that he has "gone to a better world." Meanwhile, Eliza talks of her brother's good and peaceful death and says that he makes a "beautiful corpse." She comments that she will no longer be able to care for him. Eliza also refers to him on several occasions as "poor James," lamenting his death or the reduced life that he lived as a result of his fallen stature within the church.

Roman Catholicism

Several interpretations of "The Sisters" focus on the story as a critique of Catholicism. Regardless of whether Joyce is railing against the church or merely against the unfortunate effect it has had on Father Flynn and his sisters, religious imagery (specifically Roman Catholic imagery) dominates the story. Two of the defining rituals of Catholicism are communion and confession, and the boy and the priest often discuss these rites and their meaning. These are also the two rituals that brought about Father Flynn's mental instability and his resulting fall in the church hierarchy. Father Flynn's strange smile, which bothered the boy at the onset of their relationship, is characterized by his placing his tongue over his lower lip. The behavior echoes that of a churchgoer who is about to receive communion.

On several occasions in "The Sisters," the boy notices how poor Father Flynn and his family are. Their clothing is shabby or stained, and Eliza indicates that they could not have afforded candles or flowers for the wake without Father O'Rourke's generous donation. Father Flynn's and his sisters' diminished circumstances can be seen as a direct result of the priest's failure within the church. Father Flynn's desire for redemption can also be seen in his mentoring of the protagonist. Although it is not clear that Father Flynn is training the boy to become a priest, he does teach the boy all of the things that a novice priest needs to learn; probably, he would have liked to see the boy train for the priesthood. This likely unspoken desire on the priest's part may account for the boy's surprising sense of freedom upon his mentor's passing.

In another interpretation, Father Flynn's mental breakdown is brought on by his attempts to make sense of the mystery of communion (wherein bread and wine are literally transformed into the body and blood of Jesus Christ). Such attempts may be signs that he lacked true religious faith. This lack, or, more accurately, the priest's realization of this lack, could lie at the heart of his mental instability. Eliza hints at this when she chides her brother for taking his duties too seriously.

STYLE

Lack of Detail

The stylistic technique that is most remarkable in "The Sisters" is the noticeable—and often frustrating—lack of detail. Several of the main characters are unnamed, the boy's age is not mentioned, and no explanation for why he does not live with his parents is given. It is not even clear at first who has died. Even Uncle Jack's statement, "Your old friend is gone, you'll be sorry to hear," is rather vague. The character's general connections to one another are revealed as the story develops, as are several details about them. Because these facts are revealed only slowly, the reader is not always sure of the exact nature of what is happening or why. Even the scandal that is hinted at throughout the story

is only partly explained. The lack of detail that dominates the story from beginning to end has the effect of leaving the story open to different interpretations. "The Sisters" thus invites the reader to engage with it more fully in an attempt to understand and interpret it.

Dialogue

Roughly half of the story is told through dialogue rather than narration. Notably, almost all of the conversation is held by the adults, and the boy is barely a participant. To some degree, the abundant dialogue accounts for the lack of detail. The dialogue is clipped and brief; it lacks explanation or descriptive language, and the characters tend to make vague remarks. The pacing of the story, as it switches between dialogue and the boy's observations, is also interesting. The story begins as the boy worries over an unnamed dead man and then switches to conversation as the boy, his aunt, Cotter, and Uncle Jack are in the kitchen. The boy says very little, and the adults reveal Father Flynn's death and a mysterious scandal related to him. They debate whether or not a child should spend so much time away from other children. Following this conversation, the story returns to the boy's description of his dream, his trip to Father Flynn's house, and his return trip that evening. Following the boy's reactions to the corpse, the story again gives way to adult conversation, this time held primarily between Eliza and the boy's aunt. Once more, the boy says little, and slowly, almost one sentence at a time, the reason behind the priest's downfall is revealed.

HISTORICAL CONTEXT

Modernism

Joyce wrote at the heart of the modernist movement, which began around 1890 and ended around 1940, reaching its peak during the 1920s. Modernism, a school of thought that influenced fiction, poetry, the visual arts, architecture, and other fields, valued a stripped-down style that rejected what it saw as the useless ties of the past. Modernism began in Europe and later spread to the United States, though many of its leading writers were expatriate Americans. The American poet Ezra Pound was a great proponent of the movement, and he was instrumental in Joyce's move to Paris at the end of World War I.

COMPARE & CONTRAST

- **1910s:** Nationalism and imperialism are two philosophies that cause European countries to clash, leading to the outbreak of World War I in 1914. After the war ends in 1918, the continent is divided into many new nations based on ethnic self-determination.

  Today: Europe is united under the European Union (EU), formed by the Treaty of Maastricht in 1993. Today, the EU consists of twenty-seven member countries that use a universal currency. The EU also allows its citizens to move and work freely within its members's borders.

- **1910s:** Ireland is torn by political and religious unrest. Irish citizens attempt to achieve independence from England. The Protestant minority fears that the Roman Catholic majority will in effect cause Ireland to be ruled by the Vatican. These fears result in the creation of Northern Ireland in 1922; the region holds the island's largest Protestant population, and it remains part of the United Kingdom.

  Today: The religious divide between Ireland and Northern Ireland remains amidst an often uneasy peace, and Protestants remain a minority in the Republic of Ireland. Northern Ireland's population has grown to roughly 1,685,000, and the population of the Republic of Ireland is roughly 3,370,000.

- **1910s:** The Easter Uprising of 1916 and the bloodshed it causes lead Irish members of Parliament to declare Ireland an independent republic in 1919. The declaration becomes official with the 1921 signing of the Anglo-Irish Treaty.

  Today: As a part of the EU, Irish citizens vote down the Lisbon Treaty in 2008 by a slim margin. They fear that the proposed amendments to the Treaty of Maastricht will limit Ireland's independence. Where the original treaty called for unanimous agreement in the Council of Ministers (that is, the Council of the European Union), the Lisbon Treaty requires only a double majority. The Lisbon Treaty passes in 2009.

Modernism was established as technological and scientific advances made their way into the mainstream, causing worldviews to shift. The most notable shift was the elevated importance of the individual, an idea that was brought about by new philosophies and the emerging study of psychology. Existentialist writers such as Friedrich Nietzsche and Jean-Paul Sartre challenged preconceived notions about the place of the individual in society. Psychiatrists such as Sigmund Freud and Carl Jung introduced ideas of the id, ego, and superego; the unconscious; and the collective unconscious, reframing concepts related to personality and identity. Joyce and other modernist writers, such as William Faulkner and Gertrude Stein, addressed these new ideas by experimenting with the form and structure of traditional narrative. The most prominent experimental form they developed is now known as stream of consciousness. While "The Sisters" is not told in this manner, its form is nevertheless experimental and can be described as a precursor to stream of consciousness. This can be seen in the story's vague details, the narrator's internal monologues, and the clipped dialogue. Certainly, Joyce's work in "The Sisters" and other stories in *Dubliners* can be seen as a precursor to his more characteristically modernist novels *Ulysses* and *Finnegan's Wake*.

Irish Independence

Joyce came of age as the Irish people were attempting to establish a government independent of English rule. His distaste for the political events that took place while he was a young man led him to become an expatriate, yet they also shaped his writing career. Government reform in

He was just a boy. *(Agita Leimane | Shutterstock.com)*

Ireland was a long process, beginning in 1783, when Irish citizens formed their own parliament. That parliament was destroyed in 1800, however, with the passage of the Act of Union. The act allowed for Irish political representation in England, but little else. In 1829, the Irish Catholic Church was established as an entity independent of English oversight.

Following the great famine that swept Ireland during the 1840s, the need for local government, especially in regard to land reform, became pressingly clear. Nevertheless, it was not until the bloody Easter Uprising of 1916 that true independence began to come about. It led to the 1919 decision of Irish parliament members to declare their country to be a republic in its own right. As a result, the Anglo-Irish Treaty was enacted in 1921, establishing Ireland as an independent state and full member of the United Kingdom. This treaty, however, precipitated civil war as Protestant-controlled Northern Ireland attempted to establish its own

government apart from the rest of the Catholic-controlled country. Northern Ireland was subsequently established as a division of the United Kingdom in 1922.

CRITICAL OVERVIEW

Initial critical reaction to "The Sisters" and its parent volume *Dubliners* was mostly positive, and the book launched Joyce's career as a prominent author of modernist fiction. Since its publication, however, critics have focused less on assessing the merits of "The Sisters" and more on interpreting its possible meanings. Discussing this trend in *ReJoycing: New Readings of Dubliners* Sonja Bašić notes that "one of the problems presented by the existing critical approaches . . . is overinterpretation or too literal interpretation." She adds: "On the whole, there has been too much 'irritable reaching' after verifiable facts and incontrovertible conclusions." "The Sisters," with its clipped conversations, vague detail, and brevity (it is only eight pages long), resists such treatment.

That has not stopped critics from attempting such interpretation. To Kevin J. H. Dettmar in the *Dictionary of Literary Biography*, "The Sisters" is a coming-of-age story that focuses on the strain of maintaining social conventions as a means to repress emotion. It is "a story of the initiation of a young boy into the adult world," Dettmar asserts. "Real-world experience collides repeatedly in the story with the boy's expectations, and that world comes to seem a different place from that which he has been led to expect." In the *Explicator*, John V. McDermott claims that Father Flynn's desire to plumb the mysteries of communion and confession demonstrates a "Luciferian pride that desired to know as much as his Creator. In contrast to him, the sisters stand as stalwarts of the faith." Because of this, McDermott finds that "The Sisters" may be seen as "an alleluia to the faithful and a condemnation of pride-driven intellectualism." In another interpretation, *Twentieth Century Literature* critic Thomas Dilworth focuses on the story's religious symbolism, and he states that "the biblical narrative is integral to Joyce's story. This is apparent to anyone who sees the boy as a Jesus figure and his relationship to the dead priest as potentially life-renewing."

CRITICISM

Leah Tieger

Tieger is a freelance writer and editor. In the following essay, she explores the prevailing method for establishing a critical interpretation of "The Sisters."

"The Sisters" is a remarkably vague tale. It presents the reader with unnamed characters in barely explained situations. The priest's scandal is merely hinted at, and it remains something of a mystery even after Eliza explains it. The boy's relationship with the priest and its true nature are also never fully revealed. The characters, their motivations, and even their basic connections to one another are all obscure and ambiguous. Because of this, the themes and intended or possible meanings in "The Sisters" are open to debate. The story leaves a great deal of room, perhaps too much, for interpretation. However,

WHAT DO I READ NEXT?

- To continue to explore Joyce's fiction, read his most accessible novel *Portrait of the Artist as a Young Man*. First published in serial form in 1914 and then as a novel in 1916, the book is the coming-of-age story of Stephen Dedalus. The story is largely autobiographical and reflects Joyce's own feelings and aspirations as a young writer.

- The 2002 volume *Ireland: History, People, Culture*, written by Paul Brewer, is a well-illustrated history volume replete with photographs. The book provides readers with an understanding of Ireland's unique cultural history, beginning with pre-Christian times and ending in the late twentieth century.

- For a more literary exploration of the Irish culture, read the young-adult short story collection *Thicker than Water: Coming of Age Stories by Irish and Irish-American Writers*. Edited by Gordon Snell and published in 2001, the collection features work by Vincent Banville and Chris Lynch.

- Joyce's writing owes a considerable debt to the work of Anton Chekhov. A Russian writer predominantly known for his plays and short stories, Chekhov wrote throughout the late 1800s. A good introduction to his fiction can be found in the 2000 edition of *Stories of Anton Chekhov*, translated by Larissa Volokhonsky and Richard Pevear.

- Sandra Cisneros's young-adult short story collection *House on Mango Street* was published in 1984 and has since become a classic work of Latin American literature. Like *Dubliners*, the book presents linked short stories featuring recurring characters.

- The 1994 volume *Catholicism: New Study Edition—Completely Revised and Updated* by Richard P. McBrien provides a wealth of information on the religion that dominates the themes, symbols, and plot in "The Sisters."

one somewhat unifying theory and means for interpretation has begun to emerge. This prevailing critical interpretation of the story centers on three words that appear in two sentences within the tale's opening paragraph. Stanley Sultan in *Joyce and the City: The Significance of Place*, Thomas Dilworth in *Twentieth Century Literature*, and Eric Bulson in *The Cambridge Introduction to James Joyce* have all written about the significance of these three words. They appear as the boy describes his nightly vigil outside his ailing mentor's bedroom:

> Every night as I gazed up at the window I said softly to myself the word paralysis. It had always sounded strangely in my ears, like the word gnomon in the Euclid and the word simony in Catechism.

The three words of note in this passage are *paralysis*, *gnomon*, and *simony*. In a tale told with simple vocabulary, these three words immediately stand out. Noting that "The Sisters" is the first story in *Dubliners*, Bulson and Sultan have found that these words are essential for interpreting not only the story in which they appear but also the entire collection. *Paralysis* means the inability to move, *gnomon* in Euclidean geometry is the shape that remains after a part of a parallelogram has been removed, and *simony* means the buying or selling of spiritual matters. In more symbolic or metaphoric terms, paralysis may not be physical; it can be emotional, mental, and spiritual. The gnomon is a shape relevant to its missing parts. It is also the word used for the part of a sundial that casts a shadow to tell time; thus, it is an indicator, something that reveals another thing. A more in-depth interpretation of simony is that it is an act that cheapens the sacred and holy nature of spiritual matters.

Paralysis appears in "The Sisters" both literally and figuratively. Father Flynn has been literally paralyzed by his strokes, but he is also figuratively paralyzed by his preoccupation with the mysteries of communion and confession. This figurative paralysis is the whispered scandal at the heart of the story, one that has very literal consequences. Indeed, Father Flynn is perceived as "queer"—the statement is ambiguous as to whether this means homosexual or simply odd—and mentally unstable. The perception leads to his loss of standing in the church and the effective end of his career. This end leads to the poverty in which he and his sisters must live. Paralysis also imprisons the protagonist. He

watches over his dying mentor but does not go in to see him, and he repeats this behavior again when he goes to look at the death notice posted on Father Flynn's door. Although the boy is unaware of his paralysis, he is aware of its passing. As he walks away from Father Flynn's house, he states: "I felt even annoyed at discovering in myself a sensation of freedom as if I had been freed from something by his death."

There are several gnomons within the story, and "The Sisters" can in and of itself be described as a gnomon. The story is a shape with a part (or, more accurately, many parts) removed. Where are the boy's parents? What is the actual nature of his friendship with the priest? What exactly lay at the heart of Father Flynn's scandal? Notably, even the characters' conversations are gnomons. When Cotter refers to the "queer" priest, his speech becomes filled with ellipses. Every time Cotter comes close to naming the scandal or describing the priest's specific failings, ellipses appear. The same occurs as he tries to explain why the boy should not have spent so much time with the priest or why it would be best for him and other children to spend more time exercising. Ellipses occur again when Eliza is speaking of her dead brother. They appear each time she comes close to saying anything offensive about him and whenever she is about to fully explain his downfall. Given this, Father Flynn can be seen as the part that is missing from the gnomon. His life has been removed from the characters' lives. The reader sees only the parts that remain.

The dream that the boy has about his dead mentor is also something of a gnomon, and it points to the mysterious nature of the boy's relationship to the priest. In the dream, the priest's grotesque face begs for forgiveness, and the boy attempts to grant it. Whether the dream is entirely symbolic or indicative of a darker truth underlying the relationship is unclear. The dream could even be interpreted as a repressed memory. These latter options seem more likely in light of the sense of freedom that that boy experiences when he feels the full force of Father Flynn's death.

This freedom also indicates the role of simony in the story. If one considers the theory that Father Flynn was training the boy to become a priest, then the relationship he had with the boy can be seen in terms of simony.

The priest who died had been his friend. *(Alistair Cotton / Shutterstock.com)*

This popular view of the priest's intentions for the boy represents a type of simony because the spiritual matter of friendship is undermined by the earthly goals and desires of Father Flynn. His ambition is to reenter the good graces of church, albeit through a substitute. "An ulterior motive in friendship seeks to exchange something spiritual for nonspiritual gain. Such an exchange fits the definition of simony," Sultan explains. Another, more abstract interpretation, can be found if one considers the priest's preoccupation with the broken chalice. Although the communion cup was empty when it broke, Father Flynn still feels as if he has spilled Christ's blood. Because of this, he shows himself to be overly concerned with the material objects that act as a vehicle for the spiritual. His preoccupation with the chalice cheapens the spiritual beliefs related to it.

Source: Leah Tieger, Critical Essay on "The Sisters," in *Short Stories for Students*, Gale, Cengage Learning, 2011.

> BOTH HIS EPITHETS HAVE THEIR LIMITED TRUTH, BUT BOTH OBFUSCATE; AS 'THE SISTERS' CREATES A SIGNIFICANCE FOR *PARALYSIS* DIFFERENT FROM THE ONE HE INVOKES, SO IT DOES FOR *SIMONY.*"

Stanley Sultan

In the following excerpt, Sultan explicates the meaning of several key words in "The Sisters."

I believe an important reason why the story with which James Joyce began *Dubliners* belongs in its initial place is the general declaration it makes about Dublin, through both its unnamed boy's experience and the narrative about that experience by the man the boy became. Joyce's judgment on his native city in "The Sisters" can be elicited by tracing what he did with the two memorable details he placed, one in each of its first two full paragraphs of exposition: the set of three italicized words in the story's first paragraph and, in the paragraph after the boy learns that Father James Flynn is dead, the memorable dream the boy has of the priest's disembodied smiling face confessing to him and his own responsive smile.

The three italicized words "had always sounded strangely in my ears," the man reports for him. That adverb "strangely" is not slovenly English, but describes his auditory experience when the man was the boy and signifies his actual young ears' hearing of the sounding of those three words; both memorable details indicate that things experienced by a Dublin boy constitute the essence of "The Sisters." My procedure will be to first trace out what Joyce did with the other detail, then discuss the three italicized words . . . .

II

An extensive bibliography exists of interpretations of the meaning in and for "The Sisters" of the three italicized words. My particular concern is their function for what Joyce was declaring in the story about Dublin.

While sitting in Flynn's chair, with the boy in his "usual chair in the corner" (*Dubliners, D*), Eliza is in the place of his late instructor; conducting the proceedings, she unknowingly instructs the boy. Before entering the parlor he was aware of the smiling then finally truculent Flynn's troubled history with two of the four sacraments of the church relevant to one of its priests: Holy Orders and Extreme Unction. In the parlor, she reveals Flynn's troubled history with the other two, Communion and Penance (his "nervous[ly]" dropping the chalice and laughing in his confession box). But Eliza functions for the boy there as *gnomon*, in the broad sense of "that which enables knowledge," less for this reason than for being the instrument of his learning that the adults already know, or learn with him, all he learns from her about her brother and refuse or are unable to acknowledge its significance.

He knows the adults misperceive or deny Flynn's truculent end and attribute Flynn's treatment of Communion and Penance to mental debility. Beyond the hints in "idle" and "I knew," the narrator does not reveal how he reacted, when he was the boy, to his experience of the failures of perception and understanding, or of candor, by Dublin adults, including churchmen and his own surrogate parent, with respect to Flynn's late life and death. However, he has directed his story of himself when a boy toward, and ended it with, that experience; this fact indicates how the most prominent of the three italicized words may function in "The Sisters."

At the end of its first paragraph, he reveals that the "being" whose name *paralysis* "sounded to me like" when a boy "filled me with fear, and yet I longed to be nearer to it and to look upon its deadly work" (*D*); promptly the boy hears at home that he will not succeed with the literal paralysis of Flynn's final illness.

However, he realizes during the story that Flynn was confounded—metaphorically paralyzed—by his strict (i.e., orthodox) conception of the duties of the priesthood. More to the point, the boy learns in the story that the other adults, explicitly Cotter, Eliza, and the churchmen, consider Flynn and not their church to be the cause of his predicament; they have been incapacitated for acknowledging the truth about a priest broken by his profound grasp of the extreme demands of his—and their—church. The story portrays a boy learning, as Phillip

Herring points out in "Structure and Meaning in Joyce's 'The Sisters,'" that Dublin adults are mentally immobilized—metaphorically paralyzed—by their conformity to a hegemony of Roman Catholic piety (1982). For them, the legitimacy of the Irish Church is a categorical given. Although the narrator the boy has become does not reveal whether he recognized at the time this etiology for the metaphorical paralysis of these Dublin adults, manifestly the grown man recognizes it, for what he tells is his boyhood experience of "be[ing] nearer to it"; as a boy he had, at the end of the story he has begun with the word in italics, "look[ed] upon [the] deadly work" of Catholic Dublin's intellectually paralyzing religious hegemony (*D*).

If the symbolic Eucharist that Joyce created for the story is considered in the context of this metaphorical paralysis of a community, its signification ceases to be problematic. The sherry and crackers symbolize the sacrificial wine and wafer, not to invoke Communion directly, but to effect a highly appropriate social trope on the religious rite the communion the sisters' wine and crackers admit one to, and the aunt receiving them participates in, is that of pious Dublin Catholic adults, who misperceive and misinterpret things that are contrary to the religious ideology that has absorbed them and so has immobilized their intelligence.

The narrator's report of his ambiguous response to the proffered social communion when he was the boy points to his complicated place in the story he tells. While telling his thoughts and dream in bed the previous night those many years ago, the narrator calls Flynn "the paralytic," then in the same passage makes his explicit judgment, "the simoniac." Both his epithets have their limited truth, but both obfuscate; as "The Sisters" creates a significance for *paralysis* different from the one he invokes, so it does for *simony*. After the boy has forgiven Flynn in his dream, he learns of the priest's failed struggle to perform his office and its pathetic conclusion. The narrator knows that in this context Flynn committed trivial simony; he learned it when he was the boy. I will try to show that both italicized words that the narrator obfuscates the significance of, that "had always sounded strangely in [his] ears" when a boy, Joyce's story applies to him and *gnomon* as well.

Not only Eliza, but Flynn before her and even his aunt, are gnomons for the boy in the broad sense of the term. That sense does not enrich the story particularly; "*gnomon* in the Euclid" invokes explicitly its geometric sense, of the remainder of a parallelogram after a similar one had been taken from one of its corners; the shape of the remainder reveals (provides *gnosis* of) that of the removed corner. The rich significance of *gnomon* in the story is indicated by an early instance of the functional comic wit Joyce used increasingly in *Ulysses* and the *Wake*.

In the original story, Nannie is seated not "behind her sister" but "in a corner" and the boy's location in the parlor is not specified. When Joyce revised it in 1906, the boy as well as Nannie is precisely situated. In that culminating scene, he is explicitly where he sat when being tutored by Flynn: "I groped my way toward my usual chair in the corner" (*D*). It is "in the corner" that he previously learned about the baleful effect of the church on the most admirable kind of priest, the erudite and conscientious Father Flynn; and it is there he learns about the distorted consensus of the adults. Not sharing that consensus, he is the piece taken out of the whole. "Let him learn to box his corner," his uncle specifies at the beginning of "The Sisters," and by its end he has done so.

The remainder of the parallelogram, not the removed corner, is the gnomon defined by Euclid; in the story it is the adults around the boy who reveal their nature to him precisely because he is not part of their adult Dublin Catholic "communion." Being the boy grown up, the narrator also has *gnosis* of that gnomon whose nature the boy apprehended; yet the narrator speaks as part of it. The reason is that a gnomon reveals by its own shape the shape of the removed piece. Eventually, "The Sisters" turns toward its teller, the Dublin Catholic adult the boy became.

The narrator provides reasons why both the boy's inability to pray in the dead room and his later declining the crackers of the adults' symbolic communion are innocuous actions; he preserves his own reputation as a pious Catholic boy. The reasons sound like lame excuses, but the narrator presents them as the boy's conscious reasons and specifies that he did sip his wine.

Moreover, there is a pattern of increased withholding of the boy's reactions to his four crucial experiences as the story progresses; it is the narrator of a story who reveals or withholds. Of the four components of the story's armature,

the boy's silent outrage at Cotter and subsequent ambivalence about Flynn that night and the next day are fully articulated; there is a brief account of his reaction to his memory of the sessions with Flynn. Of his reaction to his discovery that the face on Flynn's corpse is not only not smiling but "truculent," the narrator tells nothing more than that he "groped my way towards" his seat in the corner, providing only this physical symptom of his state of mind; at the end of the story, after telling that the adults shared what "I knew" about Flynn and quoting Eliza's reiteration of the almost lurid climax and conclusion of her account of her brother, he withholds almost totally his reaction when the boy.

Possibly nothing in "The Sisters" before it points as insistently to the narrator as does the conclusion of the story. In both of the other childhood stories in *Dubliners*, the boy's reaction to his culminating experience provides closure, even though the narrator knows, and has shown, more about its significance than he was aware of when a boy. In "The Sisters," the reaction of the boy to Eliza's revelation about the extent of adult misapprehension in his Catholic Dublin world can be inferred easily enough. It is the narrator's action in essentially withholding what he realized about the adults when he was the boy that calls for scrutiny. That action, his declining to articulate what he realized, relates to his conventional piety in the story and explains his inconsistency; in spite of what he knows about a priest's disablement by his church and about the intellectual paralysis of Dublin's adult Catholics when confronted with it, as an adult he has joined them. The gnomon reveals the shape of the (once-) removed piece. Hence, at the end of his narrative he refrains from disclosing his boyhood reaction to the derogatory truth about Dublin's adult Catholics that has been revealed to him. His withholding the reaction he had when the boy recalls the beggar-playwright's changing the ending of his play, also to gain public approval, in Gay's *The Beggar's Opera*; in both cases, his act makes the agent the subject.

This is why all three italicized words in the first paragraph of "The Sisters" not only relate, as critics have pointed out, to the adults in the story and to the boy, but also ultimately relate to the narrator. The adults in his world when a boy are afflicted with intellectual paralysis; they are the boy's gnomon of that fact. But excepting Flynn they are not guilty of any simony. In contrast, the grown man who tells his boyhood story accommodates himself to the hegemony of Catholic Dublin. In doing so, he subverts truth for his convenience as the simoniac does faith. He knowingly conforms to the paralysis afflicting Dublin's adults and so joins them as gnomon of it. His knowing accommodation to the pious community is prudential, of course; Joyce is signifying by it that a man could not remain in that society otherwise. But it is still self-interested, an act of metaphorical simony against the truth, however understandable. In the context of the power in Dublin of Irish Catholicism, Father James Flynn and the man the boy became are foils.

Each of the two subsequent childhood stories in *Dubliners* presents a man telling about how his Dublin Catholic environment influenced his growing self; in "An Encounter," the influence is its class snobbery and violence; in "Araby," its sexual repression. Each narrator's understanding of the formative boyhood experience he tells of is part of young Joyce's story; implicitly, the knowledge has been salutary to him. But although the narrators are characterized to different degrees, the stories essentially are about the boys' formative experiences.

While this narrator's story also is about his formative experience when a boy, Joyce made "The Sisters" eventually about him and so turned his narrative into a revelation of how he has coped with that experience. The Dublin man's prudential submission to the environmental pressure on him affirms the force of that pressure. Joyce made the inaugural story of his volume an eloquent introduction to the baneful power of the Irish Church over the minds and lives of the Dubliners the volume portrays.

Source: Stanley Sultan, "Dublin Boy and Man in 'The Sisters,'" in *Joyce and the City: The Significance of Place*, edited by Michael Begnal, Syracuse University Press, 2002, pp. 85–97.

Mamta Chaudhry-Fryer

In the following excerpt, Chaudhry-Fryer examines the role of game playing in Joyce's short fiction.

In one of *Dubliners'* most arresting observations, the boy in "Araby" says he has "hardly any patience with the serious work of life which seemed to me child's play." Reading this stunning paradox in reverse offers a way of approaching the stories through Michel Foucault's theories about power and knowledge, as well as Mikhail

Bakhtin's analysis of comedy: embodying both subversion and inversion, child's play is the serious work of life.

Foucault argues in *Power/Knowledge* that the challenge to accepted truths comes through "the insurrection of subjugated knowledges," admitting into the discourse what has been systematically excluded by the "hierarchy of knowledges." Dovetailing with Foucault's theory, Bakhtin's formulation of carnivalesque laughter allows people not only to admit what is normally excluded, but to stand it on its head. Both Foucault and Bakhtin thus argue that certain limits must be transgressed in order to shift power from where it traditionally resides into the hands of the powerless.

But where does power lie? When trying to locate it, Foucault suggests a five-fold inversion of the way that power is usually studied. One should be concerned with power not at the head, but at the extremities, where it becomes "capillary"; not with conscious intention, but with action; not as the rigid and mutually exclusive poles of those who have it and those who don't, but as links in a chain; not at a global or general level, but at a minute and particular one; not with ideological concerns, but with practical applications. Such a study yields a body of knowledge that subverts existing structures of power.

Bakhtin points out that comedy itself is subversive, because it gives us new ways of seeing situations, liberated from the blinkers of the official viewpoint. The rules of everyday life are suspended and replaced by their contraries. This suspension of the prevailing truth and established order allows one to explore "a second life, outside officialdom," in which games play an important role.

Through games, children create their own second life, outside officialdom and its rules. According to Iona and Peter Opie in their extensive studies of children's games, adults seldom realize that, even though children may need looking after, they also have their own society and their own code of jurisdiction. Children's games challenge the world of adults, puncturing the pompous shams of authority through play. Their games resist colonizing by grown-ups: the moment adults want to join in, children change the rules. In the struggle between life's serious work and childish games, subverting authority thus becomes power play.

Like the world of Rabelais, the world of Joyce is filled with games and game playing. Children at play run rampant through the streets of Dublin. They play till their bodies glow and their shouts echo in the street ("Araby"); Eveline remembers the "children of the avenue" frolicking together in the field; everywhere a "horde of grimy children populated the street. They stood or ran in the roadway, or crawled up the steps" ("A Little Cloud"), while the adults, like Chandler walking by, "gave them no thought."

When children play by themselves, without adult control or supervision, their games fall into several well-defined categories, among them chasing, seeking, hunting, racing, exerting, daring, guessing, and pretending. All of these, either singly or in combination, are represented in various *Dubliners* stories. Surprisingly, it is not just the children who play these games; the adults do, too, and they revert to being childish in the process. Reversion, inversion, and subversion all come together in the games of *Dubliners*.

The guessing game is one way of coming to knowledge, and children are fascinated by riddles and puzzles, as the first story in *Dubliners* makes clear. In "The Sisters," the unnamed young boy wishes to penetrate the world of authority, of adult knowledge. Even though it is vacation time, he "studied the lighted square of window" in the priest's house, trying to find some answers. He is a young "Rosicrucian," absorbed in solving mysteries, none more enigmatic than that of the priest's death and character. Old Cotter and the boy's father seem to understand what is going on. But the child—and, by extension, the reader—wishes to know more. The boy is told that knowing too much is bad for children; he should "run about and play with young lads of his own age and not be...." The father picks up the dropped conversational ball and lobs it back with his own set of ellipses: "Education is all very fine and large...." The boy is excluded from this back and forth because Old Cotter points out, "When children see things like that, you know, it has an effect...." The ellipses signify some hidden knowledge that needs to be excavated.

The child treats it as a game, a riddle: "I puzzled my head to extract meaning from his unfinished sentences." The buried knowledge surfaces in the boy's dreams, in which he juxtaposes strange customs and the priest's smiling face. The boy realizes something the adults do not: the mourners insist that the priest was "resigned" to his death—the word is repeated thrice—but to the boy, the corpse's face looks "truculent," subverting the role assigned to him. In life, as in death, the old priest with his queer ways breaks the rules as he has broken the chalice. What is a joke to the priest is also transgressive, an indication that the rules of normal life have been suspended. When the other priests, representing the power and authority of the church, see Father Flynn "laughing-like softly to himself," they realize "there was something gone wrong with him."

... All the games scattered throughout *Dubliners* provide a metaphor for the reading of the text, which becomes the ultimate game. Joyce is a master of word play. Not only does he link the stories through verbal motifs, he also, like Rabelais, uses figurative language borrowed from games. Corley's belligerent question to Lenehan, "Are you trying to get inside me?" in "Two Gallants," is an expression from a game of bowls (Gifford 59), while the term "a sure five" which crops up in the middle of a discussion of the Pope's infallibility, is a term from billiards (Gifford 107). The interconnected words ("paralysis," "gnomon," "simony") and images are elaborated by the stories themselves, which consist of interlocking pieces as in a jigsaw puzzle.

Games are an integral part of the comedic spirit. In writing the stories that make up *Dubliners*, Joyce wanted his countrymen to get "one good look at themselves" in a "nicely polished looking glass" (*Letters*). A mirror image is already a double and an inversion. That image is further doubled and re-doubled through themes and plots which are duplicates or opposites of each other, making the book a hall of mirrors (itself a carnivalesque image), where truth is seen from many angles, leading to the liberation of laughter. Carnival laughter is "universal in scope" (Bakhtin 11). So is truth. Joyce told a friend, "I always write about Dublin, because if I can get to the heart of Dublin, I can get to the heart of all the cities in the world. In the particular is contained the universal" (Ellmann 505). In the face of efforts by printers and publishers to silence him, the book symbolizes an act of insurrection. In Joyce's *Dubliners*, knowledge leads to power by way of language and laughter.

Source: Mamta Chaudhry-Fryer, "Power Play: Games in Joyce's *Dubliners*," in *Studies in Short Fiction*, Vol. 32, No. 3, Summer 1995, pp. 319–27.

John Fletcher

In the following excerpt, Fletcher compares Joyce and Samuel Beckett in terms of their humor and use of irony and describes Beckett's admiration of Joyce's work.

In freshmen classes, I tend to define the short story as a short prose narrative of concentrated effect, complete within its own terms, showing a firm story-line and often an abrupt ending, limited in its temporal and spatial location and in the number of characters deployed, and tending to work through understatement and humor rather than explicit comment.

Joyce's *Dubliners* is one of the greatest short-story collections ever published. Beckett's *More Pricks Than Kicks*, an early book—one he refused for many years to allow to be reissued—is far from being in the same league. Still, they are worth comparing in the light of the above definition for a number of reasons. The first, and most obvious, is that the young Beckett greatly admired his older compatriot and sought to imitate him. Secondly, they are both set in Dublin and feature Dublin people, as Joyce's title explicitly acknowledges. Thirdly, they both deploy a particular sense of humor—at once intellectual, sardonic, and self-consciously literary—which readers tend to associate with Irish writing in general.

I would like in this essay to look closely at their art of the short story with particular reference to "Ivy Day in the Committee Room" from *Dubliners* and to the second story, "Fingal," in *More Pricks Than Kicks*. I have deliberately chosen, as being more typical of their respective authors, stories that are less frequently discussed than, say, "The Dead" in Joyce's case or than "Dante and the Lobster" in Beckett's collection; because they are not perhaps the "best" story by either writer, they are, arguably, more representative of each collection taken as a whole.

"Ivy Day in the Committee Room" is set, as its full title implies, in an electoral ward committee room in Dublin as dusk falls on October 6 (Ivy Day, the anniversary of the death of Parnell) in a year early in the present century. A motley group of canvassers and election workers enter the room to warm themselves by the fire, to drink stout, and to chat. Warmed by liquor and fellowship, the half-dozen men become a trifle sentimental about their great hero, Parnell, and one of them, Joe Hynes, is prevailed upon to recite a piece of mawkish doggerel verse that he has written, being, in the eyes of his companions, "a clever chap...with the pen" (*D* [*Dubliners*. Ed. Robert Scholes. New York: Viking, 1957]). In an interesting use of what we now call intertextuality, Joyce gives the poem in extenso, all eleven stanzas of it. Deeply touched, Mr. Hynes's listeners give him a spontaneous round of applause. So moved is the poet himself that he pays no heed to the popping of the cork in his bottle of stout, and another prominent character (prominent in that he is present in the room throughout), Mr. O'Connor, starts to roll himself a cigarette, "the better to hide his emotion." Even Mr. Crofton, who represents the Conservative interest (for the men, although in temporary electoral alliance, do not belong to the same political party), agrees that Hynes's panegyric is "a very fine piece of writing." Joyce's irony is all the sharper for not being spelled out: drink and national sentiment temporarily unite these men who, otherwise, have little in common and who indeed (as their sarcastic remarks behind each other's backs reveal all too plainly) do not even greatly care for one another. They have, in other words, about as much charity as they have literary taste: precious little.

In Beckett's story, "Fingal," the hero Belacqua takes his girlfriend Winnie on a walk in the countryside near Dublin. Because she is "hot" (*MPTK* [*More Pricks Than Kicks*]) (a sexist epithet that the author did not permit himself in later years), they take advantage of the fine spring weather to make love a couple of times. When not embracing, they gaze upon the Irish landscape in general and upon the Portrane Lunatic Asylum in particular, where Belacqua declares his heart to reside, and Winnie, a doctor friend of hers; so they agree to make for there. But Belacqua, his immediate sexual needs having now been gratified, abandons Winnie to her friend Dr. Sholto. He infinitely prefers to her company—now that the baser lusts of the flesh have been satisfied—that of a bicycle, which he steals from a farmworker. Much to Winnie's annoyance, he gets clean away on it, and the author leaves him drinking and laughing in a roadside pub. This is the "memorable fit of laughing" referred to in the opening sentence of the story, a fit which, we are told, incapacitated Belacqua from further gallantry for some time.

The style throughout "Fingal"—indeed throughout the entire collection—is marked by elaborate and calculated allusiveness combined with extensively developed verbal irony. At its best this can give rise to suggestively witty prose, as in the coy way the sexual act is referred to: "They had not been very long on the top [of the hill] before [Belacqua] began to feel a very sad animal indeed." This is an erudite allusion to a saying usually attributed to Galen, the most famous physician of ancient Rome, to the effect that every creature suffers depression after intercourse ("*omne animal post coitum triste est*"); and the bawdy innuendo here is that the first act of love must have been intensely pleasurable for Belacqua since it leaves him feeling particularly sad, whereas the second embrace, on the top of another hill, makes him only plain sad. (What Winnie experiences is not specified, unless we are meant to understand something quite abstruse from the assertion that, after the first occasion, she appears to Belacqua to be in high spirits; following the same logic, the author may be implying that she did not have an orgasm and so escaped Galen's depression. But this may be carrying obscene interpretation further than even this witty author intends.)

At less than its best, this kind of writing is pedantry pure and simple, arrogantly disdaining simple formulations and cloaking a banal idea in an esoteric manner. On the second page of the story, for instance, there is elaborate and rather fatuous play on the name of the French poet Alphonse de Lamartine, and on the third, some toying with Latin and Roman history. This is neither funny nor particularly clever, unlike the rather effective joke upon Galen's aphorism.

All the stories in *More Pricks Than Kicks* are set in Dublin and its environs and are, like *Dubliners*, permeated with the atmosphere of the Irish capital. In snatches of dialogue that anticipate the elegant Irishisms of *Waiting for Godot*, we hear the authentic brogue of the people, which Beckett sometimes helpfully translates ("Now would they do him the favour to adjourn . . . ? This meant drink"), and their characteristic accent ("Dean Swift" pronounced "Dane Swift," for instance). Nevertheless, Belacqua is something of an outsider as far as ordinary Irish people are concerned: he is idle, he is educated, and above all, he is a Protestant, a "dirty lowdown Low Church Protestant highbrow." Inevitably, then, one does not find in *More Pricks Than Kicks* the same intimate familiarity with Dublin life—the sense of belonging to a society that is unique with its particular customs, humor, and myths—as one experiences in *Dubliners*. The country and its people are contemplated in Beckett's collection from a certain distance, which is perhaps not so surprising in the work of a Protestant Irishman, but, for all that, the feeling of alienation cannot be explained solely in terms of religion and ethnic origin. Belacqua is not only a member of the "Protestant Ascendancy," which ruled Ireland until independence; he is also the first in a line of Beckettian heroes whose condition of exile becomes gradually more painful. He is, in fact, the natural precursor of Molloy and of the Unnamable.

Physically, indeed, Belacqua appears a bit of a clown, an early version of the Chaplinesque figures in *Waiting for Godot*. It is easy, for instance, for Dr. Sholto to give a "brief satirical description" (*MPTK*) of his person, which would run on these lines: a pale fat man, nearly bald, bespectacled, shabbily dressed, and always looking ill and dejected (he is suffering from impetigo on his face in "Fingal," much to the disgust of Winnie, who has been kissed by him). His appearance is in fact grotesque enough to provoke comment and even laughter in all places except where he is well known. He is a total eccentric; we have already noted his habit of preferring bicycles to women. This oddity in his reactions (or, rather, his incapacity for registering the normal reactions expected of him) is coupled with a faculty for acting with insufficient motivation, which his creator maintains is serious enough to make a mental home the place for him (hence his avowal that his heart resides in the Portrane Lunatic Asylum). But, even more than a padded cell, what Belacqua really longs for is to return to the womb, where he fantasizes about lying on his back in the dark forever, free from "night sweats" (i.e., sex). In default of such a refuge, Belacqua enjoys to the full a melancholy indulged in for its own sake: landscapes, such as Fingal, are of interest to him only insofar as they furnish him "with a pretext for a long face."

Beckett uses this oddity—a person not quite at one with his fellow men, often more an onlooker than active participant in what goes on in the stories—for satirical ends. Inspired caricature fixes the less amiable aspects of a person in few words as is the case in "Fingal" with Dr. Sholto, "a pale dark man with a brow" who feels "nothing but rancour" toward Belacqua, evidently because Winnie prefers him to Sholto (which may indicate that what made Belacqua "sad" was pleasurable for her, after all). This is all the more galling to the pompous, prissy doctor in that Belacqua patently prefers his own company, laughing out loud alone in the pub, to getting "sad" with Winnie: his "sadness" falls from him "like a shift" as soon as he finds the bicycle, we are told. Despite an unsightly rash on his face, we are meant to understand that Belacqua is "sexier" than Sholto, even assisted, as the latter is, by the aphrodisiac of a glass of whiskey.

Belacqua's compulsive urge to retreat from the body and its "night sweats" into the wider freedom of the mind springs from a dualistic conviction that he shares with his successor-heroes in the Beckett canon. They, too, are lovers of bicycles; man and machine together form what Hugh Kenner calls, in an arresting phrase, a "Cartesian centaur" (Kenner 132), from Descartes, whose thought deeply influenced the young Beckett who wrote *More Pricks Than Kicks*. In all his writing, indeed, Beckett advances his own version of Cartesianism, in which the mental part of his heroes seeks continually to escape from the physical part. In this early story, therefore, there is already discernible a theme—not quite drowned by the academic wit and the tiresome allusiveness—which becomes increasingly central in Beckett's fiction: the radical split between body and mind, a disconnection that allows the mind to retreat progressively into itself, into an isolated life of its own. In the later works, the body is left to break down, like a worn-out piece of machinery, while the mind, panic-stricken at the prospect of cessation, chatters on, rehashing continually its never-changing futilities.

Thus the seeds of *For to End Yet Again* were sown forty years earlier in *More Pricks Than Kicks*, just as the long road to Finnegan's wake starts out from the committee rooms and parlors of the Dubliners whom Joyce portrays so deftly in "Ivy Day" and the other stories. Just as the bicycle that enables Belacqua to escape from Winnie is the twin of the one that leads Molloy into his disastrous encounter with *his* mitress, Lousse, so the Liffey, which the friends cross in a ferryboat in the second story of *Dubliners*, is the same "riverrun," the same Anna Livia's "hitherandthithering waters of" *Finnegans Wake*.

Both writers, then, are supremely consistent with themselves: just as both—the senior, a Catholic; the junior, a Protestant—are intensely, politically, Irish. The political dimension is less in evidence in "Fingal," but it is there, discreetly, in references to Swift and to the potato famine (the tower near which Belacqua and Winnie make love the second time was, they learn, "built for relief in the year of the Famine"). The Fingal landscape stretching out before them is, Belacqua asserts in stoutly patriotic tones, a "magic land" comparable at least to Burgundy and far superior to Wicklow.

But Beckett does not—perhaps understandably, given his background—comment upon or even reflect contemporary Irish political concerns: there is no trace in his work of any reference to the Easter Rising or to the civil war; his criticisms are purely social and cultural in nature. Developments like literary censorship or the ban on contraceptives he does satirize and debunk, but he eschews party politics and above all the bitter struggles surrounding the birth of the Irish Republic. Joyce, as a member of the majority community, feels no such inhibitions about expressing his feelings in *Dubliners*. There is telling satire in "The Dead" of the kind of nationalist virago who hurls the insult "West Briton!" at anyone who does not wear his shamrock heart on his sleeve, and in "Ivy Day in the Committee Room," as we have seen, mawkish patriotism is ridiculed in Mr. Hynes's ghastly doggerel. At the same time, the men's emotion is genuine enough, even if its expression is inflated and pretentious. The figure of Parnell himself, it is important to note, is not ridiculed; if anything, it emerges enhanced by the extremes of devotion to which his admirers will go, composing and applauding bad verse in homage to their "dead King," felt so much more truly to be their sovereign lord than Edward VII, who is about to pay a visit to his "wild Irish" subjects and who is derisively referred to as "Eddie" for his pains. Insofar as the views of the implied author can be surmised, they are those of moderate nationalism, unemphatic patriotism, and temperate republicanism. This tolerant, non-extremist position stands in sharp contrast to the intolerance of the harpy in "The Dead" and to the naïve hero-worship of Mr. Hynes in "Ivy Day in the Committee Room."

Thus far, for the purposes of comparison, I have been treating "Fingal" and "Ivy Day in the Committee Room" as more or less of equal interest, but, as I made clear at the outset, the two stories are not of equal merit. Joyce's story, even though not the finest story in *Dubliners*, is markedly superior to "Fingal." For one thing, Beckett's story is slighter, shorter than Joyce's by about a third, and it deploys fewer and less interesting characters. Belacqua engages our sympathy, no doubt because the author tends to treat him indulgently, but Winnie is not very plausible, and Sholto is no more than sketched. Joyce, by contrast, introduces seven main characters and brings them on like a competent dramatist at different points in the narrative. Old Jack and Mr. O'Connor are present as the story opens and remain in the room throughout; Mr. Hynes the poet enters, leaves, and re-enters later to deliver his composition; Mr. Henchy enters about one-third of the way through; Father Keon puts in a brief, rather sinister appearance at about the half-way mark; and Mr. Crofton and Mr. Lyons walk in shortly afterward and remain to the end. This deployment of characters gives a much tauter feel to the story than Beckett's does. The effect (to return to my simple definition of the genre outlined at the beginning of this essay) is therefore more noticeably concentrated in "Ivy Day in the Committee Room," and the story line is appreciably firmer, the end coming precisely when it should, with the emotional responses to Hynes's elegy undercut by the implied author's discreet mockery of the enterprise when he gets Mr. Crofton (normally a political opponent) to concede that it is "a very fine piece of writing." The manner in which the end of "Fingal" refers back to the beginning (confirming the previously enigmatic allusion to Belacqua's fit of laughing) is competent enough but feels rather contrived in comparison with the ending of "Ivy Day in the Committee Room."

Both stories are sensibly limited in terms of temporal and spatial location, each covering a few hours in real time and a single setting, the committee room in Joyce's case and the vicinity of the Portrane asylum in Beckett's. The closed space of the committee room symbolizes the inward-looking nature of the men's political and social concerns—parochial and mundane—just as Beckett's outing to the country in fine weather is the objective correlative of Belacqua's escaping from convention and flouting of social niceties. And, last but not least, both writers work their effects by understatement and humor rather than explicit comment, although Beckett is, rather curiously, more old-fashioned than Joyce in his occasional, admittedly muted, use of the authorial aside to the reader, a device that the modernist Joyce eschews altogether. Not only that, but the Beckettian asides reveal the writer's unease: he is not really at home in the short-story form, and rhetorical questions like "Who shall silence them, at last?" betray his discomfort. We are, after all, nearly half a century away from the great brief texts *Imagination Dead Imagine, Lessness, Still* and the others, texts that are Beckett's supreme, unique contribution to the short prose form. The classic short story, on the other hand, the kind that Chekhov, Henry James, D. H. Lawrence, and Joyce himself developed to such a high pitch of aesthetic perfection and emotional power, was never (to use an apt colloquialism) Beckett's "scene," any more than the play in several acts was: he wisely abandoned about the same time an attempt to write a stage work in four acts, one act devoted to each of the four years between the widowing and the remarriage of Mrs. Thrale, Dr. Johnson's friend. In the only section actually composed, Act One, Scene One, the tone is already at odds with the realistic, historical material that Beckett was trying manfully to shape into dramatic form. The pauses, repetitions, and formal patterns in the fragment that survives are precisely those which he was to hone later, in *Waiting for Godot*, into a style that, even as early as 1937, is characteristically Beckettian. But the form available to him in the '30s was not suitable to his purposes, and he abandoned the project (*Disjecta* 155–66). He did not abandon *More Pricks Than Kicks*, but he did, as we saw earlier, refuse for many years to have it reissued. In his eyes the book was juvenile stuff, and although that judgment was not fair, he was correct in accepting that, as examples of the short story form, his collection did not begin to match up to those of his great mentor Joyce.

Source: John Fletcher, "Joyce, Beckett, and the Short Story in Ireland," in *Re: Joyce'n Beckett*, edited by Phyllis

Carey and Ed Jewinski, Fordham University Press, 1992, pp. 20–30.

Ezra Pound

In the following excerpt, Pound offers a favorable review of Dubliners, *praising Joyce's artistry, universality, and selection of details.*

Freedom from sloppiness is so rare in contemporary English prose that one might well say simply, [*Dubliners*] "is prose free from sloppiness," and leave the intelligent reader ready to run from his study immediately to spend three and sixpence on the volume.

Unfortunately one's credit as a critic is insufficient to produce this result . . . .

Mr. Joyce's merit, I will not say his chief merit but his most engaging merit, is that he carefully avoids telling you a lot that you don't want to know. He presents his people swiftly and vividly, he does not sentimentalise over them, he does not weave convolutions. He is a realist. He does not believe "life" would be all right if we stopped vivisection or if we instituted a new sort of "economics." He gives the thing as it is. He is not bound by the tiresome convention that any part of life, to be interesting, must be shaped into the conventional form of a "story." Since de Maupassant we have had so many people trying to write "stories" and so few people presenting life. Life for the most part does not happen in neat little diagrams and nothing is more tiresome than the continual pretence that it does.

Mr. Joyce's "Araby," for instance, is much better than a "story," it is a vivid waiting.

It is surprising that Mr. Joyce is Irish. One is so tired of the Irish or "Celtic" imagination (or "phantasy" as I think they now call it) flopping about. Mr. Joyce does not flop about. He defines. He is not an institution for the promotion of Irish peasant industries. He accepts an international standard of prose writing and lives up to it.

He gives us Dublin as it presumably is. He does not descend to farce. He does not rely upon Dickensian caricature. He gives us things as they are, not only for Dublin, but for every city. Erase the local names and a few specifically local allusions, and a few historic events of the past, and substitute a few different local names, allusions and events, and these stories could be retold of any town.

That is to say, the author is quite capable of dealing with things about him, and dealing

directly, yet these details do not engross him, he is capable of getting at the universal element beneath them.

The main situations of *Madame Bovary* or of *Doña Perfecta* do not depend on local colour or upon local detail, that is their strength. Good writing, good presentation can be specifically local, but it must not depend on locality. Mr. Joyce does not present "types" but individuals. I mean he deals with common emotions which run through all races. He does not bank on "Irish character." Roughly speaking, Irish literature has gone through three phases in our time, the shamrock period, the dove-grey period, and the Kiltartan period. I think there is a new phase in the works of Mr. Joyce. He writes as a contemporary of continental writers. I do not mean that he writes as a faddist, mad for the last note, he does not imitate Strindberg, for instance, or Bang. He is not ploughing the underworld for horror. He is not presenting a macabre subjectivity. He is classic in that he deals with normal things and with normal people. A committee room, Little Chandler, a nonentity, a boarding house full of clerks—these are his subjects and he treats them all in such a manner that they are worthy subjects of art . . . .

I think that he excels most of the impressionist writers because of his more rigorous selection, because of his exclusion of all unnecessary detail.

There is a very clear demarcation between unnecessary detail and irrelevant detail. An impressionist friend of mine talks to me a good deal about "preparing effects," and on that score he justifies much unnecessary detail, which is not "irrelevant," but which ends by being wearisome and by putting one out of conceit with his narrative.

Mr. Joyce's more rigorous selection of the presented detail marks him, I think, as belonging to my own generation, that is, to the "nineteen-tens," not to the decade between "the 'nineties" and to-day.

At any rate these stories and [*A Portrait of the Artist as a Young Man*] are such as to win for Mr. Joyce a very definite place among English contemporary prose writers, not merely a place in the "Novels of the Week" column, and our writers of good clear prose are so few that we cannot afford to confuse or to overlook them.

Source: Ezra Pound, "*Dubliners* and Mr. James Joyce," in *Egoist*, Vol. 1, No. 14, July 15, 1914, p. 267.

SOURCES

Armstrong, Tim, *Modernism: A Cultural History*, Polity, 2005.

Bašić, Sonja, "A Book of Many Uncertainties: Joyce's *Dubliners*," in *ReJoycing: New Readings of Dubliners*, University of Kentucky Press, 1998, pp. 13–40.

Bradbury, Malcolm, and James McFarlane, *Modernism: A Guide to European Literature 1890–1930*, Penguin, 1978.

Bulson, Eric, "Joyce the Modernist," in *The Cambridge Introduction to James Joyce*, Cambridge University Press, 2006, pp. 17–21.

———, "Works: *Dubliners*," in *The Cambridge Introduction to James Joyce*, Cambridge University Press, 2006, pp. 35–42.

"The Countries of the UK," in *UK Statistics Authority*, November 11, 2005, http://www.statistics.gov.uk (accessed June 20, 2010).

Craig, Paul, and Grainne De Burca, *EU Law: Text, Cases and Materials*, 4th ed., Oxford University Press, 2008, p. 15.

Dettmar, Kevin J. H., "James Joyce," in *Dictionary of Literary Biography*, Vol. 162, *British Short-Fiction Writers, 1915–1945*, edited by John H. Rogers, Gale Research, 1996, pp. 160–81.

Dilworth, Thomas, "Not 'Too Much Noise': Joyce's 'The Sisters,'" in *Twentieth Century Literature*, Vol. 39, No. 1, Spring 1993, p. 99.

Doherty, Gerald, "The Art of Confessing: Silence and Secrecy in James Joyce's 'The Sisters,'" in *James Joyce Quarterly*, Vol. 35, No. 4, Summer 1998, pp. 657–64.

Gall, Timothy, L., and Susan Bevan Gall, "Ireland," in *Worldmark Encyclopedia of the Nations*, Gale, Cengage Learning, 2009.

Gibson, Andrew, and Declan Kiberd, *James Joyce*, Reaktion Books, 2006.

Joyce, James, "The Sisters," in *Dubliners*, Tutis Digital Publishing, 2008, pp. 1–8.

McDermott, John V., "Joyce's 'The Sisters,'" in *Explicator*, Vol. 51, No. 4, Summer 1993, p. 236.

Pindar, Ian, *James Joyce*, Haus Publishing, 2005.

Sultan, Stanley, "Dublin Boy and Man in 'The Sisters,'" in *Joyce and the City: The Significance of Place*, edited by Michael Begnal, Syracuse University Press, 2002, pp. 85–97.

Swartzlander, Susan, "James Joyce's 'The Sisters': Chalices and Umbrellas, Ptolemaic Memphis and Victorian Dublin," in *Studies in Short Fiction*, Vol. 32, No. 3, Summer 1995, p. 295.

Whitworth, Michael, *Modernism*, Wiley-Blackwell, 2007.

FURTHER READING

Ingersoll, Earl G., *Engendered Trope in Joyce's "Dubliners,"* Southern Illinois University Press, 1996.
    This volume provides readers with an in-depth critical analysis of gender issues and symbolism in *Dubliners*.

Joyce, James, *Ulysses*, edited by Enda Duffy, Dover, 2009.
    No study of Joyce is complete without reading his masterpiece. First published in 1922, the novel features a groundbreaking structure, graphic scenes, and language. When it was first published, it was banned throughout Europe and the United States.

Lyons, F. S. L., *Charles Stewart Parnell*, new ed., Gill & Macmillan, 2005.
    This biography of Charles Stewart Parnell explores the life and legacy of the man who not only changed late-nineteenth-century England but also heavily influenced Joyce's views and feelings toward his birthplace.

Mansfield, Katherine, *Bliss and Other Stories*, NTC/ Contemporary Publishing, 1999.
    Mansfield wrote during the same period as Joyce. First published in 1920, this collection provides readers with an introduction to a female modernist author who is not as widely known as some of her peers.

SUGGESTED SEARCH TERMS

Dubliners

James Joyce

Dubliners AND James Joyce

The Sisters AND Catholicism

The Sisters AND grief

The Sisters AND James Joyce

The Sisters AND short story

James Joyce AND modernism

James Joyce AND Catholicism

James Joyce AND Ireland

Stalking

JOYCE CAROL OATES

1972

In 1972 American author Joyce Carol Oates published the short story "Stalking" in the *North American Review*. The story later appeared in her collection of short stories *Marriages and Infidelities*, published initially in 1968 but reissued with new material in 1972. "Stalking" tells the story of Gretchen, a thirteen-year-old girl who roams her suburban community hunting her Invisible Adversary. Gretchen is not a very attractive character. She is angry, spiteful, and antisocial. During her journey she commits vandalism and theft. She chooses to make herself physically unattractive. Oates, though, portrays Gretchen in part as a victim of her environment. Her mother neglects her, and her father is frequently away, perhaps on business trips. The story is set in modern suburbia, and its implication is that the hunt for the Invisible Adversary is Gretchen's effort to fill the void in her life that the bland comforts of suburbia supply, or perhaps to hunt down a more authentic version of herself. In this way the short story is a critique of modern suburban society. "Stalking" should not be confused with another short story by Oates, "The Stalker."

"Stalking" is one of many short stories and novels Oates has written, and she is one of the most prolific authors in American literary history, perhaps in literary history anywhere. During her college years she wrote a number of novels that, she says, she happily discarded. She published her first novel in 1964, and for a

Joyce Carol Oates (*AP Images*)

number of years she published two new novels a year—for a total of nearly sixty. Additionally, she published twenty-nine collections of short stories, fifteen collections of poetry, more than a dozen nonfiction books and collections of essays, and more than twenty plays. She edited or compiled twenty-two books, and her journal grew to four thousand single-spaced pages. Joyce Carol Oates has been a dominating voice in American fiction for nearly half a century. Her fiction is often disturbing, with themes of rape, pedophilia, incest, broken homes, victimization, and violence. Her varied settings include academia, the slums of Detroit, backwoods areas of Pennsylvania, and rural areas of upstate New York. Some critics argue that she is a feminist writer in her depiction of strong female characters, but others disagree, arguing that too often her female characters become passive victims of vague unconscious forces.

AUTHOR BIOGRAPHY

Oates was born in Lockport, New York, on June 16, 1938. Her mother was a homemaker, her father a tool-and-die maker. She grew up in Millersport, New York, a farming community, and she later described her upbringing and family life in very positive terms. She first attended school in the same one-room schoolhouse her mother had attended, but she later attended suburban schools and was the first member of her family to graduate from high school. As a child she was a voracious reader, devouring the works of William Faulkner, Ernest Hemingway, Fyodor Dostoevsky, and Charlotte and Emily Brontë. As a student at Syracuse University, she was attracted to the fiction of Franz Kafka, D. H. Lawrence, Thomas Mann, and Flannery O'Connor. After completing her bachelor's degree as class valedictorian in 1960, she attended graduate school at the University of Wisconsin, completing a master's degree in 1961.

In the late 1960s, Oates combined writing with teaching. She published her first novel, *With Shuddering Fall*, at age twenty-six, and new novels, as well as collections of short stories, poetry, and nonfiction, appeared on the shelves of bookstores and libraries with astonishing frequency in the years that followed. Her 1969 novel *them* (the title is not capitalized) won the National Book Award, and three of her novels have been nominees for the Pulitzer Prize. She is the recipient of numerous other awards, including the PEN/Malamud Award for excellence in short fiction. Some of her major novels include *Garden of Earthly Delights* (1967), *Bellefleur* (1980), *We Were the Mulvaneys* (1996), *Blonde* (2000), and *The Gravedigger's Daughter* (2007). Additionally, she has published a number of novels, several of them mysteries, under the pen names Rosamond Smith and Lauren Kelly.

Shortly after completing graduate studies, Oates took a teaching job in Beaumont, Texas. She then moved to Detroit to teach at the University of Detroit. In 1968 she accepted a teaching position at the University of Windsor in Canada. Ten years later she returned to the United States to teach at Princeton University, where, as of 2010, she was the Roger S. Berlind '52 Professor in the Humanities with the Program in Creative Writing. As if all this were not enough, she edits journals, writes book reviews, gives readings of her works throughout the country, and serves on the boards of artistic foundations. She is an avid runner and reports that while running she has conceived many of her books or solved difficulties in books that were already under way.

PLOT SUMMARY

"Stalking" is set in an unnamed suburb. It follows the movements of a thirteen-year-old girl named Gretchen, who is "stalking" what she thinks of as her Invisible Adversary through the suburb on a cold "gritty" Saturday in November. The story begins abruptly as Gretchen spots the Invisible Adversary fleeing across an open field. Wearing blue jeans and white leather boots that are "scuffed and filthy with mud," she follows the Invisible Adversary across the field and then across a highway. On the other side of the highway she crosses another field with signs indicating that an office building is planned for the site. She continues to follow the Invisible Adversary, which seems to taunt her as it flees before her. At one point the Invisible Adversary is "peeking out at her from around the corner of a gas station," but then it "ducks back out of sight." Gretchen makes her way through a field filled with rocks and debris past a brand-new gas station, although the gas station appears to have been vandalized with smears of a tar-like substance, and some of its windows have been broken. The area is part of a construction zone, where detour signs direct traffic from the pavement onto the shoulder of the highway. Bulldozers stand idle, and storm sewer pipes lie about.

Gretchen continues to follow the Invisible Adversary to a shopping plaza. Again the plaza appears to be new; there are no sidewalks, and some of the buildings are vacant. After she jumps over a ditch and passes the Federal Savings Bank, she encounters a steady line of traffic leading to the shopping plaza, the Buckingham Mall. The Invisible Adversary continues to tease Gretchen as it stops at the entrance to the Cunningham Drug Store. Gretchen observes the enormous parking lot and thinks she might have spotted her mother's car. Gretchen pushes past a number of older youths who are hanging around to enter the drugstore in pursuit of the Invisible Adversary. As she observes a salesgirl showing an older woman some makeup, she steals a tube of lipstick. She then "drifts" to a newsstand and shoplifts a package; she does not know what the package contains.

MEDIA ADAPTATIONS

- Joyce Chopra directed a film adaptation of another Oates short story, "Where Are You Going, Where Have You Been?," titled *SmoothTalk*, for Spectrafilm in 1985.

- *Foxfire: Confessions of a Girl Gang*, Oates's 1993 novel, was adapted for the screen in a 1996 film titled simply *Foxfire*, starring Angelina Jolie and directed by Annette Haywood-Carter. It was released on DVD by Sony Pictures in 2000. Running time is 102 minutes.

- In 2001 National Public Radio interviewed Oates about her latest collection of short stories, *Faithless: Tales of Transgression*. Listeners can hear the interview at the National Public Radio (NPR) Web site.

- Oates's 1996 novel *We Were the Mulvaneys* was adapted as a film starring Beau Bridges and Blythe Danner and directed by Peter Werner. It was released on DVD by Lionsgate in 2004. Running time is eighty-six minutes.

- Oates's 2000 novel *Blonde*, based on the life of screen legend Marilyn Monroe, was made into a miniseries starring Poppy Montgomery and Patrick Dempsey and directed by Joyce Chopra. It was released on DVD by Allumination in 2006 and runs 240 minutes.

Gretchen continues to pursue the Invisible Adversary through the mall. She follows it to the Franklin Joseph store. She walks past the counters and dress racks to the ladies' room, where she examines the lipstick, then smears it all over the mirror. She vandalizes the rest room by filling a toilet with the lipstick tube, wads of toilet paper, the other object she stole (which turns out to be toothpaste), and wads of cloth toweling. She flushes the toilet until the items become stuck.

Gretchen leaves the store and follows the Invisible Adversary into the mall area. In front of a record store she encounters a group of boys, one of whom pushes her against a trash can, but Gretchen walks away. She enters the Sampson Furniture store, where she is distracted by the many displays until she remembers her purpose and leaves the store in pursuit of the Invisible Adversary. Her next stop is Dodi's Boutique, where a salesgirl tries to wait on her. Gretchen takes a number of dresses into the dressing room, where she deliberately smears one with mud from her boot and carelessly breaks the zipper on another.

Gretchen leaves the boutique and makes her way to Carmichael's, a department store. She observes a display of advertisements for winter homes. She goes into a Big Boy restaurant, where she has a hamburger, french fries, and a Coke. After she leaves the Big Boy, she follows the Invisible Adversary out to the parking lot and then through open, muddy fields. While crossing a road, the Invisible Adversary appears to be struck by a car. It gets up and staggers along a sidewalk, leading Gretchen into the Piney Woods subdivision. The Invisible Adversary is bleeding and walks "like a drunken man." It appears to be leading Gretchen into a randomly chosen house, but the reader learns that the house is Gretchen's. No one else is at home, so Gretchen wanders through the house, turns on the television, and sits on the sofa with a Coke. In the final sentence of the story, she dismisses the Invisible Adversary, thinking that if it appears behind her "groaning" and "weeping," "she won't even bother to glance at him."

CHARACTERS

Boy
Outside a record store Gretchen encounters a group of boys who push her against a trash can. The reader is told nothing about the one boy who says to Gretchen, "Watch it, babe!" The boy becomes part of the alien and uncaring landscape through which Gretchen moves.

Girl at the Cosmetics Counter
This unnamed character appears only briefly. She is a salesperson at the mall and is described as having "shimmering blond hair and eyes that are penciled to show a permanent exclamatory interest." She represents the type of employee one might normally encounter at a shopping mall.

Gretchen
Gretchen is the protagonist in "Stalking" and the only character the reader gets to know. She is thirteen years old, and she and her parents have lived in an unnamed suburb for about six months.

Although she is described as having an attractive face, she seems to deliberately make herself unattractive. Her "solid legs" are "crammed into old blue jeans." She has a "stern, staring look," and her face has a "blunt, neutral, sexless stillness to it." Throughout the story she is portrayed as not caring about anything. She stalks the suburb, with its stores, restaurants, mall, gas station, and parking lots, hunting her Invisible Adversary. During her journey she is depicted as antisocial and angry. She commits acts of petty vandalism and shoplifting. She is emotionally detached from her surroundings and family. She feels neglected by both her parents. Gretchen seems to hate her life, and the only way she can fill the void in her life is by hunting the Invisible Adversary.

Gretchen's Mother
Gretchen's unnamed mother appears only briefly in the story, but from Gretchen's thoughts about her, it is clear that she plays a role in the girl's anger and disaffection. The reader knows that the mother provides for Gretchen's material needs but appears to be absent and uncaring. At the shopping mall, Gretchen thinks she sees her mother's car in the parking lot. Later she thinks she sees her mother on an escalator, but "her mother doesn't notice her."

Invisible Adversary
The Invisible Adversary is not, strictly speaking, a character. It exists in Gretchen's mind as she hunts it throughout the suburban landscape where she lives. The story never makes explicit what the Invisible Adversary represents. In the process of hunting the Invisible Adversary, Gretchen seems to be filling some sort of void or emptiness in her life or using it to express her anger. The Invisible Adversary is described as "light-footed" and constantly running ahead of her, teasing her and "wagging a finger at her." Toward the end of the story the Invisible Adversary seems to be struck by a car. It gets up and appears to be bleeding and "staggering... like a drunken man" as it leads her into her own home. At the end, Gretchen concludes that if the Invisible Adversary crawls up behind her, "she won't even bother to glance at him."

Salesgirl
An unnamed salesgirl tries to wait on Gretchen at Dodi's Boutique. She has "long swinging hair and a high-shouldered, indifferent, bright manner." Like the salesgirl at the cosmetics counter, she becomes part of the suburban landscape that Gretchen despises.

TOPICS FOR FURTHER STUDY

- "Stalking" is set in modern suburbia. Conduct Internet research about the suburbanization of the United States and locate data about how the suburbs have grown, particularly after World War II. Prepare charts and tables showing your findings and be prepared to discuss the effects of suburbanization on American life, such as traffic patterns, neighborhoods, socialization, spending patterns, and consumerism. Post your graphics on a class Wikispace and compare the information to that added by your classmates.

- "Stalking" makes prominent use of setting as Gretchen moves about in her suburban community. Imagine that you were writing about your own community, whether a suburb, a city, a small town, or a rural area. Make a list of the places that would stand out for you. Take photos of the places, perhaps using a cell phone, and send the photos to your classmates or post them on your blog or social networking site to elicit their reactions to the places you have photographed. Explain in your blog how each item on your list in some way helps define the community in which you live.

- Prepare a written report on the topic of mall culture in America. Define the term "mall culture." Examine its effects on families and particularly on teenagers. Examine how the mall culture in some sense defines life for some American teenagers and how hanging around in a mall differs from doing so in a downtown or other areas. Compare and contrast mall culture in the United States with that in another nation, such as India (where the number of shopping malls has grown exponentially).

- Visit a local real estate office. Real estate agents often put notices, with pictures, on the windows so that browsers can examine properties for sale without having to enter the office. Alternatively, examine the real estate advertisements in a local newspaper or in a real estate booklet (which can frequently be found for free at the entrances to grocery stores and other businesses), or on an real estate Web site. Answer these questions: How do real estate agents attempt to idealize suburban life? What words and phrases do they use? What features of a home for sale do they emphasize? Compare this advertising material with the vision of the suburbs found in "Stalking." Develop a persuasive essay in which you argue that one vision is essentially either accurate or inaccurate.

- Sonya Harnett's 2009 young-adult novel *Butterfly* examines teenage angst and the mall culture in Australia. Read the novel and prepare a chart listing the similarities and differences in attitudes to suburbia and the mall culture in Australia with those related in "Stalking."

THEMES

Surburban Life

"Stalking" is in part an examination of suburban life from the point of view of a young teenager. The story sketches the suburban setting with great detail. As Gretchen moves about in her suburb, she comes across bulldozers, muddy fields, new buildings, parking lots, highways, and the mall.

Nothing about the suburb is attractive, pleasing, or colorful. The people who work in the stores she enters are polite to her, but nothing about them is real or genuinely personable, and the author describes them strictly in terms of their physical appearance. The environment is depicted as cold, forbidding, and alien, in many ways like a wasteland. Gretchen and her parents have lived in a large colonial house perched on an artificial hill

She discreetly grabbed the little box and quickly hid it. (*Steve Lovegrove | Shutterstock.com*)

for only about six months. Gretchen's parents seem to neglect her, and she does not appear to have any friends. In fact, she seems deliberately to avoid taking part in activities with her peers.

The short story is never explicit in condemning suburban life. Rather, it relies on suggestion and on the reactions of the reader to Gretchen's character. In stalking the Invisible Adversary, Gretchen seems to be trying to fill some void in her life, find some sort of meaning in her environment, or hunt down some sort of authentic version of herself. She is clearly angry and at odds with the world in which she lives. Thus, the short story implicitly becomes a critique of a certain kind of suburban life.

Teenage Angst

A common theme in much of Oates's fiction involves young people who feel threatened or victimized by their environment. Many of her young characters behave in antisocial ways because they do not feel that they fit in with the world surrounding them. They are isolated and angry, and they project this isolation and anger

by using drugs, perpetrating violence, or committing crimes. During her day stalking the Invisible Adversary, Gretchen steals and commits petty vandalism. She repeatedly thinks to herself that she does not care about anything. On two occasions she purposefully wipes mud from her boots on things. Although she could be attractive, she makes herself unattractive. At no point does she smile or seem to enjoy anything around her. The reader is told:

> She could be good at gym, if she bothered; instead, she just stands around, her face empty, her arms crossed and her shoulders a little slumped. If forced, she takes part in the games . . . but she runs heavily, without spirit, and sometimes bumps into other girls, hurting them.

In some ways, Gretchen might be regarded as a typical teenage girl: sometimes sullen and uncaring, unwilling to make friends, disconnected from her family, unsure where she fits in. "Stalking," though, presents a more extreme version of this angst, and the reader is invited to speculate about what type of person Gretchen will become.

STYLE

Point of View

"Stalking" is written from the third-person omniscient point of view. This means that the story is told *about* Gretchen, rather than *by* Gretchen, by an omniscient ("all-knowing") narrator. The narrator is able not only to report action but also to report Gretchen's thoughts and feelings. Sometimes omniscient narrators take an outside, objective view of their characters. Sometimes, though, they narrate the action strictly from the perspective of an individual character, recreating the character's thoughts and ways of speaking in the narration. This is the technique Oates adopted for this story. Sometimes it is clear that the narrator is reporting the actual words Gretchen is thinking. These words are often set it italic type. Thus, at one point Gretchen is represented as thinking about the Invisible Adversary: "*You'll be sorry for that, you bastard.*" At other points, Gretchen's words and thoughts are woven into the narration. For example, at one point the narration says, "Is this the bank her parents go to now?" The words are Gretchen's, although they are in the third person rather than the first person (that is, "Is this the bank my parents go to now?"). This type of narration and point of view gives the story more immediacy. Rather than viewing the character strictly from the outside, the reader is able to enter Gretchen's mind and experience her thoughts and reactions as she has them.

At some points in the story, though, Oates adopts a more objective, outside view. Gretchen's view of herself is limited, so the author finds it necessary to fill in background information the reader needs for a full understanding of the character. Thus, the story at one point says, "She has untidy, curly hair that looks like a wig set loosely on her head." Later in the same paragraph the description continues: "She has a stern, staring look, like an adult man. . . . Her facial structure is strong, pensive, its features stern and symmetrical as a statue's, blank, neutral, withdrawn." These statements do not represent Gretchen's words. These are judgments made about Gretchen by the omniscient narrator. Some writers might argue that statements such as these make the point of view in the story inconsistent. However, these observations are made as Gretchen examines herself in a mirror. Even though the words are not those that Gretchen would use, they still

represent in some sense Gretchen's perceptions of herself in the mirror. Thus, the apparent inconsistency of the point of view is actually an adept method of allowing the narrator to comment on Gretchen in a way that enhances the reader's understanding of her character.

Setting

Setting plays a crucial role in "Stalking," and it could be argued that the story is as much about the setting as it is about Gretchen. The story is set in an unnamed suburb, although the reference to the Upper Peninsula suggests that the suburb is somewhere in Michigan, possibly near Detroit. (The Upper Peninsula is the northern portion of Michigan.) Oates frequently sets her fiction in Detroit and its suburbs, and her short story "How I Contemplated the World from the Detroit House of Correction and Began My Life Over Again" is set in the Detroit suburb of Bloomfield Hills, making the Detroit location likely. The suburban location is important, for the story depicts the suburb as empty and soulless. It makes repeated reference to concrete, for example. The Invisible Adversary jumps up onto a "curb of new concrete," the gas station is all "white concrete," and "concrete pipes" are lying about. The growing suburb is a world of bulldozers, muddy fields, parking lots, roads, trash cans, and the mall. As a new and growing suburb, it has no center and no tradition. As Gretchen wanders through it, the suburb is described as an impersonal wasteland, a "bulldozed field of mud and thistles and debris that is mainly rocks and chunks of glass."

Although a number of stores are given particular names, there is little that is particular about them. They are the kinds of generic stores one might find in a new suburban mall, with little personality and nothing unique, quirky, or interesting about them; even Gretchen's lunch is a generic hamburger, fries, and Coke. Little about the larger setting is natural. Even the name of Gretchen's subdivision, Piney Woods, is ironic, for there is nothing woody or piney about it, for the houses are perched on artificial hills. The homes are large colonial homes, again suggesting a kind of artificiality and falseness, for the homes in reality are all new and modern. Yet when Gretchen arrives home "the house is empty." This emptiness is symbolic; it refers not just to the absence of Gretchen's parents but to its lack of homeyness and feeling. The furnishing are the type of furnishings that can be purchased at the Sampson Furniture store, but there is a uniformity about them; when she is in the store, "Gretchen's eyes squint to see so many displays: like seeing the inside of a hundred houses." The emphasis on stores suggests that the suburban setting is one of consumption, where people spend their time shopping or hanging out around stores. No one is playing a game or taking part in a convivial social gathering.

Symbolism

Symbolism in literature is often found in objects that take on a special significance. Symbolism can also be more general and can encompass characters and setting. "Stalking" makes extensive use of this second kind of symbolism. The setting, for example, is symbolic. Although it is particularized through the use of specific details, the setting also induces an overall feeling that is one of emptiness and artificiality. The setting is in many respects a wasteland of muddy fields, concrete, parking lots, and debris. The setting, then, can be seen as an externalization of Gretchen's state of mind. Gretchen is an angry girl. She is neglected by her parents, she does not fit in with any of her schoolmates, and she seems to hate everything about her life. She takes out her anger on the things around her: for example, by stealing, smearing mud on one of the dresses she looks at in the store, smearing mud on the carpet in her home, and vandalizing the rest room. The poet T. S. Eliot coined the term *objective correlative* to refer to this literary technique; for Eliot, the objective correlative was an outward situation, a group of objects, or a sequence of events that correspond to an inward experience and that evoke an experience in the reader.

HISTORICAL CONTEXT

"Stalking" makes no direct reference to historical circumstances, so history as the term is generally understood plays little role in the story. However, the story does embody trends in American life in the early 1970s, when the story was written. The decades after World War II were a time of prosperity and growth for the United States. Although the cold war with the Communist Soviet Union and its satellite states was continuing, and although the war in Vietnam was still under way, the period was one of expansion and optimism. In 1950, for example, the U.S. population was about 151 million; by 1970 the population was about 203 million. In 1950 the median household income was just under $24,000; by 1972 that figure had risen to nearly $47,000. (These are not the actual numbers; these numbers are calculated according to the value of the dollar in 2006 to account for inflation and to allow accurate comparisons.) Thus, household incomes had almost doubled over the preceding two decades. Given these higher incomes, many families sought new, modern houses and amenities in the suburbs, where they could live in areas with lower crime rates and lower population densities. By 1950, for the first time in American history, more people were living in the suburbs than in cities, particularly because of the large number of servicemen and women returning from World War II. These people wanted a piece of the American dream and were starting families. Developers wanted to provide low-cost housing for these people. The federal government encouraged home ownership by insuring mortgage loans and making interest paid on home loans deductible on individual income taxes. Insurance rates for suburban homes and cars were lower than they were in the cities. The result was the emergence of the suburb, a trend that continued through the 1950s and 1960s and in many respects continues today.

A number of other historical developments gave rise to the type of suburb that plays such a prominent role in "Stalking." One was the development of roads, particularly the interstate highway system, which began during the administration of President Dwight Eisenhower in the 1950s. These roads, along with commuter trains, made it easier for suburbanites to commute to work in nearby cities. Another development was the skyscraper. Although skyscrapers had been built earlier, throughout the 1950s and 1960s skyscrapers became commonplace in cities. If one imagines "Stalking" taking place in a Detroit suburb, an example of the skyscraper is Detroit's Renaissance Center, which was built during the 1970s. One of the effects of the skyscraper was to make urban land much more valuable and expensive. The high cost of urban land made it difficult for people to buy homes in the cities. For this reason, many moved to the suburbs, where land and homes were less expensive. This cheaper land also provided opportunities for retail businesses. To serve the needs of growing suburbs, malls sprung up all

COMPARE & CONTRAST

- **1972:** In response to the decay, high crime rates, and crowding of many American cities, more and more people move to the suburbs.

  Today: While suburbs continue to grow, many people, especially young married couples and empty nesters, move back into cities, where many older neighborhoods are renovated and where cultural and other activities are more readily available.

- **1972:** The war in Vietnam is beginning to wind down, although it is still being fought. Many people continue to protest the war, and many young people begin losing faith in the government and other institutions.

  Today: Many older people who grew up in the 1960s and 1970s now hold positions of authority in government, education, journalism, and other institutions. Many protest the war in Iraq, while others protest various government policies in such matters as health care, taxes, and the federal budget.

- **1972:** During the preceding two decades, median household incomes increase by nearly 100 percent, creating considerable growth and expansion in the United States and contributing to greater affluence among many Americans.

  Today: During the two decades of the 1990s and 2000s, median household income increases by only about 10 percent, limiting growth and contributing to a sense of shrinking possibilities.

---

over the suburban landscape. These malls could be sprawling affairs with ample parking and a wide range of shopping options under one roof, where the temperature was controlled and shoppers did not have to contend with weather. As malls were built in the 1960s and 1970s, many downtown shopping areas, both in major cities and in smaller cities and towns, died out.

Many sociologists and social observers decried the suburbanization of the United States during this period. They argued that the suburbs tended to isolate people, in contrast to the city, where people congregated and developed a community life and where they could attend plays, concerts, baseball games, and other events. The suburbs, critics said, induced conformity. People had to have the same green lawns, the same barbeque grills, the same furniture, and the same cars. They contributed to crowding of the roads and pollution as more people drove long distances to work, and those distances grew longer as suburbs sprawled ever farther away from city centers. Suburbs killed many traditional downtown areas, whose businesses could no longer compete with businesses in the suburbs. Most important, critics of the suburbanization typified in "Stalking" pointed to its psychological effects. Suburbanites, it was argued, were rootless, tossed into a bland, conformist, standardized world that lacked the texture and vitality of the city and the sense of belonging often found in small towns and rural areas. This sense of rootlessness could have a major impact on teenagers such as Gretchen, who become disaffected and isolated and express their emotions through antisocial behavior.

CRITICAL OVERVIEW

Oates's critical reputation has varied over time. For some critics, her best work was her earliest work, and the later work is of lesser quality. Some critics, too, have argued that her output is too large, and these critics suggest that she dashes out material without giving it enough thought. In *Critical Essays on Joyce Carol Oates*, Linda

She spotted her mom riding the escalator. *(Andre Blais | Shutterstock.com)*

W. Wagner summarizes this fluctuation in the author's critical reputation:

> Critical reaction to Oates' writing has varied unpredictably.... That reaction could serve as a barometer for changes in literary taste ... as the once respectable mode of realism fell further and further from fashion.... Critics persisted in emphasizing her early efforts, in seeing all her writing as an outgrowth of the original fiction.

Wagner concludes that "the range of Oates' critical reception has been from enthusiastic praise to the present 'faint praise' which undermines even if it does not directly attack."

Ronald De Feo expresses a lack of enthusiasm about Oates's work. In "Only Prairie Dog Mounds," originally published in the *National Review* and reprinted in Linda W. Wagner's *Critical Essays on Joyce Carol Oates*, he comments on *Marriages and Infidelities*, the collection in which "Stalking" appeared. He calls it a "disappointing volume," and he says that "she generally fails to interest us in her dreary lot,"

referring to her characters. He concludes that in the collection "we find merely efficient, colorless, flat prose; unsubtle, forgettable characterizations. We feel that the writer is hurrying along at careless breakneck speed."

Despite these criticisms, most scholars and reviewers have found much to admire in Oates's work. In *Joyce Carol Oates: A Study of the Short Fiction*, Greg Johnson comments on the author's "complex and wide-ranging engagement with literary tradition." Johnson also describes the story's connection with others in the volume: "Some relationship to 'the other,' therefore, regardless of the person's identity—spouse, lover, or child— becomes a symbiotic, usually doomed attempt at self-realization." With regard to "Stalking," he writes that in her hunt for the Invisible Adversary, Gretchen is "unconsciously projecting a wounded and unloved version of herself outward as a convenient enemy and object of her rage." In the same volume, Johnson reprints a review of *Marriages and Infidelities* by William Abrahams, who writes that the collection "confirms what has already been evident for some years: In the landscape of the contemporary American short story Miss Oates stands out as a master, occupying a preeminent category of her own." In *Understanding Joyce Carol Oates*, Johnson echoes this judgment, writing that *Marriages and Infidelities* "established her as one of America's preeminent masters of the short story."

Many critics of Oates focus on the broader social implications of her work. Mary Allen, in "The Terrified Women of Joyce Carol Oates," discusses feminist issues. In connection with "Stalking," she writes:

> Women's mortifying effects to their bodies, committed in spite against the importance placed upon appearance or as a direct design against their specific antagonists, are also a way of reacting to the genuine fear of assault.

Similarly, in *Refusal and Transgression in Joyce Carol Oates' Fiction*, Marilyn C. Wesley concludes that "Gretchen's actions in the story rebel against the alienating strictures of a system that would define her in terms—artificial, commercially attractive, thoughtlessly benign—that are appropriate to the stylized world of the salesgirl."

CRITICISM

Michael J. O'Neal

(O'Neal holds a Ph.D. in English. In the following essay, he discusses the mythical concepts of the quest and the labyrinth as a way of understanding "Stalking."

In the early decades of the twentieth century, poets and fiction writers began to explore new ways of executing their art. Many concluded that earlier literature relied too much on description, analysis, and explanation. In their view, fiction writers, for example, tended to stand outside their subject and comment on it. As a result, the reader was unable to enter into a character's life and see the world in the way the character saw it. For this reason, many novelists and short story writers began to compose fiction in a new and different way.

Fueling this search for a new form of fiction was the development of psychology as both a formal discipline and as a philosophy that explored how people come to understand their world. Sigmund Freud, of course, was one of the major names in psychology, and many writers were attracted to his view that people are driven

by unconscious forces, which could be suggested in literature. Another psychologist who had a major impact on literature was Carl Jung. Jung posited the belief that human experience was structured by a set of archetypes that have appeared over and over again in literature, art, and the culture at large. One prominent archetype Jung identified was the shadow. The shadow figure in literature is someone dark, unknown, and perhaps troubling, rather like the Invisible Adversary Gretchen pursues. The shadow archetype embodies chaos and wildness and does not follow rules. It can fascinate other characters and lead them into chaotic situations. Dark enemies, such as Darth Vader in the "Star Wars" series of novels and movies, exemplify the shadow archetype in literature.

In addition to archetypal characters, literature often features archetypal plots. One of the most prominent of these plots is the quest. In mythical literature, central characters often embarked on a quest to find something. Often the "something" was a physical object: a treasure, a religious object, perhaps a place. Usually, in the process of encountering and overcoming obstacles in the quest, the character acquires some sort of wisdom, insight, or growth. In some respects, "Stalking" can be thought of as embodying the quest archetype. Gretchen embarks on a quest to hunt down the Invisible Adversary and along the way she crosses through a wasteland that throws up obstacles in her way. Eventually, she seems to catch the Invisible Adversary, but the story leaves open the question of what she has learned from her quest. She returns home, plops down in front of the television with a Coke, and resolves not to pay attention to the bleeding and injured Invisible Adversary. The question the reader is left with is whether Gretchen has learned anything from her experience.

Another archetypal pattern that has historically been used in literature is that of the labyrinth, that is, a complex maze or system of paths or tunnels in which a person can become lost. Typically, working through a labyrinth is seen as a positive experience. Labyrinths are seen as healing and meditative tools that allow one to take part in a quest for God, self-knowledge, wisdom, serenity, truth, and the like. People who go through labyrinths frequently get lost, forcing them to start over and find their way again. But as the character moves from the

WHAT DO I READ NEXT?

- Oates has written several novels for young adults, including *Big Mouth and Ugly Girl* (2002), *Freaky Green Eyes* (2003), and *After the Wreck, I Picked Myself Up, Spread My Wings, and Flew Away* (2006). She also published a collection of short stories for young adults, *Small Avalanches and Other Stories* (2003). Additionally, her short story "How I Contemplated the World from the Detroit House of Correction and Began My Life Over Again" examines the emotionally sterile life of a fifteen-year-old girl in a Detroit suburb.

- The classic American novel of teenage angst and disaffection is J. D. Salinger's *Catcher in the Rye*, published in 1951. Salinger wrote the book for adults, but it has become widely popular with younger readers, many of whom identify with the novel's protagonist, Holden Caulfield.

- Cecily von Siegesar's *Gossip Girl* series consists of thirteen novels that appeared beginning in 2002 and spawned a television series by the same title. The books trace the lives of privileged teenage girls in a cosmopolitan urban setting.

- Bruce Duffy's 1997 novel *Last Comes the Egg* features a twelve-year-old boy driven by loss and a blend of adolescent innocence and toughness. The novel is a portrayal of a world of emptiness and uncovers the hidden side of the relentlessly optimistic view of America after World War II.

- Helen Benedict's *The Opposite of Love* (2007) is a young-adult novel about a girl name Madge who, as the daughter of a neglectful white mother and a Jamaican father, never feels as though she fits into her rural town.

- Robert Fishman's 1989 book *Bourgeois Utopias: The Rise and Fall of Suburbia* is a critical examination of suburban life from its origins in nineteenth-century London to its particular problems in the United States in the late 1980s.

outer edges of the labyrinth to the center, the character sheds cares, becomes receptive to wisdom and serenity, and is thus able to exit the labyrinth, join the outside world, and bring to that world new insight.

"Stalking" draws in part on the archetype of the labyrinth. Gretchen has been dropped into a world where she has to find her way. In her day-long quest for the Invisible Adversary, she encounters all manner of obstacles along the way. At the start of the story, for example, the Invisible Adversary, with its long legs, jumps up onto a curb of new concrete. Gretchen is not as spry as the Invisible Adversary, so she follows with difficulty. The Adversary leads her through a wasteland of roads under construction, muddy fields, driveways, unfinished or unoccupied buildings, detour signs, zigzag lines, ditches, traffic, mailboxes, and trash cans. She finally arrives at the center of the labyrinth, the shopping mall, which is described in the same geometric terms that might be used to describe a labyrinth: "The Mall is divided into geometric areas, each colored differently; the Adversary leaves the blue pavement and is now on the green." In response to her arrival and the center of the labyrinth, though, Gretchen does not achieve wisdom or serenity. Quite the contrary, her response is to go into a rest room, vandalize it, and try to flush objects down a toilet.

Part of the archetypal pattern of the labyrinth is to leave the labyrinth and return to the world changed in some way. "Stalking" follows this pattern. Gretchen leaves the mall and returns home, but she continues to stalk the Invisible Adversary, suggesting that the trip into the center of the labyrinth has not changed her in any meaningful way. Once again the Invisible Adversary, the "shadow," leads her, this time to the familiar surroundings of her home, although the narration makes it seem as though the Invisible Adversary has selected a house at random, suggesting that to Gretchen the house is not a home. Historically, one feature of the quest pattern has been that the character enters a wood or forest, there to encounter danger and overcome it. In modern suburbia, the best "forest" available to Gretchen is her subdivision, called Piney Woods. In some sense she is victorious over the Invisible Adversary, for the figure is injured and bleeding, in much the same way that, for example, the medieval character Beowulf was able to leave his antagonists (Grendel,

She didn't care that her boots got very muddy. *(Michal Durinik / Shutterstock.com)*

Grendel's mother, and a dragon) bleeding and wounded. While Beowulf becomes king because of his heroic exploits, Gretchen wanders alone in her house, following her normal routine. She turns on the television, but the show she watches is a repeat, one that she has seen before. Gretchen's routine will continue, but the reader is left wondering whether her apparent triumph over the Invisible Adversary will change her in any way.

Source: Michael J. O'Neal, Critical Essay on "Stalking," in *Short Stories for Students*, Gale, Cengage Learning, 2011.

Marilyn C. Wesley

In the following essay, Wesley explains how Oates's fiction challenges gender ideology by describing the characterization of the protagonist of "Stalking."

Although Joyce Carol Oates has frequently been labeled a non-feminist and criticized for the passivity of her female characters, her works actively challenge restrictive gender ideology. A case in point is the Oatesian figure I will define as the transgressive heroine, whose murderous

early debut is the short story "Swamps," the first story in Oates' first collection, and whose continuing truculent influence is felt in the Kali struck heroines of *The Goddess and Other Women*, in the powerful women of *Bellefleur*, and in the wilful artist of *Solstice*, and who is most fully present as the protagonist of the 1972 short story "Stalking."

A previous stage in the evolution of the transgressive heroine is the figure of the *anti-hero*—the protagonist who is "not simply a failed hero but a social misfit, graceless, weak, and often comic, the embodiment of ineptitude and bad luck in a world apparently made for others"—a commonplace in our contemporary literature. "The Hero, who once figured as Initiate, ends as Rebel or Victim," Ihab Hassan explains [in *Radical Innocence*, 1961]. The presentation of this anti-hero places him in counter-relation to the social structure which produces him. Oates' transgressive works, however, recognize the impossibility of the superimposition of an imaginary counter-structure. While the anti-hero, like Ralph Ellison's "invisible man," stages his protest by defining a metaphoric space

> GRETCHEN'S ACTIONS IN THE STORY REBEL
> AGAINST THE ALIENATING STRICTURES OF A
> SYSTEM THAT WOULD DEFINE HER IN TERMS—
> ARTIFICIAL, COMMERCIALLY ATTRACTIVE,
> THOUGHTLESSLY BENIGN—THAT ARE APPROPRIATE
> TO THE STYLIZED WORLD OF THE SALESGIRL."

of freedom and moving outside the system, the transgressive protagonist, unable to dream of lighting out for any territory, however surreal, repeatedly inscribes her discomfort from within. The victimization and ineffective rebelliousness of Oates' transgressive heroines serve to illuminate and interrogate the system which creates them.

Transgression, Michel Foucault argues [in *Language, Counter-Memory, Practice*, 1977], implies an operation more complex than the antithesis of two terms: its purpose, like the repeated violations perpetrated by Oates' transgressive protagonists, is to reveal the dysfunctional interaction between the terms:

> Transgression, then, is not related to the limit as black to white, the prohibited to the lawful, the outside to the inside, or as the open area of a building to its exposed spaces. Rather, their relationship takes the form of a spiral which no simple infraction can exhaust.

Exhibiting such transgression articulates the terms and questions the limits they impose.

In "Stalking," Gretchen, the protagonist, is female—a fact which forces us from the outset to recast the convention of the anti-hero as a problem of gender. Our first glimpse of her indicates her problematic situation:

> She is dressed for the hunt, her solid legs crammed into old blue jeans, her big, square, strong feet jammed into white leather boots that cost her mother forty dollars not long ago, but are now scuffed and filthy with mud. Hopeless to get them clean again, Gretchen doesn't give a damn.

Gretchen is uncomfortably suspended between contradictory ascriptions of gender. Unlike the male anti-hero whose failure is marked by weakness, the transgressive heroine suffers from inappropriate strength. Like the ugly step-sister at the royal ball, she cannot contract her foot to any comfortable relation to the feminine apparel whose value is defined by the social system and promoted by her mother, and hence cannot claim her feminine reward. Her size, her shape, and her manner violate clear demarcation between conventional masculine and feminine identification, an interpretation reinforced by this detailed description of Gretchen's face:

> She has untidy, curly hair that looks like a wig set loosely on her head. Light brown curls spill out everywhere, bouncy, a little frizzy, a cascade, a tumbling of curls. Her eyes are deep set, her eyebrows heavy and dark. She has a stern, staring look, like an adult man. Her nose is perfectly formed, neat and noble. Her upper lip is long, as if it were stretched to close with difficulty over the front teeth. She wears no make-up, her lips are perfectly colorless, pale, a little chapped, and they are usually held tight, pursed tightly shut. She has a firm, rounded chin. Her facial structure is strong, pensive, its features stern and symmetrical as a statue's, blank, neutral, withdrawn. Her face is attractive. But there is a blunt, neutral, sexless stillness to it, as if she were detached from it and somewhere else, uninterested.

The face is, of course, no less coded than the foot. We are used to intimately observed catalogues of features in literature. What is remarkable about the use of the tradition in this story is that Oates rarely employs her gaze in this exhaustive fashion. She sketches her characters by a brief mention of their hair color and then, typically, looks through their eyes at the closely observed world around them rather than into their eyes like a rapt admirer. The function of this sustained description is keyed to the problematics of gender. The hair suggests the familiar associations of female sexuality; but although as a turbulent "cascade," it evokes abundant "nature," which usually signifies feminine sensuality, the suggestion of wig-like appearance quickly undercuts this automatic ascription. Perhaps Gretchen is neither natural nor sensual. In effect, this description invokes the literary code of femininity only to revoke it—a strategy immediately employed again in the next two sentences, where the eyebrows are emphasized as dark and thick, a feature conventionally expressive of masculinity. And, in fact, the eyes, those symbolic windows to essence, return not the modest glance of a woman expected in this context but the provocative stare of "an adult man." Further, this contradiction of femininity is at least a partly willful undertaking of Gretchen herself. Such is the message of the mouth, which has deliberately refused the application of the cosmetic allure of color and is "pursed" in tight rejection. The cumulative effect of this manner of presentation is summarized in the climactic series of adjectives, "blunt, neutral, sexless." Gretchen's statue-like physiognomy, as Oates orchestrates its "meaning," is a complex field of reference upon which is played out the repudiation of conventional femininity.

For Gretchen is, without doubt, an "anti-heroine." At thirteen years of age, her size-fourteen body is evidently "graceless." She is a clear "misfit" in a "world apparently made for others," a world whose gender requirements are garishly evident in the people, objects, and decor of the shopping mall Gretchen visits:

> Dodi's Boutique is decorated in silver and black. Metallic strips hang down from a dark ceiling, quivering. Salesgirls dressed in pants suits stand around with nothing to do except giggle with one another and nod their heads in time to the music amplified throughout the store.... "WCKK. Radio Wonderful...."

> "Need any help?" the girl asks. She has long swinging hair and a high-shouldered, indifferent, bright manner.

Gretchen's actions in the story rebel against the alienating strictures of a system that would define her in terms—artificial, commercially attractive, thoughtlessly benign—that are appropriate to the stylized world of the salesgirl. In one store, Gretchen shoplifts a tube of pale pink lipstick, "Spring Blossom," which she takes into the "Ladies Room" to examine, destroy, and discard. As if to underscore her rejection, she also breaks the toilet into which she tosses the pilfered lipstick. And in Dodi's Boutique, Gretchen takes several dresses into the changing cubicle. She muddies one with her boots; she deliberately tears out the zipper of another.

What changes the focus of this story from Gretchen as a rebel-victim to Gretchen as a transgressive protagonist is the intriguing contest central to the action. Gretchen is not merely out shopping on a November Saturday afternoon; she is engaged in hunting down an imaginary antagonist who leads her from an open field into the mall, through several stores, and home again. "The Invisible Adversary," a male figure, is the conscious target of Gretchen's

hostility throughout the story: "*You'll be sorry for that, you bastard.*" "*You'll regret this.*" "*You'll get yours.*" Gretchen's "stalking" maneuvers finally force the Adversary out onto the highway, where he is struck by a car. He is "limping like an old man" as they both return to Gretchen's home. The story ends with Gretchen watching television: "If the Adversary comes crawling behind her, groaning in pain, weeping, she won't even bother to glance at him."

The sequence of events and attitudes demands that the reader determine who or what the Adversary represents and what his function is in the story. The thematic contest that engages Gretchen, we have already discovered, is the struggle for and against gender identity. Certainly this projection acts out a role in that struggle. In a review of a biography of Carl Jung, Oates indicates her extensive knowledge and admiration of Jungian theory, so we may identify the Adversary as an animus figure, that personification of the masculine component of a woman's unconscious typically projected in dreams and fantasies. The Jungian objective is the integration of all the unconscious elements of the personality, but what is most striking in Gretchen's story is the violence with which she strives to destroy and reject what Jung understood as her masculine nature.

The text suggests only two coded means to gender production, which do not appear to intersect. The woman may participate in the endless replication of the feminine body and her domestic accouterments through purchase encoded in the capitalistic system and epitomized in the reiterated "family rooms" Gretchen sees displayed at the furniture store:

> She wanders through Sampson Furniture....a ritual with her. Again she notices the sofa that is like the sofa in their family room at home.... All over the store there are sofas, chairs, tables, beds....People stroll around them, in and out of little displays, displays meant to be living rooms, dining rooms, bedrooms, family rooms....It makes Gretchen's eyes squint to see so many displays: like seeing the inside of a hundred houses.

Gretchen herself participates directly in the practice of a masculine code of aggression:

> Some boys are fooling around in front of the record store. One of them bumps into Gretchen and they all laugh as she is pushed against a trash can. "Watch it, babe!" the boy sings out.

Her leg hurts. Gretchen doesn't look at them but, with a cold, swift anger, her face averted, she knocks the trash can over onto the sidewalk. Junk falls out. The can rolls. Some women shoppers scurry to get out of the way and the boys laugh.

That the seemingly desultory destructiveness is really constitutive is evident in the emphatic differentiation in this encounter between the powerful males and the victimized female "babe," between the forceful Gretchen imitating the masculine mode and the flustered powerless women. Further, Gretchen's general anger and resultant vandalism are codified in the story as components of the ritualized stalking, hunting, and killing—activities of the primitive male hero. But Gretchen is not a hero, although it is her masculine capacity for anger and physical strength that compromises her participation in the feminine world "apparently made for others."

In the same way that she has tried to feminize her large feet by stuffing them into the feminine white boots purchased by her mother, only to finally react by desecrating them when the transformation proved inadequate and incompatible, Gretchen responds with distressed ambivalence to the gender definitions of her shopping-center world. Rather than embracing her masculine capabilities to define herself as a rebel contradicting, negating, restrictive feminine identification, Gretchen becomes a transgressor. Instead of claiming, like the "invisible man," some free but lunatic space outside the arena of constricting definition—the open field of the "Invisible Adversary" at the beginning of this story, for example—Gretchen compulsively enters and re-enters the mall, where she is repeatedly attracted to its signifying objects. She reaches for the lipstick and the dresses again and again, only to destroy them out of frustration at their lack of congruence with her own requirements. By fantasizing the destruction of her masculine capabilities, Gretchen reveals a maladaptive complicity with a code of feminine definition which will confine her to the characteristic but ineffective rage that her story presents.

"Stalking" illustrates the transgressive "spiral" which by repeatedly desecrating limitation exposes it to examination and interrogation. Underlying the concept of the transgressive heroine is the assumption that a rule which is "transgressed" is not destroyed but merely violated. Such violation calls attention to conditions that provoke defiance—a gender ideology which

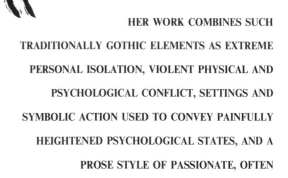

HER WORK COMBINES SUCH TRADITIONALLY GOTHIC ELEMENTS AS EXTREME PERSONAL ISOLATION, VIOLENT PHYSICAL AND PSYCHOLOGICAL CONFLICT, SETTINGS AND SYMBOLIC ACTION USED TO CONVEY PAINFULLY HEIGHTENED PSYCHOLOGICAL STATES, AND A PROSE STYLE OF PASSIONATE, OFTEN MELODRAMATIC INTENSITY."

supports economic rather than human development in this case—at the same time that it underscores their continuing existence. The repetition of this maneuver produces not reform, but the possibility of reform. "Transgression," according to Foucault, "carries the limit right to the limit. . . ; transgression forces the limit to face the fact of its imminent disappearance. . . ." The transgressive heroine of Oates' fiction, a female protagonist who repeatedly violates the forms of gender stricture without personally solving the social problem of gender restriction, promotes feminist reform, understood as literary challenge to patriarchal ideology.

Source: Marilyn C. Wesley, "The Transgressive Heroine: Joyce Carol Oates's 'Stalking,'" in *Studies in Short Fiction*, Vol. 27, No. 1, Winter 1990, pp. 15–20.

Greg Johnson

In the following excerpt, Johnson presents a favorable assessment of Oates's literary career.

In the 1980s Oates remains a major force in contemporary American writing. Aside from her fiction and her teaching, she is a prolific poet, critic, and book reviewer; several of her plays have been produced in New York; and she is an extremely popular, engaging speaker on college campuses across the country. She also serves as coeditor of the *Ontario Review*, a literary magazine which she and her husband inaugurated in 1974 in Windsor, and continue to operate from their home in Princeton. Her achievement is all the more extraordinary when one considers that she is still in her forties and may now be viewed as entering the middle stage of her illustrious career.

Joyce Carol Oates's versatility as a fiction writer relates directly to her overwhelming fascination with the phenomenon of contemporary America: its colliding social and economic forces, its philosophical contradictions, its wayward, often violent energies. Taken as a whole, Oates's fiction portrays America as a seething, vibrant "wonderland" in which individual lives are frequently subject to disorder, dislocation, and extreme psychological turmoil. Her protagonists range from inner-city dwellers and migrant workers to intellectuals and affluent suburbanites; but all her characters, regardless of background, suffer intensely the conflicts and contradictions at the heart of our culture—a suffering Oates conveys with both scrupulous accuracy and great compassion.

Her particular genius is her ability to convey psychological states with unerring fidelity, and to relate the intense private experiences of her characters to the larger realities of American life. "I think I have a vulnerability to a vibrating field of other people's experiences," she told an interviewer in 1972. "I lived through the '60s in the United States, I was aware of hatreds and powerful feelings all around me." Her frequently remarked tendency to focus upon psychological terror and imbalance thus relates directly to her vision of America, what Alfred Kazin has called "her sweetly brutal sense of what American experience is really like." Though she has been accused of using gratuitous or obsessive violence in her work, Oates has insisted that her violent materials accurately mirror the psychological and social convulsions of our time. In an acerbic essay titled "Why Is Your Writing So Violent?," she points out that "serious writers, as distinct from entertainers or propagandists, take for their natural subjects the complexity of the world, its evils as well as its goods. . . . The serious writer, after all, bears witness."

In responding to the "vibrating field of other people's experiences," Oates's imagination has created hundreds and possibly thousands of fictional characters: people coping with the phantasmagoric wonderland of American life and suffering various degrees of psychological and spiritual isolation. Her typical protagonist is tragically blinded to the possibility of the "communal consciousness" that Oates sees as a likely salvation for our culture. . . . Positing the hopeful idea that the violent conflicts in American culture represent not an "apocalyptic close" but a "transformation of being," Oates suggests that we are experiencing "a simple evolution into a higher humanism, perhaps a kind of intelligent pantheism, in which all substance in the universe (including the substance fortunate enough to perceive it) is there by equal right."

Because this epoch of cultural transcendence has not yet arrived, Oates has conceived her primary role as an artist who must dramatize the nightmarish conditions of the present, with all its anxiety, paranoia, dislocation, and explosive conflict. Her fiction has often focused particularly on the moment when a combined psychological and cultural malaise erupts into violence; and despite the notable variety of her character portrayals, there are several representative "types" that recur frequently and present distinctive facets of the turbulent American experience.

There are the confused adolescents, for instance, like Connie in "Where Are You Going, Where Have You Been?" and Jules in *them*, essentially innocent, romantic souls whose fantasies and ideals collide with the environment and with the imperatives of their own maturity. There are the young women seeking fulfillment in adulterous love, like the heroines of "Unmailed, Unwritten Letters" and "The Lady with the Pet Dog," and like Elena of *Do With Me What You Will*, all of whom seek redemption outside marriages originally based upon the expectations of others. There are the tough, earthy women like Clara in *A Garden of Earthly Delights*, Loretta in *them*, and Arlene in *Childwold*, each rising from an impoverished childhood, developing considerable resilience and cunning, and dealing shrewdly with a male-dominated society. There are the brilliant but emotionally needy intellectuals like Hugh in *The Assassins* (1975), Kasch in *Childwold*, Brigit in *Unholy Loves* (1979), and Marya in *Marya: A Life*, whose lives dramatize Oates's ironic view of a culture that values "masculine" intellect at the expense of "feminine" intuitive knowledge and that inhibits, on the individual level, a healthy integration of reason and emotion. There are the middle-aged men who control society, like the businessman Curt Revere in *A Garden of Earthly Delights*, the megalomaniac Dr. Pedersen in *Wonderland*, and the lawyer Marvin Howe in *Do With Me What You Will*. And there are the doomed, literally "mad" characters, like Allen Weinstein in "In the Region of Ice," Richard Everett in *Expensive People*, and T. W. Monk in *Wonderland*, young people whose inner conflicts drive them to the point of madness or suicide.

This bare-bones summary of the most frequently recurring character types in Oates's fiction scarcely does justice to the subtlety of individual characterization she lavishes on each, but it does suggest Oates's major fictional concerns and the distinct ways in which her work focuses upon the intense conflict between the individual and his social environment. While some aspects of her work—especially the increasingly hopeful resolutions of her more recent novels—may hint at "transcendence," she remains notable as an industrious chronicler of America's personal and collective nightmares.

Understanding the violent and frequently ironic terms of the American experience, Oates has employed a notable variety of aesthetic approaches in her attempt to convey such an immense, kaleidoscopic, and frequently grotesque reality. In a much-quoted remark Philip Roth has said that "the American writer in the middle of the 20th century has his hands full in trying to describe, and then to make credible, much of the American reality. It stupefies, it sickens, it infuriates, and finally it is even a kind of embarrassment to one's own meager imagination. The actuality is continually outdoing our talents."

Yet Joyce Carol Oates has met this challenge with increasingly bold and resourceful experiments in fiction, sharing not the postmodernist concerns of John Barth or William Gass solely with language and its aesthetic possibilities, but rather the Victorian faith of Dickens or George Eliot in the efficacy of the novel in dealing with profound social and philosophical themes. Oates has thus adhered throughout her career to the novel of ideas and to the mode of psychological realism, while at the same time producing highly experimental works of fiction that both complement her more traditional work and allow her to present the daunting American reality in terms of myth, antirealism, and other forms of literary intrigue. As John Barth noted in a seminal essay dealing with the traditional versus the experimental in fiction, "Joyce Carol Oates writes all over the aesthetical map."

. . . Some of Oates's best-known short stories published during this same period showed similar concerns, dealing with such "representative" characters as the adolescent girl from an affluent home who has a compulsion to shoplift and eventually serves as the sardonic narrator for "How I Contemplated the World from the Detroit House of Correction and Began My Life Over Again"; the reserved Catholic nun of "In the Region of Ice," suffering a crisis of faith and conscience in her dealings with an unstable Jewish student; the well-to-do businessman in "Stray Children," drawn unwillingly into a relationship with a dependent, drug-saturated girl who claims to be his daughter; and the married woman conducting a doomed love affair in "The Lady with the Pet Dog," Oates's "re-imagining" of the famous Chekhov story. These stories along with dozens of others published in *The Wheel of Love, Marriages and Infidelities* and other collections have in common both a riveting psychological intensity and an authoritative, all-inclusive vision of "what American experience is really like" for people who suffer various kinds of emotional turmoil and who, like the title characters in *them*, become emblematic of America as a whole.

Oates's attempts to dramatize this turmoil, and often to convey psychological states at the very border of sanity, have often led her into the fictional mode loosely described as "gothicism." Her work combines such traditionally gothic elements as extreme personal isolation, violent physical and psychological conflict, settings and symbolic action used to convey painfully heightened psychological states, and a prose style of passionate, often melodramatic intensity. The combination of rural settings and psychological malaise in her earlier fiction, for instance, prompted some reviewers to align Oates with the gothic tradition of Southern literature, suggesting that she had been influenced by William Faulkner, Flannery O'Connor, and Carson McCullers. Certainly her bewildered, inarticulate characters, fighting their losing battles against a backdrop of brooding fatalism, do bear a spiritual kinship to the Southern isolates of Faulkner and McCullers in particular. Oates has often stated her admiration for Southern fiction, but the dynamic, hallucinatory power of her best work recalls not only Southern gothicism but also the psychological explorations of Dostoevsky, the nightmare visions of Franz Kafka, and even the fantastic world of Lewis Carroll. . . .

To describe much of Oates's fiction as gothic in nature is not to resort to a convenient label or to suggest any limitations of theme or subject matter. The tenor of Oates's prose, however—her distinctive "voice"—often conveys the kind of extreme psychological intensity, and occasionally the outright horror, traditionally associated with gothic fiction. As Oates commented in 1980, "gothic with a small-letter 'g'" suggests "a work in which extremes of emotion are unleashed"—a description which could be applied to virtually all her novels. Whether rich or poor, cultured or uneducated, the majority of her characters live within a psychological pressure-cooker, responding to intense personal and societal conflicts which lead almost inevitably to violence. The critic G. F. Waller has discussed at length this "obsessive vision" at the heart of Oates's rendering of the American reality. As Oates herself has observed, "Gothicism, whatever it is, is not a literary tradition so much as a fairly realistic assessment of modern life."

Oates has also used the gothic tradition explicitly in short stories dealing with the paranormal, collected in *Night-Side* (1979), and in her cycle of genre novels begun in 1980, novels appropriately described by Oates as Gothic "with a capital-letter G." In *Bellefleur* (1980), *A Bloodsmoor Romance* (1982) and *Mysteries of Winterthurn* (1984), Oates combines her usual psychological realism with a free-wheeling, explicit use of fantasy, fairy tales, horror stories, and other Gothic elements; the central settings of all three novels, for instance, include a huge, forbidding mansion and such assorted horrors as a female vampire (*Bellefleur*) and a painting which comes to life and murders a couple on their honeymoon (*Mysteries of Winterthurn*). [Of *Bellefleur*, Oates said] "I set out originally to create an elaborate, baroque, barbarous metaphor for the unfathomable mysteries of the human imagination, but soon became involved in very literal events."

Her handling of these "literal events" shows a characteristic inclusiveness in her desire to present a sweeping social and philosophical vision of American history. Oates has described her specific attraction to the Gothic mode in these novels:

> To 'see' the world in terms of heredity and family destiny and the vicissitudes of Time (for all five novels are secretly fables of the American family); to explore historically authentic crimes against women, children, and the poor; to create, and to identify with, heroes and heroines whose existence would be problematic in the clinical, unkind, and one might almost say, fluorescent-lit atmosphere of present-day fiction—these factors proved irresistible....

It should be clear that despite the sheer abundance and inclusiveness of Oates's fiction,

her work does not represent an aesthetic surrender to the chaos of "real life" or the failure of a driven, highly productive artist to organize her materials; yet such well-known critics as Alfred Kazin and Walter Sullivan, accustomed to the more typical modern writer who might manage a single book every five or even ten years, leveled exactly these charges against her work in the 1970s and helped create the impression of Oates as a careless, haphazard writer, working in a trancelike state and continually pouring forth novels and stories without adequate concern for their literary integrity or coherence....

Critics in the 1980s occasionally repeat these charges, but one suspects that they cannot have read Oates's work very extensively or thoughtfully. As the late John Gardner remarked in an appreciative review of *Bellefleur*, "for pseudo-intellectuals there are always too many books," and over the years Oates has patiently responded to the charges of excessive productivity....

Late twentieth-century criticism, nourished on modernist and postmodernist works, has frequently devalued or simply lost sight of the artist as a committed, energetic craftsman, producing the kinds of ambitious, socially relevant novels that had virtually defined the genre in the Victorian era. Such esteemed nineteenth-century writers as Dickens, Balzac, Trollope and Henry James all wrote steadily, daily, and produced many volumes, unharassed by critical suggestions that they slow down or stop altogether. The modernist conception of the creative process as infinitely slow and tortuous, resulting in a single exquisite work after long years of painstaking labor, combined with the particularly American view of the writer as a hero of experience, like Ernest Hemingway or F. Scott Fitzgerald, someone who must travel the world, live as colorfully as possible, and preferably drink to excess, has perhaps influenced critical attacks on Oates, who not only writes voluminously but leads a quiet, disciplined life that she once called "a study in conventionality." And much of the criticism clearly stems, as Oates herself has noted, from simple envy.

Any reader making his way through such a skillfully paced family chronicle as *them*, or the complicated series of interlocking tales that comprise *Bellefleur*, or an intricately constructed political novel like *Angel of Light* (1981), can have little doubt that Oates is an extremely careful and deliberate craftsman.... Occasionally her patience in the face of critical attacks has worn thin. In 1979 she emphasized her dedication to craftsmanship, reacting angrily to one critic's speculation that she wrote in a trancelike state, "a fever of possession": "I revise extensively. I am passionate about the craftsmanship of writing. I am perfectly conscious when I write, and at other selected times.... Will I never escape such literary-journalism drivel? Year after year, the same old cliches."

Oates will probably never escape the "drivel" of those critics who prefer attacking her to considering thoughtfully her voluminous, carefully written works. What matters to Oates is the work itself, not its critical reception or her own notoriety. Despite her occasional remarks hinting at exhaustion, her passionate engagement with her craft continues.... Despite the occasional criticism, her reputation continues to grow not only in the United States but worldwide: she is a member of the American Academy and Institute of Arts and Letters, and has been nominated several times for the Nobel Prize for literature. Although it is pointless to speculate about which of her works future generations will consider her masterpiece—quite possibly, she has not yet written the book that will be viewed as representing the full range of her talents—it is clear that Joyce Carol Oates has already earned her place alongside the major American writers of the twentieth century.

Source: Greg Johnson, "Understanding Joyce Carol Oates," in *Understanding Joyce Carol Oates*, University of South Carolina Press, 1987.

Linda W. Wagner

In the following excerpt, Wagner declares that despite the emphasis on fact and character, the assumption that the artist is in control is absent in Oates's fiction.

To view Oates' fiction in retrospect is to be surprised that what seemed to be basically "realistic" fiction has so many variations, and shows such range of experimentation, such wealth of literary antecedent. But whether she writes a comic *Expensive People*, an impressionistic *Childwold*, or that strangely heightened realism of *them* and the short stories, her interest is less in technical innovation than it is in trying the border between the real and the illusory, in testing the space in which those two seemingly separate entities converge....

Oates' conviction—made increasingly clear in the progression of her fiction—is that people in the modern world generally pretend to be tied to the factual, the largely physical details of living (accordingly, reassuringly, she will give numerous details about a dimestore cosmetic counter or a physician's crowded dining table). But although we focus on these tangible props, our understanding of them does not necessarily help us apprehend the larger forces behind them. Oates has repeatedly been called a "realist" because her technique often does suggest that method; but for the most part, her accumulation of fact is an irony—locating and describing the easily discernible is precisely what will *not* work in any full confrontation with reality.... The fascination for Oates as writer lies in acknowledging that her readers' interest will center on character rather than on milieu ("All literature deals with contests of will"), and then working within a method which seems to emphasize the latter.

If Oates is never a simple realist, neither is she the traditional character-oriented story teller. Her insistence on the importance of character remains oblique to usual protestations of that sort. Since one of the comforts of art is that it allows the artist to create order, to impose a personal moral standard on chaotic surroundings, most writers use character to reflect those personal standards.

In Oates' fiction, for all its emphasis on fact and all its reliance on powerful character, the assumption that the artist is in control is clearly absent. Artist-as-judge has become artist-as-recorder. Her readers have sometimes expressed dismay that such unpleasant things happen to characters, while Oates as author appears to have little opinion about these reprehensible situations—little opinion, little sympathy, little outrage. What kind of moral judgment underlies Oates' fiction? So different is her approach to the use of character-to-instruct that many readers feel uncomfortable interpreting her fiction.... [Oates] tends to judge implicitly. Content to observe people in their usually mundane worlds, she presents them in their touching inarticulateness; most important, she ascribes little if any "meaning" to their suffering. Recognizing the mysteries of life—especially at this commonplace and often silent level—is Oates' accomplishment; translating that mute suffering so that readers are moved by it even when they do not fully understand it is her aim.

Oates's fascination with character has, in effect, created her prolegomenon, for her world view is one that recognizes the primacy of emotion over reason, that emphasizes the reality of human passion.... The force, the intensity of passion, is an index of a character's being able to transcend the trivial. All these details in Oates' fiction insist, more clearly than any philosophical treatise could, that the mundane will only starve us; that coherent pattern is not, in itself, adequate. Her admiration for writers such as Chekhov, Yeats, and the absurdist playwrights stems from the fact that they resist "systematic definitions"; they "remain true to their subject—life—by refusing to reduce their art to a single emotion and idea."

[Her] collection of short fiction, *Scenes from American Life*, presents a paradigm of Oates' personal movement from the ostensibly objective and factual to the strange, mysterious, fantastic—or, at least, inexplicable.

Oates' own stylistic changes, and her approaches to what have remained remarkably consistent themes, depend in large part on that kind of progression—from dealing with "lies that seem quite plausible" to "lies that exhibit themselves proudly as lies"; from the painfully serious to the near-comic or grotesque; from the halting pace of detailed realism to the flurry of surreal speed. The progression is not, of course, rigid; hints of Oates' later styles occurred in her first writings. The connotation of "progression" to suggest a linear course is somewhat misleading: Oates' later fiction moves instead toward an unfolding, an opening; its movement is circular rather than linear, hoping to lead in and down as well as out, aiming toward revealing those emotions common to every person—reader, character, author.

Most of [her characters] look for fulfillment in romantic love, although in Oates' fiction, genuine love is rare. It remains illusive, even though mentor figures deify it.... Oates' plots are often based on the search for love; perhaps that is one reason she writes frequently about teenagers, though her characters of every age and marital state are usually in quest of some idealized romance. This pervasive use of the love relationship suggests the real vacuum in the lives (and imaginations) of her characters. For example, the single-mindedness of the fifteen-year-old Connie in "Where Are You Going, Where Have You Been?" underscores the assumptions of the title—women and girls are possessions to be watched, valuable chiefly for their physical properties (beauty, chastity). In Oates' cryptic accumulation of detail, she conveys not only literal meanings but also attitudes toward the women described.... Choosing the term "psychological realism," Oates achieves her seemingly objective tone... at least partly by writing in third person. No matter how many factual details she gives about a character, the point of view distances the reader....

[Knowledge] in Oates' early novels is presented didactically. By the time of *them*, 1969, she has modified her third-person exposition enough to rely a bit more on the image and scene conveying meaning.... For all its third-person perspective, [scenes in *them* resemble] the kind of stream-of-consciousness she used in *Expensive People* and would use to a greater extent in *The Assassins: A Book of Hours* and *Childwold*.... The possessed Kasch of *Childwold* could only be believable through an interior monologue.... Oates' change to first person enables her to follow the non-rational impulses of her characters, to give her readers some insight into that mysterious world of emotion that prompts most action. For her at least, the third-person appeared to be less flexible; and those characters developed in fiction told objectively too often remained enigmas to her readers. The mixture of first and third in *Son of the Morning* works very well; this novel also has a concentration of focus on a single character that is new to Oates' fiction.

Regardless of the difference in effect between Oates' third-person and first-person narrative, her fiction continues to show patterns and oddities of contemporary life.

For a writer so dedicated to shaping our vision of American culture, and so interested in revealing the mysterious forces of human response, Oates' later novels hardly diminish the bleakness of her first fiction; but their method is somewhat changed. That her canvas remains the same is more a charge to our responsibility than to hers.

Source: Linda W. Wagner, "Oates: The Changing Shapes of Her Realities," in *Great Lakes Review*, Vol. 5, No. 2, Winter 1979, pp. xvii–xxxi.

Samuel F. Pickering, Jr.
In the following essay, Pickering compares Oates's earlier short stories to the later stories.

By the North Gate [was] Miss Oates's first collection of stories.... For the most part

> "TAKING A LONG-RANGE, AND THEREFORE SOMEWHAT DISTORTED, VIEW OF MISS OATES'S SHORT STORIES, IT LOOKS AS IF SHE MAY HAVE WRITTEN HERSELF INTO A CORNER."

describing the spare life of hill people in Eden County, the stories successfully tie their characters to the primitive, often inexplicable, rhythms of the land. Taking her cue from Eliot, who wrote in "The Hollow Men" that the shadow fell between the idea and the act, Miss Oates depicts the mysterious shadows that change lives. Men's best laid plans go astray for reasons which neither they nor the reader quite understand. Heightening readers' feelings in order to deepen an awareness of the mystery of human life, the stories successfully appeal to the sympathetic imagination. In "Why Distant Objects Please," William Hazlitt, the romantic theorist, explained the concept, writing: "Whatever is placed beyond the reach of sense and knowledge, whatever is imperfectly discerned, the fancy pieces out at its leisure." In other words a viewer is forced to complete his vision by using his imagination creatively. Similarly, Miss Oates obscures events in her stories in order to force the reader to become an imaginative participant in the narrative. The danger inherent in this technique is obvious. Concrete events become so hazy that instead of being creatively involved in the tale, the reader loses the narrative thread. In *By the North Gate*, however, unlike Miss Oates's later collections, the appeal to the sympathetic imagination rarely undermines the narrative and as a result contributes to the stories' power. A sense of mystery enhances "Swamps," "By the North Gate," and the superb "Census Taker," for example; whereas in "Spiral," "Plot," and "Where I Lived and What I Lived For" (found in *Marriages and Infidelities*, 1972) the narrative line is so tenuous and the shadow so emphasized that the stories break up on the granite rock of obscurity.

In contrast to her later tales, in which the spaces between people become bigger, *By the North Gate* conveys not only a sense of community but also the positive values conveyed by

communal living. Illustrating that a community rests on both need and duty, "Ceremonies" criticizes the self-sufficient and consequently isolated man. In "Swamps," although he is destroyed, the grandfather's personal [benevolence] is a creative force. On the other hand the violence of the drifters in "Boys at a Picnic" seems to stem in part from their lack of belonging. In her later stories, though, Miss Oates draws her villains in more heightened colors, cutting melodramatic cartoon characters from the cloth of corrupt Byronic heroes. Out of step with the conventions of all societies, these characters exist in a state of preternatural tension which they resolve only through action. Unlike the true romantic, a Childe Harold, who resolved the tension produced through his conflict with society into art, Miss Oates's characters strike out blindly and bloodily. In "The Man That Turned into a Statue" (*Upon the Sweeping Flood*, 1966), the hero, a piece of flotsam forever brushing violently against society, asserts his individuality and *Clockwork Orange* creativity by killing three people.

In Miss Oates's later volumes, the positive aspects of community disappear. More often than not suburbia takes its place. With the natural man smothered and creativity frustrated, Miss Oates's suburbanites live lives of quiet vulgarity, punctuated only by demons descending from without or rising from suppressed psychological urges within. As a result the stories flow smoothly from breakdowns and rapes to suicides and murders. Plucking a different but just as hackneyed a chord as Horatio Alger, these tales provide no surprises. Their conventions resemble those of the gothic novel with neuroses replacing skeletons in closets and the moan of sexual ecstasy drowning out the heroine's last sigh as she falls faintingly and innocently to the castle floor.

Except for the fine story from which the volume takes its name, Eden County plays a much smaller part in *Upon the Sweeping Flood* than it did in *By the North Gate*. More important in this collection are the subjects which dominate Miss Oates's later volumes: academic life, childhood, death, and Catholicism. The pictures of academic life are the stuff from which Miss Oates's weakest tales are made. There are no sentimental Mr. Chipses, no hilarious Lucky Jims, and no absurd or brilliant "Peacocky" conversations. Instead, echoing the weaknesses of Zola's "Experimental Novel," under the guise of realism, we are given dreary people with dull vices wandering in psychological mazes. Certainly such people exist, but they constitute only a part, not the whole, of any world, academic or otherwise. Moreover stories which rely on excessive detail ("The Expense of Spirit" and "Archways") in order to convey realism, yet are filled with unrepresentative characters are paradoxically unrealistic.

Aware of its power, Faulkner used *Ecclesiastes* to add depth and meaning to *As I Lay Dying*. In *The Dubliners*, Joyce not only made readers aware of the corruptions of religion but also the richness that it adds, has added, and will add to the citizens of Dublin. Miss Oates, on the other hand, seems content merely to describe the abuses of religion. Consequently her stories about Catholicism are often one-dimensional and do not strike chords that roll from soul to soul and force readers to put her stories in a larger perspective.

"Dying" is a ponderously serious tale about a man's slow death and is the ancestor of "Loving, Losing, Loving a Man." Here again, devoid of humor, Miss Oates's world is unnaturally narrow. In *Look Homeward Angel* Thomas Wolfe showed us that serious depictions of death need not be solemn. In *Pickwick Papers* Jingles' anecdote of the coach passenger whose head was knocked off by a low bridge while she ate a ham sandwich taught us that death need not be the slightest bit serious. An inability to laugh is Miss Oates's greatest limitation. Certainly her world should not be that of the Drones Club and Bertie Wooster, but the merest touch of Galahad Threepwood or the Empress of Blandings would make me, at least, take her seriousness more seriously. With broader views some of our young writers...create worlds in which man is capable of acting not only pathetically, but also humorously and tragically.

In Joyce Carol Oates's later stories, the Keats-like quest for a life of sensations, in opposition to a humdrum existence in suburbia, controls the psyches of the main characters. After granting that Miss Oates's last two volumes (*The Wheel of Love* and *Marriages and Infidelities*) are in some way about love, or at least intimate relationships, "hips jammed together in languid violence" still dominate the stories to an inordinate degree. Moreover there are no simple tumbles in the hay. Copulating becomes a terribly serious act. fraught with all sorts of psychological

bugbears....All this is not to say, though, that these volumes contain only poor stories. On the contrary, many are well-written and provocative. In particular "Shame" describing a priest's rejection of life after a confrontation with sordid fertility and "Problem of Adjustment of Survivors in Natural/Unnatural Disasters" showing the effects of mental and physical earthquakes on a small boy are first-rate. Others including "The Happy Onion" about a young girl's love for a rock idol and "Bodies" about, I think, the reality of life and the artifice of art, are not far behind.

In spite of these successes, there remains a heaviness and single-mindedness about the stories in the volumes.

Over the past decade the world of Joyce Carol Oates's stories has shifted from a comparatively objective, albeit oftentimes mysterious, reality to a subjective reality and a heavy emphasis on psychology. Over half the stories in *Marriages and Infidelities* are in some way about mentally disturbed people, or at least whose way of seeing life is not "normal."...In trying to render the peculiar worlds of these characters, the stories lean heavily on stream of consciousness technique and processes of association which are almost unfathomable. Moreover as the characters fall further into subjectivism, and deny the reality of external reality, their worlds narrow until they are left With the final reality: the body. As a result sexual activity becomes important as a proof of their existence. In "Bodies" an impoverished artist cum rejected lover, slashes his throat so that his blood spurts on a beautiful woman.... This denial of all reality except for the body is, of course, but a halfway house. The next step is the denial of the body, and in "29 Inventions" this occurs.

Taking a long-range, and therefore somewhat distorted, view of Miss Oates's short stories, it looks as if she may have written herself into a corner. Her world and its range of characters have never been broad. Moreover when all reality becomes subjective, the body, then sentence structures, finally words themselves, become too subjective to convey meaning to a wide audience. Once then the story becomes inexpressible in conventional terms, the literary alternative is to experiment with the form of the genre. This, however, is chancy; and for every successful Sterne, there are countless failures. Although exciting perhaps to the cognoscenti, Miss Oates's experiments with form in *Marriages and Infidelities*,

"Nightmusic" and "Plots" in particular, are not successful.

Source: Samuel F. Pickering, Jr., "The Short Stories of Joyce Carol Oates," in *Georgia Review*, Summer 1974, pp. 218–26.

SOURCES

Abrahams, William, "Stories of a Visionary," in *Joyce Carol Oates: A Study of the Short Fiction*, edited by Greg Johnson, Twayne Publishers, 1994, p. 164.

Allen, Mary, "The Terrified Women of Joyce Carol Oates," in *Joyce Carol Oates*, edited by Harold Bloom, Chelsea House, 1987, p. 66.

De Feo, Ronald, "Only Prairie Dog Mounds," in *Critical Essays on Joyce Carol Oates*, edited by Linda W. Wagner, G. K. Hall, 1979, p. 31.

Johnson, Greg, ed., *Joyce Carol Oates: A Study of the Short Fiction*, Twayne Publishers, 1994.

Johnson, Greg, *Understanding Joyce Carol Oates*, University of South Carolina Press, 1987, pp. 5, 8.

Oates, Joyce Carol, "Stalking," in *Marriage and Infidelities*, Vanguard Press, 1972, pp. 171–79.

Wagner, Linda W., ed., "Introduction," in *Critical Essays on Joyce Carol Oates*, G. K. Hall, 1979, p. xxiii.

Wesley, Marilyn C., *Refusal and Transgression in Joyce Carol Oates' Fiction*, Greenwood Press, 1993, p. 94.

FURTHER READING

Hayden, Delores, *Building Suburbia: Green Fields and Urban Growth, 1820–2000*, Pantheon, 2003.
This volume is an examination of suburban life in the United States. It discusses not only the facts of suburbanization but also the suburbs' cultural patterns. Rather than a critique of suburban life, Hayden emphasizes the suburbs' diversity and potential beauty.

Johnson, Greg, *Invisible Writer: A Biography of Joyce Carol Oates*, Dutton, 1998.
This biography, written with the cooperation of Oates and her family, provides unique insights into the author's life, emphasizing her upbringing in upstate New York, the violence she encountered in Detroit during the 1960s, and her comfortable teaching job at Princeton. The biography explores the ways these components of her life combined to form her unique vision of American life.

Milazzo, Lee, ed., *Conversations with Joyce Carol Oates*, University Press of Mississippi, 1989.
This volume, part of the "Literary Conversations" series, reproduces twenty-five interviews Oates gave for a variety of publications. In the interviews she discusses the craft of writing, her own work, her concepts of literature, and other topics, including the way writing tries to capture the panorama of life.

Oates, Joyce Carol, *The Journal of Joyce Carol Oates: 1973–1982*, Harper Perennial, 2008.
Oates began keeping a journal to record, among other things, the mysterious ways in which her stories and novels came to her. Readers interested in the genesis of works of the imagination will find this book candid and revealing.

SUGGESTED SEARCH TERMS

Joyce Carol Oates

Joyce Carol Oates AND Marriages and Infidelities

Joyce Carol Oates AND Stalking

suburbanization

Joyce Carol Oates AND young adult literature

mall culture

consumerism

doppelganger

teenage disaffection

teenagers AND suburbia

The Tenant

BHARATI MUKHERJEE
1988

Bharati Mukherjee, a native of India who evolved from temporary exile to perceptive immigrant author through her years of residence in Canada and the United States, has gained through her novels, short stories, nonfiction, and essays a reputation as the *grande dame* of Indian diasporic literature (literature of people living far from their homeland). Raised in a wealthy family of the elite Brahmin caste (hereditary Hindu social class) in Calcutta in the 1940s, Mukherjee was interested from childhood in becoming a writer, and her attendance at the prestigious University of Iowa Writer's Workshop sped her toward this goal. After publishing several volumes while residing in Canada, her breakout success upon relocating to America came with *The Middleman and Other Stories* (1988), which won the National Book Critics' Circle Award. Although she was initially shunned by American publishing houses for telling immigrant stories, in this virtuoso collection she demonstrates acute insight into the psyches of immigrants from a global variety of backgrounds. Of particular renown in this volume is "The Tenant," which was first published in the *Literary Review*, a small quarterly journal, and was selected for inclusion in *The Best American Short Stories of 1987*. In this story, an immigrant Indian woman—a classic protagonist in Mukherjee's early fiction—who is ensconced in academia finds herself in a state of irremediable loneliness as she uncertainly navigates from one tenancy to the next.

Bharati Mukherjee *(AP / Wide World Photos. Reproduced by permission)*

AUTHOR BIOGRAPHY

Mukherjee was born on July 27, 1940, the second daughter in a Brahmin family of the uppermost caste in Calcutta, India. She spent the first seven years of her life sharing a home with some forty members of her extended family, a traditional domestic arrangement. Her father was a distinguished chemist whose business success would allow his three daughters many opportunities and advantages. Her mother, as Mukherjee noted in her autobiographical half of *Days and Nights in Calcutta* (1977), was "a powerful storyteller" who cared not about technical details but "only about passion."

While her first language is Bengali, Mukherjee began attending a Protestant missionary school that emphasized English lessons at age three, and by age eight, when her father took the family to London, she felt she had become bilingual. During the three years she spent attending boarding schools there and in Basel, Switzerland, she started her first novel, about children in England. As she noted in an interview for the

Massachusetts Review, she always knew she would be a writer: "the world of fiction seemed more real to me than the world around me."

Her family returned to Calcutta in 1951 to inhabit a mansion on the compound of her father's factory, leaving the daughters isolated from the middle-class community around them. In turn, they were enrolled in the elite Loreto Convent School, run by Irish nuns who made the environs and education as English as possible. Mukherjee earned a bachelor of arts degree in English from the University of Calcutta in 1959 and a master of arts degree in English and ancient Indian culture—a degree requirement that reconnected her with the wonders of Hinduism—from the University of Baroda in 1961. Through letters of recommendation from academics who were informed of her talent by her father, Mukherjee traveled abroad to attend the Writer's Workshop at the University of Iowa, where she earned an master of fine arts degree in 1963. That year, during a lunch hour, she married a fellow graduate student, Clark Blaise, with whom she would have two children and collaborate on literary projects such as *Days and Nights in Calcutta*.

In 1966 the family moved temporarily to Canada, Blaise's homeland, where Mukherjee joined the faculty at McGill University. She received her doctorate from the University of Iowa in 1969. She soon published her first novels, *The Tiger's Daughter* (1972) and *Wife* (1975). Canada did not prove hospitable to Mukherjee, as she experienced persistent and oppressive racism there during the 1970s. The family moved back to the United States in 1980, and Mukherjee taught at various New York-area institutions, including Columbia University. Feeling renewed creative energy as she accepted a series of professorships, she published the story collection *Darkness* in 1985 and *The Middleman and Other Stories*, which includes "The Tenant," in 1987. She has published five novels and two nonfiction volumes since, and as of 2010, she was teaching English at the University of California, Berkeley.

PLOT SUMMARY

"The Tenant" opens with mention of Maya Sanyal's presence in Cedar Falls, Iowa. From the description of her belongings, the reader may assume that she has come alone. She is originally from India and is drinking a little bourbon with her friend Fran, who helped her find her apartment. Fran is breaking up with a man named Vern, whose pharmacist father is familiar to Maya from public appearances. Maya and Fran both teach literature at the University of Northern Iowa. Fran sympathizes with Vern's need to go somewhere new, and she is not distressed about his leaving, especially since their relationship was primarily physical.

Maya mulls over the absence of food in her refrigerator, caused by her lack of a car and the poor selection of groceries at the corner store. In considering the effects that American food will have on her skin, she recalls the notion that "no folly is ever lost." (The third-person narration can at times be understood to reflect Maya's thoughts and perceptions.) She compares history to the nets used by the trapeze artists she saw at circuses in Calcutta with her father. While Fran dallies in the kitchen, Maya frets about conceived expectations that, as an Indian woman, she be able to handily fix dishes for guests, but she has not yet found where to buy exotic spices, nor has she befriended any Bengalis who might provide culinary inspiration. She does have beer, left as a friendly gesture by her landlord, Ted Suminski, but does not drink beer herself. Maya considers Fran the most helpful person she has met in ten years in the United States; she suggests an omelet, but Fran declines.

Preparing to leave, Fran asks Maya if she has yet been called by Rab Chatterji—a Bengali name familiar to Maya from the telephone book—who teaches physics at the university. Fran assumes Chatterji's identity as a Brahmin is important to Maya, but Maya dismissively characterizes all Indian men as wife beaters, a reason for her having married an American, now in 1983, she is divorced. As Fran leaves, Maya waves to Ted, who is watching from his kitchen; he seems to live alone, and she finds him somewhat "creepy." She expresses disinterest in hearing stories about him from Fran. Fran admiringly compares the adventurous Vern to Maya, but Maya dismisses the presumed similarity. She has, however, broken with the ways of her parents, such as by exploring options that other women from her neighborhood do not explore even in thought. The opening section of text ends with a hesitant assertion of Maya's identity as an American citizen.

Two nights later, Dr. Chatterji calls, speaking respectfully. Maya accepts an invitation to tea on Sunday. While on the phone, Maya watches the large yet graceful Ted Suminski outside throwing darts in the September evening. She sees him turn and take aim at her shadow and toss a dart that hits the window—an act so strange that she cannot be sure she truly saw it; she wonders whether he might be displaying interest or aggression. On the phone, Dr. Chatterji offers to pick her up, expressing his delight at soon meeting the daughter of the esteemed Dr. Sanyal.

On Sunday, Maya is ready early for an occasion she imagines will include other guests. She is dressed in a sari, with earrings and a necklace; she does not consider herself pretty, but she attends to her appearance. At Duke University in the 1970s, her opinionated women's group had considered her too feminine; but as a girl, she was taught to fulfill a submissive role. Because of this childhood training, she considers that a bold act such as seducing Ted Suminski would be fairly heroic.

Dr. Chatterji arrives, haltingly driving a clunker, ten minutes late, as he is operating on "Indian Standard Time." Americans, he condescendingly asserts in light of his own nation's three thousand years of superior civilization, rush about too much. Maya instructs Dr. Chatterji, who at about forty is a little older than she expected, to call her by her first name, not Mrs. Sanyal—prompting her to recall her ex-husband, John. In retrospect she realizes that what they shared had not quite been love, but this did not diminish the pain she felt when he left. She tersely relates the non-Brahmin marriage and divorce to Dr. Chatterji, who sags at her unsentimentality. His wife has fixed Indian snacks, so he intends to bring her to his house; she agrees, considering that while she has been intimate with married men, she has never been so with an Indian man.

At the Chatterjis' home, in a suburban neighborhood just being developed, Mrs. Chatterji is playing with a neighbor, a young Asian boy, in the driveway. The glowing, commodified suburban scene strikes Maya as surreal. Maya is shown inside and seated in the best armchair, and, imagining that the couple might whisper in the kitchen about her "misadventures," she hopes the wife will stay to converse. On the coffee table is an expansive array of traditional Indian food. Dr. Chatterji imperiously urges his wife to fix the tea, which he assures Maya has been brought straight from India. Mrs. Chatterji has already put the kettle on; she asks their guest about accomplished members of her family, which Maya interprets as signalling that they know of her transgressions.

Some commotion upstairs, sounding to Maya like a tormented ghost dropping heavy objects, disturbs the quiet scene. The Chatterjis try to suggest nostalgic Indian music, but the commotion is overwhelming; as the kettle boils, Dr. Chatterji shouts up the stairs to Poltoo, their nephew, to quiet down. Mrs. Chatterji shows serious distress over her intelligent nephew's troubled state, but Maya knows that intelligence and good breeding are no guarantee against deviant behavior. The nephew is studying at Iowa State University but has fallen in love with a Muslim student from Ghana—an unacceptable development in his family's opinion. Maya despises Dr. Chatterji's self-isolation from the society and ideals of America; his nephew's marrying within the Brahmin caste is essential even to his own identity. She understands how serious the disruption of identity can be, as when her husband left her, her limited world turned "monstrous, lawless." She discarded her moral sense in responding as if she were not a conscientious person but a character featured in a literary plot.

Mrs. Chatterji seems to feel guilty over the nephew's effect on the afternoon. Turning spiritual, she asserts her belief that the goddess will set things right by preventing Poltoo from marrying the African woman. She then plays a harmonium (a piano-like instrument with an accordion-like sound) and sings devoutly.

Dropping Maya off that evening, Dr. Chatterji comments flirtatiously about Maya's name, leaving her embarrassed. He then expresses jealousy over her carefree divorcée's life, as marriage can be quite lonely. His inappropriately sexual behavior leads her to express her indignity and flee the car.

On Monday, Maya declines a ride from Fran after work to instead peruse the international newspapers in the periodicals room. An Indian paper has a few notable stories, with one deceptively highlighting a caste-related concern: the killing of a low-caste boy. She realizes that she craves the sense of "virtues made physical" that she knows from India and felt in the Chatterjis' home; this leads her to think of seducing someone. She steals an issue of *India Abroad*, with its matrimonial columns.

At home, she notes how professional Indian men across America are all seeking Indian women to complete their lives. She happens upon an advertisement from a virile, self-assured doctor looking for an "emancipated Indo-American woman," and she calls; his name is Ashoke Mehta. As he will be flying through Chicago, they will meet at O'Hare Airport on Saturday.

At the bustling airport, Maya and Ashoke experience a dreamlike meeting. She is awed by his attractive face and confident bearing, to the point of feeling unattractive and "unworthy" in his presence and questioning the path her life has taken. When his hand touches her back, she feels desire, and she finds herself appreciating his fine scarf and sweater. They take advantage of the hour they have to get to know each other quickly through conversation. Then their courtship is ready to enter a "second phase."

Back in Cedar Falls that night, Ted has been waiting on the porch in the cold to tell her that he left a note upstairs; he is getting remarried and requesting that Maya vacate the apartment at the end of the semester. Pouring herself a shot of bourbon, she regrets that she has no one to tell about visiting the Chatterjis and her trip to O'Hare; she has never had such a person with whom to share her most intimate thoughts. Over the next two months, she finds a new room, with a landlord named Fred, who has no arms but makes dexterous use of his feet.

Fred, who is divorced and has adult children living in Oregon, proves amiable, and over time he and Maya "settle into companionship." He sees an equivalency in their circumstances, what with them being "two wounded people," but she considers her identity as Indian a far cry from being armless.

Ashoke Mehta calls in the spring, having somehow tracked her down, assuming that she will remember him. He admits that he has his vices but assures her that he was honest with her when they met at O'Hare. When Fred asks her who is on the phone, Ashoke Mehta overhears and recognizes that she has "a problem," but he is confident that she will come to his home in Connecticut. Looking ahead to moving out, Maya tells herself that Fred will be able to go on with his life.

CHARACTERS

Dr. Rabindra Chatterji

Dr. Chatterji is an "old-fashioned" physics professor who, like Maya, is a Brahmin, a member of the elite caste, from Bengal, a region in eastern India. At tea, he and his wife naturally speak with Maya about family relations. Maya observes that he "likes to do things correctly," and she comes to consider him "pompous," "reactionary," and "a vain man, anxious to cut losses." Dr. Chatterji is thus a sort of parody of a traditional Indian gentleman. He looks down on the inferior civilization of America and defies the ideal of the melting pot, believing it impermissible for his wife's nephew to marry an African Muslim. For his failure to understand the confusion their circumstances impose on immigrants like Poltoo and her, Maya hates him. His true character is revealed when, in dropping Maya off, he expresses jealousy of her freewheeling divorcée's life; he pathetically flatters her and tries to force their brief acquaintance into the sexual realm.

Mrs. Santana Chatterji

Mrs. Chatterji comes across as benevolent and kind-hearted but conservative. She plays ball with a neighbor boy, and she has prepared a veritable banquet of Indian snacks for their lone guest. Dr. Chatterji becomes "imperious" in asking her to fix tea, but she is able to ignore him at will. Her questions about the Sanyal family lead Maya to imagine that the woman has already gossiped plenty about the family's scandalous side. As for her own family, Mrs. Chatterji is distraught over her nephew's affection for an African Muslim, her face dropping from "plump and cheery" to "flabby" when they start discussing him. She expresses a disbelief in free will, saying, "It is the goddess who pulls the strings. We are puppets." However, she does not interpret this notion as meaning that Poltoo cannot be expected to deny his feelings for the Ghanaian student; rather, she expects the goddess to pull the strings in accord with her cultural expectation that a Brahmin not marry outside his caste. The spirituality of her singing astounds Maya, who is expertly trained in music but is not "a devotee" like Mrs. Chatterji.

Chung-Hee

Chung-Hee is a small Asian boy with whom Mrs. Chatterji plays ball. His presence gives that developing corner of suburbia the feel of an enclave for wealthy immigrants.

Fred

After leaving the apartment rented by Ted Suminski, Maya finds a kindly landlord with no arms named Fred, and they become companions. Fred considers them "two wounded people," but she bristles at the direct comparison of his physical wounds with her emotional ones and her alien identity. The cause of Fred's disability is never revealed, and so his presence in the story comes across as more comic than tragic—nearly to the point of absurdity. The reader may have difficulty imagining him perform all the actions described, such as driving, pushing sacks of clothes up stairs, and shoveling snow. At a crucial moment in the story, when Ashoke has finally called Maya back, Fred happens to be "lighting a cigarette with his toes." For both Maya and the reader, then, Fred serves as a transitional distraction.

John Hadwen

Maya's ex-husband left her after only about two years of marriage for reasons not specified in the story, which devastated her. He is not described, such that he remains a generic "John Doe" sort of character to the reader. His last name could be a play on the words "had when," as in, he was a friend Maya "had back when."

Fran Johnson

A tall, Swedish brunette, Fran teaches utopian fiction and women's studies and also serves on the hiring committee at the University of Northern Iowa. She helped Maya obtain both her job and her apartment and is very friendly, but Maya recognizes that Fran is not someone with whom she can share her most intimate thoughts. Fran's attitude toward her recent relationship with Vern, which was primarily physical, reflects a low level of romantic expectations.

Ashoke Mehta

Ashoke Mehta turns out to be a sort of savior for the ever-lonesome Maya, who in the course of the story notes separately that she has never been with an Indian man and also has never found the right person to open her heart to. His advertisement in *India Abroad* for a "new emancipated Indo-American woman" depicts him as the height of sensitive masculinity. Maya is certainly drawn to his occupying the same cultural niche as her, with their both being "at ease in USA" with ethics "rooted in Indian tradition," though he repudiates the caste system, which she has also defied through her relationships. At O'Hare airport, she finds him handsome, sees in him the confident bearing of "a Hindu god," and is further swayed by his upper-class trappings, including an imported Icelandic sweater and a scarf with the colors of England's elite Cambridge University. In effect, he sweeps her off her feet for the hour. When he finally gets back in touch with her months after their rendezvous, sounding charmingly self-centered in citing "a problem" and "my vices" as having delayed him, she has not lost her affection for him, and she abruptly decides to go to him in Hartford. Whether she will find a long-term solution to her loneliness with Ashoke or whether living in Connecticut she will still be just another "tenant" is not indicated by the author.

Poltoo

Mrs. Chatterji's nephew has come from India to study agricultural science. Poltoo has fallen in love with a Muslim student from Ghana. His frustration at his family's expectation that he defy his emotions is manifest in the commotion he causes while Maya is visiting, as if he were a "clumsy ghost" dropping things on the floor. The duality in the image of Poltoo as a ghost trying to break free from the body reflects the dual existence of the immigrant as rooted in national origins but spiritually disconnected from them. Maya feels more akin to Poltoo than to any other character, in that they are both lost in "the confused world of the immigrant."

Dr. Sanyal

Maya's father, "a complicated man," is mentioned a couple of times by her and once by Dr. Chatterji, who evidently holds Maya in esteem because of his respect for Dr. Sanyal, a legendary Calcutta businessman.

Maya Sanyal

Maya is the story's central protagonist, and through third-person narration the reader is allowed glimpses of her stream of consciousness. Thus, the reader comes to understand her precisely through what she reveals of herself in her thoughts. She originally broke with her parents' culture, and presumably their Brahmin expectations, when she married a fellow American student at Duke University. His leaving her, then,

was doubly traumatic, in that she lost someone she had considered the love of her life, and yet she could not simply return to her Indian roots, having been stigmatized by both the relationship and its failure. Outside of both Indian tradition and the security of the marriage with which she had replaced that tradition, "she lost her moral sense, her judgment, her power to distinguish"—she was cast adrift. She was thus led into what the reader understands to be a prolonged series of occasional flings with little meaning. Ultimately, with the Indian expatriate community defining her by her "misadventures in America," she seems to likewise define herself by those "indiscretions." The possibility of dallying with men, whether acquaintances or strangers, is often on her mind.

The main reason for her preoccupation with forming liaisons appears to be her incurable loneliness. When she thinks of chatting with someone about her experiences at the Chatterjis' and with Ashoke Mehta, she laments that "no one she's ever met is the person" with whom to share her sentiments—not even her ex-husband, the reader assumes. This absence of genuine connection can be seen as rooted in Maya's status as an isolated immigrant who has never experienced companionship with someone from her home country. Her visit with the Chatterjis and her perusal of an Indian newspaper, which "unsettles" her, lead her to posit that what has been lacking in her life is a sense of "virtues made physical" that she associates with India but not with America. She is deeply moved by the spirituality of Mrs. Chatterji, where her own parents perhaps never instilled her with any religious sense. Her father's priorities were evidently business and his daughter's academic advancement; her mother considered states like "love" and "inner peace" to be little more than "the brain's biochemistry." Thus, while she surely values her American education and has come to adopt American mores with regard to forming temporary relationships, Maya senses and suffers from the absence of spirituality and sentimental connection in the world of academia she has come to inhabit. It seems likely that Maya's traveling to unite with Ashoke will mark a new phase in her life, although the reader can only guess as to what that new phase will entail.

Ted Suminski

Maya's landlord through most of the story, Ted Suminski is a large, bald, seemingly lonely man of at least fifty years. Fran tells Maya that there are odd stories about him. He spends his time shooting baskets and tossing darts—including one aimed at Maya's window, a gesture she does not understand. He also prunes and gardens obsessively, leaving sacks of branches lying around. It turns out that Ted will be remarrying, which forces Maya to find another apartment.

Vern

Fran talks about her departing boyfriend, Vern, a pharmacist going to film school, and classifies both him and Maya as "headstrong adventurers."

THEMES

Immigrant Life

A prominent theme in "The Tenant" is what the narration, following Maya's thoughts during her visit to the Chatterjis, refers to as "the confused world of the immigrant—the lostness that Maya and Poltoo feel." This theme is evident throughout the stories of *The Middleman* and, indeed, most all of Mukherjee's work; she has made explicit in interviews that immigrants' experiences are what she aims to write about. The Indian immigrant's confusion is characterized succinctly by Ashoke in his personal ad, where he speaks of being "at ease in USA"—that is, aligned with American values in terms of daily behavior—but still ethically "rooted in Indian tradition."

Throughout the story, Maya actually tends to downplay whatever cultural confusion she might be feeling, such that the reader does not necessarily connect her "lostness" with her status as an immigrant. Rather, her failed relationship with John Hadwen seems to be the source of her lingering discontent, and she gives no indication that this relationship failed because of her ethnic identity. When Indian cultural influences or factors do get addressed, Maya mostly seems indifferent or even in opposition to them. She feels little motivation to learn to prepare Indian cuisine, whether for guests or for herself. She sardonically refers to Indian men as all being "wife beaters," and in mentioning that she has never been with an Indian man, she seems to regard them more as curiosities than as worthy of serious attention. The narration's ironic praise of "that young chap, Manna Dey"—a prolific Indian film singer who was sixty-four years old by 1983—conveys the impression that Maya

TOPICS FOR FURTHER STUDY

- Read Mukherjee's "A Wife's Story," which is also found in *The Middleman and Other Stories*, and write an essay comparing and contrasting the female Indian protagonist with that in "The Tenant."

- With your classmates, create a Wikispace about India's caste system, providing the cultural origins and history, with a focus on how the caste system has evolved since India gained independence, both within India and as a result of the Indian diaspora.

- Mukherjee found Canada far less welcoming to immigrants than the United States. Research the two nations' immigration policies over the last century, and then write a paper considering how societal attitudes toward immigrants in the two nations have reflected these policies or have been shaped by these policies. Post your paper as a blog and invite your classmates to comment on the policies and your summarization.

- Read *Born Confused* (2002) by Tanuja Desai Hidier, which is suitable for young adults, and write an essay fully exploring Dimple's perceptions of what qualities are characteristically Indian and what qualities are characteristically American.

- Use the Internet to collect images of and musical samplings from the harmonium, tanpur, and sitar, and also research the three instruments' histories. Then create a presentation on the instruments in the form of either a Web site or a PowerPoint presentation featuring printed and recorded materials.

finds the Chatterjis' affection for his music a bit ridiculous, and she expresses disdain for the Chatterjis' enthusiasm about maintaining the integrity of their caste by marrying within it.

However, Maya's particular connections to her native culture do become evident. She takes care to dress in distinctly Indian apparel for her teatime visit. She is "astonished" by Mrs. Chatterji's spiritually inspired performance on the harmonium, and although she satirizes the Chatterjis in her thoughts during her visit, the next day, she realizes that she yearns for precisely what she felt in their home: the "familiar feeling" of "virtues made physical." This is also somewhat ironic, in that earlier the narration, presumed to be following her thoughts, had lampooned Dr. Chatterji's sense of superiority by comically inferring from his simple lateral head gesture the suggestion that the Indian immigrants "have three thousand years plus civilization, sophistication, moral virtue," over those born in America; as it turns out, "moral virtue" is indeed of consequence to Maya. Her realization is brought on when she reads the accounts in the Indian newspaper, which, in 1983—before the mass multiculturalization of America, as reflected in media like the Internet, films, and television—was likely her only means of transporting her mind back to her homeland.

Upon meeting Ashoke, Maya at last identifies how she feels to have failed: "She has changed her citizenship but she hasn't broken through into the light, the vigor, the *hustle* of the New World." That is, she is stuck somewhere in between the old world and the new. She has perhaps come to feel as though assimilating herself into American culture must entail cutting off her bonds with India, but when she reveals after the rendezvous that "no one she's ever met is the person" with whom to share her innermost feelings, the reader may suspect that when she does meet this person, he or she will be, like her, an "emancipated Indo-American"—someone who can help her sustain a connection with the home of the first nineteen years of her life while also helping her grow within the country that is her home now.

Loneliness

Maya seems through the opening pages of the story to be emotionally well balanced, but she eventually says that "she is stuck in dead space," refers again to "the dead space she lives in," and labels herself "strange, and lonely." The reader may conclude that her loneliness is perhaps the most significant motivating factor in her life and that she could even be said to be mired in depression. In this sense, it may not be surprising that Maya does not seem depressed during her conversations, as an aspect of depression can be a

Maya had tea with her Indian friends. (Pietus / Shutterstock.com)

disinterest in discussing it with others. Indeed, Maya makes clear that, if she were depressed, she would not care to tell anyone in particular about it, yet her loneliness seems to dictate her behavior, in that she almost compulsively seeks liaisons with men—as if, because her spiritual loneliness is incurable, she can only attend to her physical loneliness. In the library, the "longing" she feels for the ambience of India, a longing that cannot be resolved, leads directly to her thought of seducing someone. Back at home after her rendezvous, she is almost immediately lonely again and wishes Ashoke would call back. A reason for her engaging in a relationship with Fred is that "the dead space need not suffocate"— that is, she need not let her loneliness overwhelm her, even though this particular relationship will not address all the dimensions of that loneliness; it will not actually enliven that dead space but will only let in some air. Ultimately, Maya's loneliness may or may not be resolved through her relationship with Ashoke.

STYLE

Declaratory Sequences

One pattern in Mukherjee's writing in this story is the presence in the narration of series of simple, related declarative sentences. One such series occurs during Fran's visit: "Fran is out in the kitchen long enough for Maya to worry. They need food. Her mother believed in food." Another occurs as she awaits Dr. Chatterji, referring to her peach-colored sari: "The color is good on dark skin. She is not pretty, but she does her best. Working at it is a part of self-respect." Yet another occurs in reference to Poltoo's circumstances: "Dr. Chatterji's horror is real. A good Brahmin boy in Iowa is in love with an African Muslim. It shouldn't be a big deal." What these series of declarations have in common is that the author is not providing logical connectors between the thoughts, leaving the reader to determine exactly how the statements are connected. As such, this narrative strategy may serve to engage the reader, and it also leaves the meaning of the text open to interpretation. In each of the series above, the text begins with a statement of immediate circumstances and then progresses to a value statement, but it is not always clear where the values should be located. In the first series, what is not indicated is the extent to which Maya has been influenced by her mother's belief in food. In the second series, it is not clear whether Maya or the narrator is asserting that attending to one's appearance is related to self-respect. Similarly, in the third series, it is unclear in whose opinion Poltoo's romantic interest "shouldn't be a big deal." Throughout the story, such sequences of declarative statements leave the reader to piece together the precise rationale behind the notions expressed—or to simply absorb their sense without worrying about the logistical details behind them.

Ambiguity

As with the sequences of declarations in the narration, which leave the reader to form logical connections on his or her own, other aspects of the text are marked by ambiguity. As in the examples above, the source of the narration is often unclear, such that the reader must guess whether a statement is intended to reflect Maya's thoughts or the displaced third-person narration. A number of statements with unclear meanings appear throughout the story: "Every place has something to give," "She means it and doesn't mean it," and "Planets contained, mysteries made visible." These, too, the reader must interpret on his or her own. Also prominent are the several instances when Mukherjee ends a paragraph with the one-word statement: "But." These instances may be more interpretable than other ambiguities, since in each instance a statement related to Maya's Americanization is being hesitantly refuted. The first two preceding statements are positive: "She is an American citizen" and "She has broken with the past." The third is a negative reaction to Dr. Chatterji's Brahminism: "She hates him." Thus, the repeated use of the word "but" to end paragraphs reflects Maya's inhabiting an uncertain space between the two cultures of India and America. In general, the story's ambiguities may be seen as reflecting the notion that Maya's conscience, the voice inside her head, sometimes sees things from an American perspective and sometimes sees things from an Indian one. Where the reader is unsure of the source or meaning of the narration, Maya, too, may be unsure of which cultures or which ideals are governing her sensibilities and of how she should interpret her own thoughts and impulses.

Immigrant Fiction

In interviews, Mukherjee has differentiated herself from certain other immigrant writers—such as Anita Desai, who is also Indian, and Bapsi Sidhwa, who is Pakistani—who tend to write narratives that, whether situated in America or in South Asia, are thematically and continentally rooted not in their present home but in their past one. In speaking with Sharmani Gabriel in *Ariel*, Mukherjee classified herself and Jhumpa Lahiri as among the few Indian Americans who write "not about the India we left behind but the here and now, the daily life that we encounter and that many hundreds and thousands of other South Asians or other immigrant groups are facing." She asserts, "We are writing immigrant fiction," and she classifies herself in an unqualified way as "an American writer." In contrast, she considers that authors whose work is rooted in their homeland are writing "nostalgic expatriate fiction." Interestingly, in "The Tenant," Maya does experience nostalgia, as "a familiar feeling, a longing" for India, after visiting the Chatterjis. Based on her interview, Mukherjee might not consider this nostalgia a positive quality in her protagonist; the answer would perhaps depend on whether her relationship with Ashoke proves to be a progressive one or a regressive one.

HISTORICAL CONTEXT

The Multicultural Age in North America

The groundwork for what might be termed the multicultural age in America began in 1965, at the peak of the civil rights movement, when the Immigration and Nationality Act was signed. This act abolished the system whereby the influx of persons from other nations was limited based on existing proportions of immigrants in the U.S. population, a system that served to forestall growth in ethnic diversity. The 1965 act thus allowed an influx of labor of diverse nationalities and ethnicities to bolster the economy. While earlier waves of immigration had primarily stemmed from Europe, the coming decades would witness ever greater proportions of new immigrants from elsewhere in the world. By the end of the 1980s, when Mukherjee was writing stories for *The Middleman*, among immigrants, only 25 percent were European, while another 25 percent were Asian, and 43 percent were Latino. While those arriving over land from as close as Mexico were more likely to be Spanish-speaking migrant farmers or manual laborers, those arriving from India were more likely to already be fluent in English—since India had been colonized by Great Britain—and to be or become well-educated professionals, especially scientists, engineers, and doctors.

Mukherjee arrived to attend graduate school through a P.E.O. International Peace Scholarship in 1961, before the relaxation of U.S. immigration laws. Thus, she gained a feel for the nation when the racial discourse was conducted almost exclusively in black-or-white terms. Her experiences in Canada, her husband's home country, between 1966 and 1980 were jarring. In the early 1970s, South Asians—particularly professionals with children in private school were targets of racism, both socially and institutionally. She was once assaulted in a subway station in Toronto and had to board buses last despite being among the first in line.

When she finally returned to the United States, she had a renewed appreciation for the American ideal of the melting pot and the nation's hospitality toward immigrants. By the time she wrote *The Middleman*, she had gained enough insight to confidently write about and in the voices of immigrants not merely from India but from Pakistan, Sri Lanka, China, the Philippines, Afghanistan, Yugoslavia, Hungary, Germany, Iraq, Uganda, and Trinidad, as well as in the voices of ordinary white Americans. In "The Tenant," the year is 1983, but Maya, situated, as was Mukherjee, in the heartland of Iowa, feels profoundly isolated as an Indian immigrant. The suburbs of Connecticut, where Maya is headed at the close of the story, had been since the 1960s a popular haven for the wealthiest Indian immigrants, and so, after Iowa, she would likely benefit from the increased level of interaction with other Indian Americans.

Postcolonialism and Feminism

Although an author's associations with literary movements may not be as readily apparent in a single short story as in several works jointly considered, one may perceive in "The Tenant" that Mukherjee has positioned herself as beyond, if not opposed to, the concerns of both postcolonialist and feminist literary theory. She has made clear her relationship to postcolonialists and feminists, some of whom have critically attacked her work in interviews. *Postcolonialism* can be characterized as a literary or theoretical movement concerned primarily with portrayals symbolic of the subjugation and oppression of so-called third-world nations by Western imperialists. The movement began in the mid-twentieth century as colonized nations gained their independence, as did India in 1947.

In her interview with Gabriel, Mukherjee observed that postcolonial critics, such as the Indian scholar Gayatri Spivak, "would like me to dramatize all white people as villains and oppressors and all non-white characters as the oppressed and victimized," but Mukherjee believes that a novel with such a schematic, politicized framework makes for "fifteenth-rate literature"; she is more inclined toward truthful development of character, and so she conceives fictional circumstances that reflect not theory or a political agenda but the way people behave in real life. In "The Tenant," John Hadwen might have been portrayed as villainous, but no explanation is given for his having abandoned Maya, and so the reader cannot form a negative judgment of his character based on the failed relationship. Conflict in the story is found instead in the discrepancies between the attitudes of insulated Indian immigrants like Dr. and Mrs. Chatterji and the attitudes of ideologically modern, open-minded immigrants like Maya and Poltoo. In other words, the story does not revolve around postcolonial concerns regarding oppressors and the oppressed.

COMPARE
&
CONTRAST

- **1980s:** According to the U.S. Census Bureau, in 1980 there are 206,087 Indian immigrants living in the United States. They make up just 1.5 percent of the immigrant population and Indians are only the twelfth largest immigrant population group.

  Today: In 2006, Indian immigrants are the fourth largest immigrant population group. The 1.5 million Indians hold a 4 percent share of the foreign-born population.

- **1980s:** Very few of the Indian immigrants settle in the farm belt states of the upper Midwest.

  Today: In 2006, the American Community Survey of the U.S. Census Bureau reported that less than 0.5 percent of the Indian-born immigrant population is settled in Iowa. The largest populations are in California and New Jersey.

- **1980s:** In 1988 the Indian Business & Professional Women (IBPW) organization is founded as a support network and forum for Indian women to identify and address issues of mutual concern in the business and professional world.

  Today: The IBPW Web site links to nearly a dozen organizations that have been established to support the business and professional endeavors of women of Indian descent.

Mukherjee has similarly distanced herself from feminism, especially the second-wave feminism of the 1970s. Some feminists have criticized her work for reflecting, and thus perhaps to a certain extent condoning, the exploitation and marginalization of women rather than their empowerment. However, as Mukherjee, coming from a more traditional and conservative culture than American feminists, noted in an interview for the *Iowa Review*, "For some non-white, Asian women, our ways of negotiating power are different. There is no reason why we should have to appropriate—wholesale and intact—the white, upper-middle-class women's tools and rhetoric." In fact, Mukherjee has rendered some white feminists as antagonists in her fiction, such as in the novel *Jasmine*, which features a wife "whose feminism and professionalism are built on the backs of underemployed Caribbean or Hispanic au-pair girls."

In "The Tenant," Maya makes clear her own contrary relationship with feminism, as her women's group at Duke found her "too feminine." Like Mukherjee, Maya points to the vast differences between expectations for women in American and Indian societies. Maya came from a culture where her grandmother was married off at five, while a great aunt was burned to death because of problems with the dowry, which in India would entail money or possessions given to the groom's family by the bride's family. Such circumstances are entirely foreign to the American experience, and yet they necessarily shape even a modern Indian woman's perspective on gender roles. Maya reveals that she has considered the freedom she has exercised with regard to romantic relationships as an adult to be "miraculously rebellious," but in that wavering moment when the awe-inspiring Ashoke first stands before her, she assesses her adult life as "grim" and "perverse," as "she has accomplished nothing." From a feminist perspective, her independent renegotiation of relational boundaries and her subsequent self-assessment could both be considered positive psychic developments. What feminist critics might object to in this story is the fact that Maya ends up in a relationship, with Ashoke Mehta, where she does not feel equal to her partner but rather worships him, despite his potentially misogynist vices.

Maya wore her traditional Indian clothing when visiting Indian friends. (michaeljung | Shutterstock.com)

CRITICAL OVERVIEW

While some critics find fault with her work from certain theoretical perspectives, Mukherjee is a popular and widely acclaimed author, and *The Middleman and Other Stories* has earned much praise. In the *New York Times*, Jonathan Raban asserts that, as compared to her previous collection, *Darkness*, in this collection Mukherjee "has greatly sharpened her style" with writing that "is far quicker in tempo, more confident and more sly than it used to be." He observes that "the idiom of American in the 1980's is handled" with "rapturous affection and acuteness of ear," and he calls the collection "a consummated romance with the American language." Inspired, Raban points out that "every story ends on a new point of departure," as "for these birds of passage, America is a receding infinity of fresh beginnings; they keep aloft on luck and grace." He concludes, "The great lesson that the immigrant has to teach the born-and-raised citizen is that being on the run is a native American condition."

In his essay "From Expatriation to Immigration: The Case of Bharati Mukherjee," A. V. Krishna Rao comments that "The Tenant" is "more successful and artistically finished than some of the earlier" stories in *The Middleman*. He notes that the story ends "by dramatizing the precarious existential condition of the liberated Indian woman." He affirms that the stories in this volume "have a certain verve and vitality so characteristic of the best-known American fictional prose."

In the *Women's Review of Books*, Carol Ascher notes that with this "swift-moving collection" filled with so many distinct voices, Mukherjee shows that she is "at the forefront of immigrant chic," presenting characters who "*are* the great social transformation affecting North America." Ascher observes that the author's prose "has the flat deadpan that is very much in style." She finds "The Tenant" and one other story "particularly poignant" by virtue of their narrators being "thoughtful and torn about their experiences." Ascher concludes that a great joy of the collection is "experiencing a world that generally remains just at the edge of my consciousness."

CRITICISM

Michael Allen Holmes

Holmes is an editor and writer. In the following essay, he posits that in "The Tenant," Ashoke Mehta will fail to provide Maya with the spiritual fulfillment she craves.

The closing paragraphs of "The Tenant" find Maya "breathless" while listening to Ashoke Mehta's voice on the phone, as "the god has tracked her down." Although she says no more to him than "Yes, I remember," the last line of the narrative informs the reader that she will indeed move out to go live with him in Hartford, Connecticut. The reader might interpret this as a happy ending, that Maya seems to have met just the right person, at least for the time being. She practically swooned over him when first meeting him at the airport, and their encounter was evidently memorable, but Ashok's words on the phone are somewhat ominous. He remarks, "You know that I have my vices"—a convenient line for subconsciously preparing a romantic interest for future heartbreak. After "his laugh echoes" over the phone—a laugh that the reader may imagine as eerie, if not villainous—he comes

WHAT DO I READ NEXT?

- Soon after the publication of *The Middleman*, Mukherjee published the novel *Jasmine* (1989) about a young Indian woman who refashions her identity several times as she adapts to life in America.

- V. S. Naipaul, a Trinidadian novelist of Indian descent who won the Nobel Prize in 2001, is often mentioned alongside Mukherjee. His three stories in the collection *In a Free State* (1971) deal with Indian immigrants to the West and the sense of displacement that they feel.

- Salman Rushdie, a British-Indian author with a magical-realist style, is also frequently considered alongside Mukherjee. His most famous work is *Midnight's Children* (1981), which relates the life of a child born at the moment of India's independence who is blessed with supernatural powers.

- Paula Gunn Allen, an American author of Laguna descent, addresses the nation's hybridization from a Native American perspective. Her novel *The Woman Who Owned the Shadows* (1983) tells of a mixed-blood woman's efforts to express herself creatively.

- Mukherjee finds that her work harmonizes with that of Bernard Malamud, a Jewish American author who depicts the lives of poor urban immigrants from Eastern Europe in the stories in his first collection, *The Magic Barrel* (1958).

- Flannery O'Connor is a renowned American author whose short stories, like Mukherjee's, sometimes lead to unexpected violence, such as in her collection *A Good Man Is Hard to Find* (1955).

- Jhumpa Lahiri's *The Namesake*, which is suitable for young adults, tells of the experiences over several decades of the Ganguli family, who immigrate from Calcutta to Cambridge, Massachusetts, in the 1960s.

- Santha Rama Rau, who was born in India but was educated at a boarding school in England, relates her return to her home country in the nonfiction volume *Home to India* (1945).

---

across as arrogant when he predicts, or perhaps orders, "You will come to Hartford, I know." Indeed, in light of certain revelations from the story, one may conclude that although Ashoke will undoubtedly ameliorate Maya's loneliness, he will not provide what she truly lacks.

Maya's name surely bears significance, in that it is a concept in Hindu philosophy with which Mukherjee is surely familiar. From a simplified perspective, *maya* can be understood as the sensory world that is perceptible all around and that conceals the true fundamental reality, called Brahma, whereby all of creation is unified. *Maya* prevents people from seeing the true fundamental reality of the universe. In the Hindu conception, all people are aspects of the divine, which determines all of existence; in Mrs. Chatterji's words, "It is the goddess who pulls the strings. We are puppets." Thus, where the deity controls and determines all that people do, both free will and individual identity are illusory, but the person deluded by *maya* is, in effect, trapped in the sensory world and so is invested emotionally in his or her own identity.

As explained in the Bhagavad Gita, a sacred Hindu text, "By constantly thinking of the sense objects, a mortal being becomes attached to them. Attached thus he develops various desires, from which in turn ... comes delusion." *Maya* can be associated with emotions, desires, and self-fulfillment, in both positive and negative senses. The spiritually fulfilled person, on the contrary, may understand *maya* as inconsequential in relation to the infinite workings of the divine, with which all people are connected. That is, such a person will not be emotionally

THIS IS CERTAINLY NOT A MAN WHO CAN
PROVIDE MAYA WITH A SENSE OF SPIRITUALITY,
AND IF HE WILL PROVIDE A SENSE OF 'VIRTUES
MADE PHYSICAL,' IT WILL ONLY BE THROUGH HIS
HABIT OF TRANSLATING HIS CAPITALIST'S
VIRTUE—HIS MONEY—INTO TANGIBLE ASSETS
LIKE INTERNATIONAL VACATIONS AND
LUXURIOUS GOODS."

dependent on relationships with others and will not suffer diminished self-worth based on experiences or achievements.

In "The Tenant," Maya is highly concerned with her activity in the sensory world. With regard to her career, she has committed herself to the competitive world of academia, in which one's material accomplishments will directly determine long-term success or failure. For some professors, the joys of forging relationships with and enlightening students may provide ample professional satisfaction, but as Mukherjee well knows from experience, professors of literature, among many other sorts, must "publish or perish," producing either original work or criticism of others' work; the publications are what legitimize his or her status as a teacher of writing. These aspects of her work would certainly tend to firmly situate Maya in the production- and achievement-based sensory world. Indeed, the world of academia—outside of religious and theological schools—is typically perceived as a bastion of liberalism in which spiritual concerns may be dismissed as nonacademic and thus irrelevant. A direct association of academia with a lack of spirituality is made in "The Tenant" when Maya reflects on her scientific-minded mother: "What is love, anger, inner peace, etc., her mother used to say, but the brain's biochemistry." Maya's parents can be inferred to have channeled her energy toward academic pursuits, just as Mukherjee's parents did with her and her sisters.

Maya makes almost no mention of spiritual concerns throughout the story. She does not

profess to have any religious or spiritual routines or practices. She is evidently not spiritually invested in the food she eats, as she seems not to know how to prepare traditional Indian cuisine; at least, she cannot "whip up exotic delights to tickle an American's palate." Furthermore, although typically Hindus in India consider cows sacred and do not eat beef, when Fred asks whether she refrains from eating certain animals, she says, "it's okay, any meat."

Maya herself points to her spiritual deficit through her response to Mrs. Chatterji's musical performance. Upon hearing the woman sing "beautifully, in a virgin's high voice," Maya "is astonished." She recognizes that in contrast to her own technical training on the sitar and tanpur, which are traditional Indian instruments, Mrs. Chatterji, accompanying herself on the harmonium—an instrument that was actually brought to India by the French in the mid-nineteenth century—"is a devotee, talking to God." With this crossing of images—pairing the traditional but unspiritual in Maya and the nontraditional but spiritual in Mrs. Chatterji—Mukherjee seems to suggest that true spirituality does not stem from culture alone but is a quality inherent in the spiritual person. Maya's musical training, then, has not infused her with spirituality.

The day after visiting the Chatterjis and shortly before swiping an issue of *India Abroad* from the library, Maya seems to identify what she truly lacks: the sense of "virtues made physical" that she felt in the Chatterjis' home. This revelation is somewhat ironic, in that what Maya seemed most concerned with during her visit was not her hosts' virtues but rather her reputation, about which the Chatterjis were presumed to be gossipy and judgmental, and the Chatterjis' preoccupation with caste, which she found appalling. When Maya reads the newspaper story about the child who was formerly an "untouchable" (a member of the lowest Hindu caste, the system which has now been outlawed in India) and was stoned while drawing well water, the reader may conclude that Maya, perhaps viewing the story from an American "all men are created equal" angle, would blame the caste system for the boy's death, but the Chatterjis still believe in this system. Overall, the Chatterjis' particular sense of traditional morality and virtue seems at odds with Maya's individualistic morality. Thus, when she finds herself with "a familiar feeling, a longing" for something she felt at the Chatterjis' house, the reader might conclude that "virtues made physical" is an inaccurate description of that something; perhaps "spirituality made physical" is what she truly longs for.

Mukherjee offered a telling characterization of Maya in a 1990 interview with Beverley Byers-Pevitts in the *Iowa Review*:

> I think of Maya as a very lost, sad character, who really went out and married a white man and is so well attuned to women intellectuals, her colleagues, but at the same time there is that desire for wholeness, nostalgia, that India and Indian traditions promised. And so, she's the one who is going out and seeking an advertised, perfect Indian groom, and it works out in strange ways for her.

Mukherjee seems to confirm that Maya is "lost" in the world of physical attachments and intellectual achievement, the world of *maya*. In asserting that Maya desires all "that India and Indian traditions promised," Mukherjee leaves open the question as to whether "spiritual" might be a more appropriate term than "virtue" in Maya's conception of what she lacks; both spirituality and virtue can be seen as embodied in India's traditions. What is interesting is Mukherjee's mention of Maya's search for "an advertised, perfect Indian groom," since Maya does not seem to be looking for any particular type of man but "stops at random" while tracing her finger along the ads.

Mukherjee might be understood, then, to be describing Ashoke, who does come across as a perfectly masculine but sensitive Indian in his advertisement, yet he and Maya seem to quickly understand that they are not looking for a marital arrangement but instead are each looking for a rendezvous "in transit," with the chat proving "as easy as that." When he intones that he prefers "a neutral zone" for "these encounters," the reader gathers that they will not simply be drinking tea together, and furthermore, Ashoke seems to have experience arranging just this sort of rendezvous.

Maya's interaction with Ashoke in O'Hare proves highly commercialized, literally and figuratively. They begin by floating toward each other "as lovers used to in shampoo commercials"; before long she is fawning over his scarf, which shows the colors of an elite university, and his imported sweater, which by scent she identifies as "Icelandic," leading the reader to conclude that she must have experience smelling expensive sweaters. After they greet each other, he promptly "pushes her out of the reach of anti-Khomeini Iranians, Hare Krishnas, American fascists, men with fierce wants," such that he can be seen as differentiated from those men; perhaps not coincidentally, the three groups mentioned are all religiously or spiritually motivated (though negatively so with the fascists). In contrast, in the related description of himself, Ashoke, who is "good with facts," notably mentions no religious or spiritual dimension. He is a free-spending capitalist, which is to say he probably does not concern himself with charity; he is an omnivorous sports fan, which is to say that he devotes his spare attention to trivial televised matters rather than consequential reality-based ones, and though he "counts himself an intellectual," the authors he mentions—understood to be Robert Ludlum, Frederick Forsyth, and Helen Clark MacInnes—are known primarily for espionage thrillers. Indeed, rather than someone who will connect her with "India and Indian traditions," Maya seems to have found a thoroughly Americanized wealthy Indian male—a status-seeking, materialistic, hedonistic playboy. This is certainly not a man who can provide Maya with a sense of spirituality, and if he will provide a sense of "virtues made physical," it will only be through his habit of translating his capitalist's virtue—his money—into tangible assets like international vacations and luxurious goods.

Mukherjee commented further on her protagonist in this story in the *Iowa Review* interview: "For her, the turn comes when the guy without arms, the lover without arms, calls her May. Suddenly, she snaps. No, I'm not May, I'm Maya, and people from the outside don't understand me." Indeed, she is Maya, condemned by virtue of her name to remain lost in the sensory stimulation and self-valuation of *maya*. Ashoke, the "sensualist" who cannot resist temptations, is likewise fully invested and situated in the *maya* of the world, and he seems to understand her perfectly. As the narration states, "it is the fate of women like her, and men like him. Their karmic duty, to be loved." Although Maya seems unlikely to find true spiritual fulfillment through a relationship with this man, she has found "a Hindu god" of her very own to worship, and perhaps this quasi-spirituality will suffice.

Source: Michael Allen Holmes, Critical Essay on "The Tenant," in *Short Stories for Students*, Gale, Cengage Learning, 2011.

Maya shares loneliness and erotic cravings with several men. (Cindy Hughes | Shutterstock.com)

Arvindra Sant-Wade and Karen Marguerite Radell

In the following excerpt, Sant-Wade and Radell discuss the ways in which immigrant characters adapt to American culture in Mukherjee's The Middleman and Other Stories.

The female protagonist in one of Bharati Mukherjee's prize-winning short stories, from the collection titled *The Middleman and Other Stories*, is shocked when her landlord lover refers to the two of them as "two wounded people," and thinks to herself that "She knows she is strange, and lonely, but being Indian is not the same, she would have thought, as being a freak." The Indian woman, Maya Sanyal, who is the central figure of the story, "The Tenant," recognizes her strangeness in America and her appalling loneliness, but she resists being recognized as a "freak." No doubt this term occurs to her when her current lover, Fred, a man without arms, refers to them both as wounded. She does not see herself as being as freakish as

Fred, as bereft as Fred, though certainly the story makes clear that she has been wounded emotionally and spiritually by the struggle to come to terms with her new life in America. In one sense, Fred's assessment is accurate, for as the author indicates in all the stories in this collection, it is impossible to adapt to life in the New World without sustaining some kind of wound to one's spirit.

It is apparently a deeper wound for the women of the Third World, who are engaged in the struggle to fashion a new identity for themselves in an alien culture. Perhaps this struggle results from their sudden freedom from the bonds of superstition and chauvinism that held them fast in their old, familiar cultures, freedom that seems to leave them floating, unbalanced, in the complex, sometimes treacherous air of this new and unfamiliar culture. The irony is that this refashioning of the self is both painful and exhilarating; hence, the terrible ambivalence of the women toward their own freedom—the freedom to *become*—an ambivalence expressed by these women in the midst of arduous change, in the powerful act of rejecting the past and moving energetically toward an unknown future.

In a *Massachusetts Review* interview, Mukherjee asserts that

we immigrants have fascinating tales to relate. Many of us have lived in newly independent or emerging countries which are plagued by civil and religious conflicts. We have experienced rapid changes in the history of the nations in which we lived. When we uproot ourselves from those countries and come here, either by choice or out of necessity, we suddenly must absorb 200 years of American history and learn to adapt to American society. Our lives are remarkable, often heroic.

Mukherjee goes on to say that she attempts to illustrate this remarkable, often heroic quality in her novels and short stories. Her characters, she asserts, "are filled with a hustlerish kind of energy" and, more importantly,

> they take risks they wouldn't have taken in their old, comfortable worlds to solve their problems. As they change citizenship, they are reborn.

Mukherjee's choice of metaphor is especially apt with reference to the women in her fiction, for the act of rebirth, like birth itself, is both painful, and, after a certain point, inevitable. It is both terrible and wonderful, and an act or process impossible to judge while one is in the midst of it. So the women in Mukherjee's stories are seen deep in this process of being reborn, of refashioning themselves, so deep that they can neither extricate themselves nor reverse the process, nor, once it has begun, would they wish to. There is a part of themselves, however, that is able to stand back a little and observe their own reaction to the process, their own ambivalence. We know this because Mukherjee weaves contradiction into the very fabric of the stories: positive assertions in interior monologues are undermined by negative visual images; the liberation of change is undermined by confusion or loss of identity; beauty is undermined by sadness.

A close look at three stories from *The Middleman and Other Stories*, each with a female protagonist from the Third World, illustrates the author's technique and her success in conveying this theme of rebirth or refashioning of the self by immigrant women. The stories are "The Tenant," "Jasmine," and "A Wife's Story," and in each of them, we encounter a different woman at a different stage in the subtle, complex, and traumatic process of becoming a new woman, one who is at home in the sometimes terrifying freedom of the new American culture. In each story, the exhilarating sense of possibility clashes with the debilitating sense of loss, yet the exuberant determination of the women attracts us to them and denies the power of pity.

Perhaps this attraction without pity derives from the women's avoidance of self-pity. In "The Tenant," we first meet the protagonist, Maya, sitting over a glass of bourbon (the first one of her life) with a new colleague from her new job in the English Department at the University of Northern Iowa. The American colleague, Fran, is on the Hiring, Tenure, and Reappointment Committee, and is partly responsible for bringing

Maya to the school. While Fran chats about her own life and gossips a little about Maya's landlord, Maya contemplates the immensity of her isolation and loneliness. And although she longs to be able to confide in someone, Fran even, she realizes that Fran is unable to receive these confidences because Fran cannot see that Maya is a woman caught in the mingled web of two very different cultures. To Fran, "a utopian and feminist," Maya is a bold adventurer who has made a clean break with her Indian past, but Maya understands, as the reader does, that there is no such thing as a "clean" break.

When Maya is invited to Sunday afternoon tea by another Bengali, Dr. Rabindra Chatterji, a professor of physics at her new university, she accepts with somewhat mixed feelings but dresses carefully in one of her best and loveliest saris. Once inside the Chatterji's house, in a raw sub urban development that seems full of other Third World nationalities, Maya allows the familiar sights and smells of Indian high tea to take her back to that other world of "Brahminness":

> The coffee table is already laid with platters of mutton croquettes, fish chops, onion pakoras, ghugni with puris, samosas, chutneys. Mrs. Chatterji has gone to too much trouble. Maya counts four kinds of sweetmeats in Corning casseroles on an end table. She looks into a see-through lid; spongy, white dumplings float in rosewater syrup. Planets contained, mysteries made visible.

Maya's hostess begins to ask questions about Maya's distinguished family in Calcutta, and Maya thinks to herself that "nothing in Calcutta is ever lost." She worries that the husband and wife may retreat to the kitchen, leaving her alone, so that they may exchange "whispered conferences about their guest's misadventures in America." Apparently the story of her "indiscretions" with various men, her marriage and divorce to an American, is known to the entire Bengali community in North America, which may be one of the reasons Dr. Chatterji both speaks and acts suggestively (he has one hand in his jockey shorts) when he drives her home that evening. Maya has been marked as a "loose" woman and as a divorcée, and therefore cannot ever hope to remarry respectably in the Indian (at least not the Brahmin) community: she is both in it and out of it, forever.

She occupies the same ambiguous position in the American community; although she has become an American citizen, she does not fully belong there either. She longs for a real sense of belonging, for the true companionship and love she dares to want, and eventually brings herself to answer an ad in the matrimonial column of *India Abroad*, the newspaper for expatriates. She answers the ad that declares:

> Hello! Hi! Yes, you *are* the one I'm looking for. You are the new emancipated Indo-American woman. You have a zest for life. You are at ease in USA and yet your ethics are rooted in Indian tradition.... I adore idealism, poetry, beauty. I abhor smugness, passivity, caste system. Write with recent photo. Better still, call!!!

Maya does call the man who placed the ad, Ashoke Mehta, and arranges a meeting at Chicago's O'Hare airport, "a neutral zone" they both prefer for this emotionally risky encounter. Until she meets Mehta, another immigrant who lives a life that bridges two worlds, she feels she lives in a "dead space" that she cannot articulate properly, even to herself. At the end of the story, after their courtship has entered its final phase, and she has decided to go to Connecticut to be with him, we know she will finally be able to repudiate her own accusations that her life is grim and perverse, that "she has changed her citizenship, but she hasn't broken through into the light, the vigor, the *bustle* of the New World." At the end, she does bustle off to meet the man who will make her whole again (and whom she will make whole) in this new life.

The next story, "Jasmine," also explores some of the more appalling, perhaps even "violent and grotesque aspects of [the] cultural collisions" Mukherjee writes about. In this story, the protagonist is a young Trinidadian woman named Jasmine who has been smuggled illegally into the US, all paid for by her father ("Girl, is opportunity come only once"), and goes to work first in the motel of the Indian family who helped her get there, and later as a "mother's helper... Americans were good with words to cover their shame" for an American family. When her new American employers ask about her family and her home, Jasmine recognizes the need to deceive them:

> There was nothing to tell about her hometown that wouldn't shame her in front of nice white American folk like the Moffitts. The place was shabby, the people were grasping and cheating and lying and life was full of despair and drink and wanting. But by the time she finished, the island sounded romantic.

Jasmine must construct a suitable, tolerable narrative of her past and her roots, in the same way that she is attempting to construct a positive narrative of her life in the New World. She seems precariously balanced between what she once was and what she hopes to become. She is like other Mukherjee characters, who

> remind one of circus performers, a combination of tightrope walkers and trapeze artists, as they search for secure, even familiar, places they can claim as their home.... They try to transcend the isolation of being a foreigner not only in another country but also in their own cultures.

Jasmine tries hard to cut all ties with "anything too islandy" as she struggles to refashion herself in America. Though she cleans, cooks, and irons for the Moffitts, she never stops giving thanks for having found such "a small, clean, friendly family... to build her new life around." She is constantly thanking Jesus for her good luck. The irony is that through all the exuberance and energy we see how terribly she is exploited by the Moffitts, and how unaware she often is of this exploitation, though it is not something she could recognize, even if it were pointed out.

At Christmas time, Jasmine is taken by Bill Moffitt to see her only "relatives" in the country, the Daboos, the Indian family she had originally worked for. In her original interview, she had told Bill and Lara Moffitt that Mr. Daboo was her mother's first cousin because

> she had thought it shameful in those days to have no papers, no family, no roots. Now Loretta and Viola in tight, bright pants seemed trashy like girls at Two-Johnny Bissoondath's Bar back home. She was stuck with the story of the Daboos being family. Village bumpkins, ha! She would break out. Soon.

We never do get to see Jasmine "break out," but the sense that she is a survivor emanates from the story even when she weeps with homesickness on Christmas Day. However, Mukherjee undercuts Jasmine's enthralled sense of unlimited possibility with a poignant moment of epiphany at the end of the story. In the last scene, she is half-willingly seduced by Bill Moffitt:

> She felt so good she was dizzy. She'd never felt this good on the island where men did this all the time, and girls went along with it always for favors. You couldn't feel really good in a nothing place.... She was a bright, pretty girl with no visa, no papers, and no birth certificate. No, nothing other than what she wanted to invent

and tell. She was a girl rushing wildly into the future.... it [the love-making] felt so good, so right that she forgot all the dreariness of her new life and gave herself up to it.

In "A Wife's Story," another immigrant woman has had her share of dreariness, loneliness, confusion, and anger in the effort to reshape her life in the land of opportunity. She too is weighed down by the burdens of two cultures and the hardship of trying to balance parts of her old life with the best of the new. The wife is a woman who has left her husband temporarily to pursue a graduate degree in New York, to break the cycle begun hundreds of years before. The narration is first person this time:

> Memories of Indian destitutes mix with the hordes of New York street people, and they float free, like astronauts, inside my head. I've made it. I'm making something of my life. I've left home, my husband, to get a Ph.D. in special ed. I have a multiple-entry visa and a small scholarship for two years. After that, we'll see. My mother was beaten by her mother-in-law, my grandmother, when she registered for French lessons at the Alliance Française. My grandmother, the eldest daughter of a rich zamindar, was illiterate.

This woman has even gone so far as to befriend another lonely immigrant, a Hungarian named Imre, who also has a spouse and family back home in the old country. Their friendship, so necessary to her survival in New York, would be unthinkable in her own country: in India, married women are not friends with men married to someone else. But Imre helps her to survive assaults on her dignity and the hopelessness of not truly belonging. He comforts her after a David Mamet play (*Glengarry Glen Ross*) in which she must endure terrible lines about Indians, such as, "Their women ... they look like they've just been fucked by a dead cat." She feels angry enough and strong enough to write a letter of protest to the playwright, or at least to write it in her head.

The Americanized but still Indian wife surprises herself occasionally by literally breaking out in very un-Indian behavior (like the time she impulsively hugs Imre on the street), and when her husband arrives for a visit, she realizes how many of the changes in her own behavior she now takes for granted. She dresses in a beautiful sari and her heavy, ornate wedding jewelery to greet him at JFK Airport, but underneath the familiar costume she is not the same woman at all. She is not even sure whether she is unhappy

about it, though she can tell her husband is disconcerted.

The end of the story encapsulates both the strength of her spirited struggle to refashion herself and the difficulty of achieving wholeness when one is stretched between two cultures. On her way to bed with her husband, she stops to look at herself:

> In the mirror that hangs on the bathroom door, I watch my naked body turn, the breasts, the thighs glow. The body's beauty amazes. I stand here shameless, in ways he has never seen me. I am free, afloat, watching somebody else.

This sense of floating is the key to the immigrant woman's experience, whether it is the English professor in "The Tenant," the Indian girl from the Caribbean in "Jasmine," or the PhD candidate in "A Wife's Story." Like Bernard Malamud, with whom Mukherjee compares herself in the *Massachusetts Review* interview, and other American writers of immigrant experiences, Mukherjee writes powerfully "about a minority community which escapes the ghetto and adapts itself to the patterns of the dominant American culture," and in her own words, her work "seems to find quite naturally a moral center." This moral center she speaks of comes quite naturally to her because she is attempting the nearly sacred task of making mysteries visible, to paraphrase an expression from "The Tenant."

Source: Arvindra Sant-Wade and Karen Marguerite Radell, "Refashioning the Self: Immigrant Women in Bharati Mukherjee's New World," in *Studies in Short Fiction*, Vol. 29, No. 1, Winter 1992, pp. 11–17.

Uma Parameswaran

In the following review, Parameswaran critiques the stories in Mukherjee's The Middleman and Other Stories, *commenting on a kind of cynicism that was absent in her earlier works.*

Bharati Mukherjee's second volume of short fiction consists of eleven stories that are wide-ranging in both settings and themes. Following her self-proclaimed American identity stated in her first volume of stories, *Darkness*, she explores the American experience through various personae or protagonists, four of whom are white American males and six of whom are females (only three of the women are of Indian origin). The result is a curious mix of voices and experiences that go to make up the celebration of being American (as she states in *Darkness*) as opposed to being Canadian.

Mukherjee's explorations of male attitudes and diction are interesting as experiments. Alfred Judah, the protagonist of the title story, is a macho operator in the rough-and-tumble world of smugglers: "Me? I make a living from things that fall. The big fat belly of Clovis T. Ransome bobs above me like whale shit at high tide." This image from the Florida scenery seems to have impressed her deeply, for in the next story we find "python turds, dozens of turds, light as cork and thick as a tree, riding high in the water." One is led to see a metaphorical streak that runs through the volume: these characters may be full-blooded Americans racing with both hands grabbing at all that life has to offer, but what they grasp is rather obnoxious all the way. More disturbing is the fact that Mukherjee's control of language is as devastating as ever, but now geared to a kind of cynicism that was absent in her earlier works. The characters who appear in the American stories, especially those from India, are stark caricatures of individuals: motel owners who use underpaid fellow Indians whenever possible; highly educated professionals whose linguistic idiosyncrasies are laughed at; a Vietnam veteran who brings home his daughter Eng and "rescues" her from "our enemies," the doctor and the hospital that terrify her; a ruffian who, we are asked to believe, is driven to auto theft and rape by his feeling of betrayal by some larger entity, the state.

The final story in the collection is "The Management of Grief." It has clearly come out of Mukherjee's scintillating and controversial documentary *The Sorrow and the Terror* (co-authored with Clark Blaise), on the crash of Air India flight 182 on 23 June 1985, which killed 329 passengers, most of whom were Canadians of Indian origin. There are minor questions that come to the reader's mind. Would the Stanley Cup have been played so late in June? Would the two young Sikhs have left for India within a month of having brought over their parents, who did not know the language and had no other family members? However, the story is very poignant and improves on E. M. Forster's idea of the failure of disparate cultures to connect. Though the families of the victims manage their grief in their own ways, the Canadian government finds itself in a quandary of communication, trying ineffectually to get paperwork done through translators. Shaila, who has lost her husband and two sons in the crash, is a volunteer interpreter; when the government agent Judith takes Shaila to the old Sikh couple who had been in Canada only a month before losing both their sons, we see their intractability clashing with Judith's impatience. No amount of explanation will persuade them to accept aid, because such acceptance might "end the company's or the country's obligations to them." Or, as Judith perceptively concludes, "They think signing a paper is signing their sons' death warrants." As Judith and Shaila leave, Judith talks about the next woman, "who is a real mess." At this, Shaila asks Judith to stop the car, gets out, and slams the door, leaving Judith to ask plaintively, "Is there anything I said? Anything I did . . . Shaila? Let's talk about it." The story would have been more effective if it had ended here, but Mukherjee follows her more traditional storytelling form of tying up loose ends.

The title of the volume goes beyond the title story to imply that many of Mukherjee's personae are middlemen, moving between cultures or events that pull others or themselves in opposite directions.

Source: Uma Parameswaran, "A review of *The Middleman and Other Stories*," in *World Literature Today*, Vol. 64, No. 2, Spring 1990, p. 363.

Carol Ascher

In the following excerpt, Ascher comments on how Mukherjee writes with the voice of immigrants from the Third World in The Middleman and Other Stories.

In the United States, where women are increasingly active in turning the wheels of history, so much fiction by women seems to be intensely personal, devoted exclusively to the tangles of friendship and love. This means that I can read a well-received novel in which from cover to cover no one goes to work, reads the newspaper, makes adjustments for inflation, votes, or—God forbid!—joins a political march.

Yet somehow when the writing is from the pen of a foreign woman these austere aesthetics seem to expand and let in more various winds. This may be because politics looks less rancorous or dogmatic when it's wrapped in foreign enchantment. But it also may be that women writing about countries where female roles remain highly restricted can still bring us the eroticism of passivity even while they describe historical change.

The three books under review here are all by Indian and Pakistani women writers who have left their homelands. Bharati Mukherjee now teaches at Columbia University and City University of New York, Sara Suleri teaches at Yale in New Haven, and Gita Mehta, as the book jacket informs us, "divides her time between India, London, and New York." Although grouped here because of their geographic commonality, they are vastly different in their styles, literary precursors and points of view. At the same time, all three have a strong sense of the sweep of history, and each struggles with the narrative problem of how to unite traditionally private lives with great social transformations.

...In *The Middleman and Other Stories* Bharati Mukherjee leaves the zenana far behind as she writes with the rushed, rootless, naively cynical voices of Third World newcomers and those who get involved with them. The eleven stories in this swift-moving collection are about the immigrants filling US cities and campuses: they come from India, Iraq, Afghanistan, Trinidad, Uganda, the Philippines, Sri Lanka, Vietnam, and they are all busy creating new ties and scrambling for a living, often in the shadier niches of the economy. As the narrator of "Danny's Girls," a Ugandan living in Flushing, says of his neighbor and idol, Danny, a northern Indian,

> He started out with bets and scalping tickets for Lata Mangeshkar or Mithun Chakravorty concerts at Madison Square Garden. Later he fixed beauty contests and then discovered the marriage racket.

> Danny took out ads in papers in India promising "guaranteed Permanent Resident status in the U.S." to grooms willing to proxy-marry American girls of Indian origin. He arranged quite a few. The brides and grooms didn't have to live with each other, or even meet or see each other. Sometimes the "brides" were smooth-skinned boys from the neighborhood.

Jasmine, in the story by her name, is a Trinidadian who's come over to Detroit from Canada hidden in the back of a truck. Without a Green Card, she finds a job at the Plantation Motel, run by a family of Trinidad Indians. "The Daboos were nobodies back home. They were lucky, that's all. They'd gotten here before the rush and bought up a motel and an ice-cream parlor." For her room and a few dollars, Jasmine does the book-keeping and cleaning up, as well as working on Mr. Daboo's match-up marriage service on Sundays.

It's "life in the procurement belt," as a white Vietnam vet says in "Loose Ends," his cold rage building at the fact that native Miami-ites like him are becoming "coolie labor" to foreigners.

> So I keep two things in mind nowadays. First, Florida was built for your pappy and grammie. I remember them, I was a kid here.... The second is this: Florida is run by locusts and behind them are sharks and even pythons and they've pretty well chewed up your mom and pop and all the other lawn bowlers and blue-haired ladies.

As enraging as it may be to the "natives" that Mukherjee's immigrants are so adept at finding ways to stay afloat economically, their piecemeal assimilation is also a source of wonder. "I envy her her freedom, her Green Card politics. It's love, not justice, that powers her," says Jeff of his Filipino girlfriend, Blanquita, in "Fighting for the Rebound." Although these newcomers may insist that they're ignored, misunderstood, or even despised, and that "Here, everything mixed up. Is helluva confusion, no?" they rapidly get the local lingo, and they are voracious consumers of microwave ovens, sweat-suits, VCRs, Press-On Nails, Cuisinart machines. In fact, if Bobbie Ann Mason has made being a hick chic, as Diane Johnston once said, then Bharati Mukherjee may be at the forefront of immigrant chic. Her prose has the flat deadpan that is very much in style, and she has an unerring eye for the detritus of shopping malls that draws these lonely newcomers.

As if in a covert lesson on the power of rootlessness to server the author's own loyalties to gender as much as to homeland, Mukherjee's collection contains as many stories with male as with female narrators. Yet I found two stories about Indian women particularly poignant. This may be because the two women are also academics, and more thoughtful and torn about their experiences than are the others whose dog-eat-dog world offers them little time for reflection.

In "A Wife's Story," Mrs. Bhatt has come to New York to take a two-year course in Special Ed at Teachers College. Freed from the strict roles of Indian society, she has even become friends with a Hungarian man with whom she goes to the theatre. When her husband comes for a short visit, he seems an unlikely stranger. Still, she puts on her sari, gets tickets for a depressing package tour of the city, and obligingly takes him shopping at the discount stores.

In "The Tenant," Maya Sanyal of Calcutta is in Cedar Falls, Iowa, where she has come to teach Comparative Literature. Afraid of her bachelor landlord, Maya answers the "India Abroad" personals from Indian men, and puts on her best sari to go to tea at the home of the other Indian professor on campus, a Dr. Chatterji. There everything remains traditional, the old "virtues made physical." Yet something has snapped for Dr. Chatterji—as it has for Maya. Both experience their loneliness and anomie as erotic craving.

Although Mukherjee's characters only participate in public life to advance their narrow private interests, in total they *are* the great social transformation affecting North America. Finishing the collection, one senses that the strategy of short stories has served her well. Whether or not one might add other characters to the mosaic to form a truer, more complete picture, there is no other writer documenting these largely unseen immigrants; one of the great joys, for me, of reading *The Middleman* is experiencing a world that generally remains just at the edge of my consciousness.

Source: Carol Ascher, "After the Raj: Review of *The Middleman and Other Stories*," in *Women's Review of Books*, Vol. 6, No. 12, September 1989, pp. 17–19.

Alison B. Carb

In the following excerpt, Carb and Mukherjee discuss how The Middleman and Other Stories *was written and what Mukherjee sees as her role in literature.*

. . . Mukherjee finished the manuscript of The Middleman *during the summer of 1987, when she was on vacation from teaching at Columbia University and Queens College. At the same time she was busy with other projects: updating the introduction to the book on the Air India crash, reviewing and editing the work of immigrant writers, and participating in literary activities sponsored by PEN.*

During November of 1987, I interviewed Mukherjee at her home near Columbia University where she was in the process of moving yet again to an apartment downtown. At first she seemed shy. A small, slender woman with a cloud of dark hair and luminous eyes, she motioned me into the living room without looking at me and said in a low voice, "Just call me Bharati, it will be easier." But, after we were seated around a glass coffee table, a confident, almost masterful personality emerged. I began the interview by asking her how long it took her to complete her soon-to-be-published collection.

BHARATI MUKHERJEE: The stories were done in two intense flurries, although I had been thinking about the book for a long time. As soon as *Darkness* was published in 1985, I started working on stories for *The Middleman*. One cycle of stories was written over an eight-month period during a semester off from teaching and on an NEA grant. Then my work was interrupted while I was teaching and writing the book on the Air India crash, *The Sorrow and the Terror*, with my husband. Once that book was over, I wrote another cycle of stories for *The Middleman* over the summer of 1987. So it took me about a year and a half to write this book if one includes the break in between.

CARB: Where did you get the idea for the book?

MUKHERJEE: It grew out of an incomplete novel about a man who served in the Army in Vietnam, and who, after the war, becomes a professional soldier and hires himself out in Afghanistan and Central America. While I was working on that novel, a character with a minor role, a Jew who has relocated from Baghdad to Bombay to Brooklyn, took control and wrote his own story. He attracted me because he was a cynical person and a hustler, as many immigrant survivors have to be.

So Alfie Judah, the protagonist in *The Middleman*, travels around the world, providing people with what they need—guns, narcotics, automobiles. The story takes place in an unnamed country in Central America where he becomes involved in a guerilla war.

Incidentally, the Vietnam veteran, Jeb Marshall who comes from Miami, is featured in his own story in this collection, called "Loose Ends." A large number of these stories are told by native-born Americans, but even when I write about them I tell how their lives are affected by newly arrived or first-generation Americans.

For example, one of my stories, "Fighting for the Rebound," is narrated by an Atlanta stockbroker who falls in love with a former millionaire's daughter from the Philippines, who supports Marcos. As a writer, my voice is supple and I can enter diverse characters' lives and let each of them speak for themselves.

The new, changing America is the theme of the stories in *The Middleman*. For me, immigration from the Third World to this country is a metaphor for the process of uprooting and rerooting, or what my husband Clark Blaise in his book *Resident Alien* calls "unhousement" and "rehousement." The immigrants in my stories go through extreme transformations in America and at the same time they alter the country's appearance and psychological make-up. In some ways, they are like European immigrants of earlier eras. But they have different gods. And they come for different reasons.

CARB: What is special about this collection?

MUKHERJEE: I write about well-known American establishments, such as the family, in unique ways. In my stories, the families are not the American families which we are accustomed to reading about in fiction. The American family has become very different, not just because of social influences and new sexual standards, but because of the interaction between mainstream Americans and new immigrants.

For example, there's a story in *The Middleman* entitled "Fathering," in which the secure life of a yuppie living with his girlfriend in a small town in upstate New York is disrupted when the half-Vietnamese child he had fathered in Saigon comes to visit.

In another story, "Orbiting," a New Jersey woman of Italian origin invites her parents and her Afghan boyfriend for Thanksgiving dinner at her home and a crisis occurs over who should carve the turkey, her father or the boyfriend. My stories are discomfiting because they challenge accepted codes of behavior in this country and show the changes taking place here.

CARB: Do you see changes in your writing style in The Middleman?

MUKHERJEE: My style has changed because I am becoming more Americanized with each passing year. American fiction has a kind of energy that fiction from other cultures seems to lack right now. The stories in *The Middleman*, I like to think, have this energy and passion as well. Each character and story suggests a different style.

When I sit down in my study to write, I don't immediately say, "I have to write an experimental story." The story idea itself dictates the appropriate voice for it and how lean or fleshy a paragraph might be. I write some stories from a very authoritative third person point of view. With others I use an intimate, textured style and a first person point of view.

My first novel, *The Tiger's Daughter*, has a rather British feel to it. I used the omniscient point of view and plenty of irony. This was because my concept of language and notions of how a novel was constructed were based on British models. I had gone to school in London as a young child and later to a British convent school for elite young women in post-colonial India, where we read English writers like Jane Austen and E. M. Forster.

By the time I wrote *Darkness* I had adopted American English as my language. I moved away from using irony and was no longer comfortable using an authoritative point of view. In addition, I started to write short stories instead of novels. The short story form requires us to express our thoughts concisely and not waste a single sentence or detail.

CARB: How does your writing contrast with that of other India-born writers?

MUKHERJEE: There is a large difference between myself and these authors. Unlike writers such as Anita Desai and R. K. Narayan, I do not write in Indian English about Indians living in India. My role models, view of the world, and experiences are unlike theirs. These writers live in a world in which there are still certainties and rules. They are part of their society's mainstream. Wonderful writers as they are, I am unable to identify with them because they describe characters who fit into their community in different ways than my naturalized Americans fit into communities in Queens or Atlanta.

On the other hand, I don't write from the vantage point of an Indian expatriate like V. S. Naipaul. Naipaul, who was born in Trinidad because his relatives left India involuntarily to settle there, has different attitudes about himself. He writes about living in perpetual exile and about the impossibility of ever having a home. Like Naipaul, I am a writer from the Third World but unlike him I left India by choice to settle in the U.S. I have adopted this country as my home. I view myself as an American author in the tradition of other American authors whose ancestors arrived at Ellis Island.

CARB: Which authors do you think your writing most closely resembles?

MUKHERJEE: (Emphatically) I see a strong likeness between my writing and Bernard Malamud's, in spite of the fact that he describes the lives of East European Jewish immigrants and I talk about the lives of newcomers from the Third World. Like Malamud, I write about a minority community which escapes the ghetto and adapts itself to the patterns of the dominant American culture. Like Malamud's, my work seems to find quite naturally a moral center. Isaac Babel is another author who is a literary ancestor for me. I also feel a kinship with Joseph Conrad and Anton Chekhov. But Malamud most of all speaks to me as a writer and I admire his work a great deal. Immersing myself in his work gave me the self-confidence to write about my own community.

CARB: How does your writing differ from Malamud's?

MUKHERJEE: When you are from the Third World, when you have dark skin and religious beliefs that do not conform to those of Judaism or Christianity, mainstream America responds to you in ways you can't foresee. My fiction has to consider race, politics, religion, as well as certain nastinesses that other generations of white immigrant American writers may not have had to take into account.

I was born into a Hindu Bengali Brahmin family which means that I have a different sense of self, of existence, and of mortality than do writers like Malamud. I believe that our souls can be reborn in another body, so the perspective I have about a single character's life is different from that of an American writer who believes that he only has one life.

As a Hindu, I was brought up on oral tradition and epic literature in which animals can talk, birds can debate ethical questions, and monsters can change shapes. I believe in the existence of alternate realities, and this belief makes itself evident in my fiction.

CARB: Do you think American readers and editors have been receptive to your work?

MUKHERJEE: Yes. Americans have a healthy curiosity about new writers and new ideas. American publishing houses have been far more ready to receive my writing than have houses in Canada, where the attitude in the '60s and '70s was that if one hadn't played in snow and grown up eating oatmeal one didn't have anything relevant to say to Canadian readers.

I was touched when one of my "immigrant" stories, "The Tenant," which was printed in a small literary quarterly, the *Literary Review*, was read by people and eventually made it into *The Best American Short Stories 1987*.

Writing short stories helped too. As soon as I started writing them, my work became more available to American readers than my novels had been. The novels were not easily obtainable because initially there were no paperback editions. This past year they were reissued by Penguin Books.

Unfortunately, one of the difficulties that writers like myself face are editors of large-circulation magazines who are unwilling to risk publishing writers whose fictional worlds are not intensely familiar or overtly sellable. They say my work is "too strong" for their readers.

CARB: What other difficulties have you experienced as a writer?

MUKHERJEE: (In a low, strained voice) I had a very bad time during the 1970s when my husband and I lived and taught in Canada. I had gone there with him because his family lived there. The 70s were horrendous years for Indians in Canada. There was a lot of bigotry against Canadian citizens of Indian origin, especially in Toronto, and it upset me terribly when I encountered this or saw other people experiencing it.

There was a pattern of discrimination. I was refused service in stores. I would have to board a bus last when I had been the first person on line. I was followed by detectives in department stores who assumed I was a shoplifter or treated like a prostitute in hotels. I was even physically roughed up in a Toronto subway station.

I found myself constantly fighting battles against racial prejudice. Toronto made me into a civil rights activist. I wrote essays about the devastating personal effects of racism. For many years I didn't find the strength to turn my back on Canada and do what I really wanted to do: write fiction.

But in 1980 I did leave. We were living in Montreal at the time. I resigned my full professorship at McGill University and came to the United States with my family. I felt guilty about pulling my husband and sons away from what was home but it was a question of my own self-preservation. It was the only way I could think of removing myself from the persistent hurt.

Being in the U.S. was a tremendous relief after Canada. I suddenly felt freed to write the thousands of stories inside my head. In the U.S. I wasn't continuously forced to deal with my physical appearance. I could wear Western clothes and blend in with people on a New York City street. America, with its melting pot theory of immigration, has a healthier attitude toward Indian immigrants than Canada. Although this country has its share of racial problems there are human rights laws and ways to obtain legal redress in the courts.

CARB: Do you find it easy or difficult to write?

MUKHERJEE: I *like* to write but finding the time isn't easy. It would be ideal if I could write from nine to three or four every day. But I have so many jobs to do, teaching, lecturing, writing articles and reviews, taking care of my family, that I can't write as much as I would like. When I do sit down at the word processor in my study I'm ready to go and the writing just flows. Especially where short stories are concerned. I hear a voice inside my head and start typing. Not everything I write appears in a book though, I'm a great reviser.

My husband, Clark, also helps me with my fiction. He is an American-Canadian author. Like me, he teaches in the English Department at Columbia University. We work well on joint writing projects such as the nonfiction books we did, *Days and Nights in Calcutta*, about our year long stay with my family in India in 1977, and *The Sorrow and the Terror*.

We have an intensely literary marriage. We talk about writing and Clark is a very good audience for my work. He reads it and comments on it just as he did when we were students in the Writers' Workshop at the University of Iowa, where we first met.

CARB: Were you interested in writing before graduate school?

MUKHERJEE: Yes. I always knew I was going to be a writer. I had wanted to write since I was a child. The world of fiction seemed more real to me than the world around me. I started my first novel when I was about nine or ten. It came to seventy or eighty pages. It was about English children and was set in England.

But it wasn't until I was in high school in Calcutta that I started writing short stories for school magazines. I don't remember what these stories were about and I want to forget them

(laughs), but I recall writing one from Napoleon's point of view. My imagination was stimulated by reading about European history and Western civilization. By the time I was at college I decided that I wasn't going to be a chemist like my father. I enjoyed writing far too much.

CARB: You have come from a complex background and world. Is it hard for you as a South Asian immigrant writer to convey the immigrant experience to native-born American audiences?

MUKHERJEE: No, no, no. My task as an author is to make my intricate and unknown world comprehensible to mainstream American readers. This is what good novels and stories do. If my fiction is effective, unexplained and cultural aspects about the Indian community in Queens or the Korean community in New York will become accessible.

We immigrants have fascinating tales to relate. Many of us have lived in newly independent or emerging countries which are plagued by civil and religious conflicts. We have experienced rapid changes in the history of the nations in which we lived. When we uproot ourselves from those countries and come here, either by choice or out of necessity, we suddenly must absorb 200 years of American history and learn to adapt to American society. Our lives are remarkable, often heroic.

I attempt to illustrate this in my novels and short stories. My characters want to make it in the new world; they are filled with a hustlerish kind of energy, like Alfie Judah in *The Middleman*. Although they are often hurt or depressed by setbacks in their new lives and occupations, they do not give up. They take risks they wouldn't have taken in their old, comfortable worlds to solve their problems. As they change citizenship, they are reborn.

My aim is to expose Americans to the energetic voices of new settlers in this country, not only through my own writing but by editing and reviewing the fiction of writers from nontraditional nations, including India, Sri Lanka, Egypt, and South Africa. By doing this I hope to make editors aware of how these writers are changing the scope and structure of American fiction.

Source: Alison B. Carb, "An Interview with Bharati Mukhejee," in *Massachusetts Review*, Vol. 29, No. 4, Winter 1988–89, pp. 645–54.

SOURCES

"About Us," in *Indian Business & Professional Women*, http://ibpw.net/?q = about (accessed August 24, 2010).

Alam, Fakrul, *Bharati Mukherjee*, Twayne Publishers, 1996, pp. 1–14, 78–99.

Ascher, Carol, "After the Raj," in *Women's Review of Books*, Vol. 6, No. 12, September 1989, pp. 17–19.

Banerjee, Ranee Kaur, "'Singing in the Seams': Bharati Mukherjee's Immigrants," in *No Small World: Visions and Revisions of World Literature*, National Council of Teachers of English, 1996, pp. 189–201.

Bhatia, Sunil, *American Karma: Race, Culture, and Identity in the Indian Diaspora*, New York University Press, 2007, pp. 1–4, 12–16.

Blaise, Clark, and Bharati Mukherjee, *Days and Nights in Calcutta*, Doubleday, 1977, p. 173.

Byers-Pevitts, Beverley, "An Interview with Bharati Mukherjee," in *Speaking of the Short Story: Interviews with Contemporary Writers*, University Press of Mississippi, 1997, pp. 189–98.

Carb, Alison, "An Interview with Bharati Mukherjee," in *Massachusetts Review*, Vol. 29, No. 4, Winter 1988–89, pp. 645–54.

Carpenter, Allan, and Randy Lyon, *Between Two Rivers: Iowa Year by Year, 1846–1996*, 3rd ed., Iowa State University Press, 1997, pp. 294–97.

Chandra, Subhash, "Americanness of the Immigrants in *The Middleman and Other Stories*," in *The Fiction of Bharati Mukherjee: A Critical Symposium*, Prestige Books, 1996, pp. 130–36.

Connell, Michaek, Jessie Grearson, and Tom Grimes, "An Interview with Bharati Mukherjee and Clark Blaise," in *Iowa Review*, Vol. 20, Fall 1990, pp. 7–32; reprinted in *Conversations with Bharati Mukherjee*, edited by Bradley C. Edwards, University Press of Mississippi, 2009, pp. 37–58.

Dascălu, Cristina Emanuela, *Imaginary Homelands of Writers in Exile: Salman Rushdie, Bharati Mukherjee, and V. S. Naipaul*, Cambia Press, 2007, pp. 2–5, 65–92.

Doerksen, Teri Ann, "Bharati Mukherjee," in *Dictionary of Literary Biography*, Vol. 218, *American Short-Story Writers since World War II, Second Series*, edited by Patrick Meanor and Gwen Crane, The Gale Group, 1999, pp. 228–34.

Gabriel, Sharmani Patricia, "'Routes of Identity': In Conversation with Bharati Mukherjee," in *Ariel*, Vol. 34, No. 4, October 2003, pp. 125–38.

Gomez, Christine, "The On-going Quest of Bharati Mukherjee from Expatriation to Immigration," in *The Fiction of Bharati Mukherjee: A Critical Symposium*, Prestige Books, 1996, pp. 25–38.

Hancock, Geoff, "An Interview with Bharati Mukherjee," in *Canadian Fiction Magazine*, Vol. 59, May 1987, pp. 30–44; reprinted in *Conversations with Bharati Mukherjee*, edited by Bradley C. Edwards, University Press of Mississippi, 2009, pp. 10–24.

Imtiaz, Shagufta, "Place and Displacement in 'The Tenant,'" in *The Fiction of Bharati Mukherjee: A Critical Symposium*, Prestige Books, 1996, pp. 125–29.

Jayaram, V., "Delusion: The Power of Maya and the Nature of Reality," in *Hinduwebsite*, http://hinduwebsite.com/hinduism/h_maya.asp (accessed June 9, 2010).

Mathur, Suchitra, "Bharati Mukherjee: Overview," in *Feminist Writers*, edited by Pamela Kester-Shelton, St. James Press, 1996.

Mukherjee, Bharati, "The Tenant," in *The Middleman and Other Stories*, Grove Press, 1988, pp. 97–113.

Pati, Mitali R., "Love and the Indian Immigrant in Bharati Mukherjee's Short Fiction," in *Bharati Mukherjee: Critical Perspectives*, Garland Publishing, 1993, pp. 197–211.

Raban, Jonathan, "Savage Boulevards, Easy Streets," Review of *The Middleman and Other Stories*, in *New York Times*, June 19, 1988.

Rao, A. V. Krishna, "From Expatriation to Immigration: The Case of Bharati Mukherjee," in *The Fiction of Bharati Mukherjee: A Critical Symposium*, Prestige Books, 1996, pp. 105–15.

Sant-Wade, Arvindra, and Karen Marguerite Radell, "Refashioning the Self: Immigrant Women in Bharati Mukherjee's New World," in *Studies in Short Fiction*, Vol. 29, No. 1, Winter 1992, pp. 11–17.

Saran, Parmatma, *The Asian Indian Experience in the United States*, Schenkman Publishing, 1985, pp. 25–35.

Schwieder, Dorothy, *Iowa: The Middle Land*, Iowa State University Press, 1996, pp. 316–21.

Terrazas, Aaron, "Indian Immigrants in the United States," in *Migration Information Source*, http://www.migrationinformation.org/usfocus/display.cfm?id = 687 (accessed August 24, 2010).

Tikoo, S. K., "The American Dream: Immigration and Transformation in *The Middleman and Other Stories*," in *The Fiction of Bharati Mukherjee: A Critical Symposium*, Prestige Books, 1996, pp. 137–47.

FURTHER READING

Bhaskarananda, Swami, *The Essentials of Hinduism: A Comprehensive Overview of the World's Oldest Religion*, Viveka Press, 2002.
> This text by a Ramakrishna monk is intended to introduce Westerners to the basic tenets of Hinduism.

Forster, E. M., *A Passage to India*, Penguin Books, 1998.
> Originally published in 1924, Forster's classic tale revolves around an accusation and trial set during the Indian movement for independence in the early 1920s.

Naipaul, V. S., *An Area of Darkness*, Vintage Books, 2002.

> In this travelogue originally published in 1964, the Nobel Prize-winning Naipaul, who was born in Trinidad, relates his first trip to his ancestral homeland, India, which left him profoundly disillusioned.

Tolstoy, Leo, *Anna Karenina*, translated by Richard Pevear and Larissa Volokhonsky, Viking, 2001.

> This Russian masterpiece, which was first published in complete form in 1878, is the story of the tribulations of an aristocratic woman who for the sake of love abandons her husband and son, a move that is frowned upon by society and leads to tragic consequences.

SUGGESTED SEARCH TERMS

Bharati Mukherjee

The Middleman AND Mukherjee

The Tenant AND Mukherjee

The Middleman AND The Tenant

East Indian American AND literature

immigrant AND literature

Mukherjee AND postcolonialism

Mukherjee AND second-wave feminism

Mukherjee AND immigration

Mukherjee AND Canada AND racism

Glossary of Literary Terms

A

Aestheticism: A literary and artistic movement of the nineteenth century. Followers of the movement believed that art should not be mixed with social, political, or moral teaching. The statement "art for art's sake" is a good summary of aestheticism. The movement had its roots in France, but it gained widespread importance in England in the last half of the nineteenth century, where it helped change the Victorian practice of including moral lessons in literature. Oscar Wilde and Edgar Allan Poe are two of the best-known "aesthetes" of the late nineteenth century.

Allegory: A narrative technique in which characters representing things or abstract ideas are used to convey a message or teach a lesson. Allegory is typically used to teach moral, ethical, or religious lessons but is sometimes used for satiric or political purposes. Many fairy tales are allegories.

Allusion: A reference to a familiar literary or historical person or event, used to make an idea more easily understood. Joyce Carol Oates's story "Where Are You Going, Where Have You Been?" exhibits several allusions to popular music.

Analogy: A comparison of two things made to explain something unfamiliar through its similarities to something familiar, or to prove one point based on the acceptance of another. Similes and metaphors are types of analogies.

Antagonist: The major character in a narrative or drama who works against the hero or protagonist. The Misfit in Flannery O'Connor's story "A Good Man Is Hard to Find" serves as the antagonist for the Grandmother.

Anthology: A collection of similar works of literature, art, or music. Zora Neale Hurston's "The Eatonville Anthology" is a collection of stories that take place in the same town.

Anthropomorphism: The presentation of animals or objects in human shape or with human characteristics. The term is derived from the Greek word for "human form." The fur necklet in Katherine Mansfield's story "Miss Brill" has anthropomorphic characteristics.

Anti-hero: A central character in a work of literature who lacks traditional heroic qualities such as courage, physical prowess, and fortitude. Anti-heroes typically distrust conventional values and are unable to commit themselves to any ideals. They generally feel helpless in a world over which they have no control. Anti-heroes usually accept, and often celebrate, their positions as social outcasts. A well-known anti-hero is Walter Mitty in James Thurber's story "The Secret Life of Walter Mitty."

Archetype: The word archetype is commonly used to describe an original pattern or model from which all other things of the same kind are made. Archetypes are the literary images that grow out of the "collective unconscious," a theory proposed by psychologist Carl Jung. They appear in literature as incidents and plots that repeat basic patterns of life. They may also appear as stereotyped characters. The "schlemiel" of Yiddish literature is an archetype.

Autobiography: A narrative in which an individual tells his or her life story. Examples include Benjamin Franklin's *Autobiography* and Amy Hempel's story "In the Cemetery Where Al Jolson Is Buried," which has autobiographical characteristics even though it is a work of fiction.

Avant-garde: A literary term that describes new writing that rejects traditional approaches to literature in favor of innovations in style or content. Twentieth-century examples of the literary avant-garde include the modernists and the minimalists.

B

Belles-lettres: A French term meaning "fine letters" or" beautiful writing." It is often used as a synonym for literature, typically referring to imaginative and artistic rather than scientific or expository writing. Current usage sometimes restricts the meaning to light or humorous writing and appreciative essays about literature. Lewis Carroll's *Alice in Wonderland* epitomizes the realm of belles-lettres.

Bildungsroman: A German word meaning "novel of development." The *bildungsroman* is a study of the maturation of a youthful character, typically brought about through a series of social or sexual encounters that lead to self-awareness. J. D. Salinger's *Catcher in the Rye* is a *bildungsroman*, and Doris Lessing's story "Through the Tunnel" exhibits characteristics of a *bildungsroman* as well.

Black Aesthetic Movement: A period of artistic and literary development among African Americans in the 1960s and early 1970s. This was the first major African-American artistic movement since the Harlem Renaissance and was closely paralleled by the civil rights and black power movements. The black aesthetic writers attempted to produce works of art that would be meaningful to the black masses. Key figures in black aesthetics included one of its founders, poet and

playwright Amiri Baraka, formerly known as Le Roi Jones; poet and essayist Haki R. Madhubuti, formerly Don L. Lee; poet and playwright Sonia Sanchez; and dramatist Ed Bullins. Works representative of the Black Aesthetic Movement include Amiri Baraka's play *Dutchman,* a 1964 Obie award-winner.

Black Humor: Writing that places grotesque elements side by side with humorous ones in an attempt to shock the reader, forcing him or her to laugh at the horrifying reality of a disordered world. "Lamb to the Slaughter," by Roald Dahl, in which a placid housewife murders her husband and serves the murder weapon to the investigating policemen, is an example of black humor.

C

Catharsis: The release or purging of unwanted emotions—specifically fear and pity—brought about by exposure to art. The term was first used by the Greek philosopher Aristotle in his *Poetics* to refer to the desired effect of tragedy on spectators.

Character: Broadly speaking, a person in a literary work. The actions of characters are what constitute the plot of a story, novel, or poem. There are numerous types of characters, ranging from simple, stereotypical figures to intricate, multifaceted ones. "Characterization" is the process by which an author creates vivid, believable characters in a work of art. This may be done in a variety of ways, including (1) direct description of the character by the narrator; (2) the direct presentation of the speech, thoughts, or actions of the character; and (3) the responses of other characters to the character. The term "character" also refers to a form originated by the ancient Greek writer Theophrastus that later became popular in the seventeenth and eighteenth centuries. It is a short essay or sketch of a person who prominently displays a specific attribute or quality, such as miserliness or ambition. "Miss Brill," a story by Katherine Mansfield, is an example of a character sketch.

Classical: In its strictest definition in literary criticism, classicism refers to works of ancient Greek or Roman literature. The term may also be used to describe a literary work of recognized importance (a "classic") from any time period or literature that exhibits the traits of classicism. Examples of later works and authors now described as classical include French literature of the seventeenth century, Western novels of the nineteenth century, and American fiction of the mid-nineteenth century such as that written by James Fenimore Cooper and Mark Twain.

Climax: The turning point in a narrative, the moment when the conflict is at its most intense. Typically, the structure of stories, novels, and plays is one of rising action, in which tension builds to the climax, followed by falling action, in which tension lessens as the story moves to its conclusion.

Comedy: One of two major types of drama, the other being tragedy. Its aim is to amuse, and it typically ends happily. Comedy assumes many forms, such as farce and burlesque, and uses a variety of techniques, from parody to satire. In a restricted sense the term comedy refers only to dramatic presentations, but in general usage it is commonly applied to nondramatic works as well.

Comic Relief: The use of humor to lighten the mood of a serious or tragic story, especially in plays. The technique is very common in Elizabethan works, and can be an integral part of the plot or simply a brief event designed to break the tension of the scene.

Conflict: The conflict in a work of fiction is the issue to be resolved in the story. It usually occurs between two characters, the protagonist and the antagonist, or between the protagonist and society or the protagonist and himself or herself. The conflict in Washington Irving's story "The Devil and Tom Walker" is that the Devil wants Tom Walker's soul but Tom does not want to go to hell.

Criticism: The systematic study and evaluation of literary works, usually based on a specific method or set of principles. An important part of literary studies since ancient times, the practice of criticism has given rise to numerous theories, methods, and "schools," sometimes producing conflicting, even contradictory, interpretations of literature in general as well as of individual works. Even such basic issues as what constitutes a poem or a novel have been the subject of much criticism over the centuries. Seminal texts of literary criticism include Plato's *Republic,* Aristotle's *Poetics,* Sir Philip Sidney's *The Defence of Poesie,* and John Dryden's *Of Dramatic Poesie.* Contemporary schools of criticism include deconstruction, feminist, psychoanalytic, poststructuralist, new historicist, postcolonialist, and reader-response.

D

Deconstruction: A method of literary criticism characterized by multiple conflicting interpretations of a given work. Deconstructionists consider the impact of the language of a work and suggest that the true meaning of the work is not necessarily the meaning that the author intended.

Deduction: The process of reaching a conclusion through reasoning from general premises to a specific premise. Arthur Conan Doyle's character Sherlock Holmes often used deductive reasoning to solve mysteries.

Denotation: The definition of a word, apart from the impressions or feelings it creates in the reader. The word "apartheid" denotes a political and economic policy of segregation by race, but its connotations—oppression, slavery, inequality—are numerous.

Denouement: A French word meaning "the unknotting." In literature, it denotes the resolution of conflict in fiction or drama. The *denouement* follows the climax and provides an outcome to the primary plot situation as well as an explanation of secondary plot complications. A well-known example of *denouement* is the last scene of the play *As You Like It* by William Shakespeare, in which couples are married, an evildoer repents, the identities of two disguised characters are revealed, and a ruler is restored to power. Also known as "falling action."

Detective Story: A narrative about the solution of a mystery or the identification of a criminal. The conventions of the detective story include the detective's scrupulous use of logic in solving the mystery; incompetent or ineffectual police; a suspect who appears guilty at first but is later proved innocent; and the detective's friend or confidant—often the narrator—whose slowness in interpreting clues emphasizes by contrast the detective's brilliance. Edgar Allan Poe's "Murders in the Rue Morgue" is commonly regarded as the earliest example of this type of story. Other practitioners are Arthur Conan Doyle, Dashiell Hammett, and Agatha Christie.

Dialogue: Dialogue is conversation between people in a literary work. In its most restricted sense, it refers specifically to the speech of characters in a drama. As a specific literary genre, a "dialogue" is a composition in which characters debate an issue or idea.

Didactic: A term used to describe works of literature that aim to teach a moral, religious, political, or practical lesson. Although didactic elements are often found inartistically pleasing works, the term "didactic" usually refers to literature in which the message is more important than the form. The term may also be used to criticize a work that the critic finds "overly didactic," that is, heavy-handed in its delivery of a lesson. An example of didactic literature is John Bunyan's *Pilgrim's Progress*.

Dramatic Irony: Occurs when the reader of a work of literature knows something that a character in the work itself does not know. The irony is in the contrast between the intended meaning of the statements or actions of a character and the additional information understood by the audience.

Dystopia: An imaginary place in a work of fiction where the characters lead dehumanized, fearful lives. George Orwell's *Nineteen Eighty-four*, and Margaret Atwood's *Handmaid's Tale* portray versions of dystopia.

E

Edwardian: Describes cultural conventions identified with the period of the reign of Edward VII of England (1901–1910). Writers of the Edwardian Age typically displayed a strong reaction against the propriety and conservatism of the Victorian Age. Their work often exhibits distrust of authority in religion, politics, and art and expresses strong doubts about the soundness of conventional values. Writers of this era include E. M. Forster, H. G. Wells, and Joseph Conrad.

Empathy: A sense of shared experience, including emotional and physical feelings, with someone or something other than oneself. Empathy is often used to describe the response of a reader to a literary character.

Epilogue: A concluding statement or section of a literary work. In dramas, particularly those of the seventeenth and eighteenth centuries, the epilogue is a closing speech, often in verse, delivered by an actor at the end of a play and spoken directly to the audience.

Epiphany: A sudden revelation of truth inspired by a seemingly trivial incident. The term was widely used by James Joyce in his critical writings, and the stories in Joyce's *Dubliners* are commonly called "epiphanies."

Epistolary Novel: A novel in the form of letters. The form was particularly popular in the eighteenth century. The form can also be applied to short stories, as in Edwidge Danticat's "Children of the Sea."

Epithet: A word or phrase, often disparaging or abusive, that expresses a character trait of someone or something. "The Napoleon of crime" is an epithet applied to Professor Moriarty, arch-rival of Sherlock Holmes in Arthur Conan Doyle's series of detective stories.

Existentialism: A predominantly twentieth-century philosophy concerned with the nature and perception of human existence. There are two major strains of existentialist thought: atheistic and Christian. Followers of atheistic existentialism believe that the individual is alone in a godless universe and that the basic human condition is one of suffering and loneliness. Nevertheless, because there are no fixed values, individuals can create their own characters—indeed, they can shape themselves—through the exercise of free will. The atheistic strain culminates in and is popularly associated with the works of Jean-Paul Sartre. The Christian existentialists, on the other hand, believe that only in God may people find freedom from life's anguish. The two strains hold certain beliefs in common: that existence cannot be fully understood or described through empirical effort; that anguish is a universal element of life; that individuals must bear responsibility for their actions; and that there is no common standard of behavior or perception for religious and ethical matters. Existentialist thought figures prominently in the works of such authors as Franz Kafka, Fyodor Dostoyevsky, and Albert Camus.

Expatriatism: The practice of leaving one's country to live for an extended period in another country. Literary expatriates include Irish author James Joyce who moved to Italy and France, American writers James Baldwin, Ernest Hemingway, Gertrude Stein, and

F. Scott Fitzgerald who lived and wrote in Paris, and Polish novelist Joseph Conrad in England.

Exposition: Writing intended to explain the nature of an idea, thing, or theme. Expository writing is often combined with description, narration, or argument.

Expressionism: An indistinct literary term, originally used to describe an early twentieth-century school of German painting. The term applies to almost any mode of unconventional, highly subjective writing that distorts reality in some way. Advocates of Expressionism include Federico Garcia Lorca, Eugene O'Neill, Franz Kafka, and James Joyce.

F

Fable: A prose or verse narrative intended to convey amoral. Animals or inanimate objects with human characteristics often serve as characters in fables. A famous fable is Aesop's "The Tortoise and the Hare."

Fantasy: A literary form related to mythology and folklore. Fantasy literature is typically set in non-existent realms and features supernatural beings. Notable examples of literature with elements of fantasy are Gabriel Gárcia Márquez's story "The Handsomest Drowned Man in the World" and Ursula K. Le Guin's "The Ones Who Walk Away from Omelas."

Farce: A type of comedy characterized by broad humor, outlandish incidents, and often vulgar subject matter. Much of the comedy in film and television could more accurately be described as farce.

Fiction: Any story that is the product of imagination rather than a documentation of fact. Characters and events in such narratives may be based in real life but their ultimate form and configuration is a creation of the author.

Figurative Language: A technique in which an author uses figures of speech such as hyperbole, irony, metaphor, or simile for a particular effect. Figurative language is the opposite of literal language, in which every word is truthful, accurate, and free of exaggeration or embellishment.

Flashback: A device used in literature to present action that occurred before the beginning of the story. Flashbacks are often introduced as the dreams or recollections of one or more characters.

Foil: A character in a work of literature whose physical or psychological qualities contrast strongly with, and therefore highlight, the corresponding qualities of another character. In his Sherlock Holmes stories, Arthur Conan Doyle portrayed Dr. Watson as a man of normal habits and intelligence, making him a foil for the eccentric and unusually perceptive Sherlock Holmes.

Folklore: Traditions and myths preserved in a culture or group of people. Typically, these are passed on by word of mouth in various forms—such as legends, songs, and proverbs—or preserved in customs and ceremonies. Washington Irving, in "The Devil and Tom Walker" and many of his other stories, incorporates many elements of the folklore of New England and Germany.

Folktale: A story originating in oral tradition. Folk tales fall into a variety of categories, including legends, ghost stories, fairy tales, fables, and anecdotes based on historical figures and events.

Foreshadowing: A device used in literature to create expectation or to set up an explanation of later developments. Edgar Allan Poe uses foreshadowing to create suspense in "The Fall of the House of Usher" when the narrator comments on the crumbling state of disrepair in which he finds the house.

G

Genre: A category of literary work. Genre may refer to both the content of a given work—tragedy, comedy, horror, science fiction—and to its form, such as poetry, novel, or drama.

Gilded Age: A period in American history during the 1870s and after characterized by political corruption and materialism. A number of important novels of social and political criticism were written during this time. Henry James and Kate Chopin are two writers who were prominent during the Gilded Age.

Gothicism: In literature, works characterized by a taste for medieval or morbid characters and situations. A gothic novel prominently features elements of horror, the supernatural, gloom, and violence: clanking chains, terror, ghosts, medieval castles, and unexplained phenomena. The term "gothic novel" is also applied to novels that lack elements of the traditional Gothic setting but that create a similar atmosphere of terror or dread. The term can also be applied to stories, plays, and poems. Mary Shelley's *Frankenstein* and Joyce Carol Oates's *Bellefleur* are both gothic novels.

Grotesque: In literature, a work that is characterized by exaggeration, deformity, freakishness, and disorder. The grotesque often includes an element of comic absurdity. Examples of the grotesque can be found in the works of Edgar Allan Poe, Flannery O'Connor, Joseph Heller, and Shirley Jackson.

H

Harlem Renaissance: The Harlem Renaissance of the 1920s is generally considered the first significant movement of black writers and artists in the United States. During this period, new and established black writers, many of whom lived in the region of New York City known as Harlem, published more fiction and poetry than ever before, the first influential black literary journals were established, and black authors and artists received their first widespread recognition and serious critical appraisal. Among the major writers associated with this period are Countee Cullen, Langston Hughes, Arna Bontemps, and Zora Neale Hurston.

Hero/Heroine: The principal sympathetic character in a literary work. Heroes and heroines typically exhibit admirable traits: idealism, courage, and integrity, for example. Famous heroes and heroines of literature include Charles Dickens's Oliver Twist, Margaret Mitchell's Scarlett O'Hara, and the anonymous narrator in Ralph Ellison's *Invisible Man.*

Hyperbole: Deliberate exaggeration used to achieve an effect. In William Shakespeare's *Macbeth,* Lady Macbeth hyperbolizes when she says, "All the perfumes of Arabia could not sweeten this little hand."

I

Image: A concrete representation of an object or sensory experience. Typically, such a representation helps evoke the feelings associated with the object or experience itself. Images are either "literal" or "figurative." Literal images are especially concrete and involve little or no extension of the obvious meaning of the words used to express them. Figurative images do not follow the literal meaning of the words exactly. Images in literature are usually visual, but the term "image" can also refer to the representation of any sensory experience.

Imagery: The array of images in a literary work. Also used to convey the author's overall use of figurative language in a work.

In medias res: A Latin term meaning "in the middle of things." It refers to the technique of beginning a story at its midpoint and then using various flashback devices to reveal previous action. This technique originated in such epics as Virgil's *Aeneid.*

Interior Monologue: A narrative technique in which characters' thoughts are revealed in a way that appears to be uncontrolled by the author. The interior monologue typically aims to reveal the inner self of a character. It portrays emotional experiences as they occur at both a conscious and unconscious level. One of the best-known interior monologues in English is the Molly Bloom section at the close of James Joyce's *Ulysses.* Katherine Anne Porter's "The Jilting of Granny Weatherall" is also told in the form of an interior monologue.

Irony: In literary criticism, the effect of language in which the intended meaning is the opposite of what is stated. The title of Jonathan Swift's "A Modest Proposal" is ironic because what Swift proposes in this essay is cannibalism—hardly "modest."

J

Jargon: Language that is used or understood only by a select group of people. Jargon may refer to terminology used in a certain profession, such as computer jargon, or it may refer to any nonsensical language that is not understood by most people. Anthony Burgess's *A Clockwork Orange* and James Thurber's "The Secret Life of Walter Mitty" both use jargon.

K

Knickerbocker Group: An indistinct group of New York writers of the first half of the nineteenth century. Members of the group were linked only by location and a common theme: New York life. Two famous members of the Knickerbocker Group were Washington Irving and William Cullen Bryant. The group's name derives from Irving's *Knickerbocker's History of New York*.

L

Literal Language: An author uses literal language when he or she writes without exaggerating or embellishing the subject matter and without any tools of figurative language. To say "He ran very quickly down the street" is to use literal language, whereas to say "He ran like a hare down the street" would be using figurative language.

Literature: Literature is broadly defined as any written or spoken material, but the term most often refers to creative works. Literature includes poetry, drama, fiction, and many kinds of nonfiction writing, as well as oral, dramatic, and broadcast compositions not necessarily preserved in a written format, such as films and television programs.

Lost Generation: A term first used by Gertrude Stein to describe the post–World War I generation of American writers: men and women haunted by a sense of betrayal and emptiness brought about by the destructiveness of the war. The term is commonly applied to Hart Crane, Ernest Hemingway, F. Scott Fitzgerald, and others.

M

Magic Realism: A form of literature that incorporates fantasy elements or supernatural occurrences into the narrative and accepts them as truth. Gabriel Gárcia Márquez and Laura Esquivel are two writers known for their works of magic realism.

Metaphor: A figure of speech that expresses an idea through the image of another object. Metaphors suggest the essence of the first object by identifying it with certain qualities of the second object. An example is "But soft, what light through yonder window breaks? / It is the east, and Juliet is the sun" in William Shakespeare's *Romeo and Juliet*. Here, Juliet, the first object, is identified with qualities of the second object, the sun.

Minimalism: A literary style characterized by spare, simple prose with few elaborations. In minimalism, the main theme of the work is often never discussed directly. Amy Hempel and Ernest Hemingway are two writers known for their works of minimalism.

Modernism: Modern literary practices. Also, the principles of a literary school that lasted from roughly the beginning of the twentieth century until the end of World War II. Modernism is defined by its rejection of the literary conventions of the nineteenth century and by its opposition to conventional morality, taste, traditions, and economic values. Many writers are associated with the concepts of modernism, including Albert Camus, D. H. Lawrence, Ernest Hemingway, William Faulkner, Eugene O'Neill, and James Joyce.

Monologue: A composition, written or oral, by a single individual. More specifically, a speech given by a single individual in a drama or other public entertainment. It has no set length, although it is usually several or more lines long. "I Stand Here Ironing" by Tillie Olsen is an example of a story written in the form of a monologue.

Mood: The prevailing emotions of a work or of the author in his or her creation of the work. The mood of a work is not always what might be expected based on its subject matter.

Motif: A theme, character type, image, metaphor, or other verbal element that recurs throughout a single work of literature or occurs in a number of different works over a period of time. For example, the color white in Herman Melville's *Moby Dick* is a "specific" motif, while the trials of star-crossed lovers is a "conventional" motif from the literature of all periods.

N

Narration: The telling of a series of events, real or invented. A narration may be either a simple narrative, in which the events are recounted chronologically, or a narrative with a plot, in which the account is given in a style reflecting the author's artistic concept of the story. Narration is sometimes used as a synonym for "storyline."

Narrative: A verse or prose accounting of an event or sequence of events, real or invented. The term is also used as an adjective in the sense "method of narration." For example, in literary criticism, the expression "narrative technique" usually refers to the way the author structures and presents his or her story. Different narrative forms include diaries, travelogues, novels, ballads, epics, short stories, and other fictional forms.

Narrator: The teller of a story. The narrator may be the author or a character in the story through whom the author speaks. Huckleberry Finn is the narrator of Mark Twain's *The Adventures of Huckleberry Finn.*

Novella: An Italian term meaning "story." This term has been especially used to describe fourteenth-century Italian tales, but it also refers to modern short novels. Modern novellas include Leo Tolstoy's *The Death of Ivan Ilich,* Fyodor Dostoyevsky's *Notes from the Underground,* and Joseph Conrad's *Heart of Darkness.*

O

Oedipus Complex: A son's romantic obsession with his mother. The phrase is derived from the story of the ancient Theban hero Oedipus, who unknowingly killed his father and married his mother, and was popularized by Sigmund Freud's theory of psychoanalysis. Literary occurrences of the Oedipus complex include Sophocles' *Oedipus Rex* and D. H. Lawrence's "The Rocking-Horse Winner."

Onomatopoeia: The use of words whose sounds express or suggest their meaning. In its simplest sense, onomatopoeia may be represented by words that mimic the sounds they denote such as "hiss" or "meow." At a more subtle level, the pattern and rhythm of sounds and rhymes of a line or poem may be onomatopoeic.

Oral Tradition: A process by which songs, ballads, folklore, and other material are transmitted by word of mouth. The tradition of oral transmission predates the written record systems of literate society. Oral transmission preserves material sometimes over generations, although often with variations. Memory plays a large part in the recitation and preservation of orally transmitted material. Native American myths and legends, and African folktales told by plantation slaves are examples of orally transmitted literature.

P

Parable: A story intended to teach a moral lesson or answer an ethical question. Examples of parables are the stories told by Jesus Christ in the New Testament, notably "The Prodigal Son," but parables also are used in Sufism, rabbinic literature, Hasidism, and Zen Buddhism. Isaac Bashevis Singer's story "Gimpel the Fool" exhibits characteristics of a parable.

Paradox: A statement that appears illogical or contradictory at first, but may actually point to an underlying truth. A literary example of a paradox is George Orwell's statement "All animals are equal, but some animals are more equal than others" in *Animal Farm.*

Parody: In literature, this term refers to an imitation of a serious literary work or the signature style of a particular author in a ridiculous manner. A typical parody adopts the style of the original and applies it to an inappropriate subject for humorous effect. Parody is a form of satire and could be considered the literary equivalent of a caricature or cartoon. Henry Fielding's *Shamela* is a parody of Samuel Richardson's *Pamela.*

Persona: A Latin term meaning "mask." Personae are the characters in a fictional work of literature. The persona generally functions as a mask through which the author tells a story in a voice other than his or her own. A persona is usually either a character in a story who acts as a narrator or an "implied author," a voice created by the author to act as the narrator for himself or herself. The persona in Charlotte Perkins Gilman's story "The Yellow Wallpaper" is the unnamed young mother experiencing a mental breakdown.

Personification: A figure of speech that gives human qualities to abstract ideas, animals, and inanimate objects. To say that "the sun is smiling" is to personify the sun.

Plot: The pattern of events in a narrative or drama. In its simplest sense, the plot guides the author in composing the work and helps the reader follow the work. Typically, plots exhibit causality and unity and have a beginning, a middle, and an end. Sometimes, however, a plot may consist of a series of disconnected events, in which case it is known as an "episodic plot."

Poetic Justice: An outcome in a literary work, not necessarily a poem, in which the good are rewarded and the evil are punished, especially in ways that particularly fit their virtues or crimes. For example, a murderer may himself be murdered, or a thief will find himself penniless.

Poetic License: Distortions of fact and literary convention made by a writer—not always a poet—for the sake of the effect gained. Poetic license is closely related to the concept of "artistic freedom." An author exercises poetic license by saying that a pile of money "reaches as high as a mountain" when the pile is actually only a foot or two high.

Point of View: The narrative perspective from which a literary work is presented to the reader. There are four traditional points of view. The "third person omniscient" gives the reader a "godlike" perspective, unrestricted by time or place, from which to see actions and look into the minds of characters. This allows the author to comment openly on characters and events in the work. The "third person" point of view presents the events of the story from outside of any single character's perception, much like the omniscient point of view, but the reader must understand the action as it takes place and without any special insight into characters' minds or motivations. The "first person" or "personal" point of view relates events as they are perceived by a single character. The main character "tells" the story and may offer opinions about the action and characters which differ from those of the author. Much less common than omniscient, third person, and first person is the "second person" point of view, wherein the author tells the story as if it is happening to the reader. James Thurber employs the omniscient point of view in his short story "The Secret Life of Walter Mitty." Ernest Hemingway's "A Clean, Well-Lighted Place" is a short story told from the third person point of view. Mark Twain's novel *Huckleberry Finn* is presented from the first person viewpoint. Jay McInerney's *Bright Lights, Big City* is an example of a novel which uses the second person point of view.

Pornography: Writing intended to provoke feelings of lust in the reader. Such works are often condemned by critics and teachers, but those which can be shown to have literary value are viewed less harshly. Literary works that have been described as pornographic include D. H. Lawrence's *Lady Chatterley's Lover* and James Joyce's *Ulysses*.

Post-Aesthetic Movement: An artistic response made by African Americans to the black aesthetic movement of the 1960s and early 1970s. Writers since that time have adopted a somewhat different tone in their work, with less emphasis placed on the disparity between black and white in the United States. In the words of post-aesthetic authors such as Toni Morrison, John Edgar Wideman, and Kristin Hunter, African Americans are portrayed as looking inward for answers to their own questions, rather than always looking to the outside world. Two well-known examples of works produced as part of the post-aesthetic movement are the Pulitzer Prize–winning novels *The Color Purple* by Alice Walker and *Beloved* by Toni Morrison.

Postmodernism: Writing from the 1960s forward characterized by experimentation and application of modernist elements, which include existentialism and alienation. Postmodernists have gone a step further in the rejection of tradition begun with the modernists by also rejecting traditional forms, preferring the anti-novel over the novel and the anti-hero over the hero. Postmodern writers include Thomas Pynchon, Margaret Drabble, and Gabriel García Márquez.

Prologue: An introductory section of a literary work. It often contains information establishing the situation of the characters or presents information about the setting, time period, or action. In drama, the prologue is spoken by a chorus or by one of the principal characters.

Prose: A literary medium that attempts to mirror the language of everyday speech. It is distinguished from poetry by its use of unmetered, unrhymed language consisting of logically related sentences. Prose is usually grouped into paragraphs that form a cohesive whole such as an essay or a novel. The term is sometimes used to mean an author's general writing.

Protagonist: The central character of a story who serves as a focus for its themes and incidents and as the principal rationale for its development. The protagonist is sometimes referred to in discussions of modern literature as the hero or anti-hero. Well-known protagonists are Hamlet in William Shakespeare's *Hamlet* and Jay Gatsby in F. Scott Fitzgerald's *The Great Gatsby*.

R

Realism: A nineteenth-century European literary movement that sought to portray familiar characters, situations, and settings in a realistic manner. This was done primarily by using an objective narrative point of view and through the buildup of accurate detail. The standard for success of any realistic work depends on how faithfully it transfers common experience into fictional forms. The realistic method may be altered or extended, as in stream of consciousness writing, to record highly subjective experience. Contemporary authors who often write in a realistic way include Nadine Gordimer and Grace Paley.

Resolution: The portion of a story following the climax, in which the conflict is resolved. The resolution of Jane Austen's *Northanger Abbey* is neatly summed up in the following sentence: "Henry and Catherine were married, the bells rang and every body smiled."

Rising Action: The part of a drama where the plot becomes increasingly complicated. Rising action leads up to the climax, or turning point, of a drama. The final "chase scene" of an action film is generally the rising action which culminates in the film's climax.

Roman a clef: A French phrase meaning "novel with a key." It refers to a narrative in which real persons are portrayed under fictitious names. Jack Kerouac, for example, portrayed various friends under fictitious names in the novel *On the Road*. D. H. Lawrence based "The Rocking-Horse Winner" on a family he knew.

Romanticism: This term has two widely accepted meanings. In historical criticism, it refers to a European intellectual and artistic movement of the late eighteenth and early nineteenth centuries that sought greater freedom of personal expression than that allowed by the strict rules of literary form and logic of the eighteenth-century neoclassicists. The Romantics preferred emotional and imaginative expression to rational analysis. They

considered the individual to be at the center of all experience and so placed him or her at the center of their art. The Romantics believed that the creative imagination reveals nobler truths—unique feelings and attitudes—than those that could be discovered by logic or by scientific examination. "Romanticism" is also used as a general term to refer to a type of sensibility found in all periods of literary history and usually considered to be in opposition to the principles of classicism. In this sense, Romanticism signifies any work or philosophy in which the exotic or dreamlike figure strongly, or that is devoted to individualistic expression, self-analysis, or a pursuit of a higher realm of knowledge than can be discovered by human reason. Prominent Romantics include Jean-Jacques Rousseau, William Wordsworth, John Keats, Lord Byron, and Johann Wolfgang von Goethe.

S

Satire: A work that uses ridicule, humor, and wit to criticize and provoke change in human nature and institutions. Voltaire's novella *Candide* and Jonathan Swift's essay "A Modest Proposal" are both satires. Flannery O'Connor's portrayal of the family in "A Good Man Is Hard to Find" is a satire of a modern, Southern, American family.

Science Fiction: A type of narrative based upon real or imagined scientific theories and technology. Science fiction is often peopled with alien creatures and set on other planets or in different dimensions. Popular writers of science fiction are Isaac Asimov, Karel Capek, Ray Bradbury, and Ursula K. Le Guin.

Setting: The time, place, and culture in which the action of a narrative takes place. The elements of setting may include geographic location, characters's physical and mental environments, prevailing cultural attitudes, or the historical time in which the action takes place.

Short Story: A fictional prose narrative shorter and more focused than a novella. The short story usually deals with a single episode and often a single character. The "tone," the author's attitude toward his or her subject and audience, is uniform throughout. The short story frequently also lacks *denouement*, ending instead at its climax.

Signifying Monkey: A popular trickster figure in black folklore, with hundreds of tales about this character documented since the 19th century. Henry Louis Gates Jr. examines the history of the signifying monkey in *The Signifying Monkey: Towards a Theory of Afro-American Literary Criticism,* published in 1988.

Simile: A comparison, usually using "like" or "as," of two essentially dissimilar things, as in "coffee as cold as ice" or "He sounded like a broken record." The title of Ernest Hemingway's "Hills Like White Elephants" contains a simile.

Socialist Realism: The Socialist Realism school of literary theory was proposed by Maxim Gorky and established as a dogma by the first Soviet Congress of Writers. It demanded adherence to a communist worldview in works of literature. Its doctrines required an objective viewpoint comprehensible to the working classes and themes of social struggle featuring strong proletarian heroes. Gabriel García Márquez's stories exhibit some characteristics of Socialist Realism.

Stereotype: A stereotype was originally the name for a duplication made during the printing process; this led to its modern definition as a person or thing that is (or is assumed to be) the same as all others of its type. Common stereotypical characters include the absent-minded professor, the nagging wife, the troublemaking teenager, and the kind-hearted grandmother.

Stream of Consciousness: A narrative technique for rendering the inward experience of a character. This technique is designed to give the impression of an ever-changing series of thoughts, emotions, images, and memories in the spontaneous and seemingly illogical order that they occur in life. The textbook example of stream of consciousness is the last section of James Joyce's *Ulysses.*

Structure: The form taken by a piece of literature. The structure may be made obvious for ease of understanding, as in nonfiction works, or may obscured for artistic purposes, as in some poetry or seemingly "unstructured" prose.

Style: A writer's distinctive manner of arranging words to suit his or her ideas and purpose in writing. The unique imprint of the author's personality upon his or her writing, style is the product of an author's way of arranging ideas and his or her use of diction, different sentence structures, rhythm, figures of speech, rhetorical principles, and other elements of composition.

Suspense: A literary device in which the author maintains the audience's attention through the buildup of events, the outcome of which will soon be revealed. Suspense in William Shakespeare's *Hamlet* is sustained throughout by the question of whether or not the Prince will achieve what he has been instructed to do and of what he intends to do.

Symbol: Something that suggests or stands for something else without losing its original identity. In literature, symbols combine their literal meaning with the suggestion of an abstract concept. Literary symbols are of two types: those that carry complex associations of meaning no matter what their contexts, and those that derive their suggestive meaning from their functions in specific literary works. Examples of symbols are sunshine suggesting happiness, rain suggesting sorrow, and storm clouds suggesting despair.

T

Tale: A story told by a narrator with a simple plot and little character development. Tales are usually relatively short and often carry a simple message. Examples of tales can be found in the works of Saki, Anton Chekhov, Guy de Maupassant, and O. Henry.

Tall Tale: A humorous tale told in a straightforward, credible tone but relating absolutely impossible events or feats of the characters. Such tales were commonly told of frontier adventures during the settlement of the west in the United States. Literary use of tall tales can be found in Washington Irving's *History of New York,* Mark Twain's *Life on the Mississippi,* and in the German R. F. Raspe's *Baron Munchausen's Narratives of His Marvellous Travels and Campaigns in Russia.*

Theme: The main point of a work of literature. The term is used interchangeably with thesis. Many works have multiple themes. One of the themes of Nathaniel Hawthorne's "Young Goodman Brown" is loss of faith.

Tone: The author's attitude toward his or her audience maybe deduced from the tone of the work. A formal tone may create distance or convey politeness, while an informal tone may encourage a friendly, intimate, or intrusive feeling in the reader. The author's attitude toward his or her subject matter may also be deduced from the tone of the words he or she uses in discussing it. The tone of John F. Kennedy's speech which included the appeal to "ask not what your country can do for you" was intended to instill feelings of camaraderie and national pride in listeners.

Tragedy: A drama in prose or poetry about a noble, courageous hero of excellent character who, because of some tragic character flaw, brings ruin upon him- or herself. Tragedy treats its subjects in a dignified and serious manner, using poetic language to help evoke pity and fear and bring about catharsis, a purging of these emotions. The tragic form was practiced extensively by the ancient Greeks. The classical form of tragedy was revived in the sixteenth century; it flourished especially on the Elizabethan stage. In modern times, dramatists have attempted to adapt the form to the needs of modern society by drawing their heroes from the ranks of ordinary men and women and defining the nobility of these heroes in terms of spirit rather than exalted social standing. Some contemporary works that are thought of as tragedies include *The Great Gatsby* by F. Scott Fitzgerald, and *The Sound and the Fury* by William Faulkner.

Tragic Flaw: In a tragedy, the quality within the hero or heroine which leads to his or her downfall. Examples of the tragic flaw include Othello's jealousy and Hamlet's indecisiveness, although most great tragedies defy such simple interpretation.

U

Utopia: A fictional perfect place, such as "paradise" or "heaven." An early literary utopia was described in Plato's *Republic,* and in modern literature, Ursula K. Le Guin depicts a utopia in "The Ones Who Walk Away from Omelas."

V

Victorian: Refers broadly to the reign of Queen Victoria of England (1837-1901) and to anything with qualities typical of that era. For example, the qualities of smug narrow-mindedness, bourgeois materialism, faith in social progress, and priggish morality are often considered Victorian. In literature, the Victorian Period was the great age of the English novel, and the latter part of the era saw the rise of movements such as decadence and symbolism.

Cumulative
Author/Title Index

Bellow, Saul
  Leaving the Yellow House: V12
  A Silver Dish: V22
Bender, Aimee
  The Rememberer: V25
Benét, Stephen Vincent
  An End to Dreams: V22
  By the Waters of Babylon: V31
Berriault, Gina
  The Stone Boy: V7
  Women in Their Beds: V11
The Best Girlfriend You Never Had
  (Houston): V17
Beware of the Dog (Dahl): V30
Bierce, Ambrose
  The Boarded Window: V9
  A Horseman in the Sky: V27
  *An Occurrence at Owl Creek
    Bridge:* V2
Big Black Good Man (Wright): V20
Big Blonde (Parker): V5
The Birds (du Maurier): V16
Bisson, Terry
  The Toxic Donut: V18
Black Boy (Boyle): V14
The Black Cat (Poe): V26
Black Is My Favorite Color
  (Malamud): V16
Blackberry Winter (Warren): V8
Bliss (Mansfield): V10
Blood-Burning Moon (Toomer): V5
Bloodchild (Butler): V6
The Bloody Chamber (Carter): V4
Bloom, Amy
  Silver Water: V11
Blues Ain't No Mockin Bird
  (Bambara): V4
The Blues I'm Playing (Hughes):
  V7
The Boarded Window (Bierce): V9
Boccaccio, Giovanni
  Federigo's Falcon: V28
Boll, Heinrich
  Christmas Not Just Once a Year:
    V20
Borges, Jorge Luis
  The Aleph: V17
  The Circular Ruins: V26
  The Garden of Forking Paths: V9
  The House of Asterion: V32
  *Pierre Menard, Author of the
    Quixote:* V4
Borowski, Tadeusz
  *This Way for the Gas, Ladies and
    Gentlemen:* V13
Boule de Suif (Maupassant): V21
Bowen, Elizabeth
  A Day in the Dark: V22
  The Demon Lover: V5
Bowles, Paul
  The Eye: V17
A Boy and His Dog (Ellison): V14

Boyle, Kay
  Astronomer's Wife: V13
  Black Boy: V14
  The White Horses of Vienna: V10
Boyle, T. Coraghessan
  *Stones in My Passway, Hellhound
    on My Trail:* V13
  The Underground Gardens: V19
Boys and Girls (Munro): V5
Bradbury, Ray
  The Golden Kite, the Silver Wind:
    V28
  There Will Come Soft Rains: V1
  The Veldt: V20
Brazzaville Teen-ager (Friedman):
  V18
Bright and Morning Star (Wright):
  V15
Brokeback Mountain (Proulx): V23
Brown, Jason
  Animal Stories: V14
Brownies (Packer): V25
Burton, Richard
  The Arabian Nights: V21
Butler, Octavia
  Bloodchild: V6
Butler, Robert Olen
  *A Good Scent from a Strange
    Mountain:* V11
  Titanic *Survivors Found in
    Bermuda Triangle:* V22
B. Wordsworth (Naipaul): V29
Byatt, A. S.
  Art Work: V26
By the Waters of Babylon (Benét): V31

C

Callaghan, Morley
  All the Years of Her Life: V19
Calvino, Italo
  The Feathered Ogre: V12
  The Garden of Stubborn Cats: V31
Camus, Albert
  The Guest: V4
The Canal (Yates): V24
The Canterville Ghost (Wilde): V7
Capote, Truman
  A Christmas Memory: V2
Caroline's Wedding (Danticat): V25
Carter, Angela
  The Bloody Chamber: V4
  The Erlking: V12
Carver, Raymond
  Cathedral: V6
  Errand: V13
  Popular Mechanics: V32
  A Small, Good Thing: V23
  *What We Talk About When We
    Talk About Love:* V12
  Where I'm Calling From: V3
The Cask of Amontillado (Poe): V7

The Catbird Seat (Thurber): V10
Cathedral (Carver): V6
Cather, Willa
  The Diamond Mine: V16
  Neighbour Rosicky: V7
  Paul's Case: V2
  A Wagner Matinee: V27
*The Celebrated Jumping Frog
  of Calaveras County*
  (Twain): V1
The Censors (Valenzuela): V29
The Centaur (Saramago): V23
The Challenge (Vargas Llosa): V14
Chandra, Vikram
  Dharma: V16
Charles (Jackson): V27
Cheever, John
  The Country Husband: V14
  The Swimmer: V2
Chekhov, Anton
  The Darling: V13
  Gooseberries: V14
  Gusev: V26
  The Lady with the Pet Dog: V5
  A Problem: V29
Chesnutt, Charles Waddell
  The Goophered Grapevine: V26
  The Sheriff's Children: V11
Children of the Sea (Danticat): V1
Chopin, Kate
  Désirée's Baby: V13
  A Point at Issue!: V17
  The Storm: V26
  The Story of an Hour: V2
Christie, Agatha
  The Witness for the Prosecution:
    V31
A Christmas Memory (Capote): V2
Christmas Not Just Once a Year
  (Böll): V20
The Chrysanthemums (Steinbeck):
  V6
A Circle in the Fire (O'Connor): V19
The Circular Ruins (Borges): V26
Cisneros, Sandra
  Eleven: V27
  Little Miracles, Kept Promises:
    V13
  *My Lucy Friend Who Smells Like
    Corn:* V32
  Woman Hollering Creek: V3
Civil Peace (Achebe): V13
Clarke, Arthur C.
  Dog Star: V29
  "If I Forget Thee, O Earth . . .":
    V18
  The Star: V4
A Clean, Well-Lighted Place
  (Hemingway): V9
Cofer, Judith Ortiz
  American History: V27
  Aunty Misery: V29

Cumulative Nationality/Ethnicity Index

Mann, Thomas
  Death in Venice: V9
  Disorder and Early Sorrow: V4
Wolf, Christa
  Exchanging Glances: V14

Haitian

Danticat, Edwidge
  Caroline's Wedding: V25
  Children of the Sea: V1

Hispanic American

Allende, Isabel
  And of Clay Are We Created: V11
  The Gold of Tomás Vargas: V16
Alvarez, Julia
  Liberty: V27
Cisneros, Sandra
  Eleven: V27
  Little Miracles, Kept Promises: V13
  My Lucy Friend Who Smells Like Corn: V32
  Woman Hollering Creek: V3
Cofer, Judith Ortiz
  American History: V27
  Aunty Misery: V29
García Márquez, Gabriel
  Eyes of a Blue Dog: V21
  The Handsomest Drowned Man in the World: V1
  A Very Old Man with Enormous Wings: V6
  The Woman Who Came at Six O'Clock: V16
Morales, Alejandro
  The Curing Woman: V19
Rivera, Beatriz
  African Passions: V15
Rivera, Tomás
  The Harvest: V15
Thomas, Piri
  Amigo Brothers: V28

Indian

Chandra, Vikram
  Dharma: V16
Desai, Anita
  A Devoted Son: V31
  Games at Twilight: V28
Divakaruni, Chitra Banerjee
  Meeting Mrinal: V24
  Mrs. Dutta Writes a Letter: V18
Lahiri, Jhumpa
  A Temporary Matter: V19
  This Blessed House: V27
Manto, Saadat Hasan
  The Dog of Tithwal: V15
Mistry, Rohinton
  Swimming Lessons: V6

Mukherjee, Bharati
  The Management of Grief: V7
  The Middleman: V24
  The Tenant: V32
Naipaul, V. S.
  B. Wordsworth: V29
Narayan, R. K.
  Forty-Five a Month: V29
  A Horse and Two Goats: V5
Sharma, Akhil
  If You Sing like That for Me: V21

Indonesian

Rangkuti, Hamsad
  The Fence: V31

Irish

Beckett, Samuel
  Dante and the Lobster: V15
Bowen, Elizabeth
  A Day in the Dark: V22
  The Demon Lover: V5
Devlin, Anne
  Naming the Names: V17
Joyce, James
  Araby: V1
  The Dead: V6
  Eveline: V19
  The Sisters: V32
Lavin, Mary
  In the Middle of the Fields: V23
O'Connor, Frank
  Guests of the Nation: V5
O'Flaherty, Liam
  The Sniper: V20
  The Wave: V5
Trevor, William
  The News from Ireland: V10
Wilde, Oscar
  The Canterville Ghost: V7

Israeli

Hendel, Yehudit
  Small Change: V14

Italian

Boccaccio, Giovanni
  Federigo's Falcon: V28
Calvino, Italo
  The Feathered Ogre: V12
  The Garden of Stubborn Cats: V31
Pirandello, Luigi
  A Day Goes by: V30

Japanese

Kawabata, Yasunari
  The Grasshopper and the Bell Cricket: V29
Mishima, Yukio
  Fountains in the Rain: V12
  Swaddling Clothes: V5

Murakami, Haruki
  The Elephant Vanishes: V23
Naoya, Shiga
  Han's Crime: V5
Waters, Mary Yukari
  Aftermath: V22
Yoshimoto, Banana
  Kitchen: V16

Jewish

Asimov, Isaac
  Nightfall: V17
Babel, Isaac
  My First Goose: V10
Bellow, Saul
  Leaving the Yellow House: V12
  A Silver Dish: V22
Berriault, Gina
  The Stone Boy: V7
  Women in Their Beds: V11
Doctorow, E. L.
  The Writer in the Family: V27
Eisenberg, Deborah
  Someone to Talk To: V24
Friedman, Bruce Jay
  Brazzaville Teen-ager: V18
Helprin, Mark
  Perfection: V25
Kafka, Franz
  A Hunger Artist: V7
  In the Penal Colony: V3
  The Metamorphosis: V12
Malamud, Bernard
  Black Is My Favorite Color: V16
  The First Seven Years: V13
  The Magic Barrel: V8
Olsen, Tillie
  I Stand Here Ironing: V1
  O Yes: V32
Orringer, Julie
  The Smoothest Way Is Full of Stones: V23
Ozick, Cynthia
  The Pagan Rabbi: V12
  Rosa: V22
  The Shawl: V3
Paley, Grace
  Anxiety: V27
  A Conversation with My Father: V3
  The Long-Distance Runner: V20
Roth, Philip
  The Conversion of the Jews: V18
  Goodbye, Columbus: V12
Salinger, J. D.
  A Perfect Day for Bananafish: V17
Singer, Isaac Bashevis
  Gimpel the Fool: V2
  Henne Fire: V16
  The Son from America: V30
  The Spinoza of Market Street: V12
  Zlateh the Goat: V27

Subject/Theme Index